RISE AND DECLINE OF CIVILIZATIONS:
LESSONS FOR THE JEWISH PEOPLE

ACADEMIC
STUDIES
PRESS

www.jppi.org.il

המכון **למדיניות העם היהודי** (מיסודה של הסוכנות היהודית לא"י) **בע"מ**
The Jewish **People Policy Institute** (Established by the Jewish Agency for Israel) **Ltd.**

Library of Congress Cataloging-in-Publication Data:
A catalog record for this title is available from the Library of Congress.

ISBN 978-1-61811-276-7 (hardback)
ISBN 978-1-61811-377-1 (paperback)
ISBN 978-1-61811-277-4 (electronic)

Book design by Ivan Grave

Published by Academic Studies Press in 2014
28 Montfern Avenue
Brighton, MA 02135, USA
press@academicstudiespress.com
www.academicstudiespress.com

A Project of the Jewish People Policy Institute

RISE AND DECLINE OF CIVILIZATIONS:

LESSONS FOR THE JEWISH PEOPLE

Shalom Salomon Wald

Foreword by Shimon Peres

Boston • Jerusalem • 2014

WWJPPIW
www.jppi.org.il

המכון למדיניות העם היהודי (מיסודה של הסוכנות היהודית לא"י) בע"מ
The Jewish People Policy Institute (Established by the Jewish Agency for Israel) Ltd.

To the memory of my mother Regina-Rifka Wald-Lakser
who passed away in 1989 after a hard life of flight and survival,
and to the memory of my father Nathan Nachman Wald,
the brothers and sisters of both my parents,
their spouses and children,
and all our other close relatives
who perished in 1941 and 1942 in the Shoah.

Table of Contents

Acknowledgements xi
Foreword xiii
Introduction. A Thought Experiment xv

Part I
QUESTIONS OF DEFINITION AND METHODOLOGY

Introduction 3
Chapter 1: Civilization or Culture? 4
Chapter 2: At the Crossroads: The Trouble with "Rising," "Thriving,"
    and "Declining" 8
Chapter 3: A Selection of Historians: Three Categories 13
Chapter 4: On Philosophy of History 16
Chapter 5: Obstacles to Foresight 20

Part II
HISTORIANS ON RISE AND DECLINE

Introduction 27
Chapter 1: Thucydides, Greece, ca. 460-400 BCE 29
Chapter 2: Sima Qian, China, ca. 145-90 BCE 35
Chapter 3: Ibn Khaldun, Tunisia, 1332-1406 CE 43
Chapter 4: Edward Gibbon, UK, 1737-1794 50
Chapter 5: Jacob Burckhardt, Switzerland, 1818-1897 57
Chapter 6: Max Weber, Germany, 1864-1920 64
Chapter 7: Oswald Spengler, Germany, 1880-1936 68
Chapter 8: Johan Huizinga, Netherlands, 1872-1945 72
Chapter 9: Arnold Toynbee, UK, 1889-1975 77
Chapter 10: Pitirim Sorokin, USA, 1889-1968 83
Chapter 11: Fernand Braudel, France, 1902-1985 87
Chapter 12: Marshall G.S. Hodgson, USA, 1922-1968 92

Chapter 13: Bernard Lewis, USA, 1916– 97
Chapter 14: Jonathan I. Israel, USA, 1946– 101
Chapter 15: Paul Kennedy , USA, 1945– 106
Chapter 16: Jared Diamond, USA, 1937– 108
Chapter 17: Bryan Ward-Perkins, UK, 1952– 110
Chapter 18: Mancur Olson, USA, 1932-1998 113
Chapter 19: Peter Turchin, USA, 1957– 114
Chapter 20: Christopher Chase-Dunn, USA, 1944–
    and Thomas D. Hall, USA, 1946– 115
Chapter 21: Joseph A. Tainter, USA, 1949– 117
Chapter 22: Arthur Herman, USA, 1956– 118

Part III
MACRO-HISTORICAL CONDITIONS OF RISE,
GOLDEN AGE, AND DECLINE

Introduction 123
Chapter 1: "Challenge-and-Response" 124
Chapter 2: Windows of Opportunity 130
Chapter 3: Global Up- and Downturns 133
Chapter 4: Thriving Civilizations, or the Myth of a Golden Age 135
Chapter 5: Cultural Accomplishments of Thriving Civilizations 139
Chapter 6: Decline Has Multiple Causes 148
Chapter 7: Global Futures: "End of Civilization" or "Decline of the West"? . . . 153

Part IV
DRIVERS OF RISE AND DECLINE OF CIVILIZATIONS:
GENERAL OBSERVATIONS AND JEWISH HISTORY

Introduction 161
Chapter 1: Religion: Identity Safeguards and their Downsides 162
Chapter 2: Extra-Rational Bonds: Tacit Consensus or Group Cohesion 180
Chapter 3: Education, Science and Technology: Drivers of the Future 193
Chapter 4: Language: A Factor in Rise and Decline 211
Chapter 5: Creative Leadership and Political Elites 220
Chapter 6: Numbers and Critical Mass 242
Chapter 7: Economic Foundations of Long-Lasting Civilizations 253
Chapter 8: War: A Double-Edged Sword 278
Chapter 9: Geopolitics and Civilizational Affinities 301
Chapter 10: Internal Dissent 315
Chapter 11: "Fortune" or Chance Events 329
Chapter 12: Natural and Health Disasters 342

Part V
DRIVERS OF TRANSFORMATION:
TWO CASE STUDIES

Introduction 353
Chapter 1: Transforming a Small Country into a Great Power:
    The Dutch Republic 354
Chapter 2: Transforming Great-Power Decline into New Power Rise: Turkey . . 358

Outlook and Conclusions 362
Afterword 366

Appendix

Appendix A: A Framework for Policy-Makers 373
Appendix B: JPPI Brainstorming Participants 380

Selected Bibliography 382

Notes 403

Index 439

Acknowledgements

This book owes a lot to a lot of people. First I have to mention Yehezkel Dror, Founding President of the Jewish People Policy Institute (JPPI) and professor at Hebrew University (but from now on I will mostly omit the numerous, varied titles of my academic friends from China, France, Israel, Switzerland and the United States). Dror's creative suggestion was to look at Jewish history from a "rise-and-decline" perspective and to consult for this purpose the world's great historians. It was his idea that launched this book, but the launch would not have ended in bringing this book to print without the active interest and support through several difficult years of Dror's successor, Avinoam Bar-Yosef, and JPPI's Projects Coordinator, Ita Alcalay.

As I slowly advanced in my endeavor, the support and advice of senior policy-makers and advisers who are following JPPI's work became increasingly important. I received encouragement and helpful comments from the two co-chairs of the JPPI Board, Ambassadors Stuart Eizenstat and Dennis Ross, as well as the associate chair, Leonid Nevzlin. No less valid was the critical interest expressed by the past and current chairs of the Jewish Agency for Israel, Sallai Meridor and Natan Sharansky.

My work was also inspired and encouraged in a series of JPPI "brainstorming" meetings of senior Jewish and Israeli policy makers and intellectuals at Wye Plantation and Glen Cove in the United States and in Jerusalem, Israel. A full list of participants can be found in Appendix B.

However, no high-level support would have produced this book without the active cooperation of my colleagues in the JPPI. A long path usually separates the first version of a book from the draft that goes to the publisher. Several friends walked that path with me, or rather dragged me along it: the content editor, Rami Tal; the English language editor, Barry Geltman; the Hebrew translator, Emanuel Lottem; and Yogev Karasenty, who helped identify the original Hebrew sources mentioned in the book. These four did much more than correct language and discover errors; their impressive knowledge of history and current Israeli affairs has greatly enriched this book.

Other current and past colleagues from the JPPI have made essential contributions, some to the whole book and others to specific chapters: I should specifically mention Sergio DellaPergola, Michael Feuer, Avi Gil, Dov Maimon, Jehudah Mirsky, Steven Popper, Emmanuel Sivan, Noah Slepkov, and Chaim Waxman. It would be unfair not to add to this list the colleagues who helped me with advice on specific points or provided me with encouragement to continue my work, Naftali Elimelech, Shlomo Fischer, Inbal Hakman, Shmuel Rosner, and Einat Wilf.

Outside the JPPI, I am greatly indebted to helpful scholars from five countries. Henry Kissinger, who has arguably the deepest knowledge of world history of any twentieth-century statesman, read and commented on crucial sections of the book. I must mention a man who unfortunately will not see the completion of this work, my late friend and venerated teacher Professor David Sohlberg of Bar-Ilan University, a scholar with an immense knowledge of Greek and Roman antiquity and languages, who passed away in 2012. Very special thanks go to the historian Simon Erlanger, who read every line of this book, eliminated a few mistakes, and added more than a few brilliant insights of his own. He is closely followed by the Judaism and Talmud scholar Liliane Vana, whose approval was precious because few mistakes, if any, have ever escaped her critical eye, and Menachem Schmelzer from the Jewish Theological Seminary, who provided invaluable help with the Talmud quotations.

The most sensitive and controversial issues of this book are those regarding biology and genetics in the chapter on Extra-Rational Bonds. I could not have written this chapter without the active and critical help of experts from US medical and biological faculties: David Adler, Ron Atlas, and Marc and Babette Weksler.

Many other people offered indispensable, critical advice on individual chapters or issues, including Ofer Brand, Irene Eber, Manfred Gerstenfeld, Jonathan Goldstein, Nahum Gross, Antoine Halff, Peter Kearns, Aya Meltzer-Asher, Hagar Meltzer, Nahum Meltzer, Stefan Michalowski, Ken Robbins, Betty Roitman, Walter Rosenbaum, Bertram Schwarzbach, Bernardo Sorj, Jean-Jacques Wahl, Philip Wang, and Zhang Qianhong. In addition to Rabbi Yuval Cherlow, head of Yeshivat Hesder Petach Tikva, three Orthodox rabbis, who prefer not to be thanked by name, helped me to better understand some issues of Jewish law and tradition.

All of these experts have helped to write this book, but none of them bears any responsibility for the author's views or any possible remaining errors.

Shalom Salomon Wald
Jerusalem, July, 2013

Foreword

In these pages, Dr. Shalom Salomon Wald takes us on a fascinating journey through the writings of historians who have explored the reasons for the rise and decline of civilizations. The range of perspectives that emerges reflects the outlooks of the most fertile minds through the generations. They not only gave accounts of the events of their times, but also sought to discern the patterns and sequences of events that could serve as a compass for a better understanding of our own world, and possibly provide clearer insight into the chapters still to come.

Studying the history of the rise and decline of civilizations could make us question our power to shape our destiny. If "all is predetermined," then we have no influence over our fate, and are at the mercy of a cold determinism that governs the rise and fall of nations and peoples.

The destiny of the Jewish people significantly challenges the notion that people do not have the capacity to influence the course of history. Our people were able to recover from even the most terrible of the disasters that befell them. For the Jewish people, the phrase "from Shoah to rebirth" was no mere cliché or prayer, but a very real plan of action.

Rabbi Akiva asserted that, "all is predetermined, but we are granted freedom of choice." In this short sentence he expressed the wonderful dialectic between history and the human being. Indeed, our people have proven that there is still considerable room for humankind to shape their tomorrow, for better or for worse.

Israel's rebirth after 2,000 years of exile and after a heinous Holocaust is a glorious proof of the Jewish people's ability to defy the theory of historical determinism. It was my good fortune to work with the greatest of Israel's leaders, David Ben-Gurion. He was a man who respected and studied history while at the same time making history. He refused to accept the familiar patterns of thought. He chose "freedom of choice" over "all is predetermined."

Our perception of historical events is influenced by our changing perspectives over time. Events pass, but the values that ignite them remain unchanged.

The lessons of history are not to be taken lightly, but we should avoid making rigid conclusions based on processes and events that are almost always different from one another.

We should also guard against excessive pessimism concerning our capacity to influence the course of history. Such pessimism is not practical, nor does it stand up to the test of history.

Dr. Wald puts at our disposal the benefit of the wisdom of the finest historians, beginning with Thucydides, concerning the reasons behind the rise and decline of civilizations. This notable endeavor enables us to delineate some "Do's and Don'ts" for leaders that navigate between crises and guide their people to prosperous shores.

These practical insights should be an integral part of every leadership compass, especially in the Jewish-Israeli narrative, where history is still very much in the making. Israel's security must be strengthened through reconciliation with its neighbors, and this fact urges us to favor "freedom of choice" over "all is predetermined." Thus will Jewish civilization continue to thrive while honoring history, but at the same time consistently refuting the inevitability of decline and the principle that all is predetermined.

The readers of this book can look forward to an exciting journey through the chapters of history as penned by some of its greatest historians. Dr. Wald deserves our deepest appreciation for the excellent guidance he provides us in this learning experience and on this inspiring journey.

Shimon Peres, President of the State of Israel
Jerusalem, February 2013

A Thought Experiment

This book is a thought experiment that has not been tried before. The question of the future of the Jewish people* and Judaism attracts a lot of general interest and troubles many leaders and some members of the Jewish public. The Jewish People Policy Institute has warned that the Jewish people are at the crossroads "between thriving and decline."[1]

At the same time, new popular or scholarly books or articles on Judaism, Jewish history, Jewish culture, and Israel appear every day in one of twenty or more languages. The quantity and quality of academic research on Judaism and Jewish history has reached a historically unprecedented level. Most of the authors of these works are Jewish, and the majority of their contributions cover particular subjects, local history, unique events, or limited periods—they write specialized or "micro-histories," in line with the currently dominant trends in Western academic historiography. Much of this impressive output is written by specialists for specialists.

But something seems to be missing. The key assumption underlying this book, in line with the idea of many historians, is that learning from history is not only possible but also necessary, because human nature has changed little since remote antiquity. However, there is a mismatch between the general interest in the Jews and their future and the comprehension of the factors that explain their past and might again influence their future. The new approach, the thought experiment here, is to interrogate a number of historians who, with a few exceptions, were or are not Jewish, and did or do not specialize in Jewish history, but who have written about the rise and decline of other civilizations and nations from a long-term perspective, and then to reflect on whether their findings could be valid for the Jewish people as well. None of these historians is "interrogated" in person; all speak through their works. It is, thus important to remember that the starting point of this study is not a systematic review of the contemporary Jewish condition

---

* The term "Jewish people" will throughout this report include Israel, as a Jewish state. The term "Jewish leaders" will include Israeli Jewish leaders.

and its dynamics, but rather an examination of books about the past rise and fall of other civilizations and states. Of course, complete objectivity is not a human trait. Thus, even when we read, say, about the end of the Maya in Central America, the fate of the Jews is hovering somewhere in the background.

Perhaps this tentative trust in non-Jewish history will be criticized, but this is not a new problem. David Gans, one of the first pre-modern Jewish historians and a student of two great spiritual leaders of his time, Rabbi Moses Isserles in Krakow and the Maharal (Rabbi Judah Loew) in Prague, wrote in 1592 that "I see in advance that many will speak out against me, condemn me and consider me sinful because I have taken material from non-Jewish writers....I contend that Scripture has allowed us to search in non-Jewish books for accounts of events which can be of some use for us."[2] Critics may argue, as Heinrich Graetz,[3] Simon Dubnow,[4] and other apologetic Jewish historians have, that the longevity of the Jewish civilization under adverse conditions has no parallel in known history, and that the Jews cannot be compared to others because no other people has survived dispersion and persecution for so long without a permanent geographic homeland. Hence, goes this argument, the rise and decline of other civilizations contains no valid lessons for the Jews, who would do better to turn to their own historians. In this volume, works on Jewish history will often be quoted on specific issues, but none of them is included among its original sources, for Jewish historians generally did not look at Jewish history with an eye to the rise and decline of other civilizations.

Among non-Jews, the Jewish longevity has often been a source of wonder for some, and a source of denial, suspicion, or enmity for many others. However, it does not follow from Jewish exceptionality that the specific ups and downs of Jewish history, the successes and failures of Judaism's leaders, the victories and defeats of their collective endeavors, are also unique and incomparable to those of other civilizations. With due caution, they can be compared. The jigsaw puzzle of Jewish history may be unique when pieced together, but for many pieces of the puzzle there are analogous pieces in the puzzles of other civilizations and countries.

Our attempt to apply factors gleaned from general history to the past and present of the Jews, and the proposed hypotheses that will emerge from our effort, are unlikely to meet all the criteria of academic scholarship. Many scholars will be ill at ease with a review that calls on so many different sub-disciplines: history of religion, history of war, economics, genetics, demography, science, environmental policies, and more. Academia resents boundary-breakers, and reserves recognition and promotion to scholars who are experts within the boundaries of their own disciplines but do not often reach outside to search in foreign fields. However, respect for academic boundaries may be less and less compatible with a full understanding of Jewish history.

This book does not presume to be a history of the Jewish people. It offers suggestions and hypotheses rather than summaries of in-depth research. To write a new comprehensive history would require much more than an informed non-specialist, and is a challenge that others will have to take up. Then some of the proposed hypotheses might serve as a useful starting point for further discussion.

Perhaps the time has come to recall Ahad Haam's influential essay collection, *Al Parashat Derachim* (*At the Crossroads*), of the early twentieth century. Today, like then, the Jews stand at a crossroads of history and can take different directions. Their future trajectory depends upon themselves— on their capacity to change and their will to act—at least as much as upon external factors.

PART I

QUESTIONS OF DEFINITION AND METHODOLOGY

Introduction

The title *Rise and Decline of Civilizations: Lessons for the Jewish People* uses four terms that raise questions of definition: "Jewish," "Civilization," "Rise," and "Decline." The eternal question of "Who is a Jew?" will not be discussed here. We will adopt the expert opinion that bases the definition on different modes of Jewish self-identification. It includes people with at least one Jewish parent who declare themselves Jewish and those who have converted to Judaism, but excludes those who have converted to another religion or reject being recognized as Jews. The available data show for 2011 a Jewish "core" population of more than thirteen million Jews living around the world.[1]

CHAPTER 1

Civilization or Culture?

We call Judaism a "civilization" for lack of a better term, following a concept proposed in 1934 by Mordecai M. Kaplan and others.[1] The term "Jewish civilization" is not self-evident, because most modern, non-Orthodox Jews in the Diaspora belong to several overlapping civilizations, and the same could be said of many Jews in the late Roman Empire. Judaism is for many people a "part-time civilization": they are Americans and Jews, Frenchmen and Jews, etc.

In "Jewish civilization" we include the entire history of Israel and the Jewish people: we use to to refer to the thread of Jewish continuity through time and that of links through space. No Western language has an uncontroversial term for this changing and dispersed group of people who claim a history of more than three thousand years. Some Chinese historians use the Chinese term for civilization, finding it most appropriate for the Jews because they note the latter's longevity and compare it to their own. Until the late eighteenth century, everybody called the Jews a "people" or a "nation," albeit one without a territorial base. This nation was distinguished by a unique religion. Since the onset of the *Haskalah* and the Emancipation, the term "nation" has become problematic. It is no longer usable except for Israel because Diaspora Jews have joined the nation-states of the world as equal citizens. In the nineteenth century, "Religion" became the only politically and socially acceptable way to refer to the Jews in the West. This marker too is now questionable. "People" remains a widely accepted term for the Jews, and this study will use it interchangeably with "civilization." Kaplan and others, such as the writer Ahad Ha-am (1856-1927), recognized that many Jews wanted to remain Jews although they were no longer religious, and that Judaism had components that were not rooted in religion, or were only partly rooted in religion. Kaplan wrote in his book *Judaism as a Civilization* that these components consisted of, in addition to religion, "history, literature, language, social organization, folk sanctions, standards of conduct, social and spiritual ideals, aesthetic values," and on the next page noted that a civilization included the "accumulation of knowledge, skills, tools, arts, literature, laws,

4

religions and philosophies."[2] This second definition appears to include the material, meaning the economic and technological, factors as well. Kaplan argued that all these components of civilization could be found in the Jewish people, but in addition he postulated, like others, that the re-establishment of a national home in Palestine—as the Balfour Declaration called it—was a necessary answer to the question of how to assure the future of Judaism as a civilization. But even for Kaplan the term "civilization" was more a postulate than a reality. The Israeli sociologist Shmuel N. Eisenstadt contributed to the wider use of the term because notions of "religion," "nation," and even "people" were not adequate to understanding the history of the Jews. Their history also had to be seen as the history of a civilization, because this allowed for comparisons with other long-lasting civilizations.[3] Not surprisingly, the search for an appropriate term continues. Somewhere around the year 2000 a novel term appeared in print: "peoplehood," or its Hebrew equivalent *amiut*.[4] Time will tell whether this neologism for the Jews will make its way into spoken or written English.[5]

Civilizations, as well as the religions with which they are sometimes identical, are the largest and most enduring entities of world history. They have often outlasted states and empires. Today, interest in civilization is spreading beyond academia to governments and the larger public, whose members have been alerted by predictions that the world may be heading into a "clash of civilizations." "Global politics is the politics of civilization," says Samuel Huntington.[6] Historians and philosophers wrote comparative histories of civilizations long before the term itself was used. The most famous ancient example is the Greek "Father of History" Herodotus (ca. 484—425 BCE), whose *Histories* describe every civilization known to the Greeks of his time as well as the most consequential "clash of civilizations" of the time, the Greco-Persian wars. In the eighteenth century two great thinkers, among others, wrote world histories of civilization, never mentioning the term while still covering all the manifestations mentioned by Kaplan. One is Voltaire's *Essay on the Customs and Spirit of Nations and the Main Facts of History from Charlemagne until Today* of 1756; the other is Johann Gottfried Herder's *Ideas on the Philosophy of History of Mankind* of 1784-1791. These books, famous and widely read in their time, contain reflections on the rise and decline of nations and civilizations.

The noun "civilization" is a product of the European Enlightenment. It appeared after the middle of the eighteenth century in the main European languages—English, French, and German—and was derived form the earlier verb "to civilize."* Civilization was meant to set the world of progress apart

---

* In Italian the noun *civiltà,* meaning life in the city ("urbanity") as opposed to the primitive countryside is much older. It appears in the fourteenth century and goes

from more "primitive" people or "dark ages," a value judgment the world has partly or entirely discarded today. In English and French, civilization is generally an over-arching concept that includes both the material and cultural or non-material achievements of a people, its customs, and its political structures. In both languages, civilization has taken on a double meaning. Each people has an individual civilization or belongs to a family of closely related, say Latin, civilizations, but there is also a common civilization of mankind that includes scientific, technological, industrial, and even cultural trends and achievements in which all can take part. However, in German "Kultur" is superior to "Zivilisation." It represents spiritual and artistic achievements, which have a higher value than the merely technical and material ones that are mainly summarized under "Zivilisation." This study adopts the broad English or French use of the term, including its double meaning.

Civilizations define their own scope, according to their self-image and the goals they have set for themselves. This scope remains subject to change and is open to controversy when members of competing ideologies disagree. It can be all embracing as in the case of revealed religions claiming missions to convert the world, or more limited, as in the case of many tribal civilizations. Further, the definition of a civilization can depend on the criteria of the academic discipline asked to provide it.[7] The same civilization can express itself in many ways. It can be a *geographic space*, a *society*, an *economy*, a *collective mentality*, a *historical continuity*, or all of those put together. In the social science literature, the term *culture* is as widely used as *civilization*, but the dividing line between them is not always clear. This is true even in English: when British anthropologists began to use the term *culture* in the nineteenth century, they blurred the dividing line. When they spoke of indigenous or "primitive" cultures, they usually meant all of the groups' aspects, including the material and technical manifestations usually attributed to *civilization*.[8]

Although there is only one Jewish civilization, there are many Jewish cultures. David Biale's important 2002 book *Jewish Cultures*[9] shows that many different Jewish cultures emerged from the interactions of Jewish communities

---

perhaps back to Dante. Ancient languages such as Hebrew (see I, 2), Greek, and Latin have no exact synonym for civilization. The Chinese term for civilization is *wen ming*, literally "the beautiful writing," which conveys China's enormous respect for the written word. In Hebrew, a philologically exact synonym of *wen ming* would be *kitve kodesh*, "the holy scriptures," a term used in the Mishnah and other early rabbinic sources to refer to some books of the Bible, and much later extended to refer to the whole biblical canon. The Chinese term comes nearer to a pious Jew's understanding of the fundaments and goals of his own "civilization" than any Western term does. On *kitve kodesh* see Menachem H.Schmelzer, "How was the High Priest Kept Awake on the Night of Yom Ha-Kippurim," in *Studies in Jewish Bibliography and Medieval Jewish Poetry* (New York: Jewish Theological Seminary, 2006), 214ff.

6

with the cultures, languages, and religions of their host countries. It is important to keep this double nature of Jewish history in mind: it is one civilization and different but related cultures, or "multiple cultures operating within the apparently singular Jewish collective."[10]

Language is a problem. The Modern Hebrew *zivilisatzia* is a recent loanword taken from the Yiddish or Russian use of the term. The nearest original Hebrew term is *tarbut*, translated as culture, which appears only once in the Hebrew Bible, in a very negative sense: Moses scolds his people as "a breed (*tarbut*) of sinful men."[11] Rabbinic Hebrew continued to use the word, sometimes negatively and sometimes in a neutral sense, as "education, rearing."[12] Ahad Haam (1856-1927) was one of the most prominent Jewish writers of the early twentieth century who were concerned about the Jewish future. He generally used "people" or "nation" to describe the Jews, and worried that they may have lost their "national feeling," but semantic hair-splitting about the most appropriate term for the Jewish collective or heritage did not seem to interest him.[13] In the early twentieth century the term *tarbut* became important in Jewish cultural and Hebrew language movements in Central and Eastern Europe. More than one local cultural association or Hebrew day school has carried the name *Tarbut*. David Biale has defined Jewish culture as "the manifold expressions—written or oral, visual or textual, material or spiritual—with which human beings represent their lived experiences in order to give them meaning."[14] One would have to add that Jewish cultures express not only "lived experiences," but also the experiences of earlier generations. Otherwise, Biale's definition of culture is nearly identical to the more restricted English or French meaning of the term.

CHAPTER 2

At the Crossroads: The Trouble
with "Rising," "Thriving," and "Declining"

Calling periods "rising" or "declining," and the time between the two "thriving" (although the term will not often be used) is, at first sight, a value judgment: it reveals where the observer is coming from. The problem of personal subjectivity is never far. But rise and decline are not only value judgments. They are often objective historical trends that can be substantiated, with some caution, by eyewitness and other contemporaneous accounts, and more reliably by statistical data and/or archaeological excavations. This does not mean that it is always easy to identify rise or decline. If the period in question is near to our own time, it will be easier for a historian to gather evidence than if the period is remote. For example, Jonathan Israel, who will be discussed later, collected an enormous amount of detailed accounts and statistical data that prove the extraordinary economic, military, cultural and artistic rise and flourishing, but also the subsequent decline, of the Dutch Republic from the late sixteenth to the early eighteenth century.[1] His demonstration leaves no room for doubt. Another case, the decline and fall of the Roman Empire, was documented from the very beginning by contemporaries, but some historians challenged the conventional story in the 1970s and 1980s and replaced it with a story of peaceful "transition" and "transformation." Brian Ward-Perkins has convincingly refuted this interpretation by turning to a large number of recent archaeological discoveries that illustrate that the fall of the Western Roman Empire was indeed a bloody and catastrophic collapse.[2] But in other cases, the evidence is mixed or more difficult to obtain. Inevitably, the historian will be influenced by his or her own location in time and space, and by events that shaped his or her life or that occurred during his or her lifetime or shortly before. The historians in our sample are aware of their personal engagement in history, which reduces the risk of subjectivity in some cases but not all. The terms rise and decline have been applied to all entities enumerated above, not only civilizations but also cultures, empires, states, and more. The causes that determine rise and decline are similar for all such entities.

8

Apart from his or her own subjectivity, the historian has to cope with the subjectivity of available sources, which can also jeopardize objective judgment. There are five types of problems: contradictory trends during the same period of history, current or past ideologies, optical distortions, the difficulties of self-perception, and the transition from decline to transformation.

Contradictory Trends

Frequently there are contradictory trends within the same civilization. Rise and decline can occur simultaneously in the same geographic space. The best-known type of contradiction is a flourishing cultural and artistic life during or immediately after political decline, internal unrest, or military defeat. In fact, these cases are frequent enough to raise legitimate questions about whether there is a hidden, causal link between the two trends. Do external catastrophes stimulate cultural innovation and creativity? There are examples from ancient as well as modern history. The Chinese regarded the destruction of the Song Empire by the Mongols as a terrible national catastrophe, and the Mongol Yuan Dynasty (1279-1368) as a profound humiliation, but the Yuan also launched a period of enormous creative renewal in Chinese art, particularly in painting and ceramics. The styles and innovations introduced during the Yuan period remained authoritative over many centuries. Was this rise or decline? Likewise Venice, a city-state and a small civilization in its own right, with a unique form of government, culture, self-awareness, and dialect, began to decline from the sixteenth century on because it had to give way to the rise of other, stronger sea powers, and because international trade routes had changed. During the following three centuries Venice lost, one by one, all its trading, political, and military powers, but developed much of the beautiful literature, art, and refined living for which it has been admired ever since. Rise or decline? During the same centuries, Ottoman art and literature flourished while Ottoman armies lost battle after battle and the Empire went into steep decline. Modern examples include the amazing flourishing of French literature, music, poetry, impressionist painting, architecture, and other arts—an explosion of creativity in every direction—soon after the French defeat in the Franco-Prussian War of 1870 and the subsequent internal bloodshed, and the blossoming of literature, art, and theatre in Germany after its defeat in World War I and the economic catastrophe that followed.

Ideology

The historian has to watch out for political and religious ideologies that stamp certain periods with a "rise" or "decline" label. In such cases the value-dependence of the terms rise and decline is blatant. The defenders of rise or decline ideologies generally make sure that evidence that disagrees with them never comes to light. Ancient empires and modern dictatorships have been masters of this art. The ideological "labeling" can start at the beginning of the relevant period or many generations later, when ancient history is used as a tool for political and propagandistic purposes. In many such cases, subsequent generations will switch the label to its opposite. The Nazis called the period beginning in 1933 the greatest rise in German history, but it turned out to be its greatest fall. There are numerous examples, but most are not as clear-cut as the German case.

Civilizations do not always reach consensus on their respective pasts, even without political or religious censorship. Political and ethical criteria change over time, and that can radically modify the understanding a people has of itself and its past. What was glory and success to contemporaries might in retrospect appear to their descendants as the beginning of decline and fall, and vice versa. This is particularly true when radical changes, such as the end of imperial rule or foreign occupation, or a revolution and civil war, leave lasting discord in the collective memory of a people. Frenchmen who participated in the French Revolution and the victorious Napoleonic wars saw these periods as a time of rise and power. The following generations, particularly that of the Restoration, judged the same events with less enthusiasm. Chinese history presents an opposite case. The long reign of the powerful emperor of the Western Han dynasty, Wudi (157-87 BCE), was by most objective criteria a period of great rise. China's territory expanded, and the material culture of its elites developed conspicuously. Confucian scholarship, as well as arts and poetry, flourished. But the great Chinese historian Sima Qian, who lived at this time and knew the emperor and his court, did not consider it a great period of Chinese history. He noted the exhaustion of the economy, the suffering of the people in the wake of war, and the corruption and inhumanity of many of its officials.

Optical Distortion

The third problem, optical distortion, occurs because of the temporal relativity of the concepts of rise, thriving, and decline. Each of the three is what it is because of its relation to the two others, and each is a function of time. Rise is rise and decline is decline in comparison to what came before or what followed after. When the decline of a civilization or a nation leads to collapse and fall, the case seems clear. But some cases are not clear, particularly when periods considered as decline by later generations are long, drawn-out processes. The optical impact of a "Golden Age" can be prejudicial for all later periods: inevitably they become "decline." For Gibbon, the decline of the Roman Empire went on for many centuries, until the fall of Constantinople in

1453, but this process included centuries of Byzantine military victories and economic, cultural, and religious prosperity.

A similar observation has been made about Islamic civilization, which many see as in continuous decline since the thirteenth or fourteenth century because they compare all Islamic history to the preceding Golden Age of the Caliphate—quite erroneously, as Marshall Hodgson asserts.[3] The problem of optical distortion and the difficulty of distinguishing periods are particularly acute in a history that it is long and still continuing. "Western history will only become visible at full length...after the Western society has become extinct," as Toynbee wrote.[4] The same holds true for Jewish history. Every generation can interpret it anew and see past rise or decline in light of the most recent events, whereas most histories of civilization were written toward their end, or long after. "The owl of Minerva spreads its wings only after dusk has fallen," said Friedrich Hegel.

The Difficulty of Self-Perception

No civilization or nation can see itself in a completely objective light, just as no individual human being can do so. The difficulty of self-perception is not identical with ideology or optical distortion, although erroneous self-perception can also become an ideology. Ideology includes the deliberate re-writing and distortion of history for political or religious purposes, whereas erroneous self-perceptions are not intentional. Optical distortion can trouble the view of an observer who looks at a civilization from a distance in time, whereas erroneous self-perception is a contemporaneous, inside problem. A civilization can decline but take no notice of it because the process is slow and not easily perceptible. Gibbon noted that the Romans living between the second and fourth centuries CE were happy and unaware that their civilization was declining.[5] But the Romans were not alone in being wrong or complacent.

When a civilization reaches a peak of power and prosperity, it cannot fathom the possibility of decline and fall. Imperial China reached such a peak in the mid-eighteenth century, but began to be battered by rebellions, foreign interventions, and economic crises from the end of that century on. Its rulers and most of its intellectuals did not grasp that the Chinese empire was unraveling, and believed until late in the nineteenth century that their country was suffering only temporary mishaps.

Decline Leading to Transformation

In an ongoing history with an open future, such as Jewish history, there is an important issue beyond rise and decline: that of historic transformation. It is the events of an unknown future will decide how coming generations evaluate, for example, twentieth-century Jewish history. Did it include the greatest catastrophe since the fall of the Second Temple and the final end of a long history, delayed for only a few decades by a last, gigantic effort and a short-lived flicker of hope? Or was it the greatest catastrophe since the fall of the Second Temple, leading to a radical transformation and the greatest and longest period of national and cultural rise the Jewish people had known in nearly two thousand years? Decline and fall, or transformation and new rise? Observers looking back immediately after a major historic shift will more readily see decline, rupture, and fall than transformation. It may take a sharper historical eye and a greater distance from the event to detect old, long-lasting features reemerging in new forms. Even at a distance and after the dust has settled, historians can have different views. Jacob Burckhardt saw the Renaissance as a break with the past, the beginning of our modern world.[6] Johan Huizinga contradicted him and kept repeating that there was no sharp borderline, but a slow and profound transformation of a waning epoch, in this case the Middle Ages, into a new one.[7] There are several types of historical transformation, some slow and gradual, others fast and radical. Jewish history has known both. Part IV, chapters 13 and 14, will discuss the drivers of fast and radical transformation in two relatively modern cases, the Dutch Republic in the seventeenth century and Turkey in the twentieth century.

It should be made clear here that the difficulties caused by contradictory trends, ideologies, optical distortions, problems of self-perception, and the issue of transformation do not invalidate the objective nature of rise or decline. Rather, they point to pitfalls the historian can avoid in most cases if he or she watches out for them.

CHAPTER 3

A Selection of Historians:
Three Categories

The night before he was defeated in battle and killed himself, King Saul[1] called the ghost of the prophet Samuel back from the dead and questioned him about the future of Israel. We will ask similar questions of the ghosts of thirteen "seers" who are dead, and add nine more who are alive. Except for three (Bernard Lewis, Jonathan Israel, Jared Diamond), all are non-Jews, as far as could be ascertained, and only two, Bernard Lewis and Jonathan Israel, have competence in specific periods of Jewish history. The authors chosen include some of the most famous names of the past, but also some contemporary historians and political scientists. These historians and philosophers belong to three different categories, although a few of them are on the borderline and could be put into two of the groups.

Monographies

Eleven authors studied rise and decline in one or two civilizations. They are Thucydides (Greece), Sima Qian (China), Gibbon and Ward-Perkins (Rome), Ibn Khaldun (Islam and the Arabs), Burckhardt (Constantine the Great, the Italian Renaissance), Hodgson (Islam), Lewis (Turkey), Huizinga (North European Renaissance, Dutch Republic), Braudel (France, the Mediterranean—note, however, that Braudel could also be placed into either of the next two groups), and J.I. Israel (Dutch Republic, Jews in the seventeenth century). All of them assume that the relevance of their story goes beyond the few cases they are investigating, and that generally valid principles governing the history of many civilizations can be learned from a serious in-depth study of one. Thucydides stated this most candidly.[2] Gibbon believed the same, but said so more indirectly. To Ibn Khaldun, it was obvious that the patterns he discovered in studying the history of his people and faith applied to all civilized people.[3] Modern historians in our sample do not say this so openly, but their conclusions and generalizations leave no doubt that they too are looking for broader meaning in individual history. Over-specialized academic historians may write only for other specialists, but most historians would like their books to have a meaning beyond one particular group, city or nation.

Comparative Histories

Other authors do not start with one civilization but with a comparison of several, with the aim of discovering similar or identical patterns of development, including those of rise and decline. They argue that such similarities express patterns of history that are likely to apply to many other civilizations as well. Oswald Spengler (who could also be placed in the next group), Arnold Toynbee, Paul Kennedy, and Jared Diamond belong to this group, and so does Max Weber, with some reservation. Weber shows that religion can affect economic history in every civilization, albeit in different ways. Burckhardt and Braudel have to be included in this group as well, because in addition to monographies, they also drew comparisons.

Universal Histories Governed by a Single Principle

Authors in the third category are looking for a single principle that guides and articulates all of history. There must be a grand scheme in which every civilization has a place and all dance to the same music. The search for an overarching principle of history is old: it was born in religion and survived in philosophy of history. Our selection of authors includes several who search for a comprehensive theory of history: Pitirim Sorokin, Joseph Tainter, Peter Turchin, Christopher Chase-Dunn, Thomas D. Hall, and Mancur Olson. These authors, Jared Diamond included, are not academic historians but geographers, anthropologists, mathematicians, or economists who use a different methodology to look at rise and decline. They entered history from a side door, which is in itself a new and encouraging development that could bring new perspectives to an old discipline. Except for Sorokin, all see the history of civilizations as driven by socio-economic and other material factors, or determined by unchanging economic, mechanical, or mathematical laws. They write "quantitative" or "structural" history. Authors of this group do not recognize Judaism as a civilization because it is not visible on their geographic map and has no permanent economic sub-structure. Jewish civilization is based, *inter alia*, on spiritual continuity and creative leadership, which these authors do not acknowledge as autonomous drivers of history. There are many more theories of this kind, and the search for new ones will probably go on forever.*

---

* Among the important books of this category is William H. McNeill, *The Rise of the West: A History of the Human Community* (Chicago: University of Chicago Press, 1963), which is in many ways a variation of Hegel's theme, and more recently, Jared Diamond,

A Review of the Selection Process

What the authors of all three groups have in common is that they belong to a minority brand of "macro-historians," that is, historians who examine long-term trends and large-scale historical phenomena, such as rise and decline.

It is certainly possible to question the selection of the authors. Are they the right ones? Was a better choice possible? Nearly any selection of this nature would have included the most famous names: Thucydides, Ibn Khaldun, Gibbon, Spengler, Burckhardt, Toynbee, and Braudel. Other scholars may have included some of the modern authors in the present sample, maybe B. Lewis and J. Israel, but would have replaced others. Certainly the absence of many ancient and modern historians who described the rise and decline of major civilizations is a shortcoming. Some historians who would have been of interest are ancient Greek, Roman, Chinese, Byzantine, and Ottoman authors, but also nineteenth- and twentieth-century historians who have not followed the current specialization trend. The omission of the main Jewish world historians has already been explained: they do not apply lessons from the general history of rise and decline to the Jews, which is the purpose of this book. Instead they see Jewish history as a unique, continuous and ongoing process. The nineteenth-century philosopher Nachman Krochmal did see rise and decline in Jewish history, but his work had little impact and is today largely forgotten. In any event, it is unlikely that a different selection would dramatically change the results of the inquiry. The main factors of rise and decline appear in the works of most of the included authors. Whatever the number of additional books one might read, they are not likely to invalidate the main lessons of history derived from the selected authors. A different selection of authors might change the relative weight of some of the main factors, or add one or two more, but the overall picture would likely remain the same.

Guns, Germs and Steel: The Fates of Human Societies (New York: Norton, 1997), which sees all Eurasian history as dominated by the combined force of geography, demography, ecology and food.

CHAPTER 4

On Philosophy of History

Many historians who look at longer periods adhere to a general concept, or a philosophy of history. The two main traditional philosophies are cyclical or linear.

Cyclical and Linear Theories

A first and historically earlier strand of thought sees history forever moving in cycles, with no foreseeable end. This concept was shared by much of the ancient Orient, Greece, India, and China, among other civilizations. A second philosophy sees history not as circular but linear: it has a beginning and an end, and it has a purpose. Many believe that the Jews were the inventors of linear history, or at least its best-known adherents and most effective interpreters. The Romanian historian of religion Mircea Eliade saw the Jewish prophets as the first to overcome the long-lasting, predominant view of history as an "eternal return." The Jews discovered history as an ongoing manifestation of the will of one single divinity. Eliade regards monotheism as a precondition of linear history writing.[1] Recent philosophers of history tried to combine both theories: they believe in a beginning and an end, and in the existence of cycles between the two. Toynbee and Sorokin are among these.

All philosophy of history is originally religious, and so is the linear history concept. Human history is progressive; it is the history of salvation, the manifestation of the divine will or the human response to it. From Judaism this concept spread to Christianity and Islam, and from there it received various secular interpretations which have dominated historic and political thought during the last three centuries. In the eighteenth century, the Enlightenment saw this linearity in the apparently inexorable moral and civilizational "progress" of mankind, an idea the twentieth century has secularized a second time and converted into the currently widespread belief in economic growth rates as measures of "progress." In the nineteenth century Hegel formulated the most influential philosophical version of the linear concept of history. His *Lectures on the Philosophy of History* of

1837 described world history as a continuous progress of the spirit of reason, begun with the Greeks and Romans and carried forward by European Christianity and the German nation toward the ever-expanding victory of freedom. Christianity here remains the standard-bearer of human progress. Karl Marx adopted Hegel's linear concept and claimed that the Communist revolution he propagated would bring about the "end of history" as we know it and inaugurate an era of equality, justice, and peace.

Jewish Philosophy of History

Traditional Judaism sees history moving ahead in a linear direction, driven by religious-spiritual causes and events. This is true for the biblical, talmudic, and medieval historiographies and even for the first secular Jewish histories of nineteenth-century Germany.[2] History has a point zero, the creation of the world, and a high point, the revelation of the Torah, although the sages of the Talmud asserted that the Torah existed and was obeyed by the patriarchs long before Israel received it on Mount Sinai.[3] All following history, then, was the transmission of the divine laws. The guiding model for this concept of history is the famous first passage of the Mishnah's *Sayings of the Fathers*: "Moses received Torah from Sinai and handed it on to Joshua and Joshua to the Elders, and the Elders to the Prophets, and the Prophets handed it on to the men of the Great Assembly."[4] A thousand years later, the Spanish-Jewish historian Abraham Ibn-Daud[5] continued the story of transmission in exactly the same fashion, as if nothing else of importance had happened between the second and twelfth centuries CE: the sages of the Mishnah handed the Torah on to the sages of the Gemarah, who passed it on to the Saboraim, and the Saboraim handed it to the Geonim, and the Geonim handed it on, finally, to the Jewish sages of Spain—Ibn Daud's contemporaries.

Even in the nineteenth century, the immensely influential Heinrich Graetz (1817-1891), who wrote the first comprehensive Jewish history in modern times, saw this history as a mirror of a single religious idea. Jewish history was first and foremost the history of Judaism, not that of a physical entity. Judaism was the negation of paganism, the revelation of a transcendent spiritual God. It is in the work of the next great Jewish world historian, Simon Dubnow (1860-1941), that one can detect this old tradition breaking down. Dubnow called into question the concept of a single idea, and his main work, his world history of the Jewish people, presents a national rather than a primarily religious concept of Jewish history. His book title speaks of the "Jewish people," whereas Graetz' title speaks of "the Jews." It took a long time before he arrived at this watershed. Before reaching it, he formulated, in a small book of 1903, a philosophy of Jewish history that drove the spiritual concept to an extreme. "Jewry at all times, even in the period of political independence, was pre-eminently a spiritual nation...Jewry...cannot suffer annihilation: the body, the mold may be destroyed, the spirit is immortal."[6] He would abandon this philosophy later. In 1941, Dubnow's death in Riga, where the Nazis murdered him along with the overwhelming majority of Latvia's Jews, did not demonstrate his imaginary "Jewish immortality without Jews" but rather the danger and absurdity of such a notion.

The Galician philosopher Nachman Krochmal (1785-1840) is the only known Jewish author to propose a cyclical theory, albeit always within the traditional linear construction of a beginning and a final end. Krochmal is generally associated with the Jewish Enlightenment (*Haskalah*). He developed his cyclical idea into a new philosophy of Jewish history. His *Moreh Nebukhe ha-Zman* (*Guide for the Perplexed of the Time*)[7] explains that all nations have to first go through a stage of "germination and growth," followed by one of "power and achievement," and must end in one of "decomposition and extinction." This extinction is final—for every group but the Jews. They too have to go through this cycle, but after each end there is a "renewal." Jewish history has, so far, completed three cycles: the first from Abraham to the destruction of the First Temple in 586 BCE, culminating in the middle in the period of David and Solomon; the second from the exile in Babylonia to the fall of Betar in 138 CE, culminating in the successful Maccabean revolt; the third from 138 CE to the Chmielnicki massacres in Ukraine in 1648/49, culminating in the history of Spanish Judaism. There are, thus, three periods of "power and achievement," similar to Golden Ages, but Krochmal does not use this term. His book is unfinished; his third cycle is only a sketch, and it is not clear whether he believed that a new cycle had already begun.

The "Axial Age"

This book will occasionally mention one philosophical theory of universal history that was influential in the twentieth century. It is introduced in *The Origin and Goal of History* by the German philosopher Karl Jaspers.[8] Jaspers saw our world as an outcome of the greatest spiritual and ethical revolution in human history, an "Axial Age" from approximately 600 to 400 BCE that changed our ways of thinking and feeling more fundamentally than any other period of history had. He called this age the "axis" of world history. After 1945, Jaspers was looking for a new unifying spiritual principle of world history, common to all mankind and transcending differences of civilization. This could no longer be the Western, Christian view of world history. He quotes a famous phrase of Hegel, which underlies the Christian view: "All history moves to Christ and comes from Christ. The axis of world history is the appearance of God's Son."[9] Jaspers breaks this axis and rejects Hegel's concept of history, but retains his term. He postulates that it is the ancient

Jews with their prophets, the Chinese with Confucius and Laozi, the Indians with Buddha, and the Greeks with their great philosophers who determined, during the same two or three centuries but independently from each other, the spiritual progress of human civilization. It is because of the communality of these great philosophical and moral traditions that early historians who are their spiritual heirs, e.g. Thucydides or Sima Qian share a certain humanism, a concept of morality beyond their own ethnicity and a sensitivity to suffering that the Jewish prophets, who never heard of them but lived in the same period, could have understood and endorsed.

CHAPTER 5

Obstacles to Foresight

The selected twenty-three historians ignored some important future shaping trends and, when they attempted to look into the future, committed foresight errors. Anticipating history is extremely difficult, due to the inherently unpredictable nature of the historical process and the limits of the human mind.

The Future Will Not be Like the Past

A critical question is whether old or contemporary authors can see the new factors that will determine rise and decline in the future. In the twentieth century, the world changed faster than in any century during the preceding fifteen hundred years, and changes will only accelerate in the twenty-first century. A reader in 1900 would be shocked and confused by the world of 2000; a reader of 2000 who could take a glimpse at the world of 2100 might no longer recognize his or her planet. In 1967, Herman Kahn published a once famous but now forgotten book, *The Year 2000: A Framework for Speculation on the Next Thirty-Three Years*. It contained no reference to the environment as an issue of major relevance in 2000, and barely touched upon the beginning informatics revolution that would radically change the world's economies and societies, but did predict that by 2000 Japan's economy would be larger than America's. Needless to say, many other twentieth-century authors concerned with the evolution of civilizations could also not foresee the environmental crisis in its global historical context. In general, the increasing speed of advances in science and technology, and the unpredictability of their applications, will make foresight more and more difficult. In 1987 Paul Kennedy predicted an inevitable decline of American power because, he contended, the country's military expenditures were apparently undermining its economy.[1] He could not foresee any better than Herman Kahn that the nascent informatics revolution would greatly boost American productivity and economic growth.

What other major issues are looming today that nobody sees as factors of future rise and decline? The danger that nuclear weapons might put an end to all civilization deeply troubled Toynbee,[2] but he saw it exclusively as a consequence of the East-West confrontation and invested all his public efforts in improving the East-West relationship and accommodating the Soviet Union. The idea that the Soviet Union could disappear and that its dreaded weapons might fall into the hands of smaller, unstable countries and terrorists apparently never crossed his mind. Is this a new factor nobody could imagine before? Could a few terrorists with doomsday weapons exterminate a whole civilization? There is another, much deeper and slower-moving issue that has begun to modify our civilizations. It is the inexorable rise of women in society. The daily skirmishes about women's rights in every country of the world can easily cause one to forget how recent and revolutionary this trend is: history's first certified female doctor received her university degree in 1849, the first lawyer was admitted to the bar in 1869, and the first female chemistry student was admitted to MIT in 1873—all three in the United States. Only two of our twenty-three authors pays any attention to women. The exceptions are Jonathan Israel and Jacob Burckhardt, who saw periods of great cultural flourishing coincide with great improvements in the education and freedom of women.[3] Many policy analysts agree that the condition of women is becoming a key indicator of a society's competitiveness and success. What this may imply for the rise or decline of an entire civilization cannot yet be understood. There are already more female than male university students in several countries, and in science, engineering, law, and management the proportion of females is rising steadily. Is it likely that all major public decisions affecting the future of a civilization—regarding external and internal policies, war and peace, religion, economics, science, and more—will continue to be taken almost exclusively by men as they have been in the last 5000 years, or will women make decisions in the same way and with the same motivations as men?

Good Theories Do Not Guarantee Good Forecasts

Many assume that a good theory of civilizations will allow for a reasonably good forecast of the future. This is what the historian Fernand Braudel believed, but often this is not the case.[4] Braudel himself developed a compelling theory of history based on the "long duration" forces underlying daily events, but his own future forecasts of 1962 were mostly wrong. Some of Toynbee's theories of history, such as the "challenge-and-response" idea, are relatively convincing, but many of his predictions turned out to be far off the mark, and some are just absurd.[5] In contrast, Spengler developed no convincing theory of history. His thesis that the world consisted of eight independent cultures that were born and had to grow and die like all living organisms is not history but a poetic or biological metaphor. Yet he made some of the most accurate predictions of the future trends of our civilization of all the scholars studied here.

There are several reasons for mismatches between theories and forecasts. One is that even good theories do not include surprise developments, which by their very nature can invalidate specific forecasts. Also, making good forecasts takes exceptional intuition more than explicit theories, and may also require the forecaster to break with his cultural and intellectual milieu. Spengler broke with his milieu. Germany's powerful university professors had rejected and ridiculed him, and he despised them. In contrast, Toynbee and Braudel were celebrated in their countries' elite universities and involved themselves in various public and governmental policy issues. Intuition is not easily acquired, and breaking with one's milieu can be a costly process with no guarantee that it will lead to better historical understanding.

Cultural Bias

An axiom of this book, as emphasized in the introduction, is that Jewish history is subject to tangible factors of rise and decline. When it is examined from this angle, it is not a singularity: it has parallels in other civilizations. But not everybody accepts this axiom. The Jews were the first to discuss the matter with intensity. Traces of debates that took place in the second, third, and subsequent centuries CE can be found in the Talmud. "Said Rabbi Haninah: 'The planets (the zodiac which in ancient beliefs determines the fate of people) give wisdom, the planets give wealth, and Israel is subject to the planets.' Rabbi Yohanan said: 'Israel is not subject to the planets,' and Rabbi Yohanan was coherent in his views, because he said: 'from where (do we know) that Israel is not subject to the planets? Because it is written (quoting Jeremiah 10:2), 'Thus says the Lord, do not learn to go the way of the nations, and do not be dismayed by portents in the sky—let the nations be dismayed by them.'"[6] This and other discussions show agreement that there were laws of history, as they were then understood, but no unanimity on whether the same laws applied to the Jews. The majority opinion was that they did not. Many of the historians of Part II have no more than a limited understanding of Jewish history, and some who analyzed various civilizations ignored the Jews. Perhaps this void is due to a certain cultural bias. It is not the same kind of bias as the belief of the talmudic sages, but it has similar consequence on historical thought. Nobody could have defined the problem more frankly than Toynbee himself did toward the end of his professional life, when he made an extraordinary confession that has few parallels in historiography:

> It is difficult for anyone brought up in the Christian tradition to shake himself free of the official Christian ideology. He may have discarded Christian

22

doctrine consciously on every point, yet on this particular point (the Jews) he may find that he is still being influenced subconsciously....If I had happened to be brought up in the Muslim tradition instead of the Christian one, no doubt my outlook would have been affected correspondingly....I am aware of my neglect of Israel, Judah, the Jews and Judaism. I have neglected these out of proportion to their true importance....When Jewish critics accuse me of seeing Judaism not through Jewish eyes, but through those of the Christian Church...I have to plead guilty to the charge.[7]

One may say that historians raised in a Christian, Muslim, liberal, or left-wing cultural environment cannot be completely objective toward the Jews because Jewish history creates ideological problems for them. Similarly, it would be equally difficult for a Jewish historian to study the rise and decline of the Jewish people in complete neutrality.

PART II

HISTORIANS ON RISE
AND DECLINE

———

Introduction

Twenty-three historians have inspired this book. As two of them are co-authors (Chase-Dunn and Hall), this section contains only twenty-two chapters analyzing pertinent theories of rise and decline.

The listing order of these historians reflects their approximate importance, their influence on later and ongoing historical thought, and, until the early twentieth century, more or less also their birth year. The first fourteen, until J. Israel, have made lasting contributions which can be found all though this book. The next three (Kennedy, Diamond, and Ward-Perkins) have made additional, innovative analyses of specific rise-and-decline cases. The last five (or six if Chase-Dunn and Hall are counted separately), all of the late twentieth century, offer a variety of mono-causal explanations of rise and decline which claim universal validity. They are of little or no use for the understanding of Jewish history.

Prior to reading in depth about each of the figures discussed, let us consider each of them briefly.

1. *Thucydides (Greece, ca. 460-400 BCE)*: Author of *Peloponnesian War,* analyzing Athens' self-destruction and fall.
2. *Sima Qian (China, ca. 145-90 BCE)*: Father of Chinese historiography, upheld beliefs that history is moving in cycles and that leadership quality plays a crucial role.
3. *Ibn Khaldun (Tunisia, 1332-1406)*: Detailed theories of emergence of civilizations; believed Arab decline was due to loss of science and scholarship.
4. *Edward Gibbon (UK, 1737-1794)*: Author of *Decline and Fall of the Roman Empire,* the most famous book on decline, believed that Rome destroyed itself, mainly for internal reasons.
5. *Jacob Burckhardt (Switzerland, 1818-1897)*: Author of influential *Culture of the Renaissance in Italy,* believed that Golden Ages are short and unexplainable.
6. *Max Weber (Germany, 1864-1920)*: Author of *Sociology of Religions,* believed that religions can create or stifle a civilization.

7. *Oswald Spengler (Germany, 1880-1936)*: Author of *Decline of the West*, argued that all civilizations must rise, decline, and die, like living organisms.

8. *Johan Huizinga (Netherlands, 1872-1945)*: Author of *Autumn of the Middle Ages*, emphasizing slow transformation, not rupture, as the main mover of history.

9. *Arnold Toynbee (UK, 1889-1975)*: Believed that world history is the story of twenty-three civilizations, which emerge as "responses" to "challenges."

10. *Pitirim Sorokin (USA, 1889-1968)*: Believed that history consists of cyclical alternations between materialism and idealism.

11. *Fernand Braudel (France, 1902-1985)*: Believed that history is determined by deep forces of "long duration," more than rise or decline.

12. *Marshall G.S. Hodgson (USA, 1922-1968)*: Author of *Venture of Islam*, argued that both the rise and the "decadence" of Islam were conditioned by external forces.

13. *Bernard Lewis (USA, 1916—)*: Author of *Emergence of Modern Turkey*, describing the road from decline and collapse to transformation and new rise.

14. *Jonathan I. Israel (USA, 1946—)*: Author of *The Dutch Republic: Its Rise, Greatness and Fall*, analyzing the transformation of a small country into a great power and its subsequent decline.

15. *Paul Kennedy (USA, 1945—)*: Author of *Rise and Fall of the Great Powers*, asserting that great powers lose wars and decline for economic reasons only.

16. *Jared Diamond (USA, 1937—)*: Author of *Collapse*, describing the self-destruction of civilizations that ravaged their natural environment.

17. *Bryan Ward-Perkins (UK, 1952—)*: Believes that the fall of Rome caused the end of a great material civilization, and that this could happen again.

18. *Mancur Olson (USA, 1932-1998)*: Believed that GDP growth rates explain rise and fall.

19. *Peter Turchin (USA, 1957—)*: Believes that macro-history is subject to mathematical laws.

20. *Christopher Chase-Dunn (USA, 1944—)* and *Thomas D. Hall (USA, 1946—)*: Believe that rise and demise are determined by continent-wide or global trends.

21. *Joseph A. Tainter (USA, 1949—)*: Believes that civilizations fall due to growing complexity.

22. *Arthur Herman (USA, 1956—)*: Believes that decline theories are ideologies born of Europe's cultural pessimism.

CHAPTER 1

Thucydides
Greece, ca. 460-400 BCE [1]

The History of the Peloponnesian War by Thucydides is the earliest known descriptions of the decline and fall of the cultural center of a great civilization, and one of the most compelling such volumes ever written. This war lasted almost thirty years (431-404 BCE) and caused the destruction of a large part of Greece, including Athens and many of its enemies. Athens' impoverishment and loss of independence marked the end of what is generally considered the most creative phase of Greek culture and art, although Greek philosophy and literature continued, and Hellenic civilization survived in many forms and even expanded geographically. Athens' classical period and its power were over, and soon Macedonia would swallow all that remained of Greece.

Thucydides has been called the founder of historiography. He took history out of the realm of mythology and for the first time made it plain that the fates of men were determined by their own actions and social organization, as Sima Qian would show three centuries later in China. Thucydides belonged to the old Athenian nobility, linked by family bonds to Miltiades, who had helped defeat the Persians two generations earlier. He owned a gold mine in Thrace and described himself as rich and powerful. He was a general in the war, and had sailed with seven ships to save a city from the hands of the Spartan general Brasidas, but arrived a few hours too late. As punishment, Athens banished him for twenty years. He mentioned the episode briefly, without recrimination or self-justification, and spoke respectfully of his enemy.[2] Late Hellenistic commentators suggested that his general criticism of Athens was an act of personal revenge, but later historians refuted this suspicion as petty-minded. Thucydides' history is incomplete—it stops abruptly, which lends credence to the suspicion that he was murdered.

For Thucydides, the yearning for power dominates human nature and hence all of human history. A historian who wants to explain the fate of nations must understand the psychology of power, how it affects human thought and action, and why it so often leads to tragedy. During his banishment Thucydides sought access to all parties involved in the Peloponnesian War, interrogated all witnesses, and kept searching for the truth about it. This was very difficult, he wrote, because what the witnesses told him about the same events varied according to their political biases and memories. However, his relentless cross-examinations eventually led him to the secret reason that drove the belligerents. The warring Greek parties gave many reasons for the war, but concealed the truest and deepest one: Sparta's hidden fear of the steadily growing power of Athens. Thucydides did not write for entertainment, he said, but for the "perpetual custody"[3] of those who wanted to see the past more clearly so that they could better understand the future. There are permanent laws of history because human nature, unchangeable as it is, will ensure that similar reasons will always have similar consequences. His analysis of the human passions, deceptions, and illusions, the fear and greed that determined this war, had a long-lasting effect on Western historical thought.

Thucydides expected from the very beginning that this war would become "more memorable than all earlier ones." "It was by far the most powerful convulsion for the Greeks and a part of the Barbarians, I would even say for all of mankind,"[4] and more important than the Persian Wars, which shows how difficult it is for a contemporary to appreciate the long-term historical implications of a major event he witnesses himself. All later historians would agree that the Greek victory over the Persians was a more decisive watershed not only in Greek history, but also in European and world history, yet Thucydides apparently did not see this.

Athens' Rise and Glory

Thucydides does not elaborate on a theory of rise, thriving, and decline, but all three themes are present in his work. He begins with the rise of Attica. The richer a province, the more often it will change hands, because the high-quality soil provokes internal fights and attracts the greed of foreign invaders. Athens, by contrast, was for a long time free of internal disturbances due to the poverty of its soil. It did not attract greedy invaders but rather people who were expelled from other, troublesome provinces, and were seeking a safe haven. They became citizens and greatly increased the size and wealth of the city. Arnold Toynbee (II, 7) would take up Thucydides' theory and explain that the "arid soil" not only of Attica but also of Israel was the kind of "challenge" that could lead to the emergence of great civilizations.[5]

What Thucydides saw as the reasons for Athens' prosperity and success can be gleaned from his summary of Pericles' famous funeral oration for the city's war dead in 431 BCE.[6] Thucydides reported Pericles' glorification of the city's apogee in words he certainly approved himself—he admired Pericles as the greatest statesman the city ever had. Pericles saw Athens' greatness in its constitution, its respect for the rule of law, the freedom and equality of its citizens and the climate of tolerance between neighbors of different persuasions and lifestyles. It offered the greatest opportunities to the free development of every individual, and Pericles extols its uniqueness. Its democratic constitution does not follow any foreign laws. Public prestige accrues through merit, not origin, and poverty does not prevent anyone from contributing to the city. Athenians alone are preoccupied in equal measure with their personal well-being and that of the city, and whoever does not participate in public affairs is not called a "quiet" citizen, but a "bad" one. Even in war Athenians are different from all others: they close the city to nobody and expel no foreigners out of fear of espionage, because "we trust less in…deceptions than in our own eagerness for action and courage."[7] Pericles approves his city's imperial policy. Athens achieved access to every country and sea through its daring, and what it created in the wide world will remain as a monument to its endeavors for all times to come. For these reasons, Athens has become the model for all Greeks and attracts what is good from the rest of the world.

Thucydides' (that is Pericles') description of what would later be called Athens's "Golden Age" probably embellishes reality, but it is memorable because it does not emphasize the power, expansion, and wealth that were the trademark of most other Golden Ages, but rather the city's civic qualities. There is no dread of foreigners, but neither is there the kind of "multi-culturalism" that destroyed the Roman Empire according to Gibbon,[8] and no need is felt for safeguarding cultural borders and identity. Pericles' words show a secure faith in Athens' unquestionable superiority and attractiveness.

The Role of Leadership in Athens' Rise and Decline

Thucydides shows how his beloved city and its power and glory were destroyed. There is no doubt in his mind that leadership is the single most important factor of the rise and decline of nations and civilizations. Great leaders can save a nation and ensure its well-being; bad leaders destroy it. Athens had both. Thucydides sketches in a few phrases the nature of its two greatest leaders, and that of its most dangerous leader as well. Themistocles saved Greece from the Persians, and Pericles maintained Athens' greatness and won its first victories in the Peloponnesian War, but Alcibiades caused the city's fall. From Thucydides' biographies one could draw a typology of good and bad leadership. Of Themistocles he said, "Without prior instruction or subsequent deliberation, and thanks to his innate intelligence, he recognized without fail and after short reflection the problem that had to be settled instantaneously. His ability to assess what was likely to happen in the longer term was unmatched, and even when he lacked experience he did not lack apt judgment. Even in situations of uncertainty he was supreme in foreseeing the possibilities for good or evil. In one word: through force of genius, and almost without education, this man was excellent like nobody else in instinctively making the right decisions, guided by the inspiration of the moment."[9] Themistocles' genius was his natural instinct. World history has known other great rulers with little education but a sixth sense and exceptional intuition, particularly in conditions of crisis and war, but their appearance is rare and a matter of chance, and their skills cannot be easily acquired or recognized in advance.

Pericles' genius was of a different nature. He was a man of great culture and education, and prudent by nature. He had a sharp analytical intellect and a vast knowledge of human psychology and quantitative facts. His qualities were already apparent before the war, "when he guided his city with moderation and maintained its safety,"[10] and when the war broke out it turned out that he had "correctly calculated the balance of forces." His foresight became even clearer after his death. Thucydides is convinced that the Athenians could have won the war had they only followed the advice of Pericles, who warned them to remain cautious, not to expand their empire while the war lasted, nor to overestimate their forces, and to attack the enemy where he was weak, on sea, and not on land where he was strong. But they did exactly the opposite. As long as Pericles lived, he "dominated the masses, empowered by his prestige and intelligence, and because he was unblemished and incorruptible by money." Thucydides' emphasis on the absence of corruption as a condition of greatness and of the capacity to govern is noteworthy, for he points to a problem that has accompanied leadership all through history, to this day. But his theme is not morality; it is power politics. Only because Pericles was known to be irreproachable in his personal life and financial dealings could he speak to the people as bluntly as he did. He did not tell them what they wanted to hear just to remain in power, but had enough standing to contradict them in anger. When they were over-confident he unnerved them, and when they were over-anxious he reassured them. "In name this was a democracy, in truth it was the rule of the First Man." Pericles died in the third war year, of the epidemic that demoralized and severely weakened Athens, just when his leadership was most indispensable.

Alcibiades, his nephew, was his main successor. He was responsible for the collapse of Athens, for he convinced the Athenians to attempt the occupation of Sicily, from which they would dominate the entire Mediterranean. Alcibiades was young and handsome, but also vain, reckless, and socially outrageous. His support for the war was rooted less in deeply-felt convictions than in opportunistic calculations. Thucydides recognized Alcibiades' charisma and exceptional intelligence, but everything he attempted to do was due to his excessive personal ambition, and never by a principled commitment to the well-being of his city: "First of all he wanted to be commander because he hoped that the conquest of Sicily and Cartago, if successful, would bring him money and fame."[11] Horses were his great love, and he was also given to other luxuries. The people, fearful of his unusual life style, were concerned that he would become a tyrant. They relieved him of his power and transferred it to others while the war was in progress—a mistake with far-reaching consequences, as Thucydides admits, but one for which Alcibiades had only himself to blame. The Sicilian adventure ended in a catastrophe that broke Athens and its allies. Their expeditionary corps of fifty thousand men, including many of Athens' best youth, was annihilated. Greece fell of its own fault, not because of foreign aggression. The Peloponnesian War was fought within a single civilization, by people who spoke the same language and worshiped the same gods.

The Form of Government

The quality of leadership interacts with the form of government and the people. It was this interaction that empowered both Pericles and Alcibiades, both of whom were democratically elected, but Pericles protected Athens and Alcibiades destroyed it. It is not easy to say which form of government Thucydides' favored. He supported Pericles and admired his power over the people, unlike other members of the Athenian nobility who opposed him; he detested the demagogy of Alcibiades. He knew that the fickleness, emotionalism, and short memory of the masses were major shortcomings of democracy. Thus, Pericles had exhorted the people to persevere, fearing at every new turn of events that their mood would change. Some have read into Thucydides' oration at Pericles' funeral that Thucydides supported democracy; others, such as Thomas Hobbes, who favored the royalist cause during the English Civil War of 1642, used him as a warning against democracy and an argument for monarchy. Jacqueline de Romilly of the French Academy emphasized the difference between Pericles' devotion to a common cause and Alcibiades' unscrupulous ego-centrism, and drew comparisons to French politicians in the decades after World War II.[12] Thucydides was thought-provoking like few other historians. He stood above political parties and ideologies, and would probably have been satisfied with a moderate form of aristocracy. He knew that there was no form of government that could alone guarantee rise and prevent decline. Those depended, among other factors, on the rulers and their interactions with the people.

The Importance of Morality

Nietzsche praised Thucydides as a great Machiavellian who understood that the world was driven by power alone, but he missed an important point.[13] Thucydides described how the strains and cruelties of war were corroding traditional ethical norms. He reported in great detail on the civil war in Kerkira (Corfu) with all its terror and bloodshed. He emphasized the subversion and corruption of language—the propaganda war, as one would say today—as both a symptom and cause of Kerkira's moral collapse: "And they changed arbitrarily the hitherto valid sense of the words for various things."[14]

There are other reasons why he dwelled so extensively on the unspeakable cruelties committed by both sides and the strategically senseless mass murder of helpless civilians in this war. It is true that he rarely explicitly condemns one side or the other, but his horror is manifest, and so is his conviction that morality matters. This was not a religious morality: he did not believe in gods who rewarded ethical behavior and punished unethical behavior, and has been called one of the first Greek "non-believers." Rather, he saw how the war's savagery undermined sound judgment. Thucydides uses the brutal and unnecessary destruction of the small island of Melos as an example of Athens' arrogance of power. Melos presented no danger to Athens; its only fault was that it wanted to remain neutral. In vain the Melians implored the Athenians to treat them fairly although they were weak, pleading that it was in Athens' own interest to not establish precedents of inhumanity, for "should you ever collapse, you could yourself become for others an illustration of horrific vengeance."[15] It is no coincidence that Thucydides mentions the gratuitous massacre of the helpless Melians just before he begins the story of the reckless and ill-fated expedition to Sicily, which would culminate in the massacre of Athens' youth.

Fate and Luck

Thucydides, like all thinkers of the ancient world, knew that fate intervenes in history when men expect it least. He himself witnessed the plague that decimated Athens and killed Pericles. The infection struck him too, but he had the good luck to recover. However, soon enough he ran into bad luck again, and it changed his life, and historiography, forever. As fleet commander he failed to rescue a city from Sparta. We owe Thucydides' *History of the Peloponnesian War* to the Aegean Sea's unpredictable winds and the author's resulting exile. Thucydides was a master of political and moral history. Socio-economic and religious factors interest him only as instruments or pretexts of power politics. Thomas Hobbes admired him as the "most politic historiographer that ever writ."[16]

CHAPTER 2

Sima Qian
China, ca. 145-90 BCE [1]

Sima Qian was China's first great historian, the father of Chinese historiography. His *Shiji* (*Records of the Historian*) reviews history from the legendary "Yellow Emperor"—who reigned more than two thousand years before his time—until his own days.

Sima Qian's years of birth and death almost coincide with the reign of Han Wudi, "the Han's martial emperor" (156-87 BCE; reigned 141-87 BCE). Wudi was the most dynamic and strong-willed ruler of the Han dynasty, which lasted from 206 BCE to 220 CE. His reign, at 54 years, was the third-longest in China's dynastic history. He nearly doubled China's territory, organized a strong, centralized state, and adopted Confucianism as a state doctrine and code of ethics. Many of his achievements lasted more than two thousand years. His gravest external problem was the Turkish Xiongnu tribes, who may have been ancestors of the Huns, who roamed the steppes of Central Asia. Their unrelenting incursions—in 166 BCE a raiding party of Xiongnu horsemen almost reached the capital and was only stopped at the last moment—caused China great civilian suffering and heavy losses of resources and soldiers. For centuries China had appeased the Xiongnu with peace treaties, gifts, and marriages between the reigning families, but it had also used force. Wudi preferred to solve border problems through conquest rather than defense. He fought bitter wars of attrition to secure the approaches to Central Asia. His wars, luxury spending, and corruption weakened central control for a time and damaged the economy, and in the latter part of his reign, Wudi seemed to have become more violent and erratic, perhaps signs of paranoia. To modern observers, his personality appears to be full of contradictions. He was a learned man, fond of literature and poetry, and an occasional poet himself, but also an irascible despot. He wanted the best minds at his court, but had many of his officials, alone or with their families, executed for often minor or imagined mistakes.[2] Officially he espoused the rational this-worldly doctrines of Confucianism, but he was so obsessed with the search for immortality that he lavished fortunes on magicians and alchemists, to the dismay of his Confucian officials. Subsequent appreciations of Wudi are as contradictory as the emperor was himself.[3]

This was the reign in which the greatest of Chinese historians played a distinguished role. His father Sima Tan had been "Prefect of the Grand Scribes" of Wudi, responsible for the imperial library and the calendar. Sima Qian had promised his dying father to continue his work, the compilation of *Shiji*, a comprehensive history of China. He began writing in 109 BCE and became a senior imperial official, advising Wudi on statecraft. In 99 BCE he got involved in the controversial affair of General Li Ling who had surrendered to the Xiongnu tribes, having fought and lost an impossible battle against them. While the other government officials condemned Li Ling in order to appease their furious emperor, Sima Qian alone defended him, because in his view he had done no wrong. The emperor was deeply offended and handed Sima Qian over to the judiciary, which condemned him to castration. Sima Qian had no money to pay his way out, as was legally possible, nor could he commit suicide, as many others did in similar same situations, because he was bound by his promise to his late father. After the ordeal and three years in jail he was again given an appointment at the palace, this time with a new "privilege": as eunuch, he was now authorized to meet the emperor even in the ladies' quarters. He completed the *Shiji* in 91 BCE and died about a year later, three years before the probably senile Wudi. We will never know how Sima's personal history influenced his judgment of Wudi. His description of Wudi's reign stops short after the introductory paragraph—we do not know why—and contains no fawning. He makes clear in indirect ways what he thought of the emperor and his reign. At the end of a chapter that has no link with Confucius, he makes an unexpected comment noting that the philosopher Confucius was open when writing about earlier reigns, but when "he was writing about his own times, he did not express his judgment frankly, but used subtle and guarded language."[4] Every Chinese reader instantly understood and still understands that Sima did not mean Confucius but himself.

Generally, biographies of Sima Qian put him into the context of Chinese and East Asian history and historiography. This book reviews him together with Western and Arab historians who wrote about the rise and decline of civilizations. Sima Qian knew no foreign historians. In the absence of known contacts between Chinese and any non-Chinese thought at that time, similarities between Chinese and biblical or Greek insights into the course of history are fascinating. As suggested in Part I, Chapter 4, these similarities may be a legacy of the "Axial Age," which left a comparable spiritual and moral heritage in China, Greece, Israel, and India. This is what Tong Shijun has recently suggested, quoting Karl Jaspers' "Axial Age" theory to assert that Chinese and Jews did indeed have an old spiritual heritage in common, and mentioning Sima Qian in this context.[5]

Sima Qian organized his *Shiji* in 130 chapters, but they do not follow a direct chronological order from the earliest times to the present. Some chapters describe natural or economic conditions of the past or the present, the ethnography of foreign tribes, official sacrificial rites, music, commerce, and more. Many chapters are critical biographies of important leaders of the past or present, civilian officials, generals, and members of the dynasty, including women. Sometimes Sima Qian juxtaposes two figures for comparison, not unlike Plutarch. Others are collective biographies that allow for comparisons across the ages, or between different characters in the same era.

Long Trends and Cycles of History

Early Han philosophy sees an interaction between human and natural processes. Sima Qian, like his father, was also court astrologer. He advised on the course of government based on the stars, terrestrial events, or catastrophes. Human beings were connected to the processes of history and nature. According to the old Chinese version of humanism, the stars did not determine the fates of men, as the inhabitants of the Ancient Orient and the Greeks believed. Instead, according to this old Chinese view, portents indicated that something was wrong with the empire or the ruler. The theory of the "Mandate of Heaven"[6] explained the relationship between heavenly law and man. Dynasties fell when they lost the moral right to rule, which was given by heaven alone, an overriding cosmic force.

Sima Qian proposes no explicit grand theory of history, but history does have patterns, regularities, and laws. Change is universal and inevitable, but its depth and length are not predestined. Rise and decline are Sima Qian's persistent preoccupation. Chinese civilization as such is not in question; it is older than history and will endure. But dynasties, kingdoms, and states keep rising and falling. Must this be the case, and if so, why? If we found the reasons, could we preserve well-being and prevent decline? Many forces of history are deep and long lasting. We shall never understand all of them: "Some say that the ways of Heaven are dark and silent...."[7] But others can be identified. What Braudel would call the long waves of history, or "history of long duration," was an evident fact for Sima Qian. For example, he points out that the "virtues" of the earliest rulers, that is the ethics, arts, and skills they were teaching, remain beneficial to his day. He believes that he can detect the benign influence of the Xia kings, the rulers of the first, legendary dynasty (ca. 2100-1600 BCE), because their influence has remained in the character of the inhabitants of the region where they lived two thousand years earlier.[8] During the long period between the two eras, however, dynastic history was cyclical. All dynasties went through comparable cycles of rise, decline, and fall. "The rulers at the beginning of each new dynasty never failed to conduct themselves with awe and reverence, but...their descendants, little by little, sank into indolence and vain pride."[9] Sima Qian uses changing formulations of rise and decline, adding with each one a new element of explanation: "When a thing has reached its height it must begin to decay, and when an age has gone to one extreme it must turn again in the opposite direction; therefore we find periods of rude simplicity and periods of refinement alternating with each other endlessly."[10] The cycles can be long or very short when rulers and reigns are exceptionally evil. Sima Qian compares slow decline to "falling tiles," and the sudden collapse of a dynasty to a "landslide." The preceding Qin dynasty collapsed after a few years in a "landslide" because of its cruelty. Thus, it is not biological laws, the stars, or heaven that are setting the cycles of history, but human nature. As Thucydides had said, the same human attitudes produce the same historical results, again and again.

History is Made by Men:
Leadership and Governance

Sima Qian takes history out of mythology: "most scholars agree that there are no such things as ghosts and spirits."[11] One conclusion, repeated in various formulations, dominates his explanations of rise and decline: "If one would establish a truly worthy dynasty...nothing is more important than selecting the right generals and ministers! Nothing is more important than selecting the right generals and ministers!"[12] (repetition in the original). It was prudent not to add "the right emperors," but it is clear to Sima Qian that "survival and defeat (depend) upon the men one puts in office."[13]

Like Confucius, Sima believed that high officials had the important function of admonishing the ruler. His concept of the upright official who incurs punishment for his fearless but justified criticism has remained an important consideration to this day. He criticized Wudi indirectly by quoting poems or statements of other officials. He has a courageous official of Wudi reprimand his master: "On the surface Your Majesty is practicing benevolence and righteousness, but in your heart you have too many desires."[14] A second method was to speak in generalities: "There has never been anyone in the world who could govern others without being able to govern himself."[15] Theoretically, he was simply remembering a quote from Confucius,[16] but he had probably something else in mind that could not be mentioned directly: Wudi's violent rages. The third, classical Chinese way was to criticize emperors of the preceding dynasty, in this case the Qin, in order to warn the ruler of the current one. Who is a good emperor?, he asked. One who resembles the greatly admired founder of the Han dynasty, "who was kind and affectionate with others,"[17] one who "does not take offence at remonstrations no matter how severe, as long as they broaden his understanding,"[18] one who seeks more than "the approval and delight" of his own generations, one who brings peace to near and far, and one who "turns back a dying age from the course of decay and ruin."[19] In other words, great emperors work for the long term, ensure the rise of the nation, and turn back its decline. Has Wudi done this, in Sima Qian's judgment? The historian gives Wudi credit, because "he drove back the barbarian tribes beyond the borders and within the country put the laws and regulations into order,"[20] he enshrined Confucianism as the sole state philosophy and code of ethics, and he also searched out the best minds to serve in his government. Sima's verdict is complex and not entirely negative. He knew that Wudi was a great ruler, but could not ignore the suffering of so many to ensure the greatness of one.

However, the emperor alone does not make the empire. He has a court and a large number of officials. He defines policy, but the officials and members of the court have tremendous power in carrying it out. Sima Qian knew most of them, and despised many. *Shiji* Chapter 119, "The Biographies of the Reasonable [meaning law-abiding, righteous] Officials," describes China's good officials, and soon after, Chapter 122—"The Biographies of the Harsh Officials"—flays the bad ones.[21] It so happens that the "reasonable" officials mentioned in the earlier chapter all lived in remote antiquity, and all the "harsh" ones of the latter chapter lived in his own time under Wudi. Bad officials are sycophants, strive only for personal distinction, and are stern, arbitrary, deceitful, and corrupt. Also bad are the officials who are gentle, compliant, and "good at writing memos" (a complaint all the more surprising as it was written 2100 years ago!), but do nothing to reform the abuses of government. Good officials are lenient, refuse gifts, take responsibility for mistakes committed in their office, and do not let "personal feelings interfere with the public good."[22] Sima Qian also knows that good government is not only a question of the qualities of a few persons, but depends on the system of governance and the capacity to rule. He does not offer a comprehensive theory of governance, but his biographies and anecdotes contain many elements of such a theory. Some of his stories are memorable and indicate what he himself thought about good governance, such as when he quotes a particularly ambitious and daring high official who admonishes the emperor: "Your Majesty appoints officials just the way one stacks firewood— whatever comes to hand last is piled on the top."[23]

Geography and Economy: The Material Undercurrents of History

Sima Qian has a sharp eye for geographic and economic conditions. Alone, they do not explain rise or decline, but they can play a major role in both. Sima Qian notes many geographic details and devotes an entire chapter to rivers and dykes (*Shiji* 29), because China's fate cannot be understood without its great waterways. This is why he visits the rivers himself: "I have climbed Mt. Lu...to observe the courses which Emperor Yu opened up for the nine tributaries of the Yangtze....How tremendous are the benefits brought by these bodies of water and how terrible the damages! I was among those who carried bundles of brushwood on their backs to stem the break at Xuanfang...."[24] Sima Qian notes the professional activities and economic products of various provinces, writes about currency and wealth creation, and when he reports imperial appointments sometimes adds the salary level and other remunerations of the new officials, because such details are not irrelevant.

Economic exhaustion, resulting from military and diplomatic expansion and corruption, is a major reason for the decline and fall of dynasties. Sima Qian did not approve of the central economic control policies necessitated by Wudi's wars and luxuries. He explains that a flourishing empire needs a prosperous economy. To achieve prosperity, he calls for policies that would today be acknowledged as conditions of a *laissez-faire* or free market economy: society needs farmers, craftsmen, and merchants, "but once these exist, what need is there for government directives, mobilisation of labour or periodic assemblies?... Goods will naturally flow forth without having been summoned...and wealth and currency should be allowed to flow as freely as water."[25] Of course, only a centrally controlled economy could give Wudi sufficient resources for his wars and luxuries. Sima Qian did not say so, but could the hidden reason for his free-market philosophy be a wish to limit the emperor's resources? He seems most modern when he explains that innovation and creative thinking are the surest way to get rich. The wealthiest men did not get their money from fiefs, the government, or crime, he asserts, but from astute guesses about future conditions: they "kept a sharp eye for opportunities of the times, and so were able to capture a fat profit." "There is no fixed road to wealth, and money has no permanent master. It finds its way to the man of ability."[26]

War and Foreign Relations

Sima Qian, like China's classical philosophers, abhors disorder and chaos. Only peace, harmonious social relations, and the free flow of economic forces can prevent disorder. Sima does not share the belief of other pre-modern rulers and historians that war is a normal if not beneficial phenomenon, and a legitimate part of government business. Peace is, war is not. The supreme task of the ruler is to bring peace. Sima Qian took part in one of Wudi's military campaigns, and knew the fearful price of war. He keeps count of the losses of soldiers, animals, gold, and labor, notes the suffering of the people, and mentions by name the officers who were captured and beheaded by the enemy. War results from bad policy, causes economic crisis, and ruins dynasties. It makes no sense to attack the Xiongnu tribes; they are too widespread. "What need is there to turn the whole empire upside down and exhaust the resources of China merely to accommodate a bunch of barbarians?" he quotes a like-minded official as asking the emperor.[27]

Sima Qian has no doubt that Chinese civilization is superior to all others and that non-Chinese people share this opinion. After the Han dynasty sent envoys to Central Asia, "all the barbarians of the distant west craned their necks to the east and longed to catch a glimpse of China."[28] But the *Shiji* shows no contempt for any people. It has several chapters on foreign regions and tribes, one of them on the Xiongnu. It gives objective geographic, ethnographic, and political details of these foreigners and enemies and tells of battles and negotiations. But there is not a single defaming word against the dreaded enemies, such as could be found in the work of the Roman historian Tacitus describing the defeated Jews. Sima Qian has been compared to Tacitus—wrongly so, at least in his attitude toward enemies.* Sima Qian's humanity appears when he speaks of barbarians and enemies: according to him, China has no monopoly on good governance. "Although the Yue is a land of barbarians, its former rulers must have treated the people with great wisdom."[29] And about enemies: "Nothing brings greater misfortune than killing those who have already surrendered to you."[30]

The Role of Coincidence and Luck

Some causes of rise and decline are not subject to human foresight and intervention, and Sima Qian knows that fortune and coincidence play a great role in history. He reports the story of a whole kingdom that was destroyed by "misfortune, borne of the love for a concubine."[31] He tells of an imperial messenger sent to a land of barbarians, where he tastes some *ju* berry sauce and sees other products he wants. He likes the *ju* sauce so much that he persuades the emperor to conquer the country. "The whole affair of the Han

---

* While Tacitus' pages on the Jews are filled with absurd fairy tales about their religion, Sima Qian gives some neutral data on that of the Xiongnu, one of which has tantalized historians. In 121 BCE, a Han general defeated an enemy king, "seizing the golden man which he used in worshipping Heaven," (Sima, 152). It has been suggested that the "golden man" could have been a Buddha statue. If this was the case, Sima Qian's note would be the among documented evidence of an encounter between Confucian China and the spreading Buddhist religion. Some of the great civilizations met first on the battlefield.

relations with the South-western barbarians came about because someone saw some *ju* berry sauce in Punyu...."* Sima Qian wants to tell us that historic events can result from the caprice of a single individual. History does not always make sense. Sima Qian knows as well as Western historians do that the appearance of great men is sometimes a matter of luck. He says of one of the greatest officials of Wudi, Gongsun Hong, that he was "fortunate in having lived at the right time."[32] Fortunate were the emperor, his dynasty, and China.

---

* Sima 258. The French Sinologist Jacques Gernet, *Le monde Chinois (The Chinese World)* (Paris: Armand Colin, 1999), 120 gives a radically different interpretation of the same story, although he had no other source than Sima himself. Gernet writes in the wake of Fernand Braudel (II, 9) and adheres to a "structural" view of history. Contrary to Sima, who may have been a witness to and acquainted with some of the actors of the story, Gernet does not believe that random events can determine history. Only long-term socio-economic trends can do this. Thus he sees the anecdote of the exotic *ju* berry as an expression of the ongoing economic and military expansion of the Han dynasty. The berry confirmed the existence of yet another foreign trade route that the emperor felt compelled to conquer.

CHAPTER 3

Ibn Khaldun
Tunisia, 1332-1406 CE[1]

Many praise Ibn Khaldun as the world's greatest Arab historian. In his *Muqqadimah*, he developed some of the first general theories of the rise and decline of civilizations. He was born in Tunis, exercised many official diplomatic and scholarly functions, and traveled widely in the Arab world, particularly in Moorish Spain, North Africa and Egypt. He was active during a period of deep crisis in the Arab and Muslim world, which greatly affected his thought. He could not know that the Ottoman Turks had just begun to build the next great Muslim empire, where long after his death his work would be held in high esteem. In 1400 he made a pilgrimage to Jerusalem, Bethlehem, and Hebron. In 1401, near the end of his life, he went to Damascus to meet the dreaded Timur (Tamerlane), Sultan of the Mongols and Tartars, who had already conquered half the Muslim world. He reported that the two discussed, of all things, their different viewpoints on the Babylonian King Nebuchadnezzar who had destroyed Jerusalem![2]

Ibn Khaldun extracts from the vast and varied past of Muslim and other nations a set of general patterns of civilization. Thucydides and Sima Qian had alluded to generally valid rules when they wrote history, but Ibn Khaldun went a step beyond them, toward further systematization and generalization. His main sources are Muslim, but he was cognizant of Jewish, Greek, Persian, pre-Islamic, and some Christian history. Like Thucydides and Sima Qian, he completed his work in the last years of his life, after decades of relentless effort, and he too tells the reader how hard the search for truth has been. "The inner meaning of history...involves speculation and an attempt to get at the truth, subtle explanation of the causes and origins of existing things, and deep knowledge of the how and why of events....Little effort is being made to get at the truth. The critical eye, as a rule, is not sharp."[3]

In contrast to Thucydides, Ibn Khaldun was a religious believer. His unquestioning faith in the divine origin and superiority of Islam, and other prejudices, more than once got in the way of his better judgment. He likens black Africans to "dumb animals,"[4] looks down on post-biblical Jews and apologizes to his readers for "blackening" his pages by mentioning Christian "dogmas of unbelief."[5] But along with the prejudices of his time and place one finds amazing insights into history that were centuries ahead of his time.

The Emergence of Civilization

Ibn Khaldun replaces traditional mythologies about the onset of civilization with a rational theory, praised by Arnold Toynbee as "the greatest work of its kind that has ever been created."[6] His definition of civilization is the broadest possible. His Arab term is derived from the verb "build up," or "develop." Civilization is identical to "human social organization." No man can live completely alone. When a few people pull together out of need, they create civilization. There are various stages. The larger the size of the population, the higher the level of civilization; the highest level requires a large, stationary population. Civilization does not flourish everywhere. Ibn Khaldun examines the geographic and climatic conditions that are favorable or unfavorable, as well as the effects that different foods have on the human character.

But the key concept of his theory is biological and anthropological. The heart of civilization, the glue holding together groups, clans, and peoples is *asabiya*, translated as "group feeling," "group consciousness," or "solidarity." The stronger the group feeling, and the greater the power of the people penetrated by it, the greater also is its chance of achieving predominance over other peoples. Group feeling produces the ability to defend and protect oneself and press one's claims. The deepest group feelings result from "blood relationship or something corresponding to it...respect for blood ties is something natural among men,"[7] but later on, when a civilization or social organization is firmly established, other people who are not related can join the group and share its solidarity. Ibn Khaldun saw that civilizations depended—at least at the beginning—on some hidden consensus or "extra-rational" bond between its members, and not only on rational material interests. What he discovered intuitively was a link between kinship and "altruism." Biologists suspected such a link since Charles Darwin, and could finally demonstrate in the late twentieth century that there was a genetic-evolutionary basis for altruism in humans and in many animal species as well. Individuals can behave "altruistically" toward others of their own kin, by acting against their immediate personal interest and even sacrificing their own lives when it ensures the survival of some of their own genes.[8] Ibn Khaldun's *asabiya* requires, in its early stages, this kind of altruism.

Conditions of Success and Prosperity, Royal Authority

When a certain size is reached, maintaining social organization or civilization is only possible with the help of strong rulers, because someone has to restrain the innate aggressiveness of humans and maintain their cohesion. This is why a royal dynasty or a state emerges. The two are synonymous—when the dynasty disappears, the state collapses. "Royal authority...is absolutely necessary to mankind." [9] Group feeling, according to Khaldun, always leads to royal authority. At the beginning, the rulers must be of the same descent or "blood-line" as the people; later on when the dynasty is firmly established, this is not always necessary, and even group feeling can be dispensed with for a time. The moral quality of rule is vital; it is the prerequisite for the well-being of a people or state, among other reasons, because the customs of each people "depend on the customs of its ruler."[10] Among the main qualities of good rulers is "mildness." "Exaggerated harshness is harmful to royal authority...and causes its destruction."[11] A more problematic Islamic postulate is that political and religious rule must be united, "so that the person in charge can devote the available strength to both of them at the same time," because "holy war is a religious duty."[12]

Ibn Khaldun mentions other factors that sustain a great civilization: religion, the economy, war, science, and scholarship. He spends much time on the economic activities essential to civilization, puts agriculture at the bottom, commerce in the middle, and skill-based crafts on top—a quite modern appreciation. He asserts that the ultimate source of profit and capital is human labor.[13] It took Europeans four hundred years longer to discard mercantilist, physiocratic, and other economic dogmas and develop comparable labor theories of value (such as those of Adam Smith, David Ricardo, and Karl Marx).[14]

Warfare

War, triggered by revenge and jealousy, is "natural among human beings. No nation...is free from it."[15] Ibn Khaldun devotes many pages to war, because victory is essential to the survival of a civilization. Whatever technologies, tactics, and strategies a ruler employs, and Ibn Khaldun reviews many of them, victory in war can ultimately depend on "luck and chance." The "hidden factors" are critical, and among these "trickery" is the most decisive.[16] Even the initial victories of the Arabs, including those of Mohammed, are mainly due to such hidden causes. Ibn Khaldun's convictions echo those of many others, but it is surprising to see a pious Muslim express them so frankly.

One of the most interesting chapters is on "the different importance of...'the sword' and 'the pen' in the dynasties."[17] "Sword" and "pen" are "instruments for the ruler to use." At the beginning of a dynasty, when power is not yet established, the sword is more important than the pen, and the same is true again at the end, when the dynasty has become weak and is threatened. In the mid-term of the dynasty, when the ruler is firmly established, the "pen" will have more authority and also more efficiency as an instrument of power. Then, the "pen" will enjoy a higher rank. Sword and pen are both necessary and complementary. A good ruler has to know when to use which one. Ibn Khaldun's explanation anticipates in substance and details some of the contemporary policy discussions on the use of military power versus diplomacy.

Scholarship and Science

One of Ibn Khaldun's most visionary contributions is his insistence on scholarship, not least in the natural sciences, as a key condition of rise and creativity. More than one third of the *Muqaddimah* is devoted to the physical sciences, logic, mathematics, astronomy, mechanics, geometry, optics, medicine, agriculture, and law, but also to scholarship in metaphysics, theology, philosophy, linguistics, music, calligraphy, and poetry. Ibn Khaldun vehemently rejects astrology and alchemy as harmful, fake sciences.[18] Many pages deal with pedagogy. They cover such modern topics as "the instruction of children," "severity to students does them harm," "the right attitude to scientific instruction," "a scholar's education is greatly improved by traveling in quest of knowledge and meeting the authoritative teachers of his time."[19] Ibn Khaldun scolds those who do not understand the scientific method: "they think that scientific habit is identical with memorizing knowledge. But that is not so."[20] He also takes a swipe at scholars: they should keep out of politics because they understand it less than anybody else. He knew them well enough, as he was a scholar himself and, in addition, deeply involved in politics and diplomacy.

The Decline of Civilization

The survival of civilization depends on royal authority or "dynasty." This is the reason that no great civilization can last very long. Every civilization has a corporeal life, "just as any individual has a physical life."[21] When a man reaches forty, he stops developing and will soon decline. The same is true of civilizations, "because there is a limit that cannot be overstepped." Ibn Khaldun's view of history is "cyclical" or organic, like that of many others before and after him. No "glorious" dynasty can last longer than three or four generations.[22] Some may linger on longer, but from the fifth generation on, they are "decaying" dynasties. The "noble" Abraham, Isaac, Jacob, and Joseph are a proof of this "law of history": Joseph was the end of his illustrious "dynasty."

Ibn Khaldun was certainly influenced by the turbulent dynastic politics of the Arabs of his day, but the idea that family and royal dynasties degrade after three generations may even be correct beyond blood links and apply to political "dynasties" in totalitarian as well as democratic regimes. Twentieth-century history provides several examples. Ibn Khaldun does not formulate a completely coherent theory of decline, and one should not try to construct one for him; he offers observations and hypotheses that do not always substantiate each other.

Ibn Khaldun analyzes specific reasons for the destructions of civilizations. A very frequent one is injustice. Economic injustice, such as forced labor, confiscation of property, and excessive taxation—"brings about the ruin of civilization" because it drives people to despair and rebellion.[23] Another reason is the decay of scholarship and science as experienced by the Arabs of his day, which will be discussed below. A third reason is made up of variations in customs, coming from situations in which one people takes over another but both want to keep its own customs. Ibn Khaldun also emphasizes natural causes, because he had witnessed the terrible human destruction wrought by the bubonic plague across the world in the mid-fourteenth century, a "destructive plague which devastated nations and caused populations to vanish."[24] Both his parents had died of the plague. It is noteworthy that Ibn Khaldun does not emphasize misfortunes caused by foreign factors, which are so often at the center of today's Arab debates. He believes that the reasons for a civilization's decline and fall are always internal, not external. He mentions the Mongol invasions and growing Christian power in the Mediterranean as challenges to Arab civilization, but does not blame them for Arab decline. In 1258, the Mongol ruler Hulagu Khan, grandson of Genghis Khan, sacked Baghdad, executed the last Abbasid caliph, and exterminated the city's population, including a considerable fraction of all living Arab scholars—more than enough to cripple any civilization. But Ibn Khaldun does not complain about this or any other foreign aggression: this historian knows no self-pity.

The Arabs

Ibn Khaldun's insight into the essential role of science and scholarship is born from his despair about the state of Arab civilization, which he sees as dying because it abandoned both. Ibn Khaldun, an Arab from an illustrious family himself, has a dim view of the Arabs, and his list of recriminations is long. Where they conquer, he finds, civilization collapses. His anger focuses on the decline of the scholarly and scientific spirit among the Arabs. Their scientific activity has disappeared, save for a few remnants "controlled by orthodox religious scholars."[25] He returns several times to this complaint: "With few exceptions, most Muslim scholars, both in the religious and the intellectual sciences, have been non-Arab. When a scholar is of Arab origin, he is non-Arab in language and upbringing and has non-Arab teachers."[26] Thus, inevitably, "the days of Arab rule were over" and power was seized by the Turks, Berbers, and Europeans.*

Ibn Khaldun and the Jews

Ibn Khaldun refers more often to Jews, Judaism, and the Bible than to any other non-Muslim civilization. His views are split, almost schizophrenic. The Jews of the Bible were a great nation. The *Muqqadima's* summaries of ancient Jewish history and of Jerusalem's history are relatively unbiased, though not always accurate.[27] We read that David and Solomon were history's two most glorious rulers, and that the Hebrew language and script carry great prestige because the Torah is written in Hebrew. Ibn Khaldun does not hesitate to defend the Jews against one of the most insidious Muslim defamations: the claim that they had altered the text of their Torah is untenable because people with a revealed religion simply do not deal with their holy books in this way.[28] But post-biblical Jews do not enjoy equal respect. The best that Ibn Khaldun can say about the Jews of the Muslim world is that they are knowledgeable and skilled in many crafts and disciplines. He finds Jewish pride unacceptable, and cannot stand the "self-delusion" of Jews who claim that they are still "members of the most noble house" even in his time.[29] Their nation is defeated. Their royal authority has vanished and therefore they can have neither group solidarity nor civilization. As they fell into the yoke of others, they inevitably acquired a "bad character," including "insincerity and trickery."[30] Ibn Khaldun's contempt for the Jews of his time reflects something other than just religious bigotry; it is a logical consequence of his definition of civilization. Civilization is the material and spiritual expression of political sovereignty and royal power and leadership. Without the latter, no civilization can survive. In fact, the civilizations that Ibn Khaldun knew

---

* Ibn Khaldun, 25f. Rosenthal's English translation of Ibn Khaldun's work offended Arabists who argued that "Arab" in Ibn Khaldun's original was not an ethnic term, but meant "camel nomad." Marshall Hodgson deplored Rosenthal, saying that he made Ibn Khaldun "paradoxically to denigrate the Arabs," see *The Venture of Islam* (Chicago/London: University of Chicago Press, 1974) 2, 481, footnote 13—as if it was not typical of many great historians to be particularly critical of their own people. In accordance with Hodgson, Dawood translated the Arabic word "Arab" into "Bedouin" whenever possible. Thus, Ibn Khaldun's "Places that succumb to the Arabs are quickly ruined," reads in Dawood: "Places that succumb to the Bedouins...." In other cases, the term "Bedouin" makes no sense, e.g., in Ibn Khaldun's "Persian civilization in the Arab Iraq is likewise completely ruined." When Ibn Khaldun writes "Arab", he often does indeed mean Arab. When he deplores the decline of "Arab science," he surely does not mean "Bedouin science."

in his time, those of the Arabs, Persians, Mongols, European Christians, and Chinese, all had a territorial basis and some form of political sovereignty. The Jews were the main exception. It cannot have been difficult for such a well-read and widely traveled scholar like Ibn Khaldun to discover that the Jews still maintained other critical markers of a genuine civilization, such as a strong "group solidarity" and a distinct and strongly believed spiritual heritage, but here his power of observation yielded to his reductionist definition of civilization and to Muslim prejudice.

CHAPTER 4

Edward Gibbon
UK, 1737-1794[1]

The History of the Decline and Fall of the Roman Empire by Edward Gibbon is the longest lasting "best-seller" of all historical works in the English language. The Roman Empire represented and transmitted a great civilization whose effects have reverberated through the centuries until this day. Its fall was, in Gibbon's words "the greatest, perhaps, and most awful scene in the history of mankind."[2] Gibbon refers repeatedly to the foundations of Rome's greatness. They are not his primary subject, but he needs them as a contrast to the times of decline that were to follow. Understanding what made Rome great is also key to understanding its decline and fall. He dates Rome's rise and expansion to the four or five centuries before the Common Era, its greatest period to the first two centuries of the Common Era, and the decline as lasting from approximately 200 to 476 CE, if the end point is the fall of the Western Empire, and 1453, if it is the fall of the Eastern Empire. A decline period of more than 1200 years is exorbitant and compels the reader to reflect on the relativity of rise-and-decline concepts and their dependence on a vision of time, as mentioned in the introduction.

Gibbon's thoughts about the end of Rome have fascinated following generations because the ageing and death of a great civilization is a metaphor for human life, but also because Gibbon explains that no empire could last forever, and that ultimately Rome was not destroyed by its enemies, but by itself. Toynbee, who often referred to Gibbon, would make this conclusion his own, as shall be discussed. Gibbon differs from some of the classical historians reviewed in this book on one point: he is less driven by his own fate and that of his country, or by other major events of his time, than they are, unless we consider his visit as a tourist to the ruins of Rome and his elegiac thoughts about past greatness as an "event."[3] Also, in contrast to Thucydides, Sima Qian, and Ibn Khaldun, he played no role in any of the events he studied. During his lifetime, his native England fought four wars, the most important of which was the war with its American colonies, but these wars took place within the same civilization and did not even scratch its values and principles. There is no comparison with the end of the Roman Empire, which caused a rupture that is unique in the history of the West.

Gibbon offers no consolidated doctrine on his subject, no sharp definitions, and no comprehensive conclusions. His explanations of decline and fall can be found in many places, for example:

— In an oft-quoted summary exactly in the middle of his work, "General Observations on the Fall of the Roman Empire in the West";[4]
— At the end of his work, in a few pages that explain decline and physical ruin, but of the city of Rome rather than its entire empire;
— On the last page of his work, where he gives, in a few sentences, a final summary of eight factors;[5] and
— All over his work, in hundreds of comments on the changing reasons for Rome's strength or weakness.

Gibbon's views evolved over the course of twenty years while he worked on his *History*. When he finally submitted his book to the "curiosity and candor of the public,"[6] his views were no longer completely identical to those he had held at the start. Gibbon's changing perceptions, the absence of strict coherence in his presentation, and the variations in the identified causes of decline can be bewildering. There are objective reasons for these variations, which should be addressed. First, the causes of the decline were multiple and complex. Gibbon seeks no single, ultimate cause because there is none; nor does he construct a grand theory of rise and decline. There can be no mono-causal reason for the decline of such a vast, varied, and long-lasting entity, only a changing combination and interplay of reasons. Gibbon would ridicule some of today's simplistic, pseudo-scientific explanations that claim to find the cause of Rome's decline and fall, for example in malaria or lead poisoning. But even if different causes operated in different centuries or carried different weights, a number of them appear again and again. These can be called the "key factors." Many of them are connected, and some are complementary.

Politics and Morality of the Rulers and Elites

The most prominent reasons for the decline were political and moral. The worsening quality of Rome's rulers and elites after the second century CE had an enormous negative influence. "Almost every reign closed by the same disgusting repetition of treason and murder,"[7] and the Byzantine emperors were nothing but "a degenerate race of princes." This is a harsh judgment no historian would repeat today, considering that the military and diplomatic skills of these "princes" maintained an empire against great odds. If "the greatness of Rome...was founded on the rare and almost incredible alliance of virtue and fortune,"[8] it could not survive the destruction of the former, virtue. The consequences of the permanent, senseless "expense of blood and treasure" were disastrous.[9] The corruption and despotism of its rulers, together with the restraints they placed on freedom generally, explain the decline of Rome to a large degree.

Loss of Freedom and Republican Spirit

According to Gibbon, Rome rose to become a world power while it was a republic of equal, free citizens. Freedom was the ultimate guarantee of public and personal virtue, of good statecraft, military strength, and political power. It ensured the cohesion of Roman society apparently without coercion. As long as Rome was free and republican, "the fidelity of the citizens to each other and to the state was confirmed by the habits of education and the prejudices of religion."[10] The tyranny of many later emperors extinguished Roman freedom. Gibbon contrasts the freedom of Athens, under which "each Athenian aspired to the level of national dignity," with the "dead uniformity" of the "decaying" Eastern Empire and its "spiritual despotism which shackles not only the action but even the thought."[11] He asserts that Athens' freedom was comparable to that of early Rome, but Athens' classical glory lasted less than a hundred years, and Byzance's alleged "decay," which Gibbon treats with so much animosity, went on for more than a thousand years. Gibbon's glorification of Athens' and early Rome's freedoms is a product of eighteenth-century Enlightenment philosophy. The Enlightenment projected a modern European ideal of political freedom back onto Athens and early Rome, which did not accurately reflect the historical reality.

Loss of Military Spirit

Military miscalculation played a significant part in Rome's decline and fall. Unlike Thucydides and Sima Qian, Gibbon never participated in war, but he was convinced that no nation or empire could survive without permanent military readiness and strength. The "martial enthusiasm of the people" was an essential condition for the rise and consolidation of Rome. Its military virtues were rooted in each citizen's obligation "to draw his sword in the cause of his country" and do military service for ten years. During their best times, the Romans knew that raw military force was often unjust and could not alone manage and maintain their conquests; it had to be balanced by other qualities: "The perpetual violation of justice was maintained by the political virtues of prudence and courage."[12] But then the victorious legions began to acquire in their distant wars "the vices of strangers and mercenaries, first oppressed the freedom of the republic, and afterwards violated the majesty of the purple [the imperial color]" (meaning: murdered some emperors).[13] In the end, the legions turned into a "mercenary army of barbarians" who contributed to the demise of the empire.

The Expansion of Empire and Citizenship

A core problem driving many other issues, including those mentioned above, was imperial expansion and the extension of Roman citizenship to the inhabitants of the entire Empire. Not all expansion is detrimental: refusal to accept and integrate newcomers can do equal harm. Gibbon believes that Athens and Sparta restricted citizenship too severely and thus hastened their ruin. Rome also hastened its ruin, but for the opposite reason: it expanded empire and citizenship without moderation. "Millions of servile provincials...had received the name, without adopting the spirit, of Romans."[14] They brought "contradictory manners" to Rome—the term "multiculturalism" did not yet exist in the eighteenth century—and as a consequence the old Roman virtues disappeared. Theodor Mommsen, in the nineteenth century, wrote the most renowned German history of ancient Rome. He saw Rome's destiny as the unfolding of a natural, inevitable process: the city of Rome had to expand to the whole of Italy, and then from country to empire. Gibbon does not share this view, but he does not specify the boundaries beyond which Rome should not have gone, nor does he explain how an empire can expand without incorporating different people with contradictory manners. Rome sowed the seeds of its own destruction through its "immoderate greatness." Rome's fall was—to no small degree—self-inflicted.

The Division of the Empire

The division of the empire into Western and Eastern parts was an entirely destructive event that hastened the ruin of both. Instead of cooperating to the mutual benefit of both, the Western and Eastern empires envied, fought with, and weakened each other.

The Growth of Christianity

Religion was a decisive factor in the destiny and ultimate decline of the late Roman Empire. Gibbon is hesitant and ambivalent about Christianity. He does not hide his disdain of many representatives of the new religion, and denounces the fanaticism, lust for power, corruption, and cruelty of some of the clergy that brought the empire to the brink of disaster. He dreads religious despotism no less than the political variety: "The Roman world was oppressed by a new species of tyranny."[15] Even the most innocent expressions of Christian faith do not escape his biting sarcasm. Some of his words could have come from Voltaire's anti-clerical pen: "Wealth was consecrated to the specious demands of charity and devotion" by "useless multitudes who could only plead the merits of abstinence and chastity."[16] These were not the active virtues Rome needed to defend itself. However, in other places, perhaps at a later stage of his work, he changes tone. It is true that Constantine the Great's conversion to Christianity hastened the decline of the Empire, but at least "his victorious religion broke the violence of the fall."[17] Gibbon recognized that Christianity, once it had become the state religion, had some merit in that it sustained the Empire. The last pages of his book show a further mellowing of his initial enmity. Rome's change of religion was achieved not by "popular tumult" but peacefully and legally, by "the decrees of the emperor, of the senate, and of time." And the bishops of Rome, by which he means the early Popes, were after all, "the most prudent and least fanatic."[18] There is no similar ambivalence with regard to Islam: according to Gibbon, its impact on the Eastern Empire was entirely destructive.

The Role of the Barbarians

The role of the barbarians, in Gibbon's thought, was even more ambiguous than that of Christianity. It is true that the barbarian invasions caused enormous destruction and bloodshed and "threatened the happiness and security of each individual," but these invasions were the results of pre-existing weaknesses of the empire, perhaps more than their cause. Barbarians finally became the majority among Roman citizens, and the overwhelming majority in the Roman legions. Did they really bring about the destruction of the Empire? The barbarians ended up speaking Latin like everybody else, and were "more inclined to admire than to abolish the arts and studies of a brighter period."[19] They wanted nothing more than to be good Romans and maintain the Empire. They were "neither sufficiently savage nor sufficiently refined" to entertain ideas of "destruction and revenge."

Hidden and Remote Causes of Decline and Fall

The Romans were not aware of their decline, which in itself was a cause of decline: "It was scarcely possible that the eyes of the contemporaries should discover in the public felicity the latent causes of decay and corruption."[20] In addition, they were not able to detect geographically remote dangers. Gibbon mentions a Chinese victory over the Huns, who were thus driven in the opposite direction and invaded the Roman Empire,[21] and an Arab victory over Christian Abyssinia, which freed the Arabs for their incursions into the

Byzantine Empire. Today's historians might question the details of these stories, which are interesting because they show Gibbon's attention to indirect geopolitical moves that can have massive effects, particularly if they are not detected or understood in time.

Gibbon writes about economic, agricultural, and financial developments, but does not consider the economy one of the main causes of decline and fall. He does, however, address environmental and climatic factors. For example, he writes a long chapter about the probable influence of cold climates on the character of the Germans, and he also records natural catastrophes, but in the main parts of his work he does not believe that any of these "natural" causes had a decisive impact on the fate of the Empire. In relation to a severe earthquake he writes, "Man has much more to fear from the passions of his fellow-creatures than from the convulsions of the elements."[22] But he seems to have changed his mind when he was about to complete his work. In the end, he gives four reasons for the ruin of the city of Rome:[23]

— "The injuries of time and nature," meaning the enormous havoc wrought on the city, its people, and its material and cultural possessions over the centuries by natural catastrophes such as fires and floods;
— "The hostile attacks of the barbarians and Christians";
— "The use and abuse of the materials," meaning the long-lasting, willful destruction of Rome's physical infrastructure for conversion into new building materials and other uses; and
— "The domestic quarrels of the Romans."

The second and fourth of these reasons are well known from the earlier chapters of Gibbon's *History*. The other two are completely new and unexpected, and seem to contradict Gibbon's earlier statements. The reader is left with more questions than answers. Gibbon's inquisitive, undogmatic, and nimble mind kept searching to the end. Perhaps the last page, a quick enumeration of eight reasons of decline and fall, contains what we might call his final answer.[24] Four of the reasons are internal political factors (military despotism, foundation of Constantinople, split of the Empire, civil law— probably meaning the extension of citizenship). Three involve religion (birth of Christianity, temporal power of the Pope, Islam), and one is an external political element: the barbarians. Six internal reasons against two external ones (Islam and the barbarian invasions)—the balance, indeed, reflects Gibbon's deepest conviction.

The loss of freedom, republican spirit, military virtue, and public morality, as well as the damage inflicted by foreign manners, are not exclusive explanations, but they are central to Gibbon's reflections on decline and fall. He is obviously indebted to the classical historians of Rome, particularly those of the last republican period, Sallust (Gaius Sallustius Crispus, 86-34 BCE) and

Livy (Titus Livius, 59 BCE-17 CE).[25] Both were deeply pessimistic. However, while they deplored the decline of republican Rome, Gibbon described that of the Roman Empire many centuries later. Sallust and Livy could not foresee what Gibbon knew, namely that Julius Caesar and Augustus would transform Rome's decline into the rise of the largest, most powerful, and longest lasting empire of the West. Gibbon lived almost 1800 years after Sallust and Livy, and their perspectives on decline focused on different time periods. Yet many drivers that Gibbon identifies for Rome's decline after the second century CE are remarkably similar to the causes that Sallust and Livy had mentioned in the first century BCE. All three identified the question of moral fiber, nurtured by war but weakened by peace and prosperity, as the core of Roman history. All three asserted that peace and prosperity led to luxury, loss of public spirit, arrogance, nefarious foreign influences, and corruption, and finally to decline and fall, and all three regarded corruption as a critical and revealing cultural phenomenon, not an inherent trait of human nature.

Livy's impact was long-lasting and can be found in Gibbon's work. Between the sixteenth and eighteenth centuries, and except for Thucydides, no historian of Antiquity is said to have exerted a deeper influence on Western political thought than Livy. Machiavelli wrote *Discourses on the First Ten Books of Titus Livius,* published in 1531, one year before the *Prince,* and it was also widely read, including by rulers and their advisers.[26] The *Discourses* vigorously defended the republican form of government and urged the study of Roman history as the best guidance for resolving the chaotic political conditions of the Italian Renaissance. Livy's explanation of civilizational decline due to problems of moral fiber, corruption, and the like lived on directly but also indirectly, through Gibbon, and has made its way down to the twenty-first century. That Gibbon was influenced by Livy does not mean that his analysis of the fall of the Roman Empire was anything less than genuine and independent. Maybe both were right for their respective periods, and the causes of decline were indeed similar.

Gibbon and the Jews

Gibbon reports on Jews in many chapters, particularly in the context of Christianity. His extensive description of the birth of Christianity is not hostile to the Jewish people, and he mentions subsequent Christian persecutions of the Jews as well. But he adds nothing of substance on Jewish civilization.

CHAPTER 5

Jacob Burckhardt
Switzerland, 1818-1897 [1]

Jacob Burckhardt was born in Basel, Switzerland, the son of a Protestant minister. He began as an art historian and became known as the "father of cultural history." He was one of the first and most influential proponents of this field, and helped to establish it as an academic discipline. Burckhardt was also one of the nineteenth century's great cultural pessimists. Like Nietzsche, with whom he had intellectual links when both were university professors in Basel, he saw European culture as being in a steep decline and predicted that worse was still to come. He rejected "philosophy of history," particularly that of Hegel, who approached history with a previously established theory. But as he kept detecting parallels and repetitive, typical patterns in history, he himself became something of a philosopher of history, albeit a pragmatic and cautious one. Another contradiction can be found in his attitude toward the future. "A future known in advance is an absurdity,"[2] he cautioned, yet his work is full of prescient anticipations of future trends. All of them were pessimistic, and many have since come true.

Burckhardt's ideas on rise and decline can be found particularly in his *The Time of Constantine the Great* (1853), *The Culture of the Renaissance in Italy* (1860), which established his international fame and remains one of the most popular history books written in the nineteenth century, and his posthumous *Reflections on World History*, based on his public lectures of 1870/71. Since the demise of Marxism, and even more since the publication of Samuel P. Huntington's 1996 *Clash of Civilizations*, cultural history in general and Jacob Burckhardt in particular have enjoyed their own "renaissance" because culture is once again recognized as prime mover of world history. The historian Peter Burke recently wrote a chapter on "Burckhardt's Return," and suggested that the renewed interest in him will bring back the history of "high cultures."[3]

Burckhardt's notion of culture is fluid and does not strictly adhere to the German language tradition that separates a prestigious "culture" from a less prestigious, technical-economic "civilization." His texts include the economy, agriculture, craftsmanship, and even technology in "culture."[4] However, it is "culture" in a more restricted sense—that is, the enduring artistic, intellectual, literary, and musical creations, as well as the ethics, customs, social life, and institutions of a society—that show the true portrait of an age. Burckhardt emphasizes the "holistic" nature of a culture and the ties between its individual parts. Because culture is a "spiritual continuity," one of the most difficult tasks of cultural history is to dissect this unit in order to individually examine its separate components. This idea of a holistic unit had a long history in German philosophy. Spengler would later give this idea a dogmatic form. Burckhardt applied it casually. For example, he shows how art history can provide metaphors to illuminate the general history of a time. The Renaissance book has a chapter on "The State as a Work of Art," meaning that this period "invented" the modern state like an artwork, as a "calculated, conscious creation."[5] Another chapter analyzes "War as a Work of Art."

History's "Unknowns" and the Historian's Subjectivity

Burckhardt keeps emphasizing how little we know of the deep currents of history and how hazardous it is to try sorting out cause and effect. For example, a number of reasons have been given for late Antiquity's growing preoccupation with the afterlife, but ultimately "such new tendencies draw their essential force from unexplorable depths; they cannot be deduced from the preceding circumstances."[6] Another example is the question of why there was never an Italian Luther, since the public's disgust with Church abuses was as strong in Italy as it was in Germany. There are some good explanations, but in the end "spiritual movements, their sudden flash and expansion as well as their end, remain an enigma to our eyes because we know one or another of the driving forces but never all of them."[7] Most of the "latent forces" are hidden to us.

The problem of history's unknowns is compounded by the problem of the historian's subjectivity. Burckhardt is intensely aware that complete objectivity in historiography is impossible. Every historian belongs to a time and place that shapes his judgment. He modestly predicts that a future historian might, one day, take exactly the same data he gathered on a given period and paint a completely different picture of it. Subjective judgments are particularly inevitable when one looks at a civilization that is the "mother" of our own, such as the Italian Renaissance. A historian cannot be "value-free" as Max Weber would later demand, and in no branch of history is value-freedom more impossible than cultural history: culture expresses values and morality. Burckhardt is a conservative humanist, but not a democrat. He is revolted by tyranny, violence, and cruelty. He admits that his cultural values are those of ancient Greece, Rome, and the Renaissance. His condemnation of the crimes of bad rulers is unforgiving and sometimes vituperative. The

Roman Emperor Caracalla was "the most horrible monster," the Emperor Elagabalus "disgusting and senseless."[8] Even the most famous do not escape his condemnation. He censures King Ferdinand of Spain and Emperor Charles V for the "outrages" committed by their armies: "They knew their hordes and still unleashed them."[9]

Rise, Decline, and Transformation

The issues of rise, decline, and transformation flow through Burckhardt's entire work like watermarks. Burckhardt absolved the historian of the need to speculate about the origin and rise of civilizations, but this did not deter him from writing a brilliant description of the cultural origins of the Renaissance. Its roots, some of which went back several centuries, were the development of individualism, the resurrection of antiquity, and the discovery of the world, of nature, and of man. The glory of the Renaissance was short-lived. Later observers tended to idealize this and similar periods, which are wrongly seen as "happy," and judge them primarily by their continued impact on their own culture: we consider ourselves much more important than we really are, notes Burckhardt. He is more interested in decline than in rise, and in spite of his skepticism regarding our ability to detect its causes, keeps searching for them.

External reasons may play a role. Both *Constantine the Great* and the *Renaissance* begin with extensive chapters on the political conditions of their time, which were uncannily similar. Both periods were characterized by incompetent, criminal, and violent rulers, divisions, bloodshed, wars, and general insecurity. Can the same conditions explain cultural decline in the first case, and rise in the second? Burckhardt asks whether good rulers could have prevented the decline of the late Roman Empire and its civilization as Gibbon seemed to suggest was the case, but expresses doubts as to whether "the deepest ills of ageing nations were at all amenable to the goodwill and wisdom of even the best rulers."[10] However, for the Renaissance he concedes that the fragmentation of Italy into many small tyrannies and republics was one of the most important sources of the early development of Italian and later European individualism. He does not emphasize external causes, and economic reasons are never among them. Braudel would later criticize the omission of economic factors as one of Burckhardt's main shortcomings,[11] but this omission is deliberate and not just due to a lack of data. The ultimate driver of culture is culture. The deepest reasons for the rise and decline of civilizations, if they can be ascertained at all, are not in economic or political movements but in spiritual, cultural, and particularly religious ones, which in turn may or may not be explainable. Both *Constantine the Great* and the *Renaissance* end with lengthy descriptions of the religious situations of their times. In both cases the old faith was waning or had collapsed, to be replaced by cynicism and a proliferation of superstition, magic, and astrology. There was also a great metaphysical yearning for new religious forms and content, which Constantine the Great grasped when he made Christianity the new Roman state religion. This was the beginning of the end of ancient civilization. The end of the Renaissance culture, Burckhardt suggests, also had important religious causes: the degradation and convulsion of faith in general, followed by the beginning of the Counter-Reformation and its opposition to intellectual freedom.

In a long-term perspective, both "ends" were really transformations. Constantine's fourth century was followed by a transformation that shaped fifteen hundred years of Christian history, and the glorious fifteenth century in Italy was first interrupted but then followed by a transformation that gave birth to our modern world. Burckhardt was no less intrigued by the long duration of civilizations than Braudel would be a century later, and like him he wanted to understand when and how the forces controlling our lives started, what underpinned long-term trends, and how ancient history could explain today's history. His answers, however, were different.

Power and the State

It is often forgotten that Burckhardt was not only a cultural historian, but also a historian of hard power. His admiration of Thucydides above all other historians was no coincidence. He saw the all-embracing power and "selfishness" of the modern state as a direct legacy of the Renaissance, but "no power has ever been created without crime," and "power is evil *per se*...it is a craving and by definition unrealizable...."[12] Burckhardt is resigned that our future will be decided by issues of power and not by culture, and that the state will more and more take control of culture.

Historical Greatness

Like all historians of the classical era, Burckhardt believes that good or bad leaders can determine the success or failure of a nation. He mentions many great men, but analyzes only one extensively: Constantine the Great. Burckhardt has no illusions about the character of "this murderous egoist"[13] who, however, was also an outstanding visionary and statesman. Constantine shaped the future for centuries to come because he grasped the importance of Christianity, conquered the Roman world, reconciled it with the new religion, and reorganized it in every important aspect. Burckhardt does not believe that great men can be "raised," he knows that "true greatness is a mystery,"[14] but he nonetheless lists all the virtues that distinguish an outstanding leader: exceptional ability in analyzing and synthesizing salient issues, complete focus on one task, clear vision when others are confused, a perfect sense of reality and power without being influenced by the noise of the day, anticipation of the right moment for intervention, and more. All civilized nations have felt the need for great men. Greatness has "a magical way" of working on us through the centuries.

Harbingers of Modernity

Burckhardt's desire to detect the origin of the forces shaping our modern world gave him insights that were amazing for his time. Florence was the "model and earliest expression" of modern Europe.[15] Florence's success in all fields, including its growing wealth, was intimately linked to its universities and schools. The strongest impact of the Medici rulers on Florence, apart from in politics, was in their leadership in promoting education. Nowhere in the fifteenth century was the enthusiastic dedication to education as the highest public goal as strong as it was in Florence: education became the great equalizer of higher Renaissance society. Even more prescient was Burckhardt's finding that the development of modernity was tied to the progress of the natural sciences and mathematics. A chapter on the "Natural Sciences in Italy" suggests that modern scientific research may have first occurred in Italy, and that at the end of the fifteenth century Italy was "without comparison" first in science and mathematics.[16] Ten years later, in 1870/71, Burckhardt reiterated his assertion that the invention of mathematics was one of the most extraordinary facts of history, that science and mathematics were a "key measure of the genius of the time,"[17] and that we must ask ourselves how their growing importance will interact with the whole fate of our epoch!

Burckhardt detected another condition of cultural creativity and a source of modernity in the Renaissance: the high position of women. Renaissance philosophy saw women as equivalent to men, offered them the same education, and allowed them the same individualism. Burckhardt could not know that the Italian Renaissance also improved, for a limited time and space, the status of Jewish women.*

---

* Rabbi Abraham Farissol in Mantua wrote in 1480 a Hebrew prayer book *(Siddur Shalem Mikol Ha'Shana Kefi Minhag Italiani: An Italian Rite Siddur)* that contained a radical modification of the morning blessings. Men traditionally thanked God for "not making me a woman" while women thanked for "making me according to His will." In Rabbi Farissol's prayer book women thanked God "for making me a woman and not a man"! See R. Weiser and R. Plesser, eds., *"Treasures Revealed": From the Collections of the Jewish National and University Library in Honor of the 75th Anniversary of the Hebrew University of Jerusalem 1925-2000* (Jerusalem: R. Plesser, 2000), 99.

Jacob Burckhardt and the Jews

Burckhardt is the only antisemitic historian in this study. This is not evident in the books he published himself: the few references to Jews they contain are neutral and objective. His true feelings appear in his letters to friends, which were published after his death without his prior consent. In them he repeated the stereotypes that Jews had enormous wealth that underpinned their allegedly malicious power, and that they owned ninety percent of all German newspapers—an absurd claim. In 1872, he predicted growing European hostility to Jews, and in 1880 he predicted that "the liberals" would not always continue to defend them, that the laws giving them equal rights would change, and that they would have to pay for their "unjustified meddling into everything." Radical anti-Jewish changes could come quite suddenly and, in a free referendum, the German people would in 1882 vote with an overwhelming majority for the expulsion of the Jews.[18] In fact, all of Burckhardt's predictions and more would come true half a century later.

Burckhardt is troubling because he is representative of a perhaps continuing, but generally hidden, "high-level" antisemitism possessed by intellectuals who could not be ignorant of Judaism's contribution to the very values they profess to cherish. Burckhardt admires the Humanist Giovanni Pico della Mirandola more than any other Renaissance scholar and quotes extensively from his *Oration on the Dignity of Man* of 1486, which he calls "one of the noblest heritages" of the entire period.[19] Pico's *Oration* overflows with references to the Hebrew Bible and to rabbinic and kabbalistic works. Pico had great respect for Jews and Judaism. The Jewish scholar Elia del Medigo had introduced him to the Hebrew language and scriptures, including the Talmud, Kabbalah and perhaps the Midrash.[20] Burckhardt knew of Pico's links with the Jews, but the only comment he made was that "Pico had the entire talmudic and philosophical knowledge of a learned rabbi," which is an enormous exaggeration.[21] All credit goes to Pico, none to the Jews. The skeptical scholar of Basel, who despised the vulgarity of the crowds, fell for the most vulgar prejudices of the day. He had condemned Charles V for the brutal *Sacco di Roma* (Sack of Rome) in 1527, but justified in one of his lecture notes the medieval massacres of the Jews, with the fantastic argument that otherwise the Jews would have ended up ruling the Christian world from the seventh or eighth century on.[22] Burckhardt had no Jewish acquaintances and never directly encountered the mythical "Jewish power" about which he was fantasizing. Switzerland was the last European country to grant the Jews equal rights (1866), a change which Burckhardt opposed. His antisemitism was part of his hostility to the massive political and socio-economic transformations all around him, which were making the cozy patrician world of his youth irrelevant: in his lifetime Basel grew from a post-medieval town of 15,000 inhabitants to an industrial immigrant city of 180,000. Burckhardt was an archconservative and loathed every aspect of modernity, especially the political liberalism that had brought about the emancipation of the Jews as part of the general process of democratization and modernization. Like Toynbee later, he never freed himself of the anti-Jewish animosity that came with the Protestant education of his childhood. His main biographer Werner Kaegi argued that Burckhardt could not be held responsible for the posthumous publication of his private letters, much less the future crimes of the Nazis.[23] This is true, but he contributed to the intellectual climate that prepared the ground for the Nazis, and Albert Debrunner provides evidence that at least some prominent Nazis read and liked his letters.[24]

CHAPTER 6

Max Weber
Germany, 1864-1920 [1]

Max Weber was the founder of German sociology, and his impact extends to all of modern sociology. He was one of the most influential German scholars and intellectuals of his time and was also politically active, serving as a member of the German parliament after 1918. His books on the sociology of religion examine the "economic ethic of the world religions" and the links between religions, economic development, and social structures. Religions were important drivers of civilization. The first of his books on this topic, *The Protestant Ethic and the Spirit of Capitalism*, published in different parts from 1904 to 1906 and re-printed and translated many times, is his most often-quoted book.

Weber raised a question many others would ask after him: what explains the rise of the West? Why did all the ingredients of modern power, such as science, technology, and industry, all based on the progress of rationalism, develop in Europe and nowhere else? His answer challenged the foundational doctrine of Karl Marx, whose impact on politics and the social sciences was growing, particularly in Germany. Marx saw politics, culture, and particularly religion as a "super-structure" of the economy, manipulated by the ruling classes to defend their ownership of the means of production. Weber set out to show that the relationship between religion, the economy, and society could be the opposite of what Marx had postulated, at least in one important case, the rise of capitalism. A new religion could give birth to a new civilization by initiating radical spiritual changes that reshape social and economic conditions.

The opposite was possible too, as Weber would demonstrate in his analyses of China and India. In these cases an old religion stifled spiritual and material change and thus contributed to the decline of a civilization. Weber emphasized that the driving force of capitalist expansion was not the accumulation of money but the development of a new spirit.[2] Why did capitalism not grow in fourteenth- and fifteenth- century Florence, which was the center of Europe's capital and money markets? Weber anticipated some of his critics who would later point to Catholic Italy as the inventor of many of the tools of modern banking. These tools were not determinative. The determinant was Martin Luther's "ethical valuation of inner-worldly professional activity," one of the "most portentous achievements of the Reformation."[3] The new spirit of "ascetic rationalism" became more radical with Calvinism and a number of Protestant sects, collectively indicated by the term "Puritanism." The Puritans created a completely new relationship between religious life and worldly action. They moved ascetic ideals and lifestyles that had deep Christian roots from the monastic cell to professional life. They created a "this-worldly" religion[4] that became the basis of the "spirit of capitalism." This spirit included the idea of a "professional duty" and the ideals and habits that favored the rational pursuit of economic gain. Gain and work became the sense of life itself, not just a way of satisfying daily needs.[5] A love of saving and frugality and the rejection of luxury were part of this spirit. By giving this pursuit of gain a positive religious meaning, Puritanism responded to an urgent spiritual need. Catholicism had assured the faithful salvation of their soul by belief in the Church's sacraments, but the Reformation had removed this assurance from the common man and propelled him to look for other signs that he could be saved. This is why worldly success became a visible measure of religious salvation. It is true that a spirit of rational pursuit of economic gain is not limited to the West when considered as the attitude of individuals. However, individuals could not by themselves establish a new economic order. Such an order could only originate as a way of life common to a large group of people, and only a religious mass movement could generate such a new way of life. Weber offers evidence that a religiously-grounded spirit of capitalism existed in the New World before capitalism emerged as an economic system. This spirit was not a "super-structure" of material conditions. Weber concedes that other factors contributed to the birth of capitalism, but without the Protestant ethic the capitalism known to us would never have arisen. That capitalism began in the New World and a few places in Europe, and ended up changing the face of the world.

Weber's erudition was impressive, but his findings challenged many intellectual traditions and paradigms. Critical discussions of his book began only weeks after the first part reached the public in 1904, and continued for a century—they have still not abated. Limitations of Weber's thesis were proposed, and some errors were corrected, but few other social science studies of our time have remained topical for so long and created so much intellectual ferment. One of the main objections to the traditional presentation of Weber's thesis is that he has been "misunderstood," and that he did not want to replace Karl Marx' materialistic determinism with a new spiritual determinism.[6] At the end of his book Weber does indeed emphasize that he does not wish that result, that both material and spiritual explanations of history are possible. However, polemics against "naïve" Marxist determinism appear frequently throughout his book.[7] He felt that the original roots of religious thought are always spiritual and cannot be traced back to the economy, but the economy can have a major impact on the later historical fate of a religious thought. In at least one case, a major new economic order grew out of a new religion. Weber expected major criticism and knew from whence it would come: modern people, he argues, are simply unable to grasp how enormous the impact of religion has been on their own ways of life, the details of their cultures, and the characters of their nations.[8]

The Religion of China

Confucianism and Taoism (1916) was Weber's second major work on the sociology of religion—he regarded Confucianism as a religion, as the Chinese authorities and many Chinese historians still do today. Weber asked why dynastic China did not even possess the beginning of a modern technological and capitalist development. There were, after all, many favorable conditions, such as the diligence and business acumen of the Chinese, and also the Confucian rationalism, self-control, and sobriety that have so much in common with Protestantism. But these favorable factors were outweighed by negative ones, some of which were the result of political, social, and economic structures, whereas others were deeply rooted in Confucianism itself.

Confucianism encouraged adaptation to the cosmos and to nature, unlike Protestantism, which advocated the rational domination of the world. It did not value scientific research to better understand the workings of nature, and was suspicious of technological and economic innovation. Kinship groups based on the religious importance of family ties protected their members against economic adversity and discouraged rational work procedures and the development of legal institutions. Moreover, the Confucian scholar class, the country's elite, despised business activity and had no interest in economic policy. In the earlier part of the twentieth century, China's reformers and revolutionaries agreed that Confucianism, and probably every religion, was an obstacle to social development and economic growth that should be discarded. Such convictions still guide China's anti-religious policies.

The Religion of India: the Sociology of Hinduism and Buddhism (1916) was Weber's third major work on religion. The Hindu concepts of an immutable world order of eternal cycles of re-birth, the depreciation of the mundane world, and the caste system—all rooted in religion—hindered economic development. Weber could not foresee the rapid economic growth of China and India, as well as the growth of Japan, Korea, and Taiwan, which have been called "post-Confucian" societies. Their successes will call for more sophisticated views on the influence of religion on Asian economies and civilizations. For the time being, all Asian forms of capitalism are imitations and adaptations of Western capitalism: no radically different form has emerged from Asia's own cultural and religious traditions, so far, so Max Weber has not yet been proven wrong.

Max Weber and the Jews

Weber's fourth and last work on religion was his *Ancient Judaism* (1917; enlarged edition 1920 after his death). Weber attached great importance to the study of Judaism because the Jews "created a highly rational ethic of social conduct... free of magic and all forms of irrational quest for salvation." This ethic still underlies all Western and Islamic culture: "World-historical interest in Jewry rests upon this fact."[9] Thus, Weber draws attention to the pioneering role of a religion, Judaism, in the formation of world civilizations.

But Weber strongly opposed the view that Judaism had made an indispensable contribution to the creation of capitalism. His *Ancient Judaism* is a polemic reply to the ideas of his colleague Werner Sombart, who had defended this thesis in his widely read book *The Jews and Modern Capitalism* (1911). Weber argued that Jews were a *"pariah"* people in the Indian sense. They had freely chosen to separate themselves from their environment and developed a dualistic morality—one for internal use and the other for external use—that allegedly allowed them to have different business ethics toward Jews and non-Jews. Also, in contrast to the Protestants, Jews did not seek material success as a sign of divine grace, though success was always welcome. For these and other reasons, they apparently did not play an economic role comparable to that of the Protestants. Weber drew his knowledge of ancient Judaism from the German Old Testament scholarship of his time, but he did not read Hebrew, and his knowledge of rabbinic Judaism, which is a much more important source of Jewish economic ethics, was weak. His characterization of the Jews as a "pariah" people with a dual morality drew much scholarly criticism, and further serious historical research has since been devoted to the role of the Jews in Western economies. Max Weber died before he could complete his work on the economic ethics of ancient Judaism.

In his study of Judaism, as in those on Protestantism and Confucianism, Weber's greatest merit perhaps did not lie in his findings, which were incomplete, but in the originality of his questions. He showed that religions have had a wide variety of impacts on social and economic development because they can encourage or discourage change.

CHAPTER 7

Oswald Spengler
Germany, 1880-1936[1]

The End of the West (wrongly translated as *Decline of the West*) by Oswald Spengler was mostly written during World War I and was published in final form in 1922. Its main theses were in Spengler's mind as early as 1912, when the West's ruling elites were still sure that their political, economic, and cultural domination of the world was unshakable. *The End of the West* became, between the two world wars, one of the most widely-discussed books in Germany and beyond, in spite of its dense and difficult style, certainly because it reflected the pessimistic mood of the time. The book had considerable influence on many other thinkers. Arnold Toynbee, for example, wrote later that his destiny changed when he began reading it, because it led to his decision to devote the rest of his life to the study of history. References to Spengler as the source of some of his main ideas can frequently be found in Toynbee's work.[2] In contrast, academic historians attacked Spengler's unconventional ideas and took him to task for his copious factual mistakes. Worse, after World War II, he was considered a right-wing extremist who helped pave the way for the Nazis. The latter certainly hoped that he would join their ranks, but he did not: Spengler remained aloof from the Nazis until his death.

Spengler announces his goal right at the beginning: his book is the first "scientific" effort to predict future history.[3] This is possible because every culture (the German "Kultur" has the meaning "civilization" takes in other European languages, as noted in Part I, Chapter 2) is an organism. It emerges spontaneously and without external stimulus from a people's "soul." All cultures have to go through the same cycle: like a plant or animal (his book's subtitle, *Outlines for a Morphology of World History*, borrows "morphology" from biology), they grow and die. "Cultures are organisms....The extraordinary history of the Chinese or antique culture is morphologically an exact parallel to the modest history of an individual man, animal, tree or flower."[4] This is an extreme form of the "organic" or cyclical theory of history. Goethe compared cultures to living and growing organisms, and Spengler referred to him more often than to any other poet. But Goethe developed this idea as poetic metaphor, not as rigid historical doctrine. According to Spengler, what happened in one culture must happen in all others, including ours. By studying the rise, decline, and death of earlier cultures, we are able to accurately predict what will happen to ours. Comparison is "the key to the understanding of our own future."[5] This evolution, including the inevitable end of every culture, is immutable: All that we can do is become better aware of the inexorable nature of this process and our place in it. Spengler sees eight important "High Cultures," each lasting approximately one thousand years and most of them already dead. They are of similar construction and with identical developmental trajectories. The manifold manifestations of each individual culture are closely linked with each other, but not with those of other cultures: art, music, religion, scientific concepts, statecraft, military organization, and even mathematics and the like are animated by a singular, unique spirit that is typical only of a single culture and its "soul," not of others.

Interactions between these cultures are coincidental and inconsequential. The notion of a "world history," a history of all mankind, makes no sense. Mankind has no single history and no single goal. Only individual cultures have a history, and their histories are not connected. This is, of course, the most dubious aspect of his theory. All history shows a continuous give-and-take between cultures: they influence and modify each other. But Spengler's dogmas and eccentricities did not preclude a number of great insights or compromise his acute sensitivity for art and literature. His discussion of Europe's classical music, which he regarded as the apogee of all Western culture, still makes fascinating reading.[6]

The last, terminal stage of a culture is called "civilization," which expresses itself in dictatorship, imperialism, militarism, materialism, and giant cities. Every culture ends in "civilization." The Western World's "civilization"—that is, the terminal state of its culture—has already begun, and with it the decay of the West. It is in many respects comparable to the late Hellenistic civilization that heralded the end of the Ancient World. The final end of the Occident will come within approximately two hundred years (and since a century has passed since Spengler wrote, this means in the early years of the twenty-second century). After this period, no Western culture or nation will exist in its current shape and composition. Spengler is too cautious to predict what will follow to replace the West, but says that the Arab culture seems to be very solid. He ignores China and India completely, but he was not the only one of his generation to see them as dead cultures. If Spengler were to come back to life in 2013, a hundred years after he became convinced that the West was reaching the end of its history, he would probably conclude that his predictions have so far been vindicated and will almost certainly be fulfilled in another hundred years.

Spengler makes a number of intuitive predictions for the West's last period that have turned out to be not far from the mark. He foresees the people of the West having fewer and fewer children and their numbers decreasing, as was the case in late antiquity,[7] and their living in giant buildings in cities of ten or more million inhabitants.[8] Scientific research will no longer target the "visible world"; those studies will be replaced by studies of the invisible and infinitesimal, mathematics and the imagination. He also predicted that separate scientific disciplines will increasingly converge.[9] The last period of civilization will see the emergence of a "second religiosity"[10] as people will again want to "believe," and not "dissect." Military establishments will abolish compulsory conscription in favor of small, voluntary, and professional armies[11]—an amazing conjecture, considering that it was made during or immediately after World War I. Equally impressive is his prophecy, made in 1922 or before, that the peace conferences of 1918 were nothing but a prelude to the next wars.[12] The power of the media (only newspapers in Spengler's time) over the masses, and their capability to manipulate public opinion, will grow exponentially, to the point of completely perverting the sense of "freedom of expression." The media will also be able to impose a "censorship of silence"[13] on unwanted news that will be more effective than all past religious and political censorship.

Organic and cyclical theories of history had appeared long before Spengler. They dominated historical thought in antiquity and in many other civilizations. Nearer to Spengler was the eighteenth-century Neapolitan philosopher, Giambattista Vico (1668-1744). In contrast to Spengler, Vico was little known or appreciated in his own time, but his vision of history resembles Spengler's on so many points that one is surprised that Spengler does not mention him in his book. "For all their various and diverse customs, nations proceed with constant uniformity through three distinct ages," says Vico,[14] and he goes on to explain that each age has its own "kind of human nature," "customs," "natural laws," "government," "language," "symbols," and "authority," which are all closely linked to each other but different from their manifestations in other ages. Spengler adheres to Vico's idea of "constant uniformity" and shares his conviction that all expressions of an "age" (for Spengler, "culture") are organically linked. The two thinkers diverge completely in their visions of the future. Vico, like many Enlightenment philosophers, is an optimist. He sees a new age coming, where "good and honorable men" become rulers, inaugurating "the eternal natural commonwealth, best in its kind, ordained by Divine Providence."[15] Spengler of course harbored no such rosy utopias.

Oswald Spengler and the Jews

Spengler was greatly interested in and sympathetic to the Jews. His book contains many references and two small chapters on Jews[16] that testify to his knowledge of Jewish history and literature. He speaks with the deepest affection for the Baal Shem-Tov, the founder of Hassidism, whom he compares to Jesus. Spengler sees no independent, isolated Jewish culture. He places them in what he calls "Arab" or sometimes "Aramaic" culture. This includes the Jews, Arabs, Arameans, Persians, early Christians, early Byzantines, and others. Toynbee would later adopt this view but replace "Aramaic" with the more nebulous term "Syriac." The distinguishing sign of Spengler's "Arab" culture is its "magial" nature (*magisch* in German), a characterization that he will often apply to the Jews. He contrasts this with the "Faustian," continuously searching and expanding culture of the West. He insists that the Jews are undoubtedly a "people," because a people is a "psychological" unit that is completely unrelated to language, race, or origin—another of Spengler's little provocations, at least for most German Jews of his time.

The Jewish people are a tacit consensus,[17] which explains their "silent and self-evident cohesion."[18] This tacit consensus is without a land and free of geographic limitations. It is "magial" because it is deeply believed but is not based on rational or measurable criteria: "a completely unconscious metaphysical drive, the expression of an immediate magial sentiment." "This silent cohesion contained the idea of a "magial" nation; it was state, church, and people at the same time."[19] Although the Jews have singular qualities, they are not unique in history. Spengler mentions as parallels, not very convincingly, the Parsees in India, the Armenians and Greeks in South-East Europe, and the Chinese in California—in other words, other diasporas.

But the European Enlightenment corroded and poisoned the "consensus" (instead of "Jews," Spengler often simply says "the consensus"). "For Judaism, the Enlightenment meant destruction and nothing else....This magial nation is in danger of vanishing, together with the Ghetto and its religion. It has lost every form of internal cohesion, and only cohesion for practical questions has remained."[20] Spengler's prognosis for the Jewish people is grim, and he announces it with obvious sadness: the Jewish people's disappearance is historically inevitable. Spengler claimed that Western Judaism, which dominated all of the Jewish people, got too entangled with Western civilization and will die with it. "The fate of Judaism is completed." Spengler did not know the Jews of the Muslim world and did not grasp the potential of Zionism. He mentioned the latter only once in his book, and lampooned it as a movement of a "mentally retarded minority."[21] This was a slur that a majority of German Jews would happily have endorsed before 1914.

CHAPTER 8

Johan Huizinga
Netherlands, 1872-1945 [1]

The Dutch historian Johan Huizinga began as a student of linguistics, Sanskrit, and anthropology. From 1915 to 1942 he was professor of history at Leiden University. When the Nazis occupied the country, they were aware of his prestige but also of his hostility to them, so they kept him in detention during the last war years, and he died in detention. Huizinga is one of the founders of modern cultural history. He is often mentioned together with Jacob Burckhardt, whose work he admired. He shared Burckhardt's love of art but also his deep pessimism about the future of our world, particularly after 1933.

His body of work is not large. The two books with original insights into rise and decline are his great classic, *Autumn of the Middle Ages,* first published in 1919, and his last book, published in 1941, *Dutch Culture in the Seventeenth Century.* In 2007 a British historian called *Autumn* still "the outstanding work of cultural history in the first half of the 20th century,"[2] whereas *Dutch Culture* has since been superseded by Jonathan Israel's masterwork *The Dutch Republic.*[3]

The Portrait of a Time

The aim of Huizinga's cultural history is to portray the patterns of culture and the characteristics of the thought and feeling of an age, and to show their expressions in art, literature, and the daily life of simple people. Huizinga is not interested in the "history of events" nor in the decisions and proclamations of ruling kings, but he does not ignore the rulers. They appear all over his work, together with countless artists, poets, chroniclers, clergymen, and outlaws, cited in anecdotes and as illustrations of the typical patterns of their time.

Burckhardt begins his *Culture of the Renaissance in Italy* with a description of Italy's city-states and the characters and politics of their rulers, in order to show the background of the rising new culture. Not so Huizinga: the first two chapters of *Autumn of the Middle Ages* describe the "Tensions of

Life"—the enormous contradictions in the feelings and perceptions of late medieval men and their "yearning for a more beautiful life." These were the deep forces driving late medieval culture and history, not day-to-day politics. In contrast to Burckhardt, Huizinga knew too much anthropology to offer up quick moral judgments. He warned the reader that many of the psychological contradictions of the Middle Ages were incomprehensible in modern times, and should not be judged by present standards nor be seen as signs of hypocrisy. Purest love and crudest obscenity lived side by side in the same individual, and so did tearful compassion for some imagined poor souls burning in hell and joyful attendance at the public torture and execution of real living people. A closer look reveals that some of the apparently incoherent mentalities Huizinga describes can again be found today. Chapter V, "The Dream of Heroism and Love," shows that the ideals of medieval chivalry emphasized sexual asceticism (or deprivation) together with the yearning for a heroic death. Huizinga suggests that these two traits in young men are psychologically closely linked, an insight still valid today, though not in Christian lands.

Huizinga is both a mirror image of and a counterpoint to Braudel, who also looked for deep structures and "long waves" of history and found them in economic and other material bases of civilization. Huizinga's work contains no mention of Braudel, who began publishing later, but plenty of polemics against the inadequacy of economic explanations of history, which were already influential in his time. "The history of culture must deal with the dreams of beauty and the fantasies of a noble life no less than with population statistics and tax revenues."[4] In one case, Huizinga's indifference to "events" stretches the reader's credulity to the limits. In Chapter XI, "Image of Death," he writes, "No other epoch laid so much stress as the expiring Middle Ages on the thought of death. The call of *'memento mori'* ('remember that you will die') resonated endlessly through life."[5] Yet this colorful chapter makes not a single mention of the Black Death, one of the most devastating epidemics of human history, which swept through Europe from the late 1340s on. Huizinga could not possibly believe that the epoch's resonating *memento mori* was born of old cultural traditions alone and had no link to the "event" of the Black Death. Why did he choose to ignore it?

Transformation, not Rupture

Huizinga's *Autumn* is a respectful but critical response to Burckhardt's *Renaissance*. Again and again, Huizinga emphasizes that Burckhardt had drawn the borderline between the Middle Ages and the Renaissance too sharply, that there was no rupture, that many Renaissance characteristics were already alive in the Middle Ages, while many Middle Age features survived in the Renaissance. "Whenever one tried to work out a clear separation between Middle Ages and Renaissance, the border line receded."[6] A great period of history does not die: it is transformed into a new period that will preserve many of its elements. In the preface to the first edition of his book, Huizinga was already concerned that the term "autumn," the exact English equivalent of the Dutch "*herfstij*," could be misread as a strict metaphor for decline and death. This is not what he wanted to say. Rather, his intention was that autumn and winter always make way for a new spring.[7]

The Rise and Golden Age of Dutch Culture[8] in the Seventeenth Century

Huizingas's *Dutch Culture in the Seventeenth Century*, a small book published in 1941, was an act of intellectual resistance against the German occupation. The rise and decline of the old Dutch Republic were simply too abrupt and spectacular to be explained away as "transformations" like the transition from the Middle Ages to the Renaissance. The Dutch rise was a "miracle." Dutch power and culture reached a peak very quickly after the beginning of the fight for independence, in a trajectory unparalleled in history, and was based on a very small territory. Huizinga claims that the "innermost characteristics" of such developments were not explainable by socio-economic and/or political factors. However, he could not ignore the fact that material factors were also involved. He reviews the conditions that were favorable to the Dutch rise: the small size of the country, the sea, the rivers, competence in navigation and trading, the preponderance of cities, the absence of big social gaps, and last but not least the character of the Dutch people: its simplicity, sobriety, and thriftiness. Huizinga mentions Dutch trading power and its level of education and technology, but does not identify these as the overriding driving forces as Jonathan Israel did in his 1995 book.

The Role of Calvinism

Calvinism played a decisive role in the Dutch rise and success, asserts Huizinga. It gave Dutch culture "the force to grow"; it gave the Dutch people the "faith, courage, confidence and steadfastness,"[9] which were the ultimate bases of the country's political, military, and economic achievements. Thus, religious and cultural factors helped explain material success; it was not primarily material factors that sustained culture. J. Israel did not see the issue in quite the same way. He also did not consider Calvinism such an outstanding and unique factor in Dutch success. He admitted that Calvinism gave an orderly structure to the dogma and organization of the early Dutch reform movement and absorbed its fragmentation, which was very important,[10] but he also commented on the intolerance of the Calvinist clergy, which was culturally very constraining.

What Role for Leadership and Governance?

Huizinga does not believe that leadership and governance are essential conditions of rise and prosperity. This puts him in opposition to the other historians of this study, with the exceptions of Braudel and several of the Americans who will be discussed later. Huizinga's divergence is remarkable because, in contrast to the latter, he does not believe in long-term economic determinants of history. Huizinga's doubts were nourished by the incredibly messy and permanently fragmented nature of the Dutch government and Dutch policy. When he compared the Dutch of the seventeenth century to the surrounding great powers, he found that the strong will, vanity, and adventurism of Europe's absolutist rulers and their centralized bureaucracies had served the well-being of their respective people much less well than the Dutch system, with all its messiness, had served its own. J. Israel, too, comments extensively on the disorder and fragmentation of Dutch governance, but he is convinced that at least twice the Dutch Republic would have courted disaster without the willpower and foresight of extraordinary leaders.[11] Another historian attributed Huizinga's deep distrust of leadership and governmental power to his religious heritage and to his ancestors, who had been Anabaptist preachers since the sixteenth century.[12] The Anabaptists were radical, reformist Puritan dissenters who refused, as a matter of principle, to participate in government or public service.

Decline and End

Dutch thinkers of the eighteenth century described the decline and collapse of their country's power and Golden Age with shock and sadness, and sought moral reasons for the fall. Some of this shock and sadness can still be felt in Huizinga's analysis of the decline of the Netherlands. He notes a "waning of the true national aspirations and inspirations" and a "weakening of taste and ability," and asks, "when did the forces weaken, the flowers wither?"[13] Spiritually, Holland seemed to "dry out and fall asleep." Had the Dutch people lost some of its most essential characteristics? Huizinga believes that the eighteenth century was as financially rich as the seventeenth—he is probably wrong about this—and that only the Dutch people's new "craving for peace and quiet" could ultimately explain the end of the Golden Age and the decline of the country. The circumlocutions by which Huizinga tries to capture the cultural causes of decline are metaphors at best, and explain very little. It is true that Huizinga did not have access to the enormous wealth of relevant economic, trade, financial, and population data that Jonathan Israel's research would make available sixty years later, but it is still surprising that he has so little to say about the dramatic collapse of the Dutch world trading position, and nothing about the fast pauperization of the cities, the emigration of many highly skilled elites, the shattering military defeats, or the intellectual deterioration of the universities—which are more than enough to fully explain Holland's decline.

Johan Huizinga and the Jews

Dutch Culture in the Seventeenth Century has a small paragraph on the Jews, which is significant because Huizinga published it in 1941 during the Nazi occupation of his country. The Jews were not important to the rise and success of the Netherlands, states Huizinga; a judgment J. Israel has shown to be wrong: Jews did make an important contribution to the economic prosperity of the Dutch Republic. But Huizinga praised the Dutch Republic of the seventeenth century for offering many Jews peace, toleration, and a certain measure of respect that they did not enjoy in other parts of Europe. However, seventeenth-century Jewish immigrants from Germany did not enjoy the same respect, and Huizinga takes their side. He deplores that they had to "suffer from the unspeakable defamation of Israel."[14]

CHAPTER 9

Arnold Toynbee
UK, 1889-1975 [1]

Arnold Toynbee wrote a history of the world as a succession of civilizations. His *Study of History* in twelve volumes grew over more than thirty years. The first six volumes (1934-1939) contain the theories of civilization that made his fame. The last six volumes (1954-1961) cover many varied issues, such as theory of history, universal states and churches, contacts between civilizations, the future of the West, and more. The last, rarely-read volume, XII: *Reconsiderations*, contains, in response to his detractors, a self-critical re-examination of some of his theses, particularly a retraction of his earlier hostility to Judaism (see Part I, Chapter 5). Toynbee's intellectual universe was vast. His references show that he received much of his inspiration from the Bible, Greek mythology, and Goethe. Spengler was the philosopher of history with the greatest influence on him, and other influences were Gibbon and Ibn Khaldun. Toynbee was a Protestant Christian believer—Christianity dominated his thought as much as Islam dominated Ibn Khaldun's. He was also a convinced English pacifist who abhorred war and much else in modern technological civilization. His books are loaded with value judgments. Few historians would sin more openly against Max Weber's postulate that science had to be "value-free."

Whatever ethical values Toynbee many have professed, his judgment of contemporary political events and personalities was notoriously poor. In 1936 he went to Berlin to meet Hitler and returned deeply convinced of the Nazi dictator's sincere love for peace.[2] Not surprisingly, he disliked Churchill and supported Neville Chamberlain. During the same years, he was deeply respectful of Stalin. In 1939, after the show trials in Moscow, the mass purges, and the reports that millions were being deported to the Gulag, he wrote: "Stalin has acted with a subtlety in which he is perhaps a pioneer,"[3] and promised the red dictator a "title to fame as a statesman" for his "brilliant political homeopathy." Toynbee was not the only British intellectual of his time to sympathize with Hitler or Stalin, although it was his exclusive distinction to sympathize with both simultaneously. At the height of the cold war in the 1960s, he named not the Soviet Union but the United States (together with Israel after the Six-Day War) as being the most dangerous country in the world.

Toynbee counted twenty-one (later amended to twenty-three) civilizations, most of them extinct but five (later seven) still living: the West, Islam, the Far East (mainly Japan and Korea), Hinduism, and Orthodox Christianity. In the volumes that appeared before 1939, Toynbee did not count Judaism, modern China, Africa, or Ottoman Turkey as genuine civilizations. He openly displayed his prejudices against all of them and also the "black race," which he felt "has failed to take an active part in the enterprise of civilization."[4]

Toynbee believed that civilizations are subject to certain laws of history based on shared patterns of behavior, but these laws are not coercive and do not necessarily lead to identical outcomes. He reached some of his deepest convictions in a long internal struggle with the key ideas of his admired mentor, Spengler. One can spot Spengler's shadow even when his name does not appear. When Toynbee asserts at the beginning of his work that "we cannot see into the future,"[5] he is obviously responding to the beginning of Spengler's work, which had asserted that we can. Civilizations are not closed units. They influence each other; there is "intrinsic comparability"[6] between them because cultural achievements are transmitted from one civilization to the next. Toynbee refuted Spengler's "organic" determinism and maintained that man could always change his own fate: "The dead civilizations are not dead by fate, and therefore a living civilization is not doomed...to join the majority of its kind."[7] Therefore, to Toynbee, the end of the West was not inevitable. However, he did join Spengler in having a general feeling of pessimism about the future of the West. Marxism was another theory of history he opposed all his life, not in part but entirely. The progress of a civilization shows in not material but spiritual matters. Likewise, the decline and breakdown of a civilization is not caused by economic factors but by political mistakes and spiritual changes.

In contrast to many others, Toynbee was greatly interested in the rise and growth of civilizations, not only their decline. The contribution for which he is best remembered remains his theory of the genesis of civilizations.

The Genesis of Civilizations and the Working of "Challenge-and-Response"

A new civilization emerges as a "secession" or "differentiation"[8] from an earlier one that had lost its creative power and therefore also the adhesion of many of its members. Civilizations do not emerge because of any genetic predisposition of a people, or due to easy and inviting natural conditions, but as a response to five external or internal challenges. These can come from difficult natural living conditions, a move to a new country (conquest or migration), foreign blows and aggression, external pressures, and internal persecution or discrimination for religious or social reasons. The greater the challenge, the greater the stimulus. This principle, however, has its limits. Challenges that are too severe can break a society. The severity of the challenges cannot increase indefinitely. If it does, a "law of diminishing returns" in terms of civilizational responses sets in. Some civilizations were overwhelmed by challenges to which they had no response and disappeared; others survived in a different, often diminished form. Therefore, there is a "Golden Mean,"[9] defined as the middle ground between a challenge that is too weak and one that is excessively severe. The most stimulating challenges belong to this middle ground.

The Flourishing of Civilizations, Repetitive Challenges, the Working of Creative Leaders and Minorities, and the Movement of "Withdrawal-and-Return"

Some civilizations are born but never grow. They become, in Toynbee's terms, "arrested" or "blind alleys." Among the "blind alleys" one finds Sparta, the Eskimos (as the Inuit were called in his time), and, Toynbee's black sheep, Ottoman Turkey.[10] For a civilization to grow, it needs more than a single stimulus; a slackening of challenges can lead to stagnation and decline. There must be a "vital impulse," an *élan vital*—Toynbee liked the beautiful but not easily translatable term of the French philosopher Henri Bergson—that carries further and converts the movement into a "repetitive recurrent rhythm." If a civilization continues to thrive after a series of successful responses to external challenges, the field of action of "challenge-and-response" will shift from the external to the internal environment. After this transference, the main challenges will be internal.

Rise and thriving have specific sociological drivers. They can only be explained by tiny creative minorities and personalities who are followed by the majority that Toynbee, the Oxford don, calls contemptuously "the sluggish rearguard."[11] He is an elitist, and fascinated by the regular appearance of creative individuals. Toynbee considers a movement of "withdrawal-and-return" as essential to this process, which many political and religious leaders have undergone. With fascinating regularity, future great leaders need to disengage and temporarily withdraw from their social milieu and subsequently return to the same milieu, transfigured. To realize their potential, they must be temporarily released from their social environment and constraints. This seems to facilitate later creativity. The biographies of many, but not all, of the world's great leaders seem to confirm this theory.

The Breakdown of Civilizations and the Transformation of "Creative" into "Dominant" Minorities

Toynbee rejects deterministic explanations of decline. Civilizations die as a result of their own faults. "The moral responsibility for the breakdown of civilization is upon the heads of the leaders."[12] Those who were successful in dealing with one challenge often fail when the next arrives, because they complacently rest on their laurels. There is a loss of creative power, a "nemesis of creativity"[13] in the souls of once-creative individuals and minorities. These then turn into merely "dominant" minorities that rule by force. Other, connected reasons include the rejection of necessary changes by old institutions, militarism, and the "intoxication of victory,"[14] which can lead victorious nations and religions to commit grave mistakes. Toynbee does not mention economic or ecological factors in breakdowns, not even foreign aggression and defeat in war.

The Disintegration of Civilizations and "Schisms" in the Soul and Social Body

The breakdown of a civilization does not have to lead to its disintegration. It can simply cause the "petrification"[15] of a civilization, as in the case of Ancient Egypt. Disintegration is the terminal phase of a civilization's life. It is provoked by "schisms" or deep splits in the population—in the souls of the people—when different and contradictory modes of behavior and feeling emerge. It is significant that Toynbee chooses the disparaging religious term "schism," which comes from church history, namely the split between the Western and Eastern Church. He dislikes not only open wars but also conflict and confrontation in general. In Toynbee's thought, there is nothing positive in conflict—and this is a judgment that other historians would certainly reject. Toynbee detects all the symptoms of disintegration in our Western civilization as Spengler had done before. He characterizes his own time with the terms "barbarization," "vulgarization," "standardization," etc.[16] Fernand Braudel might have even questioned the term "disintegration": He postulated that civilizations of long duration do not simply disintegrate and disappear, they transform and their components re-appear in new places and forms.

Toynbee believed that spiritual and religious forces were driving and should continue to drive history, but not science, technology, and industry. He understood little of the latter group and deplored its importance in the modern world. After World War II, he feared for the future of civilization and argued for the establishment of a universal state or a world government. A spiritual recovery and return to religion seemed to him essential to create a better world.

Arnold Toynbee and the Jews

No other modern non-Jewish historian of civilizations was as strongly interested in the Jews and the Hebrew Bible as Toynbee was. Chapters and paragraphs on Jewish history are spread across his work and could fill several hundred pages.[17] Prior to Toynbee, no other world historian had made statements about Judaism that became so widely known in his own time, and so hotly debated and challenged, particularly by the Jews themselves. These statements provoked a flood of articles, public debates, and scholarly books and publications, which Toynbee meticulously recorded in his last volumes. Among the comments he made about the Jews and their history in his vast oeuvre, one can find many traditional anti-Jewish themes voiced in the works published before the twentieth century, but in his last years, he completely changed his mind and expressed beautiful, eloquent hopes for a new rise of the Jewish people.

Toynbee's attitude was illogical from the very beginning, explicable only as a result of his Christian malaise. He called the Jews a "fossil," comparable to the Parsees in India, and this became his best-known term apart from "challenge-and-response." He denied the Jews a place among true civilizations. But then why did he return to his "pet" fossil again and again, every few pages in his twelve volumes? The Parsees are mentioned once or twice and then disappear from his story. According to Toynbee, even in biblical times Jews did not have a truly authentic and independent civilization; they were part of an over-arching, vaguely described, "Syriac" civilization. After the destruction of the Second Temple by the Romans, they became "debris," "drifting about in the world down to this day."[18] He mentions with admiration Rabbi Yohanan Ben-Zakkai, who transformed Judaism after this catastrophe and helped it survive, but therein lies a contradiction: Toynbee recognizes the extraordinary adaptation and survival of the Jews, but does not want to acknowledge the continuity and long duration of the Jewish people and civilization. It is mainly, he believed, the response to discrimination that formed the Jewish character. Toynbee holds that the Jews are intensely aware of their difference and imbued with their "immeasurable superiority"—which, coming from his pen, is a dubious compliment.[19] When Toynbee comes to the twentieth century, he excoriates the West for the *Shoah* in the most severe terms that could be heard in the 1950s. This was the period before the Eichmann trial, when Europe tried to forget this unpleasant episode and the few available books about it did not sell and were barely known. Toynbee warns the West that it will live in "lasting infamy" for its crime. He is one of very few people who seems to have anticipated in the 1950s that the *Shoah* would one day, in fact half a century later, occupy a major place in the conscience of the world. But then he turns around and condemns Israel with equal vehemence for its alleged injustices committed against the Palestinians. His questioning of Israel's right to exist and, as he saw it, its fault in displacing Palestinians, was often associated with attacks against America and the Jewish lobby there. His words anticipated in almost identical terms the antisemitic/anti-Zionist propaganda wave in the West that started around the year 2000.

But in parallel, and prior to 1961 when the last volume of his *Study of History* appeared, something happened that made him overturn many of his old convictions, if not his anti-Zionism. There is no explanation for his radical reappraisal of the Jewish people. He admits in this final volume, for the first time, that he grew up with an anti-Jewish bias that twisted his judgment. No longer are the Jews a "fossil"; they are now praised for having created an alternative model for civilizations no less important than the Chinese or Greek model. The Jews were the first to show how a people could maintain itself after being uprooted. "The living generation of mankind and our successors" need the Jewish Diaspora model: "this pioneer achievement has proved to be the wave of the future."[20] Toynbee anticipated that many other "Diasporas" would emerge in the future, an amazing foresight in the 1950s when national borders were still closed in most of the world. There was still more to come.

Toynbee calls on the Jewish people to seek converts, to address itself to the entire world and make it Jewish. This would be "Judaism's achievement of its destiny," because "the Jewish religion is meant for all mankind."[21] He hopes that a Jewish prophet will appear to convince the Jewish people of its universal mission: "The world has been waiting for this prophet for 2500 years." Does this mean that the old English Protestant no longer believed that Jesus had been this prophet? In any event, no more demanding and lofty world mission was ever imagined for the Jews in the twentieth century. When the twelfth, last volume of Toynbee's *Study of History* appeared, Jews barely reacted. They had probably already stopped reading him.

CHAPTER 10

Pitirim Sorokin
USA, 1889-1968 [1]

Pitirim Alexandrovich Sorokin was born into a small Finnish-minority community in rural Russia. He was ten or eleven years old when he saw a town for the first time and learned to read and write. In 1906 he was arrested as an anti-Tsarist revolutionary activist, and after the Revolution of 1917 he became a member of Kerensky's provisional government and founded a Russian Peasant Soviet that was soon dispersed by the Communists. In 1918 he took up the fight again, this time against Lenin and Trotsky, and was twice arrested and then sentenced to death. Pardoned by Lenin, he was expelled from the country in 1922 and immigrated to the United States, where from 1930 to 1955 he was professor of sociology at Harvard. Pitirim Sorokin's active, high-level involvement in the violent turmoil of his time makes him comparable to Thucydides, Sima Qian and Ibn Khaldun. Apart from these four, none of the authors providing the basis of this book could claim personal participation in critical and historic world events. Sorokin, too, risked his life, lost his bet, and turned to writing and studying rise and decline in history. The personal experience of Sorokin's predecessors made them lucid about the realities and pitfalls of power politics. The same cannot be said of Sorokin: experience made him more religious.

Among modern theorists of rise and decline, Sorokin is rare. His work, which was appreciated in his time but is rarely mentioned today, shows that even in the twentieth century and under an academic veneer, the definition of "rise," "thriving," and "decline" could entirely depend on religious, in this case Christian, criteria. Like Toynbee, Sorokin was influenced by Spengler and Christian beliefs, but the comparison to Toynbee cannot go very far. Toynbee moderated and modified Spengler's dogmatic constructions: he knew too much history to accept all of them. Sorokin adopted some of them, added more of his own, and tried to buttress his theories with statistics of unclear origin. Toynbee's religious background was Protestant. Sorokin's was Russian Orthodox, but his beliefs accommodated a strong strand of eschatology, the conviction that a fiery end of the world is near, after which humankind—or what remains of it—will rise again, pristine and wholly purified. Although this is not part of Russian Orthodox mainstream theology, Sorokin was imbued with this belief, which has many roots in Jewish messianism.

Sorokin's book is an attempt to write world history as the manifestation of a single, dominant principle. His grand frame of history is spiritual. The key to his work is the idea that all expressions of a "culture" (like Spengler, he uses "culture" for civilization), that is, all thoughts, institutions, ways of life, art, etc. belong to one of two fundamentally different categories. One is spiritual or idealistic (in Sorokin's term, "ideate," or dominated by the spirit), the other corporal or materialistic (in Sorokin's term, "sensate," or dominated by the senses). There is also a mixed or intermediary category between the two where spiritual-idealistic components generally predominate. Sorokin's theory postulates a complete separation of mind and body, a dualism propagated by Christianity and philosophers such as Plato, but no longer supported by modern science and medicine (see Part IV, Chapter 2, for more on this topic). He goes to great length to prove that this separation is a historical reality. One of his many examples is the sorting of popes, Russian tsars, Austrian emperors, and English and French kings by "cultural mentality." All are said to belong to one of the three categories above. Sorokin counts 256 popes reigning between 42 CE and 1932, and calculates that 14.6% of them were materialistic, 40.1% spiritual-idealistic, and 45.3% mixed—not a bad score overall. In contrast, the 32 French kings from 938 to 1793 CE score less well: fully 62.5% were materialistic, only 25% spiritual-idealistic, and 12.5% mixed. Russian tsars—Sorokin had fought the last one—do no better: of the 32 that reigned between 1290 and 1918, he characterizes 59.3% as materialistic and only 15.6% as idealistic, which is even worse than the notoriously disreputable French, and 25.1% mixed. Austrian kings fare a little better, and the English kings do not.[2] As we know virtually nothing of the intimate lives and innermost beliefs of early popes and kings, and not enough about the later ones, these data reflect no other reality than Sorokin's strong ascetic inclinations and prejudices. To substantiate his theories he presents similar number games, because this is what it is, for political, cultural, and scientific world history. This is not exactly what Braudel and his school had in mind when they called for "quantitative history," i.e. history based on quantifiable geographic, economic, and social data.

The second main principle of Sorokin's theory is that civilizations ("cultures") are comparable to living organisms, as they are for Spengler. Cultures are "living unities." All their components, such as art, music, science, philosophy, law, ethics, and even social, political, and economic organization, are in harmony and change simultaneously in the same direction. They are not an agglomeration of independent compartments randomly placed side by side but show an "inner consistency" and "integration" of all elements.[3] Sorokin concedes that economic conditions may be less closely associated with the other components. Socio-cultural change results only from enacted laws, not external challenges. A culture "bears in itself the reason of its change."[4] Sorokin rejects "externalist" theories of change, such as Toynbee's "challenge-and-response" model. Culture "changes by virtue of its own forces...it cannot help changing even if all its external conditions are constant."[5] This idea is an emulation of the oft-quoted Spengler.

Sorokin's best-known contribution is his theory of historical dynamics. History repeats itself. There are no continuous, linear trends, only cycles. History moves in "fluctuations" or "alternations," where periods of idealistic and materialistic culture alternate and replace each other. One fluctuation can last a few decades or hundreds of years before the tide begins to turn. The last five hundred years, the years that William H. McNeill called "The Rise of the West," are in Sorokin's eyes the decline of the West. These centuries have been dominated by a growing materialistic fluctuation in all sectors of life and culture. This is glaringly visible in politics: "Who are our leaders? Successful moneymakers. It matters little how the money is made. With few exceptions, they are at the top of 'society.'...In harmony with this almost everything is for sale in our culture."[6] But this wave is now reaching "the end of the road,"[7] heralding a great crisis of materialism. The West is heading into "one of the deepest and most significant crises of its life. The crisis is far greater than the ordinary, its depth is unfathomable, its end not yet in sight."[8] However, the inevitable breakdown will not be terminal. On this point, Sorokin diverges from Spengler, who predicted that it would be. When Sorokin describes the prospects of the end-time that has just begun, he sounds more like a traditional American fire-and-brimstone preacher than a professor of sociology. "Purified by the fiery ordeal of catastrophe Western society will be granted a new charisma, and with it, resurrection."[9] From the ordeal a new spiritual-idealistic culture will emerge.

Sorokin uses the terms "rise" and "decline" only rarely, but his intention is clear. "Rise" is equivalent to the "ideate," and "decline" to the "sensate" fluctuations of history. The former are dominated by the mind, the latter by the senses. History from the fifteenth to the twentieth century is all decline, including the Renaissance, the scientific revolution, the "Rise of the West," and the fastest increases in living standards and life expectancy in human history, but also the most destructive wars and revolutions the human race has known. When was there any great creative period? In the early period of Christianity, from the sixth to the twelfth century. This period was spiritual, according to the author, and its aims and needs non-material. This is a simplification. Sorokin does not discuss the catastrophic collapse of Europe's material culture after the fall of the Roman Empire or the suffering and bloodshed accompanying foreign invasions, nor does he refer to the improvement of material conditions and the tripling of the European population between the ninth and eleventh to twelfth centuries. His criteria were different from those of other scholars and most other people of his time. Sorokin's work is an exception, but also a warning to readers not to ignore the heavy ideological baggage that can accompany the terms "rise" and "decline." Sorokin rarely mentions Jews and brings no new understanding to Jewish rise or decline.

CHAPTER 11

Fernand Braudel
France, 1902-1985 [1]

Fernand Braudel is considered the most influential French historian of the twentieth century. After World War II, he became the leader of the "Annales" school of historiography, which emphasized the role of large-scale socio-economic factors in history. Braudel became the main proponent of "structural" or "quantitative" history of his generation. He saw history as the "queen of sciences," and was actively involved in both drafting French schoolbooks and popularizing history for adults. Of all his work, three voluminous books stand out: *The Mediterranean and the Mediterranean World in the Age of Phillip II* (1949), considered his most influential book, *Capitalism and Material Life* (1967-79), and the unfinished *Identity of France* (1988-90). [2]

Braudel's Philosophy of History

Braudel's philosophy of history can be summarized by three principles:

1. The past explains the present—not only the recent past, but many "pasts," including very ancient ones. If the deep currents of the past are well understood, they can help us predict some of the future.

2. The present is not the result of "events," famous leaders, and others making the news of the day, but of long-lasting, deep developments that can go back hundreds if not thousands of years. The historian's task is to sort out this "long duration" and separate it from the circumstantial events that are only "foam" on the long waves of history. For a traditional political historian, a day or a year is an appropriate measure of time. Not so for a "long duration" historian. Only "long duration" history can really explain the present and, perhaps, the future.

3. All historical events—political, military, and cultural—have a material basis. This is why social and economic conditions are essential to grasping history. Basic socio-economic structures change very slowly over time, which explains history's "long durations." The historian of civilizations must pay great attention to quantities: geology, geography, climate, population

numbers, size and location of territory, distances, trade, and migrations, etc. Real history moves slowly because its material structures are deep and change gradually over very long periods.

Braudel revealed how deeply his personal life influenced his philosophy of history. He was born in 1902 in a small country village of 200 inhabitants that had not changed for several hundred years, a "long duration" indeed, and grew up in a house built in 1806 and untouched ever since. His life's watershed came in 1940 when he was a French soldier and fell into German captivity. He wrote his masterwork, *The Mediterranean,* during his five years as a prisoner of war, without a library or other resources save his stupendous memory. After 1940 he no longer wanted to hear of "events." "Down with 'events' particularly when they are annoying!"[3] he admitted with unusual candor. In 1940 he chose, in his own words, the "long duration observatory" as his "hiding place." He took up the Mediterranean, which fascinated him with its historical "perpetuity" and "majestic immobility."

Long Duration

Braudel's main emphasis is not on rise or decline—he barely uses the terms. What attracts his attention is how civilizations survive, transform themselves, find new expressions, and re-emerge. He has a chapter in one of his books on the "halt or decline" of the Arab civilization after the twelfth century, which is soon followed by "The Islamic civilization has survived,"[4] and then a chapter on the "renaissance" of Islam in our days. What intrigued Braudel was not so much the decline and fall of the Roman Empire, but its "permanencies" and "survivals" in European civilization until the emergence of national literatures in the fourteenth century.[5] *Capitalism and Material Life* identified the long-term cycles in capitalist systems. Such a cycle developed in the twelfth century and dominated Europe's economy from the fifteenth to the eighteenth century, for approximately 500 years. The *Mediterranean and the Mediterranean World in the Age of Phillip II* devotes hundreds of pages to the climate, civilization, economy, and demographics of the Mediterranean world, but "Events, Politics and People," the last part of the book, only mentions the King of Spain, who had ruled this world for many decades, at the very end of the book, where we find him on his deathbed![6]

Civilization

If concepts of rise or decline did not greatly interest Braudel, the concept of "civilization" did, and very much so. He went to great lengths to explain the different meanings of the term in various languages, discussing when and where it first appeared, how it evolved, and how it distinguished itself from "culture." Braudel also wrote a critical review of a number of important historians of civilization, including Jacob Burckhardt, Oswald Spengler, and Arnold Toynbee, whose works he had very attentively studied.[7]

The Role of Great Men in History

His treatment King Phillip II of Spain shows how radically Braudel downgraded the "great men" of history. His second, posthumous book on the Mediterranean has a chapter, "A Great Personality: Mediterranean Civilization."[8] This chapter title reveals and expresses the core of his philosophy. Civilizations determine history and can deservedly claim greatness; short-lived kings cannot. Of Pericles, whose critical importance Thucydides had so clearly seen, Braudel said in the same book: "Is it not an illusion to believe that great men have destiny in their hands when in reality they are carried away by it just like everybody else?"[9] While there was little risk that downgrading Pericles would earn Braudel enemies among the living, a similar historical judgment entangled him in a controversy with the French Jewish historian of antisemitism Leon Poliakoff. Braudel spoke of the expulsion of the Jews from Spain by Ferdinand and Isabella, but defended the rulers against Poliakoff's charge that they were antisemitic. "In the Spanish situation, I am therefore naturally on the side of the Jews....But such feelings...are irrelevant to the basic problem....Let me stress once more that the economic situation, a blind force...must take its share of the blame. When they expelled the Jews in 1492, Ferdinand and Isabella were not acting as individuals....Civilizations, like economies, have their long-term history: they are prone to mass movements, carried...forward by the weight of history..."[10] Don Isaac Abrabanel, the leader of the Spanish Jews, who knew his king very well, tried in vain to prevent the expulsion. He was convinced that Ferdinand could "act as an individual" and rescind the expulsion decree. Braudel did not retreat from his position when he discussed the history of the twentieth century. When he wrote about twentieth-century Europe and France, he had almost nothing to say about the Vichy regime or Hitler. He mentioned the latter once, in the same breath as Emperor Charles V of Habsburg, King Louis XIV of France, and Napoleon, three other famous European rulers who all learned the hard way that they could not unify Europe by force.[11] Were these three cut of the same cloth as Hitler? Even if Braudel's purpose was to emphasize the deep forces of history and de-emphasize individual rulers, the comparison is troubling. In his lifetime Braudel's theories were well received by French society and academia. During these years France had a strong inclination to forget the Vichy years, or have them explained away as a dark period brought about by overwhelming forces rather than France's own leaders.

The Future

In 1960-1962, Braudel tried to apply his principles to forecast future trajectories of the main contemporary civilizations, based on their "long duration" history."[12] He sees an "Arab renaissance" in the making, and describes the essence of the Arab-Israeli conflict with a quip that shows more insight than many other explanations of his time: "Two people of God at the same time—too much for diplomats and generals!" Africa will develop into a great culture of the future, he predicts, whereas China might be hobbled by its alleged cultural immobility. Europe's unification will remain tenuous if it does not include greater cultural and religious unity. The United States will have severe problems, particularly in its race relations and through its isolationism, but Soviet Russia stands at the beginning of a great transformation toward a "happy" society and "fantastic" material achievements; it has a "prodigious" future. Half a century has passed, and none of Braudel's forecasts has stood the test of time. Some of the "long duration" forces he saw seem in retrospect a mirror of contemporaneous French habits of thought and Gaullist foreign policy objectives.

Fernand Braudel and the Jews

The application of Braudel's principles to Jewish history raises particular difficulties because the material basis of Jewish life has changed often and is much less well known than religious history. When Braudel says that "civilizations, whatever their size...can always be located on a geographic map,"[13] he seems to exclude the Jews. Moreover, every civilization is supposed to have an economic basis. In a posthumous work of several hundred pages, Braudel compares the Mediterranean civilizations of the Ancient Orient, Greece, and Rome. On ancient Israel, there is less than half a page, with a mention of the Temple and the copper mines of King Solomon. And then this curious phrase at the end: "Nobody could have foreseen...the fabulous role which the future had in store for Israel's spiritual message!"[14] Indeed, nobody could if he were to look only at King Solomon's copper mines. The material basis of the country, as it turns out, was irrelevant to Israel's future impacts on the world.

Braudel probably wrestled with the question of whether or not there is a Jewish civilization, and how his theory could accommodate it. Hegel famously retorted, "Too bad for the facts!" when he was told that some facts did not confirm his philosophy of history. In the case of the Jews, Braudel did acknowledge historical facts even when they did not fit into his philosophy at first glance. The result of his reflections is an extraordinary chapter in his master work on the Mediterranean in the age of Phillip II: "One Civilization against the Rest: The Destiny of the Jews."[15] In considering the sixteenth and seventeenth centuries, Braudel could finally identify the material basis of Jewish civilization. He found that Jews "formed the leading commercial network in the world," which sustained their cultural and religious well-being, communal self-government, and political influence. Braudel makes a number of detailed observations significant beyond the age of Phillip II because they pinpoint essential conditions of Jewish success across other ages as well:

1. The Jews were essential intermediaries between civilizations, knowing many languages, printing the first books, and disseminating science, technology, and even military arts.
2. To make up for dispersion and small numbers, the Jews created strong, coherent networks through travel, letters, and books. Their small numbers were no obstacle to their effectiveness.
3. The Jews were extremely capable of adapting to the prevailing environment.
4. Intermarriage was frequent, usually to Judaism's gain.
5. When the Jews could do so, they did not hesitate to fight or threaten their enemies: they organized several successful economic boycotts of hostile cities.

The essential feature of the Jewish civilization, and of Jewish suffering as well as strength and survival, is that their civilization was moving in the opposite direction of all others. "It disputed and defied" them while they were forming their new nation-states. The Jewish Diaspora was a "single destiny," and its "theatre was the whole world." "It was a modern destiny, ahead of its time."

As though he wanted to make up for his earlier doubts, not unlike Toynbee, Braudel now pays homage to Jewish civilization:

> There was quite undoubtedly a Jewish civilization, so individual that it is not always recognized as an authentic civilization. And yet it exerted its influence, transmitted certain cultural values, resisted others, sometimes accepting, sometimes refusing: it possessed all the qualities by which we have defined civilization. True it was not or was only notionally rooted to any one place; it did not obey any stable and unvarying geographical imperatives. This was one of its most original features, but not the only one....(It is) a civilization full of vitality and movement, and certainly not inert and "fossilized" as Arnold Toynbee calls it. It was on the contrary both vigilant and aggressive, swept from time to time by strange messianic outbursts, particularly in the early modern period when it was divided between, on the one hand, that rationalism which led some toward skepticism and atheism, well before Spinoza, and on the other, the propensity of the masses to irrational superstition and exaltation....The one thing of which we can be certain is that the destiny of Israel, its strength, its survival, and its misfortunes are all the consequences of its remaining irreducible, refusing to be diluted, that is of being a civilization faithful to itself. Every civilization is its own heaven and hell.[16]

CHAPTER 12

Marshall G.S. Hodgson
USA, 1922-1968 [1]

Marshall G.S. Hodgson was a scholar of Islamic and world history at the University of Chicago. His history of Muslim civilization in three volumes was renowned in his day and has not lost its influence. The great Arabist Albert Hourani was inspired by it and praised it as an "unusual and original" book, comparable to the work of Ibn Khaldun. [2] Hodgson was a practicing Quaker with a deep understanding of religion. He wanted very much to do justice to Islam, but was also strongly aware that no historian can approach a foreign civilization with complete objectivity, unaffected by his own cultural and religious upbringing. Because Hodgson was lucidly aware of the limits of our objectivity, he was able to make a number of important observations about civilization in general.

Rise and Decline are Relative Notions

For Hodgson, the notions of rise and decline are relative, often subjective, and dependent on the self-image of a civilization. The definition of a civilization "is only partly given by the data itself. In part, it is a function of the inquirer's purpose," he writes, and "each civilization defines its own scope, just as does each religion." [3] The scope Islam defined for its civilization was all-embracing, the goals it set for itself the highest possible. The Koran had promised Muslims that they would be the best community that ever rose up in human history. Muslims could reasonably believe that this promise was nearly fulfilled, and fail to understand, to use Bernard Lewis' phrase, "what went wrong." Islam's greatest period lasted from the tenth century to the thirteenth, but even until the sixteenth and seventeenth centuries Muslim civilization "came closer than any had ever come to uniting all mankind under its ideals," [4] and remained creative on its own terms. The early flowering of Islam makes later periods look decadent in our eyes and theirs, but this is an error of perspective induced in part by the memory of Rome's decadence, which has had a deep influence on our thought. In the case of Islam, as in other examples, what is exceptional and needs explanation is this early, simultaneous flowering of all aspects of life, more than the apparent decline in later periods.

The Rise of Islam in External Context

The rise, prosperity, and decline of Muslim civilization are at the center of Hodgson's interest. He does not see civilizational rise and decline as autonomous phenomena, but as developments essentially shaped by world history, which sets the external conditions that favor either rise or decline. Hodgson's placement of Islamic rise and decline into a broader context is as topical today as it was in his own time, and adds an original perspective to general theories of rise and decline. The indirect but decisive influence of external factors on a civilization's rise was clearly operative at the birth of Islam. Hodgson points out that Islam formed in the sixth century in a historical and cultural void, a "residual" area where neither Greek nor Sanskrit traditions had any roots. This area would have changed anyway and fallen into some other hands, with or without Islam. It could have come under Persian-Sassanid influence, for example, but the Sassanid Empire was so weakened that it itself fell to Arab invaders (634-651 CE). The original cultural void of the region, together with the Persian decline, gave the Arabs their great window of opportunity. The following "classical civilization of the High Caliphate"[5] (622-1258) was a period of great cultural creativity and innovation. Islam became a mass religion riding a wave of economic expansion.

Islam's Flourishing in the Sixteenth and Seventeenth Centuries

Hodgson directs his most persistent arguments against the widespread notion that after the Mongol invasions of the fourteenth century, the Muslim world entered a period of continuous stagnation, in which it remains today. The Mongol test was certainly worse than the Christian test and, in addition, the Muslim world was severely weakened by a strong economic contraction from 1300 to 1450 caused by the "Black Death" pandemic. However, similar contractions and population declines could be observed simultaneously in much of the known world, including in Europe, Africa, and China. After 1500, a recovery set in that led Islam to a new period of political and cultural brilliance. Three great empires emerged, each developing its own form of Islamic civilization: the Persian Safavi Empire (flourished 1503-1722), the Indian Timuri Empire (flourished 1526-1707), and the Ottoman Empire (flourished 1517-1718). During these two centuries, Islam continued to expand in Europe, Asia, and Africa, until it counted around 20% of the world's population in its numbers, the same proportion that it boasts today. At the time of these three "gunpowder empires," Islam reached its peak political power and made its closest approach to the world-dominating role the West would soon take over.

The Decline of Islam in the External Context

Hodgson concedes that in this flourishing period, the sixteenth and seventeenth centuries, Islamic society began to develop an excessive conservatism. The civilization flourished within established lines of tradition, which was very different from the way the creativity of the European Renaissance developed. Toward the end of the period, it was hard to detect any Muslim creativity at all: in the eighteenth century, Islam and particularly the Arab world became "culturally barren."[6] In addition, the bitter quarrel between the Shia and Sunni sects was putting an end to Muslim cosmopolitism. After 1700, a general depression of social and cultural life, dominated by religious conservatism, set in, followed after 1800 by the dramatic collapse of Islam's world position. Hodgson justifies the term "decadence" for this decline by the fact that many negative developments appeared together, but he insists that this decadence became fatal and apparently unstoppable only because it occurred just at the time Europe entered a period of prolonged, outstanding creativity. European expansion had already begun in the late fifteenth century when the Muslim world was exposed to the unhindered, victorious Portuguese navigation of the Indian Ocean. This was a first and very bitter political and economic blow. However, what really "sapped" Islam, to use Hodgson's term, was Europe's "transmutation" and the "overwhelming suddenness" of its emergence.[7] Hodgson regarded this emergence as a unique phenomenon in human history. Until the Renaissance, Islam and the West advanced at a relatively "leisurely pace." A major point in Hodgson's argumentation is that the scientific and technological progress of Europe was not faster than that of Islam,* and that the Muslim world did not need to keep up with Europe to maintain its advantage. He agreed that the creativity of Islamic civilization

---

* There are different opinions on this critical question. Ibn Khaldun might have disagreed with Hodgson's statement: he feared that fourteenth-century Europe was already moving ahead of the Arabs. See Part II, Chapter 3. Some specialized Western science historians also disagreed with Hodgson, for example George Sarton, "Arabic Science and Learning in the Fifteenth Century: Their Decadence and Fall," in *Homenaje a Millás-Vallicrosa*, vol. II (Barcelona, 1956), 303 ff. Sarton sees the beginning of the decline of Arab science and learning as occurring as early as in the thirteenth century, and the decline accelerating in the fourteenth century, and ending in complete collapse in the fifteenth century. The rest of Islamic science could not make up for this loss and was itself afflicted by some of the same problems.

in the sixteenth and seventeenth centuries was inadequate compared to that of the West, but it was still one of the greatest eras in Muslim history. Johan Huizinga and other European historians would strongly contest this presentation of European history because they see the Renaissance as a culmination of a long developmental process beginning no later than the fourteenth century. In their view, Europe's rise was not so abruptly sudden; it had deeper and older roots.

The Crisis of Islam and the Twentieth Century

Hodgson wrote his book in the 1950s and 1960s when other observers, including Fernand Braudel,[8] believed in the imminence of Arab unity or a general Muslim renaissance. Hodgson, by contrast, had no illusions about the depth of the crisis of Islam and was deeply troubled by it, because "the hopes, triumphs and failures of any civilization concern all of us....In the moral economy of mankind they are also our own hopes and failures."[9] If Islam wanted to rise and again thrive—which is also what Hodgson wanted— it needed a new "vision."[10] Hodgson bothered little with the conventional questions raised by politicians and the media, for example regarding whether the Muslims could "modernize," acquire Western technology, win the wars against their enemies, or adopt democracy. Instead, he looked deeper and asked whether Islam still had anything substantial to contribute to mankind as a whole and to the world of the future. He found little that was encouraging. He noted the sympathy that so many Muslims had felt for Nazi Germany and linked it to anti-Jewish fanaticism. This seemed to him a bad omen, because it was more than a politically-motivated coincidence. He deplored the "deep-rooted inadequacy of the historical image which was built into Islamic dogma,"[11] and called on Muslims to reassess the meanings of their religious traditions. Yet Hodgson had himself explained earlier why this would be so difficult for a faith that "was unique among the great civilizations of its time in failing to maintain the earlier lettered tradition of its region. Elsewhere, the masterpieces of the 1st millennium BC continued to be the starting point for intellectual life," but "the coming of Islam marked a breach in cultural continuity unparalleled among the great civilizations."[12] If Islam wished to rise again, it had to transform its traditional historical vision; in this way it could improve the conditions necessary for a new Muslim renaissance. At this point Hodgson made an unexpected and daring proposal that set him apart from other Western Islam experts. He called for a radical change in the Muslim attitude toward Jews and Judaism, an attitude that had become a dominant Muslim obsession in his time.

Marshall Hodgson and the Jews

Hodgson's sympathy for Muslim civilization and history did not cause him to have any less sympathy for Judaism and Jewish history, old and new, including Zionism. Hodgson refers to the importance of Jews in Muslim history in all three volumes of his work, beginning with the time of Mohammed. When the Jews rejected Mohammed they posed a real threat, because "as interpreters of monotheism the Jews had undoubtedly seniority over the Muslims."[13] Thus, their expulsion from Medina was an "admission of defeat."

Hodgson sees the future attitude of Islam to Judaism and Jews as a critical issue for the future of the Islamic civilization itself, and for Islam's relevance to the rest of the world: "The dependence of Islam on its Irano-Semitic heritage must be seen frankly and creatively: in particular its dependence on the Jewish tradition. Surely one of the spiritual tragedies of both Christianity and Islam, and perhaps especially of Islam, has been the failure to maintain an active and vital confrontation with the Jews. Both Christianity and Islam may be seen as presenting specialized developments out from the Hebrew prophetic tradition....It must be seen as a calamity that the Muslims rejected the Hebrew Bible...and failed to respect the study of Hebrew."[14] It was a historically fateful restriction that forbade Muslims to read the Hebrew Bible; all they could know of it were corrupt and legendary fragments. Hodgson's exhortation was about Muslim rise and decline, not Jewish. He saw the Jew, or better the imaginary Jew, and his fictional role as central to the drama and crisis of contemporary Islam.

CHAPTER 13

Bernard Lewis
USA, 1916— [1]

Bernard Lewis is professor emeritus at the Institute of Advanced Studies at Princeton University, and one of the best-known Islam scholars of our time. His books on Muslim history and culture pay particular attention to the rise and decline of Islamic civilizations and their interaction with the West. His *The Emergence of Modern Turkey*, first published in 1961, has become a classic, and some experts consider it his most enduring scholarly contribution. It inspired many of his later works, including the widely read *What Went Wrong?* of 2002.

The unique interest of *The Emergence of Modern Turkey* in the context of rise-and-decline theories is that it turns the conventional narrative of the rise and decline of civilizations on its head. Historians are used to describing the "progress" of a civilization in historical sequence, from birth and rise to peak periods, and from there to decline and fall. Lewis begins instead with the decline and fall of the Ottoman Empire, which fills the entire first half of his book, and proceeds to the rise of a new state, the modern Turkish republic, from the old one. He reviews the last five hundred years of Ottoman and Turkish history as a continuum, and describes how centuries of slow reform attempts unsuccessfully tried to halt the decline, until the Turkish revolution intervened more proactively to create the conditions for Turkey's renaissance. Lewis knows that it is as hazardous to try to disentangle the many complex and interacting causes for the decline of the Ottoman as it is to do the same for the Roman Empire. For both, the peak period of great accomplishment and glory was short—in the case of the Ottomans it lasted a century, from the fall of Constantinople in 1453 to the death of Suleiman I the Magnificent in 1566, followed by a much longer period of "decline." What distinguished the Ottomans from the Romans, among many other features, is that their intellectuals, in contrast to many of their rulers, were intensely conscious of their decline almost from its beginning at the time of the death of Suleiman I. A brilliant Ottoman school of historiography in the seventeenth century saw the decline clearly, but was unable to stop it.[2] Ottoman historians kept asking three questions: "What is wrong with the

Empire?"; "Why is it falling behind the nations of the infidels?"; and "What must be done?"

Lewis sorts the causes and symptoms of decline into three groups:

Government and Military

The first cause is the quality of the rulers. The first ten sultans of the Ottoman Empire, from Osman I (1281-1324), to Suleiman I the Magnificent (1494-1566), were without exception highly able and intelligent rulers. They were followed by "an astonishing series of incompetents, degenerates and misfits,"[3] which cannot have been a coincidence. It can only be explained by "a system of upbringing and selection which virtually precluded the emergence of an effective ruler." Lewis's scornful words echo those of Edward Gibbon, who had flayed most Roman emperors for their vices and corruptions.[4] From the early seventeenth century on, a catastrophic fall in the efficiency and integrity of the Ottoman apparatus of government became obvious, ending in its virtual collapse in the nineteenth century. Whether or not this was indeed the main reason for the decline of the Roman or Ottoman empires, Lewis's warning about selection systems that prevent the emergence of capable leaders is as valid today as it ever was in the past. Hand in hand with the decline in governance came the deterioration of the armed services. Their standards of alertness, training, and equipment slipped, and their readiness to accept new technologies withered. Some individuals did make efforts to introduce better methods and technologies, but they faltered because others refused to learn from Europe's growing military superiority. They put greater trust in the assumed superiority of their Muslim faith and culture.

Economic and Social

The Ottomans' technological backwardness and lack of interest in new inventions[5] became a critical factor beyond the battlefield. It allowed superior European ships to sweep the Ottoman fleet from the oceans, which had dramatic consequences, not only for the military but for the economy. European powers now dominated the seas. At the same time, the Ottomans did not know how to cope with the cheap silver coming from the Americas, which flooded and damaged their economy. Industry and trade were in the hands of Christians and Jews, and as they were second-class citizens their occupations carried no prestige. The Ottoman unwillingness to learn from the infidels was again a result of their religious faith in the superiority of the Islamic civilization. Thus, they simultaneously faced growing government expenditures, a shrinking economy, and stagnating trade. Lewis stresses the economic drivers of decline but does not espouse the fashion of other modern historians, who attribute rise and decline primarily or exclusively to economic factors.

Cultural and Intellectual

In spite of political, military, and economic decline, the Ottoman Empire maintained a vibrant cultural and intellectual life for many centuries. The seventeenth and eighteenth centuries produced great poets, painters, architects, and musicians, not to mention the thinkers and reformers who argued about decline. A real cultural and intellectual breakdown occurred only around 1800.

Military defeats prompted the Ottomans to initiate reforms in the early eighteenth century. Naval reforms and printing, which was first permitted for Turkish books in 1727, were the beginning. Ottoman reformers knew that the reform of education, science, industry, and the legal system had to be the cornerstones of Turkey's transformation. In the years after 1815 a converted Greek Jew, Hoca Ishak Effendi, translated European mathematical and physical sciences and introduced them for the first time to Turkish schools.[6] But these and other attempts at Westernization provoked revolts, countered by renewed and broader reform efforts that again triggered religious opposition, and so on. The agitation finally bore fruit in the reform of 1876, when the first Western constitution in the Muslim world was promulgated, and in 1900, when the first modern university in the Muslim world, the University of Istanbul, opened. Finally, the "Young Turk" revolt of 1908 formally began the Turkish revolution, but it was too late for the Ottoman Empire. Turkey's defeat in World War I sealed the fate of the empire, the sultanate, and the caliphate.

Despite this long prehistory of reform attempts and actual reform, it took an acute national crisis and the emergence of an exceptional statesman, Kemal Ataturk, to achieve the "forcible transference of a whole nation from one civilization to another."[7] Ataturk had no doubt about the transformation that his country needed in order to rise again. In the past, Turkey had built its future on one of three state ideologies: "Ottomanism," "Islam," or "Turkism." The Ottoman option had disappeared with the independence of the non-Turkish nations of the former empire, but the pan-Islamic option retained great attraction. After all, for centuries the Turks had seen the expansion and defense of Islam as their main national mission and the justification of their leadership position among Islamic nations. "Turkism" or Pan-Turkism was a newer option, born of nineteenth-century nationalism, and meant that all people speaking variouis forms of Turkish—in Anatolia, the Caucasus, Central Asia, and China—were counted as members of the same family, and that this family should be united. Ataturk demanded a radical break from both options. His deepest belief was in progress and "civilization," which for him meant Western civilization; there was no other, he insisted. Only Western civilization could help Turkey rise again from the ruins of the old empire. The Kemalist revolution had the great advantage of not having been imposed by foreign occupiers, although it was responding to enormous foreign challenges. Also to be noted is the fact that its leaders were not rebels from marginal or discriminated-against population groups, but members of the old Turkish elite. This means that the transformation from one civilization to another could barely have occurred under more favorable conditions. In spite of this, Lewis knows only too well that ultimate success can still not be guaranteed: "It would be rash to state that the Turkish people have made their final choice among the different paths that lie before them."[8]

Bernard Lewis and the Jews

Lewis has written extensively about Jews, particularly their links to Muslim history. Two of his books, *The Jews of Islam* (1984) and *Semites and Anti-Semites* (1986), remain essential reading for anyone interested in these subjects. Lewis repeatedly expresses one specific thought about rise and decline in Jewish history, asserting that Diaspora Jews could flourish in a meaningful sense only under the aegis of one of their religion's two successor, Christianity or Islam.[9] He substantiates this conclusion with the finding that the Jewish community of the Ottoman Empire declined together with the empire,[10] and with the additional comment that the Jewish communities in China and India, which were not living under the aegis of Christianity or Islam, made no valuable contribution to Jewish civilization. It is true that Ottoman Jewry did not experience an educational or intellectual revival comparable to that of the Christian communities in the Ottoman Empire. Lewis's observation is indisputable for Ottoman Jewry, but his comments about Indian and Chinese Jews can be questioned.[11] Their communities were tiny and isolated from the main centers of Judaism, yet they maintained, across centuries, a vibrant and apparently happy Jewish life, interacted positively with their Hindu or Confucian environments, and looked for common cultural ground with their host countries, when possible. This too is creativity.

CHAPTER 14

Jonathan I. Israel
USA, 1946— [1]

Jonathan Irving Israel taught modern history and Dutch history in English universities and is, since 2001, professor at the Institute of Advanced Studies at Princeton. In 1995 he published his monumental work *The Dutch Republic: Its Rise, Greatness and Fall 1477-1806*, which brought him international acclaim.

His *Radical Enlightenment: Philosophy and the Making of Modernity* appeared in 2002 and led to impassioned debates among historians which have still not abated. Israel argues that radical political changes such as the abolition of Europe's monarchical order based on biblical faith needed first a radical change of mind and long intellectual preparation. He claims that Spinoza was the radical philosopher who initiated this change of mind through his uncompromising advocacy of a democratic and republican order, and believes that Spinoza had an enormous, often covert influence on nearly all Enlightenment thinkers. His book is part of a new upsurge of interest in Spinoza, and may have inspired other recent books on the philosopher. *Radical Enlightenment* breaks with the schools that explain major historic changes mainly in terms of deep socio-economic forces. Max Weber had demonstrated that religious beliefs could change a civilization and create a new world; Jonathan Israel wanted to demonstrate that a philosophical movement against religion could do the same.

But Israel's views on the drivers of history are not dogmatic.[2] When economic and other material drivers are obvious, he recognizes them. This is clear from his book on the Dutch Republic, which focuses particular attention on the drivers of rise and decline. The rise and decline of a small country close to modern times draw particular interest because it is reasonable to assume that this country's history will have relevant lessons for other small countries or civilizations of our time. Historians have a huge amount of reliable sources, eyewitness accounts, and statistical data for the sixteenth and seventeenth centuries, and so there is less need to resort to conjecture and archaeological excavation than there is in the case of earlier civilizations. The Dutch Republic's so-called Golden Age—from rise to decline—spans barely 150 years, and there were another 80 years until the final end. Still, getting to the roots of rise and decline is not eased by the enormous amount of primary sources.

The Beginnings

The year 1572, when the revolt against Spain broke out, is the starting point of an independent Dutch nation and civilization—and in this case one can treat the two terms as almost identical. The roots of the event were in a remote past, and the qualities required were building up for a long time. "A revolution, a truly great revolt of a kind which fundamentally transforms the course of history, can arise only when there has been a long gestation."[3] From the thirteenth century on, the Netherlands surpassed other parts of Europe in various respects: the country had an agricultural revolution leading to higher crop yields before anyone else, a faster urbanization, and rapid technical improvements in windmills, water-drainage infrastructure, and shipbuilding, which were all of crucial importance for later developments. J. Israel also stresses the religious and spiritual developments that set the Netherlands apart from the rest of Europe even before the revolt, such as the impact of Erasmus of Rotterdam and his criticism of the Church.

The Dutch revolt was not assured of success. In fact, it was nearly extinguished, but once it survived Dutch power rose fast. In the quarter-century beginning in 1590, "a precarious strip of rebel territory had become one of the great powers of Europe,"[4] despite its having a population of no more than two million, much smaller than any of the surrounding great powers of the time. Under unrelenting Spanish pressure and with a shrinking territory, the Dutch succeeded in carrying out a profound military, economic, and institutional restructuring, which not only became the basis of their survival but also brought them an enduring siege mentality. "Successful state-building on the scale achieved in the 1590s by the Republic occurs only rarely in history, and only when great internal changes combine with exceptionally favorable circumstances without."[5]

Two Main Factors of Rise and Greatness

Jonathan Israel attributes the rise and greatness of the Dutch Republic to two main factors that underpinned every other achievement, particularly the flourishing of Dutch culture, intellectual life, and art during the Golden Age. The first was the rise of the Dutch Republic to become the leading commercial and naval power of Europe and one of the principal military and political powers as well. After 1590, the Dutch achieved overall primacy in world commerce because they dominated the trade in high-value products and many of the connected processing industries. This primacy lasted almost 150 years, galvanized the urban population, and enabled higher wages than anywhere else in Europe and, hence, a rapid increase in prosperity. The second decisive factor in the Dutch rise was the emergence of excellence in public and university education, in science and technology, and in military, social, and institutional innovation. Few historians understood the indispensable role of education, science, and technological innovation in the rise of civilizations as well as Jonathan Israel. The Dutch Republic of the seventeenth century had the highest level of literacy anywhere in Europe—even serving maids were able to read, wrote one surprised French visitor. This observation also testified to the general educational level and social status of Dutch women, which in the seventeenth century were higher than that of women in any other part of Europe.[6] The University of Leiden was set up as a religious bulwark and training ground for the new state and became Europe's largest Protestant university, and one of the best in the sciences and humanities.[7] The importance and influence of the Dutch universities—in the seventeenth century there were five—cannot be overestimated: their intellectual achievements outstripped those of other European universities in many fields. The international reputation of Leiden shows in the composition of the student body: more than forty percent were foreigners.

These two main factors—primacy in world trade of high-value products and excellence in education, science and technology—were inter-dependent. High-value commerce and maritime trade stimulated technological skill and innovation. The Dutch corps of engineers, whose leadership was recognized in many fields, became an instrument of growing international influence. Technological and industrial advances in turn exerted an enormous pull on the sciences and mathematics and generated great public interest in new discoveries and inventions. Dutch science, in several fields, was ahead of that in the rest of Europe. Thus, the Dutch created an "elite of the skilled"[8] rare in history, and their wealth resulted from superior skills (including, for example, in naval warfare) and relentless efforts, not from "windfall" profits, as was the case with Spain, which extracted wealth from the gold and silver of its American colonies but did not put it to economic use in education or science and technology. "Affluence...came with skill."[9]

Visionary Leaders

There were other critical factors. A few visionary leaders emerged from among the more mediocre ones and steered the republic through dangerous waters. They made future-shaping decisions that may have saved the country. One of them, Johan van Oldenbarnevelt, signed a truce with Spain in 1609 against bitter internal opposition because his country was exhausted and still regarded as an "interim rebel state lacking legitimacy."[10] Though history proved Oldenbarnevelt right, he was sentenced to death and executed for his actions. Another great statesman was Johan De Witt, who ruled the Republic "at its zenith" in the 1650s.[11] He sought to secure the state and advance trade, in contrast to all other European states, which were seeking territorial gain or dynastic advantage.

Luck

Fortune played a great role too: more than once, existential dangers faded because hostile powers were diverted by other problems. When France's Louis XIV attacked the country in 1672, the "Year of Disaster," "Holland was saved, initially, by sheer luck...."[12] In fact, the Dutch stopped the fast advancing French armies at the last moment, through a desperate, extremely hazardous but successful strategy. They opened the dykes that protected them against the sea and flooded the "low-lands" of their country.

Geopolitical Alliances

Another decisive source of strength was an alliance with the other Protestant power, England, which parlayed English and Dutch resources and combined the two navies under a unified command. This was the high point of great Dutch power politics.[13] England's "Glorious Revolution" of 1688 was a successful Dutch military invasion of England, which led the Dutch ruler William of Orange to ascend the English throne (this will be discussed in greater depth in Part IV, Chapter 9). William used the greater power of England to defend Dutch interests against their common enemy, France. The "Glorious Revolution" was the last successful invasion of England. It ended all earlier seventeenth-century English attempts to subdue the Dutch by military force. Later on, however, cooperation between the two countries gave rise to increasing trade and political rivalries. World trade dominance finally shifted from the Dutch Republic to England.

The Dutch Republic showed remarkable political, economic, and religious resilience in the face of internal conflicts and external setbacks, but signs of internal discord were often worrying. Disputes over the finer points of dogma along with religious minority policies that can barely be understood today led to many serious clashes. There were also uninterrupted arguments over the size of military expenditures. In spite of these tensions, the Dutch created a highly disciplined society. The vaunted Dutch freedom was severely limited by a deep preoccupation with order and social control.

Factors of Decline

After 1690, the Dutch economy began to deteriorate, and triggered a period of decline that transfigured the country from a great power back into a small state. The main reason was the industrial development of many other parts of Europe, which sapped Dutch international trading primacy in high-value goods, and with it the urban economy and the prosperity that had sustained the Golden Age. Among the consequences were a reduction of the urban population, the emigration of skilled artisans, massive social change, and more ominously a substantial weakening of Dutch military and naval power, which could no longer match that of its neighbors once the Dutch alliance with England broke up. The Dutch maintained a selective scientific and technological lead over the rest of Europe for a little while longer, until 1740 or so, but then Dutch universities too began to decline and the intelligentsia turned inward. Dutch intellectual and scientific developments no longer influenced the progress of the European Enlightenment. Dutch intellectuals were aware of and discussed the decay of their country, which they saw as an issue of morality and values exclusively, in line with general eighteenth-century thought. In the 1770s a deep malaise affected all aspects of public life, and thus in 1795 the French revolutionary armies swept the old regime away without opposition.

Jonathan Israel and the Jews

Jonathan Israel has also shed new light on the rise and decline of the Jewish people in Europe. His 1985 *European Jewry in the Age of Mercantilism* is the best known of his monographs on Jewish history. His skillful synthesis of political events with economic, social, cultural, and religious developments was a welcome change from more traditional narratives of Jewish history. He challenges the view that the Jewish condition in Europe improved gradually from one century to the next, with the seventeenth century better than the sixteenth and the eighteenth better than the seventeenth. This view is wrong, asserts Jonathan Israel; Europe's Jews were doing well in the seventeenth century but declined in the eighteenth. Despite persecutions in the East, the seventeenth century was the last in European history in which the Jews were still a coherent "nation," enjoying a measure of self-government in some places (particularly Poland), political influence in others, and economic and population growth across all of Europe. The royal powers protected the Jews because their trading and banking skills, and because international networks were seen as essential to the wealth of nations. The eighteenth century saw the end of this protection, which led to an enormous pauperization of European Jewry. Simultaneously, the concept and reality of Jewish "nationhood" began to dissolve, and self-government was abolished. The economy was not the sole factor determining Jewish rise and decline in these two centuries, but it was an indispensable factor.

CHAPTER 15

Paul Kennedy
USA, 1945— [1]

Paul Kennedy is a history professor at Yale known for his books on strategy, global issues, and war and peace. Most influential and widely read was his book *The Rise and Fall of the Great Powers*, written during the earlier years of the presidency of Ronald Reagan (1981-89) and published in 1987. His theory of world history was directly inspired by his concern about Reagan's growing military spending on the "Star Wars" initiative, which in his opinion was overstretching America's economy and leading the country to decline and ruin. Kennedy's political agenda was shared by most of America's liberal intellectuals and media, and widely held in Europe. It continues to resonate in far-away places. In 2005, the Politburo of the Communist Party of China disclosed that it had held a top leadership study session late in 2003 on the "rise and fall of major countries in the world since the fifteenth century," which is obviously the theme of Kennedy's book,[2] and in 2006, the Chinese translation of the book could be found in bookshops all over the country and a Chinese television series on rise and decline appeared. Kennedy did not initiate these discussions, but his book may have had some influence on them.

Kennedy reviews each European war from the early sixteenth century to the twentieth and draws a conclusion of apparently universal validity. His data, some of which are disputable, show that victory in war goes to those who have the more productive economic base. History shows "a very significant correlation over the longer term between productive and revenue-raising capacities on the one hand and military strength on the other."[3] The outcomes of the great wars reflect the economic shifts between the main players. While great economic power is not always converted into military power, great military power cannot be maintained over the long term if it is not sustained by corresponding economic power. Spain, the Habsburgs, and Napoleon lost because they were over-extended and could not maintain the economic engine of a powerful military machine. It was, according to Kennedy, inevitable that victory in both world wars would belong to those who had the greater economic resources. His thesis simplifies a complex issue: "All of the major shifts in the world's military power balances have followed alterations in the productive balances."[4] Kennedy has little to say about other, equally important sources of victory, such as leadership, fighting spirit, resilience, or strategy.

No great power lasts forever, and none can be permanently ahead of all others. Kennedy believed in 1986/87 that the greatest power, the United States, had already begun to decline in relation to the rest of the world. All powers have to set priorities according to three variables: defense, consumption, and investment. Great powers typically decline and fall when they become "over-stretched" or "over-extended," two words Kennedy uses frequently, that is, when defense commitments or war expenditures can no longer be borne by the economy without drastic reductions in consumption or investment. The former could become politically unacceptable; the latter will undermine the long-term economic future of the nation.

Kennedy does note that some wars—the Vietnam War among them—have been won by the economically weaker side. He is puzzled that in 1793-95 the French revolutionary armies were able to defeat the combined, hugely superior forces of the European monarchies, and that a century earlier Spain was not able to prevail during the revolt of the Netherlands. In both cases the wealthier side lost the war. In other words, he does not ignore other factors that also affect war outcomes. However, such contradictions do not modify his mono-causal economic explanation. His analysis of the situation of the 1980s and 1990s did not pay appropriate attention to science and technology and their impact on military and economic power. Technological progress and the resulting increased productivity greatly ameliorated the constant three-way tension between defense, consumption, and investment. Defense did not constrain prosperity as it had in the past, and the predicted decline of the American economy did not materialize until 2008. On the contrary, in the 1990s the United States had entered one of the longest periods of sustained economic growth in its history.

Two other of Kennedy's predictions were mistaken as well: 1) that Japan would begin to expand faster than other major powers, and 2) that the survival of the Soviet Union was not in question despite its economic difficulties.[5] However, one cannot exclude a possible return of the linkage between military overextension, excessive spending and economic decline in new and different circumstances. Kennedy erred in his forecasts for the 1980s and 1990s, but this does not mean that he will always be wrong.

CHAPTER 16

Jared Diamond
USA, 1937— [1]

Jared Diamond is a biologist and bio-geographer of "Polish-Jewish heritage," as his Internet biography puts it. He is professor in the geography department of the University of California, Los Angeles (UCLA) and the recipient of many professional distinctions, including a Pulitzer Prize for his 1997 book *Guns, Germs and Steel*. His *Collapse*, a response to public and professional alarm about the consequences of environmental destruction and global warming published in 2005, became an instant bestseller. Diamond warns that the world is following an unsustainable course, and that many of us will have to make drastic lifestyle changes to prevent environmental overextension and the global catastrophe it could trigger. This book provides academic firepower to the most strident ecological doomsday campaigners, but it also launches a constructive, sober call for action to avoid a possible catastrophe.

Diamond reviews the environmental status of a great variety of countries, societies, and tribes, both dead and living. Some, like China and Australia, are huge; others are tiny islands in the Pacific. Some have made grave environmental mistakes and are trying to correct them, but others cannot agree on an appropriate course of action. Some, like Iceland, Tokugawa Japan, and the New Guinea Highlands, have survived well because they pursued agricultural and economic policies adapted to their environmental constraints, but others, like Easter Island and other Pacific island cultures, the Anasazi Indians, and the classical Maya, vanished long ago because their policies were suicidal from an environmental point of view, whether that was due to sheer ignorance, value-based or religious refusal to adapt to new conditions, or the pursuit of short-term gains by selfish rulers. In all the cases of collapse Diamond cites, environmental degradation by humans, e.g. deforestation, was the only reason for the extinction of the society.

Diamond draws two conclusions from the fate of this heterogeneous group of societies:

It is Possible to Avoid Collapse by Learning from the Mistakes of Vanished Societies

"The parallels between Easter Island and the whole modern world are chillingly obvious,"[2] and "the Maya warn us that crashes also befall the most advanced and creative societies."[3] Both statements are bold but questionable. Our huge, continuously interacting global society is not comparable to a few thousand stone-age people living in isolation on a remote Pacific island. The Maya, too, lived in a stone-age civilization, practiced human sacrifice, and worshipped their kings as gods. They were lost when the equally cruel, but technologically superior, civilization of Spain confronted them. Diamond may be right that our world is currently on a "non-sustainable course," and that many of us will have to make drastic lifestyle changes, but the history of Easter Island or the Maya does not prove his point.

A Society's Fate Lies in its Own Hands

The second, more reassuring, finding is that "a society's fate lies in its own hands and depends substantially on its own choices."[4] Diamond asserts that ecological catastrophes are always the result of major failures in decision-making. There is no ecological determinism; humans could have changed the course of events. The question, then, is why some societies fail to make the necessary decisions. Some do not perceive the problem; others perceive it but are unable to solve it. The latter case is, of course, the more intriguing of the two. The reader would like to learn more about the religious and cultural value systems that clash with the need to make policy changes. The survival of the planet may depend on better understanding these obstacles. Unfortunately, the long vanished societies Diamond describes do not really assist the reader in his quest for more specific answers.

Whatever shortcomings Diamond's *Collapse* may have, it came at the right time. Its public success has inspired a specialized branch of historiography. Since 2005, a number of other books and articles have appeared that examine the links between natural disasters or environmental degradation and the decline and fall of civilizations. It will probably take a long time and much more research before there is even a limited consensus among historians on this complicated question.

CHAPTER 17

Bryan Ward-Perkins
UK, 1952— [1]

Bryan Ward-Perkins teaches at Trinity College, Oxford. His research focuses on late Antiquity and the Middle Ages. His 2005 book on the fall of Rome has been met with great interest, and not only because of its bold title, *The Fall of Rome and the End of Civilization*. It is the latest of many books written on this subject, which became, thanks to Gibbon among others, a permanent source of stimulation and curiosity for the Western mind. Ward-Perkins reviews earlier books and counts no fewer than 210 possible reasons for Rome's decline and fall.

His book has twin merits. First, he demonstrates how strongly perceptions of past rise and decline can be affected by changing intellectual fashions, demands of "political correctness," prejudices, and the optical distortions of later times. Second, he re-establishes two essential conclusions of Gibbon, namely that the fall of Rome was a catastrophic event of enormous consequence for millions and a cautionary tale for all future history, and that its causes were complex and multiple. Few had questioned Gibbon before 1970, but this has not been the case in recent decades. Ward-Perkins begins with the history books written since the 1970s, where words like "collapse," "decline," "decay," and "crisis" were no longer in fashion. These words were replaced by "accommodation," "transformation," "transition," and "change," respectively.[2] What was to earlier historians the "end of the Roman Empire" became "late Antiquity." Rome did not come to an end, it "evolved." The author suggests that the European Commission funded many of these books, because the peaceful integration of the new Germany into the European Union required some re-writing of old history. Formerly "barbaric" Germanic invaders of the empire became "immigrants" who settled, more or less peacefully, among the native inhabitants. Ward-Perkins rejects this new, politically correct version of events as a falsification refuted not just by all contemporary witnesses, but also by a huge amount of new archeological evidence. The truth is that the invasions led to violent disruptions, enormous horrors of war, destruction, and suffering. Ward-Perkins quotes the Christian authors of the fifth century, who were shocked by the unfolding catastrophe. They compared it to the catastrophes that had befallen ancient Israel, quoted the Bible, and concluded that Rome, too, was punished for its wickedness and sins.

The Roman Empire had been at risk for some time and was beset by many problems. Its military edge was due to superior equipment and organization, but it was not as absolute as, for example, European military superiority in the nineteenth century was. Ward-Perkins identifies one matter that played a particular role in the unraveling of the empire. "The key internal element of Rome's success or failure was the economic well-being of its taxpayers. This was because the empire relied for its security on a professional army."[3] This sounds like another mono-causal explanation, but it is not. It is a key factor in a complex interconnected process of events. The invasions led to chaos, unrest, civil wars, rebellions, and usurpations, and to rapid transfers of power due to the introduction of large numbers of experienced foreign fighters under their own kings. The security provided by Rome and the maintenance of extensive road and other infrastructures had guaranteed economic integration and growth. The four hundred years between approximately 50 BCE and 400 CE were the longest uninterrupted period of security enjoyed by the Mediterranean in all known history. When invasions and wars destroyed this security, the ancient economy and the empire itself began to unravel. Ward-Perkins adds one additional explanation, which does not figure prominently in Gibbon's work: good or bad luck. The Empire was certainly doomed to fall one day, but it did not have to fall in the fifth century. Rome's stunning defeat at the hands of the Goths at Hadrianopolis in 378 CE greatly encouraged the barbarians to cross the Rhine and Danube in large numbers from 405 on. It was "bad luck or bad judgment."[4] Western reinforcements were already underway, and it would have taken little for Emperor Valens to achieve a stunning victory. Likewise, the survival of the Eastern Empire for almost a thousand years longer was a result of good fortune rather than inherently greater strength or better strategy. It was the Dardanelles, the small strip of sea that separated Europe and Asia, that saved the East.

Ward-Perkins describes the "death of a civilization" in stark terms, supported by an enormous amount of archaeological evidence that was not available to earlier historians. It shows a catastrophic collapse of living standards, material sophistication, economic complexity, and specialization all across the Western Roman Empire from the fifth century on. Entire industries and networks vanished. The Roman capacity to mass-produce goods and provide comfort across vast territories, which was in many respects comparable to ours, disappeared. The scale of this collapse, which included major population reductions, was such that it can reasonably be called the end of a civilization. The collapse threw post-Roman Britain and other parts of the Empire back to the level of the pre-Roman Iron Age.

Ward-Perkin's book is both fascinating and disquieting. The analysis is cool and professional. The author does not belabor the parallels between the dying Roman Empire and our Western civilization, and avoids the bombastic language or moralizing overtones of Spengler, Toynbee, and Sorokin, but the parallels enter into the reader's mind all by themselves. A highly sophisticated economy spanning half of the known world and providing considerable material comfort to millions; the growing but not always visible weaknesses and problems in the system; a series of external shocks; the failure or inability of the ruling elite to control or even understand so many interconnected events, and, finally, the unraveling and end of an international civilization that seemed the most solid and successful the world had ever known. It is only at the end of his book that Ward-Perkins issues his warning: "The end of the Roman West witnessed horrors and dislocations of a kind I sincerely hope never to have to live through....Romans before the fall were as certain as we are today that the world would continue for ever substantially unchanged. They were wrong. We would be wise not to repeat their complacency."[5]

CHAPTER 18

Mancur Olson
USA, 1932-1998 [1]

Olson was an American economist who wrote during the 1970s and early 1980s, when Western politicians and the public were preoccupied with the twin problems of economic stagnation and inflation, and the need to restore economic growth. Olson's 1982 *Rise and Decline of Nations* equates rise and decline with variations in economic growth rates: a nation is rising in every respect when it has a steady, high growth rate, and declining when its economic growth rate sputters and approaches zero. The equation may look a bit simplistic, but it was widely accepted in his time and many still tend to regard rise and decline purely as a consequence of economic growth. During those years other economists published books with titles such as "Why Growth Rates Differ," which would have been a more accurate title for Olson's book. Olson shows that the longer a society enjoys political stability and peace, the more likely it is to develop powerful special-interest lobbies that make it less efficient economically. He attributes the higher growth rates of Japan and Germany in his time, compared to those of many other Western countries, to the two nations' defeat in World War II. Their past breakdowns explain why they have less social rigidity and fewer special interest groups that dominate and stifle their government's macro-economic policies. More than ten years later, when Japanese and German growth rates dropped to lower levels than those of the United States and the United Kingdom, other social scientists began to discover, both in Japan and Germany, social rigidities and economic lobbies that Olson may have overlooked. The earlier economic success stories of Japan and Germany must, therefore, be attributed to several rather than only one reason. Olson used the economic and political problem that dominated the society and politics of his day, "stagflation," to propose a general theory of rise and decline, but the contribution he made enriched the social sciences more than world history.

CHAPTER 19

Peter Turchin
USA, 1957— [1]

Peter Turchin is an American biologist and ecologist born in Moscow, the son of a Soviet dissident who was allowed to immigrate to the United States. Turchin specializes in population dynamics and mathematical modeling. He notes that historical processes are "dynamic": populations, empires, states and religions keep growing and declining. Therefore, "we need a mathematical theory in history." The dynamics of history should be converted into hypotheses, and these should then be translated into mathematical models and predictions that can be checked against empirical patterns. Turchin applies his method to, among other matters, the territorial expansion of agrarian states and the question of why they expand and contract. He is inspired by Ibn Khaldun's concept of "group solidarity" as the initial basis of civilization,[2] and taking this idea as his starting point sets out to demonstrate that frontiers are the best "incubators" of group solidarity. They increase group cohesion independently of the ethnic origin of the inhabitants inside the borders. Turchin's training in biology opened his eyes to the possibility that group solidarity in civilizations might be based on kinship, as Ibn Khaldun had speculated long before. Whether this and other examples in his book are properly proven mathematically only mathematicians can tell. Few historians would take seriously the postulate that mathematics is indispensable to defining the laws of rise and decline. It has become indispensable to biology, but human history is much too complex for even the most advanced mathematics. Turchin is confident of his conclusion and calls for a mathematical modeling approach—"cliodynamics"—to the investigation of history.

CHAPTER 20

Christopher Chase-Dunn
USA, 1944—
and Thomas D. Hall
USA, 1946— [1]

Christopher Chase-Dunn and Thomas D. Hall, both American sociology professors, seek to identify regularities in historical processes, such as the rise and decline of civilizations. Their aim is to create a grand theory of world history that would also allow for a forecast of our future. They claim to be followers of Fernand Braudel, but their ambition is more reminiscent of Oswald Spengler's: he too wrote an all-embracing theory of history and promised that it would reveal the future.[2]

However, Chase-Dunn/Hall's vision of civilization is diametrically opposed to that of Spengler. Spengler postulated that every civilization was a closed unit that independently followed the same organic laws of rise and decline, unaffected by any other civilization. Chase-Dunn/Hall, in contrast, postulate that civilizations are part of a larger "world-system"—as they define world-systems—of overarching "social structures and processes" that determine rise and decline. This is why rise and decline occur, allegedly, more of less simultaneously in individual civilizations or polities belonging to the same "world-system." Changes in individual civilizations are not endogenous, but are consequences of complex interactions among "local, regional, societal and global processes." These interactions include trade, warfare, intermarriage, information flows and more. "World-systems" can be small or large. Chase-Dunn/Hall analyze three cases to substantiate their theory. The first is a minuscule "world-system," the native tribal societies of Northern California before the arrival of white settlers in 1849. These Indians numbered no more than 10,000 persons. Different groups were interacting with one another in intense and important ways despite the fact that all necessary food and raw materials were produced within household units. Each group's history was part of a shared, larger system. From this micro-system the authors move to a mega-system: the alleged unification of "Afroeurasia"—as they call the giant unit they have detected—between circa 500 BCE and 1400 CE. The authors' bold hypothesis sees the three continents interacting and developing in similar ways over almost 2000 years. "Afroeurasia" saw several waves of "integration," interrupted by waves of "disintegration." Integration began with trade relations between Rome and Han China, peaked between 200 BCE and 200 CE, then collapsed, emerged again between 500 and 900, and reached its greatest intensity from 1200 to 1400 as a result of the Mongol expansion. Chase-Dunn/Hall's third case, the only one they can easily defend, is the "Europe-centered" world-system that sustained the rise of capitalism. Today, this ultimate system includes all continents and people.

All "world-systems" go through "pulsations" of network growth and contraction. The spatial scale of integration first expands, and then contracts. "Rise and demise" of individual civilizations follow "centralization" and "decentralization" of the economic, political, and social power of the "world-systems" to which they belong. Chase-Dunn/Hall predict that the current world-system will destroy itself unless humanity creates a world state. "Capitalism as a system contains such massive internal contradictions that it is unlikely to continue…for more than a few centuries."[3] The *Communist Manifesto* by Karl Marx and Friedrich Engels of 1848—never mentioned by these authors—had predicted the same eventual outcome, without granting capitalism an additional lifespan of such exorbitant length.

Chase-Dunn/Hall's postulate that civilizations must not be seen in isolation but as components of a broader historic environment is a creative idea that Braudel had indeed raised before, albeit with greater prudence and better data.[4] However, the authors present this idea almost as a creed, valid for all places and periods, which does little to clarify the multiple causes of rise and decline. Equally debatable is their conviction that pre-historic tribal societies, large empires, and modern technical civilizations are all governed by the same laws of history. Chase-Dunn/Hall's theory has no place for decisive leadership, which they deride as "the great-man theory of history," none for religion and culture as driving factors, and none for internal sources of rise and decline.

CHAPTER 21

Joseph A. Tainter
USA, 1949— [1]

The anthropologist Joseph A.Tainter describes more than twenty cases of collapse, beginning with Antiquity in pre-Columbian America, the ancient Near East, archaic Greece, and the Western Roman Empire. He reviews two thousand or more years of explanations, praises those who see the reason of collapse in economic factors, and chastises those who see it in what he calls "mystical" factors. These include "value judgments," ethical factors such as the immoral behavior of rulers, and theories that compare civilizations to organisms that grow and die. Tainter accepts none of the existing theories. He attributes the collapse of civilization to the "declining productivity of increasing complexity." Civilization means complexity, which is not a natural state. As civilizational complexity increases, the "marginal returns" on new "investments" in the complexity keep declining until collapse becomes inevitable. Collapse is a return to greater simplicity, poverty, decentralization, smaller units, etc., which is a more natural state of things. There have been many collapses in history. They are the norm, not the exception, and our civilization should not feel too secure about its future either. Tainter admits that his theory leaves virtually no room for human will, statesmanship, or intervention. He refutes all external explanations of collapse: wars and invasions, for example, are "random accidents" that cannot explain the regularity of collapse.

Tainter buried the organic and ethical theories of rise and decline, only to replace them with a mechanical one. A civilization is like a piece of machinery. As it becomes more complex over time it ages, declines, and sooner or later stops functioning altogether. Collapse follows mechanical and econometric laws, not organic ones. As new features and functions are added to the machinery as it becomes more sophisticated, the probability of breakdowns requiring costly repairs increases. In the end, the most economical solution is to scrap the old machinery and acquire a cheaper and simpler model. Tainter's generalization that all civilizations have collapsed through growing complexity, and that collapse was unavoidable in every case, is simply wrong. Nonetheless, he could be right in some cases, maybe even in the case of our Western, increasingly complex civilization. His foreboding matches that of other historians, including Bryan Ward-Perkins.

CHAPTER 22

Arthur Herman
USA, 1956 — [1]

Arthur Herman is a conservative American historian who writes about British and American history. His book, *The Idea of Decline in Western History*, is not about the decline of civilization as an objective phenomenon, but about the ideology of decline in Western thought: "The idea of decline is actually a theory about the nature and meaning of time."[2] Herman looks for the roots of the pessimism that in his view has become the norm today. In the nineteenth century, the idea of progress, although still defended by Hegel, became increasingly discredited. It gave way to an opposite idea that developed a rich, value-loaded vocabulary: "decline," "decay," "decadence," and "degeneration." After 1880, the rise of antisemitism reinforced this trend and Jews were increasingly identified as Europe's main "degenerators." The general mood was not limited to Europe, but included influential American authors, such as Brooks Adams, a critic of capitalism who published his *Law of Civilization and Decay* in 1895.

Racial (Gobineau and Chamberlain) and cultural (Nietzsche and Burckhardt) pessimists predicted the decline of European civilization in which they detected fatal flaws. Since the nineteenth century, capitalist-bourgeois society has been seen as condemned to self-destruction. The twentieth century saw a tremendous upsurge of ideological pessimism. The racial variants of this pessimism comforted the extreme right in Europe and led straight to Nazism. The cultural variants stimulated French and German radical writers, often left-wingers if not Communists, such as Sartre and Frantz Fanon, but also philosophers of history such as Spengler and Toynbee, and in the United States Afrocentric black writers and white radicals. The call for "multi-culturalism" was first heard in an American Afro-centric milieu not as a call for mutual respect, but as a springboard for a new wave of anti-Western ideology. For all of these idealogues, Western civilization and particularly America became the main target. In the United States, Noam Chomsky, Edward Said, and several others are the best-known protagonists of this camp. Herman regards what he calls the current "eco-pessimism" as the latest chapter in the history of theories of decline.

Herman does not dispute that decline can be an objective reality, but he insists that there are no inevitable laws of progress or decline. He regrets that "an alternative view of society and social action, one that stems from the Enlightenment and earlier humanist tradition, is not much in evidence these days."[3] Herman speaks of a paradox: an upsurge of cultural pessimism is accompanying the triumph of capitalism, in one of the most successful periods of civilization. He does not always differentiate between the reasons for cultural pessimism. Not all of it is antisemitic or even anti-American. Neither Nietzsche nor Sartre were antisemites: on the contrary, they scorned antisemitism. Herman counts the Jewish critic Theodor Adorno among the German cultural pessimists, but does not emphasize where Adorno's pessimism was born: in Auschwitz. Some people have had good reason to be pessimistic about Western civilization.

PART III

MACRO-HISTORICAL CONDITIONS OF RISE, GOLDEN AGE, AND DECLINE

Introduction

Historians have for millennia looked for macro-historical conditions that explain in general terms why civilizations rise, thrive, or decline. The conditions are not "drivers" in the specific sense of the term adopted in Part IV, and cannot be easily be affected by policy intervention. These conditions are complementary, not mutually exclusive.

CHAPTER 1

"Challenge-and-Response"

General Observations

The rising of civilizations has attracted much less historical, literary, and artistic attention than their declines and falls. The ends of civilizations and empires have a dramatic quality generally lacking at their beginnings. In addition, the end is historically always better documented than the beginning. "The Last Days of Pompeii" was a 1960 Hollywood thriller that earned millions. No filmmaker would have produced a movie with the title "The Early Days of Pompeii." Yet the beginning and early development of civilizations are no less important to understand than the end. There are various explanations for the birth and rise of civilizations. Ibn Khaldun is the best-known early historian to offer one. Civilization, he says, emerges when a group related by blood-bonds sets up a social organization to pool and coordinate their survival efforts.[1] This theory pulls together insights from both genetics and sociology. Oswald Spengler's theory, in contrast, was modeled on biology. He saw civilizations as emerging spontaneously like living organisms, following some immanent law, but this was a metaphor, not an explanation.[2] Race theorists of the nineteenth and early twentieth century asserted that civilization was a natural, exclusive product of "racially superior" people.

Toynbee rejected racial supremacy ideas as "repulsive."[3] He proposed a new theory, "Challenge-and-Response," which became one of the best-known models of rise and decline. Civilizations are not born naturally; they rise as a collective response to a natural-geographic or human stimulus. The attraction of Toynbee's theory is that it emphasizes human will and initiative. A civilization rises as a deliberate communal reaction to a problem or threat. The weakness is that challenge-and-response can be used to cover too many historical developments. It is important to add to Toynbee's theory that a successful response always brings change. Challenge-and-response should go hand-in-hand with a theory of transformation. "Challenge-and-transformation" might explain historical processes more precisely. If transformation is included, the "challenge-and-response" theory does allow us to compare the reactions of different civilizations to similar conditions and to better understand why some rise and others decline and disappear.

Applications to Jewish History

Jewish history is a good case to use to test the challenge-and-response theory and show the importance of transformation. Judaism has survived enormous challenges—it has demonstrated an ability to respond to repeated challenges, not only to one. Other religions and civilizations put to similar tests have disappeared. At the end of his work, in the last of his twelve volumes of history, Toynbee reveals that he got the idea of challenge-and-response from the Hebrew Bible.[4] His five types of challenge look like they were chosen to fit the case of the Jews: hard living conditions (e.g., deserts); migration to or conquest of a new country; foreign blows and aggression; long-term external pressures; and finally, internal discrimination. Not surprisingly, many of the concrete examples he proposes are taken from Jewish history. Applying Toynbee's terminology, one can say that the secret of Jewish longevity lies mainly in the ability of the Jewish people to respond repeatedly to massive, life-threatening challenges and institute creative changes that make survival possible. The Jewish people has undergone three historically tangible ruptures and, according to tradition, an earlier one that has not been substantiated, and survived them all.

Jewish tradition describes Israel's "birth" as a nation emerging from Egyptian slavery as a response to great challenges. Some historians identified a foundational period of Israel lasting from approximately 1300 to 1100 BCE. This was a time of major transformations in response to external challenges.* The archaeological debate over whether or not the Exodus actually took place is irrelevant to our question. What counted in later Jewish history is the Jewish

---

* The sociologist Alfred Weber, younger brother of the more famous Max Weber (II, 6) adapted Toynbee's model of challenge-and-response, particularly the idea that repeated challenges could give a civilization a lasting impetus. He believed that a singular, dramatic event in the early history of a people shaped its culture and thought for a long time, hence the title of his main book, *Kulturgeschichte als Kultursoziologie* (*History of Culture as Sociology of Culture*) (München: Piper, 1951). Fernand Braudel recommended his book, now largely forgotten, as one of the great histories of civilizations (*Écrits* 285f.). Alfred Weber had an encyclopedic knowledge of history and, like Toynbee, used intuition and comparative analysis to write his own history of the Jews (A. Weber, 99 ff.) He suggested that an extraordinary event at the Red Sea after the Exodus shaped Judaism. The core of this event could not be completely invented, he speculated. He called the rescue at the Red Sea the "initial sociological constellation" of the Jews. A similar great challenge occurred again centuries later in 586 BCE, when the Babylonians sacked the First Temple. This time destruction could not be prevented, but it was followed by a renaissance in a new form, a "second historic constellation" which recalled the first one with its ultimate rescue and Divine promise of survival.

people's firm belief that it was freed from slavery in a divinely guided reaction to oppression. All following generations have re-enacted this story every spring and have found inspiration in it.

The next, and for critical historians the first, major transformation in response to enormous challenges can be historically verified. It is the transformation of the Jews' political reality and religious thought and practice, and even of the Hebrew script, that occurred during the seminal period from the late eighth to the fifth century BCE.[5] This period began with the appearance of two of the earliest of the twelve so-called "minor prophets," Amos and Hosea, who are usually placed in the mid-eighth century BCE, and the destruction of the Northern Kingdom of Israel by the Assyrians in 722 BCE. In 586 BCE, the destruction of the Temple of Jerusalem by the Babylonians and the Babylonian Exile followed. This event made major transformations inevitable. They were completed by two outstanding personalities, the spiritual leader Ezra and the statesman Nehemiah. The whole process of deep crisis and transformation from Amos to Nehemiah lasted, with some interruptions, between 200 and 300 years.

The third (or second historically tangible) transformation of great depth began with the destruction of the Second Temple by Rome in 70 CE, the profound modification of Judaism initiated by Rabbi Yohanan Ben Zakkai and the school of Yavneh, the suppression of the Bar Kochbah revolt in 135-138 CE, and the renewed dispersion of the Jewish people. The whole period was one of enormous change, lasting from 70 CE to almost 500 CE, when the Talmud was completed—about 400 years. During this period, the Jewish communal structure, which had already existed in the Diaspora before, emerged as a unique and dominant political and organizational framework in which almost all Jews lived until the onset of modernity. This was a self-organizing, relatively autonomous structure that had considerable power over its members. The Jewish community system and the Catholic Church are arguably the two oldest uninterrupted and still partly-functioning socio-political structures of the Western world. They have datable historical beginnings—in the case of the Jews the date is more than 2000 years ago—and differ from other social structures that are common to all humans and older than recorded history, such as family or royalty.

The fourth historical transformational period of significant consequence began late in the eighteenth century with the Enlightenment, the emancipation and assimilation of Western Jews, and the creation of the Zionist movement. This transformation also included the decline of the Jewish community and communal networks as the dominant framework of Jewish collective life, as they had been since ancient times. The period reached its two most dramatic peaks—so far—in the twentieth century, with the annihilation of most of Europe's Jews and the creation of the State of Israel in 1948. Israel is clearly the most revolutionary response to the challenge of the *Shoah* and the failure of the Emancipation to make Europe's Jews accepted by society. Calling Israel's creation a "response" to the *Shoah* is controversial, because Israel's enemies have used the apparent link between the two events to challenge Israel's location in a mainly Arab Middle East, which did not cause the *Shoah*. It should be noted that Zionism began long before the *Shoah,* and was rooted in the Jewish people's long historical memory of the land of Israel and its enduring religious hope of return. If Israel was a "response" in a short-term sense, it was already being prepared by the early Zionist leaders, the first of whom was Theodor Herzl. Zionism could well have led one day to a Jewish state in the land of Israel. However, it is undeniable that the *Shoah* alone generated the objective emergency and the iron will and relentless pressure of Zionist and Jewish leaders to establish a state without further delay.*

Israel is the result of a never-abandoned drive rooted in history, and a sudden, indispensable catalyst. Ignoring one or the other, the drive or the catalyst, is to misrepresent history. A second direct response to the *Shoah* was the galvanization of American Judaism, which became a major political force in the service of the Jewish people at the national and international level. This potential may have existed earlier, but did not manifest itself. In addition, the Nazi persecutions triggered indirect, long-term effects, in which the Jews were involved or instrumental in one way or another. As surprising as this may sound to many readers, the most consequential and dramatic of these effects was the invention of nuclear weapons. It is true that the relevant political decisions, the organizational control, the funding, and the final military application of the bomb were purely American, but within this framework Jewish scientists, including those who would have fallen into the "Jewish" category only by Nazi definition, reacted to the Nazi persecutions in Europe and played a singular and indispensable role. The bomb could arguably have been developed with fewer of them, though not without all of them, but only with great delays and difficulties. The first step on the road to the bomb was the famous letter Einstein addressed to Roosevelt in August 1939, warning the president of the danger that Hitler might develop the bomb first.

---

* In May 1942 the Zionist leaders met in the Biltmore Hotel in New York, shocked by the beginning mass-extermination of Europe's Jews. This was the first time that Zionist leaders called explicitly for the establishment of a sovereign Jewish state in Palestine (see Michael Oren, *Power, Faith and Fantasy: America and the Middle East 1776 to the Present* (New York-London: W.W. Norton, 2007), 444. The *Shoah* also triggered the international good will for Zionist aspirations that was indispensable but did not exist before 1939, and it left 300,000 Jewish survivors in "displaced persons" camps in Germany who had nowhere else to go and exerted enormous pressure for a Jewish homeland. All these external factors together made the creation of a Jewish state possible in May 1948.

This letter was discussed and drafted by three Jewish Hungarian physicists, Leo Szilard, Eugene Wigner, and Edward Teller, who three years later joined the "Manhattan" project to develop the bomb. In the end, a large number of the involved key scientists were Jewish, some of them with friends and family trapped in Europe. Their motivation and input greatly accelerated the gargantuan research and development effort that was required. Some made it clear that their determination was a reaction to the Nazi crimes.[6] Others, including the project leader Robert Oppenheimer, were more discreet about their Jewish origins or possible commitments. Edward Teller, who later played a lead role in the development of thermo-nuclear weapons and maintained a life-long close professional and personal relationship with Israel, was blunt: "No one could have had a greater influence on me than Hitler."[7] Whatever the long-term consequences of the invention of nuclear weapons, the grave dangers that they pose for humanity—and particularly for Israel—must forever be linked to the more than understandable wartime reactions of Jewish scientists to Nazi crimes.

At the present point in history, the Jews are in the midst of this fourth great transformation. We know when it began, but not how or when it will end. The current transformation began almost 200 years ago with the start of the Jewish Enlightenment. Deep transformations that modify the spiritual, material, and political expressions of a civilization often take centuries. All that can be said is that the current one is likely to be as deep and far-reaching as the earlier ones.

The capability of the Jews to survive via creative responses and transformation is critical, but difficult to explain. A number of similarities are apparent in all responses to past challenges. One feature that all deep crises and transformations of the Jewish people have in common is that they are somehow linked to the emergence of great spiritual and political leaders (as will be discussed in greater detail in IV, 5). A second feature of successful transformations is that their roots go back to a time before the critical event requiring change. Some of the new religious expressions, the new modes of thought, the new institutions, even the new leaders that would respond to the coming challenge, emerged and began to stir long before catastrophe struck.

Jews (or more precisely Judeans) after 586 BCE, when the First Temple was destroyed, looked back on a hundred and fifty years of political and spiritual turmoil, self-questioning, and the harsh public condemnation of the corruption of rulers and populace voiced by the prophets. Calls for radical reform were heard long before the fall of the First Temple. The pre-history of the transformation that followed the next catastrophe, in 70 CE, was equally long and indispensable. The reform of Judaism after 70 CE had essential roots in rabbinic debates going back to the first century BCE, in the creation of a widespread Diaspora during the same time, and in the growing practice of synagogue worship side by side with Temple service. One should not forget that the indispensable Rabbi Yohanan Ben Zakkai did not appear out of nowhere as the Temple was burning, but was already one of the main members—some even say the single most prominent member—of the school of Hillel long before 70 CE.

Obviously, the same is true of the historic watershed of 1948, which also had a long ideological, political, and institutional pre-history. "Today I founded the state (of the Jews)," wrote Herzl in his diary during the First Zionist Congress, and this "today" was in 1897. The catastrophe then greatly accelerated the nascent Zionist movement already underway, which might not have succeeded on its own. This pre-history facilitated the transformation when it became inevitable. Because transformations did have roots in earlier times, it was easier to give them religious, ideological, or political legitimation by projecting them back into the past and certifying that they had long before existed. This brought acceptance. Historians coined the term "inventions of tradition." This is a well-known practice when leaders seek legitimation for major changes they deem necessary. The historian Eric Hobsbawm writes that traditions "which appear or claim to be old are often quite recent in origin and sometimes invented."[8] Myth-making sometimes plays an essential role in historic transformations.

CHAPTER 2

Windows of Opportunity

General Observations

The challenge-and-response theory postulates that the rise and prosperity of civilizations are triggered by a direct "challenge." The term challenge implies an antagonistic intention or a material obstacle. In other words, civilizations do not rise out of historical voids or from a gentle and bountiful nature. Another theory asserts something different: that rise results simply from a historical void, not from a challenge or stimulus, and decline from a closing of this void. An external power void can open a "window of opportunity" that stimulates the emergence of a new civilization, while closing this void can suffocate the same civilization. Hodgson argued that Islam rose in a void, as the once powerful empires that had previously controlled the Middle East weakened, and centuries later Islam declined not least because of the sudden rise and expansion of Europe, which overtook and sapped the Islamic civilization.[1] There are other civilizations that could have survived and perhaps flourished for a long time had they not been left behind by a newer, more dynamic one. Competition between civilizations does not have to end in war and physical destruction: one civilization can overshadow and absorb another, as happened more than once in Chinese civilizational history.

Applications to Jewish History

The theory of a rising civilization in an external power void, or of a declining one when this power void is closed, can be applied to Jewish history, but only with caution. It is also important to remember that the external context of sovereign Jewish states with Jewish majorities in ancient and modern Israel is very different from the external context of Jewish minorities in the Diaspora.

Some historians see the rise of ancient Israel as analogous to the rise of Islam as proposed by specialists of Islam such as Hodgson. According to these historians, Israel did not rise as a response to a particular "challenge," as Toynbee postulated. The early history of the tribes of Israel, from the time of the Judges to the that of the first kings (ca. 1200-800 BCE in traditional chronology) developed in a period when the efforts of Egypt's New Kingdom to maintain military and cultural dominance of the Near East had failed, but before circa 750 BCE, when Assyria and then Babylonia emerged as the new regional imperial powers and subdued the smaller nations.[2] In 1285 BCE, Pharaoh Ramses II of Egypt lost the decisive battle of Kadesh, a battle that was fought for supremacy in western Asia, to the Hittites. After this debacle, Egyptian control of Canaan began to loosen, and after the death of Ramses III (circa 1150) it approached total collapse. Never again did Egypt gain lasting control over the land bridge to Asia. Therefore, there was an international power void, a "window of opportunity" lasting from the first Israelite settlement to the Israelite kingdoms' destructions by Assyria and Babylonia in the seventh and fifth centuries BCE, respectively. This may be comparable to the Middle Eastern power void of the fifth and sixth centuries CE, which allowed Islam to taste victory and grow. It is likewise possible to draw a parallel between the undermining of the Muslim world following Europe's rapid expansion since the sixteenth century and the sapping of Judaism that the rapid rise of a hostile Christian Church caused in the entire Eastern Roman Empire. Shortly after that sapping, the rise of Islam further undermined Judaism in the Middle East. Not only did Jews have to abandon their conversion efforts from the fourth or fifth century CE on, but large numbers of them probably converted to Christianity and later to Islam, which were stronger and more politically successful civilizations. The Israeli historian Yehezkel Kaufmann believes that many non-Jews would have joined Judaism at the end of Antiquity, but would not have joined the defeated and exiled Judaism that was oppressed by its successor religions.[3]

Diaspora history offers a more complex and contradictory picture of the influence the external context exerts on Jewish rise and decline. In the Diaspora, Jews have rarely lived in an external "power void"; they have mostly depended, directly or indirectly, on their host countries. The country where the Babylonian Talmud was written may have looked to many of its Jewish inhabitants like a "power void." They enjoyed a limited autonomy granted by the Persian Empire, which ruled Babylonia in a loose, decentralized way, and left the Jews to their own devices—most of the time. They even formed institutions of governance, ruled by the heads of the talmudic academies of Sura and Pumpedita and an "exilarch" who claimed to be a royal prince of the house of David. Diaspora history contains other examples of external power voids that allowed Judaism to expand. Later, the closing of these voids reversed the expansion. The much-discussed kingdom of the Khazars may be such a case. The Khazars were a Turkic-speaking people of nomads, traders, and warriors who lived near the Caspian Sea and kept invading some of their neighbors, for example the Persians. The Khazars, or perhaps only their leadership, converted to Judaism in the eighth century. Their kingdom flourished in a relative power void until the eleventh century, when the first Russian state was formed and expanded from its first center at Kiev to destroy the Khazars.

CHAPTER 3

Global Up- and Downturns

General Observations

A third macro-historical model of rise and decline sees the causal forces as external, like the windows-of-opportunity theory, but in diametrical opposition to the latter postulates that civilizations rise and decline together, on a global or at least continent-wide basis. Chase-Dunn and Hall assert that civilizations of the same historical period have tended to move together up and down, in parallel ways rather than alternative ways.

They speak of "Afroeurasia" as a unit or a "world-system" and claim that between circa 500 BCE and 1400 CE nearly all civilizations within this large geographic space interacted and concurrently moved up and down.[1] The philosopher Karl Jaspers saw far-reaching spiritual movements in Greece, Israel, India, and China occurring more or less simultaneously in the sixth to fourth centuries BCE, the "Axial Age." This similarity inspired historians to look for a common sociological cause, a universal driver, to explain this similarity. Jaspers considered such speculations futile, as they could never be scientifically proven.[2]

The discovery that civilizations follow identical or similar trajectories applies mainly to the twentieth century. The universal expansion of the West that began in the early nineteenth century and culminated, so far, in the economic and cultural globalization of the late twentieth century indeed created a "world-system" in Chase-Dunn and Hall's sense of the term. The two World Wars, the Great Depression, and many other events of the twentieth century involved or affected, indirectly if not directly, all people on earth.

Applications to Jewish History

In some cases, a rise or decline of the larger environment carried the Jewish people along; in other cases it did not. One often comes across the view that Jews did well when their non-Jewish environment flourished, and suffered when their environment declined. Fernand Braudel, for example, asserts that in Europe every major episode of anti-Jewish persecution was preceded or accompanied by a general economic crisis.[3] Bernard Lewis noted that Ottoman Jewry flourished when the Ottoman Empire was at its peak, and declined in the eighteenth and nineteenth centuries when the Empire receded.[4] But the historian must not ignore the fact that there were also instances when Jews fared badly while their external environment was prosperous, and others when Jews did well while their environment was in crisis. The Persian Safavi dynasty, which ruled between the sixteenth and eighteenth centuries, created a culturally rich, politically and economically powerful empire that oppressed and persecuted Jews repeatedly, greatly reducing their numbers, due to Shiite religious fanaticism. There are other, similar examples in Jewish history.

Jonathan I. Israel describes a contrary example of Jewish revival in a crisis context. In the seventeenth century, Europe's Jews were doing relatively well, their numbers and prosperity growing while the European states tore each other apart in the Thirty Years War (1618-1648) and the German lands lost a third of their population.[5]

Examples of this nature demonstrate that there is no general rule. Only in the twentieth century did the entire Jewish people become part of a globalized world. This is a radical change. It is highly likely that henceforth Jewish futures will be linked more closely than ever to global futures (see Part III, Chapter 7).

CHAPTER 4

Thriving Civilizations, or the Myth of a Golden Age

General Observations

A metaphor was invented in ancient times to describe the thriving peak period of a civilization: the Golden Age. This term goes back to Greek mythology and Roman poetry. Greeks and Romans idealized the first age of humankind; it was called the "Golden Age," and the following age was "Silver," and then "Bronze" and finally "Iron," which was meant to be the contemporary, lowest degree of civilization. The eighth century Greek poet Hesiod described the pleasures of the Golden Age: "Just like gods they spent their lives, with a spirit free from care, entirely apart from toil and distress. Worthless old age did not oppress them, but they were always the same in their feet and hands, and delighted in festivities, lacking in all evils....They had all good things: the grain-giving field bore crops of its own accord...."[1] The ideal was to live in peace and enjoy eternal youth, free food, and life-long leisure. Hesiod's ideal was plain and material. It was remote from the ideal of a happy life that Socrates and Plato would later propose, a life of understanding, truth, and responsible citizenship, but it was Hesiod's and not Socrates' ideal that kept re-emerging through later centuries, particularly in the popular medieval myth of the "fool's paradise." Whether material or spiritual, all Golden Ages from the beginning of history until today seem to have one ideal in common: peace.

Historians and popular memory transferred the Golden Age paradigm from mythology to history and attached a "gold" label to selected periods of national glory and achievement. Thus, historians call "golden" the great age of Athens, from the glorious battles in the Persian War in 480 BCE (Marathon, Thermopylae, and Salamis) to the death of Pericles in 429 or the end of the Peloponnesian War in 404. During these 50 or 80 years, Athens indeed reached the zenith of its political power and cultural creativity. The Golden Age of Rome was said to be the lifetime of Augustus, the 41 years during which Rome was more or less at peace. Others, however, speak of the "five good emperors" from Nerva to Marcus Aurelius (96-180 CE), and call their collective 84 years of reign a Golden Age. Florence, the center of gravity of the Italian Renaissance, had its own Golden Age, which began in the early fifteenth century and was brutally terminated by the iconoclastic monk Savonarola in 1492. It lasted barely 80 years. When Jacob Burckhardt commented on this quick end, he quoted the verses of the Florentine ruler Lorenzo de Medici, which are perhaps the most famous poems in the Italian language. Burckhardt read into them a nostalgic premonition that the Renaissance glory would be very short: "How beautiful is youth—though it flees away so fast...."[2] Islamic civilization too is credited with a Golden Age, but its timelines vary.

Marshall Hodgson is generous and grants Islam a period of "great cultural fluorescence," the "High Caliphal" period from 622 to 1258.[3]

One of the most recent periods of history to have been called "golden" by national consensus is the age of the Dutch Republic, circa 1590 to 1720, when it was a great power and home to most of Europe's famous painters. Johan Huizinga noted that only the Dutch had their Golden Age at the very beginning of their national history, as it appears in antique mythologies, and not in the middle, like all others. Only fifty years before Rembrandt's birth one could barely speak of a Dutch people in the modern sense.[4]

These variations in dating indicate how strongly the ideologies of contemporaries or later generations can influence the identification of Golden Ages. Equally ideological is a widespread belief that Golden Ages were periods of external peace and personal happiness. They were not. The Italian Renaissance was a time of frequent wars between the city-states, civil unrest, cruelty, and violence. For the overwhelming majority of Italians, daily life was not enviable. Periods of great political and economic power and simultaneous flourishing of all fields of culture are relatively rare, and do not always last long. The coincidence of high creativity and great achievement in many fields is difficult to explain, particularly when it occurs in small places such as Athens, Florence, or the Netherlands. "Inevitably, much remains elusive," warns Jonathan Israel after examining the Dutch case.[5] Also, all Golden Ages must end, which underlines their dramatic and exceptional nature. Western civilizations often claim only one major Golden Age. China, however, does not. Its 2200 years of dynastic history includes many periods of rise and decline, and also of political or cultural peak periods. Even at the beginning of his dynastic history, 2100 year ago, the historian Sima Qian already saw China oscillating endlessly between rise, prosperity, and decline.[6]

Applications to Jewish History

In the eighth century the Greek poet Hesiod, who was quoted above, nostalgically celebrated an imaginary past Golden Age of affluence, happiness, and peace. The biblical record, perhaps written at the same time as Hesiod was active, chose the reign of Solomon rather than the first age of humanity as the period of greatest prosperity and happiness. The Bible does not use the Golden Age metaphor, which is Greek, but pays tribute to Solomon's reign in poetic words that would occur more than once in the Bible. This, then, is probably the Hebrew equivalent of a Golden Age during the time of the First Temple, as it is glowingly described in I Kings: "Judah and Israel dwelt in safety, everyone under his own vine and under his own fig tree, from Dan to Beer Sheva, all the days of Solomon."[7] The prophet Micah, who may have lived in the same century as Hesiod, uses the same vine and fig tree metaphor as I Kings, in his case not to extol the past but to predict a coming and final "Golden Age," that of the Messiah.[8] The prophet Amos, perhaps an early contemporary of Micah, promised the same for "the end of days," though in different words: "A time is coming...when the mountains shall drip wine and the hills shall wave with grain."[9] The prophetic notion of a Golden Age was radically different from that of the Greeks. The Golden Age was to come only at the end of history. The biblical narrative of the beginning of history knows no "Golden Age." Only Adam and Eve lived, for a while, in paradise, until they committed a sin and were expelled. While later rabbinic scriptures speculated extensively about the promised messianic future, rabbinic thoughts about the course of past and ongoing history were sober and quite comparable to those of the Chinese Sima Qian. Rabbinic tradition compared the Jewish people to the moon, which is always waxing and waning. This is one of the traditional explanations of the monthly "blessing of the moon" which is part of Jewish ritual.[10] In the nineteenth century, Nachman Krochmal developed this tradition into a cyclical interpretation of Jewish history, with high and low points in every cycle.

Whatever the facts about Solomon and his exact dates are—several different ones have been proposed—this Golden Age ended, according to biblical record, with the break-up of his kingdom. It lasted no longer than 80 years or so. The only other period of Jewish history, historically more tangible, that modern historians have called a Golden Age is the high period of Jewish culture, wealth, and political influence in the Iberian Peninsula. The dating for this period varies, depending on definitions. Dating it from 912 to 1066, when the Jews were expelled from Granada, is one possibility—150 years at best. Some modern authors refer back to this age as a model for a hoped-for reconciliation between Jews and Arabs. The term

Golden Age has also been used to describe the political power and cultural creativity of American Judaism in the twentieth century.

Jewish history, like Chinese history, has had many ups and downs, but no single exceptional, historically substantiated Golden Age shining above all earlier and later periods, as was the case in Athens, Florence, or the Netherlands. The period in Jewish history that began in 1948 has many hallmarks of what other civilizations called a "Golden Age." Israel's political, military, and economic power, and the influence and cultural productivity of the Jewish people in important parts of the world, are a historically unique confluence of positive trends. Two other characteristics are typical of other "Golden Ages": today's participants do not see the "gold" in it, and the current age craves but does not achieve peace. Once again, ours is an age of war and tension.

CHAPTER 5

Cultural Accomplishments of Thriving Civilizations

General Observations

What remains of the thriving civilizations of the past and their Golden Ages for future generations to study is less their territorial expansion, the temporary wealth of their upper classes, or their military victories if there were any, and more their cultural accomplishments and creations. All Golden Ages in history have at least one thing in common: they are periods of great cultural creativity. "Culture" in our terminology includes the visual arts, music, literature, poetry, philosophy, movies, science, and more—creative endeavors that leave memorable works, or at least traces of them, to later generations. A few authors have tried to statistically measure "cultural accomplishments" in the hope that they would discover some causal relationships. One was Pitirim Sorokin, who set out to measure "art, truth, ethics, law and social relationships"—in short, culture.[1] His statistical data are dubious and have never been verified.[2] Another author is Charles Murray, best known for his 1994 book *The Bell Curve*.[3] Murray identified what he called the 4002 "most eminent" individuals in 14 areas of human accomplishment (science, literature, philosophy, arts, music, etc.) since 800 BCE, and tried to discover what they had in common and thus what could explain their eminence. Even his apparently neutral statistical approach was partly based on outdated information and old encyclopedias, and he could not eliminate subjectivity in the evaluation of cultural creations.

Many of the historians in this book—Sima Qian, Ibn Khaldun, Jacob Burckhardt, Oswald Spengler, Johan Huizinga, Pitirim Sorokin, Bernard Lewis, and Jonathan I. Israel[4]—have commented extensively on the links between cultural creativity and the rise or decline of civilizations. All are skeptical about simple causal explanations of culture, and a few, particularly Huizinga, are convinced that a culture always follows its own immanent impulses and is not shaped by external events. The portraits and interiors of Jan van Eyck (ca. 1395-1441) radiate an atmosphere of quiet peace that is completely unaffected by the permanent violence and bloodshed that filled the painter's time and place.[5]

The following is a tentative summary of the collective findings of the aforementioned historians, or their unresolved questions:

Political and Military Power: Great cultural achievement can go hand-in-hand with political success and expansion or, contrarily, with decline and military debacle. The second case has occurred more than once in history. It has already been asked whether in some cases military defeat was not a better trigger of cultural creativity than victory. Also, overwhelming and intrusive state power can hold back—or even snuff out—cultural creativity because, as Jacob Burckhardt noted, the true aim of every state is power, not culture.

Economic Wealth and Royal Patronage: Wealth, royal patronage, and financial security have often stimulated cultural productivity. Historians who lived under powerful rulers, like Sima Qian or Ibn Khaldun, naturally regarded royal patronage as indispensable to art, science, and culture. Historians cannot agree on whether economic prosperity is a condition of collective or individual cultural creativity. Huizinga was convinced that economic and other external conditions were irrelevant to the Dutch culture of the fourteenth century, the waning Middle Ages. Jonathan Israel was equally convinced that the enormous economic wealth that the Netherlands accumulated in the seventeenth century was indispensable for the Dutch culture of its "Golden Age," at least on a society-wide level. On an individual level, the relationship between money and creativity could vary enormously. Some great artists flourished without wealth or government patronage. Rembrandt lived during the peak period of the Dutch "Golden Age," but was never funded by any public authority, and was so inept at husbanding his resources that he was once forced to sell his paintings and belongings to avoid bankruptcy. The poignant sadness of his self-portraits in old age mirror all of his life's troubles, and his unbroken creativity in spite of them.

A High Level of Education of a Large Part of the Population: An education available not only to the small number of elites was typical of classical periods of cultural creativity in ancient Greece and Rome, and in Europe during the Renaissance. Broad-based literacy seemed to be a condition of cultural flourishing, at least in some cases. In the Muslim world until the thirteenth or fourteenth century, and in parts of Europe since the Renaissance, high regard for science and scientific research was part—either the cause or the result—of cultural creativity and educational achievement.

Trans-Cultural Encounters: Encounters with other cultures can greatly stimulate cultural creativity. The Italian Renaissance owes a lot to the discoveries of Antiquity and the exploration of foreign continents. The Jewish and Muslim Golden Age of Spain resulted from, among other things, a creative encounter of three civilizations.

Geographic Concentration: Most great periods of cultural creativity have been concentrated in small geographic spaces—Athens, Florence, Venice, Amsterdam, and three or four cities in China that changed depending on the dynasty. Golden Age cities have been places of big money, much political, economic and cultural exchange, and plentiful foreign visitors, but the simultaneous appearance of many creative people in the same place remains difficult to explain. The famous Florentine artist, art historian, and biographer Giorgio Vasari (1511-1574) gave a lot of thought to this question.[6] He observed in his biography of the painter Masaccio: "When nature creates a human being of exceptional talent, whatever his field of endeavor, it has the habit of creating another one at the same moment and in the same location in order to encourage mutual emulation and inspiration."[7] However, in other biographies Vasari identified another reason: the physical proximity of creative individuals and their personal contacts often lead to competition and fuel intense jealousies and rivalries that can degenerate into physical violence, as when a jealous painter attacked Vasari's friend Michelangelo and broke his nose.[8] Competition and rivalry in small places can drive creativity in the arts, sciences, and other fields.

Relative Religious and Intellectual Tolerance: Many flourishing cultures have been destroyed by religious fanaticism. According to Burckhardt, the Catholic Counter-Reformation ruined the intellectual creativity of the Renaissance.[9] Culture can only flourish when there is spiritual and political space enough for variation and experimentation, but tolerance does not imply unlimited freedom. There is no proof that great cultural creativity depends on complete freedom of belief, speech, or writing.

Women's Rights: The Golden Ages of Athens, Florence, and the Dutch Republic were somehow linked to the high status women enjoyed in these places, in comparison with other contemporaneous countries. Why this was so is not known, nor is it certain whether this finding has universal historical merit. It is certainly the case that giving women more freedom expanded the pool of creativity. Maybe greater openness to women was simply one of the indicators of an open and tolerant society.

These external conditions can encourage creativity but cannot generate it. Nor can government policies. Two points are clear: creativity is first and foremost the creativity of individuals. A "creative" culture is one that has many such individuals. Second, the ultimate reasons for creativity are a mystery. Biologists and brain-researchers are trying to unravel parts of this mystery by linking creativity to new concepts of the sub-conscious.[10] Sub-conscious thought processes, e.g., those that occur during dream sleep or relaxation, are no longer seen as irrational forces that must be controlled by the rational and therefore "superior" consciousness but as emanating from parallel brain activity that constantly monitors our internal and external environment and engages conscious thought processes. Scientists have proposed that the source of our inspiration, which is central to all forms of creativity, is our sub-conscious thinking, and that in highly creative people sub-conscious material is more likely to spill over into consciousness. Long before modern psychology invented all of these terms, Vasari illustrated how the creativity of a great artist drew its force from his sub-conscious. He told the story of Leonardo da Vinci, who received a commission to paint the fresco of the "Last Supper" in Milan's Santa Maria delle Grazie monastery. When the monastery prior saw him "standing half a day lost in thought," apparently doing nothing, he started nagging him. The painter complained to the duke of Milan: "Leonardo, knowing the prince to be acute and intelligent, was ready to discuss the matter with him, which he would not do with the prior. He reasoned about art, and showed him that men of genius may be working when they seem to be doing the least, working out inventions in their minds, and forming those perfect ideas which afterwards they express with their hands."[11]

Explanations of individual creativity still do not tell us why creativity is occasionally concentrated in specific places, periods, and human groups, and that question remains unresolved.

A last "condition" of creativity must also be mentioned: luck. Thriving high cultures can depend on a small number of exceptionally innovative artists and thinkers. The appearance of a genius is always a question of luck, a chance event, as in the case of great political leaders (as shall be discussed in Part IV, Chapter 11). Death and illness threaten all of them, and can change the course of a culture. Mozart contracted smallpox when he was eleven years old and was temporarily blinded. In his era a third of all people infected with the disease died, and some who survived remained blind. Mozart recovered completely and became one of the greatest musical composers of all time. He seems to us irreplaceable. Had he died in childhood or remained blind, the entire history of Western music would have been different.

Applications to Jewish History

The most discussed question raised by "Jewish culture" is the great number of cultural, artistic, scientific, and other contributions that Jews of modern times have made to the civilizations of the world. Yuri Slezkine, professor of history at Berkeley, has dubbed the twentieth century "The Jewish Century" for good reason.[12] Cultural "contributions," "creativity," and "accomplishments" are used synonymously in this chapter. A discussion of Jewish cultural "contribution" or "creativity" should address two questions:

Why is This Issue So Often Discussed? What is its historical and ideological context?

The Meaning of "Jewish Contributions." When we speak of "Jewish contributions," do we mean contributions of Judaism as a civilization or religion, or contributions by individuals who happen to be Jews?

As far as the historical and ideological contexts are concerned, polemical discussions about Jewish creativity are at least two thousand years old. Pagan authors of the ancient world, annoyed by Jewish pride, asserted that the Jews had no creativity, and the Jews retorted that they were more creative than any other nation. A lively echo of such controversies can be found in Flavius Josephus' (ca. 37-100 CE) book *Against Apion*. Apion (ca. 20 BCE-45 CE) was a Greek-speaking Egyptian antisemite who wrote pamphlets against the Jews that have not survived, and which we know of only through Josephus' polemical refutations. According to Apion, writes Josephus, "we Jews have not had any wonderful men amongst us, not any inventors of arts, nor any eminent for wisdom."[13] Josephus' book sets out to prove Apion wrong and demonstrate the antiquity, originality, creativity, and even superiority of the Jews. Their laws are the best of all, their law-givers the greatest, their morality unmatched by any other people, etc. "I am so bold as to say that we are become the teachers of other men, in the greatest number of things, and those of the most excellent nature only."[14] The tenor of this exchange, though in more moderate terms, would be heard again and again through Jewish history, particularly since the seventeenth and eighteenth centuries, and turned into a central theme of the anti- and pro-Jewish polemics of the nineteenth and twentieth centuries.[15] Heinrich Graetz wrote his monumental *History of the Jews* in the second half of the nineteenth century not least as a combative response to Germany's growing public and academic antisemitism. When he claimed that the civilized world owed a great debt to Jewish monotheism he walked in the footsteps of Josephus, who had preceded him by 1800 years. A large number of books and articles, by both antisemites and apologetic Jews, continued the debate in the twentieth century, and there is no end in sight.*Jewish contributions are a reality that in some cases can even be quantified, such as by counting the proportions of Jews among Nobel laureates

---

* One of the best-known Jewish books on this subject was Cecil Roth, *The Jewish Contribution to Civilization* (London: Macmillian, 1938). Roth issued a pathetic and obviously futile appeal to the Nazis to recognize that the Jews had done a lot of good to the world, and particularly to Germany. In the years after 2000, several popular, self-congratulatory book on the same subject have appeared. See, e.g., Ken Spiro, *WorldPerfect: The Jewish Impact on Civilization* (Deerfield Beech/Florida: Simcha Press, 2002); Joe King, *The Jewish Contribution to the Modern World* (Montreal: Montreal Jewish Publication Society, 2004).

and other prizewinners. But it is also important to understand the broader ideological context of this debate, and why it kept flaring up in the twentieth century and will most likely continue to do so throughout the twenty-first.

The second question to be addressed relates to the difference between "Jewish contributions" and "contributions by Jews." The two are not the same. What Flavius Josephus and Heinrich Graetz had in mind were the contributions that Judaism, the Hebrew Bible, Jewish ethics, etc., were making to the world—hence they were "Jewish contributions." "Contributions by Jews," by contrast, can enrich any field of endeavor but do not have to be derived from Judaism. The authors of these contributions may be Jewish by faith or origin, but their links to Judaism and the Jewish people are sometimes tenuous or non-existent. Marx and Freud are often mentioned in this context. A good eye can still detect Jewish heritage in their work, but that is not the heritage they wished to convey. If they had an impact on Jews, it is because the latter participated fully in the history of the twentieth century, not because they were, sometimes against their own will, seen as "fellow Jews." Many Jews became Marxists, but not because Marx was a Jew. In fact, many left Judaism under his influence. Are works necessarily "Jewish" because their authors are Jews?

The question of whether an individual work is Jewish or not could be a tricky one even in ancient times. A few rare examples will be given. The first two are works of early Diaspora artists who are unknown to a broader public, a poetess and a composer. They were unusual cases in their own time, but illustrate precisely what has become one of the main issues today. Qasmina bint Isma'il al-Yehudi (eleventh/twelfth century) is believed to have been the daughter of the famous Spanish-Jewish statesman and poet Samuel Ha-Nagid. She wrote beautiful poems that are strongly reminiscent of the lyrics of the Greek poetess Sappho: both women bewail their loneliness.[16] Unlike her illustrious father, she wrote in Arabic, not in Hebrew, and her themes are universal, not Jewish. If her creations are counted as "Jewish" it is only because her name, "al-Yehudi," and her family pedigree suggest that she was Jewish. The second case is Obadiah the Proselyte, also called Obadiah the Norman, a Norman priest who converted to Judaism in 1102.[17] He wrote the earliest-known Jewish liturgical synagogue music, which was found on a manuscript in the Cairo *Genizah*. It is likely that Obadiah had to flee Europe after his conversion and found refuge among the Jews of Egypt. His chants follow Lombardic-Italian church melodies of the twelfth century; musicologists could not detect any Jewish difference.[18] Obadiah's work is "Jewish" if one considers the history of the author, his intention, and his presumed audience, but not if one listens to his music and recognizes its origins. Similar questions must have arisen in Hellenistic Alexandria, Apion's hometown. The bulk of literary creations by Jews from Alexandria have not survived, but it can be assumed that some of them did not have Jewish themes. Separating Jewish from non-Jewish works when most Hellenistic Jews had Greek names was virtually impossible if the subject matter was not Jewish.

The story of Alexandrian Judaism and those of Qasmina al-Yehudi and Obadiah raise an additional complexity, namely that of cultural symbiosis or syncretism. Who contributed what, and to whom? Did these Jews contribute to Greek, Muslim, and Medieval Christian culture, or was it these cultures that forced the Jews into new languages and forms of expression and thus reshaped Jewish culture? There are no clear-cut answers to these questions, which will accompany the history of Western Judaism in modern times.

Baruch Spinoza (1632-1677) adds a third variant to the history of "contributions by Jews." He was Jewish, like Ha-Nagid's daughter or Obadiah the Proselyte, but his case can be seen—with greater justification—as a Jewish contribution to Western culture. His *Tractatus Theologico-Politicus* of 1670 focused on an apparently Jewish theme, the historical accuracy of the Hebrew Bible, which distinguishes him from the poetess. But the intended addressees of his book were not so much the Jews of his time as the Christians, and this distinguishes him in turn from Obadiah. The *Tractatus* attacked the historical truth of the Bible with a deadly force never seen before. Spinoza had been excommunicated by the Jews of Amsterdam in 1656. He was no longer much interested in the Jews, and knew that his book would have little or no effect on them. He challenged biblical authority so radically because he wanted to undermine the spiritual and religious basis of Europe's monarchical order, which he loathed. He could not do that in his time by directly attacking the truth of the Christian Bible, but attacking the Hebrew Bible was less dangerous and had the same effect. His Christian readers, such as Leibniz, perceived his intention correctly. According to J. Israel, his book, though banned all over Europe, had the intended political and intellectual impact.[19]

Spinoza stood at the onset of modernity. Before him, the great majority of "contributions by Jews" were in fact "Jewish contributions"—Samuel Ha-Naggid's daughter notwithstanding, as she was an exception. The Bible was written by Jews for Jews. Its universal spread was not intentional, or was only intentional in an indirect sense, as the book itself told the Jews that they had to become, by their impeccable conduct, a "light unto the nations." After Spinoza, the cases of "contributions by Jews" not intended for Jews began to rise, and from the nineteenth century on they became overwhelming. The exception became the rule. World history knows many eminent figures who affected the world more than they did their own people. Buddha was Indian, but Hinduism first rejected and then incorporated Buddhism, and his teachings subsequently flourished elsewhere as a new, independent religion. Copernicus was Polish and revolutionized the thought of the whole world, not just that of Poland. Chopin is claimed by both Poland and France, but his music belongs to the world. However, the explosion of contributions Jews made in the late nineteenth and twentieth centuries to the cultures of the world— not primarily, if at all, to Jewish culture, however defined—is historically unique and has created a dichotomy. It reflects the unique diasporic history of the Jews. It is significant that the growing contributions of Jews to other cultures often met with initial resistance, if not outright rejection. The contributions became major themes of modern antisemitism. Jacob Burckhardt acknowledged no valuable Jewish contributions to nineteenth-century German culture. He saw only the Jews' "completely unjustified meddling into everything."[20]

The dichotomy also explains why an agreed-upon definition and measurement of "Jewish" cultural creativity has so far proved elusive.[21] But this dichotomy began to change in the second half of the twentieth century. Jewish and Israeli cultures and themes are becoming an integral part of modern cultures, while the latter have continued to penetrate Jewish and Israeli consciousness and creativity. This has begun to blur the difference between internal and external influence. Is the old dichotomy waning? Maybe these developments signal a new dialectic between internal and external influence. Harold Bloom, the historian of literature at Yale, called Kafka "*the* Jewish writer" who is still haunting American and world literature. He predicted that Kafka and Freud "may yet redefine Jewish culture for us."[22] Bloom could have said almost the same of the American Jewish writers of the twentieth century. Norman Mailer, Isaac Bashevis Singer, Arthur Miller, Saul Bellow, Bernard Malamud, Philip Roth, and many others are Jews who have changed the face of American and Western literature as well as the self-perception of America, and they have done this by taking Jewish themes, problems, and characters as models. Such themes and problems do not appear explicitly in the works of Kafka, even though Bloom has proposed him as the twentieth century's quintessential Jewish writer. Kafka and others who retained their Jewishness raise a different problem than did Marx, who did not want to be a Jew. Bloom and the readers who know Kafka's life and his Central European Jewish background are aware that Jewishness was probably the most significant spiritual and emotional influence in his life. They also know that all his works keep referring metaphorically to the Jewish experience, but never mention the word "Jew." Kafka was able to anticipate the absurdities, anxieties, and horrors of the twentieth century better than any other, because he was a Jew. He left a deep and lasting influence on world literature, theater, and film. His books can be read in every major world language, including Chinese and Arabic, and he is the only twentieth-century writer whose name has transformed into a universally understood adjective: "Kafkaesque." But few non-specialized readers today will detect the hidden, pervasive Jewish presence in his work. Kafka's global presence does not indicate whether and how he contributed to

Jewish culture. Did he strengthen Jewish identity, self-respect, creativity, or survival, or generate understanding for the Jewish people? One must say that such questions are usually not asked in an evaluation of cultural creations of universal importance. It is too early to assess whether Bloom's prediction that the twenty-first century would "re-define" Jewish culture will come true. Even if he is right, it would be wise to also remember an earlier warning of the Israeli Bible scholar Yeheskel Kaufmann. He concluded from the history of Egypt, Greece, and Rome that the spiritual wealth of a culture, its universal value and greatness, cannot save a group from extinction.[23] In other words, universal influence and perceived greatness do not assure the long-term survival of a civilization. Kaufmann believed that the longevity of the Jewish people owed nothing to its spiritual contributions to the civilizations of the world, and that there is no guarantee that this will change.

His conclusion is bleak and not entirely true for Greece. The Roman conquerors treated Greece with a respect that was lacking in their relations with some other vanquished nations. Even in the nineteenth century, the Greek struggle for independence from Turkey set off a groundswell of emotional, political, and material support throughout Europe that had nothing to do with the murky Balkan politics of the time and everything to do with memories of Homer, Plato, and Pericles. Kaufmann was right in one sense: neither Rome nor nineteenth-century Europe could restore to the Greeks the lost creativity of their classical age, but they helped the Greek people to survive and kept for them an open window to the future. The "civilizational affinity" (which will be discussed later, in Part IV, Chapter 9) the great powers felt for the Greeks provided them a measure of protection. The Jewish fate was much harsher, but even the Jews benefited more than once, at least in Christian countries, from a recognition of their spiritual accomplishments. Examples can be found in the Renaissance and in Humanism, in Cromwell's England, and in the Christian Zionism of the nineteenth and twentieth centuries, among other settings. The future will tell whether the enormous increase in universal cultural contributions by the Jews of the twentieth century will continue, and if it does whether this will cancel Kaufmann's prediction and make Jews and Judaism safer.

CHAPTER 6

Decline Has Multiple Causes

General Observations

Edward Gibbon's *Decline and Fall of the Roman Empire* contains an important lesson that must be counted among the macro-historical rise and decline theories. No single cause, he notes, can explain the decline and downfall of a multi-faceted, widespread, and long-lasting civilization: there has to be a combination of causes. No single cause is responsible for the decline of the Roman or the Ottoman Empire, or of Islamic civilization in general, as other historians have suggested, but rather the historian must look for a combination of reasons. In general, the smaller and shorter-lived a civilization, the more tempting it is to identify a single or dominant cause of its decline and fall, but even in the case of one of the smallest civilizations that ever lived and died, that of Easter Island, anthropologists still cannot agree whether the death was caused by one or several reasons, and what exactly these reasons were. Even scholars who keep looking for simple, common denominators in all civilizational collapses often propose factors that do not stand alone but are causal agents, among others, in a complex chain of events.

Gibbon's work conveys another important and related conclusion about the laws of decline and fall that had enormous influence on later historical imagination. For Gibbon, no lone foreign enemy and no unexpected catastrophe destroyed the Roman Empire: it destroyed itself. Rome's ruin was the inevitable result of "immoderate greatness." "Instead of enquiring why the Roman Empire was destroyed, we should rather be surprised that it had subsisted so long."[1] Spengler and Toynbee defended the same position, which became a deeply entrenched tenet of Western historiography and philosophy. Spengler asserted that all dead civilizations had perished by self-destruction, except for one, pre-Columbian Mexico, which was annihilated by a "handful of bandits," as he called the murderous Spaniards.[2] Toynbee chose a graphic image to drive this idea home: "Civilizations do not die by an assassin's hand, they die by suicide."[3] Even Jared Diamond's 2005 *Collapse*, which ascribes the end of past civilizations to environmental degradation, blames internal

148

political and cultural factors for preventing these civilizations from saving themselves when it was still possible.

The conclusion that civilizations die for internal and not external reasons is true in the case of many civilizations, but not all. It has been said that history is written by the victors, not the vanquished, and thus destroyed civilizations and people have no voice. It is puzzling that historians pay so little attention to the many civilizations that were exterminated by stronger enemies without leaving a record or much of a trace. Did they live and die in vain? The Roman Empire wiped out scores of foreign civilizations. Almost nothing was left of Carthage, once a great Mediterranean power, after the Romans put the city and its people to the sword. The Etruscans, who had a richer and older civilization than early Rome, were defeated and completely absorbed by the Romans, who seem to have destroyed their enemies' entire written heritage. Contrary to what Spengler wrote, pre-Columbian Mexico was not alone. It is true that nothing could have saved the indigenous Mexicans from the fearsome Spanish army, which was invincible for more than a century even on European battlefields, or from the diseases the Spaniards brought to the Americas. Even if the details of their destruction and demise were unique, other civilizations in different places and epochs shared similar fates.

Applications to Jewish History

Gibbon's first finding applies to Jewish civilization. If one looks for historical, not metaphysical, reasons for the long-term survival of the Jews, it is clear that they were saved more than once by their global spread and fragmentation into different branches. No single danger or cause of decline could touch all of them simultaneously. In ancient times, their wide dispersion was already sustaining their survival. When Titus and Hadrian occupied Judea, many Jews, including Judean refugees, found peace, protection, and an opportunity for a new start in Babylon, which was under Parthian rule. Hadrian, whose suppression of the Bar Kochba revolt inflicted grievous losses on the Jewish people, had renounced his attempts to subdue the powerful empire of the Parthians and had made peace with them. No one can say with certainty how the Jewish people as a whole would have fared if Hadrian had managed to add Babylon—with its large Jewish population—in addition to Judea to his realm, as he had initially planned, but probably not well. In other parts of the empire, the Jews were sufficiently circumspect or resourceful to ensure their survival and well-being. In Rome they were already citizens in the first century BCE, and their citizenship was never revoked, not even during the revolts in their ancestral homeland in 70 and 135 CE.

Another example in Jewish history of salvation through global dispersion can be found in the Iberian Peninsula. Had Spain and Portugal in the sixteenth and seventeenth centuries dominated the entire world with the same methods they used in the Iberian peninsula and the Americas, the Jews would have had to choose between enforced conversion or death on a global, and not only Iberian, scale. Survival would have become extremely difficult, if not impossible. Obviously, the same could be said of the fate of the Jewish people in the twentieth century. If the Nazis, who destroyed a third or more of the Jewish people, had won the war and conquered the world, there could hardly be a Jewish people today. In the absence of a strong, independent Jewish state, Jews benefited on the one hand from the fragmentation of power in a divided world and the lack of powerful, centralized bureaucracies in most countries, and on the other from their widespread presence across the world. Jewish history includes some diasporas that withered and disappeared even without persecution, while others rose and flourished elsewhere. The religious and cultural fragmentation of Judaism may also have played a role in long-term survival because the competition between different branches of the religion has probably added to the Jewish people's creativity and capacity for change and adaptation. Dispersal and variation have made the Jewish people less vulnerable to monocausal impacts.

Unless one assumes that the world is about to enter an era of eternal peace, history seems to tell us that a monolithic Judaism, or a Judaism concentrated in a single place, would have a smaller chance of long-term survival than a multifaceted Judaism present in different parts of the world. A provisional conclusion to be drawn from the past is that getting all Jews into uniform ideological-religious shape or into the same country may not be the best survival strategy. There should be at least two centers with sufficient critical mass to sustain the people—a criterion very difficult to define and measure. A second center in addition to Israel might stimulate the creativity of both and could also reinforce the power base of both. This was the conviction of Elias Bickerman, a historian who wrote about Jewish survival and success between the return from the Babylonian exile and the time of the last Maccabees: "The Dispersion saved Judaism from physical extirpation and spiritual inbreeding. Palestine united the dispersed members of the nation and gave them a sense of oneness. This counterpoise of historical forces is without analogy...."[4] It is important to fully understand Bickerman's comment. Dispersion did indeed save Judaism, but it could save it only because the center, the land of Israel, remained a unifying bond, in dreams and prayers if not in reality.

However, an ex-post explanation of the survival of the Jewish people thanks to its wide dispersion cannot be used uncritically as a policy indicator for the future. The *Shoah* and the creation of Israel have modified the traditional rule according to which a dispersed Jewish civilization has better survival odds than a centralized one. In principle, the old rule is still valid, but the creation of Israel has not simply replaced one large branch of the Jewish people with another one. This new branch has, for the first time in two thousand years if not more, considerable "hard power" that can be used directly or indirectly to help Diaspora Jews who lack it. The capture of Eichmann and the rescue of Ethiopian Jewry were two completely different exercises of Israeli "hard" and other state power on behalf of the Jewish people as a whole. Both were unthinkable before Israel existed. Another example was the emergence and assertiveness of Soviet Jewry from the 1970s on, particularly their fight for the right of emigration. Coordinated Israeli and American Jewish initiatives provided Soviet Jews with information, encouragement, books, and various forms of material help, and simultaneously convinced the United States to turn the right of Jews to immigrate to Israel into an American policy objective. Without Israel's open and covert activities this would not have been possible.

Israel is a major qualitative change not only in comparison to two thousand years of Diaspora history but probably even in regard to the Second Temple period. During that time, the land of Israel—Judea—did indeed give the dispersed Jewish communities "a sense of oneness," to quote Bickerman again. The Temple was the spiritual heart of Jewish civilization, and the size of the country's population alone would have turned it into the center of gravity for the entire Jewish people. However, as far as can be known today, Judea gave little or no political, economic, or military support to the Jews of Babylon, Egypt, Rome, or any other branch of the Diaspora except, on occasion, when Jews were in trouble in the adjacent territories of Syria or Transjordan. As far as is known, Judea was unable to do anything against the murderous anti-Jewish riots that flared up in Alexandria in 38 and 66 CE, although it is reported that Judean Jews came to the aid of those in Alexandria during troubles in the early years of the Emperor Claudius (41-54 CE).[5] If there was any flow of "hard power," it probably came more often from the Diaspora to Israel, for example in the form of annual financial contributions to the Temple, which were well-known but disliked, and a few times even forbidden, by the Roman authorities. The terrible results of the Jewish revolts of 115 CE in Cyrenaica, Egypt, and Cyprus are examples of a lack of cooperation or even mutual awareness between different Jewish communities. Roman historians reported that hundreds of thousands of Jews were killed in the massacres following these revolts, but we find no trace of these events in the Mishnah or any other early rabbinic writings. Is it possible that the *tanaim*, the sages of the Mishnah, such as Rabbi Akiva who lived at this time, never heard of these revolts or had nothing to say about them?

Israel's current power position has complex ramifications in the wider Jewish world, unmatched even by the history of the Second Temple period. In 1951, Hannah Arendt published the first in-depth, comprehensive analysis of general and Nazi antisemitism after the war. She noted the enormous explosion of hatred against the French nobility at the beginning of the French Revolution and referred to Alexis de Tocqueville for an explanation. Tocqueville emphasized that the nobility's sudden loss of power was not accompanied by a parallel loss of wealth. Great wealth and visible distinctions without real power and political function are intolerable. When this combination occurs, wealth and distinctions are seen as parasitic, superfluous, and provocative.

According to Arendt, the main reason for the virulence of modern, non-religious Nazi antisemitism was the discrepancy between the enormous cultural and economic influence of the Jews in Germany and elsewhere, and their inability to back up that influence with political and military power.[6] Israel's military power has important direct and indirect impacts on the Diaspora's political and psychological position, not only on Israel's strategic position in the Middle East. Until the Yom Kippur War of 1973, Israel's victories and military power strengthened the Diaspora's sense of pride, solidarity, and security, as became particularly clear after the Six-Day War of 1967. Since the Yom Kippur War, the Diaspora effects have been more ambiguous. When Israel is not seen as victorious, or comes under criticism for its protracted occupation and use of military force, the political and psychological effects on the Diaspora can be negative. However, a severe weakening of Israel or a terminal military defeat would have catastrophic political and psychological effects on the Jews of the world.

Gibbon's second finding was that civilizations destroy themselves, that the reasons for decline and fall are internal more than external. This conclusion does not apply to Jewish history. Large parts of the Jewish people were more than once destroyed by external, not internal, enemies. Internal tensions and dissent agitated Judaism from the beginning, but did not seriously threaten its survival, as Part IV, Chapter 10 will explain. At present, the Diaspora is seriously threatened solely by internal causes, particularly assimilation, whereas Israel faces both internal and external threats. Comparing the relative weight of internal and external dangers for the Jewish people as a whole means dealing with a set of interconnected contingencies. This is a delicate task, with uncertain conclusions that can change quickly when external conditions change.

CHAPTER 7

Global Futures: "End of Civilization" or "Decline of the West"?

General Observations

Twelve of the twenty-three authors whose works were consulted for this study write extensively or speculate briefly about the future of our world. All show a deep interest in what the future will hold. In the last decades, "futurology" or "future studies" has become an academic discipline with its own professional journals, graduate classes, international conferences, and other trappings of academia. One has to ask whether the views of the twelve relevant historians in our group, which in some cases were expressed long ago, are still valid for today and tomorrow. Of the twelve, all but one, Fernand Braudel, are pessimistic or have dark forebodings. This could be a coincidence resulting from a statistically non-representative selection of authors, or it may reflect a dominant intellectual trend. Arthur Herman's *Idea of Decline in Western History*, published in 1997, supports the second hypothesis. Herman identified the idea that European society and civilization were in decline as part of the intellectual after-shock that followed the end of the Enlightenment and the French Revolution. He regarded Burckhardt, Huizinga, Spengler, Sorokin, Toynbee, and many others, who all influenced each other, as heirs of and contributors to this growing stream of cultural pessimism. It is true that many writers and intellectuals have followed these pessimistic trends, but other philosophers and historians who believed in progress and a brighter future, like those of the Enlightenment, did exist and continue to do so. The most illustrious of this latter group in the nineteenth century were Friedrich Hegel, who saw Christian Europe and the German nation leading world history to ever-greater freedom, and Karl Marx, who promised destruction to the capitalism of his day and a glorious future to the new society that would emerge from the inevitable Communist Revolution. In the twentieth century, William H. McNeill emulated Hegel, as the optimistic title of his 1963 book shows: *The Rise of the West: A History of the Human Community*. In his time, the most prolific, optimistic, widely translated, and best-selling author of books about civilization was the American Will Durant (1885-1981). Between

1935 and 1975, Durant published *The Story of Civilization* in eleven volumes. Durant opposed what he called "contemporary pessimism," and claimed that history was not made of conflict and bloody battles but of "quieter and more inspiring scenes."[1] Professional historians ignored Durant, and his soothing gospel is completely forgotten today. He was not a recognized scholar but understood very well what the reading public, at least in the United States, wanted to hear. The end of the Cold War inspired a new wave of optimism, because liberal democracy had apparently won and was seen as history's final trend. This wave reached its intellectual apogee with Francis Fukuyama's much-discussed 1992 book, *The End of History and the Last Man.* Apogee is the right term here, because events on the ground soon enough showed that history was continuing as usual, and Fukuyama's thesis lost much of its credibility.

The twelve historians who express concern about global futures emphasize different issues and causes:

A. Collapse of Civilization I: Non-Material Causes

Pitirim Sorokin predicts a collapse of "Western culture and society"[2] as a consequence of an ever-growing, unbridled materialism and the disappearance of spiritual, idealistic values. His vision is not limited to the West but is global; he does not point to another, healthier civilization that exists today and would survive. "Even the greatest cultural values of the past will be degraded," and there will be "increasing moral, mental and social anarchy" leading to the violent destruction of civilization.[3] From the ruins of the old will emerge a new and better civilization. Sorokin's vision, in the end, looks not so different from that of Marx, but the emphasis of his book is entirely on decay, catastrophe, and a "fiery end." Sorokin did not conceal the religious source of his vision. In the early twenty-first century, new secularized versions of the same old doomsday-plus-resurrection prophecy have appeared.[4]

B. Collapse of Civilization II: Material Causes

Joseph Tainter analyzes more than twenty ancient civilizations and finds that all collapsed for internal—particularly material and organizational—reasons falling under the general rubric of "increasing complexity." He derides all non-material explanations as "mystical." All civilizations, including our own, must collapse for the same reasons that demolished the ancient ones. As a civilization becomes more complex, the improvements necessary to keep it functioning become more difficult and costly. When the point of no return is reached, the system will break down.

Today, one of the most salient manifestations of the "increasing complexity" of civilizations is their global financial and economic inter-connectedness. Other authors beside Tainter have suggested that this interconnectedness could be the undoing of global civilization. The global financial and economic crisis of late 2008 has revealed that no government, economist, or banker has a complete understanding of what exactly is happening at any given time, why it is happening, how it might end, and what must be done. Central bank officials have said that they have never in their live seen so much perplexity and helplessness. Many commentators do not consider material and economic conditions the ultimate causes of the crisis, but cite ethical reasons instead. Perhaps material and spiritual factors in the decline of civilizations cannot be so easily separated.

C. Collapse of Civilization III: Environmental Causes

Jared Diamond's 2005 *Collapse* claims that a number of civilizations destroyed themselves by degrading and over-exploiting their natural environments. He greatly fears that the same will happen to our own civilization in a not-too-remote future, but feels that it does not have to happen if mankind pursues environmentally sustainable policies. All past collapses were triggered not by unsolvable material causes, but by incompetent governance, human ignorance, and selfishness.

If current greenhouse gas trends are not halted, some fear that the consequences of global warming could spin out of control even before a hypothetical global collapse occurred, and lead to unstoppable mass migrations and violent global competition for land, fresh water, and food, finally culminating in global wars (see E., below).

D. Clash of Civilizations

Edward Gibbon wrote his monumental work in the optimistic eighteenth century and completed it before the French Revolution. But having studied Rome's decline and fall, he suspected that no civilization could last forever, not even our own. While wondering what might bring about the end of our civilization, he expressed a strange foreboding, the only major speculation about the West's long-term future we were able to identify in his main book. In Gibbon's time, Europe and England felt more secure than they had for a long time: "Yet this apparent security should not tempt us to forget that new enemies and unknown dangers may possibly arise from some obscure people, scarcely visible in the map of the world. The Arabs or Saracens, who spread their conquest from India to Spain, had languished in poverty and contempt, till Mahomet [sic] breathed into those savage bodies the soul of enthusiasm."[5] This sounds like a foreboding of a "clash of civilizations" long before the term became common in the late twentieth century. Gibbon mentioned it in the context of Rome's inability to foresee some of the gravest dangers the empire would have to face. His speculation had a double sense: one was to raise the specter of a possible clash of civilizations, another and arguably more important one was to remind us of the unpredictability of history: some of the most dangerous threats to civilizations come from the most unexpected quarters.

E. Global Wars

Arnold Toynbee feared more than any of our other authors that a new world war in which thermo-nuclear weapons would be used would destroy the earth.[6] Such a war was predictable but also preventable. His fears did not materialize. In 2007, the presidents of both Russia and the United States mentioned the danger of world war publicly, perhaps for the first time since the end of the Cold War. It is currently difficult to see which combination of conflicts and follies could push mankind into a world war again, but it was equally difficult before 1914 to foresee the impending First World War. An American historian of World War I makes a cautionary observation that is in line with Gibbon's warning that some major ruptures of history are unpredictable, even inexplicable. David Fromkin's *Europe's Last Summer* paints the picture of a continent that, before 1914, shared a civilization of identical core values, enjoyed flourishing economies and open borders, and was ruled by dynasties that had blood links and were on first-name terms with each other. The 1890s and 1900s were, not unlike our own time, an age of international congresses, disarmament conferences, and economic globalization, though also of re-armament and occasional local wars in more remote places such as the Balkans. And then, in August 1914, the continent "abruptly plunged out of control, crashing and exploding into decades of tyranny, world war and mass murder."[7] Perhaps the danger of global war should also be considered in relation to Tainter's forecast that the growing complexity of civilizations will, after a certain point, become unmanageable.

F. End of the West I: Non-Material Causes

The borderline between a hypothetical end of civilization and an equally hypothetical end of the West cannot be clearly drawn. Western civilization continues to dominate and shape the world. Its disappearance would mean the end of civilization as we know it, at least for a certain period. Sorokin spoke of the "West," but meant more than just the West.

Five of our authors predict or fear a decline and fall of the West due to spiritual reasons, and some of them would agree that it would drag the rest of humanity down as well. The five are Jacob Burckhardt, Johan Huizinga, Oswald Spengler, Arnold Toynbee, and Max Weber. Burckhardt, the pessimist, had doubts that Europe's great culture—for him the only Western achievement worth preserving—would survive the century after him. State power and the dictates of economic progress would increasingly overshadow all aspects of life,[8] and the future will boil down to one question: will the human yearning for power and material gain continue to dominate everything, or will it yield to a profound change in mentalities, as it did in the third and fourth centuries CE? Johan Huizinga shared Burckhardt's doubts about the future of the West.[9] Spengler regarded its end as inevitable, and Toynbee predicted the same unless there were far-reaching spiritual and political changes.[10] Max Weber concluded his *Protestant Ethic and the Spirit of Capitalism* of 1904/1906 with a foresight and a short but still pertinent question about our future. The ascetic puritanical spirit that had created and inhabited the material framework of capitalism had left its house, "Whether definitely, who can say? Nobody knows who will in the future live in this house, and whether completely new prophets or a powerful re-birth of old thoughts and ideas will appear at the end of such an extraordinary development...."[11] Weber does not answer the question directly, but his words allow the reader to infer what his own intuition was: our capitalist civilization will not survive if we cannot restore an ethical underpinning to it, be it the old one or a new one.

G. End of the West II: Material Causes

C. Chase-Dunn and T.D. Hall predict the self-destruction of the Western capitalist system for material reasons. Those material reasons consist of capitalism's "massive internal contradictions," a conventional Marxist prophecy.[12] More original and historically compelling is a warning by the Oxford historian Bryan Ward-Perkins, who also suggests that a collapse of the West is possible for material reasons, just as the civilization of the Western Roman Empire collapsed. The Romans had a flourishing, globally interconnected consumer economy, not unlike our own. Theirs was the first Western world economy. It collapsed, however, and took the antique civilization with it to the grave. Ward-Perkins warns us not to be "complacent" in the belief that this could never happen to us. The Romans, too, were sure that it could never happen to them.[13]

H. The Long Life of Civilization

Fernand Braudel does not swim with the stream and does not share the pessimism and forebodings of any of his eleven forerunners or colleagues. "Civilizations are continuities,"[14] and "I don't believe, as far as civilizations are concerned, in ruptures or irremediable social catastrophes."[15] Civilizations can be transformed, but not extinguished. In 1963, a year after the Cuban Missile Crisis, he published his *Grammar of Civilizations*, which presents many outlooks on the future. During the Crisis, Toynbee and many others had feared a nuclear world war and an end to civilization. Braudel's *Grammar* does not say a word about this "event," but includes chapters on the long-term evolution of the Russian and American civilizations as though their permanency was unquestionable.

The forebodings and predictions of these historians are thought-provoking and deserve to be tested for their future relevance. A majority of our historians believe that the ultimate dangers to the survival of our civilization are spiritual and ethical—in which one can include the quality of governance— not material. Another recurring theme is the unpredictability of major disruptions that can cause decline and fall. Related to this is an awareness of the complexity and interconnectedness of our civilization, which can make it almost impossible to fully comprehend or influence events.

Applications to Jewish History

Oswald Spengler is the only historian in our sample who connected a forecast of global decline and fall with the future of the Jewish people. He predicts that the Jewish people will go down with the West because it has become too integrated into, and entangled with, Western civilization. The Jews have lost their cohesion and tacit consensus (see Part IV, Chapter 2).[16] The end of the West—which to Spengler still meant mainly Europe—is the end of the Jews. In the almost hundred years since Spengler first formulated these ideas, Europe has indeed declined dramatically from the peak of power it had reached before 1914, but many major developments escaped Spengler's futuristic intuition: the steep rise of the United States during the twentieth century, the beginning great rise of Asia, and the creation of an independent Jewish state. What is still valid is Spengler's understanding that the fall of a great global civilization like that of the West may take its Jews down too, or will at least have radical consequences for them.

The chapter "Decline and Fall have Multiple Causes" contends that the wide geographic dispersion of the Jews was, in the past, essential to their survival because no single hostile power could destroy all of them. This argument applied specifically to political and religious powers that wanted to extinguish the Jews spiritually or physically. It can also be applied to the past decline of civilizations and empires that were not hostile to Jews. When Jews were widespread in the world, they would often decline with a declining civilization but flourish in another, rising one. The decline and fall of the Western Roman Empire certainly impoverished many Jews in Europe and reduced their numbers, because this was the fate of the whole population, but the Jews of Babylon were not affected and remained the center of Jewish religious and intellectual creativity. In a globalized world, geographic spread does not confer the same advantage as it does in a fragmented world. The Jewish people can neither stop nor influence the downturn of a major civilization. In such a situation it is even more urgent for the Jews to strengthen the "drivers" of rise, survival, and prosperity that will be discussed in Part IV, which will help them to survive difficult times and maintain their collective identity.

PART IV

DRIVERS OF RISE AND DECLINE OF CIVILIZATIONS: General Observations and Jewish History

Introduction

Apart from general macro-historical observations and theories, it is possible to identify from the work of the selected historians a number of specific "drivers" of rise and decline. Twelve drivers that are important in universal and Jewish history appear more or less often in the works of several of our twenty-three historians. The order of the drivers as they are discussed here does not indicate a prioritized order. These twelve drivers are linked in complex ways. Some are "primary," others are "secondary," and most of them can be both. They operate in different combinations and through multiple forms of interaction. For example, war (8) can bring to the fore creative leadership (5), in which case war is a primary and leadership a secondary driver— or the opposite can be the case when bad leadership is the cause of war. Charts of the possible relationships between drivers could be drawn up, but would be of little use. Historical reality is always shaped by a multitude of inter-connected factors, and the search for "ultimate" causes belongs more to metaphysics and philosophy than to historiography.

CHAPTER 1

Religion: Identity Safeguards and their Downsides

General Observations

Religion is interwoven with the history of every civilization. It is the source of the founding myths that shaped the collective identity of all old civilizations. The historians reviewed in Part II are interested in the question of whether religion strengthens or weakens civilization. They offer every possible answer and present contradictory observations. From the Confucian Sima Qian's point of view, emperors have a "Mandate of Heaven" that includes a set of ethical principles.[1] If they do not respect their Mandate, their dynasty will fall. For the Arab Ibn Khaldun, religion is the essence of civilization—but this is true only of the one true religion, his own. At the same time, Ibn Khaldun deplores the narrow-minded Islamic orthodoxy that led to a decline in Arab science and civilization—showing that even the religion in which he believed could damage a civilization.[2] For another historian, Gibbon, the most important religion, Christianity, played a role in the fall of the Roman Empire because it was seeking worldly power.[3] This is why Gibbon shows particular sympathy for, and devotes many pages to, the incorruptible Emperor Julian, who tried in vain to stop the spread of Christianity.[4] Jacob Burckhardt's sympathy does not go to Julian but to Constantine the Great, because he was a statesman of "bright empirical intelligence," who had the merit to understand that Christianity was a "global power," made it the official religion and thus set the course of future world history.[5] Another author, Toynbee, condemns both the Protestants and the Catholics, particularly some of the early popes,[6] for resorting to force. In so doing, they betrayed the message of Christianity's founder and jeopardized the moral heritage of Western civilization. He reserves most of his scorn, however, for English Protestantism, the religion in which he grew up, because he holds it spiritually responsible for England's colonial expansion and the ensuing extermination of native populations.[7] Some predict that the world is on its way to a new religious age, but disagree completely on the deeper meaning of this development. For Spengler, the emergence of a new religiosity in a decaying Occident will accelerate the decline of science and scientific thought, that symptom of the irreversibly approaching end of our civilization.[8] Others, to the contrary (Toynbee, Sorokin), place all their hopes for a more humane future in a comeback of religion, preferably Christianity. Bernard Lewis, the expert on Ottoman history, attributes the decline of the empire to, among other things, repeated religious opposition to reforms.[9]

Max Weber's comparative sociology of religion, mainly his studies of Protestantism, Confucianism, and Buddhism show how varied and contradictory the effects of religion can be. Religions carry with them political and social ideals that can determine social structure and daily life. The impacts of these ideals on society stimulate or stifle economic development and strengthen or weaken civilizations. Even for recent and well-documented history, different historians have proposed contradictory evaluations of the impact of a specific religion on a civilization. J. Huizinga was convinced that the Netherlands owed their national resilience, cohesion, and victory over Spain in the seventeenth century essentially to their strong Calvinist faith.[10] Jonathan Israel regarded other reasons as more important, and noted that Calvinist intolerance also had many negative cultural effects.[11]

Few aspects of civilization are as inextricably linked with the personal background and values of the historian as religion, and it is unlikely that historians will ever come to an agreement on the relations between religion, socio-economic factors, and civilization, all the more so as these dynamics are objectively complex and sometimes contradictory, and change from period to period. One important development of recent years is that evolutionary biologists and psychologists have begun to shed new scientific light on the origin and effects of religion. Some biologists argue that religion emerged not at the beginning of human evolution, but relatively late in that process. It succeeded because it was apparently beneficial to evolutionary fitness— in other words, because it made people better adapted to survive and pass their genes on to the next generation. Evidence has been supplied (based on United States data) that seems to confirm this hypothesis for individuals: in comparable circumstances, actively religious people have more resistant immune systems, live longer and healthier lives, and are happier than non-religious people.[12]

Applications to Jewish History[13]

Historically, the Jews are an ancient people of Middle Eastern origin, and all known ancient peoples emerged with a religion that dominated their life and thought. Civilization and religion could not be separated. The issues and challenges dating back to their ancient origin accompany the Jews to this very day. This chapter does not discuss questions of faith, but rather of sociology and psychology. What exactly in the Jewish religion has created and preserved the Jews as a separate group, and how is modernity affecting these factors of identity? Can one identify the components of the Jewish religion that have been essential to the rise and longevity of the Jewish people? To analyze how a religion sustains a social group does not mean that the group's faith is being questioned. It is possible to approach religious tradition and practice as a "true believer," but it is also possible to believe that tradition and practice are desirable and useful in their own right. Daniel Dennet, an American philosopher, distinguishes between "believers in belief" and "true believers."* As normative Judaism puts higher value on religious practice than on declarations of faith, this distinction is less problematic for observant Jews than it might be in other monotheistic religions.

This chapter discusses religion as a driver and guardian of the Jewish people and civilization, not of the ancient or modern Jewish state. The relationship between religion and state in Jewish history was often antagonistic, and remains so today. All biblical prophets maintained a critical distance from the power-holders of the day and called first and foremost for better ethics, which alone could guarantee better governance. Biblical and rabbinic Judaism lacks a clear and coherent state tradition, despite various later efforts to extract one from history and scripture. Confusion and weakness of governance had tragic results at the end of the Second Temple period, when Judea slid into its fatal confrontation with Rome without a generally accepted government authority or national leader. The absence of a religiously recommended and realistic state tradition still affects politics in Israel and helps to prevent the increasingly urgent reform of the country's dysfunctional government system.

The bedrock of Jewish faith is the belief in a personal, almighty God who issued laws and promised his people protection and prosperity if it followed them. This is the ultimate reason why, through much of history, many Jews remained Jews. Faith is beyond the scope of this chapter, but religious laws have sociological as well as psychological impacts and dimensions that do belong to our discussion, and can be examined as specific components of Judaism. Six such components are proposed as drivers of rise and preservation. Each also has a downside that can change it into a driver of stagnation and decline. They are inter-linked and have operated differently in different contexts and periods. The main written depository of these drivers is the Jewish prayer book. The essential prayers have for a very long time been the same for all branches of the Jewish people.

---

* Daniel Dennet, *Breaking the Spell: Religion as a Natural Phenomenon* (New York-London: Viking Adult, 2006). Dennet shows evidence that a considerable number of American Christians who identify themselves as religious do not believe in all the teachings of their religion, but believe that religious belief and practice are desirable goals.

Our method of deconstructing a religion into different components and discussing each of them in isolation might appear artificial. Admittedly, this does not reflect the historical evolution of the Jewish religion or the convictions of its adherents, but it provides a useful analytical tool.

A. Ritual as Safeguard of Boundary Maintenance

The great majority of Jewish rituals are laws of separation between the permissible and the forbidden, the pure and the impure, the holy and the mundane. Among modern Westerners this is the most misunderstood aspect of Judaism. In a book that has become a classic of anthropology, Mary Douglas studied the "abominations of Leviticus," the biblical prohibitions of "defilements."[14] She concluded that the main intention of such prohibitions among many cultures with laws of separation between pure and impure was primarily neither hygienic, aesthetic, ecological, magical, nor moral, as has frequently been suggested, but stems from the need to create mechanisms of "boundary maintenance." Douglas was, like many others, strongly influenced by Emile Durkheim's famous last book, *The Elementary Forms of Religious Life*, published in 1917. When she analyzed Jewish ritual she quoted Durkheim's comment, "Religion did not exist for the saving of souls but for the preservation and welfare of society." Societies recognized and constituted themselves through public rituals. They enacted "collective representations" and constructed a collective "conscience." However, as important as the social function of rituals is, they cannot simply be reduced to intentional sociological strategies. Biblical and rabbinic texts discussed the deep moral "reasons" or "goals" of the ritual commandments from the beginning to the present day, but boundary maintenance is clearly a very important and sometimes overriding function. Repeated, adamant biblical warnings leave no doubt that the material superiority and other attractions of the surrounding civilizations, not least Egypt, were a source of great awe and temptation for early Israel. Against these dangers, rules of avoidance inspired meditation on the "otherness" of the Jewish people. Civilizations and peoples are diluted and disappear when boundaries disappear. Jews were always aware of the boundary-reinforcing function of ritual and of its role as a permanent reminder of distinction and "otherness." Sometimes they defended this role fiercely, as in a talmudic statement, which never became law and was not applied in real life, that a Gentile who kept the Jewish Sabbath laws was subject to the death penalty.[15] What may have caused this comment was rabbinic fear of the dilution and undermining of the ritual boundary safeguards in the late Roman Empire, when many Gentiles were "Judaizing"—adopting this or that Jewish law, for example those of the Sabbath, without converting to Judaism. The separation between pure/holy and impure/mundane was applied to a) the human *body*, with circumcision as its most permanent expression; b) *food*; c) *marriage*, which had to be endogenous; d) the *calendar*; and e) in a more voluntary way, the *land of Israel*. Regarding the calendar, Jews developed notions of time that differed from those of other people. This includes the counting of years from the beginning of creation, an unusual definition of the evening as the beginning of a day, in accordance with the biblical creation story: "And there was evening and there was morning, a first day,"[16] and more. Tradition created a unique Jewish calendar and holy days. The importance of this calendar as a source of boundary maintenance, of family cohesion and of collective emotions, cannot be overestimated: "More than Israel kept the Sabbath, the Sabbath kept Israel."[17] The boundary value of the calendar is strengthened by the fact that it covers both ritual and memory—in other words, it is also the repository of Jewish historical memory, the second important safeguard of identity discussed in the next point.

Mary Douglas's anthropological explanation of Jewish ritual has found a certain resonance, but it is not the only valid explanation. Other civilizations have also had future-shaping lawgivers who were addicted to ritual, though they did not share the biblical preoccupation with religious and ethnic "boundary maintenance." Confucius is one of the most prominent ancient examples. He did once refer to the barbaric tribes that were roaming beyond the borders of China, and must have known that their language and customs were different from those of the Chinese, but he was never concerned that they could affect Chinese civilization. Yet he was deeply committed to ritual, the Chinese *li*, which is a key concept in his teaching.[18] Ritual was meant to shape human relations, those between parents and children, men and women, rulers and commoners. It determined modes of dress, what to wear and when, and instructed civilized men how they had to behave toward the sick, the dying, the dead, and their mourners. Rituals determined food and drink, what to eat and what not to eat, when to eat and how to prepare food. An ancient Chinese source said of Confucius, "He did not eat food that was not in season nor did he eat except at mealtimes. He did not eat meat that was not properly cut up or meat paired with the wrong sauce."[19] Ritual, as transmitted by the ancient texts and teachers, touched all aspects of life. It was the armor protecting Chinese ethics and humanity. It guarded the boundaries of civilization not against remote strangers but against barbarity and chaos from within. Mary Douglas' "boundary maintenance" thesis misses this point: ritual might be necessary even in the absence of challenges from outside. But a twentieth-century Chinese philosopher and a Jewish sinologist saw the point and commented on the similarities between Confucius and Jewish ritual. Lin Yutang wrote, "It is easier to compare Confucius in the scope of his teaching to Moses than to any other philosopher....The religion of *li*, like Judaism, embraces both religious worship and daily life, down to the matter of eating and drinking."[20] Donald Leslie wrote a Hebrew and French translation of Confucius' *Analects*, in which he compared the *li* to the "detailed prescriptions of the Talmud."[21] Jewish ritual allows for both explanations, boundary maintenance and civilizing force; the two are not contradictory but can complement each other.

The downside of ritual lies in the details, which have been evolving across time and are today in the hands of rabbinic authorities. Since the nineteenth century, Orthodox ritual commandments and prohibitions have kept increasing, becoming more detailed and exacting. Some of this evolution was an inevitable response to rapid changes in material life. Economic growth and the rise in living standards multiplied the variety and complexity of available foodstuffs, clothing, medical treatments, household appliances, means of travel, leisure activities, and more, and each new product, opportunity, or service could raise questions of *halakha*. But equally important were a number of fundamental internal changes in Jewish religion. Orthodox Judaism responded to the challenge of the Enlightenment, the emancipation of Europe's Jews, and the new Reform Judaism by closing the gates and arming the watchtowers. An axiom of the Chatam Sofer (Rabbi Moses Sofer, 1762-1839), a protagonist of the Orthodox reaction to Reform Judaism, has often been quoted—rightly or wrongly—as a sign of the increased precaution of the traditionalists: "Anything new is forbidden by the Torah." This was a quote from the Talmud taken out of context. The talmudic prohibition was limited to a specific occasion that occurred once a year as long as the Temple stood. Forbidden was the consumption of the first ("the new") yield of the grain harvest before a precise date by which it had to be offered to the Temple of Jerusalem.[22] The Chatam Sofer seemed to extend this long-defunct statute to a prohibition with movable and, in principle, unlimited boundaries. The historian Haym Soloveitchik analyzed the subsequent ramifications and explained the hardening of religious practices that has continued to this day.[23]

Since time immemorial, Judaism has been based partly on texts and partly on established ritual practices learned from parents, friends, teachers, and the synagogue. The Jewish mass-migrations beginning in the late nineteenth century and the destruction of most of Europe's Jews in the twentieth century ruptured the chain of transmission that had kept established ritual practices, which could vary from place to place, alive. Now texts had to replace established practice. The written word called for a new rigor and accuracy in religious observance and a punctilious adhesion to the details of religious practice, which were sometimes amplified beyond the original halakhic requirements. A visible result of this change was and is a continuing explosion of Orthodox works on practical observance. One has to add to Soloveitchik's analysis the idea that the destruction of Europe's Jews has not only ruptured chains of transmission, it has also set in motion deeper psychological pressures for increased religious stringency. The catastrophe of the *Shoah* is ultimately incomprehensible, particularly to a religious mind. Some Orthodox circles today teach that only the most meticulous and extensive observance of all the divine laws will save the Jews from fresh catastrophe. The ripple effects of the *Shoah* on Jewish and Israeli psychology, religion, and politics are likely to continue for a long time.

Another result was that submission to texts also meant submission to its interpreters, the rabbinic sages. This enlarged the mantle of ritual enormously. Not only peripheral questions about personal life, but also political and social questions of national importance were now submitted to Orthodox rabbinic decision makers, particularly in Israel. This is a fundamental historical change, for the political leadership of Ashkenazi Jews was, at least since the Middle Ages, firmly in the hands of laymen. The rabbis feared that the old religious boundary safeguards were weakening, and that Jews were less and less distinguishable from non-Jews. They concluded that this called for a continuous reinforcement of the boundaries. They had to make decisions in a rapidly changing and increasingly complex world that was not always understood, or was understood only by reference to centuries-old parallels. This problem is compounded by the steadily increasing average longevity of members of Western populations, which is slowing down the generational change of rabbinic decision-makers. External change is fast, and at the same time many rabbinic decision-makers are living much longer than those of previous generations. Soloveitchik believes that there are additional, deeply spiritual reasons for the Orthodox addiction to texts, and that this addiction is a response to real psychological needs.* Looking back over the last hundred years, the increasing detail and strictness of religious laws have certainly not reduced assimilation. On the contrary, they may have increased it. They have widened the splits, but in doing so have indirectly helped to increase religious pluralism in contemporary Judaism.

There is still another, indirect downside of Jewish ritual. Many markers of ritual, particularly the calendar and its holy days and other rules, such as those relating to prayers, circumcision, and some dietary prohibitions, were adopted by one or both of the successor religions. One need not be a Jew to partake in some achievements that were originally Jewish. For example, Christianity and Islam both absorbed the Sabbath. The Sabbath and the invention of

---

* Soloveitchik's ideas are bold and based on his vast, intimate knowledge of Ashkenazi Orthodoxy in Israel and the United States, but are not easy to substantiate. He observes a fundamental change in inner convictions: "The perception of God as a daily, natural force is no longer present...in any sector of modern Jewry, even the most religious....Individual Divine Providence...is no longer experienced as a simple reality", see 351. It is the weakening of traditional religious sensibility which explains, according to Soloveitchik, the avid desire to elicit an understanding of God's will in all its details from the written texts.

a seven-day week are not based on astronomical laws and the observation of the stars but on Jewish tradition. They were not natural concepts; some intellectuals of the ancient world who saw the Jews of Rome respecting the day of rest had no intention of emulating them, but rather insulted them for it: Seneca lampooned them, suggesting they were just lazy time wasters.[24] Today, all countries have at least one weekly day of rest they regard as a positive, irreversible, and indispensable part of public and private life.

It is for this very reason that some German and English historians and theologians ill disposed to Judaism question the Jewish paternity of the Sabbath. The nineteenth and early twentieth centuries heard heated arguments about the "true" origin of the Sabbath. These arguments were part of a wider debate about the Jewish contribution to world cultures. The eminent German historian of antiquity Eduard Meyer (1855-1930) rejoiced when he heard his colleague Friedrich Delitzsch offering alleged proofs that the Babylonians rather than the Jews had invented the Sabbath: this demonstrated, he wrote, "the religious, political and intellectual inferiority of the Old Testament."[25] There still is no consensus as to when the seven-day week first appeared in history, but nobody denies that the world has taken the consecration of the seventh day for rest and celebration from the Jews.[26] When German Reform Jews decided in the 1820s to move their day of rest to Sunday in order to demonstrate their union with Germany, they did not think they had abandoned anything essential.

B. Remembering and Actualizing History: A Religious Duty

Most holy days of the Jewish calendar commemorate specific historic events that Jews are ordered to relive each year. The celebration that resonates most among a large proportion of Jews today is *Pesach* because it forges strong ties between rituals, food, historical memory, and hope (see point D), and also because the Exodus from Egypt is seen as a universal symbol of liberation. The Torah commands memory, and the commandment is unconditional. Memory flows through ritual, but goes widely beyond it. It is meant to be a life-long preoccupation: "Remember the days of old, consider the days of ages past: ask your father, he will inform you; your elders, they will tell you."[27]

The Chinese and Greeks had produced celebrated historians, but their books did not become part of the sacred canon, in contrast to those of the Jewish people, for the Jews assigned great importance to ancient history because it had eternal truths to offer. Once these truths were understood and remembered, continuous historiography became superfluous. This is why systematic Jewish history-writing stops with the completion of the Bible, except for Flavius Josephus and a few dispersed authors of later times, and starts up again in a continuous fashion only in the nineteenth century. However, the inclination to remember the past and seek meaning in Jewish history never disappeared. This certainly was a complementary safeguard of border maintenance, a way of emphasizing civilizational singularity. For many Jews of today, the memory of the *Shoah* is one of the most important historical factors of Jewish identity and solidarity. For others, historical memory has been reduced to personal family history: it is the memory of Jewish parents or grandparents that their descendants may want to preserve. These have been powerful reasons, which partly explain the survival of Russian Jewry, but they are not sufficient conditions of long-term Jewish survival.

One downside of the religious commemoration of past catastrophes, and also promises of future redemption, is that it can reduce policy options in the present, inhibit proactive policies, or encourage wrong-minded ones. The memory of past catastrophes, for example those provoked by Bar Kochba and Sabbatai Zevi, was one of the reasons for Jewish Orthodox opposition to Zionism and to settling in the land of Israel, though it was not the only reason. Part VI will return to this topic.

A very different downside could lie in an apparent split opening between Jewish collective memory and academic historiography. In 1981, the historian Y.H.Yerushalmi wrote that historiography was now challenging Jewish collective memory, but could not replace its function as an essential pillar of collective will and hope.[28] In turn, collective memory essentially ignored historical vision. It was not historiography that shaped modern Jewish conceptions of the past, but literature. Yerushalmi called for a better dialogue between collective memory and historiography. In the 30 or so years since the first version of his book appeared, critical Jewish and Israeli historians and archaeologists, with or without political or ideological agendas, have attacked the foundational myths of both ancient and modern Israel, but the pillars of collective memory have not fallen. Whether or not there is more dialogue between the two now than there was in 1981 cannot easily be assessed. In any event, collective myth—if that is what this is—has in this case, as in many others, proven to be much more resilient than its academic detractors. The main effect of the detractors makes itself felt in the wider world, where they have probably weakened the standing of the Jewish people and Israel for readers who are interested in the Bible and who would like to know whether its stories have some true historical basis.

C. Social Ethics

Max Weber saw in Judaism's "ethic of social conduct"[29] the most important Jewish contribution to world history. The question in this chapter is not what Jewish social ethics have done for the world, but what they have done for Jewish identity, preservation, and longevity. The Bible keeps asking for social justice with an insistence unmatched in the texts of other known religions, except for those influenced by Judaism. Social justice means, first and foremost, complete equality for all members of the community: "The rich shall not pay more and the poor shall not pay less...."[30] It also means concern for the poor, the weak, the sick, the day-laborer, the slave, the widow, and the orphan. The Torah demands that they be protected and seeks to guarantee their material support with a large body of statutes. Most of the great prophets called for social justice, and when they saw how the poor and weak were mistreated, they raised their voice in a rage that has echoed through the centuries: "Ah you, who crush on the ground the heads of the poor and push off the road the humble of the land!"[31] No wonder modern Israel's first leaders, particularly Ben-Gurion, quoted the harsh words of Ancient Israel's prophet Amos as their source of inspiration for social reform and justice.[32] Rabbinic Judaism regarded charity as one of the "three pillars" on which the "world stands."[33] Consequently, the rabbis translated the social commandments of the Bible and the prophetic protests into a large body of specific laws and customs that have guided Jewish charitable traditions to this day.

Mary Douglas, who had already explained the boundary maintenance value of strict Jewish rituals (see point A), clarified in another book the role of social ethics in the preservation of the Jewish people. She called the Jews an "enclave," a small civilization surrounded by many larger and stronger ones.[34] The greatest preoccupation of an enclave is retaining its members. When deserters from an enclaved religion or people cannot be punished, as was often the case in Jewish history, the most effective policy to keep them inside emphasizes the unique value of each individual member of the community, rejects discrimination, and ensures that the poor will never be driven to despair and destitution. This is what Judaism has often done. Mary Douglas gives a compelling sociological explanation but does not claim that she discovered the only true, original intention of the lawgiver (it is here important to recall that in Jewish tradition the commandments were considered divine). History shows that social ethics indeed helped to safeguard Jewish identity, solidarity, and prosperity in many periods. The historian Tacitus, no friend of the Jews, respectfully mentions their "trustworthiness" in their dealings with each other, and their readiness to always show "compassion" for fellow Jews.[35] This privileged and well-to-do Roman intellectual had no notion of "social ethics" and even less of "social justice." He called the peculiar characteristic he observed among the Jews "compassion," and it was this quality in particular that attracted non-Jews of the Roman Empire to Judaism. In the late Middle Ages, Europe's autonomous Jewish communities had a coherent social welfare policy. Jewish society was highly stratified, neither democratic nor egalitarian, but the historian Jacob Katz emphasized the fact that this social stratification did not create inseparable barriers: Jewish office holders did not constitute a ruling class that excluded outsiders, and in addition Jewish economic power was transient.[36] Jonathan Israel added corroborating evidence for the same and later periods, noting that there was much more cohesion between social classes in Jewish society than in Christian society. They depended on each other in many ways and mixed in communal and religious life. The French Bible scholar Richard Simon (1638-1712) found the Jewish "compassion for the poor" in his time remarkable, as did other Christian intellectuals.[37] Perhaps they felt the lack of this quality in Christian society.

The downside of Jewish social ethics is that it was, from the beginning, ethnic and not universal. Rabbinic Judaism preached social justice for the Jews, not for the entire world. All the Talmud asked of the nations of the world was respect for the so-called "Seven Noahide Commandments," several of which were taken from the Ten Commandments. One pertained to law and justice: the nations were simply requested to have "laws"—that is, a legal system above and beyond arbitrary political power.[38] This in itself was a very demanding request, and the pursuit of social justice was not mentioned. A fundamental change occurred when Christianity and Islam adopted the social ethics of the Jews, particularly charity, as a priority demand of their own faith and religious practice. Finally, socialism and communism turned social ethics and social justice into universal ideals, which attracted countless numbers of Jews and helped turn them away from Judaism. When the demands of social ethics spread so widely that Jewish social ethics ceased to be unique, Judaism could not continue to hold the moral high ground forever. Nevertheless, for many centuries Jewish social ethics still seemed to be more attractive or more effective than those of other faiths, as the few historical references above indicate. In the long term, ethnic social ethics did not remain the strong safeguard of Jewish identity it may have been in the past. "Leakage" became inevitable and grew to a mass-movement. In the nineteenth and twentieth centuries, Jewish authors who wanted to show the outside world an attractive image of their religion presented social ethics as the most outstanding feature of Judaism. This was and is still the case in many countries, not least in those where there has been traditional antisemitism, such as Germany before World War I[39] or in twentieth-century Argentina.[40] Others proposed the old Jewish notion of *Tikkun Olam*—repairing the world— which already existed in the time of the Mishnah, as a useful doctrine that would continue to spiritually distinguish Judaism but also demonstrate an active and dynamic concern for global justice and peace.[41] The *Tikkun Olam* idea has some attraction in the Diaspora, particularly among liberal American Jews who want to give their Judaism a new sense, but it is ignored or treated with suspicion in Israel. As Jehudah Mirsky has pointed out, the problem with *Tikkun Olam*, and with social ethics in general, is that one does not have to be Jewish to endorse it. All men and women of good will are expected to do so. If *Tikkun Olam* is not linked to other, specifically Jewish, values or practices, it will not restore the identity safeguard function of biblical social ethics for those Jews no longer interested in Judaism. Also, Judaism cannot credibly "repair the world" if its own house is not in order.

In the longer term, there is probably only one way for the Jewish people to reclaim some of its lost moral high ground in social ethics. If the State of Israel were to become a beacon of social justice, and recognized as such, the Jewish people might again be seen as an exemplar of social ethics for the world. This was the dream of Israel's founders. Its realization may be some way off, to say the least.

D. A Sense of Mission

Until the twentieth century, there has probably never been a civilization that did not believe it had a special mission and was superior to others in one way or another, if not in every way. Such beliefs underpin the long-term survival of civilizations. The Torah told the Jews that world history had a purpose, the establishment of God's kingdom on earth, and that they were "chosen" to play the central role in this process and become a "light unto the nations." It was also for this purpose that they had to keep the commandments and become an ideal nation of justice. "Justice, justice you shall pursue."[42] The ideology of being a "chosen" people is not unique to the Jews, but few have formulated it in a more assertive and detailed manner. Their sense of mission gave the Jews another powerful incentive to maintain and pass down their identity. Other civilizations have expressed a sense of purpose in a "missionary" drive to spread their rule, culture, or religion. Among Jews, the belief of having been chosen has greatly moderated this drive. Isaiah and other prophets expected that all of mankind would be attracted to Judaism and adopt its ethical message. Their aim was not that Judaism should seek to make everybody Jewish. Instead, Jews should remain different and "chosen," but inspire and improve the world with their own impeccable conduct. One passage of the Talmud[43] goes further and states that the Jews have been spread all over the world to make proselytes. The important medieval Tossafist Rabbi Moses of Coucy, the "Smag" (*Sefer mitzvot gadol*, thirteenth century), endorsed this opinion but added, significantly, that it was for this very reason, the attraction of proselytes, that Jews were enjoined to be morally perfect.[44] Many—probably most—other important authorities were and are still opposed to such "missionary" ideas, but the debate is not closed.

Postulating that Jews are a "chosen people" has raised the issue of their relationship with the other nations of the world. Renouncing missionary activities did not mean that this problem could be ignored. It also did not mean that Judaism lacked a vision and hope for humanity as a whole. However, this is what the successor religions and the Enlightenment asserted, as did many Jews who wanted to break loose from a Judaism that they resented as ethnocentric and parochial. Biblical and post-biblical Judaism contains strong elements of universalism. A memorable example from rabbinic Judaism is the interpretation of the biblical law demanding that the Jews sacrifice seventy bulls in the Temple of Jerusalem during the seven days of the *Sukkot* celebrations. The Talmud explains that the seventy sacrifices were for the seventy nations of the world as enumerated in Genesis, because it was Israel's duty to pray for the well-being of each of them. The Talmud adds a sad afterthought: the nations did not know what they lost when they destroyed the Temple, because the sacrifices offered by the Jews had atoned for them. Who would atone for them now?[45] Even secular Jews might still be proud today that their forefathers regarded it as their duty to offer sacrifices and prayers for all the nations of the world at a time when animal sacrifice was customary. This was how Jews expressed their universalism when the Temple was still standing.

The downsides of the traditional Jewish sense of mission are considerable. The old Jewish universalism looks modest and unimpressive in comparison to the far-reaching programmatic universalism of its successor religions and today's universalistic ethics, as endorsed by various international treaties and institutions. Secularized Jews usually reject the idea of a specific Jewish mission and are very uncomfortable with the pretense, as they see it, of a "chosen people." Nonetheless, a strong general sense of mission has not disappeared among Jews, nor has a secular Jewish form of universalism. Perhaps only a Jew, Ludwik Lejzer Zamenhof from Bialystock (1859-1917), could dream that he would bring eternal peace to mankind by inventing a new, artificial language, the language of "hope," Esperanto. The Soviets absorbed Jewish universalism into their international communism, and in a cruel parody of history turned against their own Jews because they were allegedly "cosmopolitan"—that is, truly universalistic and not exclusively committed to the nationalistic power politics of the Soviet state. Under Stalin and his successors, "cosmopolitism" was an insult that became synonymous with Judaism.

Today, many modern Jews reject any claim that Jews have a "mission," and few believe that they have an essentially universalistic mission, namely to improve the condition of all humanity, the *Tikkun Olam* ideal mentioned above. Some others pursue what were originally old Jewish ideals, for example the limitation and abolition of the death penalty, but present them as non-religious, humanitarian ideals. Many more Jews have chosen the patriotic causes of the countries where they are living as their "mission," or, contrarily, revolutionary causes hostile to their societies, or specific causes with no link to the Jewish heritage. Some sponsor causes that are in direct opposition to the Jewish heritage. They are combative atheists or defenders of animal rights, which are alleged to be equivalent to human rights. Judaism's originally religious sense of mission has spawned among Jews a great multitude of competing, if not contradictory, missions.

E. Messianism as "The Principle of Hope"

Messianism plays a central role in Jewish beliefs and expectations. It was, and for some it remains, a cornerstone of traditional Jewish optimism, patience, acceptance of adversity, and hope for a better future. It has encouraged Jews not to give up their identity even in the worst of times. Jewish messianism promises that in the "end times" an ideal king from the house of David will appear, save Israel from its oppressors, restore its former glory, and inaugurate an era of moral perfection, material affluence, and lasting peace. Initially the promise of a future Golden Age (as discussed in Part III, Chapter 4) was meant for Israel, but the prophets extended it to all of humanity and thus gave it an enormous revolutionary potential with a global reach. Many of the prophets—notably Amos, Isaiah, Micah, and Joel—glorified the future messianic age in words that have become part of the world's literary and moral heritage: "Nation will not take up sword against nation...."[46] Messianic core beliefs go back at least to the First Temple period. The Talmud, Midrash, and other rabbinic sources report many lively discussions and speculations about the Messiah and his times, which was obviously a topic of great interest.[47] Maimonides concludes his most important work, the codex of Jewish law (*Mishneh Torah* or *Yad Ha'khazaka*), with chapters summarizing what he considered the most profound meanings of the messianic prophecies. The messianic world will not be different from the world of today, and the laws of nature will not change, but the world of the future will be ruled by morality, justice, and wisdom, and no longer by violence, and the Jewish people will return to independence in its ancient homeland. Maimonides does not reject the materialistic aspects of the old prophecies, which promised an abundance of material goods, but for him only the spiritual promises are truly essential: "The Jews will be great in wisdom, explore the things that are hidden, and grasp the thoughts of their Creator, as far as this is possible for the human mind...."[48]

Jewish messianism conveys three powerful, symbolic messages that explain why it had such an enormous impact on Jewish and world history:

— The Messiah has still to arrive. A lasting solution to all of the world's troubles lies in the future, not in the recent or distant past. Until then the world cannot be perfect.

— Deliverance will come to this, the real world, not to a conjectural "future world."

— Salvation is for all nations on earth, not only one. This is one of the strongest expressions of ancient Jewish universalism.

Jewish messianic hopes survived in modified forms among secularized Jews. Ernst Bloch, a German Jewish philosopher and Marxist, called his main book, written in exile during World War II, *The Principle of Hope*. A positive, optimistic outlook, a sense of hope in a better future remains essential today, particularly for the young. This could be one of the reasons explaining the attraction of the Chabad movement and its metaphoric or literal messianic message.

The downsides of Jewish messianism are well known. They are both external and internal. A fatal external downside appeared when Christianity, Islam, and much later European Communism adopted the biblical prophets' promise and proclaimed themselves, at least in the first two cases, the rightful heirs of Judaism destined to fulfill the old promise. When the new creeds asked the Jews to recognize their messianic claims and agree that the fulfillment of the old promise was now at hand, they opened a rift with traditional Judaism that could not be bridged. The Jewish rejection of such claims posed a dangerous challenge that explains much of the hostility shown to Jews and Judaism through history. Marshall Hodgson regarded this initial Jewish challenge as the root cause of Muslim hostility to Jews and Judaism.[49] Had the Jews not given the world a great hope, expressed in so many beautiful words? Now they rejected the man—the savior, the "seal" of the prophets, the supreme leader of the revolution—who had come to fulfill this hope! Messianic tradition had prepared many Jews to also look outside for a savior and salvation and, hence they heeded these claims. This made it easier for Christians and Muslims to convert some Jews, and partly explains why Communism, with its message of deliverance in this world and not the next, was so attractive to so many Jews.

One internal Jewish downside of messianism is that it can inspire as much impatience as patience. Despair, particularly during or after episodes of persecution, has caused the emergence of false Jewish messiahs all throughout history. Some of these caused severe harm, including Bar Kochba in the second century CE, and Sabbatai Zevi in the seventeenth century. Most others have been forgotten. Messianic hope can also result in passivity in the face of danger, instead of inspiring thought and action to confront it. The conviction that the Messiah will one day come to save the Jews from exile and restore their political independence made the lack of a coherent state tradition in Judaism, as mentioned above, even more unsolvable.

F. The Land of Israel

The biblical story of Abraham leaves no doubt that the original idea of Judaism was not to spread the Jews across the globe but to settle them in one land, the "promised land." The first patriarch followed the divine command to break with his past, leave his country of origin, and immigrate into the country his descendants would inherit, but a turbulent history charted another route for the Jews, and the spiritual guides of Judaism had to explain and accommodate this development. Living in the land of Israel was originally one of the strongest factors of religious boundary maintenance and identity preservation. At this early stage, tribal identity, religious faith, and geographic location were fused together. During the First Temple period, when the overwhelming majority of the population consisted of farmers and travel was difficult, the land of Israel was one of the best instruments of boundary maintenance, despite the religious dangers posed by the cults of other inhabitants. But the land of Israel was not then an alternative to ritual, because religious law tied both land and ritual together, thus reinforcing the boundary protection value of both. As long as the Temple stood, many important rituals could be performed only in Jerusalem.

A change began with the Babylonian exile and became more radical after the destruction of the Second Temple. When the school of Yavneh transformed Judaism from a Temple-centered religion into a "portable" one, the boundary protection value of the land of Israel eroded, although the symbolic importance of the land did not diminish. From then on, religious doctrine had to deal with dilemmas that have never been finally resolved. There is a large body of literature that reviews the opinions of rabbinic authorities across the ages; most considered living in Israel meritorious.[50] There is no theological disagreement as to the superior religious value of living in Israel when there is a Temple in Jerusalem, and, if this is not possible, of making pilgrimages and contributions there. After the Temple's destruction, however, the law could no longer consider life in Israel a compulsory form of religious fulfillment as though nothing had happened. A great majority of the Jewish people resided outside the land and had no way or desire to return, and the Talmud took this into account.[51]

Following the Talmud's lead, Maimonides attributed greater religious value to living in Israel than to living abroad, but did not regard residence in Israel as a religious obligation. It was not a commandment equal to Sabbath observance, food prohibitions, or other laws that no observant Jew had the right to transgress, and he personally made only one short visit there. On this matter there is a difference of opinion between Maimonides (also known as the Rambam, 1135-1204) and Nachmanides (Ramban, 1194-1270) as well as many later rabbinic authorities.[52] Nachmanides was a Kabbalist. In the mystical tradition, the land of Israel held a central position in the daily prayers, the Jewish calendar, and messianic hopes, and remained firmly anchored in the people's collective memory.

Israel's creation in 1948 has just begun to influence the relationship between Jewish religion and the land of Israel. It might take the entire twenty-first century for the religious implications of the creation of a Jewish state to become clear. One should remember that it took 200 years before the political, emotional, and religious reactions to the shock of 1492, the expulsion from

Spain, began to ebb. Realities are changing. The reality of 1900, when less than one percent of all Jews lived in Israel, was very different from the reality of 2000, when the Jews of Israel comprised more than forty percent of world Jewry. Israel has already become the indispensable center of many streams of the religious Jewish world. Without the State of Israel and the religious institutions there, religious Judaism would likely not have reached the strength it enjoys today.

To sum up, after the destruction of the Temple, the land of Israel functioned as a factor of Jewish rise and survival, and as a "boundary safeguard" only in a spiritual sense. Remembering Israel was a strong boundary safeguard; living there was not, at least not until the twentieth century. The tension between absolute boundaries (body, food, marriage, calendar) and a relative and more commemorative one (land) could also be seen as a downside. This tension nourished the dichotomy between Israel and the Diaspora since the Babylonian exile and contributed to the tragedy of the twentieth century. The perceived superiority of observing the ritually binding Jewish laws over residing in the land of Israel on the one hand, and the hostility of most Orthodox rabbis to Zionism on the other, resulted in religious Jews in Eastern Europe preferring Diaspora life to emigration in spite of rampant antisemitism and economic hardship in their host countries. They did not regard Zionism as an exclusively and genuinely Jewish movement, but—justifiably—saw it as one inspired by foreign ideas such as the quest for national rights, political freedom, and self-determination. This is part of the weakness and failure of Jewish leadership generally during the *Shoah*. Part IV, Chapter 5, will return to this tragic subject.

The role religion will play in the preservation of the entire Jewish people—its identity and traditions—is arguably the most critical internal uncertainty related to the future of the Jews. This chapter mentioned six components of Judaism as essential "identity safeguards": ritual, commemoration of history, social ethics, sense of mission, messianic hope, and a link to the land of Israel. Many of these six have in one way or another influenced, if not shaped, Christianity, Islam, socialism, and modernity in general. Values that were initially Jewish were absorbed by and are now, in modified form, officially adhered to by most living civilizations. The temptation for Jews to drop their identity safeguards will intensify if the world's cultural identities and values become more homogeneous. The unresolved, long-term dilemma of Jewish civilization is that it must politically and socio-economically fit into a changing world, at least for the great majority of Jews. But if it fits too well, it will disappear, as Oswald Spengler predicted. It was not an Orthodox rabbi but Fernand Braudel, a French Catholic and materialist historian, who concluded that the "destiny of the Jews" was to be "one civilization against the rest. Its strength, its survival, and its misfortunes are all consequences of its remaining irreducible, refusing to be diluted, that is of being a civilization faithful to itself."[53] Remaining "faithful to itself" meant, in the past, swimming against the stream. Fitting into the world while remaining ready to swim against the stream once more could become Judaism's future balancing act.

For the time being, religious ritual will be sufficient to preserve the Jewish identity of religious and traditional Jews anywhere in the world. But most Jews, including Israelis, are neither religious nor traditional, and are unlikely to follow this course. On the other hand, the land of Israel alone cannot replace the identity-safeguarding function of religion. Israel's population is currently becoming more religious, which moves Israel nearer to the dominant trends in the Muslim Middle East and further away from European standards. Nobody can say how far this trend will go, but it is unlikely that it will ever suck up the overwhelming majority of Israelis.

Living in Israel will, in the long term and in the absence of other boundaries, not be sufficient to preserve the identity of its Jewish citizens. The preservation of the historic Jewish character of Israel will pose critical policy challenges. This may require a mix of ritual, memory, sense of mission, and close ties with world Judaism. Obviously, preserving Jewish identity in the Diaspora without any form of religion would be even more difficult. Historical memory (including the celebration of important holidays of the Jewish calendar and the continuation of Jewish family traditions) can preserve Jewish identity for a certain time, but it will not prevent intermarriage. A link with Israel could serve as an additional boundary safeguard helping to maintain Jewish identity.

CHAPTER 2

Extra-Rational Bonds:
Tacit Consensus or Group Cohesion[1]

General Observations

Civilizations and their rise and decline depend on more than rational, clearly identifiable factors and objective material interests. Several authors have suggested that every civilization has some unifying factor that cannot easily be defined in words and is not shared with other civilizations. This comes in addition to the understandable and partly quantifiable characteristics of each civilization. It is noteworthy that even the most un-romantic and "materialistic" historian of civilization, Fernand Braudel, shares this opinion: "There are things one cannot explain: this is perhaps the particular secret of every civilization."[2] No less significant is a comment by the Jewish historian Haym Soloveitchik, who has studied the evolution of Jewish Orthodoxy: "The will to survival of any group, its determination to maintain its singularity and transmit it undiminished to the next generation, eludes, indeed, full explanation."[3] Scholars have scrutinized that which "eludes full explanation," and have groped for words to describe the "other" factors belonging to an emotional and not easily understood realm. Among the terms proposed were "group feeling" by Ibn Khaldun,[4] "spiritual essence" by Freud (which will be discussed below), and the tacit consensus posited by Spengler (also to be discussed below).

Such ideas were popular among Europe's Romantic poets and philosophers. The notion of a hidden unity or cohesion of a people, among others things, inspired the right-wing and fascist ideas of the twentieth century. In Germany, the word *"Volk"* (people) developed a quasi-mystical quality: it was meant to portray a deeply-felt, self-evident, extra-rational unity. Similar notions of an extra-rational mystical unity of all Muslims have appeared in Arab nationalist and other Islamist circles. According to some historians, the modern expression of this notion was an import from the West.[5] How exactly this "group feeling" comes into existence is not clear, and the founding fathers of psychoanalysis wrestled with the question. Sigmund Freud did so when he tried to understand what made him Jewish (see below), and Carl Gustav Jung when he popularized the notion of a "collective unconscious." Jung's collective unconscious must be distinguished from the individual's unconscious mind. It cannot be acquired through individual experience, and is the repository of the experiences of earlier generations, which have disappeared from individual consciousness but are transmitted from generation to generation as an unconscious psychological heritage that is shared by many whose ancestors belonged to the same people or culture. The collective unconscious helps to shape patterns of behavior, culture, rituals, myths, dreams, language, art, and more. It varies between epochs, civilizations, and nations. During the Nazi era Jung, who was anything but an antisemite, suggested that the collective unconscious of Jews differed from that of the "Aryans." This shows how easily his theory could be appropriated and misused, but the idea of a collective unconscious helped the large circle of Jung's adherents understand how "group solidarity" or "the particular secret of every civilization" might have been generated and transmitted.

Applications to Jewish History

The identity and longevity of peoples and civilizations also depend on factors that cannot be reduced to education, precise external conditions, or historical events. If this is so, it must be possible to identify such factors in Jewish civilization as well. Why did Jews not all quit their religion when it was often so difficult to remain Jewish and so easy to speak another language, move out of Judaism, and convert to another faith? Was it only religious ritual and faith that kept them within their religion, or did external drivers, still to be discussed, play a part? According to Jewish mystical traditions, it was obvious that all Jews were held together by secret bonds, whether they knew it or not. According to Gershom Scholem, all Kabbalists taught the pre-existence of human souls since the creation and the interrelation of all souls through that of Adam, and most believed in the transmigration of souls. For them, a tacit consensus was easy to explain, for had not the great Kabbalist Rabbi Isaac Luria (Ha-ari) in Safed spoken of "soul relationships" and "soul families," which accounted for the instinctive sympathy that binds people together? Had not the other master of mysticism of his time, Rabbi Moses Cordovero, asserted that in everyone there was also a piece of his fellow man?[6] Eastern European Hassidism was deeply penetrated by such ideas. Martin Buber was convinced that Hassidism and its belief in a mystical bond between all Jews, and between them and the land of Israel, had played an important spiritual role in the initial phase of East-European Zionism.

Quite a number of assimilated Jews admit that they are attached to Jews or Judaism by impulses or instincts that they can't quite explain. Non-Jews are often suspicious of this instinct, considering it a part of the unexplainable "otherness" of the Jews, or resenting it as uncanny and conspiratorial. In the Hebrew edition of *Totem and Taboo*, Freud tries to explain the strength of his own extra-rational bond with fellow Jews.[7] Speaking of himself in the third person, he states that he does not know Hebrew, is completely estranged from the Jewish religion, and has no Jewish national goals, but feels that

> he is in his essential nature a Jew and…has no desire to alter this nature.
> If the question were put to him: 'since you have abandoned all these
> characteristics of your countrymen, what is there left to you that is Jewish?'
> he would reply 'a very great deal, and probably its very essence.' He could
> not express that essence clearly in words, but someday, no doubt, it will
> become accessible to the scientific mind.[8]

Oswald Spengler was fascinated by the same phenomenon and called it the tacit consensus of the Jews.[9] Spengler assigns the attribute "magial" (*magisch* in the original German) to all Middle Eastern cultures, but reserves the idea of a tacit, i.e. magial, consensus for the Jews. It explains the unconscious, metaphysical cohesion of the Jews, which in his view had no roots in geography, language, or origin.

Religious education or personal experience can explain some of this "magial consensus." Judaism asks its adherents for group solidarity: *kol Yisrael arevim ze la ze* (all Jews are responsible for each other) is a classical and frequently quoted rabbinic saying. It should also be noted that members of any group who have experienced hostility and discrimination because of their origin, or who have relatives and friends who suffered from such experiences, will often feel solidarity with any other group members that went through the same suffering. Shared suffering can create bonds that last a lifetime. For example, it is amazing how many bonds and feelings of solidarity survived among Jews in the Soviet Union in spite of or because of the suppression of Jewish religious, educational, and other activities for seventy years. The impact of a strong or shocking personal experience can explain why Freud, the Soviet Jews, and others who were victims of discrimination in various forms developed an instinctive feeling of affinity with other Jews.

But Freud was looking for more specific scientific explanations. Several are possible. This chapter will present some that are biological and imply the negation of the traditional separation of mind and body. People who adhere to this traditional mind-body dualism will not easily accept biological views when it comes to the dispositions of the mind. For them, body determines body and mind determines mind: the two are clearly separated. Some of their opposition may still be fuelled by a justified aversion to past racist theories that attributed invariable characteristics expressed in mind as well as in body to certain human groups.

However, modern neuroscientists reject this mind-body split. Their scientific work was preceded by a philosophical and conceptual revolution. Karl Jaspers, who was a clinical psychiatrist before he turned to philosophy, stated that psychiatry must be rooted in a clear philosophical concept of the human mind, and an American research psychiatrist begins his refutation of the body-mind dualism with Jaspers' statement.[10] This dualism is in fact one of the oldest philosophical paradigms. Some have called it the "Cartesian (after Descartes) dualism," but it is much older, going back to Platonic and Aristotelian philosophy as well as Christian theology. The dualism has created the standard tradition that proposes a fundamental division between biology and culture, with human behavior determined by culture and education. Spinoza opposed this dualism and argued strenuously against Descartes. His main work, *Ethics* (1677), postulates "the union of mind and body," stating that "the human mind is united to the body," and that "the human mind must perceive all that happens in the human body."[11] A recent biographer saw in Spinoza's postulate a "radical break in the history of thought," causing an upheaval widely beyond philosophy that can only now be fully understood. Spinoza anticipated "insights from the neurosciences that would be three centuries in coming."[12] But with every step of progress in understanding life, biology becomes more complex. New theories postulate that what we call the mind can no longer be simply located in the brain. It extends to the whole body and even beyond, to the environment. The human mind includes feedback loops that "criss-cross the boundaries of brain, body and the world."[13]

A. Evolutionary Psychology

The question, then, is whether religious education and personal experience alone can create bonds that, as Spengler suggested, last over many generations. Evolutionary psychology gives a different answer. This discipline is still nascent and contested. Not all of its findings are fully understood or universally accepted. This chapter takes no position on the current scientific status of evolutionary psychology, but suggests that it could point the way to a better understanding of certain types of group cohesion, as groups often favor the selection of cognitive and emotional faculties, which improve the individual's adaptation to his or her environment, increase their competitive advantages, and strengthen their survival chances.[14] This would increase the chances of survival for the entire group. Popular beliefs have often attributed to Jews certain intellectual or other faculties that apparently facilitated their survival in difficult environments, and that may have been transmitted somehow from parents to children within the group.

The question of group selection of specific traits has triggered one of the longest, most animated, and most bitter debates in the whole history of biology. During the latter part of the twentieth century, this debate focused on the genetic origin and transmission of "altruism"—the ultimate source of group cohesion and solidarity—as opposed to "selfishness." But the consideration of this quality started long before. The human capacity for compassion and self-sacrifice—altruism—had been cited as proof of a divine spark in man. Then it was discovered that other mammals exhibit altruistic behaviors too. A lead animal will warn its herd of an approaching bird of prey, but will often pay for its "altruism" with its own life.

According to Darwinian genetics, such self-sacrificing animals should have become extinct a long time ago, but every generation produces anew a certain number of "altruists." This trait evolved because every collective, whether human, wolf, or even bacterial, transmits "selfless" genes to some of its members, and does so for its own collective protection. Charles Darwin surmised that groups containing mostly altruists had a decisive advantage over groups containing mostly selfish individuals—even if selfish individuals have the advantage over altruists within each group—but how this came about was not clear to him. The debate reached a watershed with a book the Oxford biologist Richard Dawkins published in 1976. It had the provocative title *The Selfish Gene*,[15] and postulated that "goodness"—a moralistic term for altruism—and its opposite, selfishness, were genetically rooted and heritable. When the book appeared, it created a scandal and strong ethical opposition. Thirty years later, it has become academic textbook orthodoxy. Today, the great majority of biologists regard its central thesis as a well-substantiated scientific fact. Both selfishness and altruism are recognized as largely inborn. They work through biological and genetic mechanisms and can even be chemically manipulated. Dawkins never postulated, however, that selfishness and altruism were irresistible genetic compulsions. Humans are the only animals with memories that can transmit cultural values and traditions over long periods. Dawkins used the word "memes" to refer to memorized components of culture that could replicate themselves and be transmitted. "Memes," replicators just like genes, developed ways of surviving, multiplying, and spreading intact from generation to generation. Being born selfish or altruistic does not necessarily determine a person's entire life: "We have the power to defy the selfish genes of our birth.... We can even discuss ways of deliberately cultivating and nurturing pure, disinterested altruism— something that has no place in nature.... We, alone on earth, can rebel against the tyranny of the selfish replicators."[16]

It took the accumulation of many new research discoveries during the last decades of the twentieth century to reach the current scientific consensus that Darwin had intuitively anticipated. The biologists E.O. Wilson and D.S. Wilson choose a lapidary formula to express their "summary of sociobiology's new foundation": "Selfishness beats altruism within groups. Altruistic groups beat selfish groups. Everything else is commentary."[17]

Thus, trait selection is a multi-level process. It occurs inside groups ("within-group selection") and, at a higher level, between groups ("between-group selection"). Kinship provides a first explanation of within-group selection of altruism and, hence, of the genesis of group solidarity. According to this thesis, if group members are of the same origin and carry many of the same genes, some individuals who are, in addition, endowed with a "selfless" gene will be altruistic and show solidarity with the whole group, even if they risk their life in doing so. They trust that many of their own genes will survive through the group. For this reason, the group's survival is essential to them.[18] Altruism is the readiness to suffer a disadvantage, including death, without receiving a direct personal advantage in return. Kinship, even in remote forms and small degrees, can shape altruism as a beneficial trait in both animals and humans over the course of generations. In a further significant development, evolutionary scientists have stated that kinship is not an absolute condition. Altruism as a dominant trait can also evolve among non-kin group members. They call this "reciprocal altruism."[19] In other words, group selection of a beneficial trait such as altruism starts with, but is not necessarily limited to, kin-members who share the same genes.[20] The Arab historian Ibn Khaldun had intuitively arrived at the same conclusion back in the fourteenth century: the bedrock of every civilization is "group solidarity," and group solidarity always starts with "blood-bonds," that is, kinship.[21] However, as Dawkins emphasized, humans have a freedom animals lack. Sharing genes with a group does not force humans to demonstrate "altruism" or group solidarity; they can reject their next-of-kin. World history is full of civil wars between people of the same origin and genetic composition, and the myths of many civilizations, including the Jewish Bible, pay great attention to murderous fraternal conflicts.

Jews in the past were convinced that they were all of common origin, as they were told by the Bible. In some of them, group cohesion might result from a form of altruism that evolved as a beneficial trait through group selection over long periods. Religious upbringing certainly reinforced such sentiments. Of course, not all Jews are born with an altruistic disposition, and not all practice group solidarity later in life. Selection has not eliminated the "selfish gene" in favor of altruism—far from it. It is well known that persecution and discrimination have created not only solidarity among Jews, but also its exact opposite. Through the centuries, large numbers of Jews have reacted to persecution and discrimination, even in their mildest forms, by moving away from Jews and Judaism. They did not entrust the survival of their genes to their own kin or group but reckoned "selfishly" that their individual survival chances would be better served if they left their group.

Evolutionary group selection can strengthen the identity and solidarity of the Jews, and thereby contribute to the strength and survival of their civilization. This is a sensitive issue that will need extensive further discussion and research. Evolutionary psychology does not give an exhaustive explanation of Jewish cohesion or its opposite, but could in combination with other factors become a useful analytical instrument.

B. Genetics and "Affiliative" Social Behavior

Many neuroscientists, psychiatrists, and psychologists are currently studying complex social behaviors, and their conclusions match those of the evolutionary scientists. They argue that important personality differences have genetic-hereditary roots, contrary to the popular belief that they result from parental education. As in the case of evolutionary psychology, their theses have found wide public resonance but are not universally accepted by the scientific community. Adherents of this school argue that whether a person is sociable or withdrawn, calm or neurotic, courteous or rude, careful or careless, daring or conforming, altruistic or selfish rarely results from parental socialization: "The biggest influence that parents have on their children is at the moment of conception," writes Steven Pinker, one of the best-known authors in this field.[22] Pinker cites a great deal of research to substantiate his thesis. "Much of the variation in personality—about fifty percent—has genetic causes....Does this mean that the other fifty percent must come from the parents and the home?...Wrong! Being brought up in one home versus another accounts, at most, for five percent of the differences among people in personality....No one knows where the other forty-five percent of the variation comes from. Perhaps personality is shaped by unique events impinging on the growing brain....Perhaps personality is shaped by unique experiences...." In other words, complex social behavior, including "affiliative behavior," to use neuroscientific jargon, is said to have genetic roots. If this conclusion is accepted, it might take a great educational and cultural effort to instill sociability or affiliative behavior into someone not born with a genetic disposition for it, if it is possible at all, whereas if he is born with a strong positive disposition, a small educational stimulus might bring it to fruition. An inborn tendency toward affiliative behavior can find expression in altruism, group solidarity, and cohesion, but in some cases it can also express itself in exactly the opposite way. It is important to understand that a group member's negative emotional response to his group can also be characterized as a form of affiliative behavior. This may explain many cases of what has come to be known as "Jewish self-hatred," a phenomenon that has appeared all through Jewish history.

"Self-hating" or antisemitic Jews may protest against what they perceive as a broken promise or a failed utopia. Affiliative behaviors do not imply that group members must like each other; active antagonism is also a sign of a meaningful relationship. These are reactions that must be distinguished

186

from the above-mentioned passive assimilation and the quiet drifting away of members from groups that suffer persecution or discrimination.

Genetics can explain some complex social behaviors, as Pinker and others believe, but it is still not sufficient to explain the elusive "magial consensus." The ongoing progress in genomic sequencing will allow geneticists to identify many of the genes or factors of gene expression that can determine specific social behaviors. A synergy of approaches, including evolutionary psychology, genetics, and epigenetics (below) might bring an explanation nearer.

C. Epigenetics and Transgenerational Inheritance

Epigenetics has been associated with a variety of definitions.[23] A widespread modern usage refers to heritable traits that pass at least from one generation to the next through a transmission mechanism that is not well understood. This mechanism appears to be outside the well-established, DNA-based genetic inheritance. It is a mechanism of transmission that "hitchhikes" on genes but does not change them; instead, it impacts the expression of genes. The surprising, and for some still controversial, implications of epigenetic transmission become clear when this transmission is linked to a second group of findings. It is well known that the relationship between mind and brain is not a one-way street. Mind can create biology—for example, memory retrieval changes the hard wiring of the brain by reinforcing synapses and creating new ones that remain after the retrieval has been accomplished.*

It is an established fact that environmental experiences, for example extreme biological or psychological stress, can lead to long-lasting changes in one's brain and behavior. Such changes are among the epigenetic traits that may be transmittable to offspring. In fact, some epigenetically transmitted changes have been shown experimentally in animals as well as humans. Animal research suggests that inheritance may last through three or four generations, but it is not clear whether epigenetic traits are permanent, or how significant they are to the evolutionary process. In 2007 four well-known American scientists published research results in a scientific journal revealing late-onset behavioral changes in the offspring of emotionally traumatized *Shoah* victims. These changes have been transmitted biologically, not psychologically.[24] This is one example of an epigenetic research result that is of obvious relevance to the understanding of Jewish history and its possible repercussions on later generations.

---

* Synapses allow the neurons—the approximately 100 billion brain cells that send and receive electro-chemical signals—to form interconnected neural circuits. They are thus crucial to the biological computations that underlie perception and thought. They also provide the means through which the nervous system connects to and controls the other systems of the body.

Such findings risk going against popular and political wisdom, and may have a potential for abuse, and the scientific community remains cautious for a variety of reasons. Findings that overturn long-established paradigms must be replicated by much additional research before they are generally accepted. Additionally, various complementary explanations of "epigenetic" transmissions are possible. For example, viral infection has been identified as a possible cause of hereditary disease conditions. Some viral genes or other infectious agents such as prions can transmit genetic elements to future generations for a limited time or indefinitely.[25]

The popular scientific press has begun to follow these findings closely,[26] and in 2007 the BBC presented a scientific program on epigenetics and put the following text on its website dated August 31, 2007:[27]

> Biology stands on the brink of a shift in the understanding of inheritance. The discovery of epigenetics—hidden influences upon the genes—could affect every aspect of your lives. At the heart of this new field is a simple but contentious idea, that genes have a "memory." That the lives of your grandparents—the air they breathed, the food they ate, even the things they saw—can directly affect you, decades later, despite your never experiencing these things yourself. And that what you do in your lifetime could in turn affect your grandchildren....Epigenetics adds a whole new layer to genes beyond the DNA. It proposes a control system of "switches" that turn genes on or off—and suggests that things people experience, like nutrition and stress, can control these switches and cause heritable effects in humans....Genes and the environment are not mutually exclusive but are inextricably intertwined, one affecting the other....This work is at the forefront of a paradigm shift in scientific thinking. It will change the way the causes of disease are viewed, as well as the importance of lifestyles and family relationships. What people do no longer just affects themselves....

Even without its triumphal overtone, the BBC's suggestion of a nascent "paradigm shift" is thought-provoking. As in the case of psychoanalysis, it will take time and a lot more research before old patterns of thought yield and philosophers, politicians, and the larger public accept new ones. Evolutionary group selection and heredity, whether transmitted genetically or epigenetically, affected the history of the Jews in various ways and was somehow interwoven with their rise or decline. There might be policy implications, as in the case of epigenetic transmission of traumas. The many traumas of Jewish and Israeli history in the twentieth century may have left more than temporary psychological scars. If there are hereditary modifications, even if they last only for two or three generations, one would like to be aware of them because they will affect human behavior and even politics.

D. Traces of Ancient Jewish History in the Genome of the Jewish People*

Scientists have carried out more frequent and extensive genetic research on Jews than on most of the world's other religious or ethnic groups. The first and still dominant reason for this is medical, as a number of Jews have a much greater risk of developing certain genetic or genetically influenced diseases than the majority populations in their countries of residence. Some of this research has also elucidated questions of Jewish history. As early as in the 1990s, two publications in the highly respected scientific journal *Nature* disclosed genetic confirmation that the biblical story of the Jewish priests (*kohanim*) descending from one male ancestor (Aaron) is essentially correct. It was possible to determine that this person lived between 3250 and 2100 years ago. A majority of currently living *kohanim* share a common genetic signature found in only 10-15% of other Jewish males.[28] This research result was followed by a number of publications on historically interesting, country-specific, or other specialized issues of Jewish genetics.[29] Finally, in 2010, *Nature*[30] and the *American Journal of Human Genetics*[31] published the two most comprehensive genetic studies on the origin and migrations of the Jewish people that have appeared so far. They made headlines in the international media and stirred up considerable emotions. Two different teams, including a total of 32 well-known academic researchers from eight countries, investigated Jewish Diaspora communities (the *Nature* team chose members from 14 geographically separate branches, and the *American Journal of Human Genetics* took members from seven) and compared their genomic structures to those of non-Jewish groups (69 and 16 respectively). Although the two research teams chose different samples of Jews and non-Jews, their main results were identical. "Most Jewish samples form a remarkably tight subcluster...and trace the origin of most Jewish Diaspora communities to the Levant," wrote *Nature*. The other article speaks of the "distinct genetics" and "shared Middle Eastern ancestry" of most Jews. Ashkenazi, Moroccan, Italian, Greek, Turkish, Syrian, Iraqi, Iranian, and other Jews, comprising more than 90% of the Jewish people today, "represent genome similarities that are typically seen between distant cousins," wrote a scientific reviewer of these findings.[32] These communities have more genetic links with each other than with the population of their respective host countries.

---

* The genome is the entirety of an organism's hereditary information. In most organisms, including mammals, it is encoded in DNA. The genome includes both the genes and the non-coding sequences of the DNA (non-coding for proteins). The human genome consists of approx. 23,000 protein-coding genes and many non-coding ones. In 2003 the United States-based *Human Genome Project* published a complete map of the human genome. Its aim is to understand the genetic make-up of the human species. This has become an indispensable tool of medical research.

Even when some genetic proximity between Jews and non-Jews is discovered, for example between Ashkenazi Jews and southern Europeans due to conversions to Judaism in the late Roman Empire, common ancestry outweighs more recent admixture. More importantly, both studies "are concordant in revealing close relationship between most contemporary Jews and non-Jewish populations from the Levant,"[33] including Druze, Cypriots, Syrians, and Palestinians. The studies found almost no admixture from the regions where the Khazar tribes, said to have converted to Judaism in the eighth century, once lived. Others have postulated that modern Jews are not linked to the ancient Jews of Israel, but are the offspring of primarily European converts, those famous Khazars. The new scientific findings unmask these assertions as fabrications.

The professional reputation of the large number of scientists involved guaranteed that their research results found a wide, positive echo in the scientific media, and no scientific expert has challenged these results on scientific grounds. These findings would have raised no hackles until the late nineteenth century; they simply lend credibility to the major foundational myths and historical narratives of the Jewish people. In 2010, however, public intellectuals and a few religious and political figures reacted emotionally, with hostility or with enthusiasm. Some attacked the findings while others applauded them. Many misunderstood or misused the results for their own political and ideological ends. In the nineteenth and twentieth century, elitists, racists, and antisemites have frequently abused and falsified the findings of genetics, as mentioned above. As research in genetics and genomics continues, new concern—and misunderstandings as well—are likely to emerge. Moreover, for ideological or political reasons, some will continue to oppose the findings that the Jews were already a people in the time of Antiquity and that they originated in the Near East. No amount of scientific scholarship will persuade these individuals. Therefore, it is likely that the Khazar myth or similar legends will pop up again and again.

What is called for is a moral compass and a better public understanding of science in general and of the pertinent scientific facts in this inquiry. Both studies found important traces of ancient Jewish history—of common geographic origin, past migrations and conversions into Judaism—in the current genomic structure of the Jewish people; they make no other claims. They do not say that there is a "Jewish gene," a frequent and dangerous misunderstanding, or that Jews are genetically different from everybody else. The Jews may be unique, but that is not demonstrated through their genetic structure, which has much in common with that of other groups, particularly the people of the Near East. Genes do not determine whether a person is a Jew; it is, rather, a matter of family (in Orthodox Jewish tradition the family of the mother), upbringing, history, and choice.

The key question of this chapter was whether there is a scientific explanation for Jewish group feeling, for the tacit consensus Oswald Spengler attributed to the Jews. The discovery of genetic similarities between many Jews, explainable by a common Near Eastern origin, raises the question in a new way. Can awareness among Jews that they are "distant cousins,"— with the theory now based not on religious tradition but on science—create or reinforce their group solidarity? In general, awareness of common genetic origins or traits may encourage but can never guarantee common thought or action, and does not always generate "altruism" and group solidarity, to use the terminology of evolutionary psychology once again. Conflict within groups of similar genetic origin is frequent, whereas one of the most stable and cohesive nations of modern times is the United States, although its genetic make-up is extremely diverse. America is a nation of choice.

For the Jews, the answer will be mixed and ambiguous. Some individuals will be indifferent because they regard genes and genomes as irrelevant to the problems that the Jewish people and Israel have to face today. They may also see the findings as being of only historical interest. In fact, if the numbers of conversions to Judaism increase, the current genetic markers of common ancestry will become more and more diluted. Other Jews will continue to reject the findings because they do not understand them, or for more substantial reasons. They might fear that antisemites and racists will again believe that genetics and genome analysis makes it possible to identify and discriminate against Jews, or they might see a danger that some Jews will propose genetic testing as a tool to differentiate between different groups of Jews. But for a third group, scientific proof of shared ancestry might indeed encourage greater solidarity and unified action in response to growing external hostility. The non-Jews, and in a few cases Jews too, who dispute the historical reality and origin of the Jewish people often also question the legitimacy of the State of Israel. Questioning both has been a staple of some Arab propaganda. The new genetic discoveries will provide a convincing argument to support the historical narrative of the Jewish people, perhaps not in the Middle East as long as the conflict there lasts, but at least in the wider world. Ignorance about the Jews and their history among the larger global public and among elites can have political impacts that must not be underestimated. In China, for example, some books about the history of the Jews and Israel begin in Antiquity, with the biblical patriarchs or the Temple of Jerusalem. In the eyes of informed Chinese, modern Israel's legitimacy is thus to no small degree based on a history of several thousand years that began in ancient Israel. If this argument loses credibility among Chinese elites, there could be negative consequences, not only intellectual but also political.

The social sciences have long been hesitant to consider genetic explanations of social behavior, and historians have not regarded genetics as one of their research tools. Sociology looks back at a long and bitter "nature versus nurture" debate and has generally wanted to see genetics strictly limited to bio-medical research and therapeutic applications. It seems that the traditional reticence has begun to give way. The *American Journal of Sociology* recently published a supplement on genetics and social structure that asks sociologists and historians to think about the accumulating genetic discoveries as a new "archive" to dig in and think about.[34] A commentator greeted this supplement as timely: "If sociologists ignore genes, will other academics—and the wider world—ignore sociology?"[35]

Historiography and the social sciences must be open to new findings from evolutionary science, genetics, epigenetics, and genomic research. It is also important to contemplate the enormous philosophical and ethical problematics that will arise from some of these discoveries as well as their possible implications for religion, criminal law, health care, warfare, and other issues. In this regard one must reflect upon the advances of the behavioral geneticists who are researching the genetic (or epigenetic) roots of certain types of behavior, which inevitably will raise ethical and legal questions.[36] Judaism can respond to these questions, like other religions and value systems, and may have some interesting views to put forward, for example with regard to personal versus group responsibility.

CHAPTER 3

Education, Science and Technology: Drivers of the Future

General Observations

Knowledge in the broadest sense, and its accumulation and transmission through education, is an essential basis of all successful civilizations. Even if it is knowledge for knowledge's sake, it will sometimes unexpectedly turn out to be of practical value. Today the general level of education and knowledge is accepted as an indicator of the quality of a civilization and also of its strength. In the past, the role of general education in civilizations varied considerably and depended heavily on the content and purpose of the knowledge being transmitted. Oswald Spengler described the essential difference between ancient and modern times as follows: "Knowledge is virtue—this is what Confucius, Buddha and Socrates believed. Knowledge is power—this makes sense only in European and American civilization."[1]

Thucydides, Sima Qian, Gibbon, and probably most other historians before the nineteenth century paid little attention to education as a driver of civilization. In their own civilizations, general knowledge was "virtue" more than anything else, except for the knowledge of governance and warfare required of the ruling elites. The great exception is Ibn Khaldun. For him, education, knowledge, and intellectual gifts in the broadest sense, including in science, art, poetry, music, philosophy, and more, are the hallmarks and pillars of any important civilization.[2] When these pillars break, the civilization goes down with it. It is Ibn Khaldun's despair about what he saw as the decline of the Arabs and his analysis of its deep causes that opened his eyes to the education-knowledge factor. Even in the late nineteenth and the twentieth century, few Western historians emphasized general education as an essential factor in the success of a civilization. In two exceptions, Jacob Burckhardt in the nineteenth century and Jonathan I. Israel in the twentieth century linked the Golden Age of the Italian Renaissance and of the Dutch Republic respectively to general levels of education.[3] In both cases, this level was much higher than it was in any other country in Europe. Bernard Lewis[4] saw in failing education one of the reasons for the decline and end of the Ottoman

Empire, as had the Ottoman reformers who had struggled hard to introduce educational reforms. Of course, in this as in other cases, it was not so much traditional religious education that historians and reformers had in mind, but rather a broad education that would prepare the people for change.

It seems that some European rulers were a long way ahead of their historians in understanding the power implications of general education at least in one sector. It was less education as a "virtue" than education for a purpose that attracted their attention. In the first half of the nineteenth century, Prussian governments began to understand that infantrymen who had learned to read, calculate, and measure distances performed much better on the battlefield than soldiers who lacked these skills. This was one of the reasons for the various educational reforms Prussia introduced. By the 1840s, over eighty percent of all children in Prussia between six and fourteen were enrolled in formal education. In 1866, when Prussia triumphed in its battle with Austria, its victory was also a triumph of the Prussian schoolmaster.[5] "The military command could reap the rewards of Prussia's exemplary educational system."[6] Prussia's "exceptionally high rates of literacy and numeracy"[7] allowed its soldiers to fully exploit technological advances and prevail on battlefields. It was an important factor in Prussia's, and later Germany's military successes, but it was not the only one.

The economic impacts of education were discovered much later than the military ones, and this time social scientists were ahead of governments. A few economists who studied the sources of economic growth outside the academic mainstream introduced in the late 1950s and early 1960s the notion that education was an economic variable. Education, together with scientific research and technology, was the source of "technical progress." Technical progress was a "production factor" like capital and labor. This "third factor" could be measured as a residual in addition to capital and labor. This provided an economic policy justification for the public financing of education, particularly higher education and research. The drivers of technological progress, education, and research must receive government and industry support, so went the argument, because they were essential to economic growth.

Since the late 1950s and early 1960s, individual economists and the Paris-based OECD (Organisation for Economic Cooperation and Development), then the main economic advisory and policy-making body of the West, helped convince governments that there was a direct link between economic and educational growth. This conviction, as well as Cold War competition with the Soviet Union, led many countries during the following decades to strongly increase their expenditures for education.*

---

* Alexander King, *Let the Cat Turn Round: One Man's Traverse of the Twentieth Century* (United Kingdom: CPTM, 2006) 264 ff. The scientist Alexander King headed the

This chapter will not review education or knowledge in general, but will focus on the natural sciences and technology, which will be treated here as a unit, referred to as S&T.* In modern times S&T has become a much more important driver of the rise and strength of civilizations than other areas of knowledge have. It is the "hard core" of knowledge because it builds the material base of "hard power,"[8] that is the basis for superiority in war and prosperity in peace. This is what Francis Bacon had in mind in 1597 when he coined the now-famous sentence "knowledge is power," quoted by Spengler. Bacon stood at the beginning of a scientific and technological revolution that had started in Europe. It penetrated and would over time transform all sectors of intellectual, economic, social, and political life. Governments were fast to grasp its implications, because they discovered the critical value of science for improved weapons, land and naval warfare, and maritime expansion. At the beginning of the twentieth century, when czarist Russia was defeated by a technologically superior, Westernized Japanese navy (1905) and China's last imperial dynasty fell after decades of defeat at the hands of technologically superior European powers and Japan (1911), the far-reaching strategic consequences of Western superiority in science and technology were clear enough. During World War II, the main protagonists thought that science and technology (S&T) might decide not only individual aerial, submarine, and tank battles, but also the outcome of the whole war. From then on, S&T has been a major public policy concern.

In the twenty-first century, S&T is likely to change the planet even more radically and in more ways than it did in the twentieth The progress of S&T will continue in all sectors and when well funded will accelerate in many; this movement cannot be stopped in the foreseeable future. It may create many new security, ecological, and ethical problems, but it will also provide continuously improving tools to address them. S&T has also become an effective tool in the international balance of power and an essential component not only of "hard power," but also of "soft power." The soft power of S&T accrues from the prestige attached to great scientific discoveries that enrich our understanding of nature, and from the expectation that major technological innovations

---

OECD Directorate responsible for scientific and educational policies during the critical years of the Cold War. He and his colleagues pioneered the OECD effort to convince Western governments of the critical socio-economic importance of education.

  * Science and technology are conceptually different categories, and so are the activities that create science and technology, namely "fundamental" or "applied research" and "development" (R&D). OECD statistical handbooks define these categories precisely, but in practice it is often difficult to measure them separately. Today, the borderlines between science and technology, or research and development, are increasingly blurred because all technological innovation requires new science, and many scientific discoveries lead to new technology much faster than was possible in the past. This is why experts and policy-makers often treat S&T as a unit.

will help all of mankind. S&T confers an ability to influence the long-term course of history. How a country performs in S&T will be one of the main determinants of its place in the great international power alignments that lie ahead. This is why the US National Academy of Sciences in 2007 emphasized that as much as 85% of recent measured growth in US income per capita was due to technological change driven by S&T, education, and research, and that the economic and general future of the United States depended greatly on the growing strength of these factors.[9]

Many historians of earlier generations showed little understanding of the importance of S&T. They were writing as if science and technology—the importance of which they did not deny in principle—were completely external to their professional concern. The generation of Toynbee, Braudel, and Sorokin, and even later authors, was ill informed and uncomfortable with science.

Applications to Jewish History

Education is an overriding religious duty and one of the highest values in Judaism. The continuity of Judaism depended on the transmission of religious texts and practices from one generation to the next, and only a relatively extensive period of education could cope with the richness and complexity of this written heritage. A comprehensive review of the impact of Jewish education across the ages is beyond the scope of this study. Instead, this chapter will first mention, as an example, the crucial role education—not vocational education, but education in the broadest sense—played in Jewish economic history. Economic historians proposed a theory that links education and economic success in old Jewish history.[10] In the language of economics, this is a "human capital" theory. Before the eighth century CE most Jews, including those living in Babylon, were farmers, as was the overwhelming majority of people all over the world. However, Jews had become a literate people many centuries earlier, perhaps from the first century BCE on. This made them, in international comparison, probably the most highly educated people in the world. Although their education aimed at fulfilling the demands of their religion, it turned out to be quite useful for a number of other endeavors, particularly in professional life. Rabbinic scripture underlines the importance Jews attached to a formal, comprehensive education at least from the late Second Temple period on. Some regard Rabbi Shimon Ben Shetah, head of the Sanhedrin in the first century BCE, as the most important promoter of free secondary schools in Israel.[11] Others give this title to High Priest Joshuah Ben Gamla, who was active in the decade before the destruction of the Second Temple. The Talmud reports: "Joshuah Ben Gamla ordained that teachers of young children should be appointed in each district and each town and children should enter school at the age of six or seven."[12]

This ordinance is significant, although we do not know whether and when it was carried out. Joshuah Ben Gamla's intention to set up a comprehensive, nation-wide, compulsory elementary school system probably had no parallel in the ancient world. A thousand years later Rav Chai Gaon of Babylonia, the leading authority of the Jews under Muslim rule (ca. 1007-1038), decreed that "one can teach the young children in the Synagogue, while teaching Torah, Arabic script and arithmetic...."[13] Today, Rav Chai Gaon would probably have replaced the last two subjects with English and mathematics.

According to the quoted economic historians, Jews moved out of agriculture and into skilled crafts and trades hundreds of years before most other people because their higher educational level better prepared them for skilled urban occupations. While economic discrimination, for example the prohibition on owning land in Christian Europe during some periods, certainly played a role, it alone is not sufficient to explain the massive transition out of agriculture that began in the late Roman Empire and continued under Parthian and Islamic rule. These empires created no obstacles to Jewish farming. Discrimination also does not explain why this transition was so successful and gave the Jews comparative economic advantages that were to last for generations. The reason is that the Jews' higher level of education in general became a professional asset.

In regard to science and technology it must be said that Jewish attitudes were historically less uniform than they were toward education. The historians David Rudermann and Moshe Idel reviewed variations in Jewish attitudes and their evolution.[14] They distinguished four different epochs, but noted that the borderlines between them were not sharp. Attitudes of one epoch could also be found in others.

A. Bible and Talmud

Bible and Talmud did not treat nature as having a status that is independent of the divine will, but this did not lead to a principled hostility to the natural sciences, including those of the Babylonians and Greeks, the merits of which were occasionally recognized. Religious laws required practical attention to specific sciences, particularly astronomy for determining the Jewish calendar, and also to medicine, because of the high value attached to protecting human life and health. In general, the classical Jewish attitude to science can be called one of relative indifference.

B. Middle Ages

The Middle Ages saw Jewish scholars transmitting to Europe Greek scientific texts that had been translated into Arabic. Jewish sages who were influenced by Greek and Arab philosophy had an unambiguously positive inclination toward science in general and saw no contradiction between it and religion. As nature was God's creation, its study would serve to glorify his creation. This group included many of the great sages: Saadia Gaon (882/892-942), Bahya Ibn Paquda (ca. 1000-1050), Moses Maimonides (1135-1204), his son Abraham Maimonides (1186-1237), and Gersonides (1288-1344), who was an important scientist and inventor himself. The science historian George Sarton compiled a list of the top scientists across the world between 1150 and 1300, including Asia, Europe, and the Muslim world.[15] He found 626 names, of which 15 percent were the names of Jews, although at the time Jews comprised, according to his data, barely half a percent of the world's population. Jews in Spain and the Muslim world suffered much less discrimination during this short period than they would in later centuries. Another source seems to corroborate this finding, positing that one of every ten prominent medieval scientists was Jewish.[16] These data are intriguing because they seem to anticipate the developments of the twentieth century, but it is not sure that they are reliable or comparable to the Jewish contribution to twentieth-century science. Early medieval and modern sciences are different phenomena, and the sociological and working conditions of scholars of the two periods are also completely different.

C. The Renaissance and Early Modern Times

Between the sixteenth and eighteenth centuries, Jewish scientists and physicians in increasing numbers began to absorb the scientific knowledge of their Christian environment and publish Hebrew-language books about science and medicine. However, while European science advanced in giant steps, Jews made virtually no original contributions to its progress. David Rudermann attributes this mainly to discrimination, particularly the refusal of nearly all European universities to admit Jews. Some of the most important rabbinic luminaries of the time, for example Rabbi Moses Isserles (Rema, circa 1520-1572) in Krakow and Rabbi Judah Loew (Maharal, 1525-1609) in Prague, encouraged the acquisition of scientific knowledge, particularly on the topic of astronomy. The Maharal separated the Torah from natural knowledge, which according to Rudermann allowed the latter for the first time in the history of Jewish thought to have its own individual life, independent of religion. When it came to practical applications, religion raised no principled opposition to creating new technology or mastering nature. For example, Jews adopted the invention of printing with great relish. The first printed Hebrew books appeared within a few years of Johannes Gutenberg's publication of his first Bibles around 1455.

However, the acceptance of science was often not a smooth process, particularly toward the end of this period. For Enlightenment and *Haskalah* thinkers, scientific progress was a compelling manifestation of human progress in general, destined to put an end to the obscurantism of the past.

This is exactly the reason why those who were still committed to the past became suspicious.

The autobiography of Rabbi Jacob Emden (the Jabetz, 1696-1776), who was one of the most important rabbinic authorities in eighteenth-century Germany, shows the inner tensions and dilemmas to which the new sciences now exposed Jewish believers. Emden was greatly attracted to the sciences, wishing to understand them so as not "to look stupid to others." He was anxious "to better understand the existence of the human race." He had books about mineralogy, botany, medicine, geography, and more, but dared to read them "only in the one place where the study of Torah is forbidden," namely the bathroom.[17] The tension remained high through the nineteenth century, particularly in Eastern Europe, where some Hassidic rabbis, for example Rabbi Nahman of Bratzlav and Rabbi Menahem Mendel of Kozk, condemned science, whereas a few observant Jewish scholars commended and tried to popularize it.[18]

D. The Twentieth Century

When restrictions on European Jews were lifted in the late nineteenth and twentieth centuries, there was an explosive increase of Jewish achievements in all fields of S & T C. Murray listed the key or "significant" scientists credited with fundamental discoveries across the world from 1870 to 1950.[19] He found 94 Jews, compared the percentage of Jews among all significant scientists to the percentage of Jews in the general population, and calculated that the number of Jews among the key scientists in all fields was six times greater than should have been expected: twelve times greater in mathematics, nine times in physics, eight times in medicine, etc. In Germany, the ratio of Jewish to non-Jewish key scientists, in relation to population numbers, was twenty-two to one, in France nineteen to one, and in the United States before 1950 "only" five to one. A second big quantity jump occurred between 1950 and 2000, when large numbers of American Jews, who gained unrestricted access to American elite universities and research only after World War II, made their greatest contributions to the progress of S & T so far. Twenty-nine percent of the world's Nobel Prize winners in science were Jewish (other statistics cite the same percentage for science awards to Jews from 1901 onward, which would mean that the figure for 1950-2000 was higher), and in economics 39% were. Comparisons with total population numbers result in extraordinary figures.

Considering that Jews are just 0.2 percent of the world's population, they are more than a hundred times over-represented among science Nobel Prize laureates. In other words, Jews contributed to the advancement of the world's scientific and technological knowledge like no other small minority has. Their contributions to Germany from 1870 to 1933 and the United States since 1942 are particularly noteworthy because the rise of these two countries to great power status was supported and accelerated by their scientific and technological leadership. Thus, without planning to do so, Jewish scientists and engineers contributed significantly to the great power status of these two countries.

At the same time, S&T has had a dramatic impact on the history of the Jews themselves. S&T has given a small number of Jewish scientists great public visibility, professional acclaim, and new sources of income, if not wealth. In some critical cases, it gave them political influence and power. Perhaps the most consequential example of such influence was the privileged access the British government granted the Zionist leader and chemist Chaim Weizmann during World War I, thanks to his discovery of microbial fermentation in the making of acetone, which helped shift the balance of power at a critical period in the war, as it facilitated the British ability to make munitions. Weizmann did not get the Balfour Declaration as payment for his acetone, as the simplistic anti-Zionist myth would insist later on; the link was more subtle, but still significant: "The men at Whitehall and in Downing Street who had placed their faith in Weizmann the scientist to solve a problem of national magnitude were easily persuaded to extend the same support to Weizmann the Zionist leader."[20] Weizmann the scientist, helped change the fate of his people through an invention that strengthened the "hard power" of the very country that, at the time, was most critical for the future of the Jews. Albert Einstein is another example of a Jew whose scientific fame allowed him to appeal to the leader of the free world at a perilous time, and he warned President Roosevelt in 1939 of the danger that Nazi Germany might develop a nuclear weapon.

Israel inherited some of the Jewish science traditions of the twentieth century. Its early institutions of higher learning and scientific research (Hebrew University, the Technion, and the Weizmann Institute) were among the first and proudest Zionist achievements, and their creation preceded the proclamation of the State in 1948 by decades. Ever since, Israel has slowly built up its research potential.[21] Its survival against overwhelming odds owes a lot to its excellence and ingenuity in critical fields of S&T. In 2006/2007, Israel spent 4.7 % of its GDP on research and development, the largest percentage of any country belonging to the OECD and probably the largest in the world. Four of its universities are counted among the world's 200 best, and in numbers of scientific publications per capita it holds third place in the world. Israel's knowledge-based industries grew during the 1990s by 16 percent annually. The main factors behind this performance were defense and other government research funding, the independent drive of the high-tech sector, and the immigration of large numbers of highly skilled personnel.

The sudden increase of Jewish involvement in twentieth century science has no known parallels in the history of modern science. It can be seen as simply one of many signs of Jews entering and participating in the activities of the modern world, or as an exceptional development that was independent of Jewish contributions to the humanities, literature, and other fields. In either case, this explosion raises several questions. Are there particular reasons for this development? Will the Jews maintain a privileged position in the future of S&T? Was their performance based on long-lasting cultural factors—in which case the alleged prominence of Jews in medieval science was not fortuitous—or will the twentieth century turn out to have been an exceptional period because this performance was the result of temporary sociological conditions? Are there science policies that might ensure a high level of Jewish contribution to S&T in the future as well? The American sociologist Thorstein Veblen predicted that the Jewish "intellectual pre-eminence," to use his words, was temporary, and that a victory of Zionism and the creation of a Jewish homeland would normalize Jewish conditions, remove pressure on the Jews, and ultimately put an end to their pre-eminence.

Today, one century later, some believe that it might be easier to find confirmation of Veblen's predictions in America than in Israel. In America, Jews have not suffered from hostile pressures and discrimination for at least two generations. It appears that during this period the numbers of Jewish students enrolled in elite universities has remained high, but some allege that their quality and performance have declined from their high point. Jewish students abound in universities where entry depends on intellectual merit as well as other assets, such as proximity, connections and money. In a university where admission is strictly limited to merit, the renowned Caltech, the number of Jews is quite small—for whatever reason—while there are many times as many Asian students. [22]

No single reason can fully explain the phenomenon of the disproportionate Jewish performance in S&T. Several explanations can be or have been advanced, some of them are complementary, others contradictory. Not all apply to all of the countries where Jews have made above-average contributions—Germany, the United States, the Soviet Union, or Israel.

a. Religious Traditions. Judaism is not opposed to the scientific exploration of nature, as noted above, and important religious leaders had started encouraging the study of nature in the Middle Ages. However, while this may have made the road to modern science less steep for some Jews than it was for believers of other religions, Jewish religious beliefs cannot by themselves explain Jewish scientific excellence. A more convincing explanation looks not at the content of the Jewish religion but at how religion is taught and transmitted. This is what the French historian Anatole Leroy-Beaulieu studied. His 1893 book *Israel Among The Nations* condemned the antisemitic wave that swept over France following the Dreyfus Affair. To explain Jewish prominence in many fields he wrote that, "Heredity and two thousand years of intellectual gymnastics have prepared them for this....By taking up our sciences, they do not enter an unknown territory, they only return to a country already explored by their ancestors. The centuries have not only equipped Israel for stock-market battles and assaults on fortunes, they have armed it for scientific battles and intellectual conquest....The heavy volumes of the Talmud and the old Rabbinic schools have formed them early on and predestined them for the two most modern branches of scholarship...the discussion of classical language texts and the physical and natural sciences."[23]

In fact, a multi-layered thought process was necessary to determine how a law of the Torah had to be understood and applied. The Talmud quoted the primary, secondary, and even tertiary sources of transmitted interpretations. When a contradiction seemed to appear, the Talmud enquired how fundamental the disagreement was and whether it was real or only apparent: maybe two opinions differed because they were voiced in different contexts. If no solution was found, the text might end laconically with one word: "Question," reminding the readers that not all questions can be resolved. Such modesty certainly encouraged intellectual development. The Talmud's hermeneutics, that is its interpretations of religious texts, has something in common with modern scientific research methods. Even more "scientific" is the talmudic encouragement of polemics and argumentation as an appropriate method of responding to a question or resolving a contradiction. Nevertheless, one should not overemphasize the similarities. One Talmudic rabbi could invalidate the opinion of another by quoting a contradictory opinion of an earlier sage. The opposite—questioning older traditions or the opinion of a rabbinic superior by a new finding—was not recommended and not everybody's right. On the contrary, the Talmud says with characteristic hyperbole that a student who makes a statement on religious law, *halakha*, in the presence of his teacher merits the death penalty.[24]

In traditional societies the reverence for tradition grows with the passing of time, whereas in science progress depends on challenging old assumptions with new findings. There are other things in the Talmud that are not easily compatible with science if taken at face value, for example the miracle stories, but there was and still is enough common ground between talmudic and scientific methodology to lend credibility to Leroy-Beaulieu's statement. It is probable that good Talmud scholars could have become good scientists if they had chosen that path, and some learned Jews were in fact attracted to science, engineering, or mathematics, and showed excellence in one of these fields. How many? Of Jewish Nobel laureates in science and economics, one is known to be an observant Jew and familiar with Jewish scripture: the Israeli Robert Aumann, who won the prize in 2005 for his work in economics. It may be the case that a few others were in the same category, but it is unlikely that many of them ever studied a page of Talmud. Perhaps the intellectual heritage of the Talmud did somehow percolate into family life, education, and remembrance. Nobel laureate Richard Feynman, who is regarded by some as the second-greatest physicist of the twentieth century after Einstein, seems to have searched for an explanation. The novelist Herman Wouk reported his conversations with Feynman, who respected the Talmud, in his own words, as a "wonderful book" although he knew little about it. "Maybe I have a Talmudic mind," Feynman mused.[25] He could not explain how the heritage was transmitted, and Leroy-Beaulieu's beautiful quote does not explain it either.

b. Cultural Traditions and Multicultural Perspectives. Many point to the well-known Jewish respect for education and knowledge to explain Jewish eminence in S&T. This cultural tradition sustained all of the scholarly achievements of the Jews, but it does not place the natural sciences and technologies above any other field. Moreover, the same general respect for education can also be found in other civilizations. A cultured Jewish middle-class home in Western Europe or North America would traditionally groom its children to choose a respectable professional career. This could be, but did not have to be, scientific research. However, until recently at least one peculiarity of the cultured Jewish middle-class home may have promoted the "creative thought" conducive to innovation in science, technology, the economy, or the arts: the Jewish familiarity with more than one culture and language.

The sociologist Richard Florida used the concept of creative thought to explain why scientific, technological, or economic innovations flourish in some environments but not in others.[26] Creativity consists, among other things, of the ability to synthesize new and useful combinations. It grows in places that are diverse, tolerant, and open, or in other words "multi-cultural." If children learn that there are different languages to express the same idea with some variation, and different ways of thinking, looking at life, and solving problems, they will later find it easier to discard old and disproven ways in science and technology and imagine new ones. Thus the Jewish familiarity with several cultures and languages may have stimulated, among other things, scientific and technological innovativeness. Many Jewish scientists and inventors of the twentieth century were migrants or children of migrants, lived and worked in several countries, and spoke several languages.

c. Science as Ethical Substitute to Judaism. In contrast to the two earlier explanations, a third one sees the relationship between Judaism and science as competitive or adversarial. "When Judaism was left behind, science posed a highly attractive alternative to Christianity in the search for a new world view and a source of meaning."[27] The scientific ethos emphasizing the search for truth, integrity, and universalism offered assimilating Jews who had had enough of the old religion an attractive new avenue. They could "convert" to Christianity, to science, or to both. Quite a number of them, for example in late-nineteenth-century Germany, did indeed convert to both, some probably out of conviction and not just to escape academic discrimination against Jews. If some chose science because it promised truth and universalism, others looked for something more, like intellectual adventure, freedom, and the breaking of chains and boundaries. Science promised all of this too. Judaism did not; it promised stability and security—the stability of traditional ritual and the security of unquestioning faith. The personality structure of adventure-seekers differs from that of stability-seekers. This may have added to leakage from Judaism to science.

Common ground between Judaism and science might again be found at a higher, philosophical level, and Jewish philosophers have looked for this ground in Hellenistic, medieval Spanish, and modern times. The phenomenon of science as replacement of Judaism was typical of the period of the European emancipation. Today there are legions of religiously observant Jewish research scientists and engineers, particularly in Israel, who do not seem to suffer from the dilemmas of earlier times.

d. "Creative Skepticism." A fourth explanation begins with the understanding that great scientific breakthroughs are breaks with accepted theories, past "truths." It takes a particular mindset to throw long-held beliefs overboard. Freeman Dyson, one of the great physicists of our time, calls science an "inherently subversive act" and a threat to all kinds of establishments.[28] In fact, this is exactly what the Bible repeatedly castigates the Jews for—saying that they are perennial rebels—and what antisemites have been muttering since time immemorial—that they are subversive. Historically, because Jews have been discriminated against for so long they often had no stake in the political, social, or intellectual status quo of the societies in which they were living. Spinoza, Marx, Freud, and Einstein all set out to smash an intellectual status quo. This type of explanation was first proposed by the American sociologist Thorstein Veblen in 1919, when he coined the term "creative skepticism."[29]

In the past some Jews probably chose science because other professions, such as politics or army service, or even other academic disciplines, were closed to them. The awareness of discrimination can only have strengthened their skeptical minds. However, not all skepticism is the result of bitter life experience. The Talmud teaches critical thought, as mentioned above, and one does not have to go back to the Talmud to discover streaks of intellectual skepticism in Jewish history that were not just the result of discrimination and exclusion. Such streaks were shown to have been strong in the seventeenth century, particularly among some Italian Jews as well as converted or returning *(converso)* Sephardi Jews.[30]

One of the famous authors of the time was Simone Luzatto, rabbi of Venice for almost 60 years until his death in 1663. He was an outstanding representative of the "Early Modern," period when Jews became fully aware of science. Apart from composing many religious writings, he was also an avid student of all known sciences and wrote books on science and philosophy. In a book about Socrates, he praised the tentative, skeptical, and doubting spirit of the great Athenian, with whom he obviously identified, which enabled him to disprove the dogmas and assertions of presumptuous scholars. Socrates, as seen through the eyes of Luzatto, understood the unstable and capricious nature of human knowledge and the unreliability of sensory perceptions. The natural world was ultimately enigmatic, and certain questions would never be resolved with certainty. A similar mindset was found among some of the Jewish medical doctors of the time, most of Sephardi origin, who in the seventeenth century comprised a large professional community. They injected a new cultural element into the Judaism of their age, a skeptical posture calling for empiricism as the basis of knowledge.

e. Social Capital. Social capital will be discussed in the economic context (in Part IV, Chapter 7), as one of the main explanations for the exceptional educational and economic success of American Jews in the twentieth century. It is also one of the factors that foster excellence and advancement in scientific research. Social capital is created by an often unplanned accumulation of information, career inspirations, and connections that close family and community links provide. For example, when a member of a social group becomes famous, he often acts as a role model for younger members of the group. An example is David Kornberg (b. 1947), an American biochemist who received the 2006 Nobel Prize in chemistry. His father was Arthur Kornberg (1918-2007), also a biochemist, who received the 1959 Nobel Prize in physiology and medicine. David Kornberg explained that his enthusiasm for science started on the day his father took him to the Stockholm ceremony to watch the King of Sweden present the prizes to the laureates. David was twelve years old, and his dedication to science has never since faltered. Although serious data are lacking, there is anecdotal evidence that similar links continue to exist in educated Jewish families.

f. The Social and Political Standing of S&T. Emancipated Jews wanted the respect of the countries in which they were living, and also looked for rewarding professions newly open to them. In Germany and, to some degree, the United States, academia, governments, and the general public held science and technical discoveries in high regard. It was natural that Jews went into those fields, particularly when they seemed to be abstract and objective, such as mathematics or physics. There their intellectual achievements would be more easily and impartially recognized than it would be in fields that touched on entrenched, extra-scientific interests, such as constitutional law or history—

a problem already touched upon in our discussion of creative skepticism. It was politically and socially less dangerous to apply creative skepticism and attack the intellectual status quo in physics than it was to do the same in law. However, not all physicists agreed with this statement. In March of 1929, Sigmund Freud congratulated Albert Einstein on his fiftieth birthday. Einstein was lucky, he wrote, because it was much easier to secure recognition in mathematical physics than in psychology, Freud's own, strongly contested field. Freud refused to make Einstein's reply public, because the latter had reacted angrily to what he regarded as an unsympathetic view of his own difficulties in securing recognition. Freud admitted in 1930 that his letter to Einstein had been a regrettable error.[31] Moreover, even if shaking up the status quo was easier in physics than in psychology, Jews entered and excelled in many fields, including some that were politically and socially controversial. In any event, the high social and political standing of science and the ability of Jews to fully participate in scientific endeavors were indispensable preconditions of Jewish excellence in S&T. All the other reasons proposed here could only come into play when science enjoyed high standing in society and Jews were allowed to pursue careers in it. When this was the case, for example in pre-war Germany, Italy, or Hungary, or in the United States, Jews excelled in and made outstanding contributions to science. When it was not, such as in pre-war Poland, they did not, or did so much more rarely. Surely high social and political standing remains one of the most potent incentives for young people to choose S&T careers.

   g. Unknown or Controversial Reasons. Some scholars have not been satisfied with the explanations already discussed. As Jews generally shy away from discussions of their true or alleged "excellence," particularly when this raises issues of heredity, it may be more appropriate to quote a non-Jewish expert, the Cambridge scholar and trained physicist C.P. Snow (1905-1980). Snow's "political correctness" credentials are impeccable. He was a socialist, and like all socialists of his time an admirer of scientific progress. He was a lifelong supporter of the British Labour Party and the personal science adviser of Labour Prime Minister Harold Wilson. He said in 1969 that "The Jewish performance (in science) has been not only disproportionate, but also ridiculously disproportionate. The record is remarkable and quite outside any sort of statistical probabilities. This isn't arguable. The facts are plain. But why is it?... Is there something in the Jewish gene-pool which produces talent on quite a different scale from, say, the Anglo-Saxon gene pool? I am prepared to believe that that may be so. One would like to know more about the Jewish gene pool."[32] More recently, the philosopher George Steiner, who is no more suspected of any form of racism than was C.P. Snow, similarly conjectures about the possible role of genetics in Jewish scientific excellence, albeit with some hesitation. He predicted that "there may be 'illiberal' surprises in store."[33]

206

This whole subject is politically and ideologically explosive, particularly in the United States, as it hearkens back to the "nature versus nurture" debate that lasted more than a hundred years. Other academic authors who are as respected as C.P. Snow or George Steiner have seriously questioned hereditary explanations of intelligence in general, and Jewish intelligence in particular. Richard E. Nisbett, professor of psychology and member of the National Academy of Sciences of the United States, did so in a book with the programmatic title *Intelligence and How to Get It: Why Schools and Culture Count.*[34] For a short while, this book stirred up a vociferous public and academic debate, with many readers celebrating it and others putting it down as "advocacy, not scholarship."* Nisbett rejects the "hereditarian" claim that IQ is 75% to 85% heritable—the true figure is less than 50%, he states, which means intelligence owes as much to education and environment as it does to genes. Chapter nine of his book discusses the somewhat higher IQs and the much higher intellectual achievements of American Jews than those of the average American. The author suggests that Jews might actually have a small genetic advantage based on brain anatomy, but there is not enough evidence to prove that for sure. Evolutionary selection over many generations, as suggested in Part IV, Chapter 2, can provide a complementary explanation of higher Jewish IQs. However, Nisbett attributes the intellectual achievements of the Jews less to their innate endowment than to their relentless effort to get the most out of their endowment through education and hard work. Finally and most importantly, Nisbett denies a direct correlation between intelligence—the subject of his book—and creativity or genius. But exceptional scientific and other scholarly accomplishments—the subject of our chapter—are the result of creativity and genius, not simply of intelligence. Thus, while Nisbett seems to partly support several of the aforementioned hypotheses for Jewish excellence in S&T, the riddle remains to be solved.

We must leave it at that. Jewish organizations and individuals have voiced strong opposition to any form of "genetic profiling," because they fear the abuse of genetics, some of which has already occurred. However, genetic profiling is accepted and successfully used to prevent, detect, and hopefully soon cure heritable diseases and mitigate genetic disease risks. It is an undisputed medical fact that a number of specific genetic conditions causing diseases can be found more frequently among specific sub-groups of the Jewish people than in the general population,[35] or can be found only among Jews and a few other sub-groups. If one is forced to accept, via undisputable evidence, that some Jews are genetically different in ways that are evolutionarily negative and potentially life-threatening, it is illogical to deny that some Jews might

---

* This debate must be seen in the context of its time: the book was published a few weeks after the American people elected a non-white president for the first time.

also be genetically different in ways that are evolutionarily advantageous and potentially life-enhancing. Moreover, it is well known that certain specific aptitudes, for example in music or mathematics, can run in families and are to no small degree inherited. This is different from the more dubious notion of general "talent" based on "gene-pool" evoked by C.P. Snow. We will probably know considerably more in a decade or two, and should be prepared for all possible scientific outcomes.

Past Jewish and Israeli achievements in S&T could tempt one to paint too rosy a picture of the current situation as well as of the long-term trends. On one hand, a vast global reservoir of potential scientific excellence is emerging that did not develop over the last few hundred years, including scientists from China and India, women scientists, and more. Will this reservoir dilute the Jewish position in S&T? On the other hand, there are a number of specific Jewish weaknesses in this field. General public respect for S&T and its academic luminaries is not what it sometimes was in the past, and university enrollments of young American Jews in S&T programs seem to be declining in absolute or relative numbers. Young people in general seem much more attracted to disciplines that promise financial rewards than those that promise answers to the riddles of nature. Trends of declining interest in S&T are common to the entire Western world, except that the West's long-term survival is under less threat than that of the Jewish people and Israel. In Israel, other weaknesses have appeared. In spite of Israel's relative prosperity, there has been a "brain drain" of Israeli scientists and engineers to other countries, particularly the United States. Israeli university research and development (R&D) budgets have been eroded and cannot keep up with the pace of growth of business R&D. Scientists with comparable experience in other countries are warning that Israel is falling behind in certain disciplines. All this does not bode well for the future of long-term fundamental research, the ultimate basis of all scientific progress. Quite ominous are the weaknesses of Israel's school system. International data for 2007 showed Israel near the bottom of the list of Western countries when school achievements in science and mathematics are compared. In 2012, Israel's Ministry of Education published statistics indicating a considerable improvement in the scientific and mathematical performance of Israeli children. The figures do not yet show a trend, and their international comparability has been questioned, but they do indicate that policy makers are concerned about the problem and want to tackle it.

Still, in America, local Jewish journals and communities celebrate the science achievements of their youngsters in college, and there is collective public pride when a Jew receives a Nobel Prize. The long-term result of this mix between the negative trends and the positive ones mentioned above is difficult to predict.

In the coming decades, the Jewish people, Israel included, will be affected be a large number of changes which will have their origin in S&T developments, and by many changes that can be modified or controlled by S&T. S&T alone cannot guarantee the well-being and success of a civilization; many other factors have to play a role as well. But it is certain that civilizations and countries that are not at the forefront of science and technology themselves will not be able to understand and anticipate these developments and, hence, will have to bear the brunt of events they cannot control. Rapid biomedical advances will improve health levels of the Jewish people and greatly increase the average age of Jews, as well as the general world population. Equally rapid advances in military technologies, including weapons of mass destruction, will present radical new challenges to Israel but will also provide new defense opportunities. The continuous revolution in information technologies has far-reaching implications for work, education, leisure, religion, politics, and relations within the Jewish people, as well as between Jews and the rest of the world. A long-term transformation of energy technologies, perhaps a real energy revolution, has begun, and could profoundly change the global environment and its strategic balance as well as the world's economies. The growth of the knowledge-based industries will attract and reward scientific entrepreneurship and creative imagination. For Israel, as well as for the rest of the Jewish people, to not be counted among the "best and brightest" in this scientific century is simply not an option.

Not everyone shares the conviction that S&T is a critical driver of Jewish civilization and must be a priority target for public policy. Before the financial and economic crisis that erupted late in 2008, one could hear it argued that young people's preferences for the study of law or finance over S&T need not be discouraged, for committed Jews who may become wealthy or politically influential could very well do more for their people than scientists and engineers. This view may be partially valid in some cases, but it holds no validity for the state of Israel. Israel has to follow the model of other small, resource-poor countries that became wealthy thanks to high levels of education, government and industrial research, technological innovation, and specialized, high-quality manufacturing, such as Switzerland, Sweden, Finland, or the Netherlands. Germany and Japan owe much of their wealth to the same factors. Israel has made several steps in this direction, but still has a long way to go. In a small country, entrepreneurs who innovate and then sell and cash in, as some Israelis have done, will not create stable, long-term economic growth.

The situation of the United States is different: it is large enough to accommodate, in principle, any number of Jews who want to succeed in the financial sector. Nonetheless, high finance can be ephemeral and subject to catastrophe, as the financial crisis of late 2008 demonstrated. In addition, the Jewish people must be concerned about its public image in the world. As far as can be gleaned from national and international opinion polls taken prior to the crisis of late 2008, most people believe that Jews are very rich and influential. This is not always a negative view. Some see Jews as making a positive contribution to economic prosperity, but many others do not, believing instead that Jews are both too rich and too prominent. There are few who think of Jews and Israelis first as scientists and engineers who will address some of the world's urgent problems of disease, war, hunger, energy, and the environment. The public image of the Jews is rarely shaped by Einstein the physicist, Weizmann the chemist, Sabin and Salk, the inventors of the vaccines that defeated the scourge of poliomyelitis, or even Sergey Brin, the co-founder of Google. Being rich does not make Jews indispensable, and does not necessarily add to Jewish prestige and respectability. In contrast, being among the best in S&T does add to prestige and respectability, and so it is important that Jewish and Israeli contributions to S&T keep growing and become better known. S&T will give a substantial boost to the Jewish people's and Israel's "soft" power. In 2002, before the effects of the Iraq war, international opinion polls were carried out on "dimensions of American attractiveness." They show that the global admiration for American advances in science and technology was by far the most important source of American soft power across the world.*

We can now return to a question raised earlier, regarding whether public science policy initiatives can ensure a continuation of high levels of Jewish contribution to the global advancement of science and technology. S&T policy cannot restore all the conditions that may have contributed to the Jewish pre-eminence in twentieth-century S&T, but it can achieve a number of goals. Specifically, it could target three problematic areas. First, the quality and quantity of science and mathematics education in Israeli and some Jewish Diaspora schools must be elevated. Second, public science policy should fight for more generous long-term funding of basic research in Israeli universities, which will be indispensable if Israel wants to keep its best scientists. And third and perhaps most importantly, the public status and image of S&T in Israel and the Diaspora should be raised. Jewish excellence in S&T has particularly flourished in countries that award high public status to science, scientists, and discoveries. There are many political, administrative, and public relations means to improve the public status of science in Israel, and several of them do not cost much money. They would reverberate across the Jewish world as well.

---

* Joseph S. Nye, 35 ff. On a global level, almost eighty percent of the sample group admired the United States for its S&T, almost sixty percent for its movies and music, and only fifty percent for its democracy. In the Moslem world, the corresponding figures were seventy percent for S&T, less than forty percent for movies and music, and little more than thirty percent for democracy.

CHAPTER 4

Language: A Factor in Rise and Decline [1]

General Observations

"The high point of every culture is the miracle of language," wrote Jacob Burckhardt.[2] From the earliest times, historians and philosophers have mentioned language as an important factor in the rise and decline of civilizations. Thucydides lamented the corruption of Greek caused by the semantic distortions that accompanied the violence of the Peloponnesian War.[3] Another great thinker of the same "Axial Age" period, Confucius, showed a similar preoccupation with the corrosive power of incorrect language. He lived a century earlier, also in a time and place of political fragmentation and civil war. Concepts, words, and acts must be consistent with each other, he warned, otherwise civilization withers. "When concepts are not correct, words cannot be correct; when words are not correct, action cannot be successful, and morality and art do not thrive."[4] This is why Confucius considered it the first duty of government to "rectify the concepts." Concepts are the first cause, not words, but words have extraordinary power.

Ibn Khaldun devoted entire chapters of his work to the critical importance of the Arabic language in Arab history and culture.[5] Language competition has affected the rise and decline of civilizations. He wrote that the Mongol invasions had greatly damaged Arab civilization, because they eliminated the Arab language from the Asian countries converted to Islam, where it had been predominant. Edward Gibbon expressed a similar thought about Latin: "So sensible were the Romans of the influence of language over national manners, that it was their most serious care to extend...the use of the Latin tongue."[6] Rome's ability to spread the Latin language across Italy and the western part of the empire was one of its great successes, and a condition of its power. Gibbon returned more than once to the importance of this common language in ensuring peace and prosperity.[7] It has been said that Luther's translation of the Bible into German was not only the most important cultural event in German history, but also a necessary condition for the foundation of the modern German nation. Others emphasize the nexus between reform or unification of national language and the rise of the Dutch nation in the sixteenth century, or of modern Turkey in the twentieth century, etc.

But is language a "driver," or is it "driven"? Is it cause or effect? Oswald Spengler devoted a whole chapter to the relationship between language and civilization.[8] Languages migrate, and early peoples changed their language quite often, he asserts. Spengler is ambiguous about which of the two, language or civilization, drives the other. Language has shaped every great event and important institution, but it has also been strongly influenced by them. He is more certain about the effect of written language. Spengler says that the essential sign of a civilization is its relationship to its writing. This is certainly true for China. The longevity of the Chinese civilization owes as much to its distinctive script as to any other factor. This script preserves and transmits a singular way of thought and a unique written heritage. Until the twentieth century, the Chinese communicated during thousands of years and across all provinces through writing, not through spoken Chinese, which varied widely. It is significant that the Chinese word for "civilization," *wen ming*, means "brilliant writing."

Applications to Jewish History

What we know of the early history of Hebrew and the beginnings of Israel does not indicate that language played a critical role in the formation of a separate national, cultural, or religious identity. Ancient Hebrew was one of several North-West Semitic languages spoken in and around Canaan. These languages are so similar that the knowledge of one, say the ninth-century Moabite language, allows a learned person to read ancient Hebrew without much difficulty. Linguists say that the Moabite language and Biblical Hebrew are two dialects, among others, of the same language, ancient Canaanite. Moab and ancient Israel were often at war, but it was apparently not language that separated them most. Moab disappeared without leaving any influential religion or literature of universal importance. It was the content, not the language, of the Jewish scriptures that shaped a distinct Jewish fate and instilled awareness of it.

The Israeli philologist Shlomo Morag researched when and why ancient Hebrew separated from its Canaanite sister languages, and suggested that the differentiation of Hebrew was a result of the emergence of monotheism among the Jews. Thus, for Morag, early Hebrew was not a primary "driver" of Jewish identity; it was itself "driven" by other, autonomous identity factors.[9] In contrast, in the same ninth century, when the two enemies, Israel and Moab, spoke closely related languages, the Greek dialects were already completely separated from other Indo-European languages, for example Persian, and had been for many centuries. Indo-European languages are assumed to have split into independent branches long before the start of the Iron Age, which began in Greece and the Near East around the twelfth century BCE.*

The Greek language was a critical distinguishing instrument of Greek thought and self-awareness. The language border was insurmountable, and for the Greeks a source of enormous pride. Classical Greeks called non-Greek speakers "barbarians," from the Greek word "*barbaroi*," which meant people whose language was not civilized, and no Greek person could understand it because it sounded like "bra-bra-bra." The ancient Greeks, and the Chinese, were no less proud of their "otherness" and perceived superiority than were the Jews, and no less eager to remain separate. Their unique language (and, for the Chinese, script) made it easier for them to maintain their cultural separation. This was not so for the Jews. This is perhaps one of the reasons why the ancient Greeks and Chinese never developed anything comparable to the ritual rules of separation which were the Jews' essential "boundary" or "identity safeguard." The Greek and Chinese languages were apparently sufficient boundaries. It would be worthwhile to discuss this hypothesis further, although its explanatory value might still be questioned. The Bible fears the attraction Pharaonic Egypt exerted on Israel no less than that of the easily understandable Canaanites, although it was well known that Egyptians and Hebrews could not communicate because their languages were so completely different.[10]

It was apparently only after the Babylonian exile, when Aramaic partly or largely replaced Hebrew as the main daily language of the people, that Jews started to be deeply preoccupied with their language situation and admitted that language played a crucial role in preserving and transmitting their distinct culture and faith. When Nehemiah returned from Babylon, he complained bitterly that many who had stayed in Judea had married non-Jews "and did not know how to speak Judean."[11] The Talmud and Midrash saw Hebrew as indispensable and glorified its role. What was an urgent policy concern of the time was expressed in narratives evoking earlier centuries. According to the Midrash,[12] Israel kept its identity in Egypt during four hundred years thanks to three or four of reasons, one of which was that the people continued to speak Hebrew. Thus, a decline of Hebrew meant a decline of the Jewish people. The Talmud[13] called the day the Torah was

---

* Many old and current languages are derivatives of an ancient, now extinct Indo-European language that was spoken as early as 2500 BCE, probably near the Black Sea. A comparison of these languages indicates that Indo-European had no word for "iron." This indicated that the daughter languages separated before the beginning of the Iron Age, and when iron appeared each of them adopted a different word for it. In contrast, the biblical word for iron, *barzel,* exists also in Akkadian, Phoenician, Ugaritic, Arabic and other Semitic languages. Hittite is not a Semitic language but absorbed many Semitic words. According to some experts, "barzel" might be one of these.

first translated into Greek (as in the Septuagint) a day of catastrophe for the whole Jewish people.

The Babylonian exile had indeed initiated a radical change in the relationship between the Jews and their language, whose effects reverberated until very recently: the Jews—if not all of them then at least their elites— became bilingual,[14] speaking Aramaic in daily life and Hebrew for religious purposes. Two centuries later, some of the elites became tri-lingual, adding Greek to Aramaic and Hebrew. But then the bi- and tri-lingual traditions began to weaken in the Greek Diaspora. Between the third century BCE and the first century CE, a rich Greek Jewish culture flourished in Alexandria. Most of its literary production is lost forever, except, notably, for the Septuagint—which had been translated for Jews who could not read Hebrew—and the immense work of the philosopher Philo of Alexandria. Both were ignored by rabbinic tradition, if not actively frowned upon by the Talmud, as mentioned earlier. Some historians believe that Philo, who defended Judaism so eloquently, knew no Hebrew.[15] This language split between Israel and an important part of the Diaspora was a sign of things to come later in modern times.

But before modern times, Alexandria was not the rule, but rather the exception. For the 1700 years from the third to the twentieth century, Hebrew no longer was the spoken language of the Jews, but it never became a "dead" language in the commonly used sense of the term. Hebrew lived on through public Bible readings in the synagogue, and was the language of the Mishnah, the Midrash, and most importantly the daily prayers. In addition, during those 1700 years many new works were written in a Hebrew that was slowly evolving, adding new words to the traditional vocabulary. Hebrew poetry, both religious and secular, reached an apogee during the Golden Age of Spanish Judaism (tenth to twelfth or thirteenth century). Many of the poems of this time survive to this day as part of the religious liturgy. Religious works in Hebrew continued to shape Jewish identity, but also influenced the Hebrew language itself. Among these are the Bible and Talmud commentaries of Rashi and his followers, the *Tosafot,* and the main compendia of Jewish law, such as Maimonides's *Mishneh Torah.* The *Mishneh Torah,* like Maimonides' other books and letters, is written in a language that is quite close to Modern Hebrew. The kabbalists, who wrote after the 1492 expulsion from Spain, also created important new terms that entered the Hebrew vocabulary. During the same centuries a number of other Hebrew prose works responded to the Jewish public's wider intellectual interests. Some were books of Jewish history—the *Sefer Yosifon,* which will be discussed in Part IV, Chapter 8, Abraham Ibn Daud's *Sefer Ha-Qabbalah,* which will be addressed in Part IV, Chapter 10, and David Gans' *Tsemah David,* which was discussed in the Introduction, are mentioned in other parts of this book. Moreover, one must not underestimate the practical, utilitarian value of Hebrew fluency during the entire period.

Learned Jews, wherever they lived, could always communicate with each other in Hebrew. Hebrew literacy conferred substantial economic and religious advantages to them, because using it enabled them to build international Jewish networks for lucrative long-distance trade as well as cultural and religious communication.

Many Jews have heard of the religious texts written during the Middle Ages or the Hebrew poetry written in Spain. Fewer know that Diaspora Jews have, over the centuries, written Hebrew texts that have no link to Judaism, Jewish history, or religion. Much of this literature is not well explored, and some exists only in manuscript form. Two widely different types of literary products will be mentioned here. Secular Hebrew poetry did not die with the end of Iberian Judaism but continued in various places, particularly in Italy, where it had already been flourishing. Many beautiful and often explicitly erotic love poems—distinct from religious and other secular ones—flowed from the pens of Italian Hebrew poets who lived between the thirteenth and eighteenth centuries. Among the poets who wrote erotic verse are Immanuel Romano (Manuello Giudeo, 1261-after 1328), who is said to have been a friend of Dante Alighieri, Yossef Tzarfati (Giuseppe Gallo, d. 1527), Immanuel Frances (1618-1710), and the poet and physician Efraim Luzatto (1729-1792) who wrote both religious and love poetry. He scandalized the Jewish community not only with his pretty erotic sonnets in Hebrew but also with a lifestyle that his Italian translators tactfully describe as "not truly consonant with the Jewish religion."[16]

Other noteworthy examples of secular Hebrew publications are the textbooks on science and medicine that appeared between the sixteenth and nineteenth centuries. The historian David Rudermann studied many of these books and found that they offered nothing new and did not generally reach the level of scholarship of contemporaneous texts written by Christians. Jewish endeavors in this field were beset by unique difficulties, but merit respect because, with few exceptions, Jews were denied access to European universities. Tobias Cohen was the most distinguished of these Jewish scholars.* He was born in Metz in 1652, attended a *yeshiva* in Krakow, and enrolled at the University of Frankfurt an der Oder but had to flee from the violent antisemitism there. It was from the University of Padua that he graduated in 1683 in medicine and philosophy. His *Ma'aseh Tuviyya* became the most influential early Modern Hebrew textbook of science and medicine. It appeared after a long delay in Venice (1707), where it saw four

---

* Rudermann, 229-255. Tobias Cohen's portrait in the first edition of his book (1707) shows the author with a thick beard, long hair and side-locks, and a broad fur hat, exactly as Polish Jews were represented in drawings and prints of the eighteenth century. See Rudermann, Fig.7.

reprints, four more editions in Poland, two in Jerusalem, and one in New York. The *Ma'aseh Tuviyya* has no relation to Judaism or any question of Jewish religion or history, but it shows the author's rebellion against the Christian contempt for Jews in science and medicine. To judge from the book's success, it appealed to Jewish intellectuals and was probably useful to those who looked for the best rational-scientific medical advice then available. It also testified to the impressive Hebrew literacy of some of the Jewish elites, who read Hebrew even when the subject matter was complex and had nothing to do with Judaism.

These and many other Hebrew texts may have reinforced Jewish identity over the centuries and were also forerunners of the Hebrew language renaissance that began in the late nineteenth century. But from approximately the fifteenth century on, Hebrew was no longer the only, and probably not even the main linguistic, "boundary safeguard" of the Jewish people. Diaspora Jews had been polyglot even before the destruction of the Temple, but after it they became one of the most polyglot peoples that the world had ever known. The fourteenth, fifteenth, and sixteenth centuries saw large-scale Jewish migrations out of Western and Central Europe to Poland-Lithuania, the Ottoman Empire, and North Africa. These dramatic movements followed the antisemitic agitation that was sweeping Europe, and had important linguistic consequences. Two new Diaspora languages emerged that would dominate the daily life and culture of a vast majority of the Jewish people for five hundred years: Yiddish and Ladino. These languages played an enormous role in preserving Jewish identity and stimulating new cultural creativity. What distinguished these from earlier and parallel Diaspora languages is that they were radically different from the national languages of the countries where most Jews would reside until the twentieth century.[17] Whoever spoke Yiddish or Ladino was marked as a Jew with a particular historical memory and a unique culture. In contrast, Hellenistic Jews in Alexandria had spoken exactly the same Greek that was used all across the eastern Mediterranean, and Aramaic-speaking Jews had spoken, with small differences, the same language that was spoken all across the wider Middle East.

Yiddish spawned a large literature with both sacred and secular themes.[18] Several Yiddish writers, particularly Sholem Aleichem in the early twentieth century and Isaac Bashevis Singer later in the same century, have entered the pantheon of world literature. Their tales of misery, wonder, and hope were taken from the lives of the Jews in Eastern Europe and written in their language, but were recognized as images of the human condition, with universal value. Yiddish also became the focus of bitter political struggles being waged between Yiddishists and Zionists all over Eastern Europe. Many, though not all, Yiddishists were "Diaspora nationalists" who wanted to secure Jewish rights in their countries of residence and strengthen autonomous

Jewish culture there. The socialist Bund party played a major role in these efforts, particularly in Poland before World War II. Some others, who did not believe that Jews had a safe future in Eastern Europe, immigrated to Western countries, particularly the New World. Sholem Aleichem himself went to America, where he continued to write in Yiddish. The Zionists, a minority to the end, fought for Hebrew and emigration to the land of Israel because they understood much better where history was going than did the "Diaspora nationalists." Echoes of these old fights were still reverberating even after World War II. The denigration of Yiddish continued during the first years of Israel's existence, but this was a time when Israel had new and compelling concerns with nation-building, which explained its rejection of Diaspora languages.

Now that the old ideological turmoil has faded, it is possible to look beyond the old dichotomy between Hebrew and Yiddish and recognize what united them. The history of Yiddish leaves no doubt that language is a major driver of the rise and decline of civilizations. A recent author even spoke of a "Yiddish Civilization: The Rise and Fall of a Forgotten Nation."[19] Yiddish had great historical merit: it put up a border behind which Jews could fight all their fights and discard whatever they disliked of Judaism without leaving the Jewish people. They remained Jews. "Yiddish had absorbed the moral values of Jewish religion and civilization," wrote an enthusiastic American historian.[20] Yiddish permitted the rise of a vibrant secular non-religious and non-Zionist culture that remained unquestionably Jewish. A hundred years ago, this culture could still respond with a resounding "yes" to the question of whether it was possible to be a Jew without religion—at least for a time. Today the question is again an open one. Yiddish helped preserve a relatively cohesive Jewish civilization in Eastern Europe one or two generations longer than was possible in Western Europe, lasting until the 1920s and 1930s, when the Soviet Union began to crush it. Tragically, the illusions the "Diaspora nationalists" generated may have had effects similar to those of the Orthodox hostility to Zionism: it may have prevented Jews from leaving for Israel when it was still possible. But then again, a majority of the growing number of Jews who began to abandon Yiddish in the late nineteenth and twentieth centuries chose the national languages of their countries, English, Russian, Polish, Hungarian, Romanian, and German, rather than Hebrew. Yiddish had been their main identity safeguard.

The story of Ladino was in some ways similar and in other ways different.[21] It evolved in the eighteenth century into a great literary enterprise. The single most important literary work in Ladino was the *Me-am Loez* of Rabbi Jacob Hulli, who began to publish it in 1730. It developed into a multi-volume compendium of rabbinic, kabbalistic, and philosophical interpretations of the Bible that addressed the deep religious anxieties of Sephardi Judaism after the fiasco of Sabbatai Zevi. It met with extraordinary success, and can still be found in many Sephardi homes. There is no single Yiddish work that had a similarly broad impact. Through this and many other publications, Ladino had the same effect as Yiddish: it preserved the Jewish identity of those who spoke and read it. The main challenge to Ladino did not come from Hebrew but from the schools of the *Alliance Israélite Universelle*, which made many Sephardi Jews into French-speakers.

In the late eighteenth and early nineteenth centuries the Jewish Enlightenment revived Hebrew as a written language for all sorts of mundane matters, surpassing the Hebrew literacy of the Middle Ages. It was a revolutionary step that prepared the ground for the renaissance of Hebrew as a modern, spoken language, an indispensable corollary of the Zionist revolution. It can be said that in the nineteenth century CE Hebrew was an essential condition for the formation of an independent and cohesive Jewish nation in its ancient homeland, more than it was in the tenth century BCE. Today, however, three generations after the most successful language renaissance of all known history, the role of Hebrew is changing again. In Israel it is being taken for granted and has ceased to be a protector of Jewish identity. It is changing quickly, like every modern language, and some language experts foresee a time in approximately another three generations when Israelis without language training may no longer be able to understand a page of Biblical Hebrew. In contrast to Israel, in the Diaspora learning and knowing Hebrew is one of the most potent and durable forms of engaging in Jewish self-affirmation and demonstrating solidarity with the Jewish people and the Jewish state. Whether or not it is seen as Jewish self-affirmation, it is the most unassailable form of their Jewishness: most countries encourage the teaching, and applaud the knowledge, of foreign languages, whatever the language.

The changing role of Hebrew intersects with another Jewish language rupture that occurred in the twentieth century. In little more than two generations most of the old polyglot Jews have disappeared, to be replaced by a generation that knows fewer languages, and in many cases only one. If they know a second, it is often a Middle Eastern or East European language that is not among the most useful in the globalized twenty-first century. This is now rapidly changing in Israel's younger generation, a large segment of which is increasingly fluent in English in addition to Hebrew, and is following movies, TV shows, and the internet in English, but it is still true for the older generation, including many of Israel's politicians. It is also true for the overwhelming majority of English-speaking Jews. The emergence of English as the dominant world language, the concentration of half of the Jewish people in English-speaking countries, and the notorious aversion of those countries' citizens, including Jews, to learning foreign languages has brought about a situation that Jews have rarely known in Diaspora history: as the older generations pass away, more and more Diaspora Jews speak and read only one language, often English. Although an increasing number of Israelis are likely to know English, the overall result is that the Jewish people are culturally split into at least four main language groups: English, Hebrew, Russian, and French. At a superficial level, this can enrich a culture, and communication between the groups is possible, particularly among young people.

At a deeper level, the language barriers remain, and the issue concerns not only language, but also the concepts and mutual understanding that can depend on language. There is a flourishing cultural life in each of these groups, with many quality publications, and there are some translations among them. All Israeli scholars know English, and most Judaic scholars in the Diaspora know Hebrew, which allows for continuous interaction and cross-fertilization between scholars, but the same cannot be said of the Jewish people in general. Language barriers pose no danger in the near future, but could in the very long-term lead to a new "Alexandria syndrome." Jews in Alexandria knew no Hebrew, and could not communicate with Hebrew- and Aramaic-speakers who knew no Greek. Today, for example, France has an intellectually vibrant Judaism that generates many books and articles of high quality each year, but most of this work is unknown to the wider Jewish world because its members do not read French. At the same time, most French Jews do not read English or Hebrew, and are not aware of what is published in those languages.

Mordecai Kaplan asserted that the complete disappearance of Alexandrian Judaism in the second century CE, leaving virtually no traces, could not have been the result of persecution alone.[22] He attributed the radical disappearance to the complete loss of any memory of Hebrew by the Alexandrian Jews, particularly their elites. From our distant vantage point we cannot know whether the complete loss of Hebrew was the cause of assimilation or its result. The long and intense intellectual and religious life of the Jews of Alexandria, expressed entirely in Greek, indicates that causes and effects were linked in complex, reciprocal ways. In the future, knowledge of Hebrew among some of the elites, and a few basic notions of the language among Jews in general, even if they consist of only a few words or phrases, might enhance Jewish emotional connectedness.

CHAPTER 5

Creative Leadership and Political Elites

General Observations

Until the early twentieth century, most general historians agreed that the rise and fall of civilizations, empires, and nations largely depended on the actions of powerful leaders and small political elites. In many civilizations, great religious and spiritual leaders, such as the founders of new religions, were as important as political leaders, if not more so, or they were also political leaders. This chapter is limited to political leaders, though it will also allude to some Jewish leaders who were both spiritual and political. The literature on political leaders and government elites is limitless, including general history books, political biographies, and the works of philosophers and sociologists who, beginning with Plato, discussed the criteria for good leadership. The historians who have inspired this study provide some backup for these general observations. Most historians have something important to say about rulers and leaders.

In archaic times and before the writing of scholarly history even began, the unlimited power of rulers was entrenched in mythology. The civilizations of the ancient Orient and pre-Columbian America attributed their origin to specific gods or half-gods. Egyptian and Babylonian kings were "god-kings," who were themselves divine and spoke or acted on behalf of the gods. From the "Axial Age" on, beginning in China, India, Greece, and Israel between the sixth and fourth centuries BCE rulers were increasingly considered human, but also subject to transcendental moral laws. They could do right or wrong, succeed or fail. Their actions determined the rise and fall of nations. Thucydides is probably the first-known historian who strongly defended this new, disenchanted view of rulers as human beings. With nuances, his conviction is shared by Sima Qian, Ibn Khaldun, Edward Gibbon, Arnold Toynbee, and even the cultural historian Jacob Burckhardt. The modern historians Bernard Lewis and Jonathan Israel place similar emphasis on the critical role of leaders in rise and decline. Of course, these historians also know that many other factors contribute to the fates of nations.

The three classic historians, Thucydides, Sima Qian, and Ibn Khaldun, all lived through periods of historic rupture and turmoil, watched up close as the rulers of their time made history, and were themselves senior participants in critical events. Thucydides commanded a navy in the Peloponnesian War, Sima Qian advised the Emperor Wudi and participated in one of his military campaigns, and Ibn Khaldun met, as diplomatic emissary, with the powerful and dreaded ruler of the East, Timur Lenk (Tamerlane). Their life experiences certainly influenced their visions of history, but it would be a mistake to attribute their appreciations of leadership only to exaggerated views of their own experiences. Gibbon, Burckhardt, and many others had no such experience and played no role in history, but had the same convictions.

Since Karl Marx, modern historians have paid greater attention to long-term structural, particularly economic, forces as the dominant drivers of history. Marx's indirect influence can best be seen in the work of Braudel and in that of many modern theoreticians seeking general, material rules of civilizational rise and decline, including Kennedy, Diamond, Olson, Turchin, Chase-Dunn, Hall, and Tainter, among others. These American historians, all university professors with no political roles, went one step further and developed universal—and in the case of Turchin even mathematical—laws of rise and decline and rejected what Chase-Dunn/Hall called the "great-man theory" of history.[1]

But the trends of historiography may have begun to change, and more attention seems again to be given to the "great men" of history. Henry Kissinger played an important role in twentieth-century events and saw how statesmen could modify the course of history. He wrote, "It is no small irony that the 20th century—the age of popular will and of impersonal forces—should have been forged by so few individuals and that its greatest calamity might have been avoided by the elimination of a single individual."[2] John Lukacs described how another man stood against the Nazi dictator during the most critical hour of the war. In his somewhat dramatic narrative, Churchill single-mindedly opposed any compromise with Nazi Germany during five fateful days in May 1940, almost alone against the majority opinion of the British war cabinet. Lukacs believes that these five days, during which Churchill may have saved Western civilization from Hitler's tyranny, were a critical turning point of twentieth-century history.[3]

If consensus on the critical role of leadership in history is easy to reach among many historians, consensus on the specific virtues and capabilities of great leaders, or on the vices and shortcomings that might condemn other leaders to failure is less obvious. Leadership criteria vary with regimes and with external circumstances: the capabilities required for the orderly pursuits of government in peacetime are not the same as those required in a struggle for national survival. Most of the classical historians give detailed assessments of famous and infamous rulers from which one can easily extract the authors' leadership criteria, but these lists are not identical because the political and moral judgments of the authors and their times vary. All of them dread the madness and megalomania of tyrants intoxicated with their own power, and most consider martial virtues as key components of great leadership. An example of much more discordant leadership criteria are the attitudes toward the sexual adventures of leaders. Today they are often seen as scandalous and unacceptable, but in Renaissance Italy or at the royal court of seventeenth-century France they were virtues and not vices—tangible proofs of the ruler's supreme power in every domain. Many classical historians do not even raise this subject because they consider it irrelevant to leadership criteria, but Roman historians and Gibbon use it as one more illustration of the criminal depravity of some rulers. Most civilizations of the past considered great rulers to be exempt from the civil laws and ethical norms which were compulsory for common mortals, but not so Judaism. The Bible severely castigates the moral failings of even the greatest kings, David and Solomon. No contemporary of Alexander the Great and no Greek historian would have condemned Alexander for coveting someone else's wife, as King David was punished for doing in the biblical narrative, or for having many women, for which King Solomon was looked at askance.

Historians kept looking for political and sociological factors that facilitated or impeded the emergence of capable leaders and enabled them to operate. Exceptional leadership can often only be recognized when it is tested under great stress. Thucydides and Jacob Burckhardt, among others, paid particular attention to such conditions. Thucydides admired the genius of Themistocles for his instantaneous intuition, perfect judgment, and exceptional foresight, but these gifts came out only when Athens faced mortal dangers from the invading Persians and had to be saved from imminent destruction.[4] Burckhardt said: "The fate of peoples and states, the evolution of entire civilizations can depend on the ability of an exceptional man to bear at a given moment supreme psychological tensions and efforts," and "sometimes, history concentrates in one man."[5] He wrote these words in 1870 or 1871. He may have been thinking of Bismarck, who had just defeated France in war and in a masterstroke had imposed the unification of Germany. Toynbee looked for long-term sociological and psychological conditions of good leadership. He noted that leaders lose their creativity and fail when they stay in power too long, because it is uncommon for the same person to develop creative responses to two or three major challenges in a row.[6]

This chapter mentions rulers and political elites together because they are closely linked. All known governments in history have been governments by elites or minorities. Many rulers in history, even revolutionary ones, have risen from some political, socio-economic, intellectual, or religious elite or from a royal dynasty. All leaders are supported by small power and government elites, from which they choose most of their ministers, advisers and the like. No leader, not even the most dictatorial one, governs completely by himself. The actual performance of government depends on the quality not only of the leader but also of his government elite, and on the political regime of the country. The greater the transformations and challenges of a period, the more critical high quality in government elites is, and the more indispensable a political regime that allows the leader and his government to function is. In a time of peace, stability, and slow change, mediocre or incompetent leaders and elites will be able to manage. In a period of rapid change and great dangers, such as the twenty-first century, they will probably not. The absolute numbers of critical persons in a country were very small in the past and are still estimated to be very small—between 100 and 1,000, depending on the country, of which no more than ten percent are top decision makers.[7] This means that decisions made by a minuscule portion of humanity could determine the future course of history and the fate of our world, more than parliaments, "civil society," NGOs, political parties, writers, or academia, as unpalatable as such a conclusion may be to many.

Applications to Jewish History

The Jews had for almost two thousand years no "political history" in the sense that nations living in their own land have political history. But even so, with the Jews living spread across the world as minorities with no real political sovereignty, political decisions by their own political leaders, or politically astute spiritual leaders, determined an important part of their history. When Ibn Khaldun, Toynbee, and others looked for concrete examples to authenticate their leadership theories, they found many of them in the Bible and Jewish history. If there is a link between bad leadership and the decline of civilizations, as is postulated by many historians, this must have particular relevance for the Jews. Their external conditions were more tenuous than those of bigger and stronger nations, and their survival required more willpower and effort. They could rely much less on stable organizational structures or an assured geographic and economic basis, and thus could not afford bad or weak leaders. All through history, Jews paid a high price for the shortcomings and mistakes of their leaders. The main catastrophes of Jewish history were almost always directly or indirectly linked to absent, paralyzed, unlucky, or incompetent Jewish leadership. On the other hand, it was in times of national or spiritual crisis and transformation that some of the most important future-shaping Jewish leaders appeared and articulated creative and transforming "responses" to severe "challenges."

There is no world history of Jewish political leaders. Worse than that, Jewish scripture provides little coherent and practically useful guidance on governance and leadership. Maimonides wrote a well-known synthesis of governance and leadership criteria extracted from Bible and Talmud, the "Laws of Kings and their Wars," a chapter of his law codex, *Mishneh Torah*. He summarizes the laws pertaining to the appointments of kings and their rights and duties, as well as the laws of war relevant to ancient Israel. He includes civil and religious laws that have no obvious link to public policy and ends with a vision of the future messianic age. Little of this was or is pertinent in the real world of politics and power. Maimonides calls for a hereditary, absolutist monarchy with powers that today would be called totalitarian.[8] Three hundred years later, Don Isaac Abrabanel (see below) read the same scriptures as Maimonides, yet arrived at the opposite conclusion: he was a convinced anti-royalist. However, the Bible and Talmud defend at least two core principles that are enormously important for governance and have never been contested by religious authorities. Maimonides and Abrabanel are in complete agreement on both. The first is that the king, or whoever rules Israel, is not above the law but subject to the law—a law that he has not made himself.[9] According to Maimonides, the king is allowed to temporarily abrogate certain halakhic procedures and laws in order to realize the ultimate goals of government—the improvement of society and vanquishing of the wicked[10]—but ultimately he is totally bound by the laws of the Torah, a situation that is symbolized by the fact that as soon as he accedes to his throne he must write a Torah scroll that he keeps with him at all times.[11] The second core principle is that a leader must be completely free of any form of corruption, and must not accumulate excessive personal wealth. When Moses confronts the rebellion of Korach in the desert, he protests: "I have not taken the ass of anyone of them...."[12] The rabbinic sages linked his protest to that of the prophet Samuel. When Samuel is told that the people want to replace his rule with that of a king, he exclaims, "Whose ox have I taken, or whose ass have I taken? Whom have I defrauded and whom have I robbed? From whom have I taken a bribe 'to look the other way?'"[13] These and other examples show that clean hands were deemed to be as important as proven achievements, if not more so. Biblical and post-biblical condemnations of corrupt rulers may still have some influence on the Jewish and Israeli public.

In the absence of a comprehensive Jewish governance doctrine, a useful way of looking at issues of Jewish political leadership is to examine the biographies of a few prominent political leaders who acted in very different, very trying, external circumstances and intervened in Jewish history. We will attempt to draw some conclusions from their stories.

Four leaders have been chosen, the first of them Nehemia. The period of the great prophets before and after the destruction of the First Temple until the return from Babylonia under Ezra and Nehemiah was exceptionally rich in outstanding personalities. Nehemiah is the last great political leader of the biblical period. His example is useful for several reasons: first, he is historically more tangible than earlier biblical figures, and second, some of his features, for example the fact that he came from the Diaspora, already pointed to a distant future. Today, a growing number of Jews live in both Israel and the Diaspora and move back and forth. This is what Nehemiah did. The challenges and opportunities of "multi-locality," as it is now called, were apparent in his life. Third, the appreciation of Nehemiah's leadership qualities varied in Jewish history. Jews across the ages perceived Nehemiah in different ways, and their perceptions are almost as instructive as the story of Nehemiah itself.

Nehemiah[14]

For reasons that will be explained, the Talmud[15] and Masoretic tradition regarded Ezra-Nehemiah as one book, not two. Today, scholars generally agree that Nehemiah is an independent work, because they can identify literary and linguistic differences between the two books. Scholars also believe that both were written soon after the events they discuss. A part of Nehemiah, however, was apparently added by a different narrator. There is a division of responsibility between Ezra and Nehemiah, although their relationship is unclear on several points. Ezra was the religious guide. He concentrated his efforts on the restoration of Temple service and the implementation of the Torah laws. Nehemiah was the political leader who created the indispensable material basis without which no spiritual renaissance would have been possible. He was the "cup-bearer" of King Artaxerxes I of Persia (reigned 465-425 BCE), and a great-grandson of King Cyrus, who had invited the exiled Jews to return to their homeland and rebuild their temple. Nehemiah's title indicates that he was a close confidant of the King and a royal adviser of the highest rank. He recorded his deeds in history's first known autobiography written by a statesman in the first person, a remarkable document in itself:[16] "I was in the capital city of Shushan. Chanani, one of my brothers, came with some men from Judah, and I enquired of them about the Jews who had survived...."[17] When he learned of the distress of his people and the broken walls of Jerusalem, he understood that the experiment of rebuilding the Jewish homeland was in danger of collapse. Though he was born in the fifth diasporic generation and certainly enjoyed a privileged life, he wept when he heard the bitter news from Judah. His decision to intervene in Jewish history was forceful and immediate. He convinced Artaxerxes to let him return as governor of Judah, then the Persian province of "Yehud." The Greek historian Plutarch called Artaxerxes "among all kings of Persia the most remarkable for a gentle and noble spirit."[18] Nehemiah wrote that he impressed his king with his pious concern for the Jewish people. Did the cupbearer sway his sovereign with only his piety? It stands to reason that he also explained to Artaxerxes that a strong and grateful Jewish province near the troubled southwestern part of the Persian Empire would be a geo-strategic asset. In 460 Egypt had revolted against Persian rule and received military help from Athens. It took Artaxerxes four years to put down the rebellion and capture a part of the Athenian forces, and he was no geopolitical novice. Among other things, he kept intervening in Greek politics in order to weaken Athens, the enemy that had defeated his father, Xerxes.

In 445 (other dates have been proposed) Nehemiah was in Jerusalem. He wrote during that year, "I got up at night, I and a few men with me, and telling no one what my God had put into my mind to do for Jerusalem...."[19] Nehemiah seemed conscious of the enormous historic role that destiny had in store for him. In twelve years of vast endeavors and incessant fights, he subdued the combined and partly-violent opposition that a Samaritan governor, an Ammonite official, and an Arab tribal chieftain had raised against the restoration of the Jewish homeland. He armed the Jewish builders, rebuilt the walls of Jerusalem, enlarged the city's population, and bolstered the status of the Temple, but also imposed far-reaching socio-economic and religious reforms in cooperation with the priestly scribe, Ezra, who was essential in the creation of rabbinic Judaism. The internal dangers of decline seemed to Nehemiah more pressing than the external problems. He tackled the grave social polarization between the rich upper classes and the poor rural population, and ordered a debt remission to prevent further pauperization of the masses and ensure economic stability. After the twelfth year, Nehemiah returned to Persia as he had promised his king he would, but learned soon enough of new troubles threatening his reforms. Around 430 he returned to Judah to redress the situation. He did not stay as long this time, but devoted all his energy to religious reform. He had watched with dismay the rampant assimilation of a Jewish population that was woefully ignorant of its ancestral traditions and of the Hebrew language, and regarded it as the most serious threat to Jewish survival. He and Ezra forbade intermarriage with the non-Jewish women in the country and insisted on strict Sabbath observance. The two convened a large popular assembly and asked the Jews to make a solemn public commitment to the religious laws. He used persuasion no less than coercion and the crowds to whom he often spoke are said to have reacted enthusiastically. He may have had that special "charisma" Max Weber identified as an indispensable trait for any leader wanting to introduce major changes. He then went back to Persia, where we lose all trace of him.

Nehemiah appears to us to be a statesman of rare foresight, willpower, and energy. His merit in Jewish history seems enormous and unquestionable, his dedication beyond doubt and free of self-interest. No other known Jew of his time was likely to match his statesmanship and the political, military, and organizational talents acquired in the nerve center of the largest multi-ethnic empire of the time. His individuality and assertiveness appeal strongly to the modern reader. The earliest known comments about him are in the post-canonical books *Ben Sira* and the *Second Book of Maccabees*, both from around 200 BCE. They praise Nehemiah, and so does Flavius Josephus.[20] But this is not how some rabbis of the Talmud judged him two or three centuries after Josephus. In their time, his book did not go under his own name, but as "Ezra II" or "Ezra III." The rabbis did not question the existence of Nehemiah, but some spoke of him with unconcealed suspicion. They would countenance no personality cult of Nehemiah, certainly no more so than they would a personality cult of Moses, whose grave "nobody knows" as the Bible says, and whose name they had deliberately omitted from the *Pessach Haggadah*. Why was the book not called by Nehemiah's name? "Because he claimed merit for himself," "because he spoke disparagingly of his predecessors," because "he spoke thus even of Daniel, who was greater than he."[21]

The sages' disapproval of what they regarded as signs of personal vanity revealed their radically different vision of Israel's fate and their indifference to political leadership. The loss of sovereignty had strengthened a belief that only piety and ritual, as demanded by Ezra, could protect the Jewish people. Not surprisingly, other teachers were not of the same opinion, and so arguments about Nehemiah continued. A few pages later, in the same tractate, another rabbi mentions Nehemiah again and expresses the opposite opinion: if in a particular text a certain letter was deleted, it was "because of respect for Nehemiah Ben Hacaliah."[22] The book *Ezra* included Nehemiah's narrative at least until Rashi's time, and probably much longer: Rashi always wrote "Ezra" when he commented on Nehemiah.[23] As far as is known, it is the early Christian translations of the Hebrew Bible, that of Origenes into Greek and that of Jerome into Latin (the "Vulgate"), that first distinguished between the two books. The earliest Hebrew Bibles, printed in the late fifteenth century, separated them too. It seems that the Jews quietly adopted this Christian tradition because it made more sense and was not in opposition to Judaism.

Modern Jewish world historians also held different views. Heinrich Graetz in the nineteenth century and Simon Dubnow and Joseph Klausner in the twentieth recognized Nehemiah's crucial political role. Graetz greatly admired this "man of untiring energy and ingenuity,"[24] and Dubnow praised him as a "patriot."[25] But Salo W. Baron, who wrote an eighteen-volume world history of the Jewish people, inclues no more than a few words about him. Baron took a "structuralist" view of the whole period, of the kind Fernand Braudel would have approved. Baron, like Braudel, was interested in long-term socio-economic and religious trends, not in great leaders. But Baron admitted that the period after the Babylonian Exile was a very "significant" and "crucial test," which Judaism finally passed. One could argue that this was because the leaders of the time were "significant" and "crucial." Baron called Nehemiah a "nationalist," which was a dubious compliment: this modern term does not capture the great reformer's life-long hopes and struggles.[26] It is ironic that Baron's vision has more in common with that of the talmudic rabbis than with Graetz or Dubnow. The rabbis, too, were looking not for individual leaders but for long-term laws that determined Jewish history—though of course their laws were not those Baron had in mind. The mistaken belief that political leaders were and are not essential for the Jewish people's well-being and survival has lived on for a long time, and is not likely to die soon.

Some Leadership Features After the Destruction of the Second Temple

The second great transformation of Judaism following 70 CE is distinguished from the first one (following 586/7 BCE) by its apparent shortage of great political leaders. This time there was no political leader like Nehemiah. When unrest against the Romans started, King Agrippa II (27-93 CE), a moderate and a great-grandson of Herodes, saw the impending danger and tried to stem the protests, but nobody listened to him.[27] The military leaders of the rebellion, the "zealots" whom the Romans defeated and executed, are barely known today. Flavius Josephus defamed them copiously, and rabbinic sources had nothing good to say about them either. The main, truly extraordinary leader was Rabbi Yohanan Ben Zakkai (ca. 40-80 CE). He appears primarily as spiritual leader, but in a deeper sense he was also a political one. He was perhaps the first person who could imagine Judaism without a temple, and his long-term influence on Jewish history was enormous. He was moderate, may have foreseen the coming catastrophe, and sensed that neither he nor anybody else could prevent it. He put all his effort and astuteness into a single goal, saving Judaism and the Jewish people after the disaster, which required dramatic religious transformations. Legend has it that he met Vespasianus before the latter became emperor of Rome; the existence of such a legend indicates that the tradition understood the political intention and reach of his action. In him, the law-giving function of a religious leader came together with the political foresight of a statesman. This union between religious law-giving and statesmanship in the same person occurred again in Jewish history approximately a century after him. Rabbi Yehudah HaNassi (ca. 135-200/220 CE), who codified the Mishnah, was again a lawgiver and a political leader. Several rabbinic anecdotes described him as a close friend and conversational partner of Roman emperors—which demonstrates the importance of his statesmanship. It has been suggested that by emperor the rabbis referred to Antoninus Pius.[28]

In the early Middle Ages there were other cases in Europe in which religious guidance based on great scholarship and political leadership went together, and the same applied to Jews in the Muslim world. Sometimes the union of scholarship and leadership was also linked to economic wealth. Rabbenu Gershom "Meor Hagolah" ("the Light of the Diaspora," ca. 960-1028/1040) was not only the first great German-Jewish scholar but also a brilliant practical organizer who reintroduced the lawmaking function of the rabbi, helped establish Jewish self-government in Europe, and struggled to bring Europe's scattered Jewish communities into a federation.[29] He assumed authority "by sheer force of personality."[30] The ordinances that bear his name had an enormous influence on later Ashkenazi generations. Best known among these is the prohibition of polygamy, which Rabbenu Gershom propounded with the reason of a statesman who had to look after the well-being of his people in a suspicious Christian environment.

It is in pre-modern and early modern times that one encounters several outstanding, historically well-documented political leaders who were not primarily religious scholars and rabbis. Some of them emerged suddenly, almost out of nowhere. In Europe they represented a type of Jewish leadership that showed the way to the nineteenth and twentieth centuries. The three Jewish leaders discussed in the following pages, Don Isaac Abrabanel, Josel of Rosheim, and Menasseh Ben Israel, who stood at the beginning of modernity, between the fifteenth and seventeenth centuries, were selected arbitrarily: others could have been chosen. Only one of the three, Don Isaac Abrabanel, is recognized as a religious commentator and spiritual as well as political leader. Their biographies can shed light on the opportunities of Diaspora leaders and the constraints laid upon them, and show how some of them operated even when they lacked resources and means of coercion.

Don Isaac Abrabanel (1437-1508)[31]

Don Isaac was a significant and impressive figure in Jewish history. He was born in Lisbon as a scion of one of the most prestigious Jewish families of the Iberian Peninsula, which claimed to be of Davidic origin. He was rich and influential, and served the kings of Spain, Portugal, and Naples, and the doge of Venice, as minister of finance, diplomat, and ambassador. He was also a great Renaissance intellectual and rabbinic scholar. Under Afonzo V of Portugal he was head of the treasury and soon won the king's confidence, but lost his position after Afonzo's death due to internal intrigues and was forced to flee. He moved to Spain and served the Spanish crown with distinction (1484-1492). While there, he became the unofficial leader of Spanish Jews thanks to his pedigree and high office at the courts of Portugal and Spain. The year 1492, however, was the watershed of his life. King Ferdinand, whom

Machiavelli called merciless and deceitful, a man of "pious cruelty,"[32] had probably planned, long before, to expel the Jews. Three months after conquering Muslim Granada (January 1492), he signed a secret expulsion decree against all Jews of his kingdom. The head of the Spanish Inquisition, Torquemada, drafted the text.

When the fatal decree became public, Don Isaac and other Jewish leaders made three vain attempts to persuade Ferdinand and Isabella to rescind it. Don Isaac is reported to have offered the king a large amount of money, but failed. Did he read Ferdinand's intentions early enough but was unable to avert the catastrophe, or did he harbor to the bitter end the illusion that the Jews, unlike the Muslims, would be spared? He certainly must have known that the Jews of Spain had often been persecuted in the past, and he should have been suspicious, considering Ferdinand's brutality and cunning.

The Israeli historian H.H. Ben-Sasson found evidence that many Sephardi exiles were later deeply troubled by the thought that they had not mounted an armed resistance.[33] If such thoughts ever crossed Don Isaac's mind in the critical weeks before the expulsion, his realization that a major part of his people would rather convert than suffer, let alone fight, must have been very painful. Faced by overwhelming external pressure and the risk of internal disintegration, Don Isaac was completely powerless. He followed the loyal part of his people into exile, although the king apparently wanted him to convert to Christianity and stay in Spain. All his nobility, stature, money, and power of persuasion were of no avail. The king's first political imperative was the unification of Spain, and to further this end he was ready to appease the antisemitism of the clergy, the cities, and the professional classes. Don Isaac could not mobilize any countervailing power against these political and economic forces or change the country's religious fanaticism: all he could do was to write messianic and mystical interpretations of the catastrophe that had befallen his people.

Don Isaac is the author of a large number of religious books, and his commentaries on the first books of the Prophets incorporate his thoughts on governance, including his anti-royalist convictions. This is probably the only political Bible interpretation ever written by a Jewish statesman. Don Isaac wrote about the coming of the Messiah, whom he saw as a person of superhuman perfection. His biographer Benzion Netanyahu wrote that he became through his books the "father" of the messianic movements of the sixteenth, seventeenth, and eighteenth centuries, but this has been questioned by other historians.[34] If this was really his posthumous impact, it was enormous, but unintentional. False messianic movements were the last thing he would have wanted to provoke.

Josel of Rosheim (1480-1554)[35]

Josel was the great advocate of the Jews of the large German Empire during the reign of the Habsburg emperors Maximilian I and Charles V. He was a small-town rabbi from Alsace who made his living as a merchant and moneylender. His political career spanned almost half a century and took him from local, to provincial, and then to imperial responsibility. He began in 1507, at 27 years old, when he successfully argued the case of the Jews of an Alsatian village who were threatened with expulsion. He became the acknowledged spokesman of all German Jews, carried the title "Commander of Jewry in the Holy Roman Empire of German Nation," and died at the age of 74 while riding on his horse to Heidelberg to defend the local Jews against another expulsion decree. He devoted his life, often successfully, to the procuring of charters of protection for his people and to the thwarting of hostile plans against them. These included death sentences for alleged ritual murder, economic discrimination, expulsion orders, and public defamations of Judaism spread by Jewish renegades and by Martin Luther, with whom he exchanged letters. He also acknowledged that some Christian complaints about Jewish usury and other unfair business practices were justified. During the Imperial Diet of Augsburg in 1530, Josel assembled a congress of rabbis and community elders and compelled them to endorse a list of ten rules prohibiting the business practices that were raising Christian ire.

The most powerful ruler of his time was Charles V, king of Spain and emperor of the Holy Roman Empire of German Nation, and grandson of Ferdinand and Isabella of Spain. Josel wrote to the emperor to ask for an audience, and repeatedly traveled to see him in person when new dangers threatened his people. In every case Charles received him and agreed to help, in contrast to Luther, who refused to meet him. In 1544 Charles confirmed all the privileges and freedoms he and his predecessors had granted the Jews. This meeting of minds between the ruler of "the empire on which the sun never sets"[36] and the Alsatian village rabbi was born of political need. Charles had many problems, including the wars with France and the Ottomans, Spain's Conquest of the New World and particularly the German Reformation and the opposition of the local German rulers. He struggled, therefore, to re-establish the full power and privileges of the German emperors. Josel supported this endeavor and exploited Charles' goals astutely. He quickly grasped the opportunity inherent in the medieval laws that made the Jews subjects of the German emperor, not of local rulers. They owed him allegiance and taxes, and he owed them protection.

Charles welcomed his role as protector of German Jewry. He used the Jews to demonstrate his connection to his greatest predecessors on the throne of the Holy Roman Empire, and in doing so also demonstrated his unbroken

Imperial privileges. In 1236, Emperor Frederick II of Hohenstaufen had made himself protector of the Jews for the first time. His edict against anti-Jewish ritual murder accusations had read: "Since a lord is honored through his servants, whoever shows himself favorable and helpful to our serfs the Jews will surely please us. However, whoever presumes to contravene the edict of this present confirmation…bears the offense of our majesty."[37]

Josel, however, kept more than one iron in the fire. His diplomacy was innovative, versatile, and carefully attuned to the often-changing religious and political conditions of his turbulent century. To Catholics he insisted on the privileges of the Holy Roman Emperor, to Protestants he quoted proof from the Hebrew Bible, and to Jews he gave the advice to invoke the principles of Natural Law in disputes with Christians, because these stated that there were no natural differences between human beings, which implied a basic equality between Christians and Jews. But the emperor's political imperatives and Josel's diplomatic nimbleness were not the whole story. There are many signs that Charles respected the courage and devotion of this Jew and was impressed by his charisma and legendary power of speech. According to the historian Selma Stern, the emperor sensed in Josel a kindred soul, a man who shared his own asceticism and unflinching sense of duty and who was, like himself, carrying an enormous burden.

During the Imperial Diet in Augsburg in 1530 Josel was forced to agree to a public religious disputation with Germany's most dangerous antisemite, a learned, Hebrew-speaking Jewish convert. The Emperor attended in person, and is reported to have listened attentively. Josel won the contest, and the convert was expelled from the Diet. Charles' vice-chancellor, Mathias Held, wrote that it was Josel's "multiple and untiring endeavors and solicitations" that moved the emperor to maintain the rights of the Jews.[38] Simon Dubnow alluded to the financial help the emperor is alleged to have accepted from the Jews of the empire, but this was not a decisive reason for his support of Jewish claims.[39]

There was never any comparable political leader representing all of Ashkenazi Jewry after Josel. He was far from achieving all of his objectives, and some of the ones he did achieve were lost after him, but it was in his time that the Jewish emigration trend that led people out of the German provinces of the empire was reversed, and Jews began to settle again in parts of Germany.

Menasseh Ben Israel (1604-1657)[40]

Menasseh's was the son of crypto-Jewish parents, who had fled from persecution in Lisbon to settle in Amsterdam, where Menasseh lived and became a writer, printer, rabbi, and self-appointed diplomat for Jewish causes, and where Rembrandt etched his famous portrait.[41] He claimed to speak ten languages and published in five, and made a living as a Hebrew schoolteacher. According to Cecil Roth, Spinoza was among his young pupils.[42] However, he acquired his place of honor in Jewish history through his intervention with the "Lord Protector" of England, Oliver Cromwell, in 1655. Menasseh grasped the opportunities that the English revolution by the anti-Catholic, Bible-reading Puritans had opened up for the Jews. In a book he published and dedicated to Cromwell in 1650, *The Hope of Israel*, he argued the case of the Jews and asked Cromwell to annul their expulsion from England, which had been decreed in 1290. The book promised the Jews imminent redemption and release from humiliation and persecution. It invested Jewish suffering with special meaning: "And seeing our perseverance amid such great hardships, we judge that the Almighty has preserved us for great rewards to come."[43] Menasseh's fervent Messianism has uncanny similarities with that of the false messiah, Sabbatai Zevi, but a world separated the two men. One searched diligently for a new window of opportunity for his people, and when he found one struggled until exhaustion and death to open it; the other's half-demented, completely self-centered fantasies precipitated his people into a catastrophe. *The Hope of Israel*, like many of his books, showed Menasseh's enormous erudition in Jewish as well as non-Jewish fields. Lacking money or any other form of real power, he made up for his weakness with superior knowledge and information, which he used to improve the lot of his people. He read, among many other texts, the specialized travel narratives of his time and learned from Jesuit reports that Jews were living freely in China. The latest of these reports was published by the Portuguese Jesuit Alvarez Semedo in 1642. Eight years later Menasseh used this interesting piece of information in a subtle, indirect message to Cromwell: How was it possible that Jews were allowed to reside in pagan China, but not in God-fearing England?[44] Cromwell was sympathetic to Menasseh and his cause, received him kindly, and called Parliament into session to debate the question. As there was still religious opposition to letting the Jews return, the parliament did not make a decision, but the question remained on the table and Jews were informally allowed to return. Menasseh's intervention contributed to opening the doors of not only England but also the English colonies, and thus was of enormous historic significance for a people that had few options of legal residence in Europe.

Menasseh knew how to appeal to Cromwell's biblical faith, but could offer no material inducements. What may have helped his cause was the aspiration of Cromwellian England to disrupt the colonial trade of its Catholic enemies, possibly with the support of Dutch-Portuguese trading networks (run by Jewish converts) that controlled part of the European trade with Brazil and the Caribbean.

Menasseh had no explicit political mandate and no known material support from the wealthy Jews of Amsterdam. It has since become known that his scheme was secretly discussed with some of the leaders of Amsterdam's Jewish community, and they apparently liked it but were afraid to make their consent known.[45] The clear public support and financial underwriting that Menasseh might have expected was not forthcoming. He had to ask Cromwell for help, and the great Protestant ruler graciously granted the penniless Jewish intellectual a small English state pension. When Menasseh died, his impoverished widow could not pay the expenses of his burial in Amsterdam: the poor-relief fund (*Gemiluth Chesed*) of the community had to take care of it. His life and death reveal some of the problems in the relationship between the moneyed upper class of the Jews and the intellectuals or other representatives who did not belong to the establishment.

These three Jewish statesmen had several qualities in common, and most of them can also be detected in Nehemiah. Though they were all pious and believed in divine providence, as far as we can judge today, they were also profoundly convinced that the future of the Jewish people called for foresight and forceful, active interventions in worldly affairs, and not only a passive reliance on divine help. Their merits included the following:

a. A life-long, burning sense of mission and wish to rescue their people;
b. Personal courage and a readiness to risk their own freedom, health, and money;*
c. Honesty and incorruptibility: indifference to financial or other rewards;
d. A touch of asceticism and a personal life in line with traditional Jewish ethics;
e. Jewish scholarship—all three also published in Hebrew;
f. Great familiarity with the global political and spiritual environment of their time—these leaders were exceptionally well informed about the world;
g. Easy command of several languages—all conversed with the rulers of their time in their own languages, not through interpreters; and
h. Personal charisma: an innate quality, impossible to learn and difficult even to define.

Their success depended on three conditions: propitious geopolitical circumstances, an effective non-Jewish ruler with a sympathy for the Jewish predicament, and a courageous Jewish defender of his people's cause who had the backing of his community. Geopolitical and external religious conditions were good for Josel and Menasseh but not for Don Isaac, and in

---

* Don Isaac barely escaped arrest in Portugal and spent all of his immense fortune to rescue his people, Josel was once physically assaulted and on another occasion was put in jail for several months on a trumped-up antisemitic charge, Menasseh lived sometimes in a state of deprivation, and fell ill and died relatively young.

addition the counterparts of Josel and Menasseh, Charles V and Cromwell, were personally well disposed toward the Jewish people whereas Don Isaac's counterparts Ferdinand and Isabella were not. Don Isaac and Josel were backed by large communities; Menasseh was not, but Cromwell's manifest sympathy for the people of the Old Testament made up for this weakness. All three Jewish leaders were articulate apologists, but only two—Josel and Menasseh—had a measure of success. Don Isaac failed, although his political experience, pedigree, and financial backing should have better positioned him to succeed. The charisma and personal bearing of all three impressed the rulers of the day. It is unlikely that this alone would have turned the fate of the Jews around—and in Don Isaac's case it did not—but it did make a difference.

Leadership in the Late Nineteenth and Twentieth Centuries

It would be tempting, but beyond the scope of this study, to compare these Jewish leaders of old times side by side with twentieth-century Jewish leaders. The Greek historian Plutarch and the Chinese Sima Qian claimed that comparing historic personalities in similar situations but different periods can lead to a greater understanding of leadership qualities. Similarities could probably be found between these old leaders and early Zionists such as Theodor Herzl, who appeared quite suddenly and without backing or major resources, appointed himself as a statesman of the Jews, and revolutionized their history, or Chaim Weizmann or Ze'ev (Vladimir) Jabotinsky. What they all had in common, among other qualities, was a profound understanding of the political situations of their times and of the complex external and internal conditions of their people.

Since the beginning of Zionism, public leadership—its strength or weakness—has again played an increasingly important role in Jewish history. This became clear in both the fortunate and the tragic events of the twentieth century. From the beginning of the century to the aftermath of World War I, a small number of Jewish leaders intervened forcefully and at the right moments to exploit the opportunities that the war and Great Britain's conquest of Palestine had opened for the Jewish people, and these leaders were successful. The Zionist leader Chaim Weizmann (1874-1952), who lived in England, and Chief Justice Louis Brandeis in the United States (1856-1941) were two of the most outstanding of these. Both owed their initial prestige not to careers in Jewish politics but to the singular contributions they made to the well-being of their respective nations. Dr. Weizmann, a brilliant chemist, solved a critical munitions shortage that threatened the British military effort at the height of the First World War. Chief Justice Brandeis was a fighter for racial and social equality. He was the first Jew to sit on the bench of America's most prestigious court, the United States Supreme Court. Both were admired for their uncompromising dedication to the ideals they believed in, their powers of speech, their quick wit, and their personal charisma. Both were tall, and Brandeis was strikingly handsome—for better or for worse, physical appearance has never been irrelevant in politics.

In 1917, Weizmann convinced the British government to issue the Balfour Declaration (also see Part IV, Chapter 3). Brandeis had been chairman of the Zionist Federation of America since 1914. He helped orchestrate relentless Zionist pressure on the White House, and finally convinced American President Woodrow Wilson to support Zionism and the Balfour Declaration. Amercian support was essential if British Foreign Secretary Arthur Balfour was to overcome internal opposition to his policy. He called Brandeis "probably the most remarkable" American he had ever met.[46] Brandeis, too, had to overcome internal opposition. He knew very well that antisemitism was a force he had to reckon with, even at the highest levels; Wilson himself was ambivalent about Jews. However, Brandeis proclaimed in public that "there is no inconsistency between loyalty to America and loyalty to Jewry,"[47] and no mainstream American politician contradicted him.

It is still too early to judge the attitude of Jewish leaders during the *Shoah* in a completely fair, dispassionate, and informed way. Later historians living in freedom and safety may not be able to appreciate all the constraints under which these leaders operated, or fully understand how their deep moral distress and physical fears may have affected their judgments and actions. Still, a number of things are clear: Weizmann and Brandeis (who died in 1941) were ageing and had lost much of their power when the Jewish people began to face what was probably its most deadly danger ever, Nazi Germany. Weizmann, who had real influence on British policy in 1917, lost all of it in 1939. His 1949 autobiography *Trial and Error* reveals his deep despair about this loss. New Jewish leaders were now at the helm. Those in Europe— community presidents, Jewish party politicians, and rabbis of various religious streams—with some exceptions did what they could in the shadow of death to save Jews, but few could be called "leaders." They had almost no power, and little vision.

Those in pre-state Palestine, first of all David Ben Gurion, put all their energy into strengthening the *Yishuv*, the local Jewish community, and preparing it for the worst case, a German invasion, or the best case, Allied victory over Germany, which would be followed by an inevitable confrontation between the *Yishuv* and the British and Arabs. Refugees from Europe were saved whenever they could reach its shores, but the *Yishuv* and its leaders were resentful that most of Europe's doomed Jews, whom they had so often invited to join the Zionist enterprise, preferred to remain in hostile lands. In their eyes, Europe's Jews were a lost cause; it was more constructive to prepare for the future of Israel. Many of Israel's early leaders have since bitterly regretted such attitudes, although there is almost nothing more they could have done to save Europe's Jews. In his last years, Ben Gurion spoke with great emotion about the enormous historic failure of Jewish leadership in Israel and America and the tragedy that ensued.[48]

The only rescue that could have come would have been from the Jews of the United States. Their leader, Rabbi Stephen Wise (1874-1949), was both the head of American Judaism and the president of the World Jewish Congress, whose task it was to protect Jews all over the world. Wise was a decent man, an early supporter of Zionism, a staunch enemy of Nazi antisemitism, and not without charm. In contrast to Brandeis, his only professional pedigree was his training as a Reform rabbi, and his main experience was in American domestic policies, not in international power politics. Now he was suddenly confronted by evil of a magnitude he had never before imagined, and was unable to cope with it. Historians have noted a streak of naiveté in him—not a helpful character trait for a leader in times of war and existential danger. In the summer of 1942, when he was informed of the extermination campaign in occupied Europe, the US State Department advised him to refrain, for the time being, from making a public statement. He obeyed. He did not retort that he, the nominal political world leader of the Jewish people, had moral duties before God and history that were more compelling than the changing tactical requirements of America's foreign policy bureaucracy. When, later in 1942, the World Jewish Congress was flooded with corroborating reports of the ongoing extermination, Wise and others still did not seem to grasp the full dimension of what was happening, or did not always believe what they read. The historian Walter Laqueur summarized Wise's failing in a lapidary phrase. Even when Wise finally recognized the full extent and rapidly growing size of the catastrophe, "he did not shake heaven and earth...and for apparent want of another course of action, put his trust in Roosevelt whom he so much admired."*

---

* Walter Laqueur, *The Terrible Secret: Suppression of the Truth About Hitler's "Final Solution"* (New York: Holt Paperbacks, 1998), 161. Laqueur acknowledges that Stephen Wise did finally speak out, was active, and tried to help in various ways—see 78-80, 93-97, 258-164, 224-227, 232, 236-237. Laqueur is much more severe with other, secondary, Jewish leaders. He has no sympathy for Wise's second-in-command Nahum Goldmann, chairman of the WJC's executive board, who was European but waited the war out in safe America. Goldmann liked to boast that he knew every important statesman of the time, but this did not prevent him from making grave political misjudgements, 158-162, 167. Another, probably not isolated, Jewish attitude was that of Judge Felix Frankfurter, who met in 1942 with Jan Karski. Karski was a Polish Catholic courrier who had risked his life to leave Poland for America in order to inform Roosevelt and Jewish leaders of the mass-exterminations and to convey the Jews' pleas for help. Karski had witnessed one mass-killing of Jews with his own eyes, but Frankfurter told him to his face, "I can't believe you," 237.

Wise was believed to be a friend and adviser of Roosevelt. However, from 1940, before the United States entered the war, until 1945, upon the war's conclusion, Wise showed complete subservience to the priorities of his president and stifled Jewish criticism of American inaction because he feared an antisemitic backlash at home. He insisted in 1943 that no Jewish concern could come in the way of his sole true loyalty: "We are Americans first, last and at all times."[*] This was a far cry from Brandeis' erstwhile assertion, made in a less dramatic situation, that loyalty to the Jewish people and loyalty to America could go hand in hand. In his younger years, Wise was Brandeis's assistant, and maintained a life-long admiration for him, but he was no Brandeis.

From the day American airplanes had access to all of Europe's skies, the United States had the military means not necessarily to stop the *Shoah*, but to make its execution more difficult and thus save lives. If only that had been one of Roosevelt's war aims. It will never be known whether a more assertive, powerful, cunning Jewish leadership could have mitigated the greatest catastrophe in Jewish history since the Bar Kochba revolt of 135 CE, and could have rescued more of the doomed Jews, but it is clear that there was no Jewish statesman of the caliber of Nehemiah, and no advocate with the charisma and power of persuasion of Josel of Rosheim—there was no one of the caliber of these two, who had once impressed upon the most powerful rulers of their times the dangers threatening their people and who did receive their help. Nor was there an American leader with the moral and political stature of Louis Brandeis. In World War I the Jews had a few great leaders who knew how to respond to colossal challenges, and they prevailed. In World War II, the Jews had weak leaders who did not know how to respond to much more terrifying challenges, and they were overwhelmed and failed.

A failure of rabbinic foresight or leadership, already mentioned in Part IV, Chapter 1, added to the weakness of Jewish political leadership. Objective research on this subject is difficult, but the facts are slowly coming to light. In Eastern Europe, rabbinic opposition to emigration to British Palestine when the doors were still open, that is from 1919 to 1929, dissuaded many from leaving who could have survived had they departed. The rabbis did not anticipate the impending catastrophe any more than most lay leaders. Many of them were secluded from the world, had less access to information than lay leaders, and did not know or understand the politicians of their own countries or the world, in contrast to some of the famous rabbis of earlier centuries. They followed their religious instincts, which made them

---

[*] Saul Friedländer, *Nazi Germany and the Jews 1939-1945: The Years of Extermination* (New York: Harper Collins, 2007), 595. Other details about the inaction of Wise and in one case his opposition to sending food to Jewish Ghettoes appear on 85f., 304, 460ff. Friedländer criticizes Wise more severely than Laqueur does.

suspicious of Zionism as a non-religious movement with messianic overtones. Their attitude also betrayed a general unwillingness to face reality, and this unwillingness did not change even when the Nazi armies were knocking at the doors of one country after another, for example Lithuania in 1941 and Hungary in 1944.* Few could have expressed their despair about the failure of Jewish leadership more forcefully than Rabbi Joseph B. Soloveitchik, the Lithuanian-born rabbi who became a leader of American Orthodoxy: "We were witnesses to the greatest and most terrible catastrophe in our history and we were silent...this is a very sad and disturbing chapter in our history. But we all sinned by our silence in the face of the murder of millions...and when I say 'we' I mean all of us, myself included—rabbis and laymen, orthodox and freethinkers, the entire spectrum of Jewish political organizations."[49]

If there was a failure of Jewish political and religious leadership, the Free World's failure to confront the *Shoah* was even more troubling. There were few, if any leaders, comparable to King Artaxerxes I, of "gentle and noble spirit," to quote Plutarch again, or to Emperor Charles V, who were both sympathetic to Jews and determined to lend them a helping hand. The documents and private statements that have kept appearing since the end of World War II shed an ambiguous light on the attitudes and motives of many Allied and neutral leaders before and during it. One leader tried to help the Jews, and he was, after Roosevelt, the most important one: Winston Churchill. He was one of the staunchest friends the Jews had had in generations, but as leader of a parliamentary democracy he could not always impose his will even in war, or did not wish to impose his will because other priorities were more urgent. An exhaustive narrative of Churchill's life-long support of the Jews and Zionism

---

* In 1940, the legal doors to Israel were closed, but those to Shanghai were still wide open. In Lithuania, the Mizrahi leader Zerah Wahrhaftig urged the rabbinic leaders of all Talmud academies (yeshivot) to let their pupils flee Europe, but only the Mir Yeshiva followed his desperate pleas. All of the Mir pupils in Shanghai survived, while the other schools perished. See Chana Arnon, "Jews Rescuing Jews during the Holocaust: Zerah Wahrhaftig," www.yadvashem.org/education/conference2004/arnon. There is comparable evidence from Hungary: A brother of the Belzer Rebbe, one of Poland's hassidic leaders, having witnessed the annihilation of Poland's Jews succeeded in fleeing to Budapest and publicly assured the Jews of Hungary in January 1944 that they were likely to be spared. His speech was reprinted only days before the Nazi invasion of March 19, 1944. Fleeing Hungary in 1944 was extremely difficult but not impossible, as hiding in the villages and the countryside would have been possible, according to eyewitnesses. This issue is still controversial. What is not controversial is the fact that Hungary's Jews and their rabbis had no idea of what was ahead of them, while the Allies, the neutrals, the Catholic Church, the Red Cross, and the international Jewish organizations knew many of the details of the ongoing *Shoah*. For a Hungarian eyewitness report—one among many—see Menahem H.Schmelzer, "Personal Recollections," 1ff.

has revealed how often members of his cabinet and his military and diplomatic bureaucracy opposed, delayed, and subverted his pro-Jewish plans.*

The biographies of Nehemiah, Don Isaac Abrabanel, Josel of Rosheim, and Menasseh Ben Israel show some of the qualities and motives of great Jewish leaders of the past. They also identified historical contexts that from time to time brought exceptional personalities with a saving instinct to the fore. Jacob Burckhardt saw the emergence of great leaders as a response to great historical crises. Other scholars, too, look "beyond the big man" and see the "context" as a determinant in bringing the right leaders to power.[50] If these scholars are right, it remains unexplainable why this particular "context," the greatest crisis the Jewish people faced in 1900 years, failed to bring greater and more forceful personalities into leadership positions. Was lack of information the problem? In late 1941, a great variety of persons knew of the beginning extermination campaign: in the neutral countries Sweden and Switzerland, in British intelligence, in the Red Cross, in the Church, and elsewhere. It appears that Jewish leaders were less well connected and informed than is often assumed. Or was the *Shoah,* in the final analysis, a matter of enormous bad luck? Part IV, Chapter 11 will discuss fortune or chance events in Jewish history.

Today, Israel's leadership and governance conditions raise different questions. Some are similar to those of the Diaspora, but others are unique. One could argue that exceptional leadership qualities were necessary only as long as Jews had no political and military power. Hence, the personality of the leaders had to make up for severe objective weaknesses in previous eras. The continuous struggle for Israel's future leaves no doubt that national independence and political and military power are no replacement for good leadership. On the contrary, they call for more good leadership, because Israel's achievements are recent and still tenuous. A Jewish state will continue to raise open and concealed ideological and theological problems for a long time, in both the West and the Muslim world. The wish expressed by early Zionists that the future Jewish state should resemble Switzerland will not soon be fulfilled, for Switzerland never created theological problems.

There are no simple answers to the question of which political system will best facilitate the emergence of great leaders and prevent the ascendency of bad ones. One reason for this is that the appearance of exceptional leaders in politics, as in other fields, is partly a matter of luck. However, history can teach

---

* Martin Gilbert, *Churchill and the Jews: A Lifelong Friendship* (London: Henry Holt, 2008). One of many examples was Churchill's foreign secretary, Antony Eden. Eden had considerable discretionary powers to carry out or delay and thwart policies. In the diary of Eden's private secretary Oliver Harvey, Gilbert found a blunt entry dated 24.4.1943: "He loves Arabs and hates Jews," Gilbert, 190. Of the unloved Jews, three million or more had already perished when these words were written, and Eden was aware of it.

us a few things. A first conclusion can be drawn from the works of Edward Gibbon and Bernard Lewis.[51] It is of a general nature: when a civilization or people produces, for generations, only weak, demented, incompetent, or corrupt leaders, as was the case in the late Roman and Ottoman empires, something much deeper must have gone wrong, because these empires had produced outstanding leaders in earlier times. A second conclusion, which, it must be emphasized, is in no way derived from the first one, is that the current leadership situation in Israel and the Diaspora is a source of considerable concern. A third, cautionary observation is that Israel's history since 1948 is much too short for an objective and comprehensive evaluation of its leaders' performance. Some think that the most severe leadership problem of Israel and the Jewish people resides not in the non-availability of great personalities, but in their lack of desire and ability to reach and hold leadership positions, their capacity to govern. Israel's generally low quality of governance brings this into sharper focus.

The Bible and Talmud occasionally reveal an apprehension about the threat of anarchy hanging over Jewish history. This threat found an early and oft-quoted expression in the tale of a Jew in Egypt before the Exodus. When Moses reprimanded the man for beating another Jew, the man snapped back at him: "Who made you chief and ruler over us?"[52] Today, Israel's internal political fragmentation and the ensuing inefficiency and occasional paralysis of its government appears to be not the transformation of Jewish history that Zionism had promised to bring about, but as the "continuation of Jewish history by other means," to paraphrase Clausewitz.[53] The political scientist Aaron Wildavsky suggested that the political secret of Jewish longevity lies in the absence of any Jewish commitment to a single type of regime. According to Wildavsky, this absence helped the Jewish people to continuously adapt to varying circumstances.[54] It is true that the Jewish civilization and religion are not committed to any particular form of governance. However, the consequences of the absence of a Jewish state tradition for more than two thousand years are increasingly troubling today. The fourteenth-century Arab historian Ibn Khaldun was a well-read and not hostile student of the biblical history of the Jews, as far as he knew it from Jewish and Muslim sources. He wondered about the anarchic inclinations of the Jews of his times, and their inability to create and keep an effective government. He attributed this problem not to a lack of great leaders, as many like to do today, but to the basic character of the Jews themselves. His words are a warning that foreign friends and foes are drawing their own conclusions from internal Jewish governance problems: "Time after time, their royal authority was endangered....They opposed their own government and revolted against it. Thus they never had a continuous and firmly established royal authority. Eventually they were overpowered...."[55]

CHAPTER 6

Numbers and Critical Mass

General Observations

Numbers do count. Is there a critical population mass below which a civilization cannot rise but is doomed to decline? Anthropologists have described independent, functioning tribal civilizations of a few hundred persons, if not fewer, for example in the Amazon rain forest. Classical historians of rise and decline paid little or no attention to population numbers, partly because other factors were much more important to them, but also partly because such numbers were not easily available. In contrast, Fernand Braudel admired the work of the French demographer Alfred Sauvy and underscored the importance of demography.[1] Braudel noted that population increases and decreases often led to the rise and decline of a civilization, and that a large population increase not followed by an economic expansion could end badly.

A manpower surplus could also, as it has in China, make technological progress superfluous and, therefore, jeopardize innovation.[2] But this is a one-sided "structuralist" explanation of Chinese history. Max Weber, in contrast, wondered why China's enormous population growth from the seventeenth to the nineteenth century did not lead to more technological progress and innovation, as might have been expected. He saw some of the main obstacles as being Confucian traditions encouraging adaptation to the world, rather than adapting the world to the people, as was done in the Protestant West.[3]

Another author, Tainter, noted that the populations of the Roman and Mayan empires were shrinking as the civilizations declined,[4] but it is not certain whether population reductions came before decline, and thus were one of its causes, or whether they were the result of other deteriorating factors, after which general and population decline reinforced each other. China's population has oscillated for the last two thousand years in correlation with internal troubles and dynastic changes, but again cause and effect are not clear. If there is a critical population mass for the rise or decline of a civilization, the figure is likely to vary greatly according to external circumstances and the ambitions of the people concerned. In principle, large numbers do not in themselves guarantee the success of a civilization, and small numbers do not guarantee its decline: many other factors come into play. The number of members in a group can be quite small, as the case of the Parsees in India shows. The Parsees, though few, are certainly a living civilization, distinguished by a common history, religion, and language.

The Parsees are perceived in India as a very successful community politically, economically, and culturally. Yet they number only 300, 000 to 400,000 people, less than 0.03 percent of India's population. This is smaller by an order of magnitude than the percentage of Jews in the world population (0.2 percent and decreasing). One must add that the Parsees are at ease in multi-religious India. They have never had to defend their survival, but also have no ambition to be a global civilization. In spite of their small numbers, their continuity and influence in India does not seem to be threatened.

Russia is an interesting, but not yet conclusive, contemporary case in which to test possible correlations between population numbers and the rise or decline of a civilization. When Western observers discovered in the 1980s that the population of the European USSR had stagnated or declined while the population of the Asian republics increased, they predicted that troubles were ahead. For more than ten years after the breaking up of the USSR, Russia's population continued to shrink, a trend the Russian government regarded as a threat to Russia's long-term survival. One could ask whether population decrease was a major initial cause of the decline of the USSR and Russia or whether it was, alternatively, the consequence of deeper changes or policy mistakes.

To postulate that there is a "critical mass" raises questions about the links between quantity and quality that have interested historians, philosophers, demographers, and scientists. Can small numbers be made up for by higher quality, however defined, or does the link between quantity and quality work in the opposite direction? Marxism-Leninism supported the second proposition, that "quantity turns into quality," as a core precept of dialectical materialism. Whatever the links are, calculating the exact critical mass necessary to achieve a certain result is possible in physics and chemistry, but not in demography, because we do not know how to relate human numbers to quality and because quality has so many different definitions.

Applications to Jewish History

From the earliest days, demography has played a critical role in determining the history of the Jews and the shape, strength, and geographic spread of their civilization. While it was possible to forget this during the many centuries of diasporic history, the conflict between Israel and the Palestinians has brought the enormous strategic weight of demography to light once again. The "power of numbers" is not the only component of the Near East's strategic balance—far from it—but it is imperative to understanding the past, present, and possible future of the conflict.[5] The assertion that small numbers do not threaten the survival of a civilization, as demonstrated by the Parsees in India, cannot simply be applied to all of Jewish history. It has been and remains valid for some branches of the Jewish people and during some periods, but not generally.

Jewish reflection and concern about the number of Jews is as old as Judaism itself. No less than five times did the three biblical patriarchs, Abraham, Isaac, and Jacob, receive a divine promise that their progeny would be numerous, comparable to the stars in the sky, the sand on the sea shore, or the dust on the earth.[6] Talmudic commentators of the late twelfth or thirteenth centuries had a problem with these promises, particularly those made to Jacob. He gave Israel its name and is considered the ancestor solely of the people Israel, whereas Abraham's progeny also include the children of Ishmael, generally considered to mean the Arabs. As these commentators lived in Europe, they knew that the Jews were very few, and that their numbers had been further reduced not long before by the massacres the Crusaders had perpetrated against the Jewish population. The commentators explained that the divine promise was not meant literally or demographically but in a qualitative sense. They focused on the word "dust," noting, among other things, that the promise given to Jacob that his descendants would be like "dust" could only mean that Jews would always be present all over the world, like dust. Following older midrashic traditions, the commentators read it as a promise of Jewish ubiquity and permanence, not of large numbers.[7] The biblical text itself has Moses convey, toward the end of his life, a more sobering message than the promise the patriarchs had received. They were chosen "not because you are more numerous than all of the peoples...for you are the fewest of all the peoples."[8] The tradition knew early on that numbers were not everything, and that the power of numbers depended critically on the strength of Jewish identity.

Biblical narratives and Jewish laws reveal an enormous concern about the erosion of identity. Identity was less precarious in medieval times, but it was certainly a serious problem during the biblical period and in late Antiquity. When rabbinic sources[9] tell us that only a fifth of the Jews followed Moses and left Egypt, they may have been thinking of more recent historical events than those of the Exodus. A dramatic example dates to 1492-1496, when a majority of Jews facing the Catholic king's expulsion orders did not leave Spain and Portugal but converted to Christianity instead.

No demographic definition of critical mass, in relative or absolute numbers, can be valid for all times and conditions; critical mass means various things at various times. Four different requirements of Jewish civilization that can be translated into policy goals depend upon critical mass:

— Defense and physical survival;
— Numerical majority in the homeland;
— Cultural and religious creativity; and
— Political influence and power.

Critical mass varied according to needs that kept changing between periods and places. Not all periods and branches of the Jewish people had to pursue all four goals at the same time. There were differences between periods of independence and dependence, and differences according to the territorial distribution of the Jewish people. The territorial history of the Jews can be broken down into five periods. Other periodizations are possible, but this one is useful in highlighting some of the broader implications of population numbers:

A. Mono-territorial Civilization Centered in Israel (Ca. Twelfth-Eighth Centuries BCE)

From the beginnings of Israelite history until the destruction of the Northern Kingdom by the Assyrians in 722 BCE and then the destruction of the First Temple in Jerusalem by the Babylonians in 586 BCE, nearly all the members of the Israelite/Jewish people have lived together in the same territory. We can speak, thus, of a mono-territorial civilization. The most critical quantitative problem of these four centuries was the capacity to defeat external enemies. Their numbers, together with other assets, were sufficient to defeat the Philistines and Canaanites, but insufficient to withstand the much more powerful Assyrians and Babylonians. In the eighth century BCE Israel was, like all other Near Eastern kingdoms, too small to stem the Assyrian expansion alone. This is why King Ahab of Israel helped to forge an alliance of twelve Near-Eastern kings, who met the Assyrian king Shalmaneser III in 853 BCE in the battle of Qarqar (also see Part IV, Chapter 9). Together they stopped the Assyrian advance, at least temporarily. A detailed Assyrian report of this battle mentioned the chariot force of Israel as the largest of all, including 2,000 chariots.[10] The historian Nadav Na'aman rejects this figure as materially impossible, the result of a writing error. He regards 200 as a more likely figure, which would have made it one of the smallest contributions.[11] Naaman seems to assume that Israel's demographic strength was already quite modest before the foreign conquests and deportations. How small numbers affected religious and spiritual development can no longer be evaluated.

B. Multi-territorial Civilization Centered in Israel/Judah and Several Diasporas (Eighth Century BCE-135 CE)

Following the destruction of the Kingdoms of Israel and Judah by the Assyrians and Babylonians in 722 and 586 BCE respectively, a more or less substantial part of the Jewish people continued to live in the ancient homeland until it was destroyed by the Romans in 70 and 135 CE. For 800 to 900 years, Judaism was a multi-territorial civilization centered in Israel/Judah and several Diasporas. For this as well as later periods, we use the term "multi-territorial" and not "non-territorial" to describe the conditions of Diaspora Jews. Most of them lived together in the same provinces, cities, city quarters, and villages, and thus did often not always feel like a minority among foreigners, but rather, in a certain sense, like a majority. Within this long timespan, demographic conditions and needs varied in three different periods:

a. Period of Assyrian and Babylonian Expansion Eighth Century BCE— 586 BCE: Diasporas were appearing from the eighth Century BCE on, probably even before the destruction of the Kingdom of Israel in 722 BCE. We do not know how large their populations were. The prophets who appeared between the eighth and sixth centuries, some of whom were themselves exiled, attached great importance to the Diaspora issue and referred to "the strayed who are in the land of Assyria and the expelled who are in the land of Egypt,"[12] or to those "who are coming from afar, these from the North and the West, and these from the land of Sinim (southern Egypt)."[13] Whatever the population numbers, this period was one of spiritual creativity. Important parts of the biblical texts, including some of the books of the great prophets, date to this time.

b. Period of Persian Rule 586 BCE—332 BCE: During the Persian period, from the beginning of the Babylonian Exile to the destruction of the Persian Empire by Alexander the Great and his conquest of the land of Israel in 332 BCE, Jewish population numbers were irrelevant for external defense. It was the Persian Empire that governed but also protected the Jewish people both in Judah and in Babylon. This model of foreign protection would recur in Jewish history. It is a comfortable solution despite the danger of keeping Jews in a situation of dependence.

Elias Bickerman has said that only Persian protection saved Judah from being swept over by the never-ending waves of Arab nomads streaming out of Arabia. The flood would have swallowed the country, and "the rock of Zion would have been the foundation of an Arab sanctuary a thousand years before Omar's mosque."[14] However, in the decades following the destruction of the First Temple, the preservation of a numeric majority of Jews in their homeland became a problem. The partial devastation of the country by the Babylonians and the deportation of important sectors of the Jewish population encouraged other population groups, including Arab tribes, to infiltrate and settle in the country over the following seventy years.

When the Jews were freed by King Cyrus and began to return, the new inhabitants met them with violent opposition, as we know from Nehemiah. The main quandary of twentieth-century Zionism, its clash with a hostile, native population, has an old prehistory, and Israel's current concerns about a potentially unfriendly Arab minority have antecedents that go back more than 2,500 years. In the later periods of Persian rule, Jewish population numbers in the land of Israel began to increase considerably.[15] At the same time, the two and a half centuries of Persian rule following the destruction of the First Temple were among the most religiously and culturally creative in all of Jewish history. These were centuries of major transformation. The Babylonian Diaspora was, for a certain period, the main source of creativity: some of the greatest prophets, such as Ezra and Nehemiah, were in Babylon. It is possible that during these centuries Jewish Diaspora numbers had political weight for the first time in history—this would be the fourth policy goal of demography mentioned above. The historian Salo W. Baron believes—perhaps influenced by the American experience of his own time—that demography did indeed play a major role in supporting Jewish political influence in the Persian Empire, and that the Persian kings took great personal interest in Jewish affairs because the growing Jewish Diaspora had become an important element in their population.[16] He provides no corroborating data from Persian or any other sources, as would become available from later Roman sources for the Jews of the Roman Empire. The story of Nehemiah, the "cup-bearer" of King Artaxerxes I, shows that at least one Jew, and probably Ezra and a few others too, had an influential presence at the Persian court. In an autocratic and hierarchical system, the quality of one near to the throne could easily replace the quantity of many farther away.

c. Period of Ptolemaic-Seleucid and Roman Rule 332 BCE-70/135 CE: The salient demographic factor of the first half of this period was the continuation of the Jewish population growth in the land of Israel that had begun under the Persians. This was essential for the future, as under Seleucid rule the number of Hellenistic settlers also kept increasing. Jewish population growth was critical, because it gave the Hasmoneans the military manpower they needed to confront Seleucid rule after 167 BCE.[17] Following their victory, Hasmonean rulers increased Jewish numerical strength further by forcing non-Jews in newly-conquered territories to convert to Judaism. This, as far as is known, is the only historically documented case of forced collective Judaization in history. The ideological justification of the Hasmoneans was not, of course, demographic. The main reason they put forward was that they wished to prevent idolatry from profaning the sanctity of the land of Israel. Although the Jews had sufficient mass for the Hasmonean wars against the Seleucid Empire, their mass was insufficient for the later wars against the Roman Empire, all of which they lost. This does not mean that the Jews were a numerically insignificant people, but their total number in the Roman Empire, whatever it may have been, did not amount to a critical mass militarily because geographic separation, lack of communication, and different political outlooks* made the creation of a single, unified force impossible. However, there was intense religious and cultural communication, and competition too, between the main centers of Jewish life, particularly Judea and Babylon. Numbers were apparently sufficient for religious and cultural creativity. General Jewish population numbers in the Roman Empire began to have political weight during this period, and in this case non-Jewish sources corroborate the influence of Jewish numbers. Jews were so numerous in Rome that their interests could not be ignored, as Roman rulers from Julius Caesar on knew. The anti-Jewish politician Cicero (106–43 BCE), complained that it took great courage "to defy the crowd of the Jews" because they were present everywhere and very powerful**—a revealing protest that has remained a staple of antisemitic propaganda to this day.

C. Multi-territorial Diaspora Civilization (70/135—ca. 1800 CE)

During this time, the Jews were without a homeland for the longest uninterrupted period in their history, and became a multi-territorial diasporic civilization. Wherever they settled in the world, most of them lived in close territorial proximity to and in daily interaction with each other. Regular discussions and interactions between Jewish communities, often residing in different countries, brought considerable cultural and economic benefits (for a discussion of the economic benefits, see Part IV, Chapter 7). With few exceptions, the issue of Jewish self-defense, and the population numbers required for it, no longer arose. If the Christian and Muslim powers did not protect the Jews, their numbers and territorial concentration was of little help to them. However, this territoriality, albeit a territoriality split into different geographic branches, was an essential condition of achieving and maintaining sufficient mass for cultural-religious creativity and political influence. Although it is not possible to quantify this critical mass, one thought-provoking observation of Fernand Braudel (II, 11) should be quoted. He speaks

---

* The Jews of Rome and Italy are not known to have moved or protested in any way while the Romans besieged and destroyed Jerusalem.

** Goodman, 389. Cicero said this as a defense attorney in a process against Flaccus in 59 BCE. Some historians argue that his comments were only rhetorical and meant to impress the judges, but not "antisemitic" in a modern sense. However, current antisemitic internet compendia of famous Jews-haters keep quoting Cicero's words.

of the number of Jews in the seventeenth century, which he identifies like J. Israel (II, 14) as a period of cultural, economic, and political improvement for Jews. They formed the leading commercial network in the world, but their numbers were very small even in some of the most important cities, although it must be added that there were many smaller Jewish settlements in the surrounding villages which were linked to the city communities. In 1586, there were only 1,424 Jews in Venice, and a few years later there were barely 100 in Hamburg, and 2,000 at best in Amsterdam. It is often in the smaller Jewish population centers that the richest Jews could be found. All of these Jewish centers were closely connected. They were linked by education and beliefs, by an unending stream of travelers—including rabbis, merchants, and beggars—and by a continuous flow of rabbinic, business, family, and friendship correspondence. Printed Jewish books played an equally important role in Jewish cohesion. According to Braudel, the numerical basis of Jewish economic power in the seventeenth century was very small.[18]

There was, long before the sixteenth century, great intellectual and religious creativity even when numbers were small. From the eleventh to the thirteenth century, the Jewish communities of Speyer, Mainz, and Worms were very small but became, together with a few places in France, the most important centers of learning in the whole Jewish world, replacing the much larger communities in Babylon. The Jewish community of twelfth-century Worms, with no more than a few hundred members but with several dozen large families, constituted a cultural critical mass, because among them were several scholars who left a lasting religious impact and also because these Jews lived, talked, prayed, and learned together. The much larger community in late-nineteenth-century Worms was not, from a Jewish perspective, of sufficient mass, and left no intellectual or cultural impact because it had few, if any, known scholars or other culturally creative persons.

Medieval history casts doubts on modern assumptions that Jewish social cohesion and community sustainability is directly dependent on population numbers. Such assumptions imply that the cohesion and sustainability of a community weakens when its numbers decrease and strengthens when they rise. There is a link between sustainability and population numbers, but it is not a simple causal relationship except, of course, in cases when numbers become so small that there are not enough people to fulfill the most basic community functions. Other factors play a role as well. As many smaller Jewish European communities have noted in the last decades, a decline in sustainability is not only a problem of quantity. It is, even more, a quality problem, the result of the best-educated and most dynamic young people drifting away or emigrating, particularly to Israel.

Did pre-nineteenth-century Jewish Diaspora numbers have the political weight to improve the Jewish condition? It is possible that in ancient Babylonia, where a large Jewish population lived at least until the Arab invasion and possibly even later, quantity bestowed political and socio-economic power upon the Jews. It was different in Europe. In Spain before the expulsion of 1492, some estimates say that Jews represented up to ten percent of the total population. Christian Spain certainly felt and evidently resented the weight of Jewish numbers, and this was one of the main reasons for Spanish religious and economic antisemitism. Numbers became a burden. When the expulsion order was issued, their numbers could not save the Jews.

D. Non-Territorial Diaspora Civilization (Ca. 1800-1948)

With the beginning of the Enlightenment, the opening of the ghettoes, and the slow abolition of other restrictions, the Jews became a truly non-territorial civilization, at least in Western Europe and America. In Russia, Poland, and the Muslim world, this process was much slower. This new non-territoriality went hand in hand with political, economic, and cultural freedom and the possibility of nearly full interaction with the non-Jewish world, but along the way the Jews lost some of the advantages of close cultural interactions with other Jews—which had been the main cultural benefit of even a small "critical mass" in the past.

Looking at the means for self-defense in the Diaspora, Jewish history prior to 1945, at least in Europe, shows that greater numbers did not confer greater security or decisive political influence and power, even in countries with large numbers of Jews such as Poland, the Baltic states, Romania, and Hungary. The Jews of these countries constituted between seven and twelve percent of the total population, with the same results as were experienced by the Jews of Spain. Numbers increased antisemitism rather than Jewish power and influence, except for a short period in the economy and academia of some of these countries, for example Hungary. But then, these countries were not truly democratic and egalitarian, or were only nominally so, for much of that time; some pursued policies of anti-Jewish exclusion and discrimination. The situation was different in democratic countries, particularly in the United States, where the number of Jews began to swell from the late nineteenth century on. In this case, the increasing population did confer political influence.

In 1939, the 16-17 million Jews, of which approximately 8-9 million lived in Europe, represented 0.7 percent of the world's population, but rarely in history have the Jews been more helpless in the face of mortal danger. In contrast, when Israel was created in May 1948, 660,000 poorly armed Jews comprised a sufficient critical mass to defend themselves, albeit just narrowly, against a general Arab onslaught, ensuring victory and causing a radical change in Jewish and world history. Today, Jews represent only 0.2 percent of the world's population, but they are incommensurately more powerful and no less culturally influential than when they comprised 0.7 percent. At the beginning of the twentieth century, when Russian Jews, numbering five million, suffered under the tsar, they were completely powerless and barely able to protect their lives. Today the Russian Jews number fewer than 300,000, but they have more rights, freedoms, and influence than their great-grandparents could ever have dreamed of. As to cultural influence, one can say that after 1800 the Jewish contributions in all cultural fields expanded exponentially, widely beyond Jewish population numbers. Numbers were apparently not a limiting factor for this cultural creativity. Against this optimistic presentation of contemporary Jewish influence one should hold a virtual and more tragic picture of what Jewish numbers would have been today had the *Shoah* not occurred. The demographer Sergio DellaPergola has made these calculations, taking into account the relatively young population structure of the destroyed European Jewry, and the statistically predictable long-term effects of their fertility trends before 1939. He arrived at a likely global Jewish population number of between 26 and 32 million in 2000, instead of the actual 13 million.[19] A Jewish people of this size would be radically different in its geographic distribution, its political, religious, and cultural outlook, and its relations with the world. Even our discussion of the meaning and size of "critical mass" in Jewish history would be different.

E. Multi-Territorial Civilization Centered on Israel and Diaspora Communities (Since 1948)

The foundation of the State of Israel has radically modified the demographic conditions of Jewish history. Jewish civilization is again split into two different territorial parts, a mono-territorial part, Israel, and a non-territorial one, Jewish communities spread all over the world. For the first time since the Second Temple period the Jews of Israel must have sufficient critical mass to achieve all four goals together: defense, numerical majority, creativity, and political influence. Israel's present security links with the United States may have vague parallels with the protection that the Jews of Judah under Nehemiah and his followers received from the Persian Empire, but today Israel's own contribution to its defense is paramount and more indispensable. This was not the case in the late fifth and fourth centuries BCE, when Persia was the uncontested master of the Middle East.

In contrast to the Jews of Israel, Diaspora Jews strive for and achieve cultural creativity and some political influence, but they leave defense to their countries of residence. In addition, in some of the countries of the Diaspora—the United States, France, and the United Kingdom, for example—the Jews have been able to translate, by democratic means, their demographic numbers into political influence. In the United States this influence is considerable and can have important impacts on domestic and foreign policy. Perhaps for the first time since ancient Rome, Jewish numbers in a few Diaspora countries do count politically. But the steady relative decrease of Jewish population numbers risks jeopardizing this influence in both the medium- and the long-term. In many Western countries, Jews are watching the confluence of a decreasing Jewish vote and a quickly-growing Muslim vote with apprehension.

Today's demographic challenges differ from those of pre-Enlightenment times. "Demography and population cannot be confined to numbers of people, but must be meaningfully related to cultural contents and identities."[20] It is the intensity and quality of group identification that determines Jewish marriage and family-size patterns, and hence demography. In the Diaspora, this quality determines Jewish community participation and sustainability. The Jewish people's demographic challenges in Israel are different from those of the Diaspora. The demographic requirement of maintaining a clear and undisputed Jewish majority in Israel, as the core state of the Jewish people, is a critical problem. There is a numerical threshold under which the percentage of Jews in Israel should not sink. The exact figure will depend on other variables. Apart from this overriding problem, Israel faces "critical mass" issues in many specific sectors. It must maintain an army, develop an advanced economy, and provide numerous services. The main challenge for the Diaspora is the preservation of sustainable Jewish communities with social cohesion and cultural-spiritual significance, which, as said, is not solely a numerical problem. Policy makers watch the continuous shrinking of overall Diaspora numbers with concern, because they see it as a symptom of weakness and decline. The Jews maintain real political influence in some countries, and an economic, religious, or cultural presence in many. The question is how they can maintain their presence and influence with decreasing numbers. For the time being, concerns are less about the risk of cultural decline and more the fear that political influence could be eroded.

Policy measures can address the demographic challenges. It is important to raise public awareness of the crucial importance of sound population policies for the future of the Jewish people, and to create in Israel a centralized, high-level governmental body meant to design and implement a comprehensive demographic policy.

CHAPTER 7

Economic Foundations of
Long-Lasting Civilizations[*]

General Observations

The belief that economics is an autonomous factor of history, a driver of other factors, belongs to modern times. This is why mainstream historians, from Thucydides to Burckhardt in the nineteenth century, paid so little attention to the economy. Beginnings of a distinct economic theory and policy emerged with mercantilism in the sixteenth and seventeenth centuries, when Europe's newly forming nations and their rulers discovered that the economy was an instrument of national and state power. The nineteenth century brought profound change. The Industrial Revolution, which had begun in the late eighteenth century, was setting into motion powerful and apparently independent and irresistible economic forces, which were about to change the world completely.

One could say that 1800 was a watershed year in world economic history. Economic history has two main periods, one before and one after 1800. The most penetrating observer of the Industrial Revolution and its painful social consequences was Karl Marx. His work, too, became a watershed, leading to a far-reaching reconsideration of history and lasting changes in historiography. Marx stated that it was the economy, or more precisely the forces of production and the social classes that owned them, that explained the history of all ages. No economic theory and no philosophy of history has ever had more immediate and deeper political and intellectual impacts.

Many of the historians underpinning this study rejected Marx's main doctrines, particularly the materialist explanation of history. Max Weber did so,[1] and so, explicitly or implicitly, did Oswald Spengler, Johan Huizinga, Arnold Toynbee, and Pitirim Sorokin. None of them saw the economy as

* Prof. Nahum Gross, Hebrew University of Jerusalem, has graciously provided the references to many of the sources used in this chapter and has provided very valuable advice.

a decisive driver of flourishing civilizations, but Spengler had insights into this (as well as into other domains) that were decades ahead of his time: "The entire global economy is since the invention of the steam engine the creation of a very small number of outstanding brains. Without their first-rate effort there would be nothing. Their accomplishment is not one of 'quantity' but of creative thought."[2] Whether these historians mentioned Marx or not, they could not ignore him or deny that they were inspired by the fundamental questions he raised. For others, these questions were an essential component of their own approach to history. Bernard Lewis identified the economic factors that contributed decisively to the decline of the Ottoman Empire,[3] and Jonathan Israel identified those that contributed—no less decisively—to the rise of the Dutch Republic.[4] B. Ward-Perkins argued that the fall of the Western Roman Empire could only be explained by understanding the fatal economic and financial repercussions of the external shocks to which the empire was subjected.[5] Gibbon could not see these links in his time. Fernand Braudel is, of our historians, the most significant defender of the thesis that the economy is a decisive element of every civilization. He is also the only one of this group to reflect on the long-term economic basis of Jewish civilization, and he identified seventeenth-century international Jewish entrepreneurship and trade networks as this basis, at least in the Mediterranean region.[6]

Applications to Jewish History

The main Jewish historians of the nineteenth and early twentieth centuries did not ascribe to economics the importance it deserved. In the 1910s and 1920s, the two most influential scholarly books on Jewish economic history were not written by Jewish historians but German sociologists, Max Weber and Werner Sombart. Heinrich Graetz's great work contains little about Jewish economic history, in line with nineteenth-century historiography. He wanted to position the Jews as a spiritual nation, and their history as driven by their own religious ideals or by foreign oppression. This does not mean that Jewish economics did not interest nineteenth-century Europe; rather, it means that what was written about this subject was sometimes antisemitic. One memorable example is the pamphlet *On the Jewish Question*, which Karl Marx published in 1844 at the age of twenty-six. There he lampooned the Jews as "hucksters and moneygrubbers," and their religion as the faith of moneygrubbing. It is ironic that Karl Marx and Heinrich Graetz knew each other, were on friendly terms, and exchanged letters. Marx's early defamatory paper, along with similar ones by other scholars, did not, apparently, encourage more serious Jewish scholarship on economic history.* Salo W. Baron was the first scholar to write a voluminous Jewish world history, in which the economy is treated as a central pillar of Jewish life, but that wasn't until the mid-twentieth century.[7]

There can be little doubt that the economy was an important factor in the history of the Jews. Some of their history cannot be fully understood without knowing its economic background. This study does not intend to develop a new "grand theory" of Jewish economic history; doubts about "grand theories," however, must not lead one to the opposite extreme. The American scholar Rabbi Jacob Neusner attacked "this mish-mash they call 'Jewish economic history,' a subdivision of the equally fictive 'Jewish history.'"[8] The path between grand theory and "mish-mash" is narrow. We shall try to walk it cautiously, by presenting five different case studies. The aim is to discuss links between economic activity and the rise or decline of Jewish civilizations in specific periods, and then to look for possible commonalities between the Jewish economic activities of these periods.

We follow a lead by the economist Simon Kuznets, who suggested in a now-classic 1960 publication that there are "common, repeatedly observed features" in Jewish economic history, and a "historical continuity."[9] The selected case studies are success stories. Until the twentieth century, such stories were more the exception than the rule. They do not represent the average economic conditions of Jews during most of their history, but the less frequent periods of economic prosperity.

Case A: Jews as Urban Pioneers North of the Alps between the Ninth and Eleventh Centuries[10]

Jews lived along the Rhine and Mosel rivers in the Germanic provinces of the Roman Empire by the early fourth century. There was a well-established Jewish community in Cologne whose elite was asked by Constantine the Great

---

* Many later Jewish historians, political thinkers, and leaders were Marxists, communists, or Marxist Zionists. Some tried to force Jewish history into Marxist thought models, such as the class struggle, the exploitation of the proletariat by the ruling bourgeoisie, etc. A moderate example is Raphael Mahler (1899-1977), who was strongly influenced by Ber Borochov, the chief ideologue of the Socialist Zionist *Poalei Zion* movement in Eastern Europe. Mahler wrote a Hebrew *Chronicles of Israel in the last Generations* (Tel Aviv: Ha-Kibuts ha-Meuhad, 1976), partly translated into English, that is little known today. He described the *Shoah* in the spirit of the Communist ideology of the time: "With the victory of the 1917 socialist revolution in Russia, a wave of reaction swept over the capitalist world, which reached its peak during the years when fascism and Nazism were strengthening their hold on Europe.... This is the most terrible assault in our history, directed against the heart of the new socialist regime, inundating the working class with a bloody terror, and inflicting on the Jewish people calamities the like of which have never, to this day, been recorded in the annals of its suffering." see Mahler, 18.

in 321 CE to take part in the municipal government. Such new responsibilities obliged the Jews to pay taxes, which was probably Constantine's main goal. We know virtually nothing about the Jews in these provinces during the following four centuries, the "Dark Ages." For the ninth century and later, recent historical research has revealed a more precise picture of Jewish life spreading along the great river valleys and trading routes of southern and southeast Germany, and even further east. This picture is very different from the popular image of the "vale of tears," which described Diaspora history as an endless sequence of persecutions. Trade was indispensable for economic growth and development, and Jews were known to be unmatched in trading skills and connections. This is why the Carolingian and Ottonian emperors offered the Jews special charters allowing them to settle in the Rhine Valley as merchants and traders. The Jews were free and had, along with the nobility and other freemen, the right to carry weapons. They enjoyed important competitive advantages: international communal networks, language skills, and religious neutrality in an age of continuous confrontation between Islam and Christendom.

Trading was their main role, and they were widely known for their abilities in that field. Their activities regularly brought them to Baghdad and further east. In 797 CE, Emperor Charlemagne sent an ambassadorial mission to the Khalif Harun Al-Rashid in Baghdad. It is no coincidence that he appointed a Jewish trader, Isaac—apparently a rich man and possibly a community leader—as their guide and interpreter. The ambassadors died in Baghdad, but in 802 Isaac returned to Charlemagne's court in Aachen with a white elephant named Abul-Abbas, Harun Al-Rashid's gift for the great Emperor of the West, in tow. The story must have been famous in its time: Charlemagne's chronicler wrote a detailed and lively record of the extraordinary peregrination of Isaac and Abul-Abbas.* This colorful Jewish long-distance trader has recently re-emerged in European memory, after 1200 years.[11]

Babylonian Jews under the Muslims, and the Jews under the kings of the Franks and later the Carolingian Empire, were linked not only by long-distance trade but also by scholar exchanges. Charlemagne's Isaac was not known as a scholar, but Rabbi Makhir of Narbonne was. Makhir was Babylonian and,

---

* *Annales Regni Francorum ab a. 741 usque a. 829 (Records of the Kingdom of the Franks from year 741 to 829)*, Internet edition. This story is truly the stuff of fairy tales. Isaac and Abul-Abbas walked from Baghdad to Jerusalem, and from there to Kairouan, travelled by ship to Italy and then walked all the way to Aachen. Abul-Abbas lived several more years at Charlemagne's court, went once to war with the Emperor, and seems to have died after taking a bath in the Rhine. An entry for the year 801 reports: "In October of this year the Jew Isaac was back from Africa with his elephant and entered Portum Veneris (Porto Venere at the Ligurian coast). However, due to the snow he could not cross the Alps and stayed through the winter in Vercelli." DCCCI, VII. Transl. by the author.

perhaps, a former exilarch of the Jews of Babylon. Later in the eighth century, he became the leader of the Jewish community of Narbonne in Gaul and is credited with founding the then-famous Talmud academy of Narbonne, which attracted many foreign students. A nineteenth-century edition of Ibn Daud's (1110-1180) book on Jewish history reports that Harun al-Rashid chose to send Makhir to Europe in response to Charlemagne's request for a reputed Jewish scholar.* Other sources date Makhir's arrival to the time of King Pepin of the Franks, Charlemagne's father. Apparently Pepin wanted to enlist Jewish help for his efforts to destroy the Umayad Saracens who occupied Narbonne. Whatever the geopolitical reasons, it is not farfetched to assume links between Jewish trading contacts, wealth, and scholarly exchanges. It is quite unlikely that Pepin or Charlemagne, whatever their affinity for the Jews, funded the immigration of Jewish scholars or the foundation of Talmud schools with their own revenues. That money was Jewish.

The Jews traded in high value/low volume items that were easily transportable: silk, spices, incense for church services (which was available only in Yemen), and slaves.** Until the First Crusade (1096), the Jews' privileged social status was largely unchallenged, although there were a few outbreaks of violence against them. Their economic standing was on average substantially higher than that of the local farming population. Their material culture was comparable to that of the nobility and the high clergy. From the ninth century to the twelfth, Europe's climate was much warmer than it was in later centuries, which greatly boosted agricultural productivity and population growth. To accommodate this rapidly increasing population, some 120,000 new villages and cities were founded, and in a number of proven cases Jews were brought in as urban pioneers. In Speyer and Freiburg in southern Germany, in Bern and Fribourg in what is today Switzerland, and in many other cities, Jews

---

* "Then King Charles sent to the King of Baghdad requesting that he dispatch one of his Jews of the seed of royalty of the House of David. He hearkened and sent him one from there, a magnate and sage, Rabbi Makhir by name. And [Charles] settled him in Narbonne...." This quote is from Abraham Ibn Daud's *Seder Ha'chachamim Ve' Korot Ha'itim (Chronicle of Sages and Periods)*, ed. Neubauer (Oxford: Clarendon, 1887), 82. Gerson D. Cohen's edited and annotated Ibn Daud text is regarded as the most authoritative one. Cohen deleted this story, because he found it to be part of a later addition not written by Ibn Daud. The story is quoted here because it reflects old reminiscences about a Jewish dimension in the relationship between the two emperors.

** Today, slave-trading causes justified revulsion. However, this practice of the ninth and tenth century must be seen in the context of its time, not in the context of the horrific transatlantic mass trade of African slaves in much later times. Early Christian Europe regarded this trade as acceptable as long as the slaves were not Christians. As far as is known the slaves were exclusively white Europeans, mainly from the pagan regions in Northern and Eastern Europe, and Jews were certainly not the only slave-traders. Toch, 6, 96 ff. asserts that the Jewish role in early Medieval slave trade has been greatly exaggerated.

formed communities that were autonomous under talmudic and rabbinic law. Some historians believe that it was this model of Jewish self-government that was later emulated by the self-governing city communes created by merchants and craftsmen in the thirteenth and fourteenth centuries.

There was thus a solid urban basis and growing economic wealth that supported the emergence of vibrant centers of Jewish learning in the Rhineland and France.[12] Jewish scholarship before and even after the Crusades was enhanced by economic prosperity. In the tenth and eleventh centuries, "an aristocracy of scholars and wholesale traders"[13] ruled Judaism north of the Alps. For five generations the most important intellectual figures came from no more than seven socio-economically connected families that consolidated their wealth through marriage to one another. Spiritual authority, political leadership, and economic power were concentrated in the same hands. Thus began the rise of Ashkenazi Judaism.

Case B: Jews as Long-Distance Traders in the Mediterranean and China between the Tenth and the Twelfth Centuries: "Maghribis" and "Rhadanites"

In the tenth and eleventh centuries, when Jews north of the Alps were merchants and urban pioneers, Jews in the Muslim world, where 80 to 90 percent of all Jews lived, developed partly similar skills. Long-distance trading played an extremely important role there, as it did for the Jews north of the Alps, but Jews under Islam were also farmers, artisans, and craftsmen. Some worked in highly skilled professions such as medicine. A large number entered the money trade, with all its ramifications and without coercion, many centuries before European Jews were forced to do so. This field included banking, money transfers, and the minting of coins more than money lending, which would later become prevalent in Europe. Nevertheless, the role of the traders was particularly significant for several reasons, some of them cultural. One example allows us to understand the competitive advantages of the Jews more generally.

The "Maghribis" were a group of Jewish traders and business entrepreneurs who in the tenth century had emigrated from the surroundings of Baghdad to Tunis. From there they and their descendants had spread across the entire Muslim Mediterranean region. Maghribis resided and traded in the land of Israel, Lebanon, Egypt, Muslim Sicily, North Africa and Spain. About a thousand *genizah* documents from the old Cairo synagogue and many rabbinic *responsa* have allowed historians of economics to reconstruct a detailed picture of Maghribi organization and power. This research shows what the often-mentioned but vague notion of "Jewish networking" or "Jewish solidarity" meant in practice, and how it worked in a specific case.[14] Before the advent of modern information and communication channels and effective international enforcement mechanisms, long-distance trading was a lucrative, albeit very risky, venture. The key problem for long-distance traders, apart from the considerable physical dangers, was how to ensure the honesty of business partners to whom cargos had to be shipped over long distances. How could one exercise control and demand remedy when a partner hundreds or thousands of miles away was suspected to have cheated? Without certain guarantees, no long-distance commerce was possible. The absence of effective government power beyond local borders forced the Maghribis to develop original forms of self-organization, control, and coercion based on Jewish cultural habits and religious laws. The Maghribis formed a traders' coalition somewhat similar to later European merchants' guilds. The Maghribi traders and their overseas agents, all of them Jews, were members of the coalition and sworn to mutual solidarity and honesty. When a member was found cheating, a boycott could be called. All members would break off relations with him, refuse to pay their debts to him, and refuse to deliver wares they owed him. Maghribis only traded with other Maghribis. They had no other business relations, not even with the increasingly important Jewish merchants in Italy. The Maghribis communicated by a steady stream of letters, written in a sophisticated Hebrew, in which they discussed complicated economic transactions and calculations. The rulers of twelfth-century Egypt dissolved the Maghribi coalition because they wanted control over Mediterranean trade.

This did not put an end to the flourishing Jewish networks, however. The historian Shlomo Goitein found that a large proportion of the Jews in the wider Middle East was involved in international trade after the eleventh century, for example trade between Spain, Egypt and India.[15] As long-distance merchants needed permanent representatives at the courts of many local rulers and protection against the ubiquitous robbers and pirates, they could only function in close, trustful cooperation with other Jewish merchants.

All of these trading networks were of more than simply economic importance, and certainly extended beyond the local level for the Jewish people under Muslim rule. The networks had a vital cultural role. Some of the traders were also religious leaders of Jewish communities: "Being a scholar and being a merchant was often the same thing among the most educated Jews,"[16] which was not so different from the European situation described above. Maghribis and other traders were indispensable for long-distance communication between Jewish communities and scholars. It is these traders who carried written religious questions from all over the world to the Talmud academies in Babylonia and brought the rabbinic *responsa* back to the questioners. Jewish traders from France and Byzantium frequently visited Egypt, not only to buy merchandise but also to buy books and get answers to religious questions. At least one Egyptian long-distance trader merits everlasting fame for his indirect but still enormous contribution to Jewish history and scholarship: David Ben Maimon, or David Maimonides, the younger sibling of Moses Maimonides (the Rambam). David supported his brother for eight full years, allowing him to devote all of his time during his best years to study and writing. Had David not been so wealthy, generous, and aware of his brother's exceptional genius we might not have Maimonides' work today, or might have only a small fraction of it. David traded in precious stones and perished at sea on one of his dangerous travels to India, leaving Maimonides heart-broken. His despair stopped him from working for a full year.

In this era, Jews maintained trading relations widely, even beyond India. A particular story with parallels to the Maghribis and the European long-distance traders is that of the "Rhadanites" of the ninth and tenth centuries. The Rhadanites were groups of Jewish long-distance traders perhaps linked by family bonds. Some suggest that their origin was in Babylonia, while others have related their name to the Rhône River (Rodanus in Latin) in southern France, where there were early Jewish settlements. The most detailed and reliable source for the Rhadanites is in a text by the mid-ninth-century Arab official and traveller Ibn Khordadbeh, whom his contemporaries called the "post-master of Baghdad." He was responsible for mail delivery in the Abbasside Empire, and had extensive and precise geographic and ethnographic knowledge of all parts of the empire. When he described these Jewish traders, he noted first their impressive language fluency: "They speak Arabic, Persian, Greek, Frankish, Andalusian and Slavic, and they travel from the East to the West and from the West to the East, by land and by sea. From the West they carry servants, slave girls, slave boys, brocade, beaver skins, furs, sable and swords....From China they bring back musk, aloe wood, camphor, cinnamon and other commodities...."[17] Ibn Khordadbeh omits Hebrew, which the Rhadanites certainly knew, from their list of languages, nor does he mention Chinese. His story could be the first written record of the extraordinary linguistic versatility that would distinguish Jewish elites for centuries, and which lasted into the twentieth century in Central and Eastern Europe (as discussed in Part IV, Chapter 4).

The Rhadanites traded in high-value items, like other Jewish long-distance traders, but also in weapons. They must have had a vast store of knowledge, not only of languages but also of foreign cultures and markets, and of geography and seafaring skills. Their entrepreneurial skills allowed them to manage what must have been the world's most extensive trading network at that time, stretching from Spain and France to China. Like other Jewish traders, they avoided the clash between Islam and Christendom. When they crossed the Muslim Middle East, they found guidance and shelter from coreligionists, and when they chose the long and dangerous land route through the deserts of Central Asia, as Ibn Khordadbeh reported that they did, the first stretch of their journey may have taken them through the Jewish Kingdom of the Khazars where they found protection, another competitive advantage.

We do not know whether the Rhadanites were of great importance for Jewish culture and history in Central Asia or the Far East. If the beginning of the Jewish community of Kaifeng, China, which existed approximately from the eleventh or twelfth to the nineteenth century, was in any way linked to Rhadanites traders, as some have suggested,[18] they would have had a much wider importance, but we are not sure. The Jews of Kaifeng used a few Persian terms until the eighteenth century, and some of them certainly had ancestors who had arrived as traders from the Middle East and Persia. Joseph Needham, the author of the classical Western history of Chinese science and technology, attributed to the Rhadanites a role in the history of civilization that extended beyond Judaism's borders. Needham believed that they were early intermediaries, who transferred scientific and technological knowledge between China and the West.[19]

Jewish long-distance traders enjoyed competitive advantages not only through their widespread religious connections but also through their vast knowledge and manifold skills. Similar factors might have been in play in matters beyond trading. For example, in many parts of the Muslim world Jews had a prominent role in the manufacture of jewelry and dyestuff, as well as in the dying of silk and wool. Specialized literature on the arts and crafts of the Muslim world contains references to the important Jewish role in these sectors, for example in Morocco, Yemen, Persia, Afghanistan, and Central Asia. Making jewelry and dyestuff were, to some extent, highly skilled professions. Dying with natural dyes was in many cases based on sophisticated experimentation and secretly transmitted family traditions. Many skills were also required of Jews who entered the money trade, for example the minting of gold coins. When diverse coins from many foreign lands began to appear in the Muslim world, particular knowledge was necessary in order to detect defects and counterfeits.

Case C: The Economic Prosperity of European Jewry in the Age of Mercantilism, ca. 1600-1713

A long period of increasing legal and economic discrimination against Jews, which began in Europe with the Crusades, was interrupted by a major respite, the century of mercantilism. In the seventeenth century, the legal and economic conditions of the Jews improved, with far-reaching political and cultural implications. Many historians knew the relevant facts but did not pull them together into a broader vision because they consider the Enlightenment of the eighteenth century and the following Emancipation as the great breakthroughs of modern Jewish history. Jonathan I. Israel's *European Jewry in the Age of Mercantilism* questioned and overturned this traditional paradigm.[20]

The hundred years from 1470 to 1570 saw the near extinction of Jewish life in many parts of Western and Central Europe, with incalculable losses. A rising tide of antisemitic agitation across Europe led to massive expulsions and the great migration of Jews to Poland and Ottoman Turkey. Severe economic distress caused a decline in internal solidarity and the dissolution of communal institutions, and became the main reason for conversion to Christianity.[21] A turning point came in the years between 1570 and 1620, when Jews were slowly being readmitted into parts of Europe. From then until the beginning of the eighteenth century, mercantilism, as the dominant economic theory the absolutist royal powers across the continent put into practice, became one of the main forces shaping the fate of the Jewish people. It saw international trade as essential to the wealth of nations, and the Jews as essential to trade. State attitudes toward Jews thus changed fundamentally. It was state power that imposed the re-integration of the Jews on various hostile churches and populations.

The years of upheaval and migration had shifted the Jews from a narrow economic framework to a much broader one, and led them to intense interaction with the non-Jewish world. In 1550 the Jews had been virtually eliminated from most of Central Europe's economic life, except for pawn-broking and money changing, but their role in trade was rapidly growing in Poland-Lithuania and the Balkans. This prepared the ground for a larger role in the West. The picture had changed dramatically by 1650. The Jews had entered the mainstreams of economic life, and dominated the important trade routes between Germany and Poland and between Italy and the Balkans. During a period of sustained Jewish economic expansion from 1650 to 1713, there developed what one can speak of as a "Jewish economy," which stretched from Brazil and the Caribbean to Central Europe, Italy, Poland, the Balkans, and Ottoman Turkey. The spread of Jewish trading activities in these countries was impressive. It included court finance and army provisioning and the buying and selling of jewelry, precious metals, copper and iron, money, spices, drugs, tobacco, foodstuffs, livestock, wool, flax, leather, furs, and clothing. Amsterdam's Sephardim were a critical factor. It was their penetration of transatlantic and Far Eastern trade that made the Ashkenazi role in jewelry, precious metals, tobacco, and more possible. During the Thirty Years War, Jewish networks were essential to the warring parties because they could speedily and reliably transfer money and military supplies. Also impressive, and for some perhaps less expected, is the Jewish role in arts and craftwork, except in Germany where most crafts remained closed to Jews. In Prague, thirty percent of all Jews were artisans and craftsmen, engaged as tailors, furriers, tanners, leather workers, jewelers, and candle and spirits producers. In 1652, the Duke of Savoy justified the admission of Jews to his domain by emphasizing their usefulness as "inventors and introducers of new crafts."[22] Jews were involved in silk weaving and textile production, sugar refining, tobacco processing, soap and candle manufacturing, saddle-making, chocolate-making, tailoring, hat-making, leather working, diamond cutting, book binding, coral polishing (for export to India), and more.

Some of the Jews' competitive advantages were identical to those already evident centuries earlier. A Frenchman who visited Constantinople and Egypt in the sixteenth century marveled at the linguistic versatility of the local Jews, just as Ibn Kordadbeh had done in the ninth century: "They speak, it might be Greek, Slavonic, Turkish, Arabic, Armenian or Italian.... The Jews who live in Turkey ordinarily speak four or five languages, and there are several who know ten or twelve.... And so they speak every language and have been of great service to us, not only in translating for us but in communicating to us how things are in that country."[23] But even in the best times, only a minority of Jews was well off, in this case consisting of the Court Jews, princely agents, and the big merchants and manufacturers, followed by some craftsmen. More numerous were the small traders, peddlers, and hawkers, and the vagrants and beggars at the bottom of the social pyramid never disappeared.

The rise of the "Jewish economy" in the early seventeenth century had many beneficial consequences for Jewish civilization. First, the number of Jews began to increase rapidly while Europe's general population stagnated or contracted. Second, new Jewish communities were springing up and old ones were flourishing all along the main trade routes in Germany, Poland, and the Balkans, among other places. Third, and most importantly, with economic strength and royal protection came a new pride in what could be called "Jewish nationhood," an awareness of a Jewish civilization that was based on, but went beyond, religion, and an adherence to a Judaism infused with new elements of mysticism, historiography, poetry, music, and more. Jews had a viable system of autonomous judicial, financial, and welfare institutions which were stronger than the fragmented institutions of earlier centuries and the dissolving frameworks of the eighteenth century. Best known is the Jewish autonomy in the four parts of divided Poland. Jews were ruled by a "Council of the Four Lands." It had an elected leader with the proud title "Parnass (President) of the House of Israel of the Four Lands," And it was he and a tight clan of rich patricians—not rabbis—who negotiated with the king, the nobility, and the Catholic Church on behalf of the Jews.

Other scholars have substantiated Jonathan Israel's findings with additional evidence. The prosperity and relative protection Jews enjoyed in Germany in the final period of mercantilism (second half of the seventeenth century) brought about a phenomenal expansion of Hebrew and Yiddish book-printing.[24] More than twenty Hebrew presses, with the permission of the ruling monarchs, were established. Between 1650 and 1750, at least 2,500 different Hebrew and Yiddish books, including secular literature, were published, with more than two and a half million total copies in print. A third of all Hebrew books printed between the invention of printing and the late eighteenth century came from these German-Jewish presses. A large fraction of them was dispatched to Poland and Russia, where there was no Hebrew printing press until 1692. East European Jews depended entirely on these German Jewish publishers for their religious and cultural needs. The latter's mercantilist wealth and religious charity became a critical factor in the religious and cultural development of Ashkenazi Judaism in the seventeenth and eighteenth centuries.*

In 1714, King Frederic William I of Prussia re-introduced discriminatory measures against Jews and severely restricted their immigration. The tides were now slowly turning against the Jews in one country after the other. National protectionism replaced the international outlook of the mercantilist age, and anti-Jewish rulers replaced better-disposed ones. When the Jewish trade system waned, and exclusion from crafts and industry grew worse, Jewish urban centers began to falter and a dramatic pauperization set in.

In the mid-eighteenth century, about 40 percent of the once-proud Portuguese Jewish community of Amsterdam was destitute. The crumbling Jewish economy was accompanied by a population reduction and had severe cultural consequences, although the eighteenth century still produced outstanding spiritual leaders. The rejection of Jewish tradition and values was growing among Jews, and again, as it had in the fifteenth and early sixteenth centuries, economic distress increased conversion to Christianity. Jewish self-government was abolished, and the old institutional framework began to disintegrate.

According to Jonathan Israel, in the age of mercantilism the economy was a leading factor in the rise and a very important one in the decline of the Jewish civilization, but it was not the only factor. Spiritual factors were of great importance too, particularly the deep crisis following the failure of the false messiah Sabbatai Zevi and the impact of the European Enlightenment, which was fundamentally hostile to Jewish tradition and learning and disparaged the Hebrew Bible. The twin pressures of extreme poverty and "enlightened" Gentile contempt was a potent mixture that compelled large numbers of Jews to abandon their people and its traditions.

---

* An outstanding example was Brandenburg's rich court Jew Behrend Lehmann, who financed the first publication of a complete, relatively uncensored Talmud in Germany (Frankfurt an der Oder, 1697 ff.). This was considered a major event because it responded to an urgent need, and Lehmann distributed half of the edition free of charge to needy Jewish scholars. See Schmelzer 45f.

Case D: The Economic Rise of German Jewry in the Nineteenth and Early Twentieth Century[25]

In the eighteenth century, the economic life of German Jewry was a shadow of what it had been in the peak period of mercantilism. More and more Jews had lost their residence permits and were forbidden from engaging in their traditional economic activities. It is estimated that one third of all German Jews in the era lived from begging and petty crime, and at least another third from hawking, small trade, and junk dealing. Many Jews were rural vagrants. In 1800, 15 to 20 percent of Jews still had no profession and depended on charity, while only two percent belonged to the rich upper class, the exclusive focus of so much literary and antisemitic interest. After the French Revolution, and after Napoleon decreed the emancipation of the Jews, their situation began to slowly advance.

It is significant that the Jews' cultural and educational improvement preceded their economic rise by several decades. Unfettered economic rise would only be possible after the abolition of all forms of discrimination, but in any event an educational preparation came first. Jewish emancipation was meant to be a collective advancement into the middle classes thanks to acculturation to German language, dress, behavior, and work ethic. Economic integration was not the primary goal, but it was expected to accompany the general advancement. Around 1810, as soon as the ghetto walls had fallen, Jews in Dresden, among many other cities, formed a "Reading Society" to fulfill their wish "to be useful through their knowledge," because, alas, "the larger segment of our nation lacks culture and scientific knowledge."[26] By 1815, there were at least 15 Jewish schools in Germany, and countless private teachers providing general knowledge. The German Jews began to accumulate "cultural capital" before anything else. In little more than ten years, a majority of Jews became fluent in literary German, which few of them had mastered before 1800. They did not intend, nor did they foresee, that one to two generations later their eagerly-sought education would set them on the course of the fastest economic rise a large Jewish community had known in a long time.

At the beginning, socio-economic change was still slow. When Napoleon was defeated in 1815 and the laws of emancipation rescinded, the proportion of Jews who emigrated was four times higher than that of German non-Jews. Of the Jews who stayed, the proportion that moved from villages to cities was smaller than that of the Germans. The Jews who did follow the urbanization trend looked for commercial and administrative jobs, not manual and industrial ones. This is not what the incessant calls for "amelioration" of the Jews issued by prominent Germans and Jews since the end of the eighteenth century had been asking for. The Jews were exhorted to move out of commerce and choose the so-called "productive" professions in agriculture, industry, and the crafts. Instead, they stayed in the commercial sector but moved upward, for example from hawkers to owners of established shops. They remained in the sector with which they were most familiar. There they found many other Jews and could stay independent.

The statistics of self-employment are striking. In Prussia, the proportion of independent or self-employed Jews increased between 1843 and 1861 from 61.8 percent to 66.3 percent, and in commerce alone Jewish self-employment rates increased from 39.7 percent to 44.6 percent, whereas the Jewish proportion of workers and employees shrank from 29.5 percent to 27.2 percent. The professional structure of the German Jews remained inflexible to the very end. According to another calculation for Prussia, 71.1 percent of all Jews were self-employed in 1852, and that number remained 50.5 percent in 1925. For the same years, the corresponding figures for the German (rather than Prussian) population decreased from 29 to 22 percent. All efforts to "reform" the professional composition of Jews, often made in response to antisemitic prejudices, had failed. Professionally, the German Jews never "assimilated" but remained "Jewish," although most wanted to assimilate culturally and ideologically, to become Germans. They turned the model of Karl Marx on its head: their economic "substructure" did not move, but their ideological "superstructure" changed completely. This professional inflexibility was rooted both in residual discrimination, which prevented the Jews from trying their luck in all economic areas, and in an inner drive. Culturally assimilating ethnic and religious minorities often still feel a need for internal links and affiliations, and naturally also want to benefit from their inherited capacities and customs.

In the late nineteenth century, Jews began to move out of commerce, but still did not move into manual and industrial employment. Instead they adopted the free professions, with major consequences for both Germany and the Jewish people. In Prussia, the number of gainfully employed Jews increased 2.5 times between 1852 and 1925. In commerce, the increase was 2.4 times; in the free professions, 7.2 times! As a result, in 1925, 26.6 percent of all independent medical doctors in Prussia, and 15 percent of all lawyers, were Jews. Jews comprised one percent of the German population in the same year. Jewish incomes began to outpace those of non-Jewish Germans in this period. Between 1890 and 1899, Jewish taxpayers in western Germany paid three times as much money in income tax as non-Jews; between 1900 and 1914, 3.5 times (in Aachen 4.5 times) more.[27] In two to three generations, Jews had moved from a despised and downtrodden mass of small traders, hawkers, and beggars to the most affluent minority in Germany. A new German-Jewish upper class was emerging, consisting of a few thousand families. In 1900 no more than 2 to 4 percent of all Jews—10,000 to 20,000 persons—belonged to this class, but their effect was politically, economically, and culturally enormous. In 1882, 43 percent of all independent bank directors and industrial entrepreneurs in Prussia were Jews, a figure that decreased to 38 percent in 1895. Jews comprised 22 percent of all persons employed in financial services. The leaders of many Jewish communities came from this new upper class.

Historically, another development was even more important. When the modern "knowledge-based economy" began to grow in Germany in the late nineteenth century, and new technical and organizational know-how began penetrating the traditional economic, industrial, and service sectors, Jews played a role significantly beyond what might be expected based on their numerical strength. Many of the large banks founded or run by Jewish directors provided industry with the capital for expansion. Enterprising Jews also founded several new industries requiring state-of-the-art technology, e.g. in the chemical, metal works, electrical, smelting, and printing sectors. Jews established the first German aircraft factory and department store chains. Emil Rathenau, founder of the AEG Company and pioneer of the German electric industry, introduced electric lights and trams to most German cities, a major technical and social revolution. Albert Ballin became Germany's biggest shipping magnate by revolutionizing trans-Atlantic travel. Through technological and industrial entrepreneurship, German Jews acquired a professional status they had never before possessed, and with it came a certain amount of wealth.[28]

The same can be said of the German-Jewish role in science, as discussed in Part IV, Chapter 3.[29] Through their contribution to science, technology, industrial innovation, and economic organization, the Jews were prominently involved in the rise of Germany to great power status. What is best remembered of all these achievements is an explosion of talent in all fields of scholarship, in the sciences, humanities, and medicine, in philosophy, literature, art, and music, and, not least, in Judaic studies, which continue to provide intellectual inspiration to this day. Since the Spanish Golden Age of the eleventh century there had been no period of general and comprehensive cultural flourishing in Jewish history comparable to this one, but it vanished more quickly than its predecessor. It is clear that this flourishing was made possible by the preceding fifty or more years of steady economic and educational growth.

Case E. Jewish Educational and Economic Success in the United States since 1945 and the Search for Explanations

The remarkable economic and educational success of American Jewry is one of the best-known phenomena of contemporary Jewish history. The reasons for this success are less well understood. This sub-chapter focuses mainly on an analysis by the sociologist Paul Burstein, who reviewed the data and discussed possible explanations.[30] American Jews never knew the wide-ranging legal and economic discrimination and the massive pauperization that was the fate of German Jewry until the early nineteenth century: the first Jewish settlers in America started on a more or less equal footing with other immigrants.

Jewish educational and economic success has been spectacular since 1945, however it is measured. Education took off first. 1945 is the earliest year for which Burstein has statistics on the Jews' relative educational attainments, and the gap between Jewish and general attainment was not yet enormous. But in 1957 Jews had 1.7 years more education than the average, and 16 percent of them were college graduates, as opposed to 9 percent of the general population. From then on, and for approximately twenty years, Jewish educational attainments rose steeply and continuously, well outstripping the national average.* Between 1972 and 1980, Jews had 2.6 years more education than the average, and 39.3 percent were college graduates (12.6 percent nationally). By another calculation for 1983-1984, 56 percent were college graduates. This is almost three and a half times more than in 1957 (16 percent). For the next 20 years or so, that is from around 1983 to 2002, the increases leveled off and relative Jewish educational attainment remained more or less unchanged. From 1991 to 2002, Jews still had 2.6 years more education than the national average, unchanged from 1972-1980, and 61.2 percent were college graduates,[31] only slightly up from the 56 percent figure of 1983-1984. However, the Jewish earnings trend follows a different curve. In 1957, the Jews' relative income was 126 percent of Protestants', and 140 percent of Catholics'. Approximately 20 years later, that is for 1972-1980, Jews' relative income was 147 percent of that of non-Jews (another study for the same years has Jews earning 136 percent of Protestant incomes). The increase is moderate. This radically changes after 1980. Jewish relative incomes took off steeply and reached, in another twenty years (by 1999), an extraordinary 246 percent of Protestant, and 243 percent of Catholic, incomes.

One is tempted to interpret these data in light of other Jewish experiences, e.g. those in Germany. In the United States, too, there was an exceptional

---

* Burstein does not discuss the origin of this steep rise. To an economist, it looks like pent-up demand that is suddenly unleashed. It could have been caused by, among other reasons, the G.I.Bill (official title: "Servicemen's Readjustment Act"), which was passed by the US Congress in 1944. The G.I.Bill offered government-paid college or vocational education to every American serviceman returning from World War II. Around 550, 000 American Jews served in the war, and more than 530, 000 returned alive. General national university enrolments increased quickly as the *numerus clausus*, the numerical restrictions that several universities had imposed on Jews until the war, became weaker and finally disappeared. It is very likely that many Jewish veterans enrolled in the universities in the years after the war, proportionally probably more than non-Jewish ex-servicemen. This could have been the start of the great Jewish educational rise of the 1950s and 1960s. Further research would be required to substantiate this hypothesis.

educational investment first, which seems to have induced a strong economic rise, again with a time lag of two to three decades. Causal links between educational attainment and economic performance are plausible, although there may have been other causal factors as well. The future will show whether Jews will suffer economic consequences for the leveling-off of their educational growth curve over the last twenty years, compared to that of the rest of the population. As they were in Germany, the achievements of Jews in America, both economic and educational, were accompanied and followed by an explosion of talent in every field of science, literature, art, culture, economics, finance, and politics. *Who's Who in America*[32] shows a stunning trend. In 1924-1925, Jews were substantially under-represented. They were, in relative terms, 70 percent as likely to appear as another American, and just 43 percent as likely as those of English extraction. Twenty years later, this had barely changed; in 1944-1945 Jews were 79 percent as likely as the average American and 53 percent as likely as those of English extraction to appear, still a considerable under-representation. Thirty years later, the change was dramatic. The representation of Jews in *Who's Who* increased beyond their steep educational and economic rise. In 1974-1975 it reached 245 percent of the national average and 216 percent of the English, and in 1994-1995 it jumped to 468 percent of the national average and 587 percent of the English. While such extraordinary figures might also partly reflect an improved attitude of *Who's Who*'s editors toward minorities and a greater readiness to acknowledge their contributions, there is no doubt that Jewish participation in all facets of American public life greatly increased in those years. There are many books, articles, and websites that try to record Jewish contributions to every area of American civilization, but it will take a long time before a final history of this contribution, which is still continuing, can be written.

It is statistically difficult to count up and compare Jewish contributions to non-Jewish ones. For example, a specialized website tries to measure the Jewish contribution to all computer- and informatics-related fields, a backbone of American technological power and leadership.[33] Some of the comparative figures for 2007 are telling: 40 percent of the members of the Computer and Information Sciences division of the U.S. National Academy of Sciences are Jewish; 44 percent of the recipients of the John von Neumann Theory Prize in Operations Research have been Jews, and three of the six most often quoted inventors of the Internet are Jews, etc. But other data presented are simply descriptions of major discoveries, with the names of the inventors and years. Only specialists in these fields can fully appreciate the importance of these discoveries, relative to others.

The literature proposes three main "reputable" (that is, non-genetic) answers to the question of why Jews do so much better in education, business, and innovation. Most frequent is the "human capital" theory: Jews do better by getting more education and working longer hours. The second answer emphasizes Jewish particularity, in other words, it suggests that Jews do better not because of just any education, but because of an education that transmits specific Jewish values. A third answer finds the reason in Jewish marginality: Jews have a heightened drive to advance because they still fear discrimination. The empirical data confirm none of the three answers if they are presented as mono-causal explanations. Burstein offers a fourth answer, "social capital," which is the ability to secure advantages through membership in networks and other social structures. Jews develop such networks through schools, universities, family, and local Jewish communities. The "social capital" theory does not negate the importance of human capital (individual education) or Jewish particularity; on the contrary, it enhances both and puts them into a broader framework. For example, it was found that people who have attended Jewish day schools report significantly higher earnings than those who have not.[34] This could confirm the "social capital" theory, although other explanations are equally possible.

The American experience seems to confirm that there are strong and probably causal links between economic success, educational attainment, and general creativity, but these links are complex and work in different directions. Economic, cultural, and educational success are so enmeshed that it is difficult to identify which factor came first.

Communalities

If one looks for a socio-economic "long duration" structure of Jewish civilization, to use Braudel's vocabulary, one has to separate the economic history of ancient Israel and talmudic times, that is until the fifth century CE, from all later Jewish economic history. The economies of ancient Israel and the Jewish communities of Babylonia were largely agricultural. The Jewish economy from the following centuries until today has been completely different, with the exception of limited and often only temporary agricultural settlements in the Diaspora and, more importantly, in Israel. All five case studies of this chapter belong to the centuries of Jewish history when agriculture was not dominant and was in fact sometimes non-existent, the last 1500 years. During this time, something like a socio-economic "long-duration" structure of Jewish civilization formed.

Jews or Jewish elites were able to make a good living and create pockets of wealth in often quite similar ways, and thus they contributed to the social, cultural, religious, and political welfare of their group as a whole. Economic success was often linked to the rise of Jewish civilization, and economic distress sometimes to decline. However, the link was circular: often culture helped create and support an economy, and the economy in turn continued to support culture. History did not start with an economic "substructure"

270

that spawned a religious, cultural, or ideological "superstructure." Further, the economy has never been the only cause of rise or decline, though it could greatly strengthen or weaken the effects of other causes. The correlation between economic and cultural prosperity was never complete. A large majority of nineteenth-century East European Jews was poor, and some were destitute, but this did not prevent them from living a vibrant cultural and intellectual life.

The communalities emerging from these five case studies are the result, on one hand, of similar constraints and "challenges," and on the other, of similar Jewish responses to the challenges. These were the main challenges:

a. The Absence of Natural Resources. Until the gas finds in Israel's Mediteranean in 2009 and 2010, the Jewish people never owned major mineral or other natural resources that could have been a basis of regular income or stable wealth. This has been true for all of Jewish history, including in the times of ancient Israel. In Israel there was probably sufficient land for subsistence agriculture, but there was not enough for growing substantial agricultural surpluses for export over longer periods. Water shortages and famines, as we know from the Bible and Talmud, were frequent. In the Diaspora, Jews were not always allowed to hold land, and even when they were often did not want to invest their wealth in land because they feared expulsion and/or expropriation. Geographic location conferred no advantage to Israel comparable, for example, to the advantage the Suez Canal brought twentieth-century Egypt, or that which controlling the passes over the Alps brought Switzerland.

Other civilizations and countries were equally poor in natural resources, but few were as across-the-board poor as the Jews, at least for much of history and in most countries: no natural resources, no rich agricultural land, no guaranteed supply of water, and no strategic geographic advantages. Only Greece was perhaps equally poor.

b. Minority Status. Jews were perennial, mostly small, minorities during the Second Temple period in countries outside the land of Israel, and in all countries from the end of the Bar Kochba revolt (135/138 CE) to the creation of the State of Israel (1948). This is one of the most relevant economic features of Jewish history. Simon Kuznets has shown that the economic life of all small minority groups, not only the Jews, is generally different from the economic life of the majority, and significantly different when a minority strives for social cohesion.[35] Cohesion calls for geographic proximity and close links at many levels, including economic and professional connections. Therefore, the economic structure of a minority seeking to preserve its unity is rarely "normal," that is, identical to the majority structure. The economic minority structure will often be maintained by history and heritage, even when other external or internal conditions have changed. Kuznets' observations on the economic implications of minority status are certainly valid for Medieval and modern Diaspora Jews.

c. Dispersion. From the destruction of the First Temple in 586 BCE until today, Jews have lived in different lands, often very distant from each other. Dispersion and minority status are not the same issue. Jews could have been dispersed to many countries, but still maintain majorities in some of them, and in fact, as was discussed above, they sometimes were majorities in specific provinces or cities. But dispersion and minority status had similar effects. The wish for social and religious cohesion expressed itself in intense contacts at the local and international levels. This created the right conditions for economic networks.

d. Discrimination. The Jews under Christian and Muslim rule were discriminated against longer than any other people in world history, for well-known religious reasons. Discrimination always carried economic restrictions. In Christian Europe, major discrimination started after 1096, worsened in the thirteenth century when Jews were forced to take up money-lending as a main profession, and continued with interruptions and variations in some countries until the late nineteenth and early twentieth century. Under Islam, Jews had easier access to some professions than they had under Christendom, particularly in the arts and crafts, but persecution and discrimination occurred there too. Discrimination had deep psychological effects. Even when all signs of external discrimination were removed, internal constraints remained, with a stubborn longevity. The outsider status of Diaspora Jewry and its consequences partly extended to the State of Israel in new forms from the day Israel was created in May 1948. Arab and Muslim economic boycotts of Israel had various, very important effects. Some boycotts continue to this day and are occasionally echoed by boycott calls from hostile circles in the West.

e. The State as Critical Decision-Maker and Partner. During most of Jewish history, external state powers set the legal and political conditions for Jewish economic activities. State power intersected with religious and social discrimination, but must be distinguished from it. The state often went along with discriminatory trends initiated by the Church or general society, but it could also reinforce these trends, as Ferdinand and Isabella did when they used religious pretexts to expel the Jews from Spain in 1492, or it could oppose and suppress hostility, as royal powers did in the age of mercantilism.

During the Thirty Years War (1618-1648), King Gustav Adolf's fearsome Swedish infantry opened fire on German mobs about to plunder Jewish ghettoes. Such occurences are rare in Jewish history, but they did happen. The lucrative long-distance trading role of Jews north of the Alps in the early Middle Ages was assigned them by the Emperors of the Holy Roman Empire, and the trading role of the Maghribis in the Mediterranean was terminated by the Mamluk dynasty that ruled Egypt after 1250. The limited economic flourishing of European Jewry in the seventeenth century was both initiated and terminated by royal powers. The final stretch of the economic rise of German Jews required legal emancipation, which was granted in the 1860s and 1870s and terminated by the Nazis in 1933. Jews were, for a long time, essential as taxpayers in both the Muslim and Christian worlds. "The state...became the silent partner in the totality of Jewish economic enterprise."[36]

The Jews responded to these constraints in various ways, but there was a potent combination of three relevant "responses." They were not all developed for economic reasons, but were part of Judaism's old cultural and historical traditions, which turned out to be economically useful. Jews created "knowledge-based" pockets of economic prosperity long before the term "knowledge-based economy," coined in the late twentieth century, existed.[37] A study of these pockets reveals similarities that could also be relevant for the future.

A. Education or "Human Capital"

Education allowed the Jews to accumulate "human capital." This gave them a comparative advantage in urban, skilled occupations that encouraged their migration from farmlands to cities. Skill-based economic benefits in turn supported further education and culture (also see Part IV, Chapter 3).

The Jews may at present be entering a new, more difficult long-term phase in their history of educational and economic success. Their educational advantages have lasted into the twenty-first century, but could soon begin to shrink in comparison to the rest of the world. Jews already lost their domination of literate society, if not monopoly on literacy, in the nineteenth century, and their fluency in many languages in the twentieth. In the United States, the Jewish educational advantage over the general population, measured in number of years of education and proportion of college graduates, appears to have stopped growing since about 1980 and is relatively stable. Average incomes of Jews are still generally higher than those of non-Jews, but the income gap is narrowing in most Western countries.[38] One has to ask whether this development is linked to the relative leveling off of Jewish educational growth observed in the United States. To complain about alleged dangers to economic prosperity when American Jews were in 2007 still earning more than twice as much as non-Jews, and when Israel's GDP and standard of living is growing faster than that of many other Western countries, seems out of place. However, if Jewish economic history can be said to offer any guidance, a greater educational effort in the Diaspora and in Israel, even an educational revolution, appears necessary.

Waiting for economic growth to pull education out of its crisis puts the cart before the horse. In Israel, high growth rates will be sustainable in the long term only if they are preceded by considerable educational improvements or a large-scale immigration of highly educated Jews, which doesn't appear likely today. A substantial reduction in growth rates could affect the country's defense position, erode its attractiveness to highly skilled Israeli and Jewish manpower, and make the demographic position of Israel's Jews, in comparison to Israel's minorities and neighbors, more precarious. The most significant reason Israelis give for not having more children is economic.

B. Networking or "Social Capital"

The "human capital" theory alone is not sufficient to explain Jewish economic success.[39] When Jews and non-Jews with exactly the same amount and quality of education are compared, as has been done in the United States, Jews are still doing better economically than non-Jews. The success of Jewish long-distance traders from the ninth to the thirteenth centuries, and again in the seventeenth century, revealed that international networks and close cooperation across borders were essential ingredients of Jewish economic achievement. Economists speak of "social capital," and social capital goes far beyond long-distance trading. In every country where there are large numbers of Jews, experience shows that Judaism and Jewish civilization operate through impacts on Jewish organizations, communities, social and educational networks, and families. It is these impacts that create or enhance "social capital." The economic advantages created by social capital derive from better information, privileged connections, etc. Social capital is also one of the explanations for Jewish scientific and technological achievement (as discussed in Part IV, Chapter 3). Jews generally do not like such explanations, because they play into the hands of those claiming that Jews are "clannish," that they stick together and help each other. Simply put, Jews do what all minorities have always done and will continue to do.

The permanence of these international "social capital" advantages of Jews cannot be taken for granted any more than their "human capital" advantages can. In this globalized world of easy communications, virtually anyone can link up with anyone else. Recent years saw many new diasporas emerge: growing numbers of Chinese, Indians, Russians, groups of Muslims (Turks, Arabs, Pakistanis) are settling in a large number of foreign countries. Many of them are building international networks and maintain links with each other and their countries of origin. This could create new economic connections and investments. The Jewish people could lose ground in the long term, and its international "social capital" could become comparatively smaller.

C. Entrepreneurship, Innovation, and Risk-Taking

Both human and social capital are essential, but they do not generate new economic activities by themselves. Such activities are developed by entrepreneurial, innovative, pioneering, risk-taking individuals. According to the Austrian-American economist Joseph Schumpeter, it is individual entrepreneurs or inventors of new technologies working in large corporations who initiate innovation, technical change, and economic development. Their initiatives involve risk, but when they are seen to succeed, many others follow.

The five case studies above show that Jewish entrepreneurship, innovation, and risk-taking have been evident in very different epochs and countries. The early long-distance traders, from Charlemagne's Isaac to David Maimonides, were risk-taking entrepreneurs, and so are many of today's Jewish scientists, engineers, and managers who are creating new high-tech companies or developing innovation within existing ones in the United States, Israel, and elsewhere. Many Jews who are or were successful financial operators and investors have a similar risk-taking, entrepreneurial mind. Do all entrepreneurial minorities share common features, or are Jewish entrepreneurial minorities different from others? An economic historian has called European Jews and Southeast Asian Chinese "the two most prominent entrepreneurial minorities in the modern world."[40] He asserted that minorities such as the Jews have an exceptional capacity or propensity for risk-bearing and economic or technological innovation.[41] The regular emergence of Jews with this capacity is another historical response to the economic challenges Jews have faced. It is also the most enigmatic response. No single reason is sufficient to explain all cases. Historians and sociologists have proposed a number of reasons, several of which are complementary and overlap:

— Discrimination: Their exclusion from economic mainstream activities forced Jews to look for "niches," high-risk ventures and opportunities others had ignored. In some cases, the ruling powers assigned the Jews to specific entrepreneurial activities, such as long-distance trading. Jewish economic habits, shaped over centuries, do not easily disappear. This explanation is valid for large periods of Diaspora history and for stretches of Israel's technological development in response to foreign embargoes, but it is increasingly unconvincing when applied to Western countries today.

— Status incongruity:[42] When Jews have relatively unhindered access to the economy but not to careers in government, the army, and the church, some of the "best and brightest," who are often also the most ambitious, seek high-risk ventures by which they might find fame, get rich, or both. This can explain Jewish entrepreneurialism in Germany or Hungary before World War II, but not in Israel or the United States today, where no avenues are closed to Jews.

— Insider/outsider perspectives: Entrepreneurship and risk-taking, as well as scientific and technological innovativeness are forms of creativity. Creativity can typically be found in people who have mastered two or more fields, cultures, or languages, and who use the framework of one to think about the other. Such people can imagine things never available before and can, in turn, capture the imaginations of others.[43] Jews combine insider and outsider perspectives. The Internet biography of Sergey Brin, the informatics scientist and co-founder of Google, emphasizes that he is American, Jewish, and Russian, and is married to a woman who studied biochemistry in America and Israel. Four perspectives bring more to innovation than one. Again, this explanation does not cover all cases. There are very successfu, export-oriented high-tech entrepreneurs who know only one language, English, one culture, and one technical specialty.

— Subverting the economic status quo: One of the reasons proposed for the prominent role of Jews in modern science is their skepticism and willingness to challenge and subvert established "truths" and traditions. Jews have historically had less at stake in the intellectual status quo than did the majority. Exactly the same could apply to the economic status quo. This goes a step further than looking for "niches" in order to compensate for discrimination (first point above): it means actively creating new niches by undermining existing economic structures. When Jewish entrepreneurs created the first big department stores in nineteenth-century Germany, they helped to improve the general public's standard of living but also threatened many German small shop owners. They did not conceive the idea because they were excluded from small shop ownership and had to look for other opportunities—on the contrary, many Jews were small shop owners and could remain so as long as they wanted. They created this new type of store because they saw great opportunity in this innovation and were indifferent to the undermining of a social and economic status quo in which they had no general inherited interest.

— Independence and self-employment: The wish of Jews to remain self-employed and independent even in advanced industrialized countries is notorious. In nineteenth-century Germany, this wish could be explained by residual discrimination in many economic sectors, but this explanation is not plausible for today's United States, where the preference for self-employment remains higher among Jews than among non-Jews.[44] There is a link between self-employment and entrepreneurship. An attractive way to become or remain self-employed is to be an entrepreneurial innovator. A yearning for independence in combination with an aversion to working in large, hierarchical organizations likely stimulates individual entrepreneurship.

— Religious constraints and habits: This explanation intersects with the problem of independence. Sabbath prohibitions and other laws make it

276

difficult for observant Jews to work in large non-Jewish organizations. This partly explains Jewish self-employment in the Diaspora. A Jewish Hungarian sociologist also asserts that Jewish religious habits contributed to their successful entrepreneurial conduct, for example through a tradition of discipline and the control of time, space, and the body.[45] This is an interesting albeit partial explanation of past Jewish entrepreneurship in some places in Europe, but its explanatory value today, for example in Israel, is not obvious.

— Middleman Minorities: The ruling elites, for example in Poland or the Ottoman Empire, used minorities, often Jews, as economic and administrative "middlemen." When there was a large gap between the elites and the masses, as there was for instance in feudal societies, minorities often fulfilled some of the economic roles mediating between the two sides. In some countries Jews were tax collectors for feudal or national rulers. This kind of entrepreneurship did not endear the Jews to the masses. Money lending, which the Church had imposed on the Jews in medieval times, can be seen as belonging to this category. Today the middleman explanation has more historical than actual interest.

Nothing indicates that the Jews today suffer from a shortage of entrepreneurial drive. There are still many Jewish and Israeli entrepreneurs and start-up companies. The global economic and financial crisis that began in fall 2008 reduced financial backing for entrepreneurial ventures as well as charity, but will not destroy entrepreneurship. Maybe the crisis will also direct some of the Jewish entrepreneurial drive away from finance into technological sectors (see also Part IV, Chapter 3). Contributions by successful entrepreneurs to Jewish causes will continue to make a big difference to culture and education, and a major reduction in charity would seriously damage the "virtuous" cycle between education and economic prosperity that was so important in the past.

Figures for 2011/2012 indicate that Jewish charity in the United States is slowly recovering from the economic crisis, but it is still far from sufficient to respond to all social, cultural, and educational needs.

CHAPTER 8

War: A Double-Edged Sword[1]

General Observations

The professional literature on war is enormous, but our twenty-three historians have contributed little to it. Still, it is significant to see how they evaluate war and its links with the rise and decline of civilizations. Their views vary and are as contradictory as those they express on some other drivers of civilization, such as leadership.

For classical historians, war is a normal and necessary event in the history of nations. Thucydides participated in war in a senior role, as was expected of an Athenian of his social rank and economic means. He reports that Athens' leader Pericles urged his people to go to war against Sparta in order to maintain and improve the city's power: "We must realize that war is inevitable." Ibn Khaldun studied the wars inside the Arab world with great attention to technology and tactics, and regarded victory in war as indispensable for the survival of any nation.[2] Edward Gibbon expressed similar convictions. The rise of Rome depended in large measure on its vigorous military spirit, while its decline was caused by, among other things, the displacement of military virtues.[3]Among the classics of this study, China's Sima Qian was the only voice to speak out against the view that war is normative and inevitable. He witnessed war up close and saw its awful costs. For him, the greatest ruler is a peacemaker, not a warmonger.[4]

This was not the opinion of other Chinese scholars. Sun Tzu, the Chinese strategist of the third or second century BCE, begins his book *The Art of War* with the assertion that "military action is important to the nation—it is the ground of death and life, the path of survival and destruction."[5] Sima Qian knew the work of Sun Tzu and referred to him in his own work.[6] A late-nineteenth-century offshoot of the classical majority opinion that condoned war can be found in the remarks of Jacob Burckhardt. Although he never saw war himself, he felt that a long peace "favoured the emergence of a lot of miserable lives," whereas war brought out the "true forces." He noted, with considerable regret, that "a people will get to know its full national power only in war and in competitive battle with other nations...."[7]

The attitude toward war among historians of civilization changed profoundly over the twentieth century. Arguments positing the beneficial effects of war, which could still be detected in Burckhardt's comments, became unacceptable. War was perceived no longer as a driver of survival and rise but of destruction. Many historians were horrified by the two World Wars and saw them as ruptures of history. The mass killings, the destructions of so many countries, and the violent disruptions of so many lives were hitherto unseen in history. Spengler declared that militarism was the last, terminal stage of a decaying culture. Sorokin and Toynbee were lifelong pacifists. Toynbee called all militarism suicidal, because it blinded leaders and drove them to attempt to settle all disputes with military force, leading to the breakdown of civilizations.[8] He also warned of "the intoxication of victory,"[9] a typical but dangerous pitfall threatening victors. He claimed that such an intoxication had ruined ancient Rome, Spain, Portugal, and even the British Empire. Toynbee thus suggested a different, inverted relationship between war and rise or decline: victory, by "intoxication," was an agent of decline, not rise.

Finally, the work of Braudel and others seeking universal and comprehensive laws of rise and decline has little or no place for war. Braudel's *Grammaire des Civilisations* presents a broad overview of today's main civilizations. Wars are absent in this picture because Braudel did not believe that they could stop or overturn the long-term trends of civilizations. The theoreticians looking for universal, ironclad laws of rise and decline tend to ignore war as an autonomous driver of civilization. Joseph A. Tainter asserted that all civilizations collapse for internal reasons; none was destroyed by war or external aggression.

Carl von Clausewitz, the Prussian strategist, famously wrote at the beginning of the nineteenth century that "war is never an isolated act...nothing but the continuation of a political discourse by other means."[10] All important historians have understood that complex reciprocal links exist between war and other civilizational drivers, such as statesmanship, economics, science and technology, religion, and more. Further, the cultural historians Jacob Burckhardt and Johan Huizinga were more interested in civilization's impact on war, not the other way around. War was a daily occurrence in and between the city-states of the Renaissance, but Burckhardt's *Culture of the Renaissance in Italy* gives it little more than three of 560 pages.[11] He speaks of the "science and art of war-making in context," which means that in the case of the Renaissance it was not war that shaped civilization, but civilization that shaped war. Johan Huizinga took a similar position. Fourteenth-century Europe was torn by incessant wars, but his cultural history of the period barely mentions them. War making was dominated by the cultural ideals of the late Middle Ages, the ideals of chivalry.[12] His *Dutch Culture in the Seventeenth Century* conveyed the same message. During most of the seventeenth century the Dutch were fighting for survival, but Huizinga barely mentions their wars because they did not, in his view, factor into the character of the Dutch people and civilization.[13] The conviction that civilization shapes war can also be found today. The American war historian V.D. Hanson argued that the conduct and outcome of wars are essentially determined by a civilization's values. Hence, he predicted that the military predominance of the West, which began with the Greek victory over the Persians, would endure for a long time. He reasons that this predominance is based on the most fundamental aspects of Western civilization, such as political freedom, individualism, rationalism, scientific inquiry, and the like, arguing that these values are what distinguish the West from all other civilizations.[14]

Jewish history, as well as the history of many destroyed civilizations, leaves no doubt that victory in war has created civilizations or allowed them to rise and thrive, whereas defeat has destroyed or exhausted them and hastened their decline. It is difficult to identify a major civilization where war has not played a role in rise or decline.

Applications to Jewish History

Oswald Spengler was fond of making provocative statements countering conventional beliefs. He commended the martial qualities and virtues of the Jews, asserting repeatedly that they were primarily a warrior people, not only in biblical and talmudic times, but also much later.[15] To better understand the complexity and changing nature of Jewish attitudes toward war, one should distinguish three, sometimes interwoven and sometimes independent, strands of thought that existed either in parallel or in succession:

A. Obeying biblical commandments to wage war against enemy nations— now long forgotten—in ancient Canaan, as well as wars of self-defense or preemption, and the commemoration of enemy defeats in scripture and prayers.

B. Yearning for peace and obeying instructions to follow the "ways of peace" not just for pragmatic reasons, but because peace is a divine blessing and a moral value in itself.

C. Obeying the calculated, pragmatic rabbinic pacifism that emerged following the catastrophic Bar Kochbah revolt, aimed at preventing further catastrophes.

A. Obeying Biblical Commands to Wage War

All discussions on war must begin with the basic fact that the biblical religion does not validate non-violence in all circumstances, in contrast to other religious and ethical philosophies. On the contrary, a Jew is obliged to fight for his own and his people's life. Militarism is not the same issue, although the Torah and other books of the Bible, particularly Joshua, provide ample material to support Spengler's view that the ancient Jews were born militarists. But Spengler may have simplified the issue. Rabbinic exegesis distinguished between three types of war: obligatory *mitzvah* wars, to be waged against the seven Canaanite nations; wars of self-defense or preemption; and optional, non-defensive wars. Wars of *mitzvah*, that is of religious duty, are a recurring theme in the Hebrew Bible.[16] Late-nineteenth-century German Old Testament scholars called them "Holy Wars," and that label is still in use. *Mitzvah* and self-defensive wars were, according to the Torah, compulsory: every able-bodied person had a duty to fight. Optional wars to increase Israel's territory could be conducted at the discretion of the kings of Israel.

At first reading, the main biblical goal of *mitzvah* wars was not just victory but the complete annihilation of the enemy's towns and populations. Rabbinic Judaism was ill at ease with the apparent harshness of this injunction and toned it down: the rabbis did not want the *mitzvah* war to be misunderstood as "a general warrant for genocide."[17] Maimonides stressed the precaution demanded by the Bible: "When you approach a town to attack it, you shall offer it terms of peace."[18] He declared that this limitation applied even to the seven nations mainly targeted in *mitzvah* wars: their annihilation would follow only if they refused Israel's peace terms, servitude and special taxes. Maimonides' law codex, the *Mishneh Torah*, articulates the rabbinic tradition, develops a comprehensive theology of war, and reexamines the conditions of *mitzvah* wars.[19] He is explicit about the religious obligation to wage such wars under certain conditions, but in general his chapter leans toward moderation and the avoidance of bloodshed if possible. Moreover, the title of the chapter where these matters are discussed is revealing: "Laws of Kings and of their Wars." When Maimonides placed the war legislation into the laws of kings, he implied that the issue was purely theoretical. It applied to the past, when an independent Israel had a king, a temple, and serving priests who all, according to the law, played indispensable roles in the war preparations. The question of *mitzvah* wars would again become topical in the days of the Messiah. Several scholars also assert that Maimonides' interpretations of Jewish war law are often similar to Muslim war doctrines, for example those of Averroes, who lived at the same time as Maimonides and in the same town, Cordoba.[20] These scholars conclude that Maimonides borrowed some of his legal war interpretations from Islamic models.[21]

Enlightenment authors, such as Voltaire, ignored the extensive rabbinic discussions about war and read the biblical war laws and extermination stories as historical truth; today's Bible scholars and archeologists do not. He defamed the Jews as "execrable" and "assassins," for their decision to "massacre men, women and children" in Jericho.[22] In the ancient world to which the Bible belongs, the mass-killing of defeated enemies was rarely a source of opprobrium, and was widely practiced by Egyptian, Babylonian, Greek, Roman, and many other conquerors. There were some individual exceptions, however: Sima Qian, revolted by the killing of disarmed war prisoners, promised "great misfortunes" to those who commit such crimes,[23] and Thucydides was equally saddened by the massacre of Melos by Athenian forces, a symptom of the hubris that would soon cause Athens' downfall. In contrast, Flavius Josephus narrates the Bible's extermination stories, for example the wars against the Midianites or the Canaanites of Jericho, with the pride of an apologetic Jew who wanted his Roman readers to appreciate that his ancestors were not only victorious warriors but could be as tough and merciless as the Romans themselves.[24] The rabbinic qualms of later centuries did not bother him. Had he feared that his Roman audience would regard such stories as bad publicity for the Jews, he would probably have omitted them from his *Jewish Antiquities*.* Both Flavius Josephus and Philo of Alexandria tried to convince the doubtful Greeks and Romans—long before Spengler's time—that the Jews were once valiant fighters and that their leader, Moses, was a great strategic genius.[25]

B. Yearning for Peace as a Moral Value

In parallel to the war laws and battle narratives, Judaism also idealizes and yearns for peace as a major religious value, not only as a reaction to military defeat and suffering. The invocation of peace appears in the earliest known citation of a text also found in the Hebrew Bible, the famous Priestly Blessing, a high point in Jewish religious liturgy to this day. The blessing culminates in a solemn call to God "to grant you peace,"[26] and was found inscribed on a silver amulet dated to the late seventh century BCE, before the Babylonian Exile.[27] The deepest yearnings for peace, and prophecies of an end-time of peace—a final Golden Age for all mankind—appear later with the great prophets who lived before, during, or after the destruction of the First Temple.[28] This yearning and the promise of peace as the final and most noble stage of human history have become core Jewish beliefs. Parallel to the celebration of enemy defeats, the yearning for peace entered Jewish prayers and left deep impressions on Jewish thought. Whereas the Greeks and Romans had a god of war, Ares or Mars, but no god of peace, the Mishnah and

---

* Flavius Josephus removed more than one biblical episode from his Jewish history, for example the story of the bronze snake in the desert Moses erected to stop snakebites and the story of the golden calf. The reason for the second omission is obvious. An antisemitic canard, which circulated widely in Rome and was taken seriously by Tacitus, asserted that the Jews worshipped in their Temple the head of a dead donkey. The golden calf story risked reinforcing the Roman suspicion that Jews worshipped animals.

Talmud regard the Hebrew term for peace, *shalom*, as one of God's own hidden names. Consequently the Talmud asks whether the use of this name might be prohibited. Yes is the answer—for example, when one stands undressed in a public bath, "the greeting 'Peace', *Shalom,* is not permitted,"[29] because pronouncing this word in an unclean environment defiles the holy name. Thus, the political ideal of peace has divine sanctification. Peace ideals, which play such an important role in contemporary Israeli politics, have very old and deep roots in Judaism.

C. Yearning for Peace as a Pragmatic Value

Bar Kochba's defeat in 135-138 CE was also a religious watershed. Some leaders regarded the rebellion against Rome as an obligatory *mitzvah* war, but it failed completely and was followed by horrific massacres. Rabbinic Judaism now understood that waging "holy war" could be not only very dangerous, but suicidal, and the rabbis constructed mechanisms of definition that made such wars virtually unthinkable.[30] They wanted to establish an equilibrium in which the Jews were forbidden to rebel against the nations of the world or to move in large numbers to Israel without the nations' authorization and, as counterpart, the latter would treat the Jews fairly. Although these rabbinic decrees were based on necessity rather than a principled love for peace, they had a considerable impact on Jews until the twentieth century. However, neither the biblical prophets[31] nor the rabbis of the Talmud regarded Jewish defeats as a result of inferior numbers, insufficient resources, or incompetent military leadership, but rather as a temporary divine punishment. The doors to future victories were not closed forever.

During the *Shoah*, it became clear that "the nations" did not keep their part of the proposed rabbinic bargain. This was the beginning of rabbinic and broader reexaminations of the whole notion of obligatory war. After the victorious Six-Day War of 1967, national-religious rabbis and scholars in Israel began to dismantle the old, pragmatic rabbinic obstacles to obligatory war and revived the latent "holy war" ideas that have never been completely expunged from Jewish thought. Animated and often bitter arguments among political and religious leaders on this issue continue.

Jewish thought and civilization are profoundly marked by tensions between the need for war and the hope for peace that have a long and continuing history.

Ancient Israel

History explains why, during pre-exilic Israel's early periods, war and not peace seemed to dominate daily thought. Victory in war was an absolute condition of the early rise and survival of Israel. It was not the only condition, but it was an indispensable one. For centuries, Israel fought wars with many peoples and cities. The longest and most difficult one appears to have been its long confrontation with the Philistines, the proto-Greek "uncircumcised" invaders from the sea. They nearly succeeded in subduing and extinguishing Israel, judging from the anguish and abhorrence evident in the biblical record. Some archeologists believe that Israel was technologically inferior because it was still in the Bronze Age, while the Philistines used superior iron weapons. This longest war in Jewish history lasted approximately three hundred years.

The military defeats inflicted on Israel by the Babylonians and Assyrians ended the First Temple period. The two great defeats inflicted by Rome ended the Second Temple period. These defeats left a lasting impact on Jewish memory. The insurgents who confronted Rome were technologically, tactically, and strategically badly prepared for the large-scale, organized warfare in which the Romans were masters, but nevertheless are reported to have inflicted severe losses on Rome, including the destruction of entire legions in both wars. After Hadrian completed his victory in 138 CE, he did not celebrate it, and the traditional formulation that his legions were "in health" was omitted from his message back to Rome. Historians have concluded that he must have lost an enormous number of men.[32] Jewish fearlessness in the face of death impressed their enemies, as the historians Tacitus and Flavius Josephus wrote, but this was, in the end, no match for the awesome Roman war machine.

If the early wars of ancient Israel were drivers of rise and survival, were the lost wars of later centuries solely drivers of decline? The Israeli historian Joseph Klausner, quoted below, attempted to answer this question, but there are some questions no historian can answer with any certitude. The destructions of the two Temples led to major transformations that allowed Judaism to survive and rise again in a new form. Maybe they even spared the Jews a worse fate later on: nobody can say how Judaism would have developed in the absence of such ruptures. Surely, the bloodshed caused by the Judean rebellions of 70 CE and 135 CE and the Jewish revolts in the Mediterranean region in 115-117 CE was horrendous, and the loss of life devastated the Jewish people. Judged by the normal rise-and-decline criteria of our world historians, this was decline and collapse in the most dramatic sense.

The Diaspora

During the diasporic centuries, war and military virtue could not play the same role it had in ancient Israel, or has in the modern state. However, the victories marked by the Jewish calendar continued to be celebrated every year with joy and hope. Non-biblical memories of war and heroism also lingered on in the Diaspora, for example Flavius Josephus' *The Jewish War*, which was first written in Aramaic, but survived only in the Greek translation primarily intended for Roman readers. There was also an early Jewish audience that did not read Josephus but wanted to know more about the fateful year 70 CE than rabbinic sources cared to tell. For eight hundred years, the most popular and widespread Jewish history book of early medieval origin was the *Sefer Josifon,* which was written in simple Biblical Hebrew, making it accessible to a broad Jewish public.[33] It was erroneously attributed to Flavius Josephus because it incorporated and developed parts of his original narrative. Probably compiled in 953 CE in southern Italy, it survived for more than five hundred years in various manuscript forms, and was first printed in 1476 in Mantua, making it one of the first printed Hebrew books. It saw, until the twentieth century, a great number of Hebrew editions and even more translations.[34] The volume devotes significant attention to the Jewish wars against Rome and is "filled with national pride," to quote David Flusser, who published a new, complete edition in 1979.[35] More than that, there is a martial spirit in the *Josifon* Oswald Spengler would have liked because it supported his theory that the Jews were a warrior people.

Like Josephus' *The Jewish War,* the *Josifon* closes with the story of Masada, but there is a revealing difference between the two narratives. Both tell the story of the heroic last stand of the Jewish rebels in Masada, which no talmudic or other rabbinic source ever mentioned. Josephus reports how the last defenders killed their women and children and then killed one another in order to avoid falling into Roman hands. This tale is signficiantly different in the *Josifon,* which notes that the defenders killed their women and children and then "went up in the morning and came out of the city [Masada], all together like one man, in a fierce and furious mood. They fought against a multitude of Romans and killed countless numbers of them until they were all dead on the battlefield."[36] This is a fabrication, but one that obviously suited the Jewish public's appetite for tales of Jewish military bravery and fighting spirit more than stories of collective self-annihilation, suffering, and martyrdom.[37] If this is what the Jews wanted to hear, *Josifon* gave them plenty of it: "The rulers of Rome...loved our forefathers for their force, their heroism and their loyalty."[38] The enduring popularity of the book through the ages points to a continuity of Jewish interest in war and heroism about which we know little. The historian Joseph Klausner suspected as much: "Undoubtedly, Yavne saved the Jewish people from extinction. But maybe Masada saved it as well? Who knows, if in addition to the Torah, the memory of the heroism...did not save the Jewish people from stagnation and extinction?"[39]

It is impossible to know whether such collective memories had any impact on the real-life attitudes of Diaspora Jews. Heroic memories could not supersede the pragmatic pacifism decreed by the rabbis of the Talmud, nor could they change the basic powerlessness of Diaspora Judaism. Rarely were Jews able or willing to offer collective armed resistance when under physical attack, although there are cases when they tried to do so, for example during the First Crusade in the Rhineland in 1095. Yet there is an apparently unrelated historical fact that has been overlooked in Jewish and general historiography: the frequent participation of Diaspora Jews, sometimes in eminent positions, in the military services of their host nations. Jewish participation in the wars of the world from the earliest times, even when the Temple still stood, is one of the most underreported chapters of Jewish history. It does not fit with Jewish religious or Zionist historical perspectives, not to mention those of Christian or Muslim historians, who found the idea of fighting and heroic Jews after biblical times unpalatable. Nonetheless, Jews fought under many flags. Their "martial virtues" (Spengler), if this is what they were, served the powers of the world with distinction. A few examples will be given shortly. There are many more, but a comprehensive military history of the Jews has yet to be compiled.

In the context of a rise-and-decline study, one has to ask a number of questions. For example, what difference did Jewish service under foreign flags make? Even if it was not a major driver of Jewish rise and survival, did it make at least some contribution to Jewish rights, prestige, and prosperity? Then, who were the Jews who joined their countries' armies? Were they a small, marginal minority who flouted their religious laws or had left the Jewish community? Were they simply desperate for employment? Or were they perhaps forced to serve? And finally, do the examples show some historical continuity, or are they isolated cases that appear here and there in irregular intervals? The answers to these questions vary according to time and place.

Jewish soldiers operated not individually but in units outside Israel or Judah even before the destruction of the First Temple.[40] As early as in the seventh or sixth century BCE, a contingent of Jewish mercenaries appeared in Elephantine, near present-day Assuan in Egypt, to help Pharaoh Psammetich I (664-610 BCE) or Psammetich II (595-589 BCE) guard the country's southern border.[41] This Jewish force wrote and probably spoke Aramaic. We know, from the letters soldiers wrote, and from their clashes with hostile Egyptian neighbors, that they wanted to remain a part of the people of Israel.

These soldiers were hired to assist the Persians after the Persian conquest of Egypt in 525 BCE: the Persian Empire, which had freed the Jews from Babylonian exile, apparently trusted the loyalty and military valor of its professional Jewish soldiers more than that of the local inhabitants. Between the sixth and fourth centuries BCE, Persian kings protected the Jews of both Babylon and Judah, as we know from the story of Nehemiah. The presence of a Jewish army unit serving Persia in a critical border area can only have enhanced the standing of Jews in the Persian Empire. Later, and throughout the Ptolemaic period (323-30 BCE), Jews served in Egypt in every capacity, apparently in large numbers, including as top military commanders of Queen Cleopatra III (reigned 142-101 BCE). The history of Jewish armed service in Egypt from late Pharaonic times to the Roman era lasted more than 500 years.

In Europe, the longest and most famous mercenary tradition, that of the Swiss units, who fought for the kings of France and other countries, lasted from the early- or mid-fifteenth-century until the French Revolution, approximately 350 years.

Jewish service for Rome was even more critical for Jewish history than the Jewish service for Elephantine.[42] This is an often-suppressed chapter of Jewish history that needs more exploration. It does not fit well with the Jewish revolts against Rome, their suffering under Roman rule, and their indisputable hatred of Rome, but it does show the great spread, variety, and complexity of Jewish life in the larger Roman Empire. Some have called Jewish soldiers in Roman service "renegades" or "apostates," but we know from many sources that they actually thought of themselves as Jews, were members of synagogues, and commissioned gravestones with Jewish iconography.[43] Their true number will never be known because many of them had Greek or Roman names, and most sources that could reveal their Jewish origin were lost long ago.

Archeological finds in unexpected places shed, from time to time, new light on Jews in the Roman military.* In Rome, Jews boasted a military history of five hundred years, lasting, with interruptions, from Julius Caesar (100-44 BCE) to the early fifth century CE. Julius Caesar's outspoken friendship for the Jewish people had long-lasting consequences that partly survived Rome's oppression and destruction of Judea in 70 and 135 CE. The original reason for this friendship was the support Julius Caesar received from Judean military units—not individual soldiers—at a critical moment in his Egyptian campaign of 48/47 BCE. Following the death of his enemy at home, Pompey, Caesar had to vanquish Pompey's Egyptian allies if he wanted to control Rome. He landed with approximately 5,000 men, who were insufficient to defeat the Egyptian army. Then the High Priest Hyrcanus II, who had taken Caesar's side, dispatched, according to Flavius Josephus, 3,000 Judean soldiers to Egypt (in other sources the number was 1,500).[44] He also appealed to the Jews of Egypt to remember their common bonds with the Jews of Judea and support Caesar, which they did.

At the head of the Judean army and some other units was a fearless commander, Antipater, the father of Herodes.[45] Antipater's Judean fighting force decided the critical battle in the Nile Delta and put the Egyptian army to flight.

---

* Swiss archeologists found a ring with a *menorah* in the ruins of a Roman military colony near Basel. The ring was provisionally dated to the third century CE, and might have been brought there by a Jewish soldier or merchant. See *Der Menora-Ring von Kaiseraugst. Jüdische Zeugnisse Römischer Zeit zwischen Brittanien und Pannonien (The Menora Ring of Kaiseraugst, Jewish Documents of Roman Times between Brittania and Pannonia),* ed. L. Berger (Basel: Verlag Schwabe, 2005). It has been suggested that many of the Jews who settled during late Roman times in Southern Germany were soldiers and not only slaves or merchants.

Caesar relied on Antipater "in the most hazardous undertakings"[46] until the end of this war, and Antipater was wounded in one of these actions. Caesar showed extraordinary gratitude for the services Jewish soldiers and their leaders had rendered. His edicts (47-44 BCE) were confirmed by the Roman Senate and gave the Jews of the Roman provinces and Judea, in recognition of their military and other merits, a number of privileges that would later be sustained by Emperor Augustus. These included the right to keep the Sabbath and, ironically, exemption from military service in some places. It is worth noting that the first time a polytheistic civilization publicly recognized the "Jewish invention" of the Sabbath, it did so in recognition of Jewish military valor.

In Judea the benefits of these edicts were short-lived, but for Jews of the wider Mediterranean Diaspora, they were lasting. Jewish tradition and some Jewish historians give none or only scant attention to the critical battle in Egypt that saved Caesar and boosted the position of the Jewish people. Apparently, the old Jewish distaste of the criminally insane Herodes also extended to his father.*

Jews made careers in the Roman military. The most successful, but also the most troubling, of them was Tiberius Julius Alexander, born in 16 CE in Alexandria. He was a nephew of the Jewish philosopher Philo of Alexandria (20 BCE-50 CE). His Jewish father, a senior Roman official, had donated a golden door to the Temple of Jerusalem. No Jew ever rose to a higher military rank in Rome than Tiberius Julius Alexander. Between 46 and 48 CE he was Procurator of Judea, and in 69 CE he accompanied his friend, Titus, during the invasion of Judea. His position was comparable to that of chief-of-staff. He commanded two legions, and participated in the siege of Jerusalem to the very end. Flavius Josephus mentions him repeatedly and praises his leadership qualities, but refers only once to his Jewish origin, saying that Tiberius Julius Alexander was less "pious" than his father, "for he did not continue in the religion of his country."** This discreet reprimand

---

* Heinrich Graetz does not question the accuracy of Flavius Josephus's narrative and describes Antipater's victory and its critical importance for Julius Caesar, but does so with so many invectives against Antipater (who is "disloyal," "conniving," "without scruples," etc.) that a credulous Jewish reader cannot be very proud of his deeds. Heinrich Graetz, *Volkstümliche Geschichte*, 464ff.

** "Jewish Antiquities" Book 20.5.2 (100), 648. As Tiberius Julius Alexander left no writings, we can only speculate about his attitude toward his origins. Schoenfeld, 120, believes that he kept some of his religious sensitivities, because Josephus reported that he was one of the officers who followed Titus in trying to prevent the burning of the Temple. In contrast, Hadas-Lebel, who wrote a biography of his uncle Philo, sees him as an example of "Jewish self-hate," 356. See also Mireille Hadas-Lebel, *Rome, la Judée et les Juifs* (Paris: A& J Picard, 2009), 94.

is revealing: the Roman Jew, Flavius Josephus, distanced himself from his no longer faithful former "coreligionist."

Jewish participation in the Roman military seems to have increased from the reign of Caracalla (211-217 CE) on. There was even an exclusively Jewish unit with a Jewish name, the *Regii Emeseni Iudaei (Royal Emesene Jews)*, stationed in 356 in Alexandria and in 409 in Italy. Egyptian Jews are believed to have provided the Roman army with the largest contingent, followed by Jews from Syria, Asia Minor and Italy. Many were stationed in Pannonia (Hungary) and Dacia (Romania).* When Christianity became the state religion, Jewish military history in Rome came to an end. Theodosius I (reigned 379-395) barred Jews from serving as officers. In 410, and again in 418, Theodosius II expelled all of them from the army. His decree had to be repeated because it was followed only reluctantly.

The conclusion that must be reached is that military service sustained the continuity, survival, and wide dispersion of Jews in the Roman Empire. This was a real driver of Jewish civilization, and it had secondary effects long after the fall of the Roman Empire. Many Ashkenazi Jews are descendants of Italian Jews of late Antiquity, who are themselves descendants of the Jews of the Roman Empire. These Italian Jews moved north between the eighth and tenth centuries to settle in German lands. They joined other Jews who had lived there for centuries and had arrived not only as Roman slaves or merchants but, as recently suggested, also as Roman soldiers. A long chain of events led from Julius Caesar, Hyrcanus, and Antipater to the rise of Ashkenazi Judaism north of the Alps.

The best-known and proudest Jewish military leader of early Diasporic times was Samuel Hanagid (993-1055), vizier of the Muslim kingdom of Granada. He served his king not only as head of government, but also as a commander-in-chief who personally led his army into many battles. He was also a brilliant poet whose Hebrew verses in the poem *The Battle of Alfuente* glorified war and revealed his own martial excitement: "Horses speed back and forth like adders from the lair. The spears flash like lightening through the air. The arrows are drops of rain, and the swords gleam brightly."** Samuel Hanagid was also a Talmud scholar and expert in *halakha*. His prestige as both

---

* Two thirds of all Jewish gravestone inscriptions from Pannonia are those of Roman legionnaires, serving with the First Syrian Archers and the First Emesene Archers, among other units. Schoenfeld, 122.

** *A History of the Jewish People,* 456. There are other poems by Samuel Hanagid which show that he also knew the tragic sides of war. One of his shortest and most famous poems is "First War": "First war resembles a beautiful girl we all want to flirt with and believe. Later it's more a repulsive old whore whose callers are bitter and grieve." *The Dream of the Poem,* 58f.

a civil and a military leader may have added to the status and prosperity of the Jews living in his time in the Muslim kingdom.

Unexpected and largely unknown is the service of Chinese Jewish officers and soldiers in the army of the Emperors of the Yuan, Ming, and early Qing dynasties (fourteenth—seventeenth centuries CE). During these dynasties, Jews had unhindered access to military and civic careers, provided they passed the required examinations. Chinese chroniclers and historians have found and still find it noteworthy that some of the sons of this tiny community reached high ranks in the army. This "reflected the trust and attention of the Yuan government (fourteenth century)...and the close relations between the Jews and the Emperor Yuan Shizu," writes one modern Chinese historian.[47] In the seventeenth century, several Jews again reached high officer ranks,[48] and in the eighteenth a Jesuit visitor reported a Chinese text stating that Jews were "held in high esteem," among other places, "in public office and in the armed forces."[49] All respectable careers were open to these Chinese Jews and, according to some sinologists, a good civil service career conferred more public prestige than an army career. Chinese Jews are likely to have sought distinction in war by their own volition, not because they were compelled to do so.

Even more astounding, and better documented, is the military history of the Jews of India, particularly their largest group, the Bnei Israel, who claim a presence in India since 70 CE. In India, like in China, there has never been anti-Jewish discrimination or persecution, except for the violence inflicted on Indian Jews by Portuguese invaders in the sixteenth century. Members of the Bnei Israel served, in the seventeenth and eighteenth centuries, in the army and navy of the Maratha confederacy then ruling large parts of central India. After 1760, when the British defeated the Maratha, the Bnei Israel began to enlist in the army of the East India Company. In 1837, one thousand Bnei Israel, including family members, of a total population of 5,225, derived their livelihoods from army service, which is a huge proportion considering that Jews were not excluded from the civil professions open to "natives." The military was their preference, apparently in accordance with older traditions. Jews fought in Mysore, Afghanistan, Burma, and elsewhere, and many received high military honors or reached the highest rank a "native" soldier could reach under British rule.[50] When India gained its independence in 1947, this old military tradition came to life again. From the ranks of this tiny community came a disproportionally large number of distinguished senior Indian officers.[51]

Bnei Israel historians tend to glorify their people's martial achievements, whereas Western Jewish historians generally prefer to pass over Jewish military history in the Diaspora. Some Bnei Israel firmly believe that they inherited their military prowess directly from the biblical Jews. Haeem Samuel

Kehimkar wrote, in 1897, a history of the Bnei Israel that wasn't published until 1937. Chapter IX, titled "The Bene-Israel As Gallant and Faithful Soldiers," uses language describing Jewish military heroism unheard since Flavius Josephus and the *Sefer Josifon*: "Israelites have, in fact, inherited the soldier-like qualities they possess from the royal race from which they are descended...the recollection of the heroic deeds of their ancestors, the memory of their undaunted valour on fields of battle, to which is to be ascribed the production of many gallant soldiers in the ranks of the sons of Israel that have rushed forth to battle under furious charges of musketry and cannon, etc."[52] A more recent Bnei Israel historian notes with equal pride that his people were early on recognized as a "martial race" like the Sikh, and that they "pre-date the Israelis as soldiers."[53]

Beginning in the twelfth century, Jews under Christian and Muslim rule were excluded from military service. The French Revolution introduced them into the armies of Europe. From the nineteenth century on, large numbers of Jews joined the armies of Europe, often through conscription. A surprising example of Jews volunteering to serve in a Jewish military unit is known from Poland. In 1794, the revolutionary Polish leader Tadeusz Kosciuszko authorized the Polish Jewish army colonel Berek Joselewicz to raise an all-Jewish unit in order to participate in the Polish uprising against Russia and Austria.[54] Joselewicz issued a patriotic call to arms in Yiddish, to which hundreds of volunteers responded. Five hundred men were chosen for a cavalry regiment. They were allowed kosher food, were exempt from fighting on the Sabbath when possible, and could keep their beards. Nearly all of them were wiped out in battle. They were probably poor men looking for employment, but their attention to Jewish religious laws seems to indicate that they were not marginal outcasts.

Their sacrifice did nothing for the future of Polish Judaism as a whole, however. This was the new pattern everywhere. Jews were expected to fight and die for their respective homelands, but this did not improve Jewish standing or living conditions, or even reduce antisemitism. However, in countries where antisemitism in the armed forces was apparently non-existent or less pronounced than in others, a few twentieth-century Jews attained the highest military ranks. In the West, these countries include Italy,[55] Belgium,[56] India, and Australia. The most distinguished of all was Australia's greatest soldier in World War I, the commander-in-chief of the Australian and New Zealand Army Corps (ANZAC) in 1918, General Sir John Monash (1865-1931), a son of Polish Jewish immigrants. On the Western front, Monash was considered an inspiring leader, brilliant tactician, and original strategist who led his men in mobile warfare. British Prime Minister Lloyd George is reported to have called him "the only soldier of World War I with the necessary qualities of leadership."[57]

Field Marshall Bernard Montgomery, the victor of the battle of El Alamein in 1942, served in 1918 as a junior officer under Monash, and himself became a mobile warfare expert. He admired Monash and wrote of him later that he was "the best general on the Western front in Europe."[58] Monash was a committed—one source says a practicing—Jew all his life, and in 1927 he became the first president of the Zionist Federation of Australia and New Zealand. It is likely that his prestige added to that of his community.

Jews as senior military commanders in Italy, Belgium, India, and Australia—countries with very different histories, cultures, and geographies— are a curious phenomenon indeed. One would like to know whether these examples are coincidental or represent a historical tradition of the kind Spengler postulated, or were caused by similar sociological factors. But which factors? In all four countries, other prestigious and rewarding careers that were less dangerous were open to Jews. However, in the end none of the Jewish generals in these four countries left a visible mark on the fate of his country, or that of the Jewish people, or on world history. The twentieth-century knows only one Jewish military leader outside of Israel who decisively affected his country, the Jews as a whole, and world history: Leon Trotsky (1879-1940).

Near the end of his life, Lenin admitted that Trotsky more than anyone had won the Russian Civil War,[59] and so did Stalin in a 1918 (later expunged) *Pravda* article. Trotsky was born to well-to-do Jewish farmers in Ukraine as Lev Davidovich Bronstein. In 1917 he joined Lenin's Bolsheviks and became, in spring 1918, their supreme military leader, although he had never served in an army. The Communists had already suffered crushing defeats on all fronts during the Russian Civil War, and Trotsky understood that the Revolution would only survive if he imposed two major military reforms. He called thousands of willing and well-trained ex-Tsarist officers back into service and introduced mass-conscription, against strong opposition from party ideologues as well as the rank and file. Between May and October 1918, he transformed a ragtag army of three hundred thousand disorganized men into a disciplined fighting machine of one million. His organizational talent, his gift for tactics and strategy, and his extraordinary power to inspire the masses are well documented, as is his personal bravery at the front of Petrograd (St. Petersburg). Let it also be said that his ruthlessness and contempt for human life are equally well documented.

No one in the leadership came anywhere near Trotsky as a public speaker, but in 1919 his military authority began to decline; his arrogance had made him too many enemies. When Lenin died in 1924, Trotsky's fate was sealed. Stalin expelled him from the party in 1927 and in 1940 had him murdered in his Mexican exile.

Trotsky's military genius had a profound and lasting impact on Russian and world history, because he probably saved the Russian Revolution. He had an indirect, negative impact on Jewish history. Trotsky knew that antisemitism was a major factor in the hostility against him, even among revolutionary Bolsheviks, and said so publicly in October 1923, before the entire Soviet leadership, when he defended himself against the charge of "Bonapartism."[60] Although he felt no enmity against other Jews, he initially rejected the cultural demands of the Yiddish-speaking "Bund" party as well as Zionism, which he blamed for Jewish "self-isolation."[61] The rise of Nazi Germany and of antisemitism in general motivated him to reexamine his positions in exile. He conceded, "The Jewish nation will maintain itself," and reflected on the conditions for the "establishment of a territorial basis for Jewry in Palestine."[62] For the Jews this was too late. The Soviet Union, which he had prominently helped to create, diverged soon enough from everything he had imagined and turned into an implacable foe of the Jewish people and, later, Israel. Stalin's increasingly deadly distrust of Jews, though it may have preceded his struggle with Trotsky, became more paranoid as a result of this struggle. On the other hand, to the Nazis and their supporters nobody offered a clearer proof than Trotsky that Soviet Bolshevism and Judaism were essentially the same. Both were hated and condemned to perish, and thus the Jews lost on all fronts. Trotsky's unwilling but disastrous role in the Jewish fate of the twentieth century is well summarized by a memorable quip attributed to a chief rabbi of Moscow: "The Trotskys make the revolutions and the Bronsteins pay the bills."[63]

Trotsky was the Soviet Union's most important military leader of Jewish origin, but there were many others. When the Tsarist rule that had oppressed the Jews collapsed, an active minority of Jews embraced the new regime, which at first appeared intellectual and cosmopolitan. It promised Jews more freedom and dignity, and quite a few of them were eager to fight for it. For the first time in Russian history prestigious military careers opened up for Jews. Some chose this path and reached senior positions, only to be later removed or wiped out by Stalin. The best known of all is General Yona Emmanuilovich Yakir (1896-1937) who distinguished himself during the Russian Civil War. Between the two wars, he, with a few other commanders, developed the military theory of "deep operations," which is regarded as one of the great innovations in military history. He created and trained the world's first large tank and air force formations, and shared with Trotsky a penchant for military innovation and an independent, nimble mind in the prosecution of war. Appropriately, Stalin indicted him for "Trotskyism," and had him and most of his family executed in 1937. It has been suggested that some of the victorious Soviet strategies in World War II resulted from General Yakir's teachings.

Other Jewish generals were among the large number of senior commanders purged and killed by Stalin. After 1945, over three hundred Jewish generals and admirals were removed, and senior military careers were closed to Jews from then on.[64] According to one (unverified) estimate, more than 300,000 Jewish soldiers gave their lives fighting with the Red Army on all fronts from 1941 to 1945 or were murdered when they fell into German captivity.[65] This is the largest single sacrifice Jewish soldiers have ever made for a country in which they lived. But not even this reduced Soviet antisemitism. The Soviet Jewish war correspondent Vasily Grossmann reported a violent clash he had in 1941 with the antisemitic novelist and later Nobel laureate Mikhail Sholokhov, who was a protégé of Stalin. Grossmann had already seen many Jews die in combat and was outraged when Sholokhov sneered at him that "Abraham is doing business in Tashkent."[66]

In the United States, Jews did their military service like everybody else when required, but few reached senior positions. They were never known to look for military careers in the same way that they sought careers in politics and law, business and finance, the film industry, literature and art, education, science and technology, and sports. Warmaking is the only major endeavor of the American nation in which Jews have not, or have only rarely, pursued success and national repute. The well-documented antisemitism of some of America's senior commanders was, perhaps, among the reasons. An extreme case was General George S. Patton, who in 1944/45 commanded America's Third Army and was celebrated by some as "America's greatest combat general." He expressed his contempt of Jews, even of Jewish Nazi camp survivors, after the war in terms that went beyond anything that was before 1945 acceptable among America's white upper classes.[67] These and similar attitudes must have added to the distaste of anything military that Jewish immigrants may have brought with them from Tsarist Russia and Central Europe. There the military was often a stronghold of antisemitism and national chauvinism.

There is no simple explanation for the long record of often-voluntary military contributions Jews made to the nations of the world. When Jews were allowed or invited to volunteer, some always did. One must add sociological factors to Spengler's suggestion of an ingrained Jewish "martial spirit." In countries where Jews were more or less accepted and lived a decent life, most grew roots and became good patriots. It is simply not true that Jews were typically unattached, homeless, and unrooted "service nomads."[68] They preferred to demonstrate their allegiance to their host countries without reneging on their Judaism if possible. This double allegiance may help to explain their military history in the Diaspora.

But we must now return to the key questions raised above. What difference did Jewish military valor under non-Jewish flags make? Was it a driver of Jewish civilization? Did it help Jewish survival? The answer is an unambiguous yes for the ancient world, in which Jews or Judeans had a distinct identity as a nation wherever they lived. Jewish soldiers in service to Egypt, Persia, and particularly Rome most probably added to the privileges, the prestige, and the survival of their nation. Ancient China and India were different. They were not aware of the story of the Jewish people, its history and global presence, and the local Jews were too few to count. Their military service made little difference to their standing in their country or the world, but is an interesting chapter of history. Pre-Modern and Modern Europe was again different. There Jewish military sacrifices were undeniable but did not enhance the status of the Jews in general. In the Soviet Union and beyond, the prominence of Jewish military commanders paradoxically exacerbated antisemitism.

During World War II, the military experience of Diaspora Jews did little to ensure their survival.* Among the millions who were killed in the *Shoah*, many had military training but no chance to use it. But there is another important aspect to this question. The massive re-entry of Jews into the armies of the world after centuries of absence must have contributed in indirect ways to a new Jewish rise and the emergence of the State of Israel. At issue was not only the acquisition of fighting skills. Military experience in the armies of the world arguably helped to change Jewish attitudes toward fighting in general, and Jewish self-defense in particular. The life of Joseph Trumpeldor (1880-1920) is an unusual but instructive example. Trumpeldor began his career in the tsar's army. Like all Russian soldiers, he had to swear allegiance to Nicholas II as well as to the "holy gospels," as the old Russian oath said. He lost an arm in the Russo-Japanese war of 1905, and received the Cross of St. George, the patron saint of Russia, for his bravery, which made him the most highly-decorated Jewish soldier of the old Russian army. He immigrated in 1911 to Ottoman Palestine, and in 1915 helped to set up the "Zion Mule Corps" to fight alongside the British. It was not the "first all-Jewish military unit in two thousand years," as Zionist narratives have asserted, but it was the first in the old homeland that was set up with a Jewish national goal. Trumpeldor fell in a battle against Arabs in 1920. General Monash is another example. Trumpeldor and Monash can be seen as two versions of a new role model. They distinguished themselves through bravery in the wars of their nations, and rose quickly in the ranks of their armies, but remained committed, in one way or another, to the homeland of their forefathers. The

---

* This statement is not true for the Jewish soldiers of Western armies who fell into German hands and generally were not murdered, in contrast to Soviet and Polish Jewish soldiers. Thousands of French Jews survived in German prisoner-of-war camps because they wore French army uniforms although the Germans knew that they were Jews, while their families, if they were caught, were deported to the death camps. All foreign (mostly East European) Jews who joined the French Foreign Legion also survived the war unless they died in battle.

first died as Israel's first national war hero, the second as the proud president of Australia's Zionist Federation.

Modern Israel

Modern Israel owes its creation and continued survival to its readiness to fight wars. This readiness had its roots in the early Zionist ideal of the "New Jew," but it also had links to older traditions and memories. Of great importance were the above-mentioned foreign military experience of Jewish soldiers and the experience of Israel-born soldiers in the 1930s who were trained by the pro-Zionist British officer and innovative tactician Orde Wingate. But foreign experience was not suddenly transferred to the Jewish people in Israel. There was a slow, organic transitional process that lasted more than half a century, beginning with the establishment of armed Jewish self-defense groups in Tsarist Russia after the pogroms of the late nineteenth and early twentieth century. Their military effectiveness was limited, but the long-term psychological impact was important: they represented the first known Jewish effort in many centuries to use weapons in self-defense rather than in the defense of other nations. During the same years, a small number of Jewish soldiers, such as Trumpeldor, joined the Zionist movement in Russia and emigrated to what was still Ottoman Palestine. From World War I to 1948, the growing Jewish defense organization in Pre-State Israel drew strength and professional competence from every army in the world in which Jews had served, from the old Ottoman army to the French Foreign Legion, not to mention the most important of all, the British army.

In the first half of 1948, the *Yishuv*, the Jews of British Mandatory Palestine, won a decisive military showdown with the Arabs of Palestine and the armies of the surrounding countries. Most of the approximately 28,000 *Yishuv* members who had served in the Allied armies during World War II joined the *Haganah* and later the Israeli Defense Forces, which numbered 65,000 fighters in July 1948 and 88,000 in October of the same year. This means that a high proportion of Israel's soldiers already had military experience, and quite a few of them had seen real war. In addition, from May 1948 onward, approximately 4,000 foreign volunteers who were World War II veterans joined Israel's armed forces. Many of them were critically-needed specialists, such as sailors, tank troops, logistics and communications experts, air and ground crews, and medics. Israel's small air force had a total of 193 pilots, 171 of whom (90 percent) were foreign volunteers, around 100 from America. Foreign volunteers comprised approximately 20 percent of the army's medical corps.[69] Tensions emerged between *Haganah* members and World War II veterans in the military high command. In July 1948, Prime Minister David Ben-Gurion was dismissive of the military abilities of some veteran *Haganah* commanders, and wanted to appoint two World War II British Army veterans as commanders of the Central Front and the Negev over the heads of incumbent *Haganah* candidates. The general staff fomented an internal "rebellion" against Ben-Gurion to prevent this move and succeeded in curtailing his powers.[70]

Thus, the military experience the Jews had acquired in World War II under foreign flags made an inestimable contribution to Israel's 1948 victory and the nascent state's survival. One can count the numbers of experienced veterans involved, but this would not accurately measure the quality or importance of their input. Israel would have won its War of Independence even without them, but more narrowly, and probably with greater human loss and less territorial gain.

The character and politics of modern Israel were profoundly influenced, indeed formed, by war. In its sixty-five years of existence (1948-2013), Israel has fought five traditional wars (in 1948, 1956, 1967, 1973, 1982), one "war of attrition" (1968-70), three new "asymmetric" wars (2006, 2008/9, and 2012), and two Intifadas (1987-1991 and 2000-2005)—more than any other Western nation in the same period—not to speak of the almost permanent war against terror and guerilla-type attacks, which had already started in the 1920s. In a narrow tactical sense it can be said that Israel won at least eight of its ten wars. Most Israeli and Western military experts appeared to agree that the ninth, the Lebanon war of 2006, was a failure. In contrast, some Chinese and Indian military experts, who observed this war with different criteria, came to different conclusions and saw Israel as victorious. It must also be said that the internal and external consequences of this war are still unfolding several years later. The criteria by which success or failure in asymmetric wars is judged—this was Israel's first important asymmetric war, the Gaza war in 2008/2009 was the second—differ from those for traditional wars and are less clearly established.

Apart from the Intifadas, the wars that apparently left the deepest impacts on Israel were the 1948 War of Independence, the Six-Day War of 1967, and the 1973 Yom Kippur War. Apart from the War of Independence, the Six-Day War had the farthest-reaching consequences for the entire Middle East and for the international system. The first reaction to the Six-Day War was "intoxication with victory," to use Toynbee's phrase, as other countries experienced fresh on the heels of victory. This euphoria was followed by a political stalemate, which was only partly broken by the subsequent Yom Kippur War. Intoxication and traumatization may have prevented Israel from taking full advantage of the greatest victory it ever had. A historian has shown how much this well planned victory owed to sheer luck and mistakes made by the Arab side. Perhaps this is true of every great and speedy military victory.[71]

War has profoundly influenced, even formed the character of Israel, and in many ways. It touched upon every major political, socioeconomic, and psychological development of the country. Some changes came about through policies aimed at turning foreign hostility to Israel's advantage. The following areas of national interest and policy have been particularly affected by war:

National Leadership. A large number of Israeli generals and senior officers moved into politics after their military service, and several of them became future-shaping national leaders, including three who became prime ministers and several who went on to become ministers of defense and ministers of other departments of government. The Israeli public welcomed this transition from the army into politics for a long time because, at least until the Yom Kippur War, it trusted its military more than its civilian politicians. Some of these officers have probably enriched Israeli statecraft with professional competence, but there have also been more critical views of their contribution. It was said, for example, that officers who became politicians may have made historic errors because their mindset was too dominated by military experience. Another criticism claimed that the military establishment had too much influence on Israeli policy-making because its members' views were always backed up by their former army colleagues who had become government ministers. In any event, taken as a whole, officers who became politicians have probably influenced Israel's history more profoundly than any other single group of politicians has. It must be added that this influence was by no means unilateral. Some former generals had rightwing convictions, others left-leaning beliefs, and several moved from one end of the political spectrum to the opposite during their careers. More time will have to pass before it will be possible to fairly judge the long-term historical impact of former military officers becoming leaders.

Internal Cohesion. Until the 1973 Yom Kippur War, Israel's wars had reinforced the internal cohesion of the Israeli people. This was important not only in 1948 and 1967, but also in 1956. The Suez War of 1956 had a "cohesive" societal effect. It broke out after major Jewish immigration waves from Muslim countries which evinced social and cultural tensions. The Yom Kippur War and all of the following ones, including both Intifadas, may have created more internal dissent and unrest than cohesion. However, not all dissent is bad. Often it is dissent, not cohesion, that brings about essential changes.

Immigrant Integration and Education. Military service—not necessarily fighting in wars—was for decades regarded as an indispensable factor of integration, acculturation, and in many cases the education of hundreds of thousands of immigrants from dozens of countries. Many Israelis learned Hebrew in the army, some of them received professional training there, and most of them learned more about the varied social and ethnic structure of their people than civil life alone would have provided.

Economic and Technological Development. A major fallout of war and foreign hostility was the successful development of Israel's economy and modern technology. From the very beginning Israel's enemies hoped to weaken and subdue her by dissuading foreign countries from selling weapons to her and by launching a general economic boycott they tried to persuade the whole world to honor. However, Israel—not always through the government, but often also through private initiative—used external danger and the concomitant need to develop its own military industry to build a competitive high-tech economy that keeps growing and has become an integral part of its military, economic, and scientific strength. A central pillar of this high-tech economy is Israel's competence in many sectors of informatics, to a large degree an outgrowth of military R&D. Thousands of innovative managers, scientists, and engineers have transferred this ingenuity from the military sector to the civilian. Of course, military R&D has also spawned Israel's international competitiveness in weaponry and other military hardware, staples among Israeli exports. The twentieth century knows no equivalent technological success story of a small country that had to start without a modern industrial or non-military technological base.

The Search for International Links and Friends. Arab hostility has spurred Israeli governments to search out allies and friends across the world. Part IV, Chapter 9 on Geopolitics will discuss this further. Prime Minister David Ben-Gurion wanted Israel to have the support of at least one great power and to avoid confrontation with other major powers. He also wanted a secondary ring of friendly states to surround the primary ring of neighboring enemies. Thus, he and his successors invested considerable efforts in forging friendships and alliances with Turkey, Iran, Ethiopia, and sub-Saharan Africa generally. Ben-Gurion also regarded China and India as great civilizations and foresaw that they would one day emerge as great powers. He was convinced that it was essential for Israel, an Asian country, to develop the best possible links with these two giants. Ben-Gurion and his successors succeeded in some of these geopolitical endeavors but not in others, or, as in the case of Iran, they succeeded only for a limited time. Some of Israel's current international links can be traced back to these early efforts.

Cohesion with the Jewish People. Israel's wars probably did as much to reinforce links with world Jewry as peace initiatives have. The effects were spiritual, political, and also practical. Each war triggered an emotional upsurge in many Diaspora communities, followed by financial, political, and other aid. At first glance, the impacts of Israel's wars on the Jewish people globally seem to have been positive. But quick, hot wars are one thing, and permanent, stalemated tension another. The unending Arab-Israeli conflict with its bloody incidents, hostile rhetoric, frequent criticisms of Israel's human rights record, and, in some countries, the perceived links between Israel and the policy of the United States, have all had corrosive effects on Jewish Diaspora identity, solidarity, and pride. Comparing the positive and negative effects of war and tension is difficult.

Considering the state of the world generally, and that of the Middle East in particular, Israel will continue to have to live with the intractable tension between readiness for war and yearning for peace mentioned at the beginning of this chapter. It is unlikely that Israel will be allowed to forget its martial readiness anytime soon. Struggling for peace while preparing for war has been the fate of many other nations in history. Ensuring Israel's future will call for strategic, tactical, and technological innovation. Maintaining Israel's capacity to fight and win violent conflicts, and preserving the determination of its society to do so, will depend on the quality of its leadership. Innovative intellectual efforts beyond military technology and tactics must also be a part of this capacity. Such efforts could aim at encouraging a revision of current international laws of war, which were formulated for traditional wars and for opponents who agree to respect them, but not for unconventional and asymmetric wars. The threat of possible weapons of mass destruction in the hands of Israel's enemies is raising a huge challenge to Jewish survival. But this time, and for the first time in history, an existential threat to a major part of the Jewish people is also a threat to the whole world, because the use of such weapons against Israel would have incalculable consequences for the wider Middle East and beyond.

CHAPTER 9

Geopolitics and Civilizational Affinities

General Observations

This chapter will focus on civilizational or cultural affinities in the service of statecraft or geopolitics. Definitions of geopolitics abound; some overlap with definitions of geo-strategy, some contradict each other, and some are simply incomprehensible. Here, geopolitics is defined as the description or the instrument of statecraft that seeks to improve the power of a nation through geographic, economic, military, or cultural assets, and by winning foreign friends and allies. Geopolitics has to match means with goals. In many cases this requires boosting the means through the acquisition of more influence, friends, allies, territory, weapons, or economic assets. In other cases it requires limiting the goals. Thucydides reported that Pericles vainly admonished the Athenians to do both—to enhance their main military asset, which was their superiority at sea, but at the same time to keep their war aims modest.[1] Pericles was a master of geopolitics long before the term was invented.

War is the most dramatic instrument of statecraft to prevail over other nations. As indicated in the previous chapter, it must be seen in a geopolitical context. Culture, expressing the values and traditions of a civilization, can be another instrument to increase power and win friends and allies. Existing civilizational affinities can be employed and new ones can be created. Samuel Huntington asserts that civilization or culture has currently become the most important dimension of geopolitics.[2] According to his thesis, global politics is being restructured along civilizational lines. Peoples and countries with similar civilizations are coming nearer to one another. The strongest bonds between countries and peoples will be civilizational, and political boundaries will be redrawn to better reflect cultural ones. A civilization shared by a number of countries will often have a "core nation" that can represent all of them. The United States is currently the core nation of Western civilization. If countries of the same "family" lack a single accepted core nation, they have a problem. This is the case of the Islamic civilization. There are also nations, like Japan, that are the only member of a civilization and therefore stand alone. They too have a problem. Huntington believes that civilization-based geopolitics represents a major historical change that will distinguish the future from the past. Whether this will come to pass is difficult to predict. One does not have to accept all his theses to agree that civilizational affinities have always played a role in history and international power politics and will continue to do so.

However, civilizational similarity is not identical with affinity and does not necessarily create affinity. In the past, different nations belonging to closely related civilizations and languages were as often in conflict as they were at peace with each other. Russians and Poles, Serbs and Croats, Swedes and Norwegians, Chinese and Vietnamese, Thais and Laotians, and others share essential cultural and linguistic traits but have long common histories of tension and war. To outsiders or later generations their differences seem minor or incomprehensible. Despite this, in many cases Huntington is right. Civilizational similarity and familiarity can become the basis of affinity, friendship, and cooperation. All through history, peoples and civilizations have sought alliances against a common enemy. The strongest and most lasting alliances are often those for which a common strategic interest coincides with a common cultural bond. This can become a cause of strength when one people helps protect another. There are other cases in which the cultural or historical bond is strong enough to underpin an alliance even when strategic interests are not identical. The historians discussed in Part II give geopolitical examples in which common interests led to alliances and strategies based on civilizational affinities. To avoid confusion with unclear or diverging theoretical definitions of geopolitics, two concrete case studies have been chosen to show how statecraft has employed civilizational affinities. They will then be contrasted with a case where a major geopolitical initiative failed spectacularly, not least because of a complete absence of historical understanding and cultural affinity. All three cases have had far-reaching historical consequences.

Chinese Geopolitics in the Second century BCE and the Opening of the Silk Road[3]

The case of a country that is at war with another one and seeks an alliance with a third one, ideally an "enemy of its enemy," is quite common, but the far-sightedness of Chinese emperor Wu of Han, Han Wudi (reigned 141-87 BCE), and the courage and persistence of his emissary Zhang Qian in pursuing his sovereign's geo-strategy are rare. During Wudi's reign, China's worst problem was the incursions of the Central Asian Xiongnu nomads, who inflicted untold suffering on the Chinese people. The Chinese army tried to pursue them but could not negotiate the enormous expanses of Central Asia to conquer them. One day Wudi learned that the Xiongnu had killed a king in

West-Central Asia and that his people wanted revenge. He calculated that it would be useful to win the other country's friendship in order to exert joint pressure on the Xiongnu. In 138 BCE, when the emperor was 19 years of age and only three years into his long reign, he sent the explorer Zhang Qian with a large delegation to the "West" (for China, the West meant Central and West Asia or India) to establish contacts and explore new political and military options. But Zhang Qian had to cross enemy territory to get there and was arrested by the Xiongnu, who kept him in detention for ten years, until 128 BCE. He never revealed that he was an imperial envoy on a secret mission and eventually succeeded in fleeing. He reached Bactria, Sogdania, and the Parthian Empire (present-day Uzbekistan, Afghanistan, and Iran), where he discovered sophisticated urban civilizations. In the words of Sima Qian, they were "all great states rich in unusual products whose people cultivated the land and made their living in much the same way as the Chinese. All these states...were militarily weak and prized Han goods and wealth."[4] This meant that the chances of a serious military alliance against the Xiongnu were slim, but new political links and great economic opportunities opened up instead, which would strengthen the empire in many ways.

To the delight of the emperor, after twelve years of absence, that is in 126 BCE, Zhang Qian brought back not only detailed descriptions of the geography, ethnography, and economics of these countries, but also luxury goods and exotic fruit, such as grapes, unknown in China before that time. In 115 BCE, Zhang Qian made a second visit to the same countries, traveling part of the way over different roads. His, and by extension Emperor Wudi's, success did much more than open a new trade route. It pierced the nomadic barrier in the West and pushed open China's door to the rest of the civilized world. It is very significant that Zhang Qian emphasized the civilizational affinities this new world shared with China, according to Sima Qian, who is likely to have seen Zhang's written reports at court. Following the explorer's return, the "Silk Road" became a major, flourishing trade route, large Chinese missions continued to visit West Asia, and, in 97 BCE, ten years before the emperor's death, General Ban Cao established military bases near the Caspian Sea during an expedition against the Xiongnu. What began as a secret geo-strategic initiative to contain an enemy led to a major trade link that enhanced China's prestige and commercial influence for centuries. This did not destroy the Xiongnu's nuisance capacity; it is not even known if it lessened it. One could, of course, argue that some Chinese silk had been exported earlier and that more of it would have found its way to West Asia and Rome in any event. Another Chinese emperor could have discovered West Asia a century or two later. But the fact is that it was young Wudi who had—perhaps for the first time—a far-reaching vision of Central and West Asia, which he pursued during most of his 54 years in power, becoming a model for later rulers. It took a strong and exceptionally long-reining emperor to pursue such a long-term geopolitical goal. Later dynasties would renew China's interest in these regions and attempt to gain footholds there, and the Qing dynasty did so successfully in the mid-eighteenth century.[5] The currently growing Chinese engagement in the wider Middle East has very old historical roots, and Westerners who attribute it only to China's need for oil are mistaken.

William III of Orange and the "Glorious Revolution": An Exceptionally Bold Initiative that Changed History[6]

In 1685-1691, the Dutch Republic launched a successful geo-strategic and military initiative of rare daring and sophistication. The "Glorious Revolution," as it was called, changed Dutch, British and, ultimately world history in dramatic ways. The immediate impetus for this event was France's aggressive trade war against the Dutch, which raised the spectre of another military invasion by Louis XIV like that of 1672, which had nearly extinguished the Dutch Republic. In England the staunchly Catholic Stuart King James II ruled over a largely Protestant population with strong anti-Catholic sentiments. This alone created an obvious religious affinity between the English and the Dutch, but also between the rulers of the English and French. James II depended on Louis XIV. When the Dutch discovered that the two Catholic kings were conspiring against them, they feared, probably rightly, that their existence was in danger. They could not defend their small country, which had no natural borders, against the French armies, not to mention the combined might of France and England. Then Prince William III of Orange, "Stadthouder" of the Dutch Republic, made a startling decision. A nephew of King James II, he set an eye on the English throne. In a secret session of Parliament in September 1688, he revealed his decision to launch an invasion of England. In a few weeks, with stunning speed and efficiency, he pulled together an armada of nearly 500 vessels, four times the size of the Spanish armada of 1588, with 21,000 armed men, thousands of horses, and all of the Netherlands' heavy artillery. The fleet departed in early November and landed with little opposition. The forces of James II quickly crumbled, and in December 1688 William entered London in triumph.

William became the joint Protestant sovereign of England and the Dutch Republic, brought England into war against France, and thus rescued the Republic. France would not threaten the existence of the Netherlands again until 1795, when the French revolutionary armies swept over all of Europe.

Observers were awed by Prince William's organizational and military performance. "It was arguably one of the most impressive feats of organization any early modern regime ever achieved," writes Jonathan I. Israel.[7] It was also an extremely risky, if not a daredevil, geo-political venture that could have gone terribly wrong. But it did not, and the Netherlands was saved. In contrast to the initiative of China's Emperor Wudi, Prince William's success was decisive in the very short term, which was its goal, but it could not last. The bonds between the Netherlands and England could not withstand the inevitable conflicts of interest that emerged between these two unequal partners. Severe trade and political tensions later led to war between the two countries.

In both cases, a bold geo-strategic initiative, one long-term and the other short-term, was supported and justified not only by urgent military need, but also by feelings of civilizational affinity. In both cases, too, exceptional geo-political achievements were the outcome of exceptional leadership qualities, which brings us back to the question of leadership, as was discussed in Part IV, Chapter 5). Wudi and William were, in their time, outstanding leaders who combined three qualities: a far-reaching vision of history, a practical sense, and a strong will to act. Thucydides saw the same talents in Athens' savior, Themistocles. Moreover, the two rulers were ready to gamble and take risks, but not without meticulous preparation. Luck also played a great role: fortune was, in the end, on their side. However, there are probably as many cases of geo-political failures due to incompetence and faulty judgment, or to a lack of factual knowledge. Often, bad luck played a major role as well, as will be discussed in Chapter 11 of this section.

The "Zimmermann Telegram": A Failed Geopolitical Venture during World War I

An example of an incredibly clumsy geopolitical initiative that had dramatic consequences for its authors is the "Zimmermann Telegram" or "Zimmerman Note,"[8] a coded message sent by Foreign Secretary of the German Empire Arthur Zimmermann on January 16, 1917, to the German ambassador in Mexico at the height of World War I. Germany planned to begin unrestricted submarine warfare in spite of warnings by the still-neutral United States, in order to weaken the United States in case they entered the war on the side of Germany's enemies. Thus, the Germans proposed to the Mexicans a joint military alliance promising them, if they joined a war against the United States, financial aid and the return of territories that they had lost in war to the United States.

Mexico was wise enough to immediately reject the idea, but the telegram was intercepted and decoded by Britain and given to the Unites States, where it was published. This led to an outpouring of anti-German hostility and propaganda in that country. Much earlier, in 1915, German submarines had sunk the Cunard liner "Lusitania," and many American lives were lost. This had begun to turn international and American opinion against Germany, but the Zimmermann telegram—nearly two years later—was a more direct trigger hastening America's entry into World War I as it changed the formerly neutral mood of the American public. On April 6, 1917, the United States Congress declared war on Germany. The Zimmermann plan was ill-conceived and reckless. It showed a surprising ignorance of the balance of power on the American continent and a miscalculation of the Mexican mentality and its interests. It was, in fact, a bizarre example of what Henry Kissinger called "the lack of geopolitical understanding by which the Germany of Wilhelm II progressively isolated itself."[9] It should also be noted that there were no historical or cultural affinities between Germany and Mexico.

Emperor Wilhelm and his government lacked the gifted know-how Emperor Wudi was eager to acquire and William III of Orange obviously possessed. A comprehensive knowledge of the world and understanding of other nations' projects and feelings in addition to their material assets is a precondition of long-term success in geopolitics. In some cases it is simply impossible to gain all the necessary knowledge. Gibbon noted that Rome's decline and fall was, among many other reasons, partly caused by its inability to find out about fatal dangers lurking in far-away places before it was too late. According to an eighteenth-century reading of Asian history, the remote Huns moved West and invaded Eastern Europe and then the Roman Empire only after they had been defeated and driven off by the Chinese Empire.[10] What could the Romans of the fifth century CE possibly have known of past wars in the Central Asian steppes when even today we have only the most fragmentary knowledge of what happened there in the early 1950s? In many other cases, however, better understanding and foresight would be possible if leaders were not hampered by religious or, as in the case of Emperor Wilhelm, nationalistic blinders. More than one nation was defeated in war not so much because it underestimated its enemies' exact military forces as because it ignored their true motivations, fighting spirit, and culture. Geopolitics has to give attention to intangible factors as well as to material factors. This is what Samuel Huntington meant when he wrote that culture is or will become an essential component of geopolitical strategies and alliances, as quoted above.

Applications to Jewish History

Until the recent gas finds in Israel's off-shore waters, the Jews had no natural resources and no geographic advantages. Their land was small and often in danger of being overrun. For more than half of their history, they had no land of their own. Old Jewish history does not report exceptionally daring and successful geopolitical strategies like those of the Han Emperor Wudi or the Stadthouder of the Dutch Republic, Prince William III. It was, in any event, exceptionally difficult for ancient Israel to correctly assess the movements and intentions of all the great and small powers in the wider Middle East and the Mediterranean which could affect its fate. For Diaspora Jews, the difficulty was compounded by their wide geographic spread. Any major power shift in the world and any major move by a great power could affect at least a part of the Jewish people.

Ancient Israel

The first historically documented geopolitical policy decisions in Israel can be attributed to King Ahab, one of Israel's most powerful kings, who reigned, according to various calculations, from 874, 871, or 869 until 853, 852, or 850. Ahab had married Jezebel, daughter of a Phoenician king, arguably not only for love but also to secure the political and strategic support of this important neighbor to the North. As the biblical chronicler paid most attention to morality and not to Ahab's geopolitical schemes, he reviled Jezebel and the erotic and other pagan cults she brought from Phoenicia. Another of Ahab's strategic schemes, perhaps a more complicated one, was the preparation for the battle of Qarqar in central Syria in 853 BCE. The event is known from an Assyrian inscription, the "Kurkh Monolith," already mentioned in this volume in the context of demography (Part IV, Chapter 6). Archeologists regard the inscription as trustworthy *inter alia* because it does not boast of an Assyrian victory. King Ahab participated in an alliance of twelve kings to stop the advance of Assyria's king Shalmaneser III in the Near East. This alliance was based on common interests and, perhaps, on some cultural affinities, and had transitory success, at least in Qarqar.[11] The Bible does not report the event. The authors of the books of Kings were probably citizens of the rival Kingdom of Judah and not Israel. Presumably they did not wish to commend the military success of a king they severely criticized because "he did more to anger the God of Israel than all the kings of Israel who had preceded him."[12]

Ahab provides credible examples of geopolitical thought, but in general looking for geopolitics in biblical scripture is difficult because the primary purpose of the Bible is not historical analysis. Yet the two books of Kings are a treasure-trove of political and military strategies, of pacts, battles, and betrayals. It must be emphasized that this study expresses no opinion on the historical accuracy or dating of the examples that will be mentioned, nor can there be a review of the scholarly debate about these events or rulers. However, these examples show that the early historians of Israel depicted its political and spiritual leaders confronting geopolitical dangers, dilemmas, and opportunities that are not fundamentally different from those reported in ancient and modern world history. The examples also show that these leaders, or the chroniclers and editors who wrote and finalized the biblical texts, saw dangers, dilemmas, and opportunities in rational-strategic and not only religious ways; in fact, they often saw them in much the same way modern historians might see them. They did not believe that it was up to divine providence alone to intervene, but that it was also a matter of human wisdom and action, even if these were expected to not contravene religious and ethical laws. Whether Israel's rulers spoke and acted precisely as reported in the texts, or whether later editors presumed that they did, is irrelevant for our purpose. In any event, even if the latter lived as late as after the Babylonian exile, they belonged to ancient Israel and reflected some of its ways of thinking.[13]

The biblical vision of an Israel that dwells alone, and the exhortations against any closeness with idolatrous neighbors, could not have facilitated its search for friends and allies. Nevertheless, Israel's rulers did look for allies. King Solomon is reported to have initiated many trade and diplomatic relations, for example with Phoenicia and Africa, and to have married an Egyptian princess and other foreign women. Although these stories cannot be substantiated in the same way as the history of his successor, Ahab, can, they appear to reflect if not a political master plan then at least the pragmatic political intuition of the king—or of a later chronicler—regarding how to improve national security and wealth by gaining foreign allies. It is clear that severe geo-political dilemmas confronted the kings of Israel and Judah, whose countries occupied the crossroads between the fighting giants of the time, Assyria-Babylonia and Egypt. The foremost prophets of the time played important political roles in this difficult context. Isaiah's warning to his ruler was to lie low and focus on internal reform rather than foreign policy. Jeremiah warned his king not to play games between the warring powers but to remain loyal to Babylonia, to whom Judah's king had already promised allegiance. The king of Judah ignored his prophet's advice and paid a terrible price, as did his people.

Today, it looks as if the prophets' inspiration also contained a measure of a geopolitical understanding of reality. Maybe they, better than their kings, grasped what is known to historians today, that the power of Egypt in the Middle East was fast waning, and that of Assyria and then Babylonia growing even faster. They also knew the horrible brutality that the latter empires displayed when they encountered opposition or disloyalty.

The twenty years immediately preceding the destruction of Jerusalem and the First Temple are documented in several books of the Bible, as well as in Babylonian sources.[14] King Zedekiah of Judah had sworn a vassal oath to Nebuchadnezzar of Babylonia, but around 592 BCE he seems to have surreptitiously invited the Egyptians to become his ally if, in return, he could rely on their help against Babylonia. An Egyptian contingent of support apparently advanced into Judah, then suddenly withdrew and left Zedekiah and his people to face the wrath of Nebuchadnezzar alone and suffer the destruction of Jerusalem. It all looks very clear from today's perspective, but what did the kings and prophets really know in their time, and what were their constraints? King Zedekiah's dilemma, and what turned out to be his fatal mistake, would recur in world history. Weak powers that must make fateful decisions in uncertain situations are naturally tempted to improve their chances by playing double-sided games.

Then, in 539 BCE, half a century after the fall of Jerusalem, the Persian King Cyrus destroyed the Babylonian empire and created a radically new geopolitical constellation for the Jewish people, as well as many others. This gives scholars a historically tangible biblical case in which a geopolitical decision may have been supported by a feeling of civilizational affinity. The historian Bernard Lewis suggests that the Zoroastrian religion, which was extremely different from Babylonian polytheism, inculcated in Cyrus an affinity with the religious beliefs of the Jewish people, which was one of the reasons he freed them from captivity and encouraged them to return to their homeland.[15] In fact, Cyrus pursued a decentralized policy toward all of his subject nations. They were granted religious and cultural autonomy if they accepted Persia's supremacy. The Jews undoubtedly knew that all liberated nations enjoyed the same privilege, and this is why it is even more revealing that the prophet Isaiah praises Cyrus with words of respect and admiration— he calls him the Messiah—that the Bible accorded no other non-Jewish rulers and, indeed, only a few Jewish ones. The Medes and Persians did not "worship figures of gods in human shape,"[16] and the new empire-builder may indeed have felt some sympathy for the only other people in the known world with similar religious convictions. The Jews were aware of Cyrus' friendly feelings and remained, for two centuries, loyal to his dynasty and empire, until Alexander the Great destroyed it.

The geopolitical backdrop of events three and a half centuries later, under the Hasmoneans, can be better assessed. In 188 BCE, Rome had defeated the Seleucid Kingdom and imposed on it heavy indemnity payments. In around 167 BCE, the Jewish war of the Hasmoneans against Seleucid rule started for religious, but also partly financial, reasons. The Seleucids needed all the money they could extort from their provinces to pay their war debt to Rome. The Hasmoneans asked for support from the Romans, who welcomed this request because they wanted to further weaken the Seleucids. Judea received a formal treaty from the Roman Senate. "The victory of the Jews was in no small measure due to the fact that in opposing the Seleucids they had the support of a foreign power."[17] The material benefits of the treaty are not known, but it certainly strengthened the international political position of the Hasmoneans. In contrast to the situation at the time of Cyrus, religious or cultural affinity is less likely to have guided this Roman-Jewish alliance. It was pure power politics.

Unanswerable geopolitical questions arise in regard to the two catastrophic Judean wars against the Roman Empire, in 70 and 135 CE, and the Jewish revolt in many parts of the Mediterranean in 116/117 CE. In an ideal world of geopolitical foresight and calculation, a revolt against an empire of such size and strength would be preceded by a period of realistic reflection on means and goals and a search for allies. But this is looking at old history with current-day perspectives. It is most unlikely that any coherent reflection of this kind took place in Judea in the chaotic years of 66 to 70. The revolt developed spontaneously and was never controlled by a common national leadership. Also, those who did reflect, such as King Agrippas II, Rabbi Yohanan Ben Zakkai (according to rabbinic sources), and—if he can be trusted—Flavius Josephus advised strongly against the war. Josephus makes a link between the Jewish revolt and the "great disorder" he said was throwing Rome into turmoil during the same years. Already in 60 and 61 CE, Queen Boadicea in eastern Britain had launched a violent revolt against the Roman occupation, causing great casualties and leading Emperor Nero to consider withdrawing from Britain, but was finally put down. Jews almost certainly knew of this war because, again according to Josephus, Titus warned them of the fate of the Britons when he addressed them publicly in Jerusalem. Did they see Boadicea as an inspiring model? Nero was murdered in 68 and was followed by three emperors who all died or committed suicide within months of taking office, until at last Vespasianus was proclaimed emperor in 69 CE. Rome had not seen such troubles for almost a hundred years. Did the Jewish rebels consider this as the most auspicious moment to strike at their apparently paralyzed enemy? Should they not have known that an empire in severe domestic trouble often reacts more aggressively to external challenges than an empire at peace? Had they considered that Rome might have been looking for an external enemy to divert attention from its internal difficulties? This is exactly what happened. Vespasianus needed a crushing victory and the destruction of an allegedly dangerous and powerful enemy to solidify his position on the throne, and with this he had his victory. After the Jewish defeat of 70 CE, the next violent Jewish uprising took place in 116/117 not in Judea but in several parts of the Mediterranean, during the last years of Emperor Trajan. Some historians suggest that it was no accident that this coincided with other external problems facing the Roman Empire. The revolt may have been part of a joint Judeo-Parthian strategy to attack Rome together.[18]

Nothing we know of the great revolt of 135 CE, and we know very little, suggests that it was preceded or informed by any geopolitical reflection that might have compared Jewish to Roman strength. In contrast to the defeat of 70 CE, this time the Jews had a clear national leadership, that of Bar Kochba and Rabbi Akiva. Both were motivated by religious fervor, not geopolitics. It was arguably the case that a rational strategic analysis was impossible with the scanty information on Rome at their disposal; perhaps they were forced to strike lest the Romans extinguish Judaism. In addition, a belief in miracles may have silenced the kind of doubts that had existed before and during the last revolt in 70 CE. Nothing indicates that Jewish leaders were looking for foreign allies against Rome, although the Parthian Empire, which flourished between roughly 150 BCE and 224 CE, was geographically near, still hostile to Rome, and undefeated.

The Diaspora

Before modern times, Diaspora leaders had few if any hard assets with which to protect and defend their people, other than money. They had to be particularly alert to the general geopolitical (which often meant "geo-religious") constellation, adept at exploiting it to their people's advantage, and sensitive to any signs of affinity with the Jewish people that might emerge from one of the ruling powers. Several Jewish leaders had this ability and were exceptionally well informed about the world, as was shown in Part IV, Chapter 3. Nehemiah in Persia's capital Susa, Josel of Rosheim, and Menasseh Ben Israel are among them. Menasseh's intervention with Oliver Cromwell to let the Jews return to England is part of a much longer story that includes, in the end, the question of how the British came to Palestine[19] and helped to change the fate of the Jewish people just as profoundly as King Cyrus had done 2,500 years before.

In the English and perhaps also the Persian case, a geopolitical interest was reinforced by an affinity with the Jewish people. The English affinity had a long history that included ancient legends attributing to the Anglo-Saxons a Near-Eastern origin, the impact of the King James version of the English Bible of 1611, which became for a time the most important book of English culture, and finally Oliver Cromwell's Puritan movement. In 1649, at the height of Puritan rule, two English Puritans petitioned the government of England to "transport Israel's sons and daughters in their ships to the land promised to their forefathers Abraham, Isaac and Jacob...."[20] From then on, Christian Zionist utopias never completely disappeared from England's intellectual and religious scene until they finally merged with British imperial policies in the late nineteenth century.

Britain's role in the restoration of Israel had a religious and political motive: a perceived historical debt owed to the people of the Bible and an imperial strategy calling for the possession of their land. Disraeli's acquisition of the Suez Canal and of Cyprus (1874-1878) made the British conquest of Palestine more than likely, in spite of the opposition Field Marshall Lord Kitchener would raise against it in World War I. Christian Zionism would give this conquest a benign moral varnish. The early alertness of the Zionist movement to both motives, the British hope of gaining worldwide Jewish support during a difficult moment of the War, and perhaps also some unexpected luck (which will be considered in Part IV, Chapter 11) led finally to the Balfour Declaration of 1917. This was a classic case of compelling geopolitical aims supported and justified by cultural-religious affinities.

Not all geopolitical ventures by Diaspora Jews were helpful or reasonable. Jewish powerlessness in the Diaspora spawned messianic eccentrics, dreamers, and outright crooks who tried to sell fantastic geopolitical schemes to Jews and Christians. One was David Reubeni (1490-1535 or 1541), who succeeded in having audiences with Pope Clement VII, King Juao III of Portugal, Emperor Charles V of the Holy Roman Empire, and other rulers. He told them of a powerful (but fictive) Jewish kingdom in Arabia allegedly ruled by his brother, and offered them a grand alliance with the "Jews of the East" to defeat the Ottoman Empire. He also showed letters by Portuguese captains that seemed to confirm his fairy tales. He ended up in the hands of the Spanish Inquisition and was probably executed. He did not help the Jewish people; he made their life more difficult.

Modern Israel

Since the establishment of Israel, the Jewish people has again developed geopolitical strategies under similar conditions to those of other independent nations. The chapter on war (Part IV, Chapter 8) explained how Arab hostility has prompted Israeli governments, from the earliest days on, to look for contacts, friends, and allies in the wider Middle East and in the rest of the world. When appropriate, Israel emphasized civilizational or historical affinities with the country it hoped to win or had already won as a friend and ally. In the 1950s and early 1960s, France was the great power supporting Israel, and both sides liked to refer to their cultural affinities, their individualism, their shared suffering under the Nazis, and their indebtedness to the French Revolution, which began the emancipation of Europe's Jews. When the United States became Israel's main ally, the emphasis shifted to the strong ideals of freedom and democracy animating both countries. During the first decade of the twenty-first century, when the political power of Bible-reading Evangelical Christians increased in the United States, Israel's biblical heritage and the biblical promises it had received became another important element of civilizational affinity and, for some Americans, an additional reason to support Israel. There are similarities with the situation of the nineteenth and early twentieth centuries, when Bible-based feelings of affinity with the Jews contributed to Britain's sympathy for Zionism.

Currently, Jewish and Israeli leaders are well aware of both the internal and the external dangers facing the Jewish people. However, predicting possible future changes and threats is difficult. For a people as widespread and as critical to the volatile Middle East as the Jews, many known and unknown events could become important. The future of the Jewish people is still inextricably linked to that of the United States and is likely to remain so for many decades. More than forty percent of all Jews live in America, and only slightly more than that live in Israel. A geopolitical alliance with a powerful

America is an issue of life or death for Israel. Nevertheless, there should be more sustained efforts to seek links with alternative powers, such as Europe, Russia, or Japan, and particularly the new emerging powers of Asia, China and India. These efforts should involve the Jewish people generally as well as Israel specifically. China and India seem to be harbor fewer prejudices against the Jewish people than much of the Christian and Muslim world have in the past, and in some cases still have today. Jews and Israel should develop a broader and better-funded cultural cooperation and outreach policy to these countries and reinforce whatever presence they already have in the collective consciousness and imagination there. Economic, technological, and military links are essential but not sufficient. Jews have been too slow to respond to the broader, long-term opportunities that are opening up in Asia. Also, some Jewish responses have been wrong-footed. When Jews put forward their Jewish credentials to criticize the human rights record of important non-hostile countries, they should be aware that they risk damaging the interests of the Jewish people as a whole. Geopolitics is also about making hard choices and setting clear priorities.

Its alliance with the United States has given Israel great and irreplaceable advantages, but its dependence on the United States also limits Israel's own geopolitical options and can raise major dilemmas. Past tensions between the United States and Russia or China have had repercussions on the latter's policies in the Middle East and the United Nations that were detrimental to Israel and the Jewish people, although in the first decade of the twenty-first century their true reason was not hostility to Israel. Israel thus may have had to bear the brunt of Washington's global strategies, for which it was not responsible. It is an open secret that during the first decade of the twenty-first century some Muslim countries pressured Russia and China to lead a more open and aggressive anti-American alliance. Some hoped that this alliance could be joined by Muslim state and non-state actors, as was the case in the days of the Soviet Union. Parts of the military establishment of at least one of the two powers were reported to be sympathetic to such proposals.[21]

The future of the world's main religions and the evolution of their attitudes toward Jews and the Jewish state could, in the long term, be as consequential as great power politics. "Geo-religious" predictions are even more hazardous than geopolitical ones. Nothing is assured and everything is possible, in Christianity as well as in Islam. Jews must know that they have options if they are willing to reach out and seek links and partnerships or if they are ready to fight back when necessary. As Part IV, Chapter 5 has shown, Josel of Rosheim in the sixteenth century and Menasseh Ben Israel in the seventeenth played subtly on the differences between Europe' feuding Catholics, Protestants, and Puritans to extract advantages for their people.

They had a measure of success, although their assets were minute compared to what Israel and the Jewish people can put on the table today.

Israel and the Jewish people are now a key part of world history and are contributing to that history more than ever before, but Jewish perspectives remain too often short-term and local. In Diaspora conditions, long-term foresight and planning was rarely an option, and so it is not a typical Jewish trait. Instead Jews have learned to improvise, and Israel has unfortunately inherited this "gift" of Jewish Diaspora weakness and vulnerability and turned short-term improvisation into a fine art.

Too many of Israel's decisions affecting foreign policy and Israel's international legitimacy are driven by domestic party politics. A considerable proportion of Israel's population and not a few of its politicians are unable or unwilling to grasp the complex, short- and long-term interactions between government decisions and their country's geopolitical interests and needs. Maybe their lack of foresight and understanding of geopolitical complexity is no worse than that of most other Western countries, but that is faint comfort. As Israel's situation is more difficult than that of other countries, it cannot afford to not be smarter than others.

The current geopolitical situation of Israel and the Jewish people calls for the formulation of a forward-looking geopolitical vision, a concept of the Jews' place in the world. In this vision, civilizational affinities and cultural outreach should be given a choice place.

CHAPTER 10

Internal Dissent

General Observations

In early philosophy, two competing metaphors describe the natural state of the world and society. Laozi (Lao-Tse) proclaimed, "Only what stays in its place can endure," and, "The sage relies on actionless activity,"[1] while at the other end of the world but probably in the same century the Greek Heraclitus wrote, "War is what is common and conflict is the norm, and everything that happens does so through conflict and necessity."[2] Both philosophies can be seen as reflections on the violent, war-torn history of their respective countries during these centuries. Heraclitus accepted the endless wars and upheavals of the Greeks as a normal condition of human civilization. Laozi, whom Chinese tradition has dated to China's "Warring States" period, did not approve of war and saw quietness, not action, as a desirable condition. The two metaphors are poles apart. One claims harmony and consensus as the natural state, the other tension and movement. Both have shaped competing philosophies of history ever since.

There are degrees of dissent: *ideological dissent inside the same people and territory, civil war,* and *geographic partition.* Toynbee believed that harmony was the normal state of a civilization and that civilizations perished for internal, not external reasons—a failure of consensus. This is why he devoted many chapters to internal ideological dissent as undermining the cohesion of civilizations. But even when internal dissent proved fatal to a civilization, it did not need to take violent forms. Civilizations and nations have disintegrated without much bloodshed. Toynbee contended that 16 of the 19 world civilizations he had identified (in other places he counted 21 or 23) disappeared because of psychological and sociological "schisms" or incompatibilities.[3] Not only Toynbee, but Ibn Khaldun[4] and Gibbon[5] as well believed that the introduction of contradictory beliefs, values, and manners by foreign populations and religions was a main reason of internal decline. Ibn Khaldun mentioned feelings of injustice due to exploitation, gaps between rich and poor, and unjust rulers to explain the tensions that ruined civilizations.

The American historian Arthur Herman discussed the cultural pessimists of the nineteenth and twentieth centuries, who offered similar explanations.[6] When they complained about the alleged decline of their own civilization, they blamed foreigners and their allegedly corroding influence.

The second, more violent category of dissent, civil war, is often a result of such ideological and societal tensions or of power conflicts. A civil war can be attached to a revolution, although the two are not identical. Revolution is the overthrow of a ruling power or a form of government, often but not always by violent means, and its replacement by a different power or form of government. A revolution can spark a civil war—as was the case in Mexico in 1911, or in Russia in 1917—or can come at the end of a civil war. This latter was the case in China in 1949, when the Communist Party emerged victorious from a bitter civil war that had gone on more than ten years. The non-violent replacement of one form of government by another one, for example of a monarchy by a republic, can also be called a revolution. Such cases have little to do with real civil war, the main topic of this chapter.

Finally, geographic partition is the third and ultimate form of dissent. The best-known historical model for such a partition is the breakup of the Roman Empire: "The schism of Greeks and Latins...has precipitated the decline and fall of the Roman Empire."[7] Linguistic, religious, and political differences can be more easily managed when they intermingle everywhere within the same territory. This was so in pre-modern Switzerland, which was divided into two main languages, German and French; two religions, Catholicism and Protestantism; and into urban and rural elites that ruled different cantons and were often in conflict. Some historians suggest that one of the main reasons Switzerland survived as a unit is that these three dividing lines did not coincide but crossed each other. French- and German-speaking Catholics had religion in common but not language, French-speaking Catholics and Calvinists were religiously divided but could communicate in the same language, etc. If language and other differences coincide with a geographic dividing line, secession and separation can become inevitable. There are many old and modern examples of this. The most recent was the secession of South Sudan in 2011. Earlier, Czechoslovakia had been divided into two independent republics in 1993, separated by geography, language, and, to a certain degree, religion. Belgium has been mentioned as another country at risk of breaking up, as was Canada some years ago.

It is significant that Gibbon, Toynbee, and others use the term "schism" to describe internal discord that causes the decline and then fall of civilizations. This term has a religious origin. Its first use was in referring to the "Great Schism" that split the Roman Catholic and the Eastern Orthodox Church in 1054. The Great Schism was the final outcome of a long period of estrangement, a fundamental breach that split the Church along theological, political, and geographic lines. It became impossible to heal the rift after 1204, when the Pope and Venice diverted the Fourth Crusade to conquer Constantinople. Since the Great Schism, Christianity is for all practical purposes no longer a unified civilization. The two churches did not support each other even when they faced existential threats. The Great Schism weakened both sides, hastened the decline and fall of the Byzantine Empire, and became the model for future schisms, particularly the rise of Protestantism. The conviction that internal dissent or "schism" must lead to the decline of a civilization was partly rooted in Toynbee's Christian upbringing and memory. This is also true of other historians: by transferring a disapproving, value-loaded term from the history of religion to that of civilizations, they may have encouraged a reflexive negative view of all internal dissent.

Jewish History

Internal dissent, even armed struggle and civil war, do not always destroy or even damage a civilization. Jewish history knows all three forms of division: ideological dissent, civil war, and geographic partition. As argued above in Part III, Chapter 5, none of the three developed into an existential threat to Judaism's long-term survival.

Ideological Dissent

Abraham Geiger (1810-1874), a co-founder of Reform Judaism and the "Science of Judaism" in Germany, claimed that spiritual divisions were a permanent condition of Judaism, and inner struggle the main source of Judaism's "spiritual heroism" and creativity.[8] It should come as no surprise that a liberal rabbi and scholar who had abandoned traditional Judaism propagated such tolerant views of dissent. The question this chapter studies, though no answer is possible here, is whether Jewish history generally supports Geiger's view. What were the reasons for divisions, and which divisions were creative?

From the first pages of biblical history, when Cain killed Abel, to the last page of II Chronicles, which repeats the story of the destruction of the First Temple, the Hebrew Bible is a book of struggles, conflicts, rebellions, and wars. All of Jewish history is full of dissent and argumentation. The Talmud recognizes that discrepancy and ambiguity are not only facts of life, but reflect a higher metaphysical truth that the human mind cannot always understand. Thus, two apparently conflicting interpretations of a text or a commandment can both express the will of the "living God," as the Talmud says. This attitude must have affected many long-term intellectual developments.

The religious history of the Second Temple period is famous for its sectarian conflicts, particularly those between Sadducees and Pharisees, and these tensions may have had creative impacts. The Sadducees appeared in the second century BCE, probably as supporters of the Hasmonean high priests, and disappeared late in the first century CE, after the destruction of the Temple. They were an aristocratic priestly group that rejected the oral law and the idea of an afterlife. For the more numerous Pharisees who fought them successfully, the oral law and afterlife were core beliefs of Judaism. The Pharisees shaped normative Judaism, not without their own internal arguments and conflicts. These conflicts and those they had with the Sadducees were not "schisms": nobody claimed that the Sadducees were not Jewish. They may have lost their "portion in the world to come," as the Pharisees said, but they were not excluded from the synagogue. A Jew who rejected Judaism's beliefs was a "sinner," but still a Jew.

"Excommunication" or ban is meant as deterrence and punishment, not exclusion from Judaism. In current religious practice, an apostate—a Jew who has converted to another religion—remains a Jew and can always return to Judaism. The rabbis discussed apostasy in the Middle Ages particularly because it was a real problem. They concluded that the apostate, even when baptized as a Christian, does not lose his Jewish identity.[9] A sentence in the daily prayers, the *birkat ha-minim*, condemns categories of people variously translated as "heretics," "apostates," "slanderers," "wicked ones," "arrogant sinners," etc. There were numerous changes in this sentence—no other sentence in the prayer was changed so often—and there is a still-continuing historical-philological debate about the exact meaning of each term. This indicates some of the difficulties of defining a "heretic" or "schismatic" or excluding one from Judaism.[10] Until recently, a faithful Catholic knew precisely who was a heretic and who a schismatic. A conservative Sunni Muslim still knows it. Salo W. Baron and other historians wrote that Judaism's main "schism" was with Christianity. When exactly a Christian "schism" occurred and whether it is appropriate to call Christianity "The Great Schism" of Judaism[11] has been the subject of many historical and theological arguments. This book does not take a position, but simply mentions the unresolved question.

After the destruction of the Temple, the rabbis aimed at unifying the various streams of Judaism into one *halakha* under a single calendar. They knew that the persistence of sectarian splits among the Jews, after they no longer had a sole unifying religious center, would have even more calamitous consequences than it had before 70 CE. The memory of the Sadducean diversion and the Judeo-Christian episode surely and persistently reminded them of the dangers. The waning of the Sadducees in the late first century CE consecrated the victory of rabbinic Judaism. The latter had apparently supplied the only valid answer to the question of how Judaism could survive the end of the Temple.

Seven centuries later, when most Jews were firmly settled under the new Islamic empire of the Abbasids, the Karaites raised a new challenge to rabbinic Judaism that in some aspects resembled the Sadducean challenge. The origin of the Karaite doctrine is better known than that of the Sadducees, because some of the writings of its late-eighth century founder, Anan Ben David, and his successors have survived. The Karaites are known to have rejected the Talmud and oral law. More precisely, they objected to the exclusive authority of the rabbinic sages of the Talmud in interpreting the Torah, and called for rigorous textual exegesis of the Torah to be undertaken individually by every believer. They disparaged reliance on rabbinic traditions, although they too had to resort to old customs when defining details of the law.[12]

They were strongly influenced by Islamic philosophy and practice. Jacob Burckhardt said that heresy is always a sign that the dominant religion no longer satisfies the metaphysical longings of a people.[13] The Karaites were intellectually demanding, conservative, severe, and ascetic.[14] These characteristics may not have stemmed directly from the "metaphysical longings" of the Jews under the Abbasids, but scholars do agree that Karaism grew out of a "deeper political and intellectual unrest"[15] in the ninth-century Jewish world. It seems to have appealed to dissatisfied and repressed elements in Jewish society, and therefore it became for a time a major force in Jewish history. Karaites and Rabbanites fought each other bitterly, but both saw themselves, at least during the first one or two centuries, as Jewish, and did not claim that the other side was not. Until the tenth century, Karaites and Rabbanites intermarried; many *ketubot* (religious marriage contracts) have survived and testify to mixed marriages between the two sides. Some historians call the Karaite and Rabbanite break a "schism," again a transplant from the history of medieval Christianity to that of a different religion and time.

Schism or not, it is clear that the Karaite challenge also had a strongly stimulating effect on the development of Judaism until the tenth or eleventh century, even if there were negative effects as well, for example the influence that polemic Karaite writings had on medieval Islamic defamation of Jews and Judaism. The work of the greatest of the *Geonim*, Rav Saadia Gaon (882/892-942) was influenced by the achievements of Arab civilization, but it was also a response to the Karaite threat, against which he fought during much of his life. The emergence of Jewish philosophy from Saadia's time on was partly motivated by a desire to systemize arguments against the Karaites. Another important innovation came from the Karaites' pioneering role in the study of Hebrew language and grammar. Rabbinic Judaism had paid little attention to grammar before, but now could no longer ignore it. It is no coincidence that Saadia also wrote the oldest known Hebrew grammar. The Karaites spurred the development of Biblical Hebrew along more scientific lines, and indirectly also helped spur the new Hebrew poetry of Spain.[16] The first great

Hebrew poet of Spain, Dunash Ben Labrat (mid-tenth century), is said to have come from Baghdad, where he had studied under Saadia Gaon. The Karaites' literary and historical approach to the Bible influenced even later rabbinic commentators, particularly Abraham Ibn Ezra and David Kimchi, both of whom refer to Karaite sources. Last but not least, the unification of the final Masoretic text of the Hebrew Bible, recognized by all Jews, was completed in the tenth century. This was an enormous achievement, and an indispensable one for the future of Judaism. The historian Raymond Scheindlin states that it was the result of the impetus that the Karaite challenge gave this kind of work, among other factors.[17] Other historians are equally convinced that the Karaites made a substantial intellectual contribution to the future of rabbinic Judaism, obviously without planning to do so: "The Karaite challenge went to the heart of medieval Jewish identity and certainly contributed to many aspects of Jewish thought and literature, particularly in the fields of philosophy, linguistics and exegesis. These contributions had a transforming and enduring effect...."[18] Long before, Shlomo Goitein had already called the Karaites "a great rejuvenating force in Judaism."[19]

The Karaite story raises two questions that are relevant in our context. Karaism was already declining in the twelfth century, as Jewish polemics against it continued. The Spanish Jewish philosopher Rabbi Abraham ibn Daud (1110-1180) wrote one of the first Jewish "world histories," *Sefer ha-Kabbalah*. The glorious period of Andalusian-Spanish Jewry had come to a brutal end before his eyes. In 1147/48 the fanatical Almohad Berbers had invaded Spain from Morocco and wiped out the Jewish communities of Cordova, Granada, Seville, and many other cities. One would have expected ibn Daud to warn his Jewish readers of the dangers of Islamic fanaticism, but his book contains not a word of open hostility against Islam or Muslims.* Instead, his last pages are a diatribe against the Karaite heresy, which he feared as the most dangerous threat to the future of the Jewish people. When he rejoices about an event where the Karaites "remained silent like dumb dogs,"[20] his slur only reveals how much he still dreaded their bark.

The Karaites were probably never more than ten percent of the Jewish people, but in ibn Daud's time still had a visible, and for Rabbinic Jews provocative, presence in Spain. Ibn Daud's fears seem greatly overblown in hindsight. In the late twelfth century, the Karaites' power to seriously threaten rabbinic Judaism, if it ever existed, had long since dissipated. Ibn Daud's

---

* Ibn Daud avoids theological polemics against Islam, but what he really thought about the beginnings of this religion can be inferred from a tart side comment: "Muhammad, the king of Ismael, had begun to make his pretensions in 4374." See Abraham ibn Daud, 45, Hebrew text 34f. As a pious Jew he refused to call the founder of Islam a "prophet." He was simply the king of the Arabs.

concern about apparent dangers to Judaism in one place was not matched by a knowledge of Jewish strength elsewhere. He alluded to new Jewish learning in France in which he puts some faint hope, but did not mention Rashi. He would have been astounded to hear that the scholar and commentator, who would become the most influential of all and dominate Bible and Talmud study for the next thousand years, had died in France five years before his own birth, and that he hadn't worried about the Karaites at all. The emergence of Ashkenazi Judaism, which would in two centuries become the driving force of the Jewish people, buried the Karaite threat for good. There were a few Karaites in Europe, but they had no influence on Jewish communities. Ibn Daud's unwarranted fears call for an element of skepticism in regard to all dire predictions about the future of the Jews, whenever they are made. He saw one worrying trend but missed the fact that it was already declining, and he could not see other trends. Could we be subject to similar blindness today?

The second question relates to the apparent Jewish tolerance of diversity and its role as a source of creativity. We have suggested that Judaism reacted less violently than other religions to internal spiritual challenges. It called for the punishment of transgressors, but did not expel them from the Jewish people. The Rabbanites had no other choice than to be tolerant. From the very beginning the Abbasside rulers had granted the Karaites legal and communal independence from rabbinic Judaism: they had their own tribunals and scholars. In the long term, Karaism withered for spiritual reasons, not because it was suppressed by force. In any event, even if they had wanted to, the Rabbanites could not do to the Karaites what Muslims and Christians of the same and other centuries all too often did to their own "heretics." Nobody can say how the Rabbanites would have acted had they retained full political and judicial sovereignty; rabbinic Judaism's "tolerance of diversity" was after 135 CE not put to a real- life test—and perhaps the Jewish people is lucky that it was not.

Another example takes a significant place in the history of tension and dissent in Judaism:[21] the Hassidic movement founded by Rabbi Israel Ben Eliezer, the Baal Shem-Tov (1698/1700-1760), in Eastern Europe. Hassidism is, in some respects, the opposite of Karaism. It originally promoted emotional values and mystical-ecstatic practices, not intellectual efforts in scholarship or rigid discipline in prayer, as did Karaism. Gershom Scholem calls Hassidism "the latest (or last) phase of Jewish mysticism."[22] It elevated the leadership role of charismatic rabbis and valued independent study less highly. The decisive historical difference is that Hassidism caught on with a large part of the Jewish people in Eastern Europe, which Karaism had failed to do anywhere in the Jewish world.

The challenge posed by Hassidism to the dominant rabbinic elite was probably less fundamental than that which the Karaites once posed. Hassidic practices may have modified the oral law here and there, and may have omitted some traditions and added new ones, but Hassidim never rejected or questioned the oral law. Geographically, the movement exploded in all directions within two generations after its founder's death, between 1760 and approximately 1830. In a short time it produced an amazing number of exceptional and charismatic personalities, each with distinct, individual features. This rapid expansion must have been a response to the severe metaphysical and emotional crisis that engulfed East European Jewry after the collapse of the false messianic movements of Sabbatai Zevi (1626-1676) and Jacob Frank (1726-1791). It also resulted from the material misery of large parts of East-European Jewry. Jacob Burckhardt's comment about the emergence of "heresies" as a response to unfulfilled metaphysical needs can easily be applied to the successes of the Hassidic movement. It is no coincidence that Hassidism first spread in the regions of Galicia, Poland, and Ukraine where Sabbatianism had previously had large strongholds. The Baal Shem-Tov must have known former or clandestine followers of Sabbatai Zevi, who were still many in his early years. He understood the enormous attraction the messianic idea exerted on the Jewish people, but also the dangers of its precipitate and disruptive manifestation in real life, as the so-called "Holy Epistle," he wrote around 1752 to his brother-in-law in the land of Israel shows.* He and most of his followers "neutralized" messianism, to use Scholem's term, not by rejecting it but rather by embedding it into a long-term perspective, a general sense of optimism, and a joyful, anti-ascetic affirmation of life in the here and now.

Then, in 1772, Rabbi Elijah, the Gaon of Vilna (1720-1797) launched his uncompromising struggle against the Hassidim, which would absorb his and many of his supporters' energies until the end of his life. The Gaon was,

---

* Hassidic tradition attached great importance to this letter. Dubnow's *History of Hassidism* is in general very critical of all Hassidic sources and regards many as late fabrications, but argues convincingly for the authenticity of this letter. Dubnow, vol. 1, 105 f., reproduces almost the entire text of the letter. The Baal Shem-Tov reports an "elevation of the soul" in 1746 during which he met the Messiah in the Garden of Eden. He asked him "When will the lord arrive?" and received the answer: only when your teaching will be known to the entire world. The Baal Shem-Tov: "I felt great pain that the time would be removed to such a distant future...." It is clear that he choose an indirect, psychologically sensitive way to convey a difficult but necessary message to the disoriented and impatient Jews of his time. Moshe Rosman, who carried out extensive and recent research on the Baal Shem-Tov, agrees that there was an authentic letter written by the Baal Shem-Tov around 1752, but that the original has not survived. What we have are copies, each with additions and variations. Rosman argues that the long references to messianic redemption were added around 1780, twenty years after the Baal Shem-Tov died. He suggests that the additions reflect the tradition of the Baal Shem-Tov's successor, the Maggid of Mezerich. Whether or not the phrases about the Messiah were from the hand of the Baal Shem-Tov himself, they clearly show the concern that early Hasidic leaders felt about the dangers of ecstatic messianism. See Moshe Rosman, *Founder of Hasidism: A Quest for the Historical Baal Shem-Tov* (Berkeley, 1996), 99 ff.

by general agreement, the greatest rabbinic mind of the entire eighteenth century. This rationalist genius refused any rabbinic employment that would have forced him to take care of the day-to-day troubles of simple Jews. His exclusive, all-embracing interest was Judaism, not Jews. He declared the expanding Hassidic mass movement "heretic" and a threat to the survival of Judaism, and the warnings of the greatest Jewish mind of the time could not be taken lightly. He excommunicated the Hassidim several times and forbade all other Jews to meet, eat, pray, or marry with them. "All those who follow their path never return. It is heresy....If I were able I would do to them as Elijah the prophet did to the prophets of Ba'al"[23]—that is, if he meant what he wrote, he would have all of them executed.[24] The Hassidim and the Mitnagdim, his supporters, fought some vicious battles that included murder, attempted murder, and denunciations by the Mitnagdim to the Russian authorities, which led to the arrest and imprisonment of Hassidic leaders. But the Gaon lost the battle he regarded as essential for the survival of Judaism: the spread of Hassidism could not be stopped. The great majority of Hassidim became less eccentric over time, perhaps because of the Gaon's condemnations, and they left Orthodox Judaism in no greater numbers than did the anti-Hassidic Jews of Lithuania. Today, what is mostly left of this bitter discord that once pitted large numbers of Jews against each other is bantering and jokes at the popular level, some variations in prayer books and religious customs, and differences in attitude toward the State of Israel, all within Orthodox Judaism.

In a larger historical perspective, the struggle was not in vain. It had enormously stimulating consequences for both sides that none of the protagonists could have anticipated. On the Mitnagdic side, it greatly bolstered Jewish learning and led to an expansion of the Lithuanian Talmud academies that played such an enormous role in the history of normative Judaism. On the Hassidic side, it forced adherents of the new way to defend themselves and write the first coherent and systematic presentation of their doctrines. This was achieved, unsurprisingly, by the Lithuanian branch of the movement, led by Rabbi Shneur Zalman of Lyadi and his successors, who founded the Chabad movement. Most importantly, Hassidism and its emotional heritage played an essential role in maintaining Judaism against the attractions of assimilation in many parts of Galicia, Poland, and Ukraine that the Gaon did not reach. Hassidism also helped to maintain and transmit Jewish culture, folklore, and even the Hebrew language. Ahad Haam, at the start of the twentieth century, criticized the Modern Hebrew literature of his time. He wrote that as a follower of the Jewish Enlightenment he was "ashamed" to admit that if he wanted to find a "shadow of original Hebrew literature," he had to look in the books of the Hassidim, not the Enlightenment.[25] Further, the Hassidim carried the messianic idea over the dangerous abyss that had opened up after Sabbatai Zevi. They put messianism on ice, so to speak, where the Zionists found it more than half a century later and brought it back to life in a new and secularized political form.

The two main conclusions one may draw from this episode are similar to the ones suggested in regard to the struggle between Karaites and Rabbanites. First, even the most learned and best-informed contemporary thinkers are often unable to correctly foresee what is dangerous to the survival of the Jewish people and what is not. Clearly, Hassidism was not. Secondly, one of the reasons internal dissent and strife had creative impacts on Judaism was the relative political and judicial powerlessness of Jewish religious leaders in the Diaspora. They could not easily suppress their opponents. Nobody knows what the Gaon or others would have done in a sovereign Jewish state, in a period where religious persecution was the norm in other parts of the world, if they had retained real executive or judicial power. The Gaon's words, though written in anger, are scary enough.

The new challenge that the Enlightenment, assimilation, and secular Zionism raised against rabbinic Judaism is of a much more radical nature than Karaism or Hassidism. This time, it is not only the oral law and/or its interpretation that is in question but religion itself, the whole tradition. Now Judaism faces something like a Hegelian "antithesis" to the "thesis" that it has constituted for so long, but no real "synthesis" is yet in sight. The search for one is likely to continue for a long time.

It is probable that in the future, too, the creativity of the Jewish people will benefit from a capacity for non-violent debate and dissent. Jewish arguments will continue to focus on values, conflicting interpretations of truth, tradition, and ritual, and what it means to be Jewish. For the protagonists, such questions are critical to the very survival of Judaism and are often conducted with deadly seriousness and, from time to time, violence. They can appear irrelevant to later generations—often because one side has won and the other has nearly disappeared, as in the case of the Karaites—or incomprehensible to a larger public, as in the strife between Hassidim and Mitnagdim.

Civil War

Jewish history has known civil wars, a more active stage of dissent, but there is a difference between its early history and the Second Temple period. The biblical record of the time of the Judges speaks of frequent tensions and border skirmishes between the tribes, and even of an attempted extermination of one tribe, Benjamin, by the others.[26] Memories of bloody conflicts must have survived for a long time. However, these events should not be seen from a modern viewpoint but in the context of tribal history in all periods and locations. Warfare is a common feature of a people divided into related but competing tribes. The indigenous tribes of North America lived through centuries of alternating periods of war and peace with each other, as did those of Papua New Guinea, just like the tribes of ancient Israel. The term "civil war" makes real sense only in larger, post-tribal, and settled societies. The bloody skirmishes between Israelite tribes, in spite of the gruesome details reported in the book of Judges, were not comparable to the violence and magnitude of the Peloponnesian War, which lasted 30 years, precipitated most Greeks into bloodshed, and killed several hundred thousand of them, not to mention the modern civil wars in the nineteenth and twentieth centuries that exterminated, except in the United States, between five and thirty percent of the relevant countries' entire populations (China, 1852-1864 and 1945-1949; the United States, 1861-1865; Mexico, 1911-1914; Russia, 1918-1920; Spain, 1936-1939; Cambodia, 1970-1975; and Rwanda, 1994). Foreign powers in each case meddled to influence the outcome, but intervened with massive military force in some cases (China in its earlier war, Russia, Spain, and Cambodia) and not in others (China in its later war, the United States, Mexico, and Rwanda). In the former cases, foreign military intervention influenced the outcomes, except in Russia.

The last two centuries of the Second Temple period differed both from Israel's earlier tribal wars and from the world's mass civil wars of the nineteenth and twentieth centuries. The two centuries saw a sequence of civil war events, from the uprising of the Maccabees against Syrian rule in 167-164 BCE, which was also partly a civil war, to the destruction of the Temple in 70 CE. Between the two events, the despotic Hasmonean King Alexander Yannai (ruled 103-76 BCE) fought a civil war of six years during which, according to Flavius Josephus, he slaughtered 50,000 Jews. The cruelty of the reported massacres between Jews equaled those of the worst outrages of the Peloponnesian War. Another case, a war of succession between two Hasmonean princes, Hyrkanos and Aristoboulos, lasted from 67 to 63 BCE and was terminated only when Pompey of Rome stepped in and effectively ended Jewish independence. These wars between Hasmonean pretenders were fought for reasons of power, not faith or principle. In the war of the Hasmoneans against the Seleucids and in the revolt of 66-70 CE, religion played a dominant, though not exclusive, role.

The whole period was politically inglorious, and Jewish tradition prefers to remember it for its portentous spiritual and religious developments rather than its political ones. The great revolt of 66-70 CE destroyed not only Jewish independence but also the Jewish nation in its homeland and its religious center. Civil war and Roman military intervention, religious strife, and internal power politics were so closely interwoven that it is almost impossible to neatly tease out internal and external elements. Flavius Josephus, a participant, went to great lengths to have the revolt and the destruction of Jerusalem remembered as a civil war provoked by Jewish fanaticism. He writes that "it was a rebellious temper of our own that destroyed it and that there were the tyrants among the Jews who brought the Roman power upon us, who unwillingly attacked us and occasioned the burning of our holy temple."[27]

He began his book with the promise that he would describe a war that "has been the greatest of all those, not only that have been in our times, but, in a manner, of those that ever were heard of," which was for a reader of the time a transparent rhetorical imitation of the beginning of Thucydides' *Peloponnesian War*. He had personal reasons to forge a comparison between the Peloponnesian War and the Jewish War, minimize the Roman responsibility, and incriminate his own camp: he had to justify why he had deserted his own people to join the Romans. This was a civil war conducted with great brutality, but there is still a huge difference between the Jewish War and the violent Greek convulsion of the Peloponnesian War. No foreign army participated in the Peloponnesian War or burned the temples of Athens or Sparta. It is impossible to know how the Jewish War would have ended without Roman intervention, or even if there could have been a full-fledged war in the absence of Rome, but it is not likely that any of the warring parties would have burned down the Temple.

The talmudic sages attributed the destruction of both the First and Second Temples to Jewish faults, idolatry and fraternal hate respectively.[28] In other words, they, like Flavius Josephus, regarded the internal causes as paramount. A historical lesson to be drawn from this period for today, if it is relevant at all, is that a hypothetical Jewish civil war would almost certainly lead to great power intervention, with huge risks to Jewish independence. The geographic location of Israel and the strategic importance of its Middle Eastern neighborhood, then and now, invite such interventions.

Geographic Partition

Partition is the most radical result of dissent. It must again be emphasized, as in the earlier chapter on geopolitics (Part IV, Chapter 9), that the following quotations of biblical examples imply no judgment about their historical accuracy. It does, however, enhance the credibility of the historians of ancient Israel and their editors that they described the tumultuous events of the time in mostly rational, non-mythic terms and thus made them comparable to similar events described by Thucydides, Gibbon, and many other historians.

The biblical narrative says that under Solomon's son Rehoboam, Israel split into the Northern Kingdom of Israel with ten tribes, and the Southern Kingdom of Judah, with two. Partition certainly weakened both kingdoms, but it may have saved Judah. When the Assyrians destroyed the Northern Kingdom in 720 or 722 BCE, they left Judah alone. The fall of Israel was followed by a stream of refugees to Judah who greatly increased its population and strengthened its statehood. If the kingdom had remained united, it is still most unlikely that it could have defeated Assyria. Rather, Assyria would have destroyed all of it, particularly the capital, Jerusalem. In 720/722 a hypothetical destruction of Jerusalem might have had more terminal consequences than Jerusalem's later destruction by the Babylonians in 586 BCE. Perhaps all that would be left to history are some legends of "Twelve Lost Tribes" instead of ten. With the passing of time, what first appears to be bad luck in history, in this case the partition of the kingdom, may contain auspicious seeds of future good fortune.

The Bible reports cooperation as well as tensions, skirmishes, and military conflicts between the two kingdoms. The second book of Kings contains a number of instructive and keenly observed episodes. Many of them tell stories of dissent, internal strife, and war—the eighth and seventh centuries are full of them. For example, in 784/785 BCE King Amaziah of Judah decided to provoke King Joash of Israel into a military confrontation. Joash replied with a memorable appeal that reveals a lot about the spirit of the time as seen by a contemporary chronicler or later editor: "Because you have defeated Edom you have become arrogant. Stay home and enjoy your glory rather than provoke disaster and fall, dragging Judah down with you."[29] Joash's taunt shows a contempt bred by familiarity, not ethnic or religious hatred. The battle took place in Beit Shemesh and Amaziah was defeated and captured. Joash breached the walls of Jerusalem—the first destruction of the capital walls reported in the Bible was the deed of Israel, not of Assyria or Babylonia. He is reported to have plundered the Temple thoroughly (though rather impiously) and carried its treasures back to his capital, Samaria. Apparently no other harm was done to Judah.

In another case, this one with more dangerous geopolitical implications, it was Israel that provoked Judah. In 733/732 BCE King Pekah Ben Remaliah of Israel plotted an attack against Judah and advanced on Jerusalem.[30] Judah's desperate King Ahaz appealed to King Tiglat-Pileser of Assyria for help. Tiglat-Pileser welcomed the opportunity, invaded Israel, apparently annexed Galilee, and dragged a part of its population into exile. History knows many other wars between closely related countries in which the losing side in despair called on a common external enemy for help. A very similar story would repeat itself during the already-mentioned civil war Hyrkanos and Aristoboulos fought in Judea from 67-63 BCE, which ended with Roman intervention. The conflicts between Israel and Judah during the first temple period were quite different from the wars of destruction that real foreign enemies would soon wage against both. Their civilizational commonalities never disappeared.

Today, territorial partition of the kind known in the First Temple period is not an issue in Israel, but geographic partition in a broader sense is a permanent experience of Diaspora history. It has helped the Jewish people to survive, but it always carries the risk that the separated sides will grow apart. The possibility of a growing partition between Israel and the Diaspora does exist today. The statistical evidence of how Israelis and Diaspora Jews view each other is variable and sometimes contradictory. According to some data, a large majority of young Israelis know little or nothing of Diaspora Jews and are not interested in knowing more.

Other data suggest that the Israeli people's general appreciation of the importance of Diaspora Jewry is growing, but most Israelis who emigrate abroad are not active in Jewish communities, and many do not wish to meet local Jews, yet according to recent polls, they maintain strong contacts with their families, friends, and professional colleagues back home. Many would return to Israel if the conditions were right. The future of Israel-Diaspora relations is open and not predictable. Silent indifference can be more damaging to Jewish civilization than active, vocal dissent. A controversial issue in this respect is the attitude of young American Jews toward Israel. Israelis and Jews critical of Israeli policies assert that young American Jews are turning away from Israel because of these policies. The data do not support this view.

Young Jews at the start of their studies or professional careers have always been less interested in Israel than the older generation, and Jews who marry non-Jews are generally also less interested. These two phenomena are not new. Aside from them, a 2008 meta-analysis of twenty years' worth of opinion polls showed that there were no fundamental changes in attitudes toward Israel as such over the course of that time (which must be separated from attitudes toward specific Israeli policies). Opinion polls taken in 2012 were a real novelty: they showed a noticeable increase in the attachment to Israel among members of the 18-35 age group. This group's attachment is higher today than that of older age groups. This may be the result of the Taglit-Birthright project, which has allowed hundreds of thousands of young American Jews to visit Israel, and it shows that occasionally and in critical times the far-sighted initiative and commitment of private philanthropists can affect the future of the Jewish civilization more profoundly than public government policies. In the longer term, the threat of silent indifference will not vanish as long as there is a Diaspora. Even now, it is as credible a threat as the still-hypothetical danger of a civil war in Israel. The 1995 assassination of Prime Minister Yitzhak Rabin and the riots by settlers were a warning that the ingredients for civil war exist in Israel. Severe and even violent disagreements over the peace process could emerge again. If Jewish history teaches us anything, it is that ideological and religious tensions will not disappear. Current disagreements are not signs of an exceptional crisis but rather a continuation of the rocky history of the Jewish people, in which dissent has always been the norm, not the exception. However, in the coming decades, the dangers and challenges that might confront the Jews may require not unanimity but a greater unity of purpose than the Jewish people has often been able to muster.

CHAPTER 11

"Fortune" or Chance Events

General Observations

The conviction that luck or fortune intervenes in human history is thousands of years old. Greeks and Romans were convinced that luck was the ultimate arbiter of the fates of nations and individuals: luck had more power than even the gods, who were themselves subject to the vagaries of luck. Thus, ancient civilizations elevated luck to the status of a superior goddess, *Tyche* in Greek, *Fortuna* in Latin. Ancient and modern historians have shared a conviction that unexpected chance events interfere with history in major ways, and their historical judgment was not necessarily related to their religious or non-religious beliefs. Thucydides, a non-believer, and Ibn Khaldun, a believer, both knew that good or bad luck in war could tip the balance from victory to defeat, and vice versa.[1] "There is often no more logic in the course of events than there is in the plans of men, and this is why we usually blame luck when things happen in ways we did not expect," wrote Thucydides.[2] Sima Qian also saw that chance events played a role in China's geographic expansion.[3]

Edward Gibbon did not attribute the fall of Rome to chance, because he viewed it as inevitable in the long run. The modern Oxford historian Bryan Ward-Perkins conceded that the Roman Empire could not have survived forever, but the Western Empire did not have to die in the early fifth century, considering that the Eastern Empire lived a thousand years longer. The beginning of the end of the Western Empire was a battle in 378 CE for which a Roman army had arrived a day too late.[4] Historians who believe that political or spiritual leadership plays a decisive role in the fate of nations are also aware of the potential impacts of unexpected chance events. Other authors, who see history as driven by long-term material or sociological forces, pay no attention to chance events. For Marx, history is determined by ironclad laws, and chance events are irrelevant. The final word on this issue may still belong to the West's first political scientist, Niccolò Machiavelli (1469-1527), who was convinced that history was made by good and evil, wise and ignorant men, but at least as much also by "Fortune":

I am not unaware that many believe that the things of this world are governed to such an extent by Fortune and God that men, with all their foresight, cannot change them; that in fact there is no improving them. Those who believe this deem that they need not toil and sweat, but can let themselves be governed by Fortune. This opinion has been more prevalent in our time because of the great upheavals that we have witnessed....Fortune seems to be the arbiter of half of our actions, but she does leave us the other half, or almost the other half in order that our free will may prevail. I would compare Fortune to one of those violent torrents that flood the plains, destroying trees and buildings, hurling earth from one place to another....Man should not neglect to prepare himself with dikes and dams in times of calm, so that when the torrent rises it will gush into a channel, its force neither so harmful nor so unbridled. The same is true with Fortune, who unleashes her forces in places where man has not taken skillful precautions to resist her....In my view, however, it is better to be impetuous than cautious....If you want to dominate her (Fortune) you must beat and batter her. It is clear that she will let herself won by men who are impetuous rather than by those who step cautiously.[5]

The first part of Machiavelli's prescription, his advocacy of anticipation and long-term systematic preparation is persuasive. The second part, however, is not without dangers. The borderline between boldness and recklessness is not easily discerned: it can take considerable self-control and intuition to not overstep it. All history's rulers encountered or feared unpredictable chance events, and some tried to prepare for them. More than a few put their hopes in religion, astrology, or magic. Even the twentieth century knew world leaders who consulted astrologers. Others followed Machiavelli's first or second piece of advice, or both, whether they had read him or not. Some leaders made extensive preparations to reduce the potential scope of the unpredictable; others tried to take fortune "by the horns" and acted boldly.

Otto von Bismarck, one of the most successful leaders of modern times, embodied both inclinations. His policies indicated caution and boldness, but also the fear of unexpected bad luck. In his memoirs, Bismarck commented on all three factors and how they influenced him.[6] Of course, the autobiography of every retired statesman contains some measure of self-justification, and so does Bismarck's. However, on this issue there is no need to be particularly suspicious, for Bismarck's career as a war leader was extraordinarily successful. He did not need to emphasize his reluctance and fears. Had he failed, his public image would have been quite different and his belated explanations would have to be read with much greater vigilance.

Bismarck triggered and waged three decisive wars, all of which he won. His autobiography conveys his belief in meticulous preparation, but also his extreme caution. He writes that for twenty years he strenuously opposed all ideas of preemptive war suggested by Prussian generals even when it seemed that, sooner or later, war was inevitable and better waged while the enemy was still weak. He insisted that even victorious wars could only be justified when they were imposed, because "we cannot look into the cards of providence in order to preempt historic developments by our own calculations." This was the basis for his caution in normal times. However, in 1870 he reached a watershed in history. He spotted a unique chance to turn the centuries-old dream of German unity into a reality under Prussian leadership.

One of Bismarck's greatest gifts was his unfailing ability to assess power and power relationships, and a critical part of this gift was his equally unfailing sense for the character, competence, and weaknesses of his colleagues and opponents in the European concert of nations. This quality of keen judgment underpinned his caution as well as his boldness. He seemed to understand his opponent, French Emperor Napoleon III, better than all other observers. Napoleon was called "the sphinx" because his plans seemed so enigmatic, but Bismarck saw through him from the beginning. "His intelligence is overrated at the expense of his sentimentality," he had already mocked in the 1850s.[7] Napoleon's passion was foreign policy, but he lacked insight. He was erratic, contradictory, and sometimes reckless. He did not grasp the realities of power and overestimated that of France. When Prussia went to war against Austria in 1866, he foolishly and publicly predicted that Prussia would lose. Prussia won quickly and decisively. In 1870 Bismarck lured Napoleon into declaring war on Prussia, then defeated him decisively with the support of all the other German states. Victory allowed him to impose unification on his German war allies and create a new German empire. This was the most important event in European history between the defeat of Napoleon I in 1815 and the start of World War I in 1914. Machiavelli would have given Bismarck high grades for his meticulous preparations, including his intensive study of power and of his opponents' character. He also would have extolled his readiness to "batter Fortune," to strike boldly once the critical moment arrived. However, it is interesting that Bismarck revealed in his memoirs, twenty-eight years after his greatest victory, how much he had feared that "misfortune" or unforeseen chance events might have thwarted all his plans. In writing about the Franco-Prussian War of 1870, he recounts his deep anxiety about the "possibility of diseases and unforeseen setbacks due to misfortune or ineptness."[8]

If one reviews the cases of major unexpected chance events reported in history, it appears that most belong to one or more of the following three categories:

a. *Events Related to Critically Important Leaders*: their fortuitous appearances and surprising careers, their sudden deaths by assassination or illness, their unpredictable, criminal or "abnormal" decisions.

b. *Events Related to War*: the unanticipated vagaries of war, tactical and strategic errors, technical mishaps, new weapon systems, major mistakes in assessing the balance of power, unforeseen third party interventions, and more.

c. *Natural and Health Disasters*: volcanic eruptions, earthquakes, tsunamis, floods, droughts, and major epidemic diseases, which are still enormously destructive (consider modern diseases like HIV/AIDS). Many such disasters are not predictable, but some are. When they are unpredictable, they are genuine chance events and logically belong to this chapter. We follow a different, equally valid logic and will review these issues in detail with predictable disasters in Part IV, Chapter 12. Both types of disaster form one category that has only recently been recognized as an independent driver of civilizations. A partial overlap between these two drivers, chance events and catastrophes, is therefore unavoidable.

A new, fourth category was added in the late twentieth century:

d. *Health and Safety Catastrophes Due to Technical Accidents*: Some are due to human error, others to technical mishaps. Parts are unpredictable and thus chance events, but other parts can be anticipated and prevented. This category is again an overlap between chance and disasters. It belongs to both but will be discussed under disasters.

Several categories of unexpected chance events can fuse into one major episode of bad luck. For example, Athens' indispensable war leader Pericles died suddenly in a fatal epidemic during the third year of the Peloponnesian War. This tipped the balance of war against Athens. Ancient myths knew that luck—or miracles—protected the births and upbringing of great heroes, but that dangers too were threatening them from the beginning. Historians knew the same. Had Alexander the Great not died suddenly at the age of thirty-three but had lived and ruled twenty years longer, the history of Europe and Asia after his time may well have been very different. If Julius Caesar had not been assassinated in 44 BCE, the history of Rome, the Roman Empire, and the whole Occident would probably have been quite different, and the future of the Jewish people radically different. No other Roman leader had a deeper and longer-lasting influence on Roman history, and none was a more open and resolute friend of the Jews. Similar reflections are possible for all centuries that modified the course of world history. Had Lenin, Stalin, Hitler, or Churchill died twenty or thirty years younger than they had, only specialized historians, if anyone, would remember their names, and the history of the twentieth century, including that of the Jewish people, would have been radically different. Machiavelli's calculation that half of all historic events are due to fortune may not be far off the mark.

Today, many sciences, including psychology and political science, have means to detect, prevent, or divert at least some, though never all, chance events. History seems unpredictable and dominated by chance, but it may be possible to reduce this dominance in sectors where prediction and prevention are possible, and this is what Machiavelli had in mind for his own time. Today, steadily increasing scientific, medical, geological, climatological, technological and other knowledge, including a better understanding of governance and human psychology, can help to partly anticipate and lessen the impact of chance on history. Complexity theory, another branch of applied mathematics, sometimes treated as identical with chaos theory, studies chance events and potential methods for controlling some of them. Other sciences are researching how to improve cognitive processes in the face of uncertainty, and how to better cope with uncertainty's psychological effects. Last but not least, government systems can be better prepared to react to unexpected crisis situations.

If the progress of science and general knowledge seems reassuring, the impact of chance events is not the same in all periods. As Machiavelli noted in the fifteenth century, turbulent and dynamic periods of history are more susceptible to unexpected chance events than stable and quiet ones. The twenty-first century looks like it is becoming a very turbulent period. Worse than that, not everything that could be improved by better science or better governance will be improved in time—Machiavelli knew this too. The obstacles are many. But in principle, a rising wave of chance events is likely to encounter a rising wave of scientific answers to cope with such events. Only history will tell whether such answers will be implemented.

Applications to Jewish History

Judaism has developed specific attitudes toward chance events, and Jewish history has been impacted by many of them. These are two different issues. In regard to the first issue, the Israeli scholar Ephraim Urbach has written a long chapter on classical Jewish attitudes toward magic and miracles as a means to influence events, particularly chance events. The biblical and rabbinic postulate that God's all-embracing power and foresight leaves no place for "chance events."[9] The Roman idea of a goddess called *Fortuna*, to whom other gods had to defer, is anathema to normative Judaism: there can be no source of power that is separate from and independent of divine power. The old belief in the power of *Fortuna* or "fate" inevitably led to the spread of numerous practices that were expected to positively influence fortune and protect against or banish bad luck: the sorcery, magical practices, and mystery cults that dominated the daily life of millions in the late Roman Empire and throughout the Orient. As luck or fate was also thought to be determined by the stars, belief in luck often encouraged the worshipping of stars, which Maimonides condemned as the core of all idolatry: "It is the object and the center of the whole Law to abolish idolatry and utterly uproot it, and to overthrow the opinion that any of the stars could interfere for good or evil in human matters, because it leads to the worship of stars."[10]

Biblical and rabbinic Judaism believed firmly that God had performed wonders and miracles to demonstrate his power. The Talmud reports miracles from as late as the fifth century CE, the time of its completion. Roman intellectuals knew that Jews believed in miracles and ridiculed them for their "superstitions." While the rabbis never excluded the possibility of future miracles, they prohibited any intentional reliance on them to cope with mundane fears and dangers. Still, some rabbinic ambiguity on this issue remained,[11] and it is not surprising that some believers found it—and still find it—impossible to respect the fine line between belief in past miracles and reliance on future ones.

The relationship between the laws of nature and miracles did not seem to greatly worry the rabbinic sages. A widespread view among them was that the laws of nature showed the order of creation, and thus represented a much greater divine miracle than any individual miracle that may have appeared to breach these laws. The logical consequence of Judaism's rejection of any power source other than divine power were religious condemnations of all forms of sorcery and magic used to divert bad luck and attract good. However, this was never the accepted view among the broad masses of the Jewish people. Many talmudic discussions show that sorcery and magical practices were widespread among Jews, and sometimes the rabbis attempted to give these a religious varnish to make them more acceptable to normative faith. Even today, such beliefs and practices seem to have a fair number of adherents, in not only religious but also non-religious circles. The Israeli anthropologist Eli Yassif documented in 2002 "widespread evidence of magical belief" extending into Israel's army and navy.[12] Of course, such beliefs are common even in the Western world, but they probably spread more easily when there are high levels of traumatization, feelings of powerlessness, doubts in leadership, and concerns about an uncertain future.

It is questionable whether historians should engage in "virtual" history writing, because it is already difficult enough to describe and explain the history that has actually taken place. However, the compulsion to speculate about what would or would not have happened in the absence of a known, history-shaping event is irresistible and quite common. The problem with such speculations is that the non-occurrence of a dramatic event does not mean that other events in history would have continued as before. Other, perhaps more radical events might have interfered and changed the course of history in even more significant ways. We cannot know. Jewish history certainly has known many chance events with profound consequences. Five examples will be presented, three "positive" and two "negative" ones. They should be read as no more than speculative illustrations of Machiavelli's paradigm.

Sennacherib's Invasion of Judah in 701 BCE

An early example of a chance event that has intrigued historians since the nineteenth century is the reportedly abrupt return of the Assyrian ruler Sennacherib to Assyria after invading and devastating much of Judah, but not its capital, Jerusalem. Most critical scholars have agreed on the date, 701 BCE, but on little else. This war has led to an enormous amount of research and discussion. The Assyrian stone reliefs illustrating how Sennacherib conquered the city of Lachish in southern Judah and killed or took away his Judean captives are among the most famous Near Eastern antiquities displayed in London's British Museum. The story is best known from the biblical records, which tell of Sennacherib besieging Jerusalem while Isaiah prophesized to King Hezekiah that the Assyrian "shall not enter the city: he shall not shoot an arrow at it."[13] The next night "an angel" struck down the enemy camp and when day broke "they were all dead corpses." Some historians accept the biblical record and speculate about the nature of the epidemic that must have struck Sennacherib's army—was it bubonic plague?[14] Another author, R.S. Bray, who is not a biblical historian, rejects the entire story from beginning to end as a fabrication because it does not concord with the typical pattern of bubonic plague outbreaks as known today.[15]

Most scholars oscillate between these two extremes. It was noted that a key part of the biblical story is remarkably consistent with Sennacherib's own written statements.[16] Generally, three facts are not contested by most scholars: i) Several cities of Judah were conquered and destroyed, not least Lachish, perhaps the second-largest city after Jerusalem, and the countryside was devastated; ii) Judah was forced to pay tribute to Assyria, though it is not agreed when these payments were made; and iii) Sennacherib retreated back to Assyria without destroying Jerusalem; it is significant that he never mentioned a victorious or completed siege. There is no agreement on whether the Assyrians fully attacked and besieged Jerusalem or simply cut the city off by blocking its access roads. The Assyrian inscription in which Sennacherib boasts that he was holding King Hezekiah "like a bird in a cage" can mean either one.[17]

Why Sennacherib spared Jerusalem is unclear. Among the reasons advanced, apart from the often discarded plague theory, are: a palace revolt back home; troubles in occupied and hostile Babylonia; and doubts about whether Jerusalem was really worth the fight. Whatever the reason may have been, the Assyrian retreat appeared so miraculous to Isaiah—or the author writing under his name—that he could only see it as divine intervention. It was probably a lucky "chance event" of enormous historic consequence. The torture and massacre of Lachish's population is amply documented by the gruesome reliefs in the British Museum, and by the skeletons of women and children found during excavations there. There is little doubt about the fate that would have befallen the inhabitants of Jerusalem had Sennacherib conquered the city. It is true that the Babylonian Nebuchadnezzar destroyed Jerusalem 115 years later, but in the interim many long-lasting and irreversible political and spiritual developments had taken place. Had Sennacherib wiped out Jerusalem, the first Isaiah was hardly likely to survive, and thus none of his words would likely be known today. There might never have been a second Isaiah, a Jeremiah, or an Ezekiel. The fate of Judah as well as the future of the Jewish people, if indeed they had one, would have been radically different. Isaiah's prophecies are essential to Judaism. Jews loved him more than all other prophets,[18] and Christians greatly cherished him too.

Jerusalem could have been destroyed even before Sennacherib, but was spared. This is why Part IV, Chapter 10, reflects on a similar hypothetical question: what if Assyria had, in 722/720 BCE, conquered not only the Kingdom of Israel but that of Judah and its capital Jerusalem as well?

The Burning of the Second Temple in 70 CE

A second incident was an equally dramatic and better-known chance event: the burning of the Second Temple in 70 CE. The edifice was torched by first one, and then several, of Titus' soldiers. Flavius Josephus describes in great detail how and when Titus decided that he would not, under any circumstance, destroy the Temple. He made this perfectly and publicly clear to his six chief staff-officers as well as to others whom he had assembled to discuss strategy. When he was told that a fire was starting, he desperately attempted to avert it, "rose up in great haste [this wording probably means that he was exhausted and sleeping], and as he was ran to the holy house in order to have a stop put to the fire."[19] He called loudly upon his soldiers to quench it, but it was too late: he had lost all control over his excited legionnaires. This story, too, is the subject of an enormous amount of research and debate. In 1861, the historian Jacob Bernays, followed by Theodor Mommsen, questioned the veracity of Josephus. Most scholars followed in their footsteps and gave more credence to a Christian historian of the early fifth century CE, who asserted that Titus ordered the Temple to be burned, assuming that Josephus manipulated the truth to flatter Titus.

In the early twenty-first century, two Roman history scholars exposed the prejudices clouding a more objective appreciation of Josephus on this question. Tommaso Leoni from the University of York in Toronto studied all available sources as well as the preceding scholarly discussions and called Josephus' narrative "unequivocally clear, consistent and substantially trustworthy,"[20] because, among other reasons, it would have been very risky for him to publish a book including a major falsehood while Titus, his brother Domitian who followed him as emperor after his death in 81 CE, and many Roman veterans who witnessed the burning were still alive.

The Oxford historian Peter Goodman advanced additional compelling reasons to accept Josephus' version of events.[21] It was in fact not usual Roman practice to wipe out the sanctuaries of rebellious nations once they were defeated. Titus was probably still Rome's emperor when Josephus published his book, and was among its first readers. Josephus would have been unwise to pretend that Titus wanted to save the Temple if he did not, because Titus had no public reason to appear magnanimous toward the Jews. On the contrary, once the deed was done, Titus had no choice but to celebrate it. Rome's public celebration of his victory, which included a parade of the captured temple vessels, was one of the most exuberant the city had ever seen. It was impossible for the Roman Empire to admit publicly that an event of such magnitude had resulted from nothing more than a breakdown of discipline in the Roman army. Of course, neither Jewish nor Christian tradition would accept this as a random—rather than divinely ordained—event. A historian too has to ask himself whether a small random event, if this is what it was—a single Roman soldier disobeying his commander-in-chief and throwing the first torch—could change the course of history for the next two thousand years. It is futile to speculate on what would have happened if the Temple had been saved, and its worship continued under a "moderate" Jewish leadership controlled by Rome after the revolt's defeat. We might have a very different Judaism today, and Christianity and Islam would also have taken a different course—or perhaps would never have come into existence.

Sabbatai Zevi

Another chance event was the appearance of the false messiah Sabbatai Zevi from Smyrna (1626-1676) and the disastrous upheaval he created all across the Jewish world. Gershom Scholem wrote the defining classical biography of Sabbatai Zevi.[22] He was the first important scholar to discuss Sabbatai Zevi's case with medical specialists and identified a specific, severe psychiatric illness as an indispensable key to understanding Zevi's personality. He also discovered hitherto unknown firsthand personal recollections by Zevi's immediate entourage. Several who met him refused to believe his messianic claims because they realized that he was "mad," a "lunatic." A large number of contemporaneous witness accounts, including many by people who did believe in him, leave no doubt that he represented "an extreme manic-depressive case, a person whose condition is periodically oscillating between the most severe depression and melancholy, and frenzied rapture, limitless enthusiasm, and euphoria."[23] In severe cases this disease, today more accurately called "bi-polar disorder," can be clearly distinguished from other psychiatric illnesses. It often follows a regular rhythm of ups and downs interrupted by periods of relative calm, and can end in suicide. It is caused by several risk genes and environmental influence, but until modern times it was not recognized as a disease. In contrast to other severe mental disorders, the personality of the patient does not disintegrate, and his intelligence and memory are unimpaired. Afflicted persons most often acknowledge the pathology of their depressive phases, but are often reluctant to describe their ecstatic periods as part of the illness. A follower of Sabbatai Zevi said that "God's face was hid from him" when he found him in his depressive phase.[24]

Part IV, Chapter 3 mentioned that some sections of the Jewish population are more susceptible to some genetically heritable diseases than the general population. According to research in Western countries, bi-polar disorder is one of the ailments more prevalent among Jews.* Today the disorder can, to some degree, be medically and pharmacologically treated.[25] If Sabbatai Zevi appeared in modern times, he and his family might very well keep his condition private, as many in the same situation do, and ask for medical treatment. The Jewish masses' belief in miracles was strong in the seventeenth century, and has not disappeared among today's religious believers. Nevertheless, Sabbatai Zevi would probably find few public followers today. His repeated claims of levitation—floating through the air— and his aggressive reaction when these claims were challenged[26] would give him away. The delusion of levitation is a typical and well-known symptom during extreme manic phases of the disease, and a very dangerous one for the afflicted person.[27] The story of Sabbatai Zevi and the extraordinary and destructive impact he had on the Jewish world was a rare and unfortunate coincidence. The deep messianic yearnings that spread among Jews after the expulsion from Spain coincided with the sudden appearance of a charismatic, highly intelligent, and physically attractive man who proclaimed that he

---

* Scholem, in *Mystik*, chapter VIII, p. 447, footnote 4, refers to the psychiatric handbooks of Bleuler and Lange. The philosopher Karl Jaspers, who began his career as clinical psychiatrist, referred to a number of research papers to confirm in 1913 that manic-depressive disease was more often found among Jewish than non-Jewish patients. See his *Allgemeine Psychopathologie (General Psychopathology)* (Berlin-Heidelberg-New York: Neunte Aufl., 1973), 562.

was the answer to their yearnings. That he was delusional due to a severe psychiatric disease could not be understood in his time. Had he not appeared, the Jewish people's craving for rescue from persecution and expulsions would have expressed itself in other, perhaps more constructive, ways.

The Death of Lord Kitchener in 1916

Did chance play a role in the dramatic Jewish history of the twentieth century? An early-twentieth-century random event that may have had considerable consequences on Jewish history was the unexpected death of Field Marshall Lord Kitchener of Khartoum. The legendary and immensely popular war hero was asked to join the British cabinet as war minister in 1914. Kitchener's views of the desirable post-war structure of the Middle East were very different from those that ultimately prevailed. His long residency as British representative in Cairo had formed his opinions. He proposed that a new Arab caliphate rule the whole Middle East, replacing the Ottoman caliphate, and believed that Palestine should eventually be annexed to Egypt. He repeatedly voiced strong opposition to a British conquest and protectorate of Palestine. In his view, Palestine had no strategic value.[28]

He was not known for particular hostility to the Jews, but he obviously considered them irrelevant and took no interest in their old biblical claims and new national aspirations. His influence in the war cabinet was waning in 1916, and many of his colleagues wanted him out of the way, but nobody can guarantee that his power would not have risen again at a later stage of the war. If it had, the British government would have found it difficult to ignore his views on the future of the Middle East. In that case, the Balfour Declaration of 1917 might not have come to light at all, or not at the right time, or it might have been much less favorably worded. The final text of the Declaration was a compromise, which angered Chaim Weizmann and his Zionist supporters. A first, more pro-Zionist, draft had been considerably watered down at the last moment to satisfy the objections of Edwin Montague, a minor Jewish government official and stout anti-Zionist who was publicly supported by a small but vocal group of other anti-Zionist English Jews. Montague's stature in British society and politics was minuscule, compared to that of Lord Kitchener.

The predictable objections of England's most prestigious soldier, even if he was politically weakened, would have done more and perhaps irremediable harm to Zionist aspirations had he lived, but he did not live. On June 5, 1916, a torpedo from a German submarine, or a mine it had laid, sank the armored cruiser *Hampshire* on which he was traveling. Kitchener's body was never recovered. Maybe Zionist aspirations, sooner or later, would have been successful by other means. But if it is true, as is generally agreed today, that the Balfour Declaration was indispensable for the British Mandate, the creation of the national home of the Jewish people, and ultimately the State of Israel, and that the declaration had to come before the end of the war, then the Jews owe their independence to a number of important factors, and a German torpedo was one of them. Inevitably, antisemitic conspiracy theorists linked Kitchener's death with Zionist aspirations.[29] As far as they were concerned, his death was no chance event but a murder plotted by the "International Jew," the "Elders of Zion," some Rothschild, or Winston Churchill, allegedly in the pay of the above.

The Death of Joseph Stalin

There were other positive and negative chance events in the twentieth century. One with enormous implications for the Jewish people and others was Joseph Stalin's sudden death in 1953. Before the war, Stalin's attitude toward Jews had been a mix of old-fashioned prejudice, suspicion of a widespread people without a homeland, and feelings of distrust because some Jews, such as Trotsky, had been among his main enemies, although a few others had become close associates. After 1945, the aging dictator turned into a "vicious and obsessive anti-Semite," to quote Stalin's biographer, Simon Sebag Montefiore.[30] On January 13, 1953, Stalin announced the arrest of a number of eminent Jewish professors of medicine and doctors whom *Pravda*, repeating Stalin's own words, called "ignoble spies and killers." During the following wave of hysterical public antisemitism, Stalin concocted a letter prominent Jews were ordered to sign. They were instructed to beg the authorities for the deportation of the country's Jews from the cities where almost all of them lived, allegedly to protect them from an imaginary pogrom. This letter has never been found, but several of Stalin's closest associates, among them Anastas Mikoyan and Lazar Kaganovich, confirmed that a mass-deportation of the Jews was indeed being prepared. New concentration camps were already being set up. In his last days, Stalin avidly read the arrested doctors' "confessions," which the secret police had extracted under torture. Then, on March 1, 1953, he was felled by a severe stroke. He died four days later. On the same day, March 5, 1953, *Pravda* stopped its antisemitic campaign.

Would Stalin have carried out his paranoid project? Toward the end, the Soviet bureaucracy no longer automatically followed all his orders, but they had already begun to implement this one. A vast, well-tested machinery set up to deport millions to their deaths or the Gulag was ready, and there was no shortage of willing executioners. Against a mad Stalin, the Jews had no effective defenders. It is not far-fetched to assume that they escaped catastrophe—a second catastrophe in the wake of the Nazi occupation—by a hair. It may have been a matter of only weeks, if not days.

Looking to the Future

If it is true that the twenty-first century will experience more turbulence and witness more chance events than earlier, calmer periods of history, as said before, the same will be even more true for the Middle East. In other words, Jewish history will continue to be impacted by unpredictability and chance. This does not mean that the future of the Jewish people, Israel included, will mostly depend on external factors beyond its control. Rather, it means that the factors that the Jews can control, such as identity preservation, quality of governance, leadership in education, science, and technology, and the ability to win friends and allies will be more important than they would be in the absence of chance events. The drivers that mainly depend on the Jews themselves may help them to partly anticipate and sometimes control chance events or their effects.

CHAPTER 12

Natural and Health Disasters [1]

General Observations

Of the twelve drivers, natural and health disasters have only recently been recognized as a potential cause of civilizational decline. Among the historians who inspired this study, two—Sima Qian and Gibbon—touched on this question briefly. Another, Jared Diamond, made it the issue of his book *Collapse: How Societies Choose to Fail or Succeed*. Sima Qian commented on the immense influence China's great waterways had on the history of the country: "How tremendous are the benefits, and how terrible the damages!"[2] When Gibbon described a devastating Mediterranean tsunami (discussed in greater detail below), he noted that the "convulsions of the elements" did not affect the history and decline of the empire.[3]

However, a belief that violent natural events had dramatic impacts on history, even causing the destructions of entire civilizations, is much older. Plato's story of Atlantis, which was swallowed by the ocean, and the biblical story of the flood may reflect real prehistoric memories of civilizations that were destroyed by natural catastrophes without leaving a trace. Many of these myths insist that human transgression necessitating divine punishment caused catastrophes. Assertions about past catastrophes and predictions of future ones generally had and still have an ideological and moral agenda. In the 1950s, the Russian Jewish author Immanuel Velikovsky published a number of books with sensational titles such as *Worlds in Collision* (1950) and *Ages in Chaos* (1952). He claimed that a series of violent global events caused by celestial objects had shaken human history thousands of years earlier, but collective amnesia had obliterated any memory of them, except for some of the miraculous narratives in the Hebrew Bible.

By claiming that certain miraculous Bible stories reflected scientifically provable events, Velikovsky disclosed his own ideological agenda.[4] More seriously, in 1972, the Club of Rome published its *Limits to Growth* report, which attracted enormous public attention and sold more than 30 million copies. The book stated that current economic growth patterns were unsustainable and would in the end destroy the earth's natural environment. The environmentalist movements of the Western world have continued to grow, have increased their influence on politics and ideas, and have kept warning of the dangers ahead. In 2005, Jared Diamond published *Collapse*, in which he attributes the decline and collapse of a number of civilizations to their suicidal environmental practices. A large number of people have begun to regard natural and environmental events as drivers of the rise, decline, and fall of civilizations, not only in the past but in the present as well. *Collapse* has inspired other authors. Brian Fagan, the American anthropologist and author of popular archaeology books, has linked three major contemporaneous historic developments, two of them civilizational collapses, to the global warming period of the tenth to thirteenth centuries CE: the bumper harvests in Europe, which led to a population explosion and the building of many new cities north of the Alps; the collapse of the Tang Dynasty in China; and the collapse of the Mayan civilization in Central America.[5]

Since World War II, leading scientists have voiced concern not only about limited catastrophes, but also about the dangers to the survival of humankind if not all life on earth.[6] A lot of scientific research is now devoted to environmental impact questions and natural catastrophes. Several areas are attracting scientific and policy interest as well as public concern: global warming, catastrophic geological events, and microbiological pandemics.

Global Warming

The current bout of global warming is not a chance event, but—in the view of most experts—man-made. The dangers of global warming are attracting enormous public and governmental attention. At the time Diamond's book appeared, climate change campaigners began to speak of a "point of no return" or a "tipping point" for global warming: "Global warming may soon spiral out of control...[and] plunge Western Europe into freezing winters and threaten climate systems worldwide."[7] Widespread alarm about global warming is now shared by the overwhelming majority of the international scientific community. A comprehensive and authoritative report of the Intergovernmental Panel on Climate Change (IPCC 2007) notes that "warming of the climate system is unequivocal, as is now evident from observations of increases in global average air and ocean temperatures, widespread melting of snow and ice, and rising global average sea level." It further states that "most of the observed increase in globally-averaged temperatures since the mid-20th century is very likely due to the observed increase in anthropogenic greenhouse gas (GHG) concentration. It is clear that global warming caused by civilization poses real risks, but we are not yet sure how these can be reduced by exactly calibrated mitigation policies."[8]

343

Some experts see the greatest threat of climate change as the destabilization of the massive ice sheets of Greenland and the Antarctic. It is no longer disputed that they are melting, and while the effect on global sea levels is still small, it may accelerate. A future rise in sea levels will partly depend on increased greenhouse gasses. The speed of these developments is not predictable, but early earth history reveals cases in which the sea level, once ice sheets began to melt, rose one meter every twenty years for centuries. A 2007 OECD study assumes a much more modest mean sea level rise of 0.5 meters by 2070. This estimate includes the contributions from melting ice sheets that have proven important over recent decades and is consistent with a medium to high-risk scenario. By ranking 136 port cities of more than one million inhabitants, which are highly exposed and vulnerable to climate extremes, the study finds that almost four times more people could be exposed to a once-in-a-century coastal flood event by 2070 as are today. The estimated financial impact of such an event would rise to 35 trillion US dollars by 2070, up from three trillion in 2007.[9] The great majority of the most exposed populations live in the coastal mega-cities of China, India, Bangladesh, Thailand, Myanmar, and Vietnam.

A few senior scientists do not agree with the more alarmist global warming predictions. The physicist Freeman Dyson is among these. He does not believe that global warming presents as grave a danger as the great majority of scientists fear, and warns that in the history of science the great majority has often been wrong.[10] Policy-makers have no way of knowing the scientific truth, which in any event is open to continuous change; they only know that they cannot afford to discount the possibility of really serious dangers. The direct consequences of global warming, which can be partly predicted and even calculated, look bad enough, but there are many secondary consequences of great geopolitical concern, which are difficult to imagine in any detail and impossible to predict. These could be as bad or worse. They include uncontrollable population movements and large-scale violence and wars over shrinking resources, as mentioned in Part III, Chapter 7.

Catastrophic Geological Events

These include earthquakes, which are frequent in many regions, not least the Middle East, tsunamis, volcano eruptions, and meteorite or other space impacts. Scientific prediction methods for such events are making progress and will slowly increase the possibilities of anticipation and control. Since December 26, 2004, when one devastated South Asia, tsunamis are attracting popular interest. Except for the destruction of Pompeii in 79 CE, the Mediterranean region's suffering of major volcanic eruptions, but also underwater quakes followed by major tsunamis has until now been little known. Several have devastated the eastern shores of the Mediterranean.

Ancient historians reported a big one in 365 CE, which Edward Gibbon's described in gripping terms.* Geologists have identified a steep, still-active fault near Crete as the most probable source of that tsunami. In 551 CE, another quake, no less massive, triggered a huge tsunami that devastated Lebanon's coast, including Beirut. In 1303, another mega-tsunami hit Crete, Rhodes, Alexandria, and Acre in Israel, among other places. Earthquake experts say such events will happen again.[11] Much more frequent are the smaller tsunamis created by volcanic events in southern Italy. The latest one occurred in 1908, when a seven-magnitude quake created a tsunami that almost destroyed the Italian cities of Messina and Reggio di Calabria.[12] But even these smaller tsunamis can reach North Africa, Egypt, and the Near East. It has been calculated that tsunamis originating from geological events near southern Italy or Greece occur approximately once a century. The Mediterranean has been quiet since 1908. Catastrophic earthquakes, tsunamis, and volcanic eruptions, as well as meteor impacts, will continue to pose partly unpredictable risks to civilization.

Microbiological Pandemics:_

Historians tell us of plagues that ravaged countries and continents and changed the course of history. The "Black Death," or bubonic plague, which crossed through much of the world in the mid-fourteenth century, is estimated to have annihilated between one third and two thirds of Europe's population, not to mention the deaths in China, Africa, and the Middle East. In recent years, interest in health disasters has begun to grow, following the bird flu epidemic in Asia and the fears that it created in governments and the scientific community. There are concerns that a pandemic comparable to the "Spanish flu" of 1918, which killed more people than the ten million soldiers who lost their lives during World War I, could strike the world again, and the "swine flu" outbreaks in 2009 reinforced these concerns.

---

* "The greatest part of the Roman Empire was shaken by a violent and destructive earthquake. The impression was communicated to the waters; the shores of the Mediterranean were left dry by the sudden retreat of the sea; great quantities of fish were caught by the hand; large vessels were stranded in the mud, and a curious spectator amused his eye, or rather his fancy, by contemplating the various appearance of valleys and mountains, which had never, since the formation of the globe, been exposed to the sun. But the tide soon returned, with the weight of an immense and irresistible deluge, which was severely felt on the coast of Sicily, of Dalmatia, of Greece and of Egypt; large boats were transported, and lodged on the roofs of houses or at the distance of two miles from the shore; the people with their habitations were swept away by the waters; and the city of Alexandria annually commemorated the fatal day on which fifty thousand people had lost their lives in the inundation. This calamity...astonished and terrified the subjects of Rome....They recollected the preceding earthquakes which had subverted the cities of Palestine and Bithynia...." (Gibbon, 791).

Health and Safety Catastrophes Due to Technical Accidents

Technical accidents that harm people are by definition man-made and have always been known. Low-probability/high-impact accidents that can affect millions of people and change the course of history, however, are new. Several technologies may now have this potential, although the only one for which potential nearly became reality is the use of nuclear energy for power generation. Among a substantial number of nuclear accidents, three have had considerable national and international repercussions: the reactor accident on Three-Mile Island in the United States in 1979, the accident in Chernobyl in the Soviet Union in 1986, and the 2011 damage to Fukushima in Japan. The enormous public fear and outrage created by the Chernobyl accident and its initial denial by the authorities is believed to have contributed to the demise of the Soviet Union.

A second, widely pervasive technology that its detractors suspect of carrying great health and safety risks is genetic modification, particularly the deliberate release of genetically modified organisms into the environment for agricultural production, or the accidental releases of such organisms. During decades of use in many parts of the world, no accident caused by this technology has been reported, and the scientific consensus is that, when regulated, it is safe. The law obliges technological innovators and industries to pay great attention to risk avoidance. A major human catastrophe, caused by a technical accident, that could affect the future of civilization is a low-probability chance event, but it can never be completely excluded from consideration.

Jewish History

The Jewish people suffered several major disasters in its long history, but none of them originated from a specific geological or other natural catastrophe. The most devastating earthquakes and tsunamis to strike the land of Israel occurred in pre-historic times or during the centuries of dispersion, when few Jews lived in Israel. However, the threat of drought and famine has always loomed over the land of Israel. This was the main natural calamity affecting the Jewish people in ancient times. The Bible is full of drought and famine narratives, prayers for rain in the land of Israel are still said by Jews even in countries with abundant rain, and there is an entire Talmud tractate, *Taanit*, "Fasting," that discusses the timing and conditions of fast days which were called for when the absence of rainfall risked causing a local or national disaster. The only response to drought and famine the Bible mentions apart from prayer is temporary emigration. There is no important reference to technological responses, such as water-saving techniques or the cultivation of crops suited to arid areas, so it is unclear whether such responses existed or not.

In the twenty-first century, the environment and geology will become more salient for the Jewish people. Wherever they live, they will be affected by environmental degradation and global warming one way or another, and in addition almost half of them live in a small and environmentally fragile country, Israel. However, the Jewish people can do very little to influence global environmental trends and policies except, perhaps, through major scientific discoveries and technological innovations.

Global Warming

The consequences of global warming will affect Jews in various degrees. The above-quoted OECD report notes that among the most exposed populations of Western mega-cites are those of greater New York and South Florida, including Miami. This could affect more than two million Jews. The top ten urban areas in terms of exposed assets include New York, Miami, Virginia Beach, Amsterdam, and St. Petersburg. If the most pessimistic—but not unanimously agreed-upon—forecasts come true, the expected sea level rise could also harm other Jewish populations. Seventy-seven percent of all Jews live in 20 major urban areas of the world, and almost half of them are on or near an ocean. While the geographic locations of many Jews may pose particular long-term problems if the dangers are ignored, most Jews will likely be able to cope with them because they have a long tradition of mobility and migration, and are usually well informed and connected.

For Israel, the consequences of global warming could be quite serious. In 2007, the Israel Union for Environmental Defense, a non-governmental lobby group, studied the quoted Intergovernmental Panel on Climate Change Report of the United Nations for its implications for Israel, and warned that Israel could see its entire coastline flooded and lose its seaports if global warming continues unchecked. The report offered a second, less alarmist scenario based on the assumption that the world makes a concerted effort to reduce greenhouse gas emissions, a policy that U.S. President Barack Obama has promised to pursue.[13] In August 2008, Israel's Environmental Protection Ministry released a more sober yet still disquieting report: Israel was unprepared for the coming global climate crisis, and its water supply was at risk. If precautions were not taken, Israel would suffer enormous economic losses by 2020.[14] Obviously, Israel was and is too preoccupied with its political, foreign policy, and defense problems to pay adequate attention to climate change, but Israel's political and defense problems might also become entangled with climate change, which is predicted to have enormous consequences for the Middle East. It is likely that wet regions will get wetter, and dry regions drier. Future weather maps show that Middle East's water scarcity will likely worsen. How this will affect Middle Eastern conflicts will greatly depend on large-scale technological improvements and the policies of the countries concerned.

Catastrophic Geological Events

Israel's geological situation is unfavorable. Geological catastrophes have occurred in the Middle East in the past and will occur again. The most dangerous event would be an earthquake of seven or greater magnitude on the Richter scale, with its epicenter in or near Israel. Some geologists believe a major earthquake in Israel is overdue. Israel is not considered to be well prepared for this danger, as many of its older buildings have not been retrofitted for earthquake safety. The cost of retrofitting all of them would be enormous and would require a rejuggling of national priorities. Since approximately 2010, the Israeli government has begun to sensitize the public to the potential earthquake danger. First aid teams have conducted disaster preparedness exercises testing their readiness and equipment, and earthquake drills have been conducted in schools and workplaces. Still, a large majority of Israelis probably has no idea what to do in the case of a serious earthquake, in contrast to the citizens of other threatened countries, such as Japan. Tsunamis are almost sure to hit Israel's coast again, as they have in the past. Nothing can be done to prevent tsunamis, but early warning systems could help minimize damage.

Microbiological Pandemics

Pandemics are much more amenable to preemptive and protective policies by a small country than climate change or geological disasters are. Microbiologists fear that pandemics will happen again, whether triggered by nature or biological terrorism, and Jews need to be well prepared because, in addition to the risks they share with everybody, they could become a specific target of biological terrorism and warfare. Of particular concern is the fact that according to concerned microbiologists pandemics are likely to have their greatest impacts in large urban areas, where the majority of the world's Jews are concentrated. Israel is said to be preparing for such eventualities.

Health and Safety Catastrophes Due to Technical Accidents

No technical accident with far-reaching human consequences has yet struck Israel or a Jewish community. Israel has a small nuclear reactor for research and a larger, well-publicized one in Dimona. Since 2004, Israeli and foreign sources have expressed occasional concerns about the safety of the Dimona reactor and have speculated about the danger of leaks. The most alarmist statements have been orchestrated by foreign sources hostile to Israel, and Israeli authorities have dismissed them as unfounded.

Israel has been carrying out research on genetic modification and has used genetically modified products for decades. No negative side effects have been reported, and the Israeli public has shown little concern about genetic modification, in contrast to the European public.

Potential dangers are numerous and diverse, and many are unpredictable. Natural and health disasters could become a future driver of rise and decline within the Jewish civilization. This means that Israel and the Jewish people need to do serious long-term thinking and make preparations for such events.

PART V

DRIVERS OF TRANSFORMATION: TWO CASE STUDIES

Introduction

The following two chapters summarize the emergence of the Dutch Republic in the seventeenth century and that of modern Turkey in the twentieth. They identify some of their salient drivers and look for possible parallels with modern Israel. The intention is not to impose artificial comparisons on countries belonging to different epochs, regions, and historical environments, but to study one country's history in the hopes that it may allow us to better assess another country's performance. The successes or failures of one country could serve as encouragement or warning for others.

The Dutch Republic is the first case that is tentatively placed in parallel not to the Jewish people but to the State of Israel. This story shows how a small country fighting for survival was able to radically transform itself and reach great-power status in a short time. It would hold this status for more than a century, until its survival was no longer threatened. Turkey, the second case, shows how decline and collapse can in some cases lead to deep transformation and new rise. Eyewitnesses of collapse are rarely able to see this effect; it only becomes visible to later generations. The decline and fall of the Ottoman Empire was not the end of Turkish history but an extraordinary challenge that led to a new rise. This story has some metaphoric similarities with modern Jewish history, which has also moved from catastrophe to rebirth. Both the seventeenth-century Dutch Republic and twentieth-century Turkey faced life-threatening challenges by foreign powers. At the beginning, their existence was in doubt, and they responded not only with military victories but also with profound changes that assured that their survival would last.

CHAPTER 1

Transforming a Small Country into
a Great Power: The Dutch Republic [1]

The Dutch case study takes up some of the drivers of rise and decline reviewed in other chapters—leadership, war, religion, internal dissent, science, and technology—but looks at them from a small country's perspective. History has known a number of small countries or cities that grew into great powers or civilizations Some lasted a very long time—Rome is arguably the most illustrious case. Others shrank back to a small size or disappeared completely. The Mongol empire is an outstanding case. The Mongols appeared from the steppes of Central Asia from, in terms of history, a void or "nowhere," conquered China and most of Asia, organized the largest contiguous empire ever known, terrorized Europe, and than drifted back to "nowhere."

Drivers of the rise and decline of small states are not always identical to those of big nations or large civilizations. Of particular interest to us are drivers of rise that can transform a small country into a great power. In Europe, several small countries or cities held great-power positions for longer or shorter times, were able to compete with much larger countries, and left an important mark on European civilization. They include Italian city-states such as Venice and, for a shorter time, Florence, and also Sweden and the Dutch Republic.

The Dutch Republic is the most interesting case because it started on a small, fragile piece of land with no natural resources, in contrast to Sweden, which had rich iron ores for export. The main difference between the Italian city-states and the Dutch Republic is that the latter forged a new, independent civilization with its own language, literature, and art, with many old roots for sure, but not as part of a greater overarching civilization. The Dutch Republic enables us to make a few fascinating analogies, not to the Jewish people as a whole, but to the State of Israel. The rise and fast growth of the Republic by force of arms resulted from the fact that the Dutch had no choice: they had to reach beyond their "smallness" if they wanted to be independent and survive the hostility of powerful Spain, as well as the indifference of others who did not wish to offend the Spaniards. Today's Netherlands, however, also shows that rise and decline are relative terms. Compared to the great-power status of the seventeenth-century Dutch Republic, all subsequent Dutch history must appear to be "decline." Yet it makes no sense to apply the rise-and-decline perspective beyond the eighteenth century in the Dutch case. Today's Netherlands is a prosperous and secure European country that has neither need nor great ambitions to reach beyond its size.

The drivers that transformed this small strip of land threatened by the sea into a great power are:

1. Global trading primacy in high-value products, which was built up over a long period and created enormous wealth;

2. Leadership in important sectors of science and technology and in social and organizational innovation, which underpinned economic strength;

3. Outstanding universities and European leadership in popular literacy and education, which buttressed scientific and technical excellence;

4. Exceptional artistic creativity, which turned the Dutch Republic into the recognized center of European painting and other arts;

5. Supremacy in naval power and great strength in land power based on wealth, technological superiority, patriotism, and an unflagging will to fight;

6. Enormous political, economic, and religious resilience of the masses and the elites across long periods and against great odds: the Dutch war for independence lasted, with interruptions, for eighty years. Spain's resistance to accepting Dutch independence was fierce, but Dutch faith and patience outlasted Spanish pride and fanaticism;

7. Exceptional statesmanship by a few Dutch rulers: Dutch institutions and decision-making structures were essentially collective, which made it very difficult for visionary figures to emerge. The Twelve Years' Truce of 1609-1621, an example of extraordinary foresight, was proposed by Spain and accepted by Dutch rulers but vigorously opposed by fundamentalists who demanded full—and clearly unobtainable—Spanish recognition. The republic's material and diplomatic position improved conspicuously under the truce, turning the balance of power in its favor; and

8. A political and military alliance with England, one of the great powers of the time: there was even, as discussed above, a short-lived project of merging the two Protestant powers into a union after 1650. The alliance multiplied the effective power of the Dutch and allowed them to defeat the French, but it ultimately dissolved into hostility.

Against these eight drivers of Dutch rise, one might mention two factors that played a role in its decline:

1. Lack of internal unity: from the beginning to the end of the Republic, about 230 years, the Dutch never stopped their internal quarrelling about religious and political questions, even when the very survival of the Dutch Republic was in danger. These fights were bitter, and some ended in violence and political assassination. Internal disunity was the rule, not unity; and
2. Lack of agreed-upon borders: during the same 230 years, the borders of the Dutch Republic expanded and contracted, fluctuating with victories and defeats. The country's final borders were agreed upon only in the nineteenth century.

The Dutch case indicates that a small country will need outside help and a relentless internal effort, innovativeness, qualitative superiority, and, occasionally, luck to maintain a great-power position, or even to survive.

Applications to Jewish History

The Dutch Republic cannot be compared to the much older, transnational civilization of the Jews. Even a comparison with Israel alone has to take the transnational element of Israel into account. Israel is supported by the world's main superpower, the United States, and the dynamic and influential American Jewish community. The Dutch, too, needed allies, but lacked the asset of a Diaspora.

Despite these and other limitations, there are a few possible parallels. Is it possible to measure Israel's current strengths and weaknesses against the eight drivers that transformed the Dutch Republic into a great power? A comparison with the Dutch can only be tentative, but it may confirm that small countries that have to prevail over numerous enemies must develop a number of similar assets and will encounter a number of similar problems and constraints.

1. Israel's economy is small but its competitiveness is improving. World primacy in a major sector, of the kind that the Dutch enjoyed, is remote but not completely out of reach. It is not clear that Israel could hold such primacy for long, however, and it might even be dangerous to put too many eggs into one basket.
2. Israeli scholars and researchers have a world-class position in some scientific and technological disciplines, but Israel cannot claim a global leadership role in any major sector of science or technology, as the Dutch

could at their peak. Perhaps reaching that position today is only possible for the largest advanced countries. Israel's capacity for technological innovation is impressive, but the country seems to be falling behind its earlier pioneering performance in social and institutional innovations such as those at which the Dutch excelled.

3. Israel's universities are ranked among the better ones globally, but its primary and secondary education system is deficient in comparison to other advanced small countries. The level of modern education of the average Israeli is superior to that found on average in the wider Middle East, but it is not equivalent to that of other advanced countries, and it does not meet the requirements of a small "great power" and could not match the old Dutch in comparative educational achievements: in the seventeenth century, the Dutch were the best-educated people in Europe.

4. Israel's cultural and artistic creativity is not inferior to that of other small countries, but it cannot be compared to the enormous Dutch creativity of the seventeenth century, in painting for example.

5. Israel enjoys an air superiority in the Middle East comparable to the former Dutch naval supremacy. It is also said to be unsurpassed in classical land wars, but not necessarily in asymmetric conflicts.

6. The patience and resilience of the Israeli people in the face of adversity has been questioned by some and confirmed by others. Israel has shown resilience over short periods of time. Conditions are too different to compare modern Israeli resilience to the enduring Dutch resilience of the seventeenth century, but it is clear that this driver of survival was critical to the Dutch Republic and will remain so for Israel as well.

7. In its short history, Israel has had a small number of good leaders who made critical, future-shaping decisions. The Dutch had few more, even in two hundred years. Israel's institutions and collective decision-making apparatus may hinder the emergence of great leaders, as was the case in the Dutch Republic.

8. Israeli-American relations were cold in the 1950s, but the two countries slowly developed a strong alliance, to Israel's considerable benefit, not unlike the development of the Anglo-Dutch alliance. In both cases, strains and rivalries between the allies never disappeared.

CHAPTER 2

Transforming Great-Power Decline
into New Power Rise: Turkey[1]

In discussing Turkey, we must flip our perspective from "rise-and-decline" to "decline-and-rise." This country went through a crisis and revolution, which accelerated historical processes that might have developed more slowly under quieter circumstances. Turkey's new power rise had a number of notable characteristics:

1. Turkey's revolutionary transformation, formally beginning with the "Young Turk" rebellion of 1908, had a very long pre-history. Knowing that their empire was in decline, several of the Ottoman Empire's rulers and reformers repeatedly proposed and introduced reforms during the preceding two hundred years.

2. This slow evolution was a necessary but insufficient preparation for a broad and thorough transformation. The profound post-1918 national crisis that followed the defeat and dismemberment of the Ottoman Empire and the threat of a foreign invasion of Anatolian Turkey demanded a radical response, a break with the past.

3. This response and the revolutionary break required a strong and charismatic leader ready and able to slice through a series of "Gordian knots." Mustafa Kemal Ataturk was this leader.

4. The ill-advised Greek invasion of Turkey led to the Greek-Turkish war of 1919-1922, which ended in Ataturk's military triumph over the interloping forces. Military victory played a crucial role in the establishment of the new Turkey. The invasion was supported by Turkey's World War I enemies, Great Britain and France, who saw the country as being in utter disarray. Once the invasion began, however, any doubts that may have persisted in Turkish and foreign minds about the viability of the new state were swept away. Without intending to do so, the Greeks played right into Ataturk's hands.

5. The transformation from a traditional empire rooted in religion to a modern Western republic included, it is true, the adoption of democratic institutions, but this was certainly not the only change, and it was perhaps not even the most important one. Other societal, cultural, and linguistic modernizations and other radical breaks with the past imposed by Ataturk were equally important. Only time will tell whether the AKP party, in power since 2002, and Turkey's current government will succeed in whittling away Ataturk's critical reforms and turn Turkey back into a profoundly Muslim and expansionist power, as it was in the past when it felt strong. According to many observers, this seems to be the real, though not publicly admitted, long-term intention of the Turkish government.

6. Turkey's transformation was driven by the inescapable fact that the Turks had no alternative. The option of leading a Muslim empire had vanished with the Arab revolt, and the possibility of creating a federation of all Turkish-speaking nations disappeared when the Soviet Union absorbed the Caucasus and Central Asia. The Turks of Anatolia were committed to their land, language, and independence, and needed a new, future-oriented national project. An Israeli historian compared Turkey's and Austria's predicament in 1918: both had lost a thousand-year-old empire, but only Turkey underwent a true transformation and embarked upon a radically new national project. Austria did not, because it had an alternative in *Anschluss*, the pan-Germanic option that lurked in the background until becoming a reality in March 1938, when Nazi Germany annexed the country.[2]

7. Ataturk believed he had achieved the necessary, deep transformation of Turkey. However, in the ninety years since the Turkish war for independence, trends favoring a partial religious restoration have emerged more than once, and the possibility—and for some the danger—of a slow Islamic counterrevolution has never been completely excluded. Since the start of the twenty-first century, Islam has been making a gradual, steady political comeback. In 2008 and 2009, Turkey began to seek greater political and military distance from the West and Israel, and strengthen instead its relations with its Muslim neighbors. This indicates a wish to regain the leadership role the Ottoman Empire traditionally had in the Middle East. Turkey is still a history in the making. Ninety years is not a long time, considering that the Turks embraced Islam and began to build an empire a thousand years ago. Its future remains wide open.

Applications to Jewish History

It might, at first glance, seem far-fetched to compare any period of Jewish history with the end of empires and the revolutions of the twentieth century. But with a closer look, metaphoric similarities begin to appear with the Turkish revolution. The Jewish national movement emerged in the nineteenth century, at the same time the national and revolutionary movements were beginning in Turkey. The Jewish movement called for the Jewish people's return to its ancient homeland, which made it incomparable to any other movement, but it was also a response to centuries of discrimination and persecution that made the impulse comparable to the awareness of defeat and humiliation that permeated the dying Ottoman Empire. Political Zionism had deep roots in the Jewish past, including in earlier yearnings and attempts to return to the Holy Land, but it was also a revolutionary movement because it called for a break with Jewish religious traditions, just as Ataturk called for a break with Islam and Pan-Islamism.

But just as was the case in Turkey, the long pre-history of Zionism was not sufficient to achieve a transformation. It took a profound existential crisis and challenge to Jewish survival—the *Shoah*—and the emergence of outstanding and strong-willed leaders, such as Ben-Gurion, to impose a break with the past and move a part of the Jewish people from one form of civilization to another—an appropriate way of describing the creation of Israel. Israel's 1948 military victory over hostile neighbors determined to extinguish it had a lot in common with Turkey's 1922 victory over the Greek invaders, with similar political and psychological results. Even the two refugee problems (but not their solutions) that resulted from the two wars are comparable: both could appropriately be called enforced population exchanges. In Israel and in Turkey, many vestigial roots of the old civilization remained and were revitalized. In the last two decades: domestic politics and cultural debates in both countries have partly been dominated by the entry of religious parties and politicians into mainstream politics, and by the fears and opposition this development triggered in the non-religious population and its representatives. Tugs-of-war between religious and less religious parties will affect the future of both countries. How this future will look is unpredictable in both countries, but otherwise the comparison must end there. A great majority of Jews and Israelis have accepted and internalized modernity and will not return to the past, and even a part of the ultra-Orthodox camp is making steps toward modernity, at least in professional matters.

Such metaphoric similarities suggest that some components of the Zionist revolution are not unique. However, one should not overlook major differences between the Jewish and Turkish experience. One is that the surviving Jews of 1945 had some alternatives. In contrast to the Turks of

Anatolia, they could walk away from their countries of birth, mother tongue, religion, and culture and assimilate into the general population or disappear into far-away continents. Quite a number of them in fact did so. Nonetheless, many others chose Israel, which showed the strength of the two-thousand-year-old dream.

A second difference is that Israel's links with Jews all over the world remain of overriding emotional importance and have significant political consequences. The community of millions of Turkish workers in Europe has no role comparable to that of the Jewish Diaspora; the Turkish Diaspora can give Turkey little to no political or strategic help. It remains to be seen whether Turkey's Muslim neighbors will begin to offer the country greater political and other support. It is currently difficult to see Turkey again becoming the heart of the Sunni Muslim world as it was during the Ottoman Empire and the Caliphate. In contrast, Israel is likely to remain the heart of the Jewish people.

Outlook and Conclusions

A reader who was patient enough to read to the end of the last chapter might feel confused. He has had to review twenty-three historians of the last 2500 years, assess twelve drivers of rise and decline, and then go through a search for the impact of these drivers on Jewish history, old and new. At this point, the reader might ask two questions:

1. Surely not all factors are equally important. Which are the most decisive ones? Which ones could tip the balance?

2. Suppose one could bring these twenty-three historians, the dead and the living, into the same conference room and ask them to discuss the future rise and decline of the Jewish people, what would their verdict be? Which future would they see for the Jews? Which comprehensive, long-term policies would they recommend? How might a summary record of their fictitious debate read?

Both questions are linked and can be answered together. At the beginning we called this book a "thought experiment." What the reader might ask for is a thought experiment within a thought experiment, which would be more hazardous by an order of magnitude. Hence, the following is the imaginary "executive summary" of a fictitious debate of twenty-three dead and living, mostly non-Jewish, historians about the likely future of the Jewish people:

The Current State and Possible Future of the Jewish People and Civilization

The Jews formed a distinct civilization probably more than three thousand years ago, and have maintained it in changing forms ever since. Some historians describe civilizations as "continuities." They change but do not disappear, and even when they do change much of the old survives and re-emerges in the new. A living civilization of the age and distinction of that belonging to the Jews may weaken and lose some, or even many, of its adherents, but it will not die unless the overwhelming majority of its members are physically eliminated. Destroying the Jews was tried in the past and failed. It may be tried again, and it is likely to fail again as long as Jews are vigilant, defend themselves, and have a global presence, and as long as the world is not dominated by a single political center or ideology hostile to the Jewish people. Hostility to Judaism and Jews is, like Judaism itself, also a civilizational continuity. In many Muslim, Christian, and formerly Christian countries it is so old and ingrained that it cannot entirely disappear, even if its outward manifestations change or become more discreet.

Civilizations of great age and resilience tend to oscillate, go up and down like the moon, expand and contract, in response to changing external and internal constraints. The current state of the Jewish people is a high point in its entire history, although not all Jews are prepared to see this. Never in two thousand years, and perhaps never in history, have Jews been simultaneously a leading military and economic power in the Middle East, a politically effective minority in the world's main superpower, and a strong intellectual, cultural, and scientific influence in many other parts of the world. If history follows a "normal" course, the Jewish people will come down from this peak as it has in the past after other historic peaks, whether through internal factors such as accelerated assimilation, an inability to change and respond to new needs, or other self-inflicted injuries, or through external factors such as a major economic or other crisis of worldwide proportions, a catastrophic military or natural event striking Israel, a radical change in the internal or external situation of the United States, or a major wave of global antisemitism. Several of these factors could combine with a devastating synergy.

But history does not have to, and must not be allowed to, follow a "normal" course. Jewish history has, more than once, avoided following the general stream of history. Conditions for intervention to prevent decline and boost rise are better now than in earlier times because many Jewish leaders and a significant part of the Jewish public are aware of and concerned about the danger of decline, and also because the Jewish people has many political, economic, military, and intellectual resources. But nothing is assured, and for this reason the Jewish civilization is currently at a crossroads.

Rise and decline must be seen in the context of the global environment. The twenty-first century is likely to witness ruptures of history on a scale yet unknown, whether they are a long-lasting global depression that will fundamentally re-shape politics and finance, wars with weapons of mass destruction, terror attacks with or without such weapons, global environmental or health disasters, and social upheavals leading to major shifts of global power. If a decline of the Jews coincides with and is reinforced by such a rupture, the future of Jewish civilization will become difficult, and it could take a very long time before a new rise begins. This is why it is vital to stem decline now and prevent the Jews from being dragged into the maelstrom of history that has swallowed up many other peoples. Addressing four priority areas will help the Jews if they want to strengthen their civilization and prevent it from declining. To end these introductory comments with a positive note: all four areas depend on the will and wisdom of the Jews, not on external powers. "If you will it, it is no dream," as Theodor Herzl famously wrote when he promised the Jews that they could and would have a state.

First: Commitment to a Living History

Most traditional Jews who study their past and scriptures are relatively well armed to survive the possible future maelstroms of history and preserve their identity. The others, who are the great majority, will survive as Jews only if they maintain the knowledge of their people's long history and a commitment to its continuity, and if they transmit both to the next generation. Knowledge and commitment go with a sense of mission. A strong feeling that it is important to continue Jewish history and not let it come to an end is needed now, because Jews have contributed to a better world in the past and they must continue to strive for a better world in the future as well. In a world in which many people are losing touch with their history and cultural memory, those who do not will have a long-term competitive advantage in the global political and cultural realignments that lie ahead.

Second: High-Quality Leadership and Long-Term Policies

The Jews must solve their leadership and governance problems, which many call a crisis. This crisis has been festering for many years. Israel and the Diaspora must develop a high-quality leadership that is morally and intellectually unassailable, ready to rally a large part of the public behind vital goals, and able to implement long-term policies. Israel's current political selection and governance mechanisms can apparently not generate such leadership, nor can they ensure the implementation of long-term policies. The inability or unwillingness of potentially good leaders to reach and hold leadership positions, along with obstacles to their capacity to govern, are of grave concern. In the absence of better leaders, governance systems, and long-term policies, Israel and the Jews may not make it through the twenty-first century unscathed.

Third: Staying on Top of the Knowledge Revolution

One of the main reasons Jews have achieved their current global position is that they have been on top of the knowledge revolution that has changed the world since the nineteenth century. They have been at the vanguard of social science, economic innovation, political activism, knowledge of languages, sciences, technology and more. In the future, knowledge will increasingly be the basis of every type of power, if not physical survival. Everyone in the world knows this and is competing for more knowledge. Many are running on this playing field; the Jews are not alone. Will Israel and the Jews stay on top? The signs are mixed: some are positive and others negative. Economic, educational, and cultural policies should ensure that Jews continue to strive for the highest levels of education and remain innovative leaders in the continuing knowledge revolution.

Fourth: A Long-Term Geopolitical Vision

The most creative responses to past challenges and catastrophes of Jewish history were guided by political and spiritual leaders who had a long-term view of the Jewish fate and a comprehensive understanding of the surrounding world and the Jews' place in it. These leaders were able to take their people, or at least part of it, along on the road to survival and new rise. Some current leaders may have broad, long-term geopolitical perspectives, but even when they do there is a mismatch between their perspectives and the more local, provincial, or at best national perspectives of too many Jews in Israel and the Diaspora. Correcting this mismatch will not be easy and will partly depend on the second condition, leadership. Rarely in history has it been more necessary for Jews to take a long-term global view of the future and see themselves not as locals pursuing local interests, but like some non-Jews see or want to see them: as a global presence and a significant partner in the shaping of a common global future, and also as coordinated, proactive, and fearless challengers of their enemies in the world.

Afterword

Rise and Decline of Civilizations: Lessons for the Jewish People was begun in 2004/5; a first draft was completed late in 2009. The "writing history" of the book lasted five years, but it also has a prehistory. In fact, the book was a long time in the making, and it has many layers, built one upon the other, like some famous antique cities, Jericho or Troy.

History—both world and Jewish history—was part of my life from the moment I was born in Italy, long before it became my preferred field of study. As I was being born, *Il Duce*, Benito Mussolini, addressed the Italian people by radio, bragging that their country had won the war he had provoked against Ethiopia. It took several more years before I could observe history in a conscious manner. In 1944 or early 1945, when still a small boy, I was excited to watch the bomber squadrons of the US Air Force, the F-17 "Flying Fortresses," crossing a clouded sky into Nazi Germany. For many years I continued to hear the deep roar of their engines in my dreams.

But these and other war memories remained a bit vague. Also vague and strangely detached was my understanding in 1945 that I had almost no family left—they were nearly all gone, vanished. What remains vivid in my memory is the exact moment Jewish history hit me for the first time, never to let me go.

The date was July 22, 1946, when Menachem Begin's *Irgun* blew up a wing of the King David Hotel in Jerusalem, the military and civilian headquarters of the British Mandate authority in Palestine. I ran from my refugee camp to town to glimpse the daily paper displayed in a public showcase, but I was too small to squeeze myself into the crowd of readers. I raised the topic of the bombing with a Swiss man who lived nearby, hoping he would know more details. I told him that I wanted to live in Palestine one day, and he strongly advised against this. A very bad idea, he said: "they" had no chance, what "they" were trying to do there would fail and could not survive. That country "stinks"—I cannot forget that word.

Hence, two years before the Jewish state was created, and before anyone had an idea what its name would be, I had heard of its inevitable decline and fall. Was this a decline without rise? Sixty years later, prodded by Prof.

Yehezkel Dror, I took up *Rise and Decline*, but in the meantime I had already discovered that only the Jews had founded a civilization that began life with an international death certificate *plus* an obituary already attached, three thousand and two hundred years ago. The earliest mention of the term "Israel" outside of biblical sources is found on the victory stele of Pharaoh Merneptah (reigned 1213-1203 BCE), son of Ramses II. Merneptah celebrated his victories, particularly in Canaan, and we read on his stele that "Israel is laid waste and his seed is not." So my Swiss neighbor was only following a time-honored tradition, although he was not aware of it! After hearing these mistaken reports of Israel or Judaism's demise, when I keep hearing announcements of the approaching decline and end of Israel or of Judaism, I have two reactions. One is, "There you go again—how often have we already heard this?" The other is, "maybe there is a danger—what must we do?"

I completed the first draft of this book in 2009 by pointing out that the Jews were living in a historically unprecedented "Golden Age." Unprecedented is their power and prosperity in the Middle East, as is their influence in the world's main superpower and other countries. However, history teaches us that all "Golden Ages" come to an end one day.

Internal factors, such as civil strife or assimilation, or external ones, such as a major military defeat, a severe decline of the United States, or a rise of global antisemitism could sap the Jewish people and Israel of their strength. If this was the "normal" course of history, I added, history must not be allowed to follow a normal course. If the many great historians of rise and decline, dead and living, whom I consulted for this book could give the Jews advice, it would be that they have to concentrate their efforts on four priority issues:

1. Maintaining their identity and history;
2. Ensuring high-quality political leadership and governance;
3. Staying on top of the world's knowledge revolution, particularly in education, science, and technology;
4. Improving their international position by a better understanding of, and a proactive outreach to, the world, and a long-term geopolitical vision.

So much for 2009. One year later, the Jewish People Policy Institute's *Annual Assessment of the Situation and Dynamics of the Jewish People*, began with the following significant statement:

In 2010 the Jewish People started to face challenges which seem to be qualitatively different than those with which it had been confronted hitherto.

Negative developments began to accumulate. Some of these had already cast their shadow ahead or had been rumored before, but now they became evident to everybody. The United States is Israel's indispensable supporter and home to forty percent of the Jewish people. Since the Vietnam War, America's alleged decline has been a favorite subject of jealous European pundits, unemployed politicians, and jaded American left-wing intellectuals, but now everyone began to debate the issue, because it seemed all too real.

As America slipped into a financial and economic crisis in 2008, it was predictable that its defense spending would have to be cut. America had not won the wars in Iraq and Afghanistan according to the terms it had set itself, and would cut down its military presence in the Middle East. Worst of all, the willpower and international commitment of America's people was waning, and the country was more deeply divided than it had been at any time in the last forty years. The election of Barack Obama was greeted by short-lived excitement, but soon enough it only confirmed the impression that America was a declining power governed by a weak president—an impression that was widespread particularly in the Middle East and Asia.

Partly as a result of these developments, but also based on much older political trends, signs of distancing between the United States and Israel emerged. These signs were avidly discussed and amplified, particularly by those who always advocated for the United States to reduce support for Israel and become more "even-handed" in the Middle East. Particularly jarring for official Israel was the participation of Jewish publicists in the distancing campaign, and the latter's' assertion—thrown into considerable doubt since—that they represented the growing consensus of American Jews, particularly the young, who allegedly were increasingly indifferent to or critical of Israel.

The question in everybody's mind was whether there was a country that could replace America. All eyes were on China, America's rising counterpart, but it quickly became clear that China had every intention of exploiting the decline of America, a country it continued to fear, but no intention of taking on America's peace-stabilizing role in the Middle East or anywhere else in the world. The effect of this selfish double-tenet of China's global policy was very detrimental to Israel, although China bore Israel no ill will.

China's support for Iran in the United Nations Security Council, together with Russia's, made it impossible for the international community to stop Iran's nuclear weapons development without war between 2008 and 2011. During those years, it would have been much easier than it is now, in 2013. China's support for Iran was not directed against Israel but against America: China identified Iran as America's main Achilles heel, and therefore considered a strong Iran to be in China's national interest, as it had neither the intention nor the power to confront America directly in the Far East. Israel became "collateral damage" of this policy, which is one more negative trend since 2009.

More widely noticed was the fast-growing de-legitimization, defamation, and boycott campaigns against Israel and partly also the Jewish people in the West, particularly in Europe but even in Latin American countries, South Africa, and elsewhere. Nominally, these campaigns were directed against Israel's occupation of Palestinian territories and Israel's military actions against attacks from Gaza, but it became increasingly clear that for many campaigners the issue was not the year 1967, when Israel occupied these territories, but the year 1948, when it had been created.

This campaign has been driven by Arab and Muslim—particularly Palestinian—leaders, and for most of them it is Israel itself that is illegitimate, not only the occupation. Hatred of the Jewish people and state has reached a fever pitch in many Muslim countries. This is yet another war the Arab world is waging against Israel; it follows the lost military wars of 1948, 1967, and 1973, the lost economic boycott war from the 1950s to the 1970s, and the equally lost terror war that peaked during the first decade of the twenty-first century. The novelty is that this new war enjoys the support of a part—some believe a large part—of international public opinion and has begun to damage Israel's standing and its diplomatic, cultural, scientific, and economic interests. The most ominous aspect is that the campaign draws its strength from a growing antipathy to Jews and their state. This antipathy, and the double standards that are advanced to justify it, can be found in every part of the world. As such double standards are applied to no other country in the world beside Israel, it is obvious that their source was the age-old antisemitism that had never completely disappeared in the Western world and that emerged in open and crude form in the Muslim world whenever Israel is mentioned. Every week or so, Jews and Israel have to get used to a public attack or insult by a political, cultural, or media personality who generally offers "regrets" afterward or complains that he or she was quoted "out of context."

Much of this hostility would have been unthinkable in the West twenty, thirty, or fifty years ago. Are these small volcanic eruptions, fuelled by a rising, still-hidden sea of molten lava? Or are these no more than superficial expressions of a rapidly changing public mood, inflamed by media campaigns that will quiet down as soon as Israel makes a few apparently overdue concessions?

The third and most important negative trend after America's decline and Israel's de-legitimization is the turmoil that has engulfed the Arab world since 2010 and 2011. Few if any had foreseen this, in contrast to the other two trends. The familiar Middle East has collapsed. The contours of a new, more hostile, and more unstable and unpredictable Middle East are slowly emerging. Direct talks with the Palestinians are, at best, intermittent. Turkey has at least temporarily curtailed political and strategic bonds with Israel that had lasted for decades. The future of Egypt, which was briefly ruled by the

Muslim Brotherhood, whose founders took inspiration from and supported Nazi Germany, remains anything but certain. And Syria is falling to pieces while its main patron, Iran, continues its relentless drive to develop nuclear weapons. Nobody can tell where the Middle East is headed. The troubles could last decades and may include not only asymmetric wars but also wars between states.

Is this the end of the Golden Age of the Jewish people and Israel? History does not know "automatic" sequences in which a period must end after a predetermined number of years. As explained in the four conditions for a thriving Jewish civilization above, much depends on how the Jews and Israel react. The four years from 2009 to 2013 constitute too short a time to draw definitive conclusions about Jewish and Israeli responses to the new challenges, but a few things can be said. Identity and tradition are not in danger; on the contrary, in Israel there is a trend toward greater religiosity, and in the United States, contrary to what some critics have said, the younger generation's attachment to Israel (which does not necessarily mean agreement with Israeli policies) is stronger than that of the older generation. On the other hand, it cannot be denied that disapproval of Israel and of religious Orthodoxy is driving some Jews away from Judaism and Israel. The balance for the moment, however, appears to be positive.

Regarding the Jews' and Israel's place in the global "knowledge revolution," the third condition for thriving mentioned above, the signs are mixed. Israel is still producing first-class science and technology, but average levels of education are lower than they should be in an advanced high-tech country. Various authorities are aware of the problem and are seeking means to remediate it. In the United States, in elite schools where admission is based on merit alone, Jews are less prominent than they were in previous decades. This has not yet affected Jewish wealth or Jewish prominence in science and technology, but in the longer term it will. The fourth condition of a thriving Jewish civilization is its global position, and this seems to have been degraded for the reasons mentioned.

The second condition which is indispensable for Israel's long-term survival, that is good leadership and governance, remains problematic. No great improvement seems to be on the horizon. It is "politics as usual," in Israel as well as in world Jewry, unaffected by the endless stream of criticisms and reform proposals that flow from the pens of politicians, experts, and journalists.

Rise and Decline of Civilizations has a chapter on leadership that analyses the qualities of four distinguished Jewish leaders, one from the biblical period and three from late medieval and early modern times. It identifies common traits among the four presented as model traits for good Jewish leadership: dedication to their own people in difficult times; a complete lack of interest in financial gain; an excellent understanding of the complexities of the non-Jewish world; the fluency in several languages that allowed them to speak with the rulers of their times in their own languages, and more.

One of the reproaches one could make to my book is that it does not analyze the early Zionist leadership—an enormous task that could in its own right be the subject of an entire book. The history of Zionist leaders from Theodor Herzl and his supporters to Chaim Weizmann, Nahum Sokolow, Ze'ev Jabotinsky, and others, and finally to David Ben-Gurion, is a unique chapter in history. The appearance of so many outstanding individuals in a period of less than two generations is a rare occurrence and not one easily imitated. Perhaps the founders of the United States of America in 1776, with George Washington at the center, offer a comparable example.

The Jews did not have a state tradition for two thousand or more years, and some still do not understand what is required of a people that wants to run and maintain a functioning state. This explains Israel's dismal governance and the behavior of so many of its politicians. Their hunger for power, if not financial gain, and their petty jealousies are not often matched by patriotic abnegation or exceptional foresight. Surely Israel in this respect is no worse off than many other democratic countries, but no other country is threatened with annihilation by a neighbor state on a daily basis. Will the newly elected Knesset of 2013 bring major change, a visible improvement of Israel's governance? Political commentators remain skeptical. We will see.

Between 2009 and 2013, I followed events, revised the text of this volume, and added a new finding or insight here and there. However, my concern in ensuring that the text remains up-to-date points to a fundamental problem and a contradiction. Fernand Braudel, the dominant French historian of the twentieth century, said that it is the historian's task to uncover the "history of long duration," the "long waves of history" and to separate these from the plethora of circumstantial events that float along the surface and fill the daily news. What I have tried to do is identify the "long waves" of Jewish history until our own days. Israel is a genuine revolution, but it is also a continuation. Clausewitz might have said that "Israel is a continuation of Jewish history by other means." If the history I have written is that of "long duration," though, why is there a need to follow events and update the text? Because too often we simply do not know which event indicates a deep, lasting trend and which is temporary and soon to be forgotten.

Braudel himself made a number of long-term forecasts based on his understanding of history's long waves, but today we know that most of his forecasts were wrong. Statesmen, too, need to be able to distinguish in their own time between events that herald deep, lasting changes and ones that are but "foam" on the long waves of history, to use another of Braudel's images. Only the statesmen with the sharpest eye for reality and the deepest intuition had the ability to do so, and they were very few. Maybe Bismarck was one of them, and Ben Gurion too.

It seems that the decline of the United States as a super-power, and the rise of Asia, is an unstoppable "long wave," but can we be sure that no unexpected political, technological, or ecological developments will slow down, if not reverse, one or both of these trends? Also, the Muslim Middle East seems doomed to decades of turmoil, violence, and fragmentation, but who says that this is an ironclad law that nobody and nothing can mitigate? As for the de-legitimization trend against Israel that seems so widespread and rooted in old prejudices, counter-measures have already had some success. Is it not possible that this trend will run out of steam in a few more years?

Some of the greatest historians have known that history cannot be easily predicted. "The ways of Heaven are dark and silent," said the first Chinese historian, Sima Qian, who lived in the second and first centuries BCE, and Jacob Burckhardt repeated in the nineteenth century that many trends of history "draw their essential force from unexplorable depths; they cannot be deduced from the preceding circumstances." The wisdom of these men should temper our inclination to quickly separate the "epoch-making" events from "passing" ones, and to extrapolate trends into the long-term future. When Ze'ev Jabotinsky, the founder of Revisionist Zionism, heard of the outbreak of the Russian Revolution in 1917, he is reported to have commented, "The Russian bear has slept five hundred years on his right side. Now he has woken up, will turn soon on his left side and fall again asleep." Can we say with certainty whether he was right or wrong, or partly right or wrong?

This uncertainty is one of the reasons why this book does not speak of the Arab-Israeli conflict, and particularly the Palestinian conflict. This silence is likely to become one of the more conspicuous criticisms of this book. I have already heard it. "How could you forget the Palestinian conflict, the single most important issue for the future of Israel and the Jewish people?" I do not think that it is. There are no inevitable long-term trends in this conflict; it will develop according to the decisions that leaders on both sides will make. This is why first-class, realistic, and forward-looking leadership is a precondition for coping with this problem, and so is first-class knowledge, science, and technology. And then, while every sane person should fervently hope to see a peaceful solution to this conflict, every thinking person must remember what history has taught us: war and enduring tensions do not necessarily destroy a civilization, and long-lasting peace does not guarantee the thriving of a civilization. The opposite can also be true.

We cannot be sure about the future, but we can hope that realistic confidence in the future is an agent likely to bring good results. As the prophet tell us in 1 Samuel 15:29, "Israel's Eternity will not be denied."

APPENDIX

A Framework for Policy-Makers

The book *Rise and Decline of Civilizations: Lessons for the Jewish People* provides an intellectual framework—one among others—for those who believe that they can learn from history for the future. History can be an important ingredient for making complex, future-shaping decisions. This book was not written with a prior policy catalogue in mind, but it supports a number of broad-based policy priorities for a prosperous Jewish future. Jewish and Israeli policy makers might read this as a balanced and comprehensive starting point for more specific policy recommendations.

Terminology

Jewish Civilization

As neither "religion" nor "nation" can today fully describe all aspects of the Jewish people, we call Judaism a "civilization." The term postulates a degree of unity of Jewish history. In Jewish civilization we include the entire history of Israel and the Jewish people: it is the thread of continuity through time and of links through space. The "Jewish people"—or "peoplehood," a recently coined term—is the bearer of Jewish civilization. The term "Jewish culture" is more limited in time and space, referring to the ways of life and thought of a specific branch of the Jewish people during a certain period. It includes everything that is said, written, or done if it is connected, even loosely, to Jewish identity. There are various Jewish cultures that emerged from the interaction of Jewish communities with the culture, language, and religion of their respective environments.

Rise and Decline

Designating a period as "rising" or "declining," and that in-between "thriving" can be a value judgment linked to a political agenda. However, rise and decline can in many cases be substantiated by eyewitnesses, statistical data, or archaeological excavations. Impressionistic definitions of rise and decline and empirical, data-based definitions can overlap and complement each other. All history can be examined from the angle of "rise and decline." Civilizations, religions, nations, states, and cities have been rising, declining, and vanishing through thousands of years. We have looked at Jewish history from this angle. The Bible and Rabbinic tradition regard some periods as rise and others as decline. For many civilizations and nations, decline and fall was terminal. For others, such as the Jews, decline and fall in the past initiated deep transformations that ensured a new rise.

"Thriving" Civilization

A "thriving" civilization is one in which, ideally, political and military power, economic prosperity, and cultural creativity coincide. Such periods are often called a "Golden Age." Golden Ages are rare, do not last long, and often end in internal decay, upheaval, or war. The people living in such ages rarely recognize them as "golden." Some keep pining for a mythical Golden Age of the past that on closer inspection, turns out not to have been so golden. Today, there are many signs that the Jews, at least a great majority of them, entered into a new Golden Age period after 1948.

Driver

A driver is a factor that can affect or determine the rise and decline of a civilization. It is a term borrowed from informatics.

Twelve Drivers That Determine Rise or Decline of Jewish Civilization

Based on a review of twenty-three ancient and contemporary historians of civilization, we have identified twelve critical drivers of rise and decline. While many of these have been important in general history, this particular mix of drivers is specifically relevant for the Jews of today because it targets their current strengths and weaknesses. Except for a possible loss of identity and the enormous dangers raised by weapons of mass destruction, no single driver will be decisive in isolation from all others. It is the synergy of these drivers and the way they are affected by deliberate policies that will decide the future of the Jewish people.

1. Identity and Tradition

The century of globalization has put the identity and traditions of many civilizations into question. In the past, Jewish identity was guaranteed by religion, namely a mix of rituals, beliefs, and annual celebrations of critical historic events. This is no longer so for a majority of Jews.

The question of how to define and preserve identity and tradition while adjusting effectively to the world's changing realities is, and will for a long time continue to be, the most important Jewish policy challenge. Preserving Jewish identity in Israel—where it is not automatically guaranteed—and in the Diaspora calls for various policy initiatives, some of them similar and some different. Strengthening the links between Israel and the Jewish world will help safeguard the identity of both sides. Issues of conversion to Judaism, such as the constraints imposed by religious orthodoxy but also the dangers that intermarriage may pose to identity, will become increasingly critical.

2. Quality of Political Leadership and Governance

Many historians assert that the fate of civilizations and nations rests in the hands of their leaders. They bear a great part of the responsibility for rise, decline and fall, as the history of the twentieth century has again revealed. This was also often so in Jewish history, for better or worse.

Today, the quality of the Jewish people's political leaders and also their capacity to govern is a source of concern. Israel and the Jewish people cannot afford inadequate or paralyzed leaders as their external situation remains tenuous. There are serious problems with the political selection processes, flawed electoral systems, the ability of exceptional leaders to reach and hold power, the general quality of governance, the pervasiveness of corruption, and the implementation of essential long-term policies.

3. Leadership in Education, Science and Technology

The future of our world will to a large degree be determined by the nations that have the highest educational levels and command the progress of science and technology. Jews have been among the best educated since Antiquity, and in the twentieth century were leaders in science and technology. Their comparative advantages may be shrinking now. However, Israel's achievements in scientific and technological innovation will affect its future position in the geopolitical power alignments that lie ahead. The achievements of Jews across the world—which some measure by the number of Nobel laureates—will strongly affect their global standing.

Improving the level of general education in all branches of the Jewish people, particularly in Israel, and maintaining a leadership role in science and technology should be a major policy priority. Israeli policies should increase the appeal of science and technology for the young.

4. Friends, Allies, and Global Perspectives

A small people in a difficult situation needs friends and allies. The Jews had friends in the past, from King Cyrus of Persia to England's Lord Balfour. They and others supported them at critical moments. The Jews also have powerful friends today, but their political perspectives are, as in the past, often still too limited, local, and short-term.

As the global balance of power is shifting, the Jews and Israel must seek out new friends and allies in addition to the traditional ones, e.g. among the emerging powers of Asia. Among others, cultural assets ("soft power") can be useful for this purpose.

5. Economic Prosperity

Economic prosperity is an essential basis of many drivers, such as demography, military supremacy, and science and technology. It has also helped sustain Jewish religious and cultural creativity. Past prosperity was often based on a high level of knowledge and skills, international networks and a gift for innovative entrepreneurship. Education sustained prosperity, and prosperity financed education. Today again, economic prosperity is both cause and effect of education, science and technology. Education is improving all over the world and international networks are spreading widely, which will affect and could reduce the competitive advantage of the Jews and Israel.

Economic and educational policies must aim at maintaining and improving competitive advantages. Israel's long-term economic growth cannot be assured without massive educational reforms that must begin soon.

6. Demography, the Power of Numbers

Jewish population numbers are slowly growing in Israel and appear to be shrinking in the Diaspora. The net result is stagnation. Jews need more critical mass, in Israel for defense and maintaining a majority, and everywhere for cultural creativity and political influence.

Population stagnation is a critical weakness that can be addressed. Israel should create a high-level government position in order to signal the urgency of this problem. Demography today is not limited to numbers of people but includes also qualitative criteria, such as identity and spiritual significance.

7. Solidarity and Emotional Bonds

The philosopher of history Oswald Spengler called the Jews a "Magial (Tacit) Consensus." He said that they were kept together by emotional bonds that could not be explained by purely rational factors such as a common language or territory. These bonds, so he argued, began to weaken with the European Enlightenment and would vanish completely as the Jews were inextricably linked to a terminally declining West. Jewish history has, so far, not borne out his prediction. There are many educational, psychological, evolutionary and biological factors that can form a "Magial (Tacit) Consensus."

Strengthening emotional or extra-rational bonds would go a long way toward ensuring Jewish identity (see driver 1), but we do not yet know how to do this or even how to explain such bonds. Policy makers must remain open to new scientific discoveries in this field.

8. Military Supremacy

Military supremacy is directly vital for Israel and only indirectly for World Judaism. Jews showed their military prowess all through Antiquity and have again in modern Israel. During the long periods when Jews had no military power they were often exposed to enormous threats that finally culminated in the *Shoah.* Given the state of the world today, Israel will not be able to give up its martial qualities any time soon. Struggling for peace while preparing for war has been the fate of many nations.

Israel must continue to live with the tension between yearning for peace and preparing for war, and must strengthen the resilience of its society. While continuous research and innovation are called for to respond to the technological challenges of defense, two broader challenges must also be taken up: the international laws of war that in effect favor non-state actors, and the global security frameworks that are inadequate to stop the spread of weapons of mass destruction.

9. Unforeseen Events

Machiavelli said that unforeseen "fortune," or chance events, dominated half of history. Therefore, he added, it is even more important to prepare oneself for the other half, which can be anticipated and partly controlled. Like many others, Jews have often been surprised by unforeseen events. They got so used to short-term improvisation that some of them have celebrated this as a commendable national gift rather than a shortcoming.

A people in a tenuous situation such as the one in which Jews find themselves should look for ways to reduce their exposure to unforeseen events. Their political habits and organizational capacity to prepare for such events and crises are inadequate.

10. Internal Dissent

Internal dissent has helped to destroy many civilizations, but not that of the Jews. Dissent and argumentation have accompanied Jewish history from early Biblical times on. Dissent has been a source of religious and cultural creativity. The reason is that Jewish religious leaders, in contrast to Christians and Muslims, have generally lacked the political and judicial powers to destroy internal dissent. But dissent can also be destructive when it prevents joint action in a time of crisis.

Currently, there are various manifestations of dissent. One is the tension between the religious and non-religious in Israel. Another, with political and other consequences that must be faced, is a possible growing apart of Israel and American Judaism, particularly among the young.

11. The Status of Women

There is growing awareness that the future strength and influence of a civilization will to no small degree depend on the status of women in society. How exactly the ongoing gender revolution will affect rise or decline of civilizations cannot be known because there are no clear historical precedents.

Many agree that the status and place of women in Jewish society must be improved. This might include political representation and power, religious rights, labor market participation, educational attainment, and more.

12. The Power of Nature: Catastrophe Prevention

This driver is crucial for Israel but not for the entire Jewish people. No major natural disasters are known to have affected past Jewish history, but this could change. Israel is a geologically unstable region where major earthquakes and even tsunamis can be expected. Rising sea levels could affect the Eastern shores of the Mediterranean. Growing water shortages are predicted for the Middle East, and natural or biological warfare epidemics are possible.

It is necessary to improve predictive capabilities and preparations for natural catastrophes, particularly earthquakes.

Jewish civilization, like all others, has been and will continue to be affected by global problems and dangers it cannot influence directly. The emergence of global dangers does not mean that measures to strengthen an individual civilization will be ineffective and, thus, less urgent. On the contrary, in conditions of global crisis and turmoil, policies to enhance identity, solidarity, military might, education, science and technology, etc. will become even more important.

How to Estimate the Current State of Rise or Decline

No simple answer can be given to the question: "Are the Jews rising or declining?" They have reached a high point in their history in terms of political, economic, and military power in the Middle East, combined with significant political power and a strong cultural presence in the United States as well as influence in many other countries. As rise and decline have alternated in the past, the danger that the Jewish people could slip from its current high point must not be discounted, but it can partly be anticipated and limited, if not prevented. Where an effort toward this goal might begin depends on the relative importance of each driver compared to the others, and the individual strength or weakness of each of them. Relative importance as well as strength or weakness are continuously changing and, in addition, are subject to different evaluations by policy makers and experts. It is therefore impossible to give an objective, long-term ranking of drivers by degree of importance. The twelve drivers should be read as a general matrix derived from a macro-historic approach. They should give policy makers a comprehensive perspective for their own assessments.

Is it possible in principle to objectively assess the current state and likely trend of each driver? For three drivers, precise statistical measurements and comparisons over time are possible: Science and Technology, Economics, and Demography. Three others can be evaluated, although not always with the same precision, by qualified experts and international comparisons: Political leadership, Allies, and Military Supremacy. For two more, public opinion polls are providing some answers: Identity and Solidarity. The other four drivers are extremely difficult to estimate: Unforeseen Events are by definition unpredictable. Internal Dissent is a mixed bag with both creative and destructive trends, and so are Catastrophes, with some that can and others that cannot be anticipated. Finally, for the effects of the growing impact of women on civilization, there are too few historical precedents from which to learn. A civilization where all twelve drivers were "positive" has probably never existed, except in utopias. A civilization where all twelve drivers were "negative" may have existed, but only for a short time, as such a civilization was necessarily heading to imminent collapse. As to the current and likely future state of Jewish civilization, policy makers and experts may wish to reflect on this matrix, evaluate the trends of each driver and draw their own conclusions.

JPPI Brainstorming Participants

Wye River, Maryland; Glen Cove, New York; Jerusalem, Israel

Jehuda Reinharz
Dennis Ross
John Ruskay
Shalom Saar
William Safire, z"l
Len Saxe
Steven Schwager
Dan Shapiro
Natan Sharansky
Zalman Shoval
Rene Samuel Sirat
Alan Solow
Hermona Soreq
Michael Steinhardt
Suzanne Last Stone
Lawrence Summers
Shmuel Trigano
Moshe Vigdor
Tzvi Hersh Weinreb
Ariel Weiss
Aharon Yadlin
David Young

Dan Halperin
David Harris
Roger Hertog
Malcolm Hoenlein
Steve Hoffman
Jeremy Issacharoff
Richard Joel
Henry Kissinger
Bernardo Kliksberg
Howard Kohr
Charles Krauthammer
Alisa Rubin Kurshan
Morlie Levin
Glen Lewy
Daniel Liwerant
Edward Luttwak
Dan Mariaschin
Sallai Meridor
Isaac Molho
Steven Nasatir
Leonid Nevzlin
Steven Popper

Elliott Abrams
Marcos Aguinis
Jacques Attali
Judit Bokse Liwerant
Charles Burson
Leslie Cardin
Yuval Cherlow
Irwin Cotler
Lester Crown
Ruth Deech
Alan Dershowitz
Stuart Eizenstat
David Ellenson
Rachel Fish
Abe Foxman
Sami Friedrich
Misha Galperin
Ruth Gavison
Todd Gitlin
Charles Goodman
Stanley Greenberg
Nicole Guedj

JPPI Staff Participants

Ita Alcalay	Barry Geltman	Arik Puder
Zvika Arran	Avi Gil	Emmanuel Sivan
Avinoam Bar-Yosef	Yogev Karasenty	Rami Tal
Sergio DellaPergola	Dov Maimon	Shalom Salomon Wald
Yehezkel Dror	Yehudah Mirsky	Chaim Waxman
Michael Feuer	Sharon Pardo	Einat Wilf

Selected Bibliography

The following list is not a comprehensive list of publications on Jewish and/or world civilizations. It includes only the books and articles that have been used for this study and are mostly quoted in the main text, as well as additional publications that were consulted because they had some link with the work in progress. Hebrew scriptural sources—the Bible, the Babylonian Talmud, rabbinic commentaries to both, Maimonides' religious law codex (*Mishneh Torah*) and the *Shulchan Aruch* are left out of the Bibliography. The scriptural quotes and citations in the text are taken from various Hebrew editions and translations.

Adams, Susan M., Elena Bosch, et al. "The Genetic Legacy of Religious Diversity and Intolerance: Paternal Lineages of Christians, Jews and Muslims in the Iberian Peninsula." *The American Journal of Human Genetics* 83, no. 6 (2008): 725–36.

Agi, Marc, ed. *Judaisme et droits de l'homme (Judaism and Human Rights)*. Paris: Des idées & des hommes, 2007. [French original]

Ahad Ha'am. *Am Scheidewege, Gesammelte Aufsätze* (At the crossroads, collected articles), Bd. 1. Translated by I. Friedländer-H.Torczyner. Berlin: Jüdischer Verlag, 1925. [Hebrew original]

------. *At the Crossroads.* Tel Aviv and Jerusalem: Dvir/Hozaah Ivrit, 1964. [Hebrew original]

Alexander, Philip S. "Mysticism." In *The Oxford Handbook of Jewish Studies*, edited by Martin Goodman, 705-32. Oxford and New York: Oxford University Press, 2002.

Annales Regni Francorum ab a. 741 usque a. 829 (Records of the kingdom of the Franks from year 741 to 829). Internet Edition, http://archive.org/details/annalesregnifran00anna. [Latin original]

Appelbaum, Diana Muir, and Paul S. Appelbaum. "Genetics and the Jewish Identity." *Jerusalem Post*, February 12, 2008.

Arendt, Hannah. *Elemente und Ursprünge totaler Herrschaft (Origins of Totalitarianism)*, 12. Aufl., München. Zürich: Piper, 2008. [German original]

Arnon, Chana. "Jews Rescuing Jews during the Holocaust: Zerah Wahrhaftig." Jerusalem, Yad Va'shem, 2004. http://www.yadvashem.org/yv/en/education/conference/2004/39.pdf

Attali, Jacques. *Les Juifs, le Monde et l'Argent (Jews, the World and Money)*. Paris: Fayard, 2002. [French original]

Atzmon, Gil, Li Hao, et al. "Abraham's Children in the Genome Era: Major Jewish Diaspora Populations Comprise Distinct Genetic Clusters with Shared Middle Eastern Ancestry." *The American Journal of Human Genetics,* vol. 86 (2010): 1-10.

Avneri, Zvi, and Eric Lawee. "Abrabanel, Isaac Ben Judah." In *Encyclopaedia Judaica,* second edition, vol. 1. New York: Macmillan Reference, 2007.

Babel, Isaac. *The Complete Works of Isaac Babel.* Edited by Nathalie Babel, translated by Peter Constantin. New York: W.W. Norton & Company, 2002. [Russian original]

Barclay, John M.G. *Jews in the Mediterranean Diaspora: From Alexander to Trajan (323 BCE: 117 CE).* Edinburgh: T&T Clark, 1999.

Barkai, Avraham. *Jüdische Minderheit und Industrialisierung (Jewish Minorities and Industrialization).* Tübingen: J.S.B. Mohr (P. Siebeck), 1988. [German original]

Barkay, Gabriel, et al. "The Amulets from Ketef Hinnom: A New Edition and Evaluation." *Bulletin of the American Schools of Oriental Research,* no. 334 (2004): 41-71.

Barnavi, Eli. *A Historical Atlas of the Jewish People: From the Time of the Patriarchs to the Present.* New York: Schocken, 2003.

Baron, Salo Wittmayer. *A Social and Religious History of the Jews.* 18 Vols., 2nd ed. New York and London: Columbia University Press, 1952-1983.

------, Shalom M. Paul, and S. David Sperling. "Economic History." in *Encyclopaedia Judaica,* second edition, vol. 6. New York: Macmillan Reference, 2007.

Battenberg, Friedrich. *Das Europäische Zeitalter der Juden: Zur Entwicklung einer Minderheit in der nichtjüdischen Umwelt Europas. (The European Age of the Jews: The Development of a Minority in Europe's non-Jewish Environment),* vol. 1. Darmstadt: Wissenschaftliche Buchgesellschaft, 2000.

Bearman, Peter, ed. "Exploring Genetics and Social Structure." *American Journal of Sociology* 114, no. S1 (2008): v-x.

Behar, Doron M., Metspalu Ene, et al. "Counting the Founders: The Matrilineal Genetic Ancestry of the Jewish Diaspora." *PLoS ONE* 3, no. 4 (April 2008)

Behar, Doron M., Bayazit Yunusbayev, et al. "The Genome-Wide Structure of the Jewish People." *Nature,* no. 466 (2010): 238-42.

Ben-Barzilai, Yehudah Ha-Barzeloni, *Sefer Ha-Itim (Book of the Ages).* Originally printed in Krakow, 1903; reprinted Jerusalem: Institute to Encourage the Study of Torah, 2000. [Hebrew original]

Ben David, Yohanan (Samson John David). *Indo-Judaic Studies.* New Delhi: Northern Book Centre, 2002.

Ben Israel, Menasseh. *Esperance d'Israel (The Hope of Israel, 1650).* Translated into French by H. Mechulan and G.Nahon. Paris: Librairie philosophique J. Vrin, 1979. [Spanish original]

Ben-Sasson, Haim Hillel, ed. *A History of the Jewish People.* Cambridge, MA: Harvard University Press, 1976.

------. "The Middle Ages." In *A History of the Jewish People.* Cambridge, MA: Harvard University Press, 1976.

Bensimon, Doris, ed. *Judaisme, Sciences et Techniques (Judaism, Science and Technology).* Actes du colloque organisé les 14/15 Nov. 1988 par l'INALCO. Paris, 1989. [French original]

"Berek Joselovich." In Jewish Encyclopedia. New York: Funk and Wagnalls, 1901-1906. Online verson http://jewishencyclopedia.com/articles/3044-berek-joselovich.

Berger, David. "The 'Jewish Contribution' to Christianity." In *The Jewish Contribution to Civilization: Reassessing an Idea*, edited by Jeremy Cohen and Richard I. Cohen. Oxford: Littman Library of Jewish Civilization, 2012.

Berger, L. *Der Menora-Ring von Kaiseraugst. Jüdische Zeugnisse Römischer Zeit zwischen Brittanien und Pannonien (The menorah ring of Kaiseraugst, Jewish testimonies from Roman times between Britain and Pannonia).* Augst: Römerstadt Augusta Raurica, 2005. [German original]

Berlin, A., M. Z. Brettler, and M. Fishbane, eds. *The Jewish Study Bible (JSB)*, Jewish Publication Society. Oxford: Oxford University Press, 1999.

Biale, David, ed. *Cultures of the Jews: A New History.* New York: Schocken, 2002.

Bickerman, Elias. *From Ezra to the Last of the Maccabees: Foundations of Post-Biblical Judaism.* New York: Schocken Books, 1968.

Bismarck, Otto von. *Gedanken und Erinnerungen (Thoughts and Memories).* München: Droemersche Verlagsanstalt, 1952. [German original]

Bloch, Ernst. *The Principle of Hope.* Cambridge, MA: The MIT Press, 1986.

Bloom, Harold. "Foreword," in Yoseph Hayim Yerushalmi, *Zakhor: Jewish History and Jewish Memory.* Seattle: University of Washington Press, 1996.

Boot, Max. *War Made New: Technology, Warfare and the Course of History 1500 to Today.* New York: Gotham Books, 2006.

Botticini, Maristella, and Zvi Eckstein. "Jewish Occupational Selection: Education, Restrictions or Minorities?" *Journal of Economic History* 65, no. 4 (2005): 922-48.

------. "From Farmers to Merchants, Conversions and Diaspora: Human Capital and Jewish History." *Journal of the European Economic Association* 5, no. 5 (2007): 885-926

Braudel, Fernand. *Civilisation Matérielle, Economie et Capitalisme (Material Civilization, Economy and Capitalism).* Paris: Armand colin, Le livre de poche références, 1979. [French original]

------. *The Mediterranean and the Mediterranean World in the Age of Phillip II*, vol. II. Translated by S. Reynolds. Suffolk, NY: Collins, 1982.

------. *Grammaire des civilisations (Grammar of Civilizations).* Paris : Arthaud, 1992. [French original]

------. *Écrits sur l'histoire (Historic Writings)*, vol. I, Paris: Flammarion, 1969; vol. II, Paris, Flammarion, 1994 [French original]

--------. *Les Mémoires de la Méditerranée (The Memoirs of the Mediterranean).* Paris: Bernard de Fallois, 1998. [French original]

Bray, R. S. *Armies of Pestilence: The Impact of Disease on History.* Cambridge: James Clarke & Co., 2004.

Buber, Martin. *Israel und Palästina—Zur Geschichte einer Idee (Israel and Palestine: The History of an Idea).* Zürich, Artemis-Verlag, 1950. [Hebrew original]

Buganim, Ami. *Jewish Peoplehood in an Age of Globalization.* Jerusalem: Jewish Agency for Israel, 2007. [Hebrew original]

Burckhardt, Jacob. *Briefe an seinen Freund Friedrich von Preen (Letters to his Friend, Friedrich von Preen), 1864-1893.* Berlin, Stuttgart: Deutsche Verlags-Anstalt, 1922. [German original]

------. *Die Kultur der Renaissance in Italien* (*The Culture of the Renaissance in Italy*). Edited by W. von Bode. Berlin: Th. Knaur, 1928. [German original]

------. *Weltgeschichtliche Betrachtungen* (*Reflections on World History*). Edited by W. Kaegi. Bern: Verlag Hallwag, 1947. [German original]

------. *Die Zeit Constantins des Grossen* (*The Time of Constantine the Great*). Frankfurt: G.B. Fischer, 1954. [German original]

Burke, Peter. *What is Cultural History?* (Cambridge: John Wiley & Sons, 2004).

Burrow, John. *A History of Histories: Epics, Chronicles, Romances and Inquiries from Herodotus and Thucydides to the Twentieth Century*. London and New York: Penguin Adult, 2007.

Burstein, Paul. "Jewish Educational and Economic Success in the United States: A Search for Explanations." *Sociological Perspectives* 50, no. 2 (2007): 209-28.

Buruma, Ian, and Avishai Margalit. *Occidentalism: The West in the Eyes of Its Enemies*. New York: Penguin, 2004.

Cahill, Thomas. *The Gifts of the Jews: How a Tribe of Desert Nomads Changed the Way Everyone Thinks and Feels*. New York, London, and Toronto: Cengage Gale, 1998.

Capelle, Wilhelm, ed. *Die Vorsokratiker* (*The Presocratics*). Translated into German by Wilhelm Capelle. Stuttgart: A. Kröner, 1968. [Greek original]

Chase-Dunn, Christopher K., and Thomas D. Hall. *Rise and Demise: Comparing World-Systems*. Boulder, CO: Westview Press, 1997.

Chasidah, Yishai. *Encyclopedia of Biblical Personalities, Anthologized from the Talmud, Midrash and Rabbinic Writings*. Jerusalem: Mesorah Publication Ltd, 1994.

Chin Annping. *Confucius: A Life of Thought and Politics*. New Haven, London: Yale University Press, 2008.

Chiswick, Barry R. "The Occupational Attainment of American Jewry: 1990 to 2000." Institute for the Study of Labour (IZA), *IZA Discussion Papers*, no. 1736 (2005).

Chirot, Daniel. "Conflicting Identities and the Danger of Communalism." In *Essential Outsiders: Chinese and Jews in the Modern Transformation of Southeast Asia and Central Europe*, edited by Daniel Chirot and Anthony Reid. Seattle: University of Washington Press, 1997.

------, and Anthony Reid, eds., *Essential Outsiders: Chinese and Jews in the Modern Transformation of Southeast Asia and Central Europe*. Seattle: University of Washington Press, 1997.

Clark, Christopher. *Iron Kingdom: The Rise and Downfall of Prussia, 1600-1947*. London and New York: Penguin, 2007.

Clausewitz, Carl von. *Vom Kriege* (*About War*). Reinbek bei Hamburg: Rowohlt, 1963. [German original]

Coe, Michael D. *The Maya*, 5th edition. New York: Thames & Hudson, 1993.

Coghlan, Andy. "'Gene Link to Jews' Middle Eastern Origins." *New Scientist* 12 (June 2010):

Cohen, Jeremy, and Michael I. Cohen, eds. *The Jewish Contribution to Civilization: Reassessing an Idea*. Oxford: Littman Library of Jewish Civilization, 2008.

Cohen, Steven M., and Arnold M. Eisen. *The Jew Within: Self, Family and Community in America*. Bloomington: Indiana University Press, 2000.

Cohn-Sherbok, Dan. *Fifty Key Jewish Thinkers*, 2nd ed. New York and London: Taylor & Francis, 2007.

Cole, Peter. *The Dream of the Poem: Hebrew Poetry from Muslim and Christian Spain, 950-1492*. Translated and edited by Peter Cole. Princeton: Princeton University Press, 2007.

Confucius. *Analects* (numerous translations).

------. *Confucius*. Translated into French by Daniel Leslie, 3rd ed. Paris: Seghers, 1970.

Daojiong Zha. "Can China Rise?" *Review of International Studies* 31, no. 4 (2005): 775-85.

Dawkins, Richard. *The Selfish Gene*, 30th Anniversary Ed. Oxford: Oxford University Press, 2006.

Debrunner, Albert M. "Die antisemitischen Äusserungen Jacob Burckhardts: Eine verdrängte Seite (The Antisemitic Comments of Jacob Burckhardt: A Suppressed Aspect)." In *Israelitisches Wochenblatt der Schweiz*, No. 8, 20 Feb., 1998 [German original]

De Lange, Nicholas. *An Introduction to Judaism*. Cambridge: Cambridge University Press, 2002.

DellaPergola, Sergio. *World Jewry Beyond 2000: The Demographic Prospects*. Oxford: Oxford Centre for Hebrew and Jewish Studies, 1999.

------. *Israele e Palestina: la forza dei numeri—Il conflitto mediorientale fra demografia a politica (Israel and Palestine: The Power of Numbers—The Middle East Conflict Between Demography and Politics*. Bologna: Il Mulino, 2007. [Italian original]

------. "World Jewish Population 2008." *American Jewish Yearbook 2008*. New York: AJC, 2008.

------. *Jewish Population Policies: Demographic Trends and Interventions in Israel and in the Diaspora*. Jerusalem: JPPI, 2011.

Dennet, Daniel. *Breaking the Spell: Religion as a Natural Phenomenon*. New York and London: Viking Adult, 2006.

Diamond, Jared. *Guns, Germs and Steel: The Fates of Human Societies*. New York: Norton, 1997.

------. *Collapse: How Societies Choose to Fail or Succeed*. London: Penguin Books Ltd., 2005.

Douglas, Kate. "The Other You: Meet the Unsung Hero of the Human Mind." *New Scientist*, December 1, 2007.

Douglas, Mary. "The Fears of the Enclave." In *In the Wilderness: The Doctrine of Defilement in the Book of Numbers*. New York: Oxford University Press, 2001.

------. *Purity and Danger*. London: Routledge, 2002 (first edition London: Routledge, 1966).

Dror, Yehezkel. *The Capacity to Govern: A Report to the Club of Rome*. Portland, OR: Frank Cass, 1994.

Dubnow, Simon. *Weltgeschichte des jüdischen Volkes, von seinen Uranfängen bis zur Gegenwart (World History of the Jewish People from the Earliest Beginnings to the Present)*, 10 Vols. Berlin, Jüdischer Verlag, 1925 ff. [German and Russian original]

------. *Geschichte des Chassidismus (History of Hassidism)*. 2 Vols. Reprint of 1st edition, 1931. Berlin: Jüdischer Verlag, 1982. [German original]

------. *Jewish History: An Essay in the Philosophy of History.* Reprint of 1903 edition. Honolulu, HA: University Press of the Pacific, 2003.

Dugatkin, Lee Alan. *The Altruism Equation: Seven Scientists Search for the Origins of Goodness.* Princeton and Oxford: Princeton University Press, 2006.

Dunbar, Robin. "We Believe." *New Scientist,* January 28, 2006.

Durant, Will. *The Story of Civilization.* 11 vols., 1935-1975. New York: Simon and Schuster, 1975.

Dyson, Freeman. *The Scientist as Rebel.* New York: New York Review of Books, 2006.

------. "The Question of Global Warming." *The New York Review of Books* 60, no. 10 (June 12, 2008).

Eger, Akiva. *Gilyon HaShas.* (*Marginalia to the Talmud*) [Hebrew original]

Einstein, Albert, and Sigmund Freud. *Pourquoi la guerre?* (*Why War?*). Translated from the original German by B. Briod. Paris: Rivages, 2005.

Eisenstadt, Shmuel N. *Political Systems of Empires.* London: Transaction Publishers, 1963.

------. *The Origins and Diversity of Axial Age Civilizations.* Edited by Shmuel Eisenstadt. New York: SUNY Press, 1986.

------. *Jewish Civilization: The Jewish Historical Experience in a Comparative Perspective.* New York: SUNY Press, 1992.

Eliade, Mircea. *Le mythe de l'éternel retour* (*The Myth of Eternal Return*). Paris: Gallimard, 1969. [French original]

Elias, Norbert. *The Civilizing Process: Sociogenetic and Psychogenetic Investigations.* Rev. edition. Oxford: Basil Blackwell, 1994.

Elon, Amos. *The Pity Of It All: A Portrait of Jews in Germany 1743-1933.* New York: Henry Holt, 2002.

Emden, Jacob. *Mémoires de Jacob Emden, ou l'anti-Sabbatai Zewi* (*Memoirs of Jacob Emden or the Anti- Sabbatai Zewi*). Translated by Maurice-Ruben Hayoun. Paris: Editions du Cerf, 1992. [Hebrew original]

Encyclopedia Judaica. Edited by Yeshayahu Leibowitz. Jerusalem: Keter Publishing House, 1971 (reprint 1973). Second edition edited by. F. Skolnik and M. Berenbaum. New York: Macmillan Reference, 2007.

Erlanger, Simon. *Die jüdische Gemeinde des Mittelalters: Geschichte, Struktur und Einfluss auf die Stadtentwicklung vom 9. bis 13. Jahrhundert mit besonderer Berücksichtigung des Rheinlandes* (*The Jewish Community of the Middle Ages: History, Structure and Influence on Urban Development from the 9th to 13th Century, with Special Emphasis on the Rhineland*). MA Thesis, University of Basel, 1992. [German original]

Ettinger, Shmuel. "The Modern Period." In *A History of the Jewish People,* ed. Hayim Ben-Sasson. Cambridge: Weidenfeld & Nicolson, 1976.

Ezra, Nehemiah (The Anchor Yale Bible). Edited by Jacob M. Myers. New York: Doubleday, 1965.

Fagan, Brian. *The Great Warming: Climate Change and the Rise and Fall of Civilizations.* New York: Bloomsbury Press, 2008.

Fairbank, John King, and Merle Goldman. *China: A New History,* enlarged edition. Cambridge, MA: Belknap Press, 1998.

Farissol, Abraham ben Mordecai. *Sidur Shalem Mikol Ha'Shana Kephi Minhag Italiani (An Italian Rite Siddur)*, Mantua, 1480, Manuscript, Treasures Revealed- From the Collections of the Jewish National and University Library in Honor of the 75th Anniversary of the Hebrew University of Jerusalem 1925-2000. Edited by R. Weisser. Jerusalem: R. Plesser, 2000. [Hebrew original]

Feldman, Louis H. *Jew and Gentile in the Ancient World: Attitudes and Interactions from Alexander to Justinian*. Princeton: Princeton University Press, 1993.

Feldman, Noah. "War and Reason in Maimonides and Averroes." In *The Ethics of War: Shared Problems in Different Traditions,* edited by Richard Sorabji and David Rodin. Hampshire: Ashgate Publishing Limited, 2006.

Ferguson, Niall. *The War of the World: Twentieth-Century Conflict and the Descent of the West*. London and New York: Penguin Press, 2006.

Figes, Orlando. *A People's Tragedy: The Russian Revolution 1891-1924.* New York: Penguin Books, 1996.

Finkelstein, Louis, ed. *Jewish Self-government in the Middle Ages.* Philadelphia: Greenwood Press, 1924.

------. *The Jews: Their History, Culture and Religion,* 3rd ed., 2 vols. New York: Harper & Row, 1960.

Firestone, Reuven. "Holy War in Modern Judaism? 'Mitzvah War' and the Problem of the 'Three Vows.'" *Journal of the American Academy of Religion* 74, no. 4 (2006): 954-82.

Flanagan, Owen. "Where in the World is the Mind?" *New Scientist,* January 17, 2009.

Flavius, Josephus. "Against Apion." In *The New Complete Works of Josephus,* translated by William Whiston and Paul L Maier. Grand Rapids, MI: Kregel Academic, 1999.

------. "Jewish Antiquities." In *The New Complete Works of Josephus,* translated by William Whiston and Paul L Maier. Grand Rapids, MI: Kregel Academic, 1999.

------. "The Jewish War." In *The New Complete Works of Josephus,* translated by William Whiston and Paul L Maier. Grand Rapids, MI: Kregel Academic, 1999.

------. *The New Complete Works of Josephus.* Translated by William Whiston and Paul L Maier. Grand Rapids, MI: Kregel Academic, 1999.

Florida, Richard. *The Rise of the Creative Class: And How It's Transforming Work, Leisure, Community and Everyday Life.* New York: Basic Books, 2002.

Flusser, David. "Jossipon." *Encyclopaedia Judaica.* Jerusalem: Keter Publishing House, 1971.

------. *Jesus.* 3rd ed. Jerusalem: Magnes Press, 2001.

Freud, Sigmund. *Totem and Taboo: Some Points of Agreement between the Mental Lives of Savages and Neurotics.* Great Britain: W.W. Norton & Co., 1950. [German original]

Friedländer, Saul. *Nazi Germany and the Jews 1939-1945: The Years of Extermination.* New York: Harper Collins, 2007.

Friedman, Isaiah. *The Question of Palestine: British-Jewish-Arab Relations 1914-1918.* 2nd expanded ed. New Brunswick: Transaction Publishers, 1992.

Friedman, Ron. "Israel Urged to 'Act Now' or Face Global Warming Disaster." *Jerusalem Post,* July 6, 2007.

Fromkin, David. *A Peace to End All Peace: The Fall of the Ottoman Empire and the Creation of the Modern Middle East.* New York: Avon Books, 1989.

------. *Europe's Last Summer: Who Started the Great War in 1914?* New York: Vintage, 2005.

Fukuyama, Francis. *The End of History and the Last Man.* UK: Penguin Books, 1992.

Gans, David. *Sefer Tsemah David* (The Offspring of David). First printing Prague, 1592. Jerusalem: Magnes, 1983. [Hebrew original]

Geiger, Abraham. "A History of Spiritual Achievements." In *Ideas of Jewish History*, edited by Michael A. Meyer. Detroit: Wayne State University Press, 1974.

Genetic Testing: Policy Issues for the New Millenium. Paris: OECD, 2000.

Gibbon, Edward. *The History of the Decline and Fall of the Roman Empire.* 3 vols. Edited by John Bagnell Bury. New York: Heritage Press, 1946.

Gernet, Jacques. *Le monde Chinois* (*The Chinese World*). Paris: Armand Colin, 1999. [French original]

Gilbert, Martin. *Churchill and the Jews: A Lifelong Friendship.* London: Henry Holt, 2008.

------. *Israel: A History.* Rev. and updated. London: Black Swan, 2008.

Gitelman, Zvi Y. *A Century of Ambivalence: The Jews of Russia and the Soviet Union 1881 to the Present*, 2nd ed. Bloomington: Indiana University Press, 2001.

Glick, David, and Hermona Soreq. "Ethics, Public Policy and Behavioral Genetics." *Israel Medical Association Journal* 5 (2003): 83-86.

Goetschel, Roland. *Isaac Abravanel, Conseiller des princes et philosophe* (*Isaac Abravanel, Adviser of Princes and Philosopher*). Paris: Albin Michel, Presences du Judaisme-poche edition, 1996. [French original]

Goitein, S. D. *Jews and Arabs: Their Contacts through the Ages.* New York: Schocken Books, 1974; first ed., 1955.

------. *A Mediterranean Society: The Jewish Communities of the Arab World as Portrayed in the Documents of the Cairo Geniza.* 5 Vols. Los Angeles: University of California Press, 1967-1988.

Golb, Norman. "Obadiah the Proselyte: Scribe of a Unique Twelfth-Century Manuscript Containing Lombardic 'Neumes.'" *The Journal of Religion* 45, no. 2 (1965): 153-56.

Goodman, Martin. *Rome and Jerusalem: The Clash of Ancient Civilizations.* London: Alfred A. Knopf, 2007.

------, ed. *The Oxford Handbook of Jewish Studies.* Oxford: Oxford University Press, 2002.

Goodnick, J. Westenholz, ed. *The Jewish Presence in Ancient Rome.* Jerusalem: Bible Lands Museum, 1994.

Grabbe, Lester L., ed. *"Like a Bird in a Cage": The Invasion of Sennacherib in 701 BCE.* Sheffield: Continuum International Publishing Group, 2003.

Graetz, Heinrich. *Geschichte der Juden von den ältesten Zeiten bis auf die Gegenwart, 1853-75* (*History of the Jews from the Earliest Times to the Present, 1853-75*). 11 Vols. Leipzig: Leiner, 1902. [German original]

------. *Volkstümliche Geschichte der Juden* (*Popular History of the Jews*). 3 Vols. Berlin-Wien: B. Harz, 1923. [German original]

Grayzel, Solomon. *A History of the Jews from the Babylonian Exile to the Present.* Philadelphia: Jewish Publication Society of America, 1968 (earlier ed., 1947).

Greif, Avner. "Contract Enforceability and Economic Institutions in Early Trade: The Maghribi Traders' Coalition." *The American Economic Review* 83, no. 3 (1993): 525-48.

------, Paul Milgrom, and Barry R. Weingast. "Coordination, Commitment and Enforcement: The Case of the Merchant Guild." *The Journal of Political Economy* 102, no. 4 (1994): 745-76.

------. "Cultural Beliefs and the Organisation of Society: A Historical and Theoretical Reflection on Collectivist and Individualist Societies." *The Journal of Political Economy* 102, no. 5 (1994): 912-50.

Gross, Nachum T. "Enterpreneurship of Religious and Ethnic Minorities." *Jüdische Unternehmer in Deutschland im 19. und 20. Jahrhundert*, 11-23. Stuttgart: F. Steiner, 1992.

Grossman, Vassily. *A Writer at War: With The Red Army 1941-1945*. Edited by Antony Beevor and Luba Vinogradova. London: Pimlico, 2006. [Russian original]

Gruen, Erich S. *Diaspora: Jews amidst Greeks*. Cambridge, MA: Harvard University Press, 2002.

Guttmann, Julius. *Die Philosophie des Judentums* (*The Philosophy of Judaism*). München: Ernst Reinhardt, 1933. [German original]

Hadas-Lebel, Mireille. *L'Hébreu: 3000 ans d'histoire* (*Hebrew: 3000 Years of History*). Paris: Albin Michel, 1992. [French original]

------. *Philo d'Alexandrie, un penseur en diaspora* (*Philo of Alexandria, a Diaspora Thinker*). Paris: Fayard, 2003. [French original]

------. *Rome, la Judée et les Juifs* (*Rome, Judea and the Jews*). Paris: Editions A & J Picard, 2009. [French original]

Halevi, Judah. *The Kuzari: An Argument for the Faith of Israel*. Revised edition, translated by Hartwig Hirschfeld. Jerusalem: Sefer Ve Sefel Publishing, 2003. [Hebrew/Arabic original]

Hazony, Yoram. *The Jewish State: The Struggle for Israel's Soul*. New York: Basic/New Republic Books, 2000.

Hammer, Michael F., Karl Skorecki, Sara Selig, et. al. "Y-Chromosomes of Jewish Priests." *Nature* 385 (1997): 32.

Hanson, Victor Davis. *Carnage and Culture: Landmark Battles in the Rise of Western Power*. New York: Doubleday, 2001.

Hecht, Jeff. "Fault Found for the Mediterranean 'Day of Horror.'" *New Scientist*, March 15, 2008.

Hegel, Georg Wilhelm Friedrich. *Vorlesungen über die Philosophie der Geschichte* (*Lectures on Philosophy of History*). Leipzig: P. Reclam junior, 1924. [German original]

Herman, Arthur. *The Idea of Decline in Western History*. New York: Free Press, 1997.

Hesiod. "Works and Days." In *Hesiod: Theogony Works and Days Testimonia*, edited by Glenn W. Most. Cambridge, MA: Harvard University Press, 2006. [Greek original]

Heuck, Sigrid. *Der Elefant des Kaisers* (*The Emperor's Elephant*). Stuttgart, Wien: Thienemann, 2006. [German original]

Hobsbawm, Eric, and Terence Ranger. *The Invention of Tradition*. Cambridge: Cambridge University Press, 1992.

Hodgson, Marshall G. S. *The Venture of Islam: Conscience and History in a World Civilization*; vol. 1: *The Classical Age of Islam*; vol. 2: *The Expansion of Islam in the Middle Periods*; vol. 3: *The Gunpowder Empires and Modern Times*. Chicago and London: University of Chicago Press, 1974.

Homer-Dixon, Thomas. *The Upside of Down: Catastrophe, Creativity and the Renewal of Civilization*. Toronto: Knopf Canada, 2006.

Hooper, Rowan. "Men Inherit Hidden Costs of Dad's Vices." *New Scientist*, January 7, 2006.

------. "Inheriting a Heresy." *New Scientist*, March 4, 2006.

Hourani, Albert. *Islam in European Thought*. Cambridge: Cambridge University Press, 1991.

Horowitz, Elliott. "Days of Gladness or Days of Madness: Modern Discussions of the Ancient Sabbath." In *The Jewish Contribution to Civilization: Reassessing an Idea*, edited by Jeremy Cohen and Richard I. Cohen. Oxford: Littman Library of Jewish Civilization, 2012.

Huizinga, Johan. *Herbst des Mittelalters: Studien über Lebens—und Geistesformen des 14. und 15. Jahrhunderts in Frankreich und in der Niederlanden* (Autumn of the Middle Ages: A Study of the Forms of Life and Thought in 14th and 15th Century, France and the Netherlands), 7th ed. Edited by K. Köster. Stuttgart: Alfred Kroner, 1953. Translated into German from the original Dutch, *Herfstij der middeleeuwen*, published in Leiden, 1923. [Dutch original]

------. *Homo Ludens: vom Ursprung der Kultur im Spiel (Man the Player)*. Leiden, 1938, translated by H. Nachod, Reinbek bei. Hamburg: Rowohlt, 1956. [Dutch original]

------. *Holländische Kultur im Siebzehnten Jahrhundert* (Dutch Culture in the Seventeenth Century). Edited by W. Kaegi. Basel: B. Schwabe, 1961. Originally written in German in 1932 and published in Dutch in 1941 as *Nederlands's beschaving in de zeventiende eeuw*. [German and Dutch original]

Huntington, Samuel P. *The Clash of Civilizations and the Remaking of World Order*. London: Simon & Schuster, 1998.

Ibn Daud, Abraham. *Seder Ha'chachamim Ve'Korot Ha'itim* (*Chronicle of Sages and Periods*). Edited by A. Neubauer. Oxford: Clarendon, 1887. [Hebrew original]

------. *Sefer Ha-Qabbalah* (*The Book of Tradition*). Critical Edition with a Translation and Notes by Gerson D.Cohen. Philadelphia: Jewish Publication Society, 1967. [Hebrew original]

Ibn Khaldun. *The Muqaddimah: An Introduction to History* (1381). Translated by Franz Rosenthal. 3 Vols. Princeton: Princeton University Press, 1958. [Arabic original]

------. *The Muqaddimah: An Introduction to History*, reduced edition in 1 vol. Edited by N. J. Dawood. Princeton: Princeton University Press, 1967. [Arabic original]

Intergovernmental Panel on Climate Change (IPCC). *Fourth Assessment Report*, UNEP, 2007.

Isenberg, Shirley Berry. *India's Bene Israel: A Comprehensive Inquiry and Sourcebook*. Berkeley: Judah L. Magnes Museum, 1988.

Israel, Jonathan I. *The Dutch Republic: Its Rise, Greatness and Fall 1477-1806*. Oxford: Oxford University Press, 1995; paperback with corrections Oxford: Oxford University Press, 1998.

------. *European Jewry in the Age of Mercantilism 1550-1750*. 3rd ed. Portland, OR: Littman Library of Jewish Civilization, 1998.

------. *Radical Enlightenment: Philosophy and the Making of Modernity*. New York: Oxford University Press, 2002.

Israel, Rachael Rukmini. *The Jews of India: Their Story*. New Delhi: Mosaic Books, 2002.

Jablonka, Eva, and Marion J. Lamb. *Evolution in Four Dimensions: Genetic, Epigenetic, Behaviourial and Symbolic Variation in the History of Life*. Cambridge, MA: MIT Press, 2005.

Jaspers, Karl. *Vom Ursprung und Ziel der Geschichte (On Origin and Goal of History)*. Frankfurt am Main: Fischer Bücherei, 1955. [German original]

------. *Allgemeine Psychopathologie (General Psychopathology)*. 9. Aufl. Berlin: Springer-Verlag, 1973 (1st ed. 1913). [German original]

Jastrow, Marcus. *A Dictionary of the Targumim, the Talmud Babli and Yerushalmi, and the Midrashic Literature*. London: Luzak & Co., 1903.

Jewish Peoplehood and Identity: The Peoplehood Papers. United Jewish Communities. General Assembly, Nashville TN, 2007.

Jewish People Policy Planning Institute. *The Jewish People between Thriving and Decline*. Annual Assessment 2004-2005. Jerusalem: JPPI, 2005.

JINFO.org. *Jews in Computer and Information Science*, 2004-2013. http://www.jinfo.org/Computer_Info_Science.html

Johnson, Paul. *A History of the Jews*. New York: Weidenfeld and Nicolson, 1987.

Kaegi, Werner. *Jacob Burckhardt: Eine Biographie (Jacob Burckhardt: Biography)*. 1947-1982, 7 vols. Basel: Schwabe, 1947. [German original]

Kahn, Herman, and Anthony Wiener. *The Year 2000: A Framework for Speculation on the Next Thirty-Three Years*. New York and London: Macmillan, 1967.

Kandel, Eric R. *In Search of Memory: The Emergence of a New Science of Mind*. New York and London: W. W. Norton & Company, 2006.

Kaplan, Mordecai M. *Judaism as a Civilization: Towards a Reconstruction of American Jewish Life*. Philadelphia and Jerusalem: Jewish Publication Society of America, 1994.

Karady, Victor. "Jewish Entrepreneurship and Identity under Capitalism and Socialism in Central Europe: The Unresolved Dilemmas of Hungarian Jewry." In Chirot and Reid, *Essential Outsiders: Chinese and Jews in the Modern Transformation of Southeast Asia and Central Europe*. Seattle: University of Washington Press, 1997.

Karpin, Michael. *The Bomb in the Basement*. New York: Simon and Schuster, 2006.

Katz, Jacob. *Exclusiveness and Tolerance: Jewish–Gentile Relations in Medieval and Modern Times*. New York: Schocken Books, 1962. [Hebrew original]

------. *The"Shabbes Goy": A Study in Halakhic Flexibility*. Philadelphia: The Jewish Publication Society, 1989. [Hebrew original]

------. *Tradition and Crisis: Jewish Society at the End of the Middle Ages*. New York: New York University Press, 1993. [Hebrew original]

Kaufmann, Yehezkel. *Golah ve-Nekhar (Diaspora and Foreign Countries)*. Tel-Aviv: Dvir, 1929. [Hebrew original]

------. "On the Fate and Survival of the Jews." In *Ideas of Jewish History*, edited by Michael A. Meyer. Detroit: Wayne State University Press, 1974. [Hebrew original]

------. *History of the Religion of Israel*, vol. IV. New York: Ktav Publisher House, 1977. [Hebrew original]

Kehimkar, Haeem Samuel. *The History of the Bene Israel of India*. Preface 1897. Tel-Aviv: Dayag Press, 1937.

Kendler, Kenneth. "Toward a Philosophical Structure for Psychiatry." *American Journal of Psychiatry* 162, no. 3 (2005): 433-40.

Kennedy, Paul. *The Rise and Fall of the Great Powers: Economic Change and Military Conflict from 1500 to 2000*. New York: Random House, 1987.

King, Alexander. *Let the Cat Turn Round: One Man's Traverse of the Twentieth Century*. UK: CPTM, 2006.

King, Joe. *The Jewish Contribution to the Modern World*. Montreal: Montreal Jewish Publication Society, 2004.

Kissinger, Henry. *Diplomacy*. New York and London: Simon & Schuster, 1994.

Klausner, Joseph. *History of the Second Temple*, vol. 5. Tel-Aviv: Achiasaf, 1952. [Hebrew original]

Kleiman, Yaakov. *DNA and Tradition: The Genetic Link to the Ancient Hebrews*. Jerusalem: Devora Publishing, 2004.

Kligsberg, Bernardo. *Social Justice: A Jewish Perspective*. Jerusalem: Gefen Books, 2003.

The Knowledge-Based Economy. Paris: OECD, 1996.

Köhler, Kaufmann, and Herman Rosenthal. "Caesar, Caius Julius." In *Jewish Encyclopedia*. New York: Funk and Wagnalls, 1901-1906. Online version http://jewishencyclopedia.com/articles/3886-caesar-caius-julius

Kriwaczek, Paul. *Yiddish Civilization: The Rise and Fall of a Forgotten Nation*. New York: Vintage, 2006.

Krochmal, Nachman. "Guide for the Perplexed of Our Time." In *Ideas of Jewish History*, edited by Michael A. Meyer. Detroit: Wayne State University Press, 1974. [Hebrew original]

Kupfer, Peter, ed. *Youtai: Presence and Perception of Jews and Judaism in China*. Frankfurt am Main: Peter Lang, 2008.

Kuznets, Simon. "Economic Structure and Life of the Jews." In *The Jews: Their History, Culture and Religion, 1597-1666*, vol. II. Philadelphia: Jewish Publication Society of America, 1960.

Kuznitz, Cecile E. "Yiddish Studies." In *The Oxford Handbook of Jewish Studies*, edited by Martin Goodman. Oxford and New York: Oxford University Press, 2002.

Laotse. *Laotse*. Edited by Lin Yutang. Frankfurt: Fischer Bücherei, 1955.

Laozi. *Daodejing* (numerous translations).

Laqueur, Walter. *The Terrible Secret: Suppression of the Truth About Hitler's "Final Solution."* New York: Holt Paperbacks, 1998.

Lässig, Simone. "How German Jewry Turned Bourgeois: Religion, Culture and Social Mobility in the Age of Emancipation." *GHI Research, German Historical Institute Washington, GHI Bulletin*, no. 37 (Fall 2005).

Leoni, Tommaso. "'Against Caesar's Wishes': Flavius Josephus as a Source for the Burning of the Temple." *Journal of Jewish Studies* 58, no. 1 (2007): 39-51.

Leroy-Beaulieu, Anatole. *Les Juifs et l'Antisémitisme: Israel chez les nations (The Jews and Anti-Semitism: Israel among the Nations)*. Paris: Calmann Levy, 1893. [French original]

Leslie, Donald Daniel. *Jews and Judaism in Traditional China: A Comprehensive Bibliography*. Sankt Augustin: Monumenta Serica Institute, 1998.

Lewis, Bernard. *The Jews of Islam*. Princeton: Taylor & Francis, 1984.

------. *Semites and Anti-Semites: An Inquiry into Conflict and Prejudice*. New York: W.W Norton, 1986.

------. *Islam and the West*. New York: Oxford University Press, 1993.

------. *The Middle East: A Brief History of the Last 2,000 Years*. New York: Scribner, 1995.

------. *The Emergence of Modern Turkey*, 3rd ed. New York: Oxford University Press, 2002.

------. *What Went Wrong? Western Impact and Middle Eastern Response*. Oxford: Oxford University Press, 2002.

------. *The Crisis of Islam: Holy War and Unholy Terror*. New York: Random House Publishing Group, 2003.

------. *From Babel to Dragomans: Interpreting the Middle East*. London: Oxford University Press, 2004.

Lin Yutang. *The Wisdom of Confucius*. New York: Carlton House, 1938.

Livni, Abraham. *Le retour d'Israel et l'espérance du monde (Israel's Return and the World's Hope)*. Monaco: Éditions du Rocher, 1984. [French original]

Lorito, S., et al. "Earth-quake Generated Tsunamis in the Mediterranean Sea: Scenarios of Potential Threats to Southern Italy." *Journal of Geophysical Research* 113 (2008): 113.

Lukacs, John. *Five Days in London May 1940*. New Haven: Yale University Press, 2001.

Machiavelli, Niccolò. "Discourses on the First Ten Books of Titus Livius." In *The Essential Writings of Machiavelli*, edited by Peter Constantine. New York: The Modern Library, 2007. [Italian original]

------. *The Essential Writings of Machiavelli*. Edited by Peter Constantine. New York: The Modern Library, 2007. [Italian original]

------. "The Prince." In *The Essential Writings of Machiavelli*, edited by Peter Constantine. New York: The Modern Library, 2007. [Italian original]

McNeill, William H. *The Rise of the West: A History of the Human Community*. Chicago: University of Chicago Press, 1963.

Mahler, Raphael. "The Modern Era in Marxist-Zionist Perspective." In *Ideas of Jewish History*, ed. Michael A. Meyer. Detroit: Wayne State University Press, 1974.

------. *Chronicles of the Jewish People: The Last Generations from the Late 18th Century until Today*. Tel Aviv: Ha-Kibuts ha-Me'uhad, 1976. [Hebrew original]

Maimonides, Moses. *The Guide of the Perplexed*. Translated by M. Friedländer. 2nd ed. New York: Dover Publications, 1956. [Arabic original]

Malamat, A. "Part I: Origins and the Formative Period." In *A History of the Jewish People*, ed. Ben-Sasson. Cambridge: Weidenfeld & Nicolson, 1976.

Margolis, Max L., and Alexander Marx. *A History of the Jewish People.* Philadelphia: Jewish Publication Society of America, 1927.

Marx, Karl. *Zur Judenfrage (On the Jewish Question).* Paris: Au bureau des annales, 1844. [German original]

-----, and Friedrich Engels. *Das Manifest der Kommunistischen Partei (The Communist Manifesto).* Berlin: Dietz Verlag, 1848. [German original]

Meadows, Dennis, et al. *The Limits to Growth.* Club of Rome. New York: New American Library, 1972.

Meyer, Michael E., ed. *Ideas of Jewish History.* Detroit: Wayne State University Press, 1974.

Mirsky, Jehudah. "Tikkun Olam: Basic Questions and Policy Directions." In *Facing Tomorrow: Background Policy Documents,* provisional ed. Jerusalem: JPPI, 2008.

"Monash, Sir John." *Encyclopaedia Judaica,* second edition, vol. 14. New York: Macmillan Reference, 2007.

Montefiore, Simon Sebag. *Stalin: The Court of the Red Tzar.* New York: Knopf, 2004.

Morag, Shlomo. *Studies in Biblical Hebrew.* Jerusalem: Magnes Press, 1994. [Hebrew original]

Morris, Benny. *1948: The First Arab-Israeli War.* New Haven: Yale University Press, 2008.

Moshe Ben Jacob, Rabbi of Coucy. *SMAG: Sefer Mitzvoth Ha-Gadol* (The Great Book of Commandments). Venice, 1574. [Hebrew original]

Murray, Charles. *Human Accomplishment: The Pursuit of Excellence in the Arts and Sciences, 800 BC to 1950.* New York: Harper Perennial, 2004.

Myers, David N. "Discourses of Civilisation: The Shifting Course of a Modern Jewish Motive." In *The Jewish Contribution to Civilization: Reassessing an Idea,* edited by Jeremy Cohen and Richard I. Cohen. Oxford and Portland, OR: Littman Library of Jewish Civilization, 2012.

Myers, Jacob B., ed. *The Anchor Bible, Ezra-Nehemiah.* New York: Doubleday, 1965.

Na'aman, Nadav. *Ancient Israel and Its Neighbours: Interaction and Counteraction.* Collected Essays, vol. 1. Winona Lake, IN: Eisenbrauns, 2005.

Najman, H. "Introduction to Ezra and Nehemiah and Commentaries." In *The Jewish Study Bible: Jewish Publication Society Tanakh Translation,* edited by Berlin, Brettler, and Fishbane. New York: Oxford University Press, 2004.

Needham, Joseph. *Science and Civilization in China.* 10 vols. Cambridge: Cambridge University Press, 1954.

"Nehemia." In *Encyclopaedia Judaica,* second edition. New York: Macmillan, 2007.

Netanyahu, Benzion. *Don Isaac Abrabanel: Statesman and Philosopher.* New York: Varda Books, 2001.

Neusner, Jacob. *The Making of the Mind of Judaism: The Formative Age.* Atlanta: Scholars Press, 1987.

------. *Why Does Judaism Have an Economics?* New London, CT: Connecticut College, 1988.

------. *Introduction to Rabbinic Literature.* New York: Doubleday, 1994.

Nisbett, Richard. *Intelligence and How to Get It: Why Schools and Cultures Count.* New York and London: W.W. Norton, 2009.

Nye, Joseph S. *Soft Power: The Means to Succeed in World Politics.* New York: Public Affairs, 2004.

------. "Picking a President." *Democracy: A Journal of Ideas,* no. 10 (2008): 19-28.

Olson, Mancur. *The Rise and Decline of Nations: Economic Growth, Stagflation and Social Rigidities.* New Haven: Yale University Press, 1982.

Oren, Michael. *Six Days of War: June 1967 and the Making of the Modern Middle East.* Oxford: Oxford University Press, 2002.

------. *Power, Faith and Fantasy: America and the Middle East 1776 to the Present.* New York and London: W.W. Norton, 2007.

Paludan, Ann. *Chronicle of the Chinese Emperors: The Reign-by-Reign Record of the Rulers of Imperial China.* London: Thames & Hudson, 2003.

Pan Guang, ed. *The Jews in Asia: Comparative Perspectives.* CJSS Jewish & Israeli Studies Series, vol. I. Shanghai: Shanghai Sanlian, 2007.

Parfitt, Tudor. *The Lost Tribes of Israel: The History of a Myth.* London: Weidenfeld & Nicolson, 2002.

Perdue, Peter D. *China Marches West: The Qing Conquest of Central Eurasia.* Cambridge, MA: Harvard University Press, 2005.

Phillips, Helen. "How Life Shapes the Brainscape." *New Scientist,* November 26, 2005.

Pico della Mirandola, Giovanni. *Oratio de hominis dignitate: De la dignité de l'homme* (A Speech about the Dignity of Man). Translated by Y. Hersant. Paris: Éd. de l'Éclat, 2005. [Latin original]

Pinker, Steven. *How the Mind Works.* New York: W.W. Norton, 1997.

------. *The Blank Slate: The Modern Denial of Human Nature.* New York: Viking, 2002.

Plutarch. "Artaxerxes." 75 BCE. Translated by John Dryden. *The Internet Classics Archive.* http://classics.mit.edu/Plutarch/artaxerx.html.

Pollak, Michael. *Mandarins, Jews and Missionaries: The Jewish Experience in the Chinese Empire.* Philadelphia: Jewish Publication Society of America, 1980.

Polliack, Meira. "Medieval Karaism." In *The Oxford Handbook of Jewish Studies,* edited by Martin Goodman. Oxford and New York: Oxford University Press, 2002.

Preston, D.L. "Science, Society and the German Jews: 1870-1933." PhD diss., University of Illinois, 1971.

Rabkin, Yakov, and Ira Robinson, eds. *The Interaction of Scientific and Jewish Cultures in Modern Times.* Lewiston and New York: Edwin Mellen Press, 1995.

Radosh, Allis, and Ronald Radosh. *A Safe Heaven: Harry S. Truman and the Founding of Israel.* New York: Harper Collins, 2009.

Rainey, Anson F. "Stones for Bread: Archeology versus History." *Near Eastern Journal of Archaeology* 64, no. 3 (2001): 140-49.

------. *Ranking Port Cities with High Exposure and Vulnerability to Climate Extremes: Exposure Estimates.* OECD. Environment Working Papers No.1, ENV/WKP, 2007.

Ravilious, Kate. "Major Quake, Tsunami Likely in Middle East, Study Finds." *National Geographic News,* July 26, 2007.

Rees, Martin J. *Our Final Hour—A Scientist's Warning: How Terror, Error and Environmental Disaster Threaten Humankind's Future in this Century on Earth and Beyond.* London: Basic Books, 2003.

Reinharz, Jehuda. "Chaim Weizmann, Acetone and the Balfour Declaration." In *The Interaction of Scientific and Jewish Cultures in Modern Times,* edited by. Yakov Rabkin and Ira Robinson. New York: Edwin Mellen Press, 1995.

Rinat, Zafrir. "Report: Israel unprepared for global climate crisis." *Haaretz,* May 8, 2008.

Rising Above the Gathering Storm: Energizing and Employing America for a Brighter Economic Future. National Academy of Sciences, National Academy of Engineering and Institute of Medicine, Washington, 2007.

Robinson, Ira. "Hayyim Selig Slonimsky and the Diffusion of Science among Russian Jewry in the Nineteens Century." In *The Interaction of Scientific and Jewish Cultures in Modern Times,* edited by Yakov M. Rabkin and Ira Robinson. New York: Edwin Mellen Press, 1995.

Rodrigue, Aron. "The Ottoman Diaspora: The Rise and Fall of Ladino Literary Culture." In *Cultures of the Jews: A New History,* edited by David Biale. New York: Schocken, 2002.

Rofé, Alexander. *Introduction to the Literature of the Hebrew Bible.* Jerusalem: Simore, 2009. [Hebrew original]

Romilly, Jacqueline de. *Alcibiade.* Paris: De Fallois, 1995.

Rosenberg, Stephen G. "The Jewish Temple at Elephantine." *Near Eastern Archaeology* 67, no. 1 (2004): 4-13.

Rosman, Moshe. *Founder of Hassidism: A Quest for the Historical Ba'al Shem Tov.* Berkeley, CA: University of California Press, 1996.

Roth, Cecil. *A Life of Menasseh Ben Israel: Rabbi, Printer and Diplomat.* Philadelphia: Jewish Publication Society of America, 1934.

------. *The Jewish Contribution to Civilization.* London: Macmillan, 1938.

Rubin, Alexis, ed. *Scattered Among the Nations: Documents Affecting Jewish History 49 to 1975.* Northvale, NJ: J. Aronson, 1995.

Rudermann, David D. *Jewish Thought and Scientific Discovery in Early Modern Europe.* Detroit: Wayne State University Press, 2001.

Sachar, Howard. *The Course of Modern Jewish History.* New Revised Edition. New York: Vintage, 1990.

Sacks, Jonathan. *Radical Then, Radical Now: The Legacy of the World's Oldest Religion.* London: HarperCollins, 2000.

Saey, Tina Hesman. "Dad's Hidden Influence: A Father's Legacy to a Child's Health May Start before Conception and Last Generations." *Science News,* March 29, 2008.

------. "EpiGenetics." *Science News,* May 24, 2008.

------. "DNA Packaging Runs in Families: Epigenetic Shifts Also Continue Through-out Life." *Science News,* July 19, 2008.

------. "Genome Maps Trace Jewish Origins: Roots of Far-flung Populations Reach Back to the Levant." *Science News,* July 3, 2010.

Safrai, Shmuel. "Elementary Education, Its Religious and Social Significance in the Talmudic Period." In *Social Life and Social Values of the Jewish People, Journal of World History,* edited by UNESCO, vol. XI, 1-2. Neuchatel, 1968.

Salin, Edgar. *Politische Ökonomie: Geschichte der Witschaftspolitischen Ideen von Platon bis zur Gegenwart* (Political Economy: A History of Economic Policy Theories from Platon to the Present), 5th ed. Tübingen: Mohr Siebeck, 1967. [German original]

Salomon, Jean-Jacques. *Une civilisation à hauts risques* (Civilization at high risks). Paris: Éditions Charles Léopold Meyer, 2006.

Sarton, George. "Arabic Science and Learning in the Fifteenth Century: Their Decadence and Fall." In *Consejo Superior de Investigaciones Científicas, Homenaje a Millás-Vallicrosa*, vol. II, Barcelona: Consejo Superior de Investigaciones Científicas, 1956.

Schalit, Abraham. "Antipater II, or Antipas." *Encyclopedia Judaica*, second edition, vol. 2. New York: Macmillan Reference, 2007.

Scheindlin, Raymond P. "Merchants and Intellectuals, Rabbis and Poets." In *Cultures of the Jews: A New History*, edited by David Biale. New York: Schocken, 2002.

Schmelzer, Menachem H. *Studies in Jewish Bibliography and Medieval Jewish Poetry*. New York: Jewish Theological Seminary of America, 2006.

Schoenfeld, Andrew J. "Sons of Israel in Caesar's Service: Jewish Soldiers in the Roman Military." *Shofar: An Interdisciplinary Journal of Jewish Studies* 24, no. 3 (2006): 115-26.

Scholem, Gershom. *Die Jüdische Mystik in ihren Hauptströmungen* (Major Trends in Jewish Mysticism). Zürich: Suhrkamp, 1957. [German original]

------. *Sabbatai Sevi: The Mystical Messiah, 1626-1676*. Princeton: Princeton University Press, 1973.

Schwarzbach, Bertram Eugene. "Nicolas-Sylvestre Bergier: Historien révisioniste de Judaisme" (A Revisionist Historian of Judaism). In *La république des lettres et l'histoire de Judaisme antique, XVIe–XVIII siècles*, edited by C. Grell, Paris: Presses de l'Universite Paris-Sorbonne, 1992. [French original]

Segrè, Cesare, and Sara Ferrari, eds. *Forte come la morte è l'amore: Tremila anni di poesia d'amore ebraica* (Strong like the Death and Love: Three Thousand Years of Hebrew Love Poetry). Livorno: Belforte, 2007. [Italian and Hebrew original]

Seitz, Christopher R. "Account A and the Annals of Sennacherib." *Journal of the Study of the Old Testament (JSOD)* 58 (1993).

Shea, Christopher. "The Nature-Nurture Debate, Redux: Genetic Research Finally Makes Its Way into the Thinking of Sociologists." *The Chronicle of Higher Education: The Chronicle Review*, September 1, 2009.

Shterenshis, Michael. *Tamerlane and the Jews*. London: Routledge, 2002.

Silverstein, Adam. "From Markets to Marvels: Jews on the Maritime Route to China ca. 850-ca. 950 CE." *Journal of Jewish Studies* LVIII, no. 1 (2007): 91-104.

Simes, Dimitri. "Losing Russia: The Costs of Renewed Confrontation." *Foreign Affairs* (2007): 36-52.

Singer, D., and D. Grossman, eds. *American Jewish Yearbook*. New York: AJC, 2008.

Sivan, Emmanuel. *Mythes Politiques Arabes (Arab Political Mythmaking)*. Paris: Fayard, 1995. [Hebrew original]

Slezkine, Yuri. *The Jewish Century*. New York: Princeton University Press, 2004.

Sofer, Moshe Ben Shmuel. *Responsa of the Chasam Sofer*. Bratislava, 1841. [Hebrew original]

Solomon, Norman. "The Ethics of War: Judaism." In *The Ethics of War: Shared Problems in Different Traditions*, edited by Richard Sorabji and David Rodin, Hampshire: Ashgate Publisher, 2006.

Soloveitchik, Haym. "Rupture and Reconstruction: The Transformation of Contemporary Orthodoxy." In *Jews in America: A Contemporary Reader*, edited by Roberta R. Farber and Chaim I. Waxman, Hanover and London: University Press of New England for Brandeis University Press, 1999.

Soloveitchik, Joseph B. *Fate and Destiny: From the Holocaust to the State of Israel*. Hoboken, NJ: Ktav, 1992.

Sombart, Werner. *Die Juden und das Wirtschaftsleben* (The Jews and the Economy). Leipzig: Duncker und Humblot, 1911. [German original]

Sorabji, Richard, and David Rodin, eds. *The Ethics of War: Shared Problems in Different Traditions*. Hampshire: Ashgate Publishers, 2006.

Sorokin, Pitirim Aleksandrovič. *Social and Cultural Dynamics: A Study of Change in Major Systems of Art, Truth, Ethics, Law and Social Relationships*, 4 vols. 1937-1941; rev. and abridged in 1 vol. by the author. Boston: Transaction Publishers, 1957.

Spengler, Oswald. *Der Untergang des Abendlandes: Umrisse einer Morphologie der Weltgeschichte* (The Decline of the Occident: A Morphology of World History). 1922, 16. Ausg. München: Deutscher Taschenbuch Verlag, 2003. [German original]

Spinoza, Benedictus de. *Spinoza: Complete Works*. Translated by S. Shirley. Edited by M. L. Morgan. Indianapolis: Hackett, 2002. [Latin original]

------. "Ethics." In *Spinoza: Complete Works*, translated by S. Shirley, edited by M. L. Morgan. Indianapolis: Hackett, 2002. [Latin original]

------. "Theological-Political Treatise." In *Spinoza: Complete Works*, translated by S. Shirley, edited by M. L. Morgan. Indianapolis: Hackett, 2002. [Latin original]

Spiro, Ken. *WorldPerfect: The Jewish Impact on Civilization*. Deerfield Beech/Florida: Simcha Press, 2002.

Ssu-ma Ch'ien [Sima Qian, Se-Ma Ts'ien]. *Records of the Grand Historian of China, vol. I: Early Years of the Han Dynasty 209 to 141 B.C.* Translated from the Shih chi of Ssu-ma Ch'ien by Burton Watson. New York: Columbia University Press, 1961. [Chinese original]

------. *Les Mémoires Historiques de Se-Ma Ts'ien*. Trad. et annotés par Edouard Chavannes, 6 vols., 1895-1905. New print: Paris: Librairie d'Amérique et d'Orient Adrien Maisonneuve, 1967. [Chinese original]

------. *Records of the Grand Historian*. Han Dynasty II. Translated by Burton Watson. Rev. ed. Hong Kong: Renditions Press, 1993. [Chinese original]

Steiner, George. *My Unwritten Books*. New York: New Directions Publishing, 2008.

Steinsalz, Adin. *We Jews: Who Are We and What Should We Do?* San Francisco: Jossey-Bass, 2005.

Stern, Menahem. "The Period of the Second Temple." In *A History of the Jewish People*, edited by Ben-Sasson. Cambridge: Weidenfeld & Nicolson, 1976.

Stern, Selma. *Josel von Rosheim: Befehlshaber der Judenschaft im Heiligen Römischen Reich Deutscher Nation* (Commander of Jewry in the Holy Roman Empire of German Nation). Stuttgart: Deutsche Verlags-Anstalt, 1959. [German original]

------. *L'Avocat des Juifs: Les tribulations de Yossel de Rosheim dans l'Europe de Charles Quint* (Attorney of the Jews: The Tribulations of Yossel of Rosheim in the Europe of Charles Quint). Edited by F. Raphaël and M. Ebstein. Strasbourg: La Nuée bleue, 2008. [German original]

Stewart, Matthew. *The Courtier and the Heretic: Leibniz, Spinoza and the Fate of God in the Modern World*. New York: W.W. Norton, 2006.

Strassler, R., R. Thomas, and A. Purvis, eds. *The Landmark Herodotus: The Histories*. New York: Pantheon, 2007.

Sun Tzu. *The Art of War*. Translated by Thomas Cleary. Boston: Shambhala, 1991. [Chinese original]

Tadmor, H. "The Period of the First Temple, the Babylonian Exile and the Restoration." In *A History of the Jewish People*, edited by Ben-Sasson. Cambridge: Weidenfeld & Nicolson, 1976.

Tainter, Joseph A. *The Collapse of Complex Societies*. Cambridge: Cambridge University Press, 1988.

Thomas, Mark G., Karl Skorecki, Haim Ben-Ami, et al. "Origins of Old Testament priests." *Nature* 394 (1998): 138-40.

Thorstein, Veblen. "The Intellectual Pre-Eminence of Jews in Modern Europe." *Political Science Quarterly* 34, no. 1 (1919): 33-42.

Thucydides, *History of the Peloponnesian War*. Translated by R. Warner. London: Penguin Books, 1972. [Greek original]

------. *Hobbes' Thucydides*. Edited by R. Schlatter. New Brunswick, 1975. [Greek original]

Thukydides. *Geschichte des Peloponnesischen Krieges* (History of the Peloponnesian War). Translated by G. P. Landmann. Zürich, 1960. [Greek original]

Toch, Michael. *Juden im mittelalterlichen Reich* (Jews in the Medieval Empire). München: R. Oldenbourg, 1999.

Toynbee, Arnold. *A Study of History*, 12 vols. London and New York: Oxford University Press, 1934-1961.

Trigano, Shmuel. *L'Avenir des Juifs de France* (The Future of the Jews in France). Paris: Grasset, 2006. [French original]

Trotsky, Leon. "On the 'Jewish Problem.'" *Class Struggle* 4, no. 2 (February 1934), available at The Albert and Vera Weisbrod Internet Archives, www.weisbord.org.

Tuchman, Barbara. *Bible and Sword: How the British Came to Palestine*. London: Macmillan, 1957.

------. *The Zimmermann Telegram*. New York: Ballantine Books, 1958.

Turchin, Peter. *Historical Dynamics: Why States Rise and Fall*. Princeton and Oxford: Princeton University Press, 2003.

Tylor, Edward Burnett. *Primitive Culture: Researches into the Development of Mythology, Philosophy, Religion, Art, and Custom*. Cambridge: J. Murray, 1871.

Unz, Ron, "The Myth of American Meritocracy: How Corrupt are Ivy League Admissions?", *The American Conservative*, November 28, 2012.

Urbach, Ephraim E. *The Sages, Their Concepts and Beliefs*, 2 vols. Translated by Israel Abrahams. Jerusalem: Magnes Press, 1975. [Hebrew original]

------. *The Halakhah, Its Sources and Development*. Translated by Raphael Posner. Ben Sheman: Modan, 1986. [Hebrew original]

Vana, Liliane. "La birkat ha-minim est-elle une prière contre les Judéo-Chrétiens?" (Is the birkat ha-minim a prayer against Judeo-Christians?) In *Les Communautés réligieuses dans le monde Gréco-Romain: Essai de définition*, edited by N. Belayche et al. Turnhout: Brepols, 2003. [French original]

Vasari, Giorgio. *Vies des artistes: Vies des plus excellents peintres, sculpteurs et architects (Life of the Artists: Lives of the Most Excellent Painters, Sculptors and Architects)*. Trad. L. Leclanché et Ch. Weiss. Paris: Grasset, 2007. [Italian original]

Verband der Deutschen, Juden, ed. *Soziale Ethik im Judentum (Social Ethics in Judaism)*. Frankfurt am Main: J. Kauffmann, 1914.

Vico, Giambattista. *New Science: Principles of the New Science Concerning the Common Nature of Nations*. 3rd ed., 1744. Translated by D. Marsh. New York: Penguin, 2001. [Italian original]

Voltaire. "Sermon des cinquante" (1752). In *Mélanges*, Paris: Gallimard, 1961. [French original]

------. *Essai sur les moeurs et l'esprit des nations* (An Essay about National Customs and Mentalities) (1756). Edited by R. Pomeau. Paris: Garnier, impr., 1963. [French original]

Volkman, Ernst. *Science Goes to War: The Search for the Ultimate Weapon, from Greek Fire to Star Wars*. New York: Wiley, 2002.

Wald, Shalom Salomon. *Geschichte und Gegenwart im Denken Alfred Webers: Ein Versuch über seine soziologischen und universalhistorischen Gesichtspunkte* (History and the Present in the Reflexion of Alfred Weber: An Essay about his Historical and Sociological Perspectives). Zürich: Polygraphischer Verlag, 1964. [German original]

------. *China and the Jewish People: Old Civilizations in a New Era*. Jerusalem and New York: Gefen Publishing House Ltd, 2004.

------. "'Studies on the Confucianisation of the Kaifeng Jewish Community': A Critical Commentary." *Journal of Jewish Studies* 62, no. 2 (Autumn 2006).

------. "Chinese Jews in European Thought." In *Youtai: Presence and Perception of Jews and Judaism in China*, edited by Peter Kupfer. Frankfurt am Main: Peter Lang, 2008.

Ward-Perkins, Bryan. *The Fall of Rome and the End of Civilization*. New York: Oxford University Press, 2005.

Warhaftig, Zorach. *Refugee and Remnant: Rescue Efforts during the Holocaust*. Jerusalem: Yad Va'Shem, 1984. [Hebrew original]

Watson, Burton. *Ssu-ma Ch'ien, Grand Historian of China*. New York: Columbia University Press, 1958.

Weber, Alfred. *Kulturgeschichte als Kultursoziologie* (History of Culture as Sociology of Culture). München: Piper, 1951. [German original]

Weber, Max. *Die Wirtschaftsethik der Weltreligionen* (The Economic Ethics of World Religions). Teil 1: *Konfuzianismus und Taoismus*; Bd. 2, Teil 2: *Hinduismus und Buddhismus*; Bd. 3, Teil 3: *Das Antike Judentum*, 4. Aufl. Tübingen: J.C.B. Mohr, 1947.

------. *Gesammelte Aufsätze zur Religionssoziologie*, Bd. 1: *Die Protestantische Ethik und der Geist des Kapitalismus* (Collected Essays on the Sociology of Religion). Edited by Dirk Kaesler. München: Verlag C.H. Beck, 2006. [German original]

Weiser, R., and R. Plesser, eds. *Treasures Revealed: From the Collections of the Jewish National and University Library in Honor of the 75th Anniversary of the Hebrew University of Jerusalem 1925-2000*. Jerusalem: R. Plesser, 2000.

Weizmann, Chaim. *Trial and Error: The Autobiography of Chaim Weizmann.* Westport, CT: Greenwood Publishing Group, 1972.

Wellhausen, Julius. *Geschichte Israels* (Prolegomena about the History of Israel). Berlin: Reimer, 1878 ff. [German original]

Westenholz, J. Goodnick, ed. *The Jewish Presence in Ancient Rome.* Jerusalem: Bible Lands Museum, 1994.

Wildavsky, Aaron. *Moses as Political Leader.* Jerusalem: Shalem Press, 2005.

Wilson, David Sloan, and Edward O. Wilson. "Survival of the Selfless." *New Scientist,* November 3, 2007.

Wisse, Ruth R. *Jews and Power.* New York: Knopf Group, 2008.

Wolfe, Irving. "Velikovsky and Catastrophism: A Hidden Agenda?" In *The Interaction of Scientific and Jewish Cultures in Modern Times,* edited by. Yaakov Rabkin and Ira Robinson. New York: Edwin Mellen Press, 1995.

Wouk, Herman.*The Language God Talks: On Science and Religion.* New York: Little Brown, 2010.

Yassif, Eli. "The 'Other' Israel." In *Cultures of the Jews: A New History,* edited by David Biale, New York: Schocken 2002.

Yehuda, Rachel, W. Blair, E. Labinsky, and L.M. Bierer. "Effects of Parental PTSD on the Cortisal Response to Dexamethasone Administration in Their Adult Offspring." *American Journal of Psychiatry* 164, no. 1 (Jan. 2007).

Yerushalmi, Yoseph Hayim. *Zakhor: Jewish History and Jewish Memory.* Seattle and London: University of Washington Press, 1996.

Zerubavel, Yael. *Recovered Roots: Collective Memory and the Making of Israeli National Tradition.* Chicago and London: University Of Chicago Press, 1997.

Zhang Ligang. "The Understanding and Attitude of Chinese Society Towards the Kaifeng Jews." In *Youtai: Presence and Perception of Jews and Judaism in China,* edited by Peter Kupfer. Frankfurt am Main: Peter Lang, 2008.

Zlotogora, Joel, Gideon Bach, and Arnold Munnich. "Molecular Basis of Mendelian Disorders among Jews." *Molecular Genetics and Metabolism* 69, no. 3 (2000): 169-80.

Zobel, Moritz. *Gottes Gesalbter: Der Messias und die Messianische Zeit in Talmud und Midrasch* (God's Anointed: The Messiah and Messianic Times in Talmud and Midrash). Berlin: Im Schocken Verlag/Judischer Buchverlag, 1938. [German original]

Notes

Introduction:
A THOUGHT EXPERIMENT

1 The Jewish People Policy Planning Institute Annual Assessment 2004-2005, *The Jewish People between Thriving and Decline* (Jerusalem: JPPI, 2005), and other publications. See www.jppi.org.il.

2 David Gans, *Tsemah David* (Offspring of David) (Jerusalem: Magnes, 1983; first printing Prague, 1592).

3 Heinrich Graetz, *Geschichte der Juden von den ältesten Zeiten bis auf die Gegenwart, 1853-75 (History of the Jews from the Earliest Times to the Present, 1853-75)*, 11 vols. (Leipzig: Leiner, 1902), and Heinrich Graetz, *Volkstümliche Geschichte der Juden (Popular History of the Jews)*, 3 vols. (Berlin-Wien: B. Harz, 1923).

4 Simon Dubnow, *Weltgeschichte des jüdischen Volkes, von seinen Uranfängen bis zur Gegenwart (World History of the Jewish People from the Earliest Beginnings to the Present)*, 10 vols. (Berlin: Jüdischer Verlag, 1925), and Simon Dubnow, *Jewish History: An Essay in the Philosophy of History* (Honolulu: University Press of the Pacific, 2003, reprint of 1903 edition).

PART I

Introduction

1 Sergio DellaPergola, *Word Jewry beyond 2000: The Demographic Prospects* (Oxford: Centre for Hebrew and Jewish Studies 1999), 9 ff. See also DellaPergola, "World Jewish Population 2008," in *American Jewish Yearbook 2008*, ed. D. Singer and D. Grossman (New York: AJC, 2008), 569-620. This article includes a critical review of other, variant demographic calculations that try to prove that the total number of Jews, particularly in the United States, is larger than generally indicated. Also see JPPI's 2011-12 *Annual Assessment* (Executive Report No. 8), (Jerusalem: JPPI, 2012).

Chapter 1:
CIVILIZATION OR CULTURE?

1 Mordecai M. Kaplan, *Judaism as a Civilization: Toward a Reconstruction of American Jewish Life* (Philadelphia/Jerusalem: Jewish Publication Society of America, 1994).

2 Kaplan, 178, 179.

3 S.N. Eisenstadt, *Jewish Civilization: The Jewish Historical Experience in a Comparative Perspective* (New York: Suny Press, 1992) 5.

4   Ami Buganim, *Jewish Peoplehood in an Age of Globalization* (Jerusalem: Jewish Agency for Israel, 2007). Hebrew.

5   "Peoplehood" does not currently exist in the English vocabulary and cannot be translated into French, German, or Italian, among other languages. The term an observer chooses for the Jews reveals his agenda. Those who want to strengthen communalities and solidarity between Jews invoke their "Jewish peoplehood" because this also emphasizes the singularity of the Jews. In fact, no other people or civilization calls itself a "peoplehood." Those who want to better understand the history and the present of the Jews call them a civilization, in order to make them analytically comparable to other civilizations and thus make their salient characteristics better visible.

6   Samuel P. Huntington, *The Clash of Civilizations and the Remaking of World Order*, (London: Simon & Schuster, 1998), 28.

7   On the origin of the Western term "civilization" see Norbert Elias, *The Civilising Process*, rev. edition (Oxford: Basil Blackwell, 1994); Fernand Braudel, *Ecrits sur l'histoire* (Paris: Flammarion, 1969), 258ff.; and David N. Myers, "Discourses of Civilisation: The Shifting Course of a Modern Jewish Motive," in *The Jewish Contribution to Civilization: Reassessing an Idea*, ed. Jeremy Cohen and Michael I. Cohen (Oxford: Littman Library of Jewish Civilization, 2008), 25ff.

8   See on definitions Fernand Braudel, *Grammaire des civilisations* (*Grammar of Civilizations*) (Paris: Flammarion, 1993) 40 ff., and Braudel, *Écrits sur l'histoire* (*Historic Writings*) I, (Paris: Flammarion, 1969), 256 ff.

9   The English anthropologist Edward Tylor published in 1871 his influential *"Primitive Culture"* and wrote that culture includes "knowledge, beliefs, art, morals, law, custom and any other capabilities and habits acquired by man as a member of society." The equally famous Melanesia expert Bronislaw Malinowski defined culture as "artefacts, goods, technical processes, ideas, habits, values," which includes every imaginable component of civilization. See Peter Burke, *What is Cultural History?* (Cambridge: John Wiley & Sons, 2004), 29.

10 David Biale, ed., *Cultures of the Jews: A New History* (New York: Schocken, 2002).

11 David N. Myers, 35.

12 Numbers 32:14.

13 See Marcus Jastrow, *Dictionary of the Targumim, the Talmud Babli and Yerushalmi, and the Midrashic Literature*.

14 Ahad Haam usually used the Hebrew expression *ben tarbut*, "a cultured person," in the broad German sense of "a civilized person."

15 Biale, *Cultures*, XVII.

Chapter 2:
AT THE CROSSROADS: THE TROUBLE WITH "RISING," "THRIVING," AND "DECLINING"

1   Jonathan I. Israel, *The Dutch Republic: Its Rise, Greatness and Fall, 1477-1806* (Oxford: Clarendon Press, 1995; paperback with corrections, 1998).

2   Bryan Ward-Perkins, *The Fall of Rome and the End of Civilization* (New York: Oxford University Press, 2005).

3   He called it an "optical illusion." See Marshall G.S. Hodgson, *The Venture of Islam* (Chicago-London: University of Chicago Press, 1974), 2, 380. The term "distortion" is more appropriate because "optical illusion" refers to the image of something that does not exist.

4   Arnold Toynbee, *A Study of History* (London: Oxford University Press, 1934-1961), I, 37.
5   Edward Gibbon, *The History of the Decline and Fall of the Roman Empire*, 1776-1787, 3 vols., ed. J.B. Bury (New York: The Heritage Press, 1946).
6   Jacob Burckhardt, *Die Kultur der Renaissance in Italien* (The Culture of the Renaissance in Italy), ed. W. von Bode (Berlin: Th. Knaur, 1928), 1 ff.
7   Huizinga, Johan, *Herbst des Mittelalters: Studien über Lebens- und Geistesformen des 14. und 15. Jahrhunderts in Frankreich und in der Niederlanden* (Autumn of the Middle Ages: A Study of the Forms of Life and Thought in 14th and 15th Century, France and the Netherlands), ed. K. Köster, 7th ed. (Stuttgart: Alfred Kroner Verlag, 1953), translated into German from the Dutch *Herfstij der middeleeuwen* (Leiden, 1923).

Chapter 3:
A SELECTION OF HISTORIANS: THREE CATEGORIES

1   I Samuel 28:14-19.
2   Thukydides, *Geschichte des Peloponnesischen Krieges*, trans. G.P. Landmann (Zürich-Stuttgart, 1960).
3   Ibn Khaldun, *The Muqaddimah: An Introduction to History* (1381), trans. Franz Rosenthal, complete ed. in 3 vols. (Princeton: Princeton University Press, 1958).

Chapter 4:
ON PHILOSOPHY OF HISTORY

1   Mircea Eliade, *Le mythe de l'éternel retour* (The Myth of Eternal Return) (Paris: Gallimard, 1969), 121 ff.
2   The following analysis is partly based on Michael E. Meyer, ed., *Ideas of Jewish History* (Detroit: Wayne State University Press, 1974), particularly the Introduction, and Yoseph Hayim Yerushalmi, *Zakhor: Jewish History and Jewish Memory* (Seattle and London: University of Washington Press, 1996).
3   Rashi and Ramban on Genesis 26:5, based on Babylonian Talmud Yoma 28a.
4   Mishnah Abot 1:1.
5   Abraham Ibn Daud, *Sefer Ha-Qabbalah* (*The Book of Tradition*), Critical Edition with a Translation and Notes, by Gerson D. Cohen (Philadelphia: Jewish Publication Society, 1967).
6   S.M. Dubnow, *Jewish History: An Essay in the Philosophy of History* (Honolulu-Hawaii: University Press of the Pacific, 2003, reprinted from the 1903 edition), 177.
7   Nachman Krochmal, "Guide for the Perplexed of Our Time," in *Ideas of Jewish History*.
8   Karl Jaspers, *Vom Ursprung und Ziel der Geschichte* (*On Origin and Goal of History*) (Frankfurt am Main and Hamburg: Fischer Bücherei, 1955).
9   Jaspers, 14.

Chapter 5:
OBSTACLES TO FORESIGHT

1   Paul Kennedy, *The Rise and Fall of the Great Powers: Economic Change and Military Conflict from 1500 to 2000* (New York: Random House 1987), 389, 515, 521, 527, 531.
2   Arnold Toynbee, *A Study of History*, IX, 518.
3   Jacob Burckhardt, *Die Kultur der Renaissance in Italien* (The Culture of the Renaissance in Italy).

4   Fernand Braudel, *Grammaire des civilisations* (Grammar of Civilizations), and Fernand Braudel, *Écrits sur l'histoire* (Historic Writings), I, II.

5   Many of his predictions are in VIII, IX, and X of his work *A Study of History*, 1954. Among the more quirky forecasts are that there will be a growing militarisation of the peasantry all across the non-Western world, and that countries such as Egypt and India will emerge as great military powers because of their large numbers of peasants. See IX, 503 ff.

6   Babylonian Talmud Shabbat 156a.

7   Toynbee, XII, 478, 569.

PART II
Chapter 1:
THUCYDIDES

1   *Hobbes' Thucydides* (New Brunswick: R. Schlatter, 1975); Thukydides, *Geschichte des Peloponnesischen Krieges*, trans. Georg Peter Landmann (Zürich-Stuttgart: Artemis Verlag, 1960); Thucydides, *History of the Peloponnesian War*, trans. Rex Warner (London: Penguin Books, 1972). Quotes marked "Landmann" are re-translations from Landmann's German, which is very near to the Greek original, made by the author in consultation with Warner's English text. The figures in brackets refer to the chapters in Thucydides' Greek text.

2   Landmann, 12.

3   Ibid., 36.

4   Ibid., 23 (I 1).

5   Toynbee, I, 53, note 4.

6   Landmann, 139-147 (II, 35-46).

7   Ibid., 141 (II, 39).

8   Gibbon, Edward, *The History of the Decline and Fall of the Roman Empire*.

9   Landmann 107 (I, 138).

10 This and the following quotes Landmann, 161-2, (II, 65).

11 Landmann, 454 (VI, 15).

12 Jacqueline de Romilly, *Alcibiade* (*Alcibiades*) (Paris: Livre de Poche, 1995).

13 Landmann, *Introduction,* 16.

14 Ibid., 250 (III, 82)

15 Ibid., 433 (V, 90)

16 *Hobbes' Thucydides*, 7.

Chapter 2:
SIMA QIAN

1   *Les Mémoires Historiques de Se-Ma Ts'ien* (The Historic Memoirs of Se Ma-Ts'ien) trad. et annotés par Edouard Chavannes, 6 vols. (Paris: Librairie d'Amerique ed d'Orient Adrien Maisonneuve, 1895-1905; new print, 1967) (this is the most complete translation existing in a Western language); *Records of the Grand Historian of China, Vol. I: Early Years of the Han Dynasty 209 to 141 B.C.*, trans. from the *Shih chi* of Ssu-ma Ch'ien by Burton Watson (New York: Columbia University Press, 1961); Sima Qian, *Records of the Grand Historian of China, Vol. II: Han Dynasty II*, trans. Burton Watson, (Hong Kong: Renditions Press, 1993). (This volume covers Sima Qian's own time. All references to "Sima" without other details refer to this book); *Biography of Sima Qian*, www.reference.com/browse/wiki/Sima_Qian (4.8.2006), drafted mainly by Chinese scholars;

and *Emperor Wu of Han*, www.en.wikipedia.org/wiki/Emperor_Wu_of_Han (2.12.2007), an extensive and detailed biography also drafted mainly by Chinese scholars.

This biography of Sima Qian has been reviewed by Prof. Zhang Qianhong, vice president of the University of Zhengzhou, Henan, professor and director at the Institute of Jewish Studies at Henan University in Kaifeng, China, Prof. Irene Eber of the Hebrew University of Jerusalem, and Philip Wang from the Chinese Academy of Sciences (CAS), Beijing.

2   K. Fairbank and M. Goldman wondered whether later historians did not underestimate the "transcendental role" of the Chinese emperor. The Son of Heaven granted life and death like a divinity. See John King Fairbank and Merle Goldman, *China: A New History,* enlarged edition (Cambridge, MA: Belknap Press, 1998) 69.

3   Early Chinese historians after Sima Qian did not contradict his criticism, which has been taken as a sign of approval. The current popular Chinese view of Wudi is full of admiration. Sima Qian's French translator E. Chavannes (1895) calls Wu's reign "marvelous," "happy," and "glorious"; his American translator B.Watson (1961, 1993) calls it "somber."

4   Sima, 162.

5   Tong Shijun, "Preface II: To Our Common Ideal," in *The Jews in Asia: Comparative Perspectives,* CJSS Jewish & Israeli Studies Series Vol. I, ed. Pan Guang (Shanghai: Shanghai Joint Publishing Co., 2007).

6   Sima, 3. B.Watson emphasizes the great importance of the "Mandate of Heaven" for the Han period; see Burton Watson, *Ssu-ma Ch'ien, Grand Historian of China,* 45.

7   Sima, 303.

8   Sima, 224 and footnote 3.

9   Sima, 6.

10   Sima, 84.

11   *Records,* I, 150.

12   Sima, 162.

13   *Records,* I, 398.

14   Sima, 309.

15   Sima, 191.

16   Confucius, *Analects* 13:13: "He who cannot govern himself, how can he deal with the government of others?"

17   *Records,* I, 77.

18   Sima, 193.

19   Sima, 292.

20   *Records* I, 375.

21   Sima, 373 ff., 379 ff.

22   Sima, 328.

23   Sima, 312. Not surprisingly, this official ended his career in a remote province where he complained bitterly that he had been excluded from the deliberations of the court.

24   Ibid., 60.

25   Ibid., 434, 437.

26   Ibid., 453 f.

27   Ibid., 312.

28   Ibid., 231.

29   Ibid., 224

30   Ibid., 124

31   *Records,* I, 207.

32   Sima, 206.

Chapter 3:
IBN KHALDUN

1 Ibn Khaldun, *The Muqaddimah: An Introduction to History,* reduced ed. in 1 vol., ed. N.J. Dawood (Princeton: Princeton University Press, 1967). The page numbers following "Ibn Khaldun" refer to Dawood's edition. When they are preceded by I, II, or III they refer to Rosenthal's edition.

2 Michael Shterenshis, *Tamerlane and the Jews* (London: Routledge 2002) 47. We do not know what these different views were, but we do know that Timur did not advance to capture Jerusalem, which would have presented no military problem for his army.

3 Ibn Khaldun, 5.

4 Ibid., 59, 117.

5 Ibid., 188.

6 Ibid., quoted on the back of the book.

7 Ibid., 98.

8 Lee Alan Dugatkin, *The Altruism Equation: Seven Scientists Search for the Origins of Goodness* (Princeton: Princeton University Press, 2006).

9 Ibn Khaldun, 47.

10 Ibid., 25

11 Ibid., 153

12 Ibid., 183

13 Ibid., 298

14 Edgar Salin, *Politische Ökonomie—Geschichte der Witschaftspolitischen Ideen von Platon bis zur Gegenwart* (Political Economy: History of Economic Policy Ideas from Platon to the Present), 5th ed. (Tübingen: Mohr Siebeck, 1967)

15 Ibn Khaldun, 223.

16 Ibid., 229, 253.

17 Ibid., 213.

18 Ibid., 397, 405, 409.

19 Ibid., 414 f., 424, 426.

20 Ibid., 341.

21 Ibid., 285.

22 Ibid., 106, 136.

23 Ibid., 238-242.

24 Ibid., 30.

25 Ibid., 375.

26 Ibid., 428.

27 Rosenthal I, 473-478.

28 Ibid., I, 20.

29 Rosenthal, II, 481, footnote 13; I,.275.

30 Rosenthal, III, 306.

Chapter 4:
EDWARD GIBBON

1 Edward Gibbon. *The History of the Decline and Fall of the Roman Empire,* 1776-1787, in three volumes and seventy-one chapters, ed. J.B. Bury (New York: The Heritage Press, 1946). In this edition, the numbering is continuous through all three volumes.

2 Gibbon, 2441.

3 Ibid., 2426 ff.

4 Ibid., 1218 ff.

5   Ibid., 2442.
6   Ibid., 2442.
7   Ibid., 248.
8   Ibid., 964.
9   Ibid., 345.
10   Ibid., 1218.
11   Ibid., 1605.
12   Ibid., 1219.
13   Ibid., 1220.
14   Ibid., 152.
15   Ibid., 1221.
16   Ibid., 1221.
17   Ibid., 1221.
18   Ibid., 2432.
19   Ibid., 2431.
20   Ibid., 43.
21   Ibid., 801 ff.
22   Ibid., 792.
23   Ibid., 2428 ff.
24   Ibid., 2441 f.
25   On Sallust and Livy, see John Burrow, *A History of Histories: Epics, Chronicles, Romances, and Inquiries from Herodotus and Thucydides to the Twentieth Century* (London: Penguin Adult, 2007), 83-116.
26   "Selections from the Discourses," *The Essential Writings of Machiavelli*, ed. Peter Constantine (New York: The Modern Library 2007), 101 ff.

Chapter 5:
JACOB BURCKHARDT

1   Jacob Burckhardt, *Die Zeit Constantins des Grossen* (The Time of Constantine the Great) (Frankfurt: G.B. Fischer, 1954); W. von Bode, ed., *Die Kultur der Renaissance in Italien* (The Culture of the Renaissance in Italy) (Berlin: Th. Knaur, 1928); W. Kaegi, ed., *Weltgeschichtliche Betrachtungen* (Reflections on World History) (Bern: Hallwag, 1947); *Jacob Burckhardt's Briefe an seinen Freund Friedrich von Preen 1864-1893* (J.B.'s Letters to his Friend F.v.P.) (Berlin/Stuttgart: Deutsche Verlags-Anstalt, 1922). English quotations are translations from the German original by the author.
2   Burckhardt, *Reflections*, 57.
3   Peter Burke, 101 f.
4   This is why Burckhardt's English translators who rendered the German title *Die Kultur der Renaissance*...as "The Civilization of the Renaissance..." were substantially correct.
5   Burckhardt, *Renaissance*, 3.
6   Burckhardt, *Constantin*, 158.
7   Burckhardt, *Renaissance*, 458.
8   Burckhardt, *Constantin*, 18.
9   Burckhardt, *Renaissance*, 102.
10   Burckhardt, *Constantin*, 7.
11   Braudel, *Écrits* I, 268 ff.
12   Burckhardt, *Reflections*, 149 ff., 166.
13   Burckhardt, *Constantin*, 289.

14   Burckhardt, *Reflections*, 316.
15   Burckhardt, *Renaissance*, 85.
16   Ibid., 283 ff.
17   Ibid., 69.
18   Burckhardt, *Letters*, 58, 137, 188, 224. More antisemitic comments have come to light from his student days, that is long before the antisemitic wave of late nineteenth-century Germany, from other letters and from the notebooks for his lectures.
19   Burckhardt, *Renaissance*, 354.
20   Giovanni Pico della Mirandola, *Oratio de hominis dignitate-De la dignité de l'homme* (A Speech about the Dignity of Man), transl. Yves Hersant (Paris: Ed. de l'Eclat, 2005). The translator, Hersant, refers to a commentary by Pico on Hiob which he asserts could only have come from the Midrash. See 22.
21   Burckhardt, *Renaissance*, 196.
22   Albert M. Debrunner, "Die antisemitischen Äusserungen Jacob Burckhardt's—Eine verdrängte Seite" (The Anti-Semitic Comments of Jacob Burckhardt: A Suppressed Aspect), in *Israelitisches Wochenblatt der Schweiz*, Nr.8, 20. Feb. 1998, 6 f. This is one of several articles on Burckhardt's hitherto hushed-up antisemitism.
23   Werner Kaegi, *Jacob Burckhardt: Eine Biographie*, 7 vols. (Basel: Schwabe, 1947-1982).
24   Debrunner, 7.

Chapter 6:
MAX WEBER

1   Max Weber, *Gesammelte Aufsätze zur Religionssoziologie*, Bd. 1: *Die Protestantische Ethik und der Geist des Kapitalismus* (The Protestant Ethics and the Spirit of Capitalism), ed. Dirk Kaesler (Munchen: Beck C. H.; Auflage: Vollständige Ausgabe., 2006). See also Max Weber, *Die Wirtschaftsethik der Weltreligionen* (The Economic Ethics of World Religions), Teil 1 *Konfuzianismus und Taoismus*; Bd. 2 Teil 2: *Hinduismus und Buddhismus*; Bd. 3 Teil 3: *Das Antike Judentum*, 4. Aufl. (Tübingen: J.C.B. Mohr, 1947). "Weber—Kaesler" refers to the latest and most complete edition of *Die Protestantische Ethik* of 2006. Translations into English are by the author.
2   Weber-Kaesler, 89 f.
3   Ibid., 98.
4   Ibid., 152. Weber's term is "innerweltlich," "inner-wordly."
5   Ibid., 78, 184.
6   Dirk Kaesler, who in 2004/2006 edited the latest, revised, and most complete version of the book, supports the "misunderstanding" theory but adds that Weber was himself partly to blame for it. In that case, maybe it was not a misunderstanding and Weber really meant what his readers understood? See Weber-Kaesler preface, 8 ff.
7   Weber-Kaesler, 79, 80, 94, 202.
8   Ibid., 202.
9   Max Weber, *Das Antike Judentum*, Potsdamer Internet Ausgabe (PIA), 6.

Chapter 7:
OSWALD SPENGLER

1   Oswald Spengler, *Der Untergang des Abendlandes—Umrisse einer Morphologie der Weltgeschichte* (The End of the West: A Morphology of World History) 1922 (München: Deutscher Taschenbuch Verlag, 2003). Translations into English by the author.
2   Toynbee, I, 135, footnote 2, and parallels.
3   Spengler, 3-4.

4   Ibid., 140.
5   Ibid., 36.
6   Ibid., 293 ff.
7   Ibid., 450; 681-2.
8   Ibid., 675.
9   Ibid., 552, 550.
10   Ibid., 942.
11   Ibid., 1098.
12   Ibid., 1100.
13   Ibid., 1140.
14   Giambattista Vico, *New Science: Principles of the New Science Concerning the Common Nature of Nations*, third ed. 1744, transl. D.Marsh (London: Penguin Classics, 2001), 395.
15   Vico, 483 f.
16   Spengler, 804-814; 948-960.
17   See Part IV, Chapter 2, for the different nuances of these two terms in German and English.
18   Spengler, 767.
19   Ibid., 951.
20   Ibid., 958.
21   Ibid., 812.

Chapter 8:
JOHAN HUIZINGA

1   Johan Huizinga, *Herbst des Mittelalters—Studien über Lebens- und Geistesformen des 14. und 15. Jahrhunderts in Frankreich und in den Niederlanden* (Autumn of the Middle Ages: A Study of the Forms of Life and Thought in Fourteenth- and Fifteenth-Century France and the Netherlands), ed. K. Köster, 7th edition (Stuttgart: Alfred Kröner Verlag, 1953), translated from the Dutch *Herfstij der middeleeuwen* (Leiden, 1923, with Huizinga's cooperation); Johan Huizinga, *Holländische Kultur im Siebzehnten Jahrhundert* (Dutch Culture in the Seventeenth Century), ed. W.Kaegi (Basel: B.Schwabe, 1961), first written in German in 1932 and published in Dutch by the author in 1941 *(Nederlands's beschaving in de zeventiende eeuw)*; *Homo Ludens* (Man at Play) (Leiden, 1938; German trans. H.Nachod, Reinbek-Hamburg: Rowohlt, 1956). English translations in the text are by the author.
2   John Burrow, *A History of Histories: Epics, Chronicles, Romances and Inquiries from Herodotus and Thucydides to the Twentieth Century* (London: Penguin Adult, 2007), 479.
3   Jonathan I. Israel, *The Dutch Republic: Its Rise, Greatness and Fall 1477-1806* (Oxford: Clarendon Press, 1995; paperback with corrections Oxford: Oxford University Press, 1998).
4   Huizinga, *Autumn*, 95. A similar polemic on 15.
5   Ibid., 143.
6   Ibid., 301. Many similar comments can be found on, 35, 67, 69, 290, 347.
7   There are several English translations of his book. Those written after World War II changed the title from *The Autumn* into *The Waning of the Middle Ages*, perhaps in an effort to respond to Huizinga's concern.
8   The term "beschaving" in the Dutch original would have better been translated as "civilization." It is a broader term than "culture," which is also used in Dutch. Huizinga's book in fact speaks of much more than art and poetry.
9   Huizinga, *Dutch Culture*, 78 f., 82 f.

10   Jonathan I. Israel, *The Dutch Republic: Its Rise, Greatness and Fall 1477-1806* (Oxford: Clarendon Press 1998), 73.
11   Israel, *Dutch Republic,* 405, 727 ff. and others.
12   Kurt Köster, "Foreword" to Huizinga, *Autumn,* IX.
13   Huizinga, *Dutch Culture,* 138, 140 f., 142 f. , 144.
14   Ibid., 70.

Chapter 9:
ARNOLD TOYNBEE

1   Arnold Toynbee, *A Study of History,* 12 volumes (London: Oxford University Press, 1934-1961).
2   Arthur Herman, *The Idea of Decline in Western History* (New York: Free Press, 1997), 282.
3   Toynbee, VI, 107, 111.
4   Toynbee, I, 235.
5   Ibid., 39.
6   Ibid., 147 ff.
7   Toynbee, III, 39.
8   Toynbee, II, 335.
9   Ibid., 259 ff.
10   Toynbee, III, 88 ff.
11   Ibid., 242.
12   Toynbee, IV, 129.
13   Toynbee, III, 245.
14   Toynbee, IV, 505.
15   Toynbee, V, 3.
16   Ibid., 480 ff.
17   Among many others, see "The Modern West and the Jews," VIII 272-313; "A Jewish Alternative Model for Civilisations," XII, 209-217; "Fossils," XII, 292-300; "Was There One Only, Or More Than One Civilisation, in Syria in the Last Millennium BC?," XII, 411-430; and "The History and Prospects of the Jews," XII, 477-517.
18   Toynbee, II, 286.
19   Toynbee, I, 246.
20   Toynbee XII, 215, 217, 414.
21   Ibid., 517.

Chapter 10:
PITIRIM SOROKIN

1   Pitirim Sorokin, *Social and Cultural Dynamics: A Study of Change in Major Systems of Art, Truth, Ethics, Law and Social Relationships.* Revised and abridged in one volume by the author (Boston: Transaction Publishers, 1957; Original edition in four volumes 1937-1941).
2   Sorokin, 256 ff.
3   Ibid., 8.
4   Ibid., 639.
5   Ibid., 633.
6   Ibid., 427.
7   Ibid., 703 ff.
8   Ibid., 622-628, 699-703.
9   Ibid., 702.

Chapter 11:
FERNAND BRAUDEL

1   Fernand Braudel, *Grammaire des civilisations* (Grammar of Civilizations) (Paris: Flammarion, 1993); Fernand Braudel, *Écrits sur l'histoire*, (Historic Writings), I, II (Paris: Flammarion 1969; Paris: Flammarion, 1994); and Fernand Braudel, *The Mediterranean and the Mediterranean World in the Age of Phillip II*, translated from French by Sian Reynolds (Suffolk/New York: Collins, 1982). See also Bernand Braudel, *Les Mémoires de la Méditerranée* (The Memoirs of the Mediterranean) (Paris: Bernard de Fallois, 1998). Except for *The Mediterranean* where the English version is used, the translations from French by Sian Reynolds and by the author.

2   *The Mediterranean and the Mediterranean World in the Age of Phillip II*; *Civilisation Matérielle, Economie et Capitalisme* (Material Civilization, Economy and Capitalism) (Paris: Armand Colin, 1979); and *L'Identité de la France* (The Identity of France) (Paris: Flammarion, 1986-9).

3   Braudel, *Écrits* II, 9, 15.

4   Braudel, *Grammaire*, 120.

5   Braudel, *Écrits* I 51.

6   "The Death of Phillip II, 13th September 1598," *The Mediterranean*, 1234 ff.

7   Braudel, *Écrits* I, 258-288.

8   Braudel, *Mémoires*, 332.

9   Ibid., 276.

10 Braudel, *Mediterranean*, II, 823.

11 Braudel, *Grammaire*, 456.

12 Ibid..

13 Ibid., 40.

14 Braudel, *Mémoires* 188.

15 Braudel, *Mediterranean* II 802-826.

16 Braudel, *Mediterranean* 804, 809, 826.

Chapter 12:
MARSHAL G.S. HODGSON

1   Marshall G.S. Hodgson, *The Venture of Islam: Conscience and History in a World Civilization. 1: The Classical Age of Islam. 2: The Expansion of Islam in the Middle Periods. 3: The Gunpowder Empires and Modern Times* (Chicago: University of Chicago Press, 1974).

2   Albert Hourani, *Islam in European Thought* (Cambridge: Cambridge University Press, 1991), chapter 3, 74 ff.

3   Hodgson, I, 30, 33.

4   Ibid., 71.

5   Hodgson, I, 233 ff.

6   Hodgson, III, 135 f.

7   Ibid., 136.

8   Braudel, *Grammaire*, 120.

9   Hodgson, I, 99.

10 Hodgson, III, 425 ff.

11 Ibid., 439.

12 Hodgson, I, 103.

13 Ibid., 177.

14 Hodgson, III, 439.

Chapter 13:
BERNARD LEWIS

1 Bernard Lewis, *The Emergence of Modern Turkey*, 3rd ed. (New York/Oxford: Oxford University Press 2002).
2 Lewis, 35.
3 Ibid., 23.
4 Gibbon, 248, and others.
5 Lewis, 32.
6 Ibid., 86 ff.
7 Ibid., 267.
8 Ibid., 327.
9 Bernard Lewis, *The Jews of Islam* (Princeton: Taylor & Francis, 1984), Foreword IX, and Bernard Lewis, "Palimpsests of Jewish History: Christian, Muslim and Secular Diaspora," in *From Babel to Dragomans: Interpreting the Middle East* (London: Oxford University Press, 2004), 53.
10 Lewis, 454.
11 Shalom Salomon Wald, "'Studies on the Confucianisation of the Kaifeng Jewish Community': A Critical Commentary," *Journal of Jewish Studies*, The Oxford Center for Hebrew and Jewish Studies, LVII, no. 2, Autumn 2006, 325.

Chapter 14:
JONATHAN I. ISRAEL

1 Jonathan I. Israel, *The Dutch Republic: Its Rise, Greatness and Fall 1477-1806* (Oxford: Clarendon Press, 1995; paperback with corrections, Oxford: Clarendon Press 1998). J.I. Israel, *European Jewry in the Age of Mercantilism 1550-1750*, 3rd. ed. (London: Littman Library of Jewish Civilization, 1998). J.I. Israel, *Radical Enlightenment: Philosophy and the Making of Modernity* (New York: Oxford University Press, 2002).
2 J. Israel does not argue with Braudel's belief in the primacy of socio-economic forces except once when a rare and unusually nasty remark reveals his irritation. He dismisses the thoughts of "Braudel on the subject of the Jews (as on so much else)...without more ado, as nonsense." *European Jewry*, 224.
3 Israel, *Dutch*, 169 f.
4 Ibid., 253.
5 Ibid., 241.
6 Ibid., 671 ff.
7 Ibid., 198, 577, 899 and others.
8 Ibid., 348.
9 Ibid., 350.
10 Ibid., 405.
11 Ibid., 727 ff.
12 Ibid., 798.
13 Ibid., 841 ff.

Chapter 15:
PAUL KENNEDY

1 Paul Kennedy, *The Rise and Fall of the Great Powers: Economic Change and Military Conflict from 1500 to 2000* (New York: Random House, 1987).
2 Daojiong Zha, "Can China Rise?," *Review of International Studies (RIS)*, Cambridge, 31, no. 4 (Oct. 2005).

3 Kennedy, XVI.
4 Ibid., 439.
5 Ibid., 513 f.

Chapter 16:
JARED DIAMOND

1 Jared Diamond, *Collapse: How Societies Choose to Fail or Succeed* (New York: Penguin Books, 2005).
2 Ibid., 119.
3 Ibid., 159.
4 Ibid., 341.

Chapter 17:
BRYAN WARD-PERKINS

1 Bryan Ward-Perkins, *The Fall of Rome and the End of Civilization* (New York: Oxford University Press, 2005).
2 Ibid., 4.
3 Ibid., 41.
4 Ibid., 57.
5 Ibid., 183.

Chapter 18:
MANCUR OLSON

1 Mancur Olson, *The Rise and Decline of Nations: Economic Growth, Stagflation and Social Rigidities* (New Haven/London: Yale University Press, 1982).

Chapter 19:
PETER TURCHIN

1 Peter Turchin, *Historical Dynamics: Why States Rise and Fall* (Princeton: Princeton University Press, 2003).
2 Ibn Khaldun, 98.

Chapter 20:
CHRISTOPHER CHASE-DUNN AND THOMAS D. HALL

1 Christopher Chase-Dunn and Thomas D.Hall, *Rise and Demise: Comparing World-Systems* (Boulder, CO: Westview Press, 1997).
2 Spengler, 3-4.
3 Chase-Dunn, 239.
4 Braudel, *Grammaire,* 45 ff. and parallels.

Chapter 21:
JOSEPH A. TAINTER

1 Joseph A. Tainter, *The Collapse of Complex Societies* (Cambridge: Cambridge University Press, 1988).

Chapter 22:
ARTHUR HERMAN

1 Arthur Herman, *The Idea of Decline in Western History* (New York: Free Press, 1997).
2 Herman, 13.
3 Ibid., 449.

PART III

Chapter 1:
"CHALLENGE-AND-RESPONSE"

1   Ibn Khaldun, 98.
2   Spengler, 140.
3   Toynbee, I 214.
4   Ibid., XII 255.
5   Dates and other details are from Haim H. Ben-Sasson, ed., *A History of the Jewish People* (Cambridge, MA: Weidenfeld & Nicholson, 1976), particularly Part II by H.Tadmor, "The Period of the First Temple, the Babylonian Exile and the Restoration," and Part III by M.Stern, "The Period of the Second Temple." Other dates as proposed by other historians are possible but would not change the basic arguments of this chapter.
6   One of them was the British Jewish physicist Joseph Rotblat, who later founded the "Pugwash" peace movement. He wanted to resign and did so later when he understood at the end of 1944 that Nazi Germany was not developing the bomb. He was willing to work on a nuclear bomb to defend against Nazi Germany, but not any other country.
7   Michael Karpin, *The Bomb in the Basement* (New York: Simon & Schuster, 2006), 287.
8   Eric Hobsbawm and Terence Ranger, *The Invention of Tradition* (Cambridge: Cambridge University Press, 1992) Introduction.

Chapter 2:
WINDOWS OF OPPORTUNITY

1   Hodgson, I 114, and III 176 ff.
2   A. Malamat, "Part I: Origins and the Formative Period," in *A History of the Jewish People* 21, 23, 25, 27; Alfred Weber, 100 ff., and others. One of the first proponents of this thesis was Julius Wellhausen, author of *Prolegomena zur Geschichte Israels (History of Israel)* (Germany: G. Reimer, 1878), and other works.
3   David Berger, "The 'Jewish Contribution' to Christianity," in *The Jewish Contribution to Civilization: Reassessing an Idea,* ed. Jeremy Cohen and Michael I. Cohen (Oxford: Littman Library of Jewish Civilization, 2008), 91.

Chapter 3:
GLOBAL UP- AND DOWNTURNS

1   Chase-Dunn, 149 ff.
2   Jaspers, 25-30.
3   Braudel, *Mediterranean,* 820.
4   Lewis, *Turkey,* 454.
5   Israel, *European Jewry,* 72 ff.

Chapter 4:
THRIVING CIVILIZATIONS,
OR THE MYTH OF A "GOLDEN AGE"

1   Hesiod, "Works and Days," in *Theogony, Works and Days, Testimonia,* ed. Glenn W. Most (Cambridge, MA: Harvard University Press, 2006), 97.
2   Burckhardt, *Renaissance,* 426.
3   Hodgson, I 233 ff.

4   Huizinga, *Dutch Culture*, 11.
5   J. Israel, *Dutch Republic*, 5.
6   Sima 84 and parallels.
7   I Kings 5:5.
8   Micah 4:4.
9   Amos 9:13.
10   The text of the Kiddush Levanah blessing is in Babylonian Talmud Sanhedrin 42a. For comparisons of the Jewish people's history with the moon's rise and decline, see Midrash Exodus Rabbah 15 and parallels.

Chapter 5:
CULTURAL ACCOMPLISHMENTS
OF THRIVING CIVILIZATIONS

1   Pitirim Sorokin in the sub-title of his book.
2   As an example of absurd data: The grand total of scientific discoveries between the years 3500 BCE and 1908 CE is given as exactly 12, 761, of which ca. 9000 were made after 1800. Sorokin, 278 f.
3   Charles Murray, *Human Accomplishment: The Pursuit of Excellence in the Arts and Sciences, 800 BC to 1950* (New York: Harper Perennial, 2004).
4   Sima, 41 ff., 259 ff., 355 ff.; Ibn Khaldun, 314 ff., 333 ff.; Burckhardt, *Renaissance*; Spengler, *Reflections*, 234 ff., 282 ff., 330 ff.; Huizinga, *Middle Ages*; Pitirim Sorokin, 256 ff.; Lewis, *Turkey*, 1 ff., 401 ff.; J. Israel, *Dutch Republic*, 41 ff., 328 ff., 547 ff., 863 ff.
5   Huizinga, *Middle Ages*, 285 and parallels.
6   Giorgio Vasari, *Vies des artistes—Vies des plus excellents peintres, sculpteurs et architectes* (Life of the Artists: The Life of the Most Excellent Painters, Sculptors and Architects), trad. L.Leclanché et Ch.Weiss (Paris: Grasset, 2007).
7   Vasari, 67, translation into English by the author.
8   Vasari, on Cimabue and Giotto 21, on Mantegna 162, on Michelangelo 353, 388.
9   Burckhardt, *Renaissance*, 197.
10   Kate Douglas, "The Other You: Meet the Unsung Hero of the Human Mind," *New Scientist*, 1st December 2007, 42 ff.
11   Vasari, 185. English translation from www.fordham.edu/halsall/basis/vasari/vasari-lives.html.
12   Yuri Slezkine, *The Jewish Century* (New York: Princeton University Press, 2004).
13   Josephus Flavius, "Against Apion," Book 2, 13 (135), *The New Complete Works of Josephus*, trans. W.Whiston, Paul E. Maier (Grand Rapids, MI: Kregel Publications 1999), 968.
14   Josephus, 978 f.
15   See *The Jewish Contribution*, 12, 18, 59, 154, 160, 185, 196, et al.
16   Cole translates two of her poems, "On Seeing Herself in the Mirror," and "Ah, Gazelle." Peter Cole, *The Dream of the Poem: Hebrew Poetry from Muslim and Christian Spain, 950-1492*, trans. and ed. Peter Cole (Princeton: Princeton University Press, 2007), 364.
17   Norman Golb, "Obadiah the Proselyte: Scribe of a Unique Twelfth-Century Manuscript Containing Lombardic 'Neumes'," *The Journal of Religion* 45, no. 2, April 1965, 153 ff.
18   Records of Obadiah's music are kept in the Diaspora Museum in Tel-Aviv and can be played there.

19   See J. Israel, *Enlightenment.* On Spinoza, 159-174, 230-241, 275-285.

20   *Burckhardt's Briefe,* 137.

21   Murray presents interesting data on Jewish scientific creativity, which will be used in Part IV 3.

22   H. Bloom, Foreword to Yosef Chaim Yerushalmi, *Zakhor: Jewish History and Jewish Memory* (Seattle and London: University of Washington Press, 1996), xxii.

23   Yeheskel Kaufmann, *Golah ve-Nekhar (Diaspora and Foreign Countries),* I (Tel Aviv: Dvir 1929), 166, 168-71, 204-207.

Chapter 6:
DECLINE HAS MULTIPLE CAUSES

1   Gibbon, 1219 f.

2   Spengler, 607.

3   Toynbee, IV 120.

4   Elias Bickerman, *From Ezra to the Last of the Maccabees: Foundations of Post-Biblical Judaism* (New York: Schocken Books, 1968), 3.

5   M. Stern, *Ben-Sasson,* 281.

6   Hannah Arendt, *Elemente und Ursprünge totaler Herrschaft* (Origins of Totalitarianism, 12. Aufl.) (München-Zürich: Piper, 2008), 31 ff. This is Ahrendt's own extended translation of the first American edition of her book, *The Origins of Totalitarianism.*

Chapter 7:
GLOBAL FUTURES: "END OF CIVILIZATION"
OR "DECLINE OF THE WEST"?

1   There is a Will Durant Foundation that continues to spread the optimism of the founder. Durant's deepest motives were religious. One of his last messages was, "Love one another: my final lesson of history is that of Jesus." www.en.wikiquote. org./wiki/Will_Durant.

2   Sorokin, 699.

3   Ibid., 701.

4   For example, Thomas Homer-Dixon, *The Upside of Down: Catastrophe, Creativity and the Renewal of Civilization* (Toronto: Knopf Canada, 2006), which predicts that the convergence of energy, environmental, and political crises might cause a breakdown of global order and argues that this breakdown can and should be turned into an opportunity for a bold reform of our civilization.

5   Gibbon, 1222.

6   Toynbee, IX 518 et al.

7   David Fromkin, *Europe's Last Summer: Who Started the Great War in 1914?* (New York: Vintage, 2005), 4.

8   Burckhardt, *Reflections,* 212 ff., 294 ff., 311.

9   Huizinga, *Autumn,* IXff.

10   Toynbee, IX 441 et al.

11   Max Weber, 201. Translation by the author.

12   Chase, 239.

13   Ward-Perkins, 183.

14   Braudel, *Grammaire,* 56.

15   Braudel, *Écrits,* II, 303 ff.

16   Spengler, 958, et al.

PART IV

Chapter 1:
RELIGION: IDENTITY SAFEGUARDS AND THEIR DOWNSIDES

1 Sima 3.
2 Ibn Khaldun, 375.
3 Gibbon, 1221.
4 Ibid., 528-737.
5 Burckhardt, *Constantin*, 289, 297.
6 Toynbee, IV, 538 580.
7 Toynbee, I, 465.
8 Spengler, 942.
9 Lewis, *Turkey*, 114 ff., 123 ff., 215 ff. and others.
10 Huizinga, *Dutch Culture*, 78 f., 82 f.
11 Israel, *Dutch Republic*, 73.
12 Robin Dunbar, "We Believe," in *New Scientist*, 28.1.2006. Dunbar is a biologist and anthropologist.
13 Dr. Dov Maimon has reviewed the chapter on Jewish religion and provided valuable references.
14 Mary Douglas, *Purity and Danger* (London: Routledge, 1966; reprint London: Routledge, 2002).
15 Babylonian Talmud Sanhedrin 58b.
16 Genesis 1:5
17 Ahad Ha-am, *Al Parashat Derakhim* (At the Crossroads) (Tel Aviv and Jerusalem: Dvir/Hozaah Ivrit, 1964), 11, 139.
18 *Analects*, Chapter 10 and many additional references in other chapters.
19 Annping Chin, *Confucius: A Life of Thought and Politics* (New Haven: Yale University Press 2008), 173.
20 Lin Yutang, *The Wisdom of Confucius* (New York: Carlton House, 1938), 46.
21 *Confucius*, par Donald Leslie, 3rd ed. (Paris: Seghers, 1970), 46.
22 Babylonian Talmud Kiddushin 38b.
23 Haym Soloveitchik, "Rupture and Reconstruction: The Transformation of Contemporary Orthodoxy," in *Jews in America: A Contemporary Reader*, ed. Roberta R. Farber and Chaim I. Waxman (Hanover, NH: University Press of New England for Brandeis University Press, 1999), 320-376.
24 Martin Goodman, *Rome and Jerusalem: The Clash of Ancient Civilizations* (London: A. Knopf, 2007), 390 f.
25 Elliott Horowitz, "Days of Gladness or Days of Madness: Modern Discussions of the Ancient Sabbath," *The Jewish Contribution*, ed. Cohen-Cohen, 63.
26 For a popular rather than scholarly presentation of the Jewish merit in inventing the seven-day week and the Sabbath, see Thomas Cahill, *The Gifts of the Jews: How a Tribe of Desert Nomads Changed the Way Everyone Thinks and Feels* (New York: Cengage Gale, 1998), 144.
27 Deuteronomy 32:7.
28 Yerushalmi, Chapter 4: "Modern Dilemmas: Historiography and its Discontents."
29 *Max Weber, Das Antike Judentum*, Potsdamer Internet Ausgabe (PIA), 6.
30 Exodus 30:15.
31 Amos 2:7. The translation is the Jewish Study Bible's emendation of the difficult Hebrew original. See *The Jewish Study Bible (JSB)*, ed. A. Berlin, M.Z. Brettler, M. Fishbane (Oxford: Jewish Publication Society, 1999), 1180.

32   *Jewish Study Bible*, 1176.

33   Mishnah Abot 1:2.

34   Mary Douglas, "The Fears of the Enclave," in *In the Wilderness: The Doctrine of Defilement in the Book of Numbers* (New York: Oxford University Press, 2001), 51 ff.

35   Louis H. Feldman, *Jew and Gentile in the Ancient World: Attitudes and Interactions from Alexander to Justinian* (Princeton: Princeton University Press, 1993), 227.

36   Jacob Katz, *Tradition and Crisis: Jewish Society at the End of the Middle Ages* (New York: New York University Press, 1993), 170 ff., 237 et al.

37   Israel, *European Jewry*, 190, 191.

38   Babylonian Talmud Sanhedrin 56 a/b.

39   *Soziale Ethik im Judentum*, ed. Verband der Deutschen Juden, 2nd ed. (Frankfurt am Main: J. Kauffmann, 1914). This volume contains nine contributions by well-known German Jewish scholars, who discuss all the standard topics of Jewish social ethics: love for one's neighbour, laws and justice, charity, the position of women, the Sabbath as social institution, and so on.

40   Bernardo Kligsberg, *Social Justice: A Jewish Perspective* (Jerusalem: Gefen Books, 2003). Kligsberg explains Judaism's responses to poverty, inequality, lack of solidarity, etc.

41   Jehudah Mirsky, "Tikkun Olam: Basic Questions and Policy Directions," in *Facing Tomorrow: Background Policy Documents*, provisional ed. (Jerusalem: JPPI, 2008), 213-229.

42   Deuteronomy 16:20.

43   Babylonian Talmud Pessahim 87b.

44   "Thus, the Holy One, may He be blessed, dispersed the Children of Israel across the world so that converts would gather around them; but who will trust them if they behave dishonestly towards the Non-Jews?" SMAG (*Sefer Mitzvoth Ha-Gadol*, The Great Book of Commandments of Rabbi Moshe Ben Yaakov of Coucy), (Venice, 1574) 152b.

45   Babylonian Talmud Sukkah 55b.

46   Isaiah 2:4. Micah 4:3 repeats exactly the same words in his great peace prophecy. He probably lived, like the first Isaiah, in the second half of the eighth century BCE, before the destruction of the First Temple, but may have experienced the devastation that the Assyrian Sennacherib inflicted on Judea in 701 BCE (see Part IV, Chapter 11).

47   Moritz Zobel, *Gottes Gesalbter—Der Messias and die Messianische Zeit in Talmud und Midrasch* (God's Anointed: The Messiah and Messianic Times in Talmud and Midrash) (Berlin: Schocken, 1938). As the Nazi persecutions accelerated in Germany shortly before World War II, in Berlin Zobel translated and published this comprehensive compendium of rabbinic comments on the coming of the Messiah.

48   Maimonides, *Mishneh Torah, Hilkhot Melakhim* 12:5.

49   Hodgson I, 177.

50   Abraham Livni, *Le retour d' Israel et l'espérance du monde* (Israel's Return and the Hope of the World) (Monaco: Editions du Rocher, 1984) gives an extensive list of rabbinic quotations that consider the return to Israel as a religious commandment.

51   In spite of this, the Talmud did raise the importance of living in Israel in various contexts. One Talmudic passage struck a chord with the leading medieval commentators and led to precise legal dispositions: "A man may compel all (his household) to go up to the land of Israel but none may be compelled to leave it, etc."

(Babylonian Talmud Ketubot 110b). Rashi (1040-1105) refers to this passage at least twice in his commentary to the Torah (in his notes on Genesis 17:8 and Leviticus 25:38) and so does Maimonides (1135-1204) in his own work (*Mishneh Torah, Hilkhot Melakhim* 5:11/12). Four centuries later, the *Shulchan Aruch* (published 1550-1559) would codify these opinions and statutes into a detailed and stringent religious law (*Even Ha-ezer* 75).

52   The starting point of this difference was a short but critical verse in the Torah: "And you shall take possession of the land and settle in it, for I have assigned the land to you to possess" (Numbers 33:53). To Nachmanides, this was a religious commandment that remained valid for all time. He himself left for Israel and stayed there until the end of his life. Maimonides, by contrast, did not emphasize this verse. For him this was a legally binding commandment only at the point in history in which Israel was about to cross the Jordan and enter the Promised Land.

53   Braudel, *Mediterranean*, 804, 809, 826.

Chapter 2:
EXTRA-RATIONAL BONDS:
TACIT CONSENSUS OR GROUP COHESION

1   This chapter has been reviewed by Dr. David Adler, clinical psychiatrist and professor of psychiatry at State University of New York, Downstate Division, and Dr. Ronald Atlas, professor of biology and public health at the University of Kentucky, Louisville.

2   Braudel, *Grammaire*, 189.

3   Haym Soloveitchik, 343.

4   Ibn Khaldun, 26 ff., 35, 71, 169 f.

5   Ian Buruma and Avishai Margalit, *Occidentalism: The West in the Eyes of its Enemies* (New York: Penguin, 2004).

6   Gershom Scholem, *Die Jüdische Mystik in ihren Hauptströmungen* (Major Trends in Jewish Mysticism) (Zürich: Suhrkamp, 1957), 267 ff.

7   This paragraph does not exist in the German original: Freud added it for the Hebrew translation only.

8   *Cultures of the Jews*, Biale, 741.

9   Spengler, 767 ff, 950 ff. The German terms have a different shade than their English equivalents. "Magisch" is more than superstitious: it means "enchanted," as opposed to rational or disenchanted. "Consensus" can mean "harmony" rather than unanimity. The term *"Magischer Consensus"* is attractive because it describes an elusive phenomenon in words that appeal to the imagination.

10   Kenneth Kendler, "Toward a Philosophical Structure for Psychiatry," *Am J Psychiatry* 162, no. 3 (March 2005).

11   Benedictus Spinoza, "Ethics," in his *Complete Works*, trans. S. Shirley, ed. M. L. Morgan (Indianapolis, IN: Hackett, 2002), Part II, Proposition 13, 251, and Proposition 14, 255.

12   Mathew Stewart, *The Courtier and the Heretic: Leibniz, Spinoza and the Fate of God in the Modern World* (New York: W.W. Norton, 2006) 167, 181. Stewart attributes these and other insights of Spinoza to older rabbinic traditions.

13   Owen Flanagan, "Where in the World is the Mind?," *New Scientist*, 17.1.2009.

14   Steven Pinker, *The Blank Slate: The Modern Denial of Human Nature* (New York: Viking, 2002), 51 ff.

15   Richard Dawkins, *The Selfish Gene*, 30th Anniversary Edition (Oxford: Oxford University Press, 2006).

16 Dawkins, 200 f.

17 David Sloan Wilson and Edward O.Wilson, "Survival of the Selfless," *New Scientist*, 3 Nov. 2007, 42-46.

18 Lee Alan Dugatkin, *The Altruism Equation: Seven Scientists Search for the Origin of Goodness* (Princeton: Princeton University Press 2006).

19 Steven Pinker, *How the Mind Works* (New York: W.W. Norton, 1997), 402 and other pages.

20 Other scientists have since challenged this conclusion and reported animal experiments in which altruism appeared to be strictly limited to kin and thus was a function only of genetic relatedness. The debate on this important question will certainly continue.

21 Ibn Khaldun, 98.

22 Pinker, *Mind*, 448 f. In *The Blank Slate*, Pinker explains why important findings of modern biology are often met with denial, fear, and loathing.

23 Epigenetics is supported by scientific publications, symposia, and specialized research networks, such as The Epigenome Network of Excellence, and the Human Epigenome Project, created in 2003 in Europe by the Welcome Trust. The leading US research journal *Science* published a special issue on epigenetics as early as 10 August 2001. An expert who has written about epigenetics for a broader public is the Israeli Eva Jablonka of the University of Tel Aviv. See Eva Jablonka and Marion J.Lamb, *Evolution in Four Dimensions: Genetic, Epigenetic, Behaviourial and Symbolic Variation in the History of Life* (Cambridge, MA: MIT Press, 2005).

24 R. Yehuda, W. Blair, E. Labinsky, and L.M. Bierer, "Effects of Parental PTSD on the Cortisal Response to Dexamethasone Administration in Their Adult Offspring," *American Journal of Psychiatry* 164, no. 1 (Jan 2007): 163-6. A month later the *New England Journal of Medicine* published research results confirming other cases of epigenetic inheritance in humans. See Megan P. Hitchins, Justin J.L. Wong, Graeme Suthers, et. al., "Inheritance of a Cancer-Associated MLH1 Germ-Line Epimutation," *New England Journal of Medicine* 356, no. 7 (Feb. 15, 2007): 697-705. References provided by Prof. David Adler, New York.

25 Explanation provided by Prof. Ronald Atlas, Louisville.

26 Helen Phillips, "How Life Shapes the Brainscape," *New Scientist*, 26 Nov. 2005, 12 f.; Rowan Hooper, "Men Inherit Hidden Cost of Dad's Vices," *New Scientist*, 7 Jan 2006, p.10 f.; Rowan Hooper, "Inheriting a Heresy," *New Scientist*, 4 March 2006; Tina Hesman Saey, "Dad's Hidden Influence: A Father's Legacy to a Child's Health May Start before Conception and Last Generations," *Science News* 173 (29 March 2008); T.H. Saey, "EpicGenetics," *Science News* 173 (24 May 2008); T.H. Saey, "DNA Packaging Runs in Families: Epigenetic Shifts Also Continue Throughout Life," *Science News* 173 (19 July 2008).

27 http://www.bbc.co.uk/sn/tvradio/programmes/horizon/ghostgenes.shtml

28 Michael F. Hammer, Karl Skorecki, Sara Selig, et.al., "Y-Chromosomes of Jewish Priests," *Nature* 385 (2 January1997); and Mark G.Thomas, Karl Skorecki, Haim Ben-Ami, et al., "Origins of Old Testament Priests," *Nature* 394 (9 July 1998).

29 Among others, Doron M. Behar, Ene Metspalu, et al., "Counting the Founders: The Matrilineal Genetic Ancestry of the Jewish Diaspora," *PLoS ONE* 3, no. 4 (April 2008): e2062; Susan M. Adams, Elena Bosch, et al., "The Genetic Legacy of Religious Diversity and Intolerance: Paternal Lineages of Christians, Jews and Muslims in the Iberian Peninsula," *The American Journal of Human Genetics* 83, no. 6, (April 12

2008): 725 ff. A summary of these scientific findings can be found in Diana Muir
Appelbaum and Paul S. Appelbaum, "Genetics and the Jewish Identity," *The Jerusalem
Post*, Internet Edition, 11 Feb. 2008.

30 Doron M.Behar, Bayazit Yunusbayev, et al., "The Genome-Wide Structure of the
Jewish People," *Nature*, Letters doi:10.1038/nature09103, 1-5, online 9 June 2010.

31 Gil Atzmon, Li Hao, et al., "Abraham's Children in the Genome Era: Major Jewish
Diaspora Populations Comprise Distinct Genetic Clusters with Shared Middle Eastern
Ancestry," *The American Journal of Human Genetics* 86 (June 2010): 850-859.

32 Tina Hesman Saey, "Genome Maps Trace Jewish Origins: Roots of Far-Flung
Populations Reach Back to the Levant," *Science News* (July 3, 2010): 13.

33 Doron M. Behar, et al., "The Genome-Wide Structure of the Jewish People.

34 "Exploring Genetics and Social Structure," *American Journal of Sociology* 114, no. S1
(2008): Introduction vii ff.

35 Christopher Shea, "The Nature-Nurture Debate, Redux: Genetic Research Finally
Makes Its Way into the Thinking of Sociologists," *The Chronicle of Higher Education—
The Chronicle Review*, Issue of 9.1. 2009.

36 There is a growing literature on this question. See, e.g., *Genetic Testing: Policy Issues
for the New Millenium* (Paris: OECD, 2000); David Glick and Hermona Soreq, "Ethics,
Public Policy and Behavioral Genetics," *IMAJ* 5 (Feb. 2003): 83-86.

Chapter 3:
EDUCATION, SCIENCE, AND TECHNOLOGY:
DRIVERS OF THE FUTURE

1 Spengler, 940.

2 Ibn Khaldun, 333-459.

3 Burckhardt, *Renaissance*, 85, 283 ff; Israel, *Dutch Republic*, 271 ff., 569 ff., 686 ff.

4 Lewis, *Turkey*, 83 ff.

5 Christopher Clark, *Iron Kingdom: The Rise and Downfall of Prussia, 1600-1947*
(London: Penguin, 2007).

6 Clark, 539.

7 Ibid.

8 On "soft" and "hard" power, see Joseph S. Nye, *Soft Power: The Means to Succeed in
World Politics* (New York: Public Affairs, 2004).

9 *Rising Above the Gathering Storm: Energizing and Employing America for a Brighter
Economic Future*, by Committee on Prospering in the Global Economy of the 21st
Century: An Agenda for American Science and Technology, National Academy of
Sciences, National Academy of Engineering and Institute of Medicine (Washington,
2007).

10 Maristella Botticini and Zvi Eckstein, "Jewish Occupational Selection: Education,
Restrictions or Minorities?," *Journal of Economic History* 65, no.4 (Dec. 2005): 1 ff.
Botticini and Eckstein, "From Farmers to Merchants, Conversions and Diaspora:
Human Capital and Jewish History," *Journal of the European Economic Association* 5,
no. 5 (Sept. 2007): 885-926.

11 Botticini-Eckstein, "Occupational...," 9.

12 Babylonian Talmud Baba Batra 21a. See Shmuel Safrai, "Elementary Education,
its Religious and Social Significance in the Talmudic Period," in *Social Life and
Social Values of the Jewish People, Journal of World History*, ed. UNESCO, vol. XI, 1-2
(Neuchatel: UNESCO, 1968), 149 f.

13 Botticini-Eckstein, "Occupational...," 13; and Ben-Barzilai, Yehudah Ha-Barzeloni, *Sefer Ha-Itim (Book of the Ages)*, (originally printed in Krakow 1903; reprinted in Jerusalem, Institute to Encourage the Study of Torah, 2000), Section 175.

14 David D.Rudermann, *Jewish Thought and Scientific Discovery in Early Modern Europe*, Foreword by Moshe Idel (Detroit: Wayne State University Press, 2001).

15 Charles Murray, 275 ff.

16 *The Interaction of Scientific and Jewish Cultures in Modern Times*, ed. Yakov Rabkin and Ira Robinson, (Lewiston, NY: Edwin Mellen Press, 1995), 4.

17 *Mémoires de Jacob Emden, ou l'anti-Sabbatai Zewi*, trad. Maurice-Ruben Hayoun (Paris: Editions du Cerf, 1992), 216. Jacob Emden wrote the first detailed autobiography written by a rabbi.

18 Ira Robinson, "Hayyim Selig Slonimsky and the Diffusion of Science among Russian Jewry in the Nineteenth Century," *The Interaction*, 49 ff.

19 Murray, 275 ff.

20 Jehuda Reinharz, "Chaim Weizmann, Acetone and the Balfour Declaration," *The Interaction*, 214.

21 *The Jewish People Policy Planning Institute, Annual Assessment 2006* (Jerusalem: JPPI, 2006).

22 Thorstein Veblen, "The Intellectual Pre-Eminence of Jews in Modern Europe," *Political Science Quarterly* 34, no. 1 (March 1919).

23 Anatole Leroy-Beaulieu, *Les Juifs et l'Antisémitisme: Israel chez les nations* (The Jews and Antisemitsm: Israel among the Nations) (Paris: Calmann Levy, 1893), 221. Translation by the author.

24 Babylonian Talmud Berakhot 31b and parallels.

25 Herman Wouk, *The Language God Talks: On Science and Religion* (New York: Little, Brown, 2010), 8, 153.

26 Richard Florida, *The Rise of the Creative Class: And How It's Transforming Work, Leisure, Community and Everyday Life* (New York: Basic Books, 2002).

27 D.L. Preston, *Science, Society and the German Jews: 1870-1933*. Ph.D. diss., University. of Illinois, 1971, 218. Quoted in *The Interaction*, 9.

28 Freeman Dyson, *The Scientist as Rebel* (New York: New York Review Books, 2006).

29 Thorstein Veblen, 33 ff.

30 David Ruderman, particularly Chapter Five, "Science and Skepticism" and Chapter Ten, "The Community of Converso Physicians," 153 ff., 273 ff.

31 Albert Einstein and Sigmund Freud, *Pourquoi la guerre?*, transl. by B. Briod from the original *Warum Krieg?* Preface by C. David (Paris: Rivages, 2005), 16 f.

32 Ruderman, 1.

33 Georg Steiner, "Zion," in *My Unwritten Books* (New York: New Directions Publishing, 2008), 101 f.

34 Richard E. Nisbett, *Intelligence and How to Get It: Why Schools and Culture Count* (New York: W.W. Norton, 2009).

35 Joel Zlotogora, Gideon Bach, and Arnold Munnich, "Molecular Basis of Mendelian Disorders among Jews," *Molecular Genetics and Metabolism* 69 (2000): 169-180. This paper identifies almost one hundred genetic or genetically linked diseases that are more typical for Jews than for non-Jews. Many of these diseases are concentrated only in one or a few geographic branches of the Jewish people. A few genetic diseases have been found only among Jews.

Chapter 4:
LANGUAGE: A FACTOR IN RISE AND DECLINE

1 This chapter has been reviewed by Dr. Aya Meltzer-Asher, senior lecturer at the Faculty of Linguistics, Tel Aviv University, and by the late Professor David Sohlberg of the University of Bar-Illan.

2 Burckhardt, *Reflections,* 114.

3 Thukydides, 250 (III, 82).

4 Confucius, *Analects* XIII, 3.

5 Ibn Khaldun, 422 ff., 431 ff.

6 Gibbon, 29.

7 Gibbon, 43.

8 Spengler, 385, 689-741.

9 Shlomo Morag, *Mekhkarim ba-lashon ha-mikra* (Biblical Language Research (Jerusalem: Magnes Press, 1995), 33.

10 Joseph in Egypt spoke to his brothers through an interpreter. They could not know that he understood their Hebrew. See Genesis 42:23.

11 Nehemiah 13:24.

12 Midrash Mechiltha Bo, chapter 5.

13 Minor Tractate Soferim, chapter 1, ed. M.Higger, 101 f., with parallel sources.

14 The correct linguistic term would be "diglossic," not "bilingual." "Bilingual" refers to a person who has two mother tongues, "diglossic" to a society that uses two different languages for different functions.

15 Mireille Hadas-Lebel, *Philo d' Alexandrie, un penseur en diaspora* (Paris: Fayard, 2003).

16 *Forte come la morte è l'amore: Tremila anni di poesia d'amore ebraica* (Strong like Death and Love: Three Thousand Years of Hebrew Love Poetry), ed. Cesare Segrè and Sara Ferrari, Hebrew and Italian, (Livorno: Belforte, 2007), 92 ff., 96 ff., 102 ff., 108 f., 235.

17 Judeo-Arabic dialects played an equally important role in the culture of Jews in Arab countries, but apart from specific words that Jews used among themselves so that Arabs would not understand them these dialects were Arabic.

18 Cecile E. Kuznitz, "Yiddish Studies," in *The Oxford Handbook of Jewish Studies,* ed. Martin Goodman. (Oxford: Oxford University Press, 2002), 514 ff.

19 Paul Kriwaczek, *Yiddish Civilization: The Rise and Fall of a Forgotten Nation* (New York: Vintage, 2006).

20 Ruth R.Wisse, *Jews and Power* (New York: Knopf, 2008), X.

21 Aron Rodrigue, "The Ottoman Diaspora: The Rise and Fall of Ladino Literary Culture," in *Cultures of the Jews,* 863 ff.

22 Kaplan, 193.

Chapter 5:
CREATIVE LEADERSHIP AND POLITICAL ELITES

1 Chase, see II 18c.

2 Henry Kissinger, *Diplomacy* (New York: Simon & Schuster, 1994), 351.

3 John Lukacs, *Five Days in London May 1940* (New Haven, CT: Yale University Press, 1991).

4 Thukydides, 107 (I, 138).

5 Burckhardt, *Reflections,* 347, 341.

6 Toynbee, III, 245 ff.

7 Yehezkel Dror, *The Capacity to Govern: A Report to the Club of Rome* (London: Frank Cass, 1994), 116 f.

8   Maimonides, *Hilchot Melachim ve-Milkhamot* (Laws of Kings and of their Wars), 1-3. See, among parallel laws, 3:8: "Anyone who embarrasses or shames the king may be executed by the king."

9   Maimonides, *Mishneh Torah*, "Laws of Kings and Their Wars," 3:9.

10 Ibid., 3: 10.

11 Ibid., 3:1-2.

12 Numbers 16:15.

13 I Samuel 12:3.

14 *Jewish Study Bible*, Introduction to Ezra and Nehemiah and commentaries by H. Najman, 1666 ff. and 1688 ff.; *The Anchor Bible, Ezra-Nehemiah*, trans. Jacob B. Myers (NewYork: Doubleday, 1965); H. Tadmor, "The Period of the First Temple, the Babylonian Exile and the Restoration," in *A History of the Jewish People*, 175 ff.; Yehezkel Kaufmann, *History of the Religion of Israel*, IV (New York: Ktav, 1977); and Elias Bickerman.

15 Babylonian Talmud Baba Batra 15a.

16 Tadmor, *A History of the Jewish People*, 175. Ezra too writes a few times in the first person.

17 Nehemiah 1:1

18 Plutarch, *Artaxerxes: The Internet Classics Archive*, transl. John Dryden, http.classics. mit.edu/Plutarch/artaxerxes.html, 1; see also *Artaxerxes I, Jewish Encycplopedia. com.*

19 Nehemiah 2:11.

20 "Nehemia," *Encyclopaedia Judaica*, second edition (New York: Macmillan Reference, 2007), 15, 60 f.

21 Babylonian Talmud Sanhedrin 93b.

22 Babylonian Talmud Sanhedrin 103b. Yishai Chasidah quotes a Midrash (*Midrash Hagadol Leviticus* 320) stating that Nehemiah is considered as important as the Messiah himself! Yishai Chasidah, *Ishei Ha-Tenach, Encyclopedia of Biblical Personalities, Anthologized from the Talmud, Midrash and Rabbinic Writings* (Jerusalem: Mesorah Pub., 1994) 415 ff.

23 *Gilion Ha-Shass* by Rabbi Akiva Eger (*Marginalia to the Talmud*) on Babylonian Talmud Succah 12a.

24 Graetz *Volkstümliche* 2, second half, fourth Chapter, 160.

25 Dubnow, *Weltgeschichte*, I, 374 f.

26 Baron I, 118.

27 Goodman, 12 f., 68 ff.

28 J. Goodnick Westenholz, ed., *The Jewish Presence in Ancient Rome* (Jerusalem: Bible Lands Museum, 1994), 71.

29 Louis Finkelstein, *Jewish Self-Government in the Middle Ages* (Philadelphia: Greenwood Press, 1924), 20 ff.

30 H.H. Ben-Sasson, "The Middle Ages," in *A History of the Jewish People*, 433.

31 Benzion Netanyahu, *Don Isaac Abrabanel: Statesman and Philosopher* (New York: Varda Books, 2001), and Roland Goetschel, *Isaac Abrabanel, Conseiller des princes et philosophe* (Paris: Albin Michel, Presences du Judaisme-poche edition, 1996).

32 Machiavelli, "The Prince," Chapter 21 in *The Essential Writings of Machiavelli*, ed. Peter Constantine (New York: The Modern Library, 2007), 84.

33 BenSasson, *A History of the Jewish People*, 691.

34 Zvi Avneri, Eric Lawee, "Abrabanel, Isaac Ben Judah," *Encyclopaedia Judaica*, second edition (New York: Macmillan Reference, 2007), 1, 276 ff.

35 Selma Stern, *Josel von Rosheim—Befehlshaber der Judenschaft im Heiligen Römischen Reich Deutscher Nation* (Commander of Jewry in the Holy Roman Empire of the German Nation) (Stuttgart: Deutsche Verlags-Anstalt, 1959). This biography—the only one that exists about this important leader—was for the first time translated into a second language in 2008. It appeared in French, with the support of the small Alsacian city of Rosheim, which wanted to honor its greatest son. See Selma Stern, *L'Avocat des Juifs—Les tribulations de Yossel de Rosheim dans l'Europe de Charles Quint* (The Attorney of the Jews: The Tribulations of Yossel of Rosheim in the Europe of Charles Quint), ed. F.Raphaël et M.Ebstein (Strasbourg: La Nuée bleue, 2008). Also, "The Middle Ages," in *History of the Jewish People*, 651 f, 687 f., 708.

36 The original Spanish term—*el imperio en el que nunca se pone el sol*—was first used for the empire of Charles V and became four hundred years later a standard description for the British Empire.

37 Alexis Rubin, ed., *Scattered Among the Nations: Documents Affecting Jewish History 49 to 1975* (Northvale, NJ: J. Aronson, 1995), 113 ff.

38 Selma Stern, *Josel von Rosheim*, 76.

39 Dubnow, 206-217.

40 Cecil Roth, *A Life of Menasseh Ben Israel: Rabbi, Printer and Diplomat* (Philadelphia: Jewish Publication Society of America, 1934), and Menasseh ben Israel *Esperance d'Israel* (Hope of Israel, 1650) trad. H.Mechulan et G.Nahon (Paris: Librairie philosophique J. Vrin, 1979).

41 Art historians have recently expressed doubts as to whether the portrait is really that of Menasseh.

42 Roth, *Menasseh*, 71.

43 I. Israel, *European Jewry*, 70 f.

44 Salomon Wald, "Chinese Jews in European Thought." in *Youtai: Presence and Perception of Jews and Judaism in China*, ed. Peter Kupfer (Frankfurt am Main: Peter Lang, 2008), 227 ff.

45 I. Israel, *European Jewry*, 130 f.

46 Oren, *Power*, 361.

47 Oren, *Power*, 355.

48 Personal communication by Mr.Rami Tal, who as a high school student visited Ben Gurion in his retirement in 1964.

49 Rabbi Joseph B. Soloveitchik, *Fate and Destiny: From the Holocaust to the State of Israel* (Hoboken, NJ: Ktav, 1992), 64.

50 Joseph Nye, Jr., "Picking a President," *Democracy: A Journal of Ideas* 10 (Fall 2008).

51 Gibbon, 248 and parallels; Lewis, *Turkey*, 23.

52 Exodus 2:14.

53 Clausewitz's often-quoted saying is "War is the continuation of politics by other means." The exact quote is given in Part IV, Chapter 9.

54 Aaron Wildavsky, *Moses as Political Leader* (Jerusalem: Shalem Press, 2005; first published in 1984), 258 ff.

55 Ibn Khaldun, 131.

Chapter 6:
NUMBERS AND CRITICAL MASS

1 Braudel, *Écrits II*, 207 ff.

2 Braudel, *Grammaire*, 236 ff.

3 Max Weber, *Konfuzianismus und Taoismus*, 341, 521, 534.

4   Tainter, 150, 167.
5   Sergio DellaPergola, *Israele e Palestina: la forza dei numeri—Il conflitto mediorientale fra demografia e politica* (Israel and Palestine: The Power of Numbers: -The Middle East Conflict between Demography and Politics) (Bologna: Il Mulino, 2007), 13 ff.
6   Genesis 13:16; 15:5; 22:17; 26:5; 28:14.
7   Tosafoth to Babylonian Talmud Berakhoth 17a, beginning words: *ve-nafshi* and parallels.
8   Deuteronomy 7:7.
9   Rashi on Exodus 13:18 and sources in the Midrash.
10   Tadmor, *A History of the Jewish People,* 120 f.
11   Nadav Na'aman, "Ahab's Chariot Force at the Battle of Qarqar," in his *Ancient Israel and Its Neighbours:—Interaction and Counteraction, Collected Essays* 1 (Winona Lake, IN: Eisenbrauns, 2005), 1-13.
12   I Isaiah 27:13, presumably eighth century BCE.
13   II Isaiah 49:12, presumably sixth century BCE. Other references are Hosea 11: 5, 11; Jeremiah 43:6, 7, and 44:12.
14   Elias Bickerman, 10.
15   M. Stern, *A History of the Jewish People,* 191.
16   Baron, I, 131.
17   M. Stern, *A History of the Jewish People,* 206 f.
18   Braudel, *Mediterranean,* 817.
19   Sergio DellaPergola, *Word Jewry beyond 2000,* 14 ff.
20   Sergio DellaPergola, *Jewish Demographic Policies: Population Trends and Options in Israel and in the Diaspora* (Jerusalem: JPPI, 2011), 87, and DellaPergola, *World Jewry.*

Chapter 7:
ECONOMIC FOUNDATIONS OF LONG-LASTING CIVILIZATIONS

1   *Max Weber,* Protestant 79, 80 94, 202.
2   Spengler, 1177.
3   Lewis, *Turkey,* 28 ff. and parallels.
4   Israel, *Dutch Republic,* 307 ff. and parallels.
5   Ward-Perkins, 41 and parallels.
6   Braudel, *Mediterranean,* 802-826.
7   Baron, particularly IV, *Meeting of East and West,* 1957, and XII, *Economic Catalyst,* 1967. See also Salo W. Baron, Shalom M. Paul, S. David Sperling, "Economic History," in *Encyclopaedia Judaica,* second edition, 95-139.
8   Jacob Neusner, *Why Does Judaism Have an Economics?* (New London: Connecticut College, 1988), 28.
9   Simon Kuznets, "Economic Structure and Life of the Jews," in *The Jews: Their History, Culture and Religion,* 3rd ed., ed. Louis Finkelstein (New York: Harper & Row, 1960), 1597-1666. Quotes from 1597 and 1659.
10   Friedrich Battenberg, *Das Europäische Zeitalter der Juden—Zur Entwicklung einer Minderheit in der nichtjüdischen Umwelt Europas* (The European Age of the Jews: The Development of a Minority in the Non-Jewish Environment of Europe) (Darmstadt: Wissenschaftliche Buchgesellschaft, 2000); Simon Erlanger, *Die jüdische Gemeinde des Mittelalters—Geschichte, Struktur und Einfluss auf die Stadtentwicklung vom 9. bis 13. Jahrhundert mit besonderer Berücksichtigung des Rheinlandes* (The Jewish Community of the Middle Ages: History, Structure and Influence on Urban Development from the Ninth to the Thirteenth Century, with Special Emphasis on the Rhineland), MA

thesis, University of Basel, 1992; Michael Toch, *Juden im mittelalterlichen Reich* (Jews in the Medieval Empire) (München: R. Oldenbourg, 1999); Louis Finkelstein, *Jewish Self-Government in the Middle Ages* (Philadelphia: Greenwood Press, 1924).

11   The German writer Sigrid Heuck turned the story into a popular children's book, *Der Elefant des Kaisers* (The Emperor's Elephant) (Stuttgart-Wien: Thienemann, 2006). In autumn 2007, the cathedral and townhall of Aachen organised an exhibition to make Isaac, his elephant, and their times better known to a large German public.

12   The life story of the great commentator Rashi (Rabbi Shlomoh Yitzhaki, 1040-1105) is a significant example. He studied in the Talmud academy of Worms and returned to Troyes in France, where he is reported to have earned a good living as a wine-grower and -merchant.

13   Toch, 16.

14   Avner Greif, "Contract Enforceability and Economic Institutions in Early Trade: The Maghribi Traders' Coalition," *The American Economic Review* 83, no.3 (1993): 525 ff.; Avner Greif, Paul Milgrom, Barry R. Weingast, "Coordination, Commitment and Enforcement: The Case of the Merchant Guild," *The Journal of Political Economy* 102, no.4 (1994): 745 ff.; Avner Greif, "Cultural Beliefs and the Organization of Society: A Historical and Theoretical Reflection on Collectivist and Individualist Societies," *The Journal of Political Economy* 102, no.5 (1994): 912 ff.

15   S.D. Goitein, *Jews and Arabs: Their Contacts through the Ages* (New York: Schocken, 1974; 1st ed. 1955), 111 ff.

16   Maristella Botticini and Zvi Eckstein, "Jewish Occupational Selection," 14. The authors base this statement on the path-breaking work of Shlomo Goitein, *A Mediterranean Society: The Jewish Communities of the Arab World as Portrayed in the Documents of the of the Cairo Geniza*, 5 vol.s, (Los Angeles: University of California Press, 1967-1988).

17   Adam Silverstein, "From Markets to Marvels: Jews on the Maritime route to China ca. 850-ca. 950 CE," *Journal of Jewish Studies* LVIII, no. 1 (spring 2007): 96. A list of ancient Arab and Iranian authors who mention Jews in China appears in Donald Daniel Leslie, *Jews and Judaism in Traditional China: A Comprehensive Bibliography* (Sankt Augustin: Nettetal, 1998).

18   Michael Pollak, *Mandarins, Jews and Missionaries: The Jewish Experience in the Chinese Empire* (Philadelphia: Jewish Publication Society of America, 1980), 266.

19   Joseph Needham, *Science and Civilization in China* (Cambridge: Cambridge University Press, 1954). Needham returns in several volumes of his large work to the intermediary role of Jewish travelers and merchants, e.g. in. 3, 575 f., 681 ff., 4, 231, 236, 347 f.

20   J. Israel, *European Jewry in the Age of Mercantilism 1550-1750*, 3rd ed. (London: Littman Library of Jewish Civilization, 1998).

21   Toch, 87, 124.

22   Israel, 148 .

23   Braudel, *The Mediterranean*, 809 .

24   Schmelzer, 38-57.

25   Avraham Barkai, *Jüdische Minderheit und Industrialisierung* (Jewish Minority and Industrialization), (Tübingen: J.S.B. Mohr—Siebeck, 1988). All statistics in this chapter are taken from Barkai's book and his tables if not indicated otherwise. Simone Lässig, "How German Jewry Turned Bourgeois: Religion, Culture and Social Mobility in the Age of Emancipation," *GHI Research, German Historical Institute Washington, GHI Bulletin* 37 (Fall 2005), 59 ff.

26 Lässig, 65.

27 Tax revenues are not an exact reflection of incomes, but they are a good indicator.

28 Barkai quotes an estimate according to which Jews in the 1930s owned approximately 3% of all German capital. This is a respectable figure, as Jews represented only 1% of the German population, but it is not overwhelming. The greatest German fortunes always remained in the hands of the industrial tycoons.

29 Howard Sachar, *The Course of Modern Jewish History*, New Revised Edition (New York: Vintage, 1990), particularly Chapter 19, "The Impact of the Jews on Western Culture," 472 ff. A popular description also appears in Amos Elon, *The Pity Of It All: A Portrait of Jews in Germany 1743-1933* (New York: Penguin Books , 2002), 265 ff. and other references.

30 Paul Burstein, "Jewish Educational and Economic Success in the United States: A Search for Explanations," *Sociological Perspectives* 50, no. 2 (2007): 209 ff. If not indicated otherwise, all statistics are from Burstein's article or are calculations by the author based on Burstein's statistics.

31 The *Jewish People Policy Planning Institute Annual Assessment, Jerusalem, 2007*, 63, gives the proportion of college graduates for 2001 as 67%, which more or less corroborates Burstein's data.

32 *Who's Who in America* was originally published independently by Albert Nelson Marquis in 1899. It changed owners several times in the late twentieth century and was acquired by News Communications, Inc., in 2003.

33 *Jews in Computer and Information Science*, www.jinfo.org/Computer_Info_Science. html 21.10.2007. The distinction between scientific discovery and technical or industrial application has disappeared in many cases, but this is the general trend of modern science and technology. Some scientific discoveries are quickly useful to technology and industry.

34 *JPPPI Annual Assessment, Jerusalem, 2007, Societal Aspects*, 71.

35 See Kuznets.

36 Baron, IV, *Meeting of East and West*, 226.

37 *The Knowledge-Based Economy*, (Paris: OECD, 1996). This report was widely read in government circles.

38 *JPPPI Annual Assessment, Jerusalem, 2007*, 69 f.

39 Burstein, 214, 221.

40 Daniel Chirot, "Conflicting Identities and the Danger of Communalism," in *Essential Outsiders: Chinese and Jews in the Modern Transformation of Southeast Asia and Central Europe*, ed. Daniel Chirot and Anthony Reid (Seattle: University of Washington Press, 1997), 3

41 Nachum T. Gross, "Enterpreneurship of Religious and Ethnic Minorities," Zug Beiheft 64, *Jüdische Unternehmer in Deutschland im 19. und 20. Jahrhundert* (Jewish Entrepreneurs in Nineteenth- and Twentieth-Century Germany) (Stuttgart: F. Steiner, 1992), 15.

42 The term is from Victor Karady, "Jewish Entrepreneurship and Identity under Capitalism and Socialism in Central Europe: The Unresolved Dilemmas of Hungarian Jewry," in *Essential Outsiders: Chinese and Jews in the Modern Transformation of Southeast Asia and Central Europe*, ed. Daniel Chirot and Anthony Reid (Seattle: University of Washington Press, 1997), 126.

43 Richard Florida, *The Rise of the Creative Class: And How It's Transforming Work, Leisure, Community and Everyday Life* (New York: Basic Books, 2002).

44 In 1990, Jewish male self-employment in the United States was 27% and in 2000, 23%, as against a national figure of 14% in both years (Barry R. Chiswick, "The Occupational Attainment of American Jewry: 1990 to 2000," *Institute for the Study of Labour (IZA), IZA Discussion Papers* Nr. 1736, 2005, Tables A-1, B-1, C-1, C-2, D-1). In Israel, the proportion of self-employed individuals is less than 15%, which is significantly lower than in many Diaspora countries (*JPPI Annual Assessment 2007,* 67). For Israel's Jewish majority population, the challenge of discrimination has disappeared. It would be interesting to study the ethnic and religious composition of those 15% of Israelis who are self-employed.

45 Karady, in *Essential Outsiders: Chinese and Jews in the Modern Transformation of Southeast Asia and Central Europe,* ed. Daniel Chirot and Anthony Reid (Seattle: University of Washington Press, 1997), 130.

Chapter 8:
WAR: A DOUBLE-EDGED SWORD

1 Mr. Yogev Karasenty from the JPPI in Jerusalem has reviewed the biblical history references in this and other chapters, added additional findings and provided valuable advice.

2 Ibn Khaldun, 223 and parallels.

3 Gibbon, 1223 and parallels.

4 Sima Qian, 124, 312 and parallels.

5 Sun Tzu, *The Art of War,* transl. T.Cleary (Boston: Shambhala, 1991), 1.

6 Sima, 177.

7 Burckhardt, *Reflections,* 253 ff.

8 Toynbee, III, 150, IV, 465 ff.

9 Toynbee, IV, 505 ff.

10 Carl von Clausewitz, *Vom Kriege* (On War) (Reinbeck bei Hamburg: Rowohlt, 1963), 15, 216.

11 Burckhardt, *Renaissance,* 99-102.

12 Huizinga, *Autumn,* 96.

13 Huizinga, *Dutch Culture,* 45, 47.

14 Victor Davis Hanson, *Carnage and Culture: Landmark Battles in the Rise of Western Power* (New York: Doubleday, 2001).

15 Spengler, 796 ff. and other references.

16 Deuteronomy 3:3-7; 7:1-2; 20; Joshua 6:17; 10:28-40 and parallels. See Reuven Firestone, "Holy War in Modern Judaism? 'Mitzvah War' and the Problem of the 'Three Vows'," *Journal of the American Academy of Religion* 74, no. 4 (Dec. 2006).

17 Norman Solomon, "The Ethics of War: Judaism," in *The Ethics of War: Shared Problems in Different Traditions,* ed. Richard Sorabji and David Rodin (Aldershot: Ashgate, 2006), 110.

18 Deuteronomy 20:10.

19 *Hilchot Melachim ve-Milkhamot* (Laws of Kings and of their Wars), 5-8.

20 Noah Feldman, "War and Reason in Maimonides and Averroes," in *The Ethics of War,* 92 ff.

21 Feldman, 96; Solomon, 116. Solomon states that on some issues Maimonides echoes the Islamic *Jihad* or holy war doctrine.

22 Voltaire, "Sermon des cinquante" (1752), *Mélanges* (Paris: La Pléiade, 1961), 256 ff., with many parallels in other works

23 Sima, 124.

24 Josephus, "Jewish Antiquities," Book 4.7.1 (159-162); Book 5.1.7 (28), in Josephus Flavius, *The New Complete Works of Josephus,* trans. Wiliam Whiston and Paul L. Maier (Grand Rapids, MI: Kregel Pub., 1999), 152 and 168. These are two of many examples.

25 Louis H. Feldman, *Jew and Gentile in the Ancient World: Attitudes and Interactions from Alexander to Justinian* (Princeton: Princeton University Press, 1993), 220 ff.

26 Numbers 6:26.

27 Gabriel Barkay et al., "The Amulets from Ketef Hinom: A New Edition and Evaluation," *Bulletin of the American Schools of Oriental Research,* no. 334 (May 2004): 41-71, publ. by The American Schools of Oriental Research.

28 For example, Isaiah 2:24 and 11:1-9; Micah 4:1-5.

29 Babylonian Talmud Sabbath 10 a/b.

30 Firestone, 954-982

31 See, for example, Jeremiah 32 on Nebuchadnezzar: "Therefore this is what the Lord says: I am about to give this city into the hands of the Babylonians and to Nebuchadnezzar, King of Babylon, who will capture it."

32 Goodman, 489 ff.

33 *Sefer Josifon,* Text and Commentary (Hebrew), ed. David Flusser (Jerusalem: Mossad Bialik, 1981); David Flusser, "Jossipon," in *Encyclopaedia Judaica,* ed. Y.Leibowitz (Jerusalem: Keter Pub. 1971/73), 10; "The Sefer Josippon," *Wikipedia,* the Free Encyclopedia, 25.12.2008

34 Hebrew editions (list incomplete): Constantinople 1510, Basel 1541, Venice 1544, Cracow 1588, Frankfurt-a.M. 1689, Gotha 1707 and 1710, Amsterdam 1723, Prague 1784, Calcutta 1841, Warsaw 1845 and 1871, Zhitomir 1851, Lvov 1855. Translations (list incomplete): One manuscript in Ethiopian ca. 1300, at least four in Yiddish (Zürich 1546, Prague 1607, Amsterdam 1661 and 1771, Cracow 1670), one in classical and one in Yemenite Arabic, also translations in Latin, French, English (1558 and so popular that it was re-printed in 1561, 1575, and 1608), German, Czech, Polish, Russian. The book was known in Persia in the fourteenth century.

35 Flusser, "Jossipon," 297.

36 *Sefer Josifon,* 431. Translation by the author.

37 Yael Zerubavel, *Recovered Roots: Collective Memory and the Making of Israeli National Tradition* (Chicago and London: University of Chicago Press, 1997) 208.

38 *Sefer Josifon,* 174.

39 Quote from Zerubavel, 202.

40 See Bickerman, *From Ezra to the Last of the Maccabees.* Stephen G.Rosenberg, "The Jewish Temple at Elephantine", *Near Eastern Archaeology,* 67, No 1, March 2004, 4-13, publ. by The American Schools of Oriental Research.

41 Bickerman, 34 ff.; Hadas-Lebel, *Philo,* 60 f.

42 Andrew J.Schoenfeld, "Sons of Israel in Caesar's Service: Jewish Soldiers in the Roman Military," *Shofar: An Interdisciplinary Journal of Jewish Studies* 24, no. 3 (2006): 115 ff. Kaufmann Kohler and Herman Rosenthal, "Caesar, Caius Julius," *Jewish Encyclopedia.com.,* 20.11.2007. On Caesar: M. Stern, "The Period of the Second Temple," in *A History of the Jewish People,* 224 f, 280 f., 366.

43 Schoenfeld, 116, 126.

44 Josephus, "Jewish Antiquities," Book 14.8.1 (128), 464, in *The New Complete Works of Josephus.*

45 Abraham Schalit, "Antipater II. or Antipas," *Encyclopaedia Judaica,* second ed., eds. F. Skolnik and M. Berenbaum (New York: Macmillan, 2007), 2, 205.

46 Josephus, "Jewish Antiquities," Book 14.8.2 (133), 465.
47 Zhang Ligang, "The Understanding and Attitude of Chinese Society Toward the Kaifeng Jews," *Youtai*, 143.
48 Michael Pollak: 320 f. "Li Yao (a Jew), Company Commander, died in action, fighting against the rebel Li Tzu-ch'eng, in 1643."
49 Salomon Wald, "Chinese Jews," *Youtai*, 223.
50 Shirley Berry Isenberg, *India's Bene Israel: A Comprehensive Inquiry and Sourcebook* (Berkeley: Judah L. Magnes Museum, 1988), 162 f.
51 Among others are Vice-Admiral Benjamin A. Samson, who was commander-in-chief of the Indian navy under Prime Minister Nehru, Major-General Jonathan R. Samson, and Lieutenant-General J.F.R. Jacob, who in 1971 accepted the surrender of the Pakistani army in Dacca (Bangla-Desh), after Pakistan's defeat in its third war with India. See also Rachael Rukmini Israel, *The Jews of India: Their Story* (New Delhi: Mosaic Books, 2002), 15 f., 61.
52 Haeem Samuel Kehimkar, *The History of the Bene Israel of India* (Preface 1897; Tel Aviv: Dayag Press, 1937), 187 f.
53 Yohanan ben David (Samson John David), *Indo-Judaic Studies* (New Delhi: Northern Book Center , 2002), 91.
54 "Berek, Joselewicz," *Jewish Encyclopedia.com*, 20.11.2007; Berek Joselewicz, www. wikipedia.org. 18.11.2007.
55 During and after World War I, Italy had senior Jewish officers and several admirals. One of them, naval architect General Umberto Pugliese, rebuilt the Italian fleet, and two Jewish admirals were among Italy's senior navy commanders even under Mussolini.
56 General Bernheim played a key role in Belgium's defense in World War I. He commanded the First Army Division of Flanders and reached the highest grade in the Belgian army.
57 "Monash, Sir John," *Encyclopaedia Judaica*, second edition (New York: Macmillan Reference, 2007), 14, 432.
58 www.awm.gov.au/1918/people/genmonash.htm, 24.12.2007.
59 Orlando Figes, *A People's Tragedy: The Russian Revolution 1891-1924* (New York: Penguin Books, 1996), 794.
60 Figes, 803 f.
61 Leon Trotsky, "On the 'Jewish Problem'," *Class Struggle*, no. 2 (February 1934), can be found in The Albert and Vera Weisbrod Internet Archives.
62 Trotsky, "Jewish Problem."
63 Figes, 141.
64 Zvi Y. Gitelman, *A Century of Ambivalence: The Jews of Russia and the Soviet Union 1881 to the Present* (Bloomington, IN: Indiana University Press, 2001), 258.
65 This number is taken from a list of Jewish Word War II casualties on display in the Museum of the Israeli Defense Forces Tank Corps in Latrun, Israel. Other sources gave somewhat smaller numbers.
66 Vassily Grossman, *A Writer At War: With The Red Army 1941-1945*, ed. Antony Beevor and Luba Vinogradova (London: Pimlico, 2006), 243.
67 Allis Radosh and Ronald Radosh, *A Safe Heaven: Harry S. Truman and the Founding of Israel* (New York: Harper& Collins, 2009), 73.
68 Slezkine, 1 ff.
69 Benny Morris, *1948: The First Arab-Israeli War* (New Haven: Yale University Press, 2008), 84, 85, 86. 207, 268. All figures are from this book.

70   Morris, 273.
71   Michael Oren, *Six Days of War: June 1967 and the Making of the Modern Middle East* (Oxford: Oxford University Press, 2002).

Chapter 9:
GEOPOLITICS AND CIVILIZATIONAL AFFINITIES

1   Thucydides, 113.
2   Huntington 21-29, and parallels.
3   Sima; *Emperor Wu of Han*; Ann Paludan, *Chronicle of the Chinese Emperors: The Reign-by-Reign Record of the Rulers of Imperial China* (London: Thames & Hudson, 1998), 36 ff, 56 f.; Introductions to the English and French translations of Sima Qian's work by Watson and Chavannes. This portion of the text has been reviewed by Prof. Irene Eber, Hebrew University of Jerusalem.
4   Sima, 236.
5   Peter D. Perdue, *China Marches West: The Qing Conquest of Central Eurasia* (Cambridge, MA: Harvard University Press, 2005).
6   Most of this description is based on the work of J.Israel, in *The Dutch Republic.*
7   J. Israel, *The Dutch Republic,* 850.
8   Barbara W.Tuchman, *The Zimmermann Telegram* (New York: Balantine Books, 1958).
9   Henry Kissinger, 179.
10   Gibbon, 801 ff.
11   Tadmor, *A History of the Jewish People,* 120 f.
12   I Kings 16:33.
13   According to modern scholars, the present biblical texts on Israel's royal history were completed in the fifth or fourth century, but parts of them are much older. The history of Israel's first three kings are said to be among the oldest texts and may go back to the eighth century BCE. See Alexander Rofé, *Mevoh Le-Sifruth Ha-Historith Be-Miqrah* (Introduction to the Historical Literature of the Hebrew Bible) (Jerusalem, 2001), 55 ff.
14   II Kings 24-25. For more see Tadmor, *A History of the Jewish People,* 152 ff.
15   Bernard Lewis, *The Middle East: A Brief History of the Last 2000 Years* (New York: Scribner, 1997), 27 f.
16   Baron, I 103.
17   M. Stern, *A History of the Jewish People,* 207
18   Goodman, 479.
19   Barbara Tuchman, *Bible and Sword: How the British Came to Palestine* (London: Macmillan, 1957).
20   Tuchman, *Bible,* 121.
21   Dimitri Simes, "Losing Russia," *Foreign Affairs* (Nov./Dec. 2007): 51 ff.

Chapter 10:
INTERNAL DISSENT

1   Laozi, *Daodejing,* first quote chapter 33, second quote chapter 2.
2   *Die Vorsokratiker (The Pre-Socratics),* ed. W.Capelle, (Stuttgart, 1968), 135.
3   Toynbee V, 17 ff., 376 ff. and parallels.
4   Ibn Khaldun, 238 ff.
5   Gibbon, 152.
6   Herman, 83, 135, 142 and parallels.
7   Gibbon, 2102.

8   Abraham Geiger, "A History of Spiritual Achievements," in *Ideas of Jewish History*, ed. Michael A.Meyer (Detroit, Behrman, 1974), 168.

9   Jacob Katz, *Exclusiveness and Tolerance*, chapters VI and XII.

10 The *birkat* is the twelfth of the "Eighteen Blessings", an early Rabbinic part of the daily Jewish prayer ritual. It is not a blessing but a composition of imprecations against several categories of "heretics,""apostates," or "sinners." Who are they? The words were often believed to be directed against early Judeo-Christians, allegedly with the aim of excluding them from the synagogue at the time when the *birkat* became a compulsory part of the prayers between 85 and 100 CE. There have been several arguments against this thesis. It can be shown that a *birkat* existed before the fall of theTemple in 70 CE and that it did not aim at excluding Judeo-Christians or any other Jewish movement from the synagogue. The terms have been modified more often than any other part of the "Eighteen Blessings" in order to adapt the "curses" to changing circumstances. Their original sense was apparently a warning against Jewish sectarianism. Liliane Vana presents an exhaustive summary of the scholarly debate on this question. L. Vana, "La birkat ha-minim est-elle une prière contre les Judéo-Chrétiens?" (Is the birkat ha-minim a prayer against the Judéo-Christians?), in *Les Communautés réligieuses dans le monde Gréco-Romain—Essai de définition* ed. N.Belayche et al. (Turnhout: Brepols, 2003), 201-241.

11 Baron II, "Christian Era: The First Five Centuries," 57 ff.

12 Meira Polliack, "Medieval Karaism," in *The Oxford Handbook of Jewish Studies* (Oxford: Oxford University Press, 2002), 295 ff.; Raymond P.Scheindlin, "Merchants and Intellectuals, Rabbis and Poets," in *Jewish Cultures*, 321 ff., 359 ff.

13 Jacob Burckhardt, *Reflections,* 105.

14 Baron notes that the "literal biblicism" of the Karaites led them to reject the thousand-year-old humanitarian evolution of Judaism. For example, they demanded an unstinting application of the death penalty and a literal application of the biblical "eye-for-an-eye" commandment, in stark contrast to the Talmud. See Baron, vol. V, "Religious Controls and Dissension," "Karaite Schism," 209 ff.

15 Polliack, 305.

16 *The Dream of the Poem,* notes to 214 f., 475.

17 Scheindlin, 322.

18 Polliack, 312.

19 Goitein, *Jews and Arabs,* 175.

20 Ibn Daud, 94, in the Hebrew text 68.

21 Simon Dubnow, *Geschichte des Chassidismus (History of Hassidism),* 2 vols. (Berlin, 1982; reprint of 1st edition, 1931); Shmuel Ettinger, "The Modern Period," in *A History of the Jewish People,* 727 ff.; Philip S. Alexander, "Mysticism," *The Oxford Handbook,* 722 ff.

22 Scholem, 356. Scholem wrote most of his seminal book first in German, which uses the same word for "latest" and "last." His ambiguity may have been deliberate.

23 Ettinger, 773.

24 See I Kings 18:40, *Jewish Study Bible,* 716: "Then Elijah said to them 'Seize the prophets...let not a single one of them get away' They seized them, and Elijah took them down to the Wadi Kishon and slaughtered them there."

25 Ahad Haam, "Techijjat ha-ruach" (The Renewal of the Spirit), in *Al Parashat Derachim* (At the Crossroads) II, 129.

26 Judges 17-21.

27   Josephus, "The Jewish War," in *The New Complete Works of Josephus,* first quote 1(1), second quote 1(4), 667.

28   Babylonian Talmud Yoma 9b and parallels.

29   II Kings 14:10, *Jewish Study Bible,* 752. See also A. Malamat, "The Decline, Rise and Destruction of the Kingdom of Israel," in *A History of the Jewish People,* 127.

30   II Kings 16:5 and Isaiah 7:1. See also A. Malamat, 135.

Chapter 11:
"FORTUNE" OR CHANCE EVENTS

1   Thucydides, 344 ff.; Ibn Khaldun, 229, 253.

2   Thucydides, 109.

3   Sima Qian, 258.

4   Ward-Perkins, 40, 57 f., 62.

5   Machiavelli, "The Prince," in *The Essential Writings of Machiavelli,* ed. Peter Constantine (New York: ModernLibrary, 2007), 94 ff.

6   Bismarck, *Gedanken und Erinnerungen* (Thoughts and Memories) (München, 1952), 365. Translations by the author. The analysis of Bismarck is based on Bismarck's own book and on Henry Kissinger, *Diplomacy* (New York: Simon and Schuster, 1994), 103-136.

7   Kissinger, 105.

8   Bismarck, 377.

9   Ephraim E. Urbach, *The Sages, Their Concepts and Beliefs,* 2 vols., trans. Israel Abrahams (Jerusalem: Magnes Press, 1975), particularly Vol. 1, Chapter VI, "Magic and Miracle," 97 ff.

10   Moses Maimonides, *The Guide of the Perplexed,* trans. M. Friedländer, second ed. (New York, 1904; reprinted New York: Dover Publications, 1956), 333.

11   Urbach, 103.

12   Eli Yassif, "The 'Other' Israel," in *Cultures of the Jews,* 1090.

13   II Kings 18:13-37 and 19:32. The same story is repeated in modified form in Isaiah 36-39, probably borrowed from *Kings.* Although the first Isaiah played a major role in this drama, some do not regard him as the author of Chapters 36-39. See *Jewish Study Bible,* 782.

14   For various possible reasons the Bible and later historians put forward to explain Sennacherib's sudden retreat, see Tadmor, *A History of the Jewish People,* 142 ff.

15   R.S. Bray, *Armies of Pestilence: The Impact of Disease on History* (Cambridge: James Clark & Co., 2004), 4 f.

16   Lester L. Grabbe, *"Like a Bird in a Cage": The Invasion of Sennacherib in 701 BCE* (Sheffield: Sheffield Academic Press, 2003). See also Christopher R. Seitz, "Account A and the Annals of Sennacherib," *Journal of the Study of the Old Testament (JSOD)* 58 (1993): 49 f.

17   Complete text in Seitz, 51.

18   Isaiah is cited more often in rabbinic literature than any other prophet, and nineteen *haftarot* (Sabbath readings) are taken from Isaiah, more than from any other book of the Bible. See *The Jewish Study Bible,* 780.

19   Josephus, "The Jewish War," in *The New Complete Works of Josephus,* Book 6, 4:6, 896.

20   Tommaso Leoni, "'Against Caesar's Wishes': Flavius Josephus as a Source for the Burning of the Temple," *Journal of Jewish Studies* LVIII, no.1 (spring 2007), 39 ff. Hadas-Lebel, *Rome,* 121, mentions an earlier paper of Leoni (2000) but suggests that the question remains open.

21   Goodman, 441 ff.

22 Gershom Scholem, *Sabbatai Sevi, the Mystical Messiah* (Princeton: Princeton University Press, 1973).

23 Scholem, *Die Jüdische Mystik*, 318.

24 Scholem, *Sabbatai*, 132.

25 Scholem wrote in 1973 that there was and still is no remedy for this disease. The original Hebrew version was less emphatic. It says that the patient's condition "does not change for the rest of his life." See *Sabbatai*, 126. This is no longer true, and was already not true in 1973, according to information the author received from Prof. David Adler of New York.

26 Scholem, *Sabbatai*, 127.

27 Some presumed suicides by manic-depressive persons who fell from a roof or window to their death were not in fact suicides during a depressive phase but delusional attempts to levitate during a manic phase. Information from Prof. David Adler, New York.

28 David Fromkin, *A Peace to End All Peace: The Fall of the Ottoman Empire and the Creation of the Modern Middle East* (New York: Avon Books, 1989), 96 ff., 140 ff., 217, 270, 278. Isaiah Friedman, *The Question of Palestine: British-Jewish-Arab Relations 1914-1918*, 2nd ed. (New Brunswick: Transaction Publishers 1992), 16 f. confirms Fromkin's analysis and adds more details on Kitchener's position.

29 As of this writing there are still antisemitic websites which maintain the conspiracy theory about Kitchener's death.

30 Simon Sebag Montefiore, *Stalin: The Court of the Red Tzar* (New York: Knopf, 2004), 574, 559, 621, 633 f. Footnotes 5 and 6 to Chapter 57, 739, give Montefiore's numerous sources, including interviews conducted after the end of the Soviet Union.

Chapter 12:
NATURAL AND HEALTH DISASTERS

1 This chapter has been reviewed and revised by Dr. Peter Kearns from the Environment, Health and Safety Division of the Environment Directorate of the OECD, Paris.

2 Sima, 60.

3 Gibbon, 793 f.

4 Irving Wolfe, "Velikovsky and Catastrophism: A Hidden Agenda?," in *The Interaction*, 229-262.

5 Brian Fagan, *The Great Warming: Climate Change and the Rise and Fall of Civilizations* (New York: Bloomsbury Press, 2008). Fagan has written several other books ascribing major historic changes to global climates.

6 Sir Martin Rees, Britain's "Astronomer Royal" and since 2005 President of the Royal Society, has warned that humankind has no more than a fifty percent chance of surviving to the end of this century, but that concerted human action could still avert disaster. See Martin J. Rees, *Our Final Hour: A Scientist's Warning: How Terror, Error and Environmental Disaster Threaten Humankind's Future in this Century on Earth and Beyond* (London: Basic Books, 2003).

7 *The New Scientist* and *Science News*, Dec. 2005.

8 *Intergovernmental Panel on Climate Change (IPCC), Fourth Assessment Report* (UNEP, 2007), http://www.ipcc-wg2.org

9 *Ranking Port Cities with High Exposure and Vulnerability to Climate Extremes: Exposure Estimates*, OECD, Environment Working Papers No. 1, ENV/WKP (2007) 1.

10 Freeman Dyson, "The Question of Global Warming," *The New York Review of Books* LV, no.10 (June 12, 2008), 43 ff.

11 Kate Ravilious, "Major Quake, Tsunami Likely in Middle East, Study Finds," National *Geographic News*, July 26, 2007. "Fault Found for the Mediterranean 'Day of Horror,'" New Scientist, 15 March 2008, p. 16.

12 S.Lorito, M.M. Tiberti, R.Basili, A.Piatanesi, G.Valensise, "Earth-quake generated tsunamis in the Mediterranean Sea: Scenarios of potential threats to Southern Italy," *Journal of Geophysical Research*, (January 2008): 113.

13 Ron Friedman, "Israel Urged To 'Act Now' Or Face Global Warming Disaster," *Jerusalem Post*, 6.7.2007, 1, 8, 19.

14 Rinat Zafrir, "Report: Israel Unprepared for Global Climate Crisis," *Haaretz.com*, 5.8.2008, www.haaretz.com/hasen/pages/1008468.html.

PART V

Chapter 1:
TRANSFORMING A SMALL COUNTRY INTO A GREAT POWER: THE DUTCH REPUBLIC

1 This is mainly based on Jonathan I. Israel, *The Dutch Republic*. See also Part II, Chapter 14.

Chapter 2:
TRANSFORMING GREAT POWER DECLINE INTO NEW POWER RISE: TURKEY

1 This is mainly based on Bernard Lewis, *Turkey*. See also Part II, Chapter 13.

2 Emmanuel Sivan, *Mythes Politiques Arabes* (Arab Political Mythmaking) (Paris: Fayard, 1995), 20 f.

Index

A

Abel 317
Abrabanel, Don Isaac 89, 224, 229-230, 234-235, 240
Abraham 18, 46, 176, 244, 311
Absolutist Monarchy, Royal Powers 224
Adams, Brooks 118
Adler, David xii, 421n1, 422n24, 437n25
Adorno, Theodor, 119
Affiliative Social Behavior 186-187
Afonzo V, 229
Afrocentrism, Afrocentric 118
Afroeurasia 115-116, 133
Agrippa II, 228
Ahab, King of Israel 245, 307-308
Ahaz, King 327
Akiva, Rabbi xiii, 151, 310
Alcibiades 31-33
Alexander the Great 222, 246, 309, 332
Alexandria Syndrome 219
Alliance Israélite Universelle (France) 218
Alliance(s) 104-105, 218, 245, 299, 302-303, 305-307, 309, 312-313, 355, 357
Alliance, Israel-US 313, 357
Altruism 44, 184-185, 191
Altruism, Reciprocal, 185
Amaziah, King of Judah 327
American Jewish Educational and Economic Success 199, 205-208, 267-277
Amos 126, 137, 171, 175
Anarchy, Anarchic Inclination 154, 241
Antipater 287-289
Antiquity xiii, xv, 39, 56, 58-59, 70, 110, 117, 131, 140, 169, 190-191, 244, 289, 375, 377
Anisemitism, Antisemitic 62, 82, 89, 100, 118-119, 143, 151-152, 172, 178, 186, 201, 215-216, 230, 234, 236-238, 248, 250, 254, 262, 265-266, 282, 291, 293-295, 340, 363, 367, 369, 410n18, 410n22, 437n29
Anti-Zionism, Anti-Zionist 82, 200, 339
Antoninus Pius 228
Apion 143-144
Apologetics, Apologetic xvi, 143, 282
Apostasy, Apostate 287, 318
Arab Caliphate 93, 95, 339
Arab Civilization 47, 88, 211, 319
Arab Minority in Israel 247
Arab/Muslim Renaissance 90
Aramaic Culture 71
Arendt, Hannah 151-152
Aristoboulos 325, 327
Arnon, Chana 239
Artaxerxes I, 225, 239, 247
Arts and Crafts, Jews in 272
Asceticism 73, 232, 234
Assimilation 126, 152, 168, 187, 219, 226, 323-324, 363, 367
Asymmetric Wars 297, 300, 357, 370
Ataturk, Kemal 99, 358-360
Atheism 91
Atlas, Ron xii, 421n1, 422n25
Augustus 56, 135, 288

B

Baal Shem-Tov 71, 321-322
Babylonian Exile, Diaspora 43, 125-126, 150, 177-178, 213-214, 227, 246-247, 256, 282, 286, 308
Babylonian/Assyrian Expansion 246, 284, 309
Babilonian Talmud 131
Balance of Power 195, 200, 306, 332, 355, 376
Balfour, Arthur 236, 375

Balfour Declaration (1917)   5, 200, 236, 311, 339
Ballin, Albert   267
Ban Cao   303
Bar Kochba   126 (Kohbah), 149, 170, 176, 238, 271, 280 (Kohbah), 283, 310
Bar Kochba Revolt   126, 149, 170, 238, 271, 280, 283
Barbarian(s)   30, 39, 41-42, 53-55, 111, 213
Barkai, Avraham   430n28
Bar-Yosef, Avinoam   xi
Battle of Qarqar   245, 307
Begin, Menachem   366
Bellow, Saul   146
Belzer Rebbe   239
Ben David, Anan   319
Ben Eliezer, Israel (Baal Shem-Tov)   see Baal Shem-Tov
Ben Gamla, Joshuah   196-197
Ben Labrat, Dunash   320
Ben Remaliah, Pekah, King of Israel   327
Ben Shetah, Shimon   196
Ben Zakkai, Yohanan   22, 81, 126, 129, 228, 310
Ben-Sasson, H. H.,   230, 416n5
Berger, Louis   287
Bergson, Henri   79
Bernays, Jacob   336
Bernheim, Louis   433n56
Biale, David   6-7
Bible, Christian   77, 111, 145, 198, 233, 311-312
Bible, Hebrew   6-7, 48, 62, 81, 96, 125, 137, 144-145, 169, 171, 185, 197, 214, 217, 224, 227, 232, 264, 281-282, 317, 320, 342
Bible, Hebrew, Translations of,   211, 227, 311-312
Bickerman, Elias   150-151, 246
bint Isma'il al-Yehudi, Quasmina   see Quasmina
Bismarck, Otto von   222, 330-331, 372
Black Death   73, 93, 345
Bleuler, Eugen   338
Bloch, Ernst   175
Bloom, Harold   146-147
Boadicea   310
Bolshevik   292-293
Book Printing, Hebrew and Yiddish   263

Boundary Maintenance (safeguard)   165-167, 171, 177-179, 216
Brand, Ofer   xii
Brandeis, Louis   235-238
Brasidas, General   29
Braudel, Fernand   13-15, 21-22, 28, 37, 42, 59-60, 73, 75, 80, 84, 87-90, 95, 115-116, 125, 133, 153, 157, 178, 180, 196, 221, 227, 242, 248-249, 254, 270, 279, 371
Bray, R.S.   335
Brin, Sergey   210, 276
Bronstein, Lev Davidovich   see Trotsky, Leon
Bronze Age   135, 284
Buber, Martin   181
Buddha   19, 41, 145, 193
Buddhism   66, 145, 163
Bund (Party)   217, 293
Burckhardt, Jacob   12-15, 21, 27, 57-63, 72-73, 89, 118, 136, 139-141, 146, 153, 156-157, 162, 193, 211, 220-222, 240, 253, 278-279, 319, 322, 372
Burke, Peter   57
Burstein, Paul   267-268, 270, 430n30-31

C
Cain   317
Calvinism   65, 74-75
Canaan, Canaanites   131, 212, 245, 280-282, 367
Canaanite Languages   212-213
Caracalla   59, 289
Chai Gaon, of Babylonia   197
Challenge, Hassidic   321-324
Challenge-and-Response (Toynbee)   21, 28, 30, 78-81, 85, 124-130, 222-223, 238, 271, 275, 370
Chamberlain, Neville   77, 118
Chance Event(s)   142, 329-341, 343, 346, 377
Chance Events Controlling Half of History: Macchiavelli   333
Charity   54, 171-172, 264-265, 277, 420n39
Charlemagne   5, 256-257, 275
Charles V   59, 62, 89, 231-232, 235, 239, 312, 427n36
Charters, for Jews   231, 256
Chase-Dunn, Christopher   14, 27-28, 115-116, 133, 157, 221

Chasidah, Yishai 426n22
China's Engagement in the Middle East 304
Chinese Jews 100, 290
Chinese Civilization 37, 41, 130, 166, 212
Chinese Ritual (*li*) 166
Chmielnicki, Bogdan 18
Chomsky, Noam 118
Chopin, Frédéric 145
Chosen People (choseness) 173-174, 244
Christianity (Christian Tradition, Ideology) 16, 22-23, 53-55, 60, 77-78, 84-85, 96, 100, 131, 162-163, 168, 172, 176, 178, 183, 203, 227, 230, 244, 262, 264, 289, 313, 317-319, 337
Churchill, Winston 77, 221, 239-240, 332, 340
Cicero 248
Cimabue 417n8
Civilization, American 157, 193, 296
Civilization, Decline of 46, 59, 97, 115, 118, 139, 155, 158, 211, 217, 223, 278, 378
Civilization, Jewish, Current State of and Future of xiv, xvi, 4, 6, 14, 56, 90-91, 100, 149-151, 178, 181, 209, 217, 241, 245, 251, 254-255, 263-264, 270, 274, 289, 294, 328, 349, 363, 370, 373-374, 378-379
Civilization, Mono-Territorial 245
Civilization, Multi-Territorial 246, 251
Civilization, Russian 157
Civilization, Western 71, 80, 100, 112, 118-119, 136, 156, 158, 162, 221, 280, 301
Civilizational Affinities 301-314
Civilizations, Interconnectedness of 154, 158
Clash of Civilizations 5, 57, 155
Clement VII 312
Cleopatra III 286
Climate, Climatic Factors 44, 55, 87-88, 257, 333, 343-344, 347-348
Cliodynamics 114
Cohen, Gerson D. 257
Cohen, Tobias 215
Cold War 77, 154, 156, 194-195
Collective Judaization 247

Collective Memory 10, 170, 177
Collective Unconscious 181
Commemoration 170, 178, 280
Communism, Communist 17, 83, 106, 116, 118, 153, 172, 174, 176, 255, 292, 316
Communist Manifesto 116
Communist Revolution see Revolution, Communist
Community System, Jewish 126
Competitive Advantage 183, 256, 258, 261, 263-264, 376
Complexity 111, 117, 145, 154, 156, 158, 167, 196, 280, 287, 314, 333
Conflict Sadducees-Pharisees 317-319
Confucianism 35, 39, 66-67, 163
Confucius 19, 36, 38, 166-167, 193, 211
Consensus, Magial, Tacit, Silent 71, 158, 180-182, 187, 191, 376, 421n9
Constantine the Great 13, 54, 57-60, 162, 255-256
Conversion to Christianity 54, 131, 150, 262, 264
Conversion, Convert 54, 131, 144, 150, 190-191, 262, 264, 375
Copernicus, Nicolaus 145
Cordovero, Moses 181
Corruption 10, 32, 34-35, 39- 40, 52-54, 56, 98, 128, 211, 224, 375
Council of the Four Lands 263
Creative Minorities 79-80
Creative Skepticism 204-206
Creative Thought 40, 203, 254
Creativity (Cultural Creativity) 9, 46, 61, 78-80, 93-94, 96, 100, 135-136, 138-147, 150, 158, 207, 216, 222, 245-249, 251-252, 270, 276, 317, 321, 324, 355, 357, 374, 376-377, 418n21
Crisis of Islam 95
Critical (Population) Mass 150, 242-245, 248-252, 376
Cromwell, Oliver 147, 233-235, 311
Cultural Accomplishments/Creativity/ Contributions 6, 9, 61, 78, 93, 135, 138-147, 216, 245-247-249, 251, 357, 374, 376-377
Cultural Bias 22
Cultural History (historian) 57-58, 72, 84, 220, 279

Cultural Pessimism 28, 57, 118-119, 153, 316
Cyclical History/Theory, Cyclical Historian
   16, 18, 27-28, 37-38, 46, 66, 68, 70, 85,
   88, 137
Cyrus 225, 247, 309, 311, 375

D

da Vinci, Leonardo 142
Daniel 227
Dante Alighieri 6, 215
Dark Ages 6, 256
Darwin, Charles 44, 184, 131, 175, 222,
   257
Darwinian Genetics 44, 184
David 18, 48
Dawkins, Richard 184-185
Dawood, N.J. 48
de Medici, Lorenzo 136
de Romilly, Jacqueline 33
de Tocqueville, Alexis 152
De Witt, Johan 103
Debrunner, Albert M. 63
Decadence 92, 94, 118
Decentralization 116-117
Decline, a Relative Concept 8-12
Decline/End/Collapse, of the West 68-71,
   78, 85, 153, 156-158, 376
Degradation/Catastrophes/Suicide/
   Mistakes, Environmental and Eco-
   logical 20, 108-109, 148, 155, 343,
   347-349, 363
Democracy 32-33, 95, 154, 210, 239, 312
del Medigo, Elia 63
De-Legitimization of Israel and Jews 369,
   372
Delitzsch, Friedrich 169
DellaPergola, Sergio xii, 251
Demography (Demographic) xvi, 15, 88,
   242-247, 251-252, 274, 307, 376, 379,
   403n1
Dennet, Daniel 164
Descartes, René 183
Destruction, Destroyed 9, 18, 27-29, 34,
   45, 47, 52-55, 71, 81, 108, 110, 125-126,
   130-131, 148-149, 153-154, 167, 177-
   178, 196, 209, 216, 222, 228, 245-247,
   278-279, 282, 284, 287, 300, 325-327,
   342, 344, 363, 374, 377

Destruction, of First Temple 18, 126, 222,
   245, 247, 272, 282, 284, 286, 308, 310,
   317, 326, 420n46
Destruction/Burning of Second Temple
   81, 126, 177-178, 196, 216, 228, 284,
   318, 325-326
Development, Technological, Industrial
   104, 209, 299
Diamond, Jared 13-14, 27-28, 108-109,
   148, 155, 221, 342-343
Diaspora History 131, 151, 218, 256, 275,
   327
Diaspora(s) 4, 71, 82, 91, 100, 126, 129-131,
   144, 150-152, 172, 178-179, 189, 210,
   214-217, 225, 229, 240-241, 246-252,
   256, 270-277, 284-286, 288, 290, 294-
   295, 299-300, 306, 311-312, 314, 324,
   327-328, 356, 361, 364-365, 375-376
Dimona Nuclear Reactor 348
Disraeli, Benjamin 311
Dissent, General 75, 152, 298, 315-317,
   354, 377, 379
Dissent, Internal, Jewish 298, 317-328, 377
Divine Providence 70, 168, 234, 307
Domitian 337
Douglas, Mary 165-166, 171
Dreyfus, Alfred 201
Dror, Yehezkel xi, 367
Dual Morality (Max Weber) 67
Dualism, Mind-Body 84, 182-183
Dubnow, Simon xvi, 17-18, 227-228, 232,
   322
Durant, Will 153-154, 418n1
Durkheim, Emile 165
Dutch Culture 72, 74-76, 102, 140-141, 279
Dutch Golden Age (and Decline) 8, 12-13,
   74-76, 101-102, 136, 140-141, 193, 254,
   354-357
Dutch Revolt 102
Dynasty/Dynasties 9-10, 35-42, 45-47,
   66, 103, 134, 141, 162, 195, 223, 273,
   290, 304, 309, 343
Dyson, Freeman 204, 344

E

Earthquakes/Tsunamis 55, 332, 342, 344-
   346, 348, 378
Eber, Irene xii, 407n1, 434n3
Economic Distress, of Jews 262, 264, 270

Economic History, Jewish   196, 254-255, 270, 273
Economic Prosperity, of Jews   210, 255, 258, 261-270, 273, 277, 376
Eden, Antony   240
Eichmann, Adolf   81, 151
Eisenstadt, Shmuel N.   5
Eizenstat, Stuart   xi
Elagabalus   59
Elders of Zion (Protocols of)   340
Eliade, Mircea   16
Elias, Norbert   404n7
Elijah   323, 435n24
Elimelech, Naftali   xii
Emancipation, Jewish   4, 63, 126-127, 167, 204, 261, 265, 273, 312
Emden, Jacob (Javetz)   199
Empire, Byzantine   55, 317
Empire, Chinese   9, 11, 35-40, 306
Empire, German   231, 305, 331
Empire, Holy Roman   231-232, 273, 312
Empire, Persian, Sassanid   93, 131, 226, 246-247, 251, 254, 286-287
Empire, Roman   4, 8, 10, 27, 31, 50-56, 59, 86, 88, 97, 110-112, 131, 148-149, 157, 162, 165, 171, 190, 197, 241, 242, 246-248, 255, 289, 306, 309-310, 329, 332, 334, 337, 345
Empire/Dynasty, Indian-Timuri   93
Empire/Dynasty, Ottoman   9, 43, 93, 97-100, 134, 148, 163, 194, 216, 241, 277, 312, 353, 358-361
Empire/Dynasty, Safavi   93, 134
Engels, Friedrich   116
Enlightenment   5, 16, 52, 70-71, 101, 105, 119, 126, 153, 167, 173, 198, 250, 252, 261, 264, 281, 324, 376
Enlightenment, Radical   101
Entrepreneurship   209, 254, 267, 275-277, 376
Epigenetics   187-188, 192, 422n23-24
Erlanger, Simon   xii
Erotic/Love Poems/Poetry   215
Esperanto   174
Evolutionary Fitness   163
Evolutionary Psychology   183-187, 191
Evolutionary Selection   188, 207
Exodus   125, 169, 241, 244
Expulsion   62, 96, 231, 233, 262, 271, 339

Expulsion Decree, from Heidelberg   231
Expulsion, from Spain   89, 177-178, 214, 230, 244, 250, 338
Extermination   Campaign   (by   Nazi Germany)   237-240
Ezekiel (Yehezkel)   336
Ezra   126, 225-227, 247

F
Fagan, Brian   343
Fairbank, John King   407n2
False Messiah(s)   233, 264, 337
Fanaticism, Fanatic (religious)   53-54, 95, 134, 141, 230, 320, 325, 355
Fanon, Frantz   118
Ferdinand, King of Spain   59, 89, 229-231, 235, 272
Feuer, Michael   xii
Feynman, Richard   203
Fischer, Shlomo   xii
Flaccus   248
Florida, Richard   203
Flusser, David   285
Foundation (origin) Myth(s) (Jewish)   170, 190
Fourth Crusade(s) (Crusaders)   244, 257-258, 261, 286, 317
Fragmentation, Political   59, 74-75, 149-150, 211, 241, 372
Frances, Immanuel   215
Frank, Jacob   322
Frankfurter, Felix   237
Frederic William I of Prussia   264
Frederick II of Hohenstaufen   232
Freedom (political)   17, 30, 52, 60, 141, 153, 178, 236, 250, 280, 312
Freud, Sigmund   144, 146, 180, 182, 204, 206
Friedländer, Saul   238
Fromkin, David   156, 437n28
Fukuyama, Francis   154

G
Gans, David   xvi, 214
Gaon of Vilna   322-324
Geiger, Abraham   317
Gene, Selfish   184-185
Gene, Selfless   184-185
Genetic proximity   190

Genetic(s) xiii, xvi, 44, 78, 124, 187-192, 206-208, 269, 338, 346, 349, 422n20, 424n35
Genghis Khan 47
Genocide 281
Gentile (Christian) Contempt 216, 264
Geographic Concentration 141
Geographic Partition, General 315-317
Geographic Partition, Israel/Judah 317, 326-328
Geopolitics, Chinese in the 2nd Century BCE 302-304
Geopolitics, Dutch Republic 104, 304-305
Geopolitics, Geopolitical 55, 104, 226, 234, 257, 299, 301-314, 326-327, 344, 365, 367, 375
Geopolitics, Jewish Diaspora 311-312
Geopolitics, Modern Israel's 299, 312-314
Geopolitics, of Ancient Israel 307-311
Gernet, Jacques 42
Gersonides 198
Gerstenfeld, Manfred xii
Ghetto 71, 238, 250, 265, 273
GI Bill, US 268
Gibbon, Edward 10-11, 13, 15, 27, 31, 50-56, 59, 77, 98, 110-111, 148-149, 152, 155-156, 162, 193, 211, 220-222, 241, 254, 278, 306, 315-316, 326, 329, 342, 345
Gil, Avi xii
Gilbert, Martin 240
Giotto 417n8
Global Warming, General 108, 155, 343-344, 347
Gobineau, Joseph-Arthur 118
Goethe, Johann Wolfgang 68, 77
Goitein, Shlomo 259, 320, 429n16
Goldman, Merle 407n2
Goldmann, Nahum 237
Goldstein, Jonathan xii
Gongsun Hong 42
Goodman, Martin 248
Goodman, Peter 337
Governance 38-39, 41, 75, 98, 131, 155, 158, 164, 193, 224, 230, 240, 333, 341, 364, 367, 370-371, 375
Governance, Israel's 240-241, 364
Graetz, Heinrich xvi, 17, 143-144, 227-228, 254, 288

Great Schism (between Catholicism and Orthodoxy) 316-318
Great-Man Theory of History 116, 221
Greek Struggle for Independence 147
Gross, Nahum xii, 253
Grossman, Vasily 294
Group Consciousness 44
Group Feeling 44
Group Solidarity/Cohesion 48-49, 114, 170-171, 181-186, 191, 259, 262, 376, 404n5
Gulag 77, 340
Gustav Adolf 272
Gutenberg, Johannes 198

H
Hadas-Lebel, Mireille 288
Hadrian 149, 284
Hakman, Inbal xii
Halff, Antoine xii
Hall, Thomas D. 14, 27-28, 115-116, 133, 157, 221
Hanagid, Samuel 144-145, 289
Haninah, Rabbi 22
Hanson, Victor Davis 280
Hard Power 60, 151, 195, 200, 423n8
Harun Al-Rashid 256-257
Harvey, Oliver 240
Haskalah (Jewish Enlightenment) 4, 18, 128, 198, 218, 323
Hassidim, Hassidism, Hassidic 71, 181, 199, 239, 321-324
Hebrew, (Biblical and Modern) 5-7, 48, 61-62, 67, 96, 126, 144, 166, 182, 198, 212-219, 226, 232-234, 259-260, 263-264, 283, 285, 289, 298, 319-320, 323
Hegel, Georg Wilhelm Friedrich 11, 14, 16-18, 57, 90, 118, 153, 324
Held, Mathias 232
Heraclitus 315
Herder, Johann Gottfried 5
Heresy, Heretic 318-323
Herman, Arthur 28, 118-119, 153, 316
Herodes 228, 287-288
Herodotus 5
Hersant, Yves 410n20
Herzl, Theodor 127, 129, 235, 364, 371
Hesiod 135, 137
Heuck, Sigrid 429n11

Hezekiah 335
High Cultures 57, 69, 142
Hillel 129
Hinduism 66, 78, 145
Historiography xv, 22, 27, 29, 34-36, 58, 87, 97, 109, 148, 161, 169-170, 192, 221, 253-254, 263, 286
History, Long Trends of 37-38
History, Materialist Explanation of 253
Hitler, Adolf 77, 89, 127-128, 221, 237, 332
Hobbes, Thomas 33-34
Hobsbawm, Eric 129
Hodgson, Marshall G.H. 11, 13, 28, 48, 92-96, 130, 136, 176
Homer 147
Hosea 126
Hourani, Albert 92
Huizinga, Johan 12-13, 28, 72-76, 95, 136, 139-140, 153, 156-157, 163, 253, 279-280
Hulagu Khan 47
Hulli, Jacob 217
Human Capital 196, 269-270, 273-274
Huntington, Samuel P. 5, 57, 301-302, 306
Hyrkanos 325, 327

I
Ibn Ezra, Abraham 320
Ibn Khaldun 13, 15, 27, 43-50, 77, 83, 92, 94, 114, 124, 139-140, 162, 180, 185, 193, 211, 220-221, 223, 241, 278, 315, 329
Ibn Khordadbeh 260, 263
Ibn Paquda, Bahya 198
Ibn-Daud, Abraham 17, 214, 257, 320-321
Idel, Moshe 197
Idolatry 248, 326, 334
Imperial Diet of Augsburg 231-232
Income Tax, Germany 266
Industrial Revolution 253
Information Technologies 209
Innovation 9, 40, 66, 93, 103, 195, 203, 209, 242, 267, 269, 275-277, 293, 300, 319, 347, 355, 357, 364, 375, 377
Inquisition, Spanish 230, 312
Insider-Outsider Perspective 276
Integration 85, 110-111, 116, 265, 298
Intelligence, Hereditary Explanation of 207

Intermarriage 91, 115, 179, 226, 375
Intermediaries 91, 261
International Trade 9, 259, 262
Intifadas 297-298
Intoxication of Victory 80, 279
Invasion of Sennacherib 335-336
Invasions 54-55, 86, 110-111, 117
Invasions, Mongol 47, 93, 211
Invention 61, 98, 103, 127-129, 142, 168, 198, 200, 254, 264, 288
Iron Age 111, 135, 213
Islam, Islamic (civilization, culture) 11, 43, 54-55, 67, 78, 88, 92-100, 130-131, 136, 148, 162, 168, 172, 176, 178, 180, 197, 211, 256, 258, 260, 272, 281, 301, 313, 319-320, 337, 359-360
Isaac 46, 244, 311
Isaac the Jew 256, 275
Isabella of Spain 89, 230-231, 235, 272
Isaiah 173, 175, 308-309, 335-336
Ishmael 244
Islam, Florishing of 93-94
Israel, Jonathan I. 8, 13, 15, 21, 27-28, 72, 74-76, 101-106, 134, 136, 139-140, 145, 163, 171, 193, 220, 249, 254, 261, 263-264, 304
Israel's Generals as National Leaders 292, 298, 310
Israel's High-Tech 200, 275-276, 299, 370
Israel's Universities 200, 210, 355, 357
Israel's Wars since 1948 296-299, 357, 360-361, 369-370
Isserles, Moses (Rema) xvi, 198

J
Jablonka, Eva 422n23
Jabotinsky, Ze'ev 235, 371-372
Jacob 46, 244, 311
James I 311
James II 304
Jaspers, Karl 18, 36, 133, 183, 338
Jeremiah 22, 308, 336
Jerome 227
Jesuit(s) 233, 290
Jesus Christ 18, 71, 82
Jewish "Otherness" 165, 182, 213
Jewish Calendar 166, 169, 177, 179, 197, 284
Jewish Charity 171-172, 264-265, 277, 420n39

Jewish Civilization xiv, xvi, 4, 6, 14, 56, 90-91, 100, 149-151, 178, 181, 209, 217, 241, 245, 251, 254-255, 263-264, 270, 274, 289, 294, 328, 349, 363, 370, 373-379

Jewish Communities, Autonomous 6, 100, 151, 171, 229, 248-252, 259, 263, 267, 270, 320-321, 328, 273

Jewish Community/Communal Structure 126

Jewish Contribution(s) 143-146, 170, 198, 201, 210, 251, 269

Jewish Diaspora Model 82

Jewish Doctors Arrested by Stalin 340

Jewish Economic History 196, 254-264, 270, 272-275

Jewish Farming, Agriculture 177, 196-197, 258, 265, 270-271, 292

Jewish Gene 190, 206

Jewish Genetic Diseases 242n35

Jewish History, Marxist Models of 255, 65

Jewish Linguistic Versatility 260-263

Jewish Messianism 84, 175-176, 233, 322-323

Jewish Mystical Tradition 177, 181

Jewish Orthodox Commandments/Prohibitions 165-168, 171-173, 177, 229, 276

Jewish Physicians 198, 205, 266, 340

Jewish Proselytism 173-174

Jewish Revolts 151, 284, 287, 309-310

Jewish Ritual 137, 165-168, 171, 232

Jewish Self-Hatred 186

Jewish Social Ethics 170-173, 178, 420n39

Jewish State Tradition, Absence of 164, 176, 241, 371

Jewish Universalism 174-175, 203-204

Jewish Usury 231

Jews, Public Image of 209-210

Jezebel 307

Joash 327

Joel 175

Josel of Rosheim 229, 231-232, 234-235, 238, 240, 311, 313

Joselewicz, Berek 291

Joseph 46, 425n10

Josephus Flavius 143-144, 169, 227-228, 282, 284-289, 291, 310, 325-326, 336-337

Joshua 17, 281

Juao III 312

Judaism, Reform 167-169, 237, 317

Judeo-Christians 435n10

Julian 162

Julius Caesar 56, 248, 287-289, 332

Jung, Carl Gustav 180-181

K

Kabbalah, Kabbalist 62, 177, 181, 214, 217, 320

Kaegi, Werner 63

Kaesler, Dirk 410n6

Kafka, Franz 146

Kaganovich, Lazar 340

Kahn, Herman 20

Kaplan, Mordecai M. 4-5, 219

Karady, Victor 430n42

Karaites, Karaite Challenge 319-321, 324, 435n14

Karasenty, Yogev xi, 431n1

Karski, Jan 237

Katz, Jacob 171

Kaufmann, Yehezkel 131, 147

Kearns, Peter xii, 437n1

Kehimkar, Haeem Samuel 291

Kennedy, Paul 14, 20, 27-28, 106-107, 221

Kerensky, Alexander 83

Kimchi, David 320

King David Hotel Bombing 366

King, Alexander 194

King, Joe 143

Kinship 44, 66, 114, 185

Kissinger, Henry xii, 221, 306, 436n6

Kitchener, Horatio Herbert 311, 339-340, 437n28-29

Klausner, Joseph 227, 284-285

Kligsberg, Bernardo 420n40

Korach 224

Knowledge-Based Economy (industries) 200, 209, 267, 273

Koran 92

Kornberg, Arthur 205

Kornberg, David 205

Kosciuszko, Tadeusz 291

Krochmal, Nachman 15, 18, 137

Kuznets, Simon 255, 271-272

L

Ladino 216-218

Landmann, Georg Peter 406n1

Lange, Johannes 338

Language Barrier 219

Language, Corruption of 34
Languages, Indo-European 212-213
Languages, Semitic 212-213
Laozi (Lao-Tse) 19, 315
Laqueur, Walter 237-238
Leadership 14, 27, 31-33, 38, 48, 61, 75, 99, 103, 106-107, 116, 132, 161, 168, 200, 220-241, 258, 269, 278, 283, 288, 291-293, 298, 300, 305, 310, 321, 329, 331, 334, 337, 341, 354-356, 359, 364-367, 370-372, 375, 379
Lebanon War 2006 297
Lehmann, Behrend 264
Leibniz, Gottfried Wilhelm 145
Lenin, Vladimir 83, 292, 332
Leoni, Tommaso 337
Leroy-Beaulieu, Anatole 201-203
Leslie, Donald Daniel 166
Lewis, Bernard 13, 15, 28, 92, 97-100, 134, 139, 163, 193, 220, 241, 254, 309
Li Ling 36
Li Tzu-ch'eng 433n48
Li Yao 433n48
Lin Yutang 166
Linear History/Theory, Linear Historian 16
Literacy 103, 140, 194, 215-216, 273, 355
Literacy, Hebrew 216, 218
Livni, Avraham 420n50
Livy (Titus Livius) 56
Lloyd George, David 291
Loew, Judah (Maharal) xvi, 198
Long-Distance Trade (traders) 215, 256, 258-261, 273-275
Lottem, Emanuel xi
Louis XIV 89, 104, 304
Lukacs, John 221
Luria, Isaac 181
Luther, Martin 58, 65, 211, 231
Luzzatto, Simone 204-205
Luzzatto, Ephraim 215

M
Machiavelli, Niccolo 33, 56, 230, 329-333, 337
Maghribi Traders 258-260
Magic/Miracles in Jewish Tradition 67, 165, 333-334
Mailer, Norman 146
Maimon, Dov xii, 419n13

Maimonides, Abraham 198
Maimonides, David (David Ben Maimon) 260, 275
Maimonides, Moses (Rambam) 175, 198, 214, 224, 260, 281, 334
Makhir of Narbonne, 256-257
Malamud, Bernard 146
Mandate of Heaven (theory) 37, 162, 407n6
Manhattan Project 128
Mantegna 417n8
Marcus Aurelius 135
Martial Qualities/Spirit of Jews 280, 285-286, 289-290, 294, 377
Marx, Karl 17, 45, 64-65, 116, 144, 146, 153-154, 204, 221, 253-254, 266, 329
Marxism, Marxist 57, 65, 78, 144, 157, 175, 243, 255
Masaccio 141
Masada, Siege of 285
Materialism 69, 85, 154, 243
Mathematical-Physical Sciences 99, 206
Maximilian I 231
McNeill, William H. 14, 85, 153
Meltzer, Hagar xii
Meltzer, Nahum xii
Meltzer-Asher, Aya xii, 425n1
Memes 184
Menahem Mendel of Kozk 199
Menasseh Ben Israel 229, 232-235, 240, 311, 313
Mercantilism 105, 253, 261-265, 272
Meridor, Sallai xi
Merneptah 367
Messiah 137, 175-176, 230, 233, 264, 281, 309, 322, 337, 420n47, 426n22
Messianism see Jewish Messianism
Meyer, Eduard 169
Micah 137, 175
Michalowski, Stefan xii
Michelangelo 141, 417n8
Middle Ages 12, 28, 72-74, 110, 140, 168, 171, 197, 201, 215, 218, 229, 273, 279, 318, 428n10
Middleman Minorities 277
Midrash 62, 175, 213-214, 244
Mikoyan, Anastas 340
Militarism 69, 80, 279, 281
Miller, Arthur 146
Miltiades 29

Mirsky, Yehudah xii, 172
Mishnah 6, 17, 151, 172, 214, 228, 282
Mitnagdim 323-324
Mitzvah Wars 281, 283
Modernity 61-62, 101, 126, 145, 164, 178, 229, 360
Mohammed (Muhammad) 45, 96, 320
Mommsen, Theodor 53, 336
Monash, John 291-292, 295
Mono-Causal Explanation(s) 27, 107, 111, 270
Monotheism 16, 96, 143, 212
Morality 19, 32-34, 51, 54-55, 143, 175, 211, 307
Montague, Edwin 339
Montefiore, Simon Sebag 340
Montgomery, Bernard 292
Morag, Shlomo 212
Morality, Dualistic 67
Moses 7, 17, 166, 224, 227, 241, 244, 282
Moses of Coucy (Smag) 173
Mozart, Wolfgang Amadeus 142
Multiculturalism 31, 53, 203
Murray, Charles 139, 199, 418n21
Mussolini, Benito 366, 433n55
Mythology 29, 38, 77, 135, 220

N
Na'aman, Nadav 245
Nahman of Bratzlav 199
Nachmanides (Moshe Ben Nachman, Rambam) 177, 421n52
Napoleon Bonaparte 89, 106, 265, 331
Napoleon III 331
Nationhood, Jewish 105, 263
Natural/Health Disasters, General 109, 332, 342-349, 378
Nazi, Nazi-Germany, Nazism 10, 18, 63, 68, 72, 76-77, 118, 127, 143, 150-152, 181, 200, 221, 236-239, 255, 273, 293-194, 312, 340, 359, 366, 370, 416n6, 420n47
Nazi crimes 63, 128
Nebuchadnezzar 43, 308, 336, 432n31
Needham, Joseph 261, 429n19
Nero 310
Nerva 135
Netanyahu, Benzion 230
Network 111, 116, 233, 270, 272, 422n23
Networking, Jewish 91, 126, 215, 249, 254-256, 258-259, 262, 270, 272, 274, 376

Neusner, Jacob 255
Nevzlin, Leonid xi
Nietzsche, Friedrich 33, 57, 118-119
Nisbett, Richard E. 207
Nobel Prizes/Awards/Laureates 143, 199, 202, 205, 208, 294, 375
Non-Violence 280
Nuclear Weapons/Bombs 20, 127-128, 156, 200, 368, 370, 416n6
Nye, Joseph S. 210

O
Obadiah the Proselyte, Obadiah the Norman 144
Obama, Barack 347, 368
OECD: Organisation for Economic Cooperation and Development 194-195, 200, 344, 347, 437n1
Old Testament 67, 169, 235, 281
Oldenbarnevelt, Johan van 103
Olson, Mancur 14, 28, 113, 221
Oppenheimer, Robert 128
Oren, Michael 127
Origenes 227
Osman I 98

P
Paganism, Pagan 17, 143, 233, 257, 307
Palestine, Palestinians, Palestinian Conflict 5, 82, 127, 150, 190, 235-236, 238, 243, 293-296, 311, 339, 345, 366, 369, 372
Patton, George S. 294
Pauperization 76, 105, 226, 264, 268
Peoplehood 5, 373, 404n5
Pepin, King of Franks 257
Peres, Shimon xii-xiv
Pericles 30-34, 89, 135, 147, 278, 301, 332
Pessimism, Pessimist xiv, 28, 56-57, 68, 72, 78, 118-119, 153-156, 316, 347
Phillip II 87-91
Philo of Alexandria 214, 282, 288
Pico della Mirandola, Giovanni 62, 410n20
Pinker, Steven 186-187, 422n22
Plague 34, 47, 335, 345
Plato 84, 135, 147, 183, 220, 342
Plutarch 37, 225, 235, 239
Poetry, Hebrew 6, 144-145, 214-215, 263, 289, 319-320

Poliakoff, Leon 89
Pompey 287, 325
Popper, Steven xii
Population 3, 47, 73, 76, 80, 86-87, 93-94,
102-105, 114, 140, 149, 151, 162, 168,
177, 179, 189-190, 198-199, 207, 209,
226, 242-252, 257, 262-269, 273, 281,
290, 304, 314-315, 325-327, 336, 338,
343-345, 360-361, 376
Population Decline 47, 93, 111, 134, 158,
242, 264, 266
Population Growth 105, 242, 257, 326,
343, 376
Printing 91, 99, 198, 263-264, 267
Propaganda 34, 82, 191, 248, 305
Prosperity 11, 30, 40, 44-45, 56, 75-76,
93, 102, 104, 107, 130, 134, 136-140,
158, 164, 171, 195, 208, 210-211, 255,
258-263, 271-273, 277, 286, 290, 367,
374, 376
Protectionism, National 264
Protestantism, Protestant Ethics 64-67,
82, 157, 162-163, 234, 316-317
Psammetich I 286
Psammetich II 286
Public Opinion 70, 369, 379
Pugliese, Umberto 433n55
Puritanism 65

Q
Quasmina bint Isma'il al-Yehudi 144-145
Quantitative History 84, 87

R
Rabbenu Gershom (Me'or Hagolah) 229
Rabbinic (Orthodox) Decision Makers 168
Rabbinic Debates 128
Rabin, Yitzhak 328
Ramban see Nachmanides
Ramses II 131, 367
Ramses III 131
Rashi (Shlomo Itzhaki) 214, 227, 321,
421n51, 429n12
Rathenau, Emil 267
Rationalism 64-66, 91, 280
Reagan, Ronald 106
Rehoboam 326
Religious Pluralism 168
Rembrandt van Rijn 136, 140, 232

Renaissance, Italian 12-13, 27, 56-62, 72-74,
85, 95, 136, 140-141, 147, 193, 222, 279
Republicanism, Republican Spirit 52-56
Research and Development (R&D) 128,
195, 200, 208
Responsa, Rabbinic 258-259
Reubeni, David 312
Revolution (revolutionary) 10, 18, 20, 66,
85, 102, 175-176, 183, 195, 209, 218,
222, 235, 253, 267, 274, 291-293, 316,
358-360, 364-367, 370-372, 378
Revolution, Communist (socialist, Russian)
17, 83, 153, 255, 292-293, 372
Revolution, English 104, 233, 304
Revolution, French 10, 105, 107, 152-153,
155, 265, 287, 291, 304, 312
Revolution, Turkish 97, 99-100, 360
Rhadanite Traders 258-261
Ricardo, David 45
Ritual Murder 231-232
Robbins, Kenneth xii
Roitman, Betty xii
Roman Empire see Empire, Roman
Romano, Immanuel (Manuello Giudio) 215
Roosevelt, Franklin D. 127, 200, 237-239
Rosenbaum, Walter xii
Rosenthal, Franz 48, 408n1
Rosman, Moshe 322
Rosner, Shmuel xii
Ross, Dennis xi
Rotblat, Joseph 416n6
Roth, Cecil 143, 233
Roth, Philip 146
Rothschild (family) 340
Royal Authority 44-48, 241
Royal Patronage 140
Royal Protection 263
Rudermann, David D. 197-198, 215
Russian Revolution see Revolution, Com-
munist

S
Saadia Gaon 198, 319-320
Sabbatai Zevi 170, 176, 218, 233, 264,
322-323, 337-338
Sabbath 165-169, 177, 226, 276, 288, 291,
419n26, 420n39
Sabbatianism 322
Sabin, Albert 210

Sacco di Roma (Sack of Rome) 62
Said, Edward 118
Salk, Jonas 210
Sallust (Gaius Sallustius Crispus) 55-56
Samson, Benjamin A. 433n51
Samson, Jonathan R. 433n51
Samuel 13, 224, 372
Sappho 144
Sarton, George 94, 198
Sartre, Jean-Paul 118-119
Saul 13
Sauvy, Alfred 242
Savonarola 136
Scheindlin, Raymond P. 320
Schism(s) 80, 315-319
Schmelzer, Menachem H. xii, 6, 239, 264
Schoenfeld, Andrew J. 288-289
Scholarship xvi, 10, 27, 45-47, 67, 190,
    202, 207, 215, 229, 234, 254, 258-260,
    264, 267, 321
Scholem, Gershom 181, 321-322, 337-338,
    435n22, 437n25
Schumpeter, Joseph 275
Schwarzbach, Bertram xii
Science and Technology (S&T) 20, 102-
    103, 107, 193-210, 261, 279, 294, 341,
    354-355, 367, 370, 372-379
Script (letters and characters) 48, 126,
    197, 212-213
Self-Defense 248, 250, 280-281, 295-296
Self-Destruction 118, 148, 157
Semedo, Alvarez 233
Seneca 169
Sennacherib 335-336, 436n14
Septuagint 214
Seven Noahide Commandments 172
Shalmaneser III 245, 307
Sharansky, Natan xi
Shneur Zalman of Lyadi 323
Shiite Religion, Shiah 94, 134
Shoah/Holocaust xiii, 81, 127, 150, 167-
    168, 170, 178, 187, 236, 238-240, 251,
    255, 283, 295, 360, 377
Sholem Aleichem 216-217
Sholokhov, Mikhail 294
Silk Road 302-303
Sima Qian 10, 13, 19, 27, 29, 35-43, 50, 52,
    83, 136-137, 139-140, 162, 193, 220-
    221, 235, 278, 282, 303, 329, 342, 372

Sima Tan 36
Simon, Richard 172
Singer, Isaac Bashevis 146, 216
Sivan, Emmanuel xii
Slezkine, Yuri 142
Smallpox 142
Smith, Adam 45
Snow, C.P. 206-208
Socrates 135, 193, 205
Sofer, Moses (Chatam Sofer) 167
Soft Power 195, 210, 376
Sohlberg, David xii, 425n1
Sokolow, Nahum 371
Solomon 18, 48, 90, 137, 222, 308, 326
Solomon, Norman 431n21
Soloveitchik, Haym 167-168, 180
Soloveitchik, Joseph B. 239
Sombart, Werner 67, 254
Sorj, Bernardo xii
Sorokin, Pitirim Alexandrovich 14, 16,
    28, 83-86, 112, 139, 153-154, 156, 163,
    196, 253, 279
Spengler, Oswald 14-15, 21-22, 28, 58, 68-
    71, 77-78, 80, 83-85, 89, 112, 115, 118,
    124, 139, 148-149, 153, 156-158, 162,
    178, 180-183, 191, 193, 195, 212, 253-
    254, 279-282, 285-286, 292, 294, 376
Spinoza, Baruch 91, 101, 145, 183, 204,
    233
Spiro, Ken 143
Stagnation 79, 93, 113, 164, 285, 376
Stalin, Joseph 77, 174, 292-294, 332, 340
Statecraft 36, 52, 69, 298, 301-302
Statesmanship 117, 227-228, 279, 355
Steiner, George 206-207
Stern, Selma 232, 427n35
Stone Age 109
Structuralist, Structural History 14, 42,
    87, 221, 227, 242
Suleiman I the Magnificent 97-98
Sun Tzu 278
Sunni, Sunnite 94, 318, 361
Survival 38, 44-46, 81, 88, 91, 102, 107,
    109, 111, 124-125, 147, 150-152, 158,
    170, 173, 180-185, 200, 208, 221, 223,
    226, 228, 243-245, 278-280, 283, 286,
    289, 294-297, 300, 317, 323-324, 343,
    353, 356-357, 360, 365, 370
Szilard, Leo 128

T

Tacitus 41, 171, 282, 284

Taglit-Birthright project 328

Tainter, Joseph A. 14, 28, 117, 154, 156, 221, 242, 279

Talmud (Talmudic) xii, 17, 22, 62, 126, 131, 165, 167, 172-177, 196-197, 202-203, 213-214, 224-228, 241, 244, 257-259, 264, 271, 283, 285, 289, 317, 319, 321, 326, 334, 346

Talmud Academy, Academies 131, 239, 257, 323

Talmud's Hermeneutics 202

Taxation, Taxpayer, Taxes, Income Tax 47, 73, 111, 231, 256, 266, 273, 277, 281, 430n27

Technical Accidents/Catastrophes 332, 346-348

Technical Progress/ "Third Factor" Theory 194

Teller, Edward 128

Themistocles 31-32, 222, 305

Theodosius I 289

Theodosius II 289

Thucydides xiv, 13, 15, 19, 27, 29-34, 38, 43, 50, 52, 56, 60, 83, 89, 193, 211, 220-222, 253, 278, 282, 301, 305, 326, 329

Tiberius Julius Alexander 288

Tiglat-Pileser 327

Tikkun Olam 172, 174

Timur (Tamerlane) 43, 221, 408n2

Titus 149, 288, 310, 336-337

Toch, Michael 257

Tolerance of Diversity, Jewish 321

Tolerance/intolerance 30, 75, 141, 163

Tong Shijun 36

Torquemada 230

Toynbee, Arnold 11, 14-16, 21-22, 28, 30, 44, 50, 63, 68, 71, 77-83, 85, 89, 91, 112, 118, 124-125, 131, 148, 153, 156-157, 162-163, 196, 220, 222-223, 253, 279, 297, 315-317

Trading 9, 74, 76, 104-105, 233, 256-262, 273-275

Trading Network 233, 259-260

Trading Primacy 104, 355

Trait Selection 185

Trajan 310

Transformation, Transforming 8-12, 28, 59-62, 73-74, 80-81, 90, 99-100, 110, 124-129, 209, 223, 228, 241, 247, 284, 320, 351-379

Transgenerational Inheritance 187

Transmigration of Souls 181

Trotsky, Leon (Bronstein, Lev Davidovich) 83, 292-293, 340

Trumpeldor, Joseph 295-296

Turchin, Peter 14, 28, 114, 221

Tylor, Edward 404n9

Tyranny 52, 54, 58, 156, 184, 221

Tzarfati Yossef (Giuseppe Gallo) 215

U

Unity, Arab 95, 180

Universal, Global, World History xii, 5, 14, 17-18, 20, 28-32, 57, 68-69, 77, 84, 92-93, 106, 113, 115, 133-134, 141, 145, 154-162, 170-173, 185, 224-225, 255, 272, 279, 292, 304, 307-308, 314, 342, 376-379

University Education, Degree, Professors, Students 21-22, 57, 102, 221

University(ies) 22, 61, 72, 76, 92, 97-99, 101, 103-105, 108, 198-201, 208-210, 215, 268, 270, 355, 357

Urbach, Ephraim 333

US Flying Fortresses F17 366

V

Valens 111

Value-Free (History, Science) 77

van Eyck, Jan 139

Vana, Liliane xii, 435n10

Vasari, Giorgio 141-142

Veblen, Thorstein 201, 204

Velikovsky, Immanuel 342

Vespasianus, 228, 310

Vichy Regime 89

Vico, Giambattista 70

Vietnam War 107, 368

Vital Impulse, Elan Vital 79

Voltaire 5, 54, 281

von Clausewitz, Carl 241, 279, 371, 427n53

W

Wahl, Jean-Jacques xii

Wahrhaftig, Zerah 239

Wang, Philip xii, 407n1
War(s) of Attrition 35, 297
War, Civil, General 10, 33-34, 111, 185, 211, 315-317, 325
War, Civil, Jewish 317, 324-328
War, Civil, Russian 292-293, 325
War, Holy 45, 281, 283
War, Italian-Ethiopian
War, Peloponnesian 27, 29, 31-34, 135, 211, 221, 325-326, 332
War, Thirty Years' 134, 262, 272
Ward-Perkins, Bryan 8, 13, 27-28, 110-112, 117, 157, 254, 329
Warner, Rex 406n1
Warring States Period of China 315
Warrior People 280, 285
Washington, George 371
Water Shortage 271, 378
Watson, Burton 407n6
Waxman, Chaim xii
Weapons of Mass Destruction (WMD) 209, 300, 363, 374, 377
Weber, Alfred 125
Weber, Max 14, 27, 58, 64-67, 77, 101, 125, 156-157, 163, 170, 226, 242, 253-254
Weizman, Chaim 200, 210, 235-236, 339, 371
Weksler, Babette xii
Weksler, Marc xii
Wen Ming (Chinese: Civilization) 6, 212
Westernization 99
White Elephant, Abul-Abbas, Charlemagne's Gift 256
Wigner, Eugene 128
Wildavsky, Aaron 241
Wilf, Einat xii
Wilhelm II 306
William III of Orange 104, 304-306
Wilson, David Sloan 184
Wilson, Edward O. 184
Wilson, Harold 206
Wilson, Woodrow 236
Window of Opportunity 93, 130-131, 233
Wingate, Orde 296
Wise, Stephen 237-238

Women's Rights, Status, Conditions 21, 37, 61, 103, 141, 166, 208, 226, 285, 308, 378
World Jewish Congress 237
World War I 9, 68, 70, 99, 156, 172, 200, 235, 238, 291, 296, 305, 311, 331, 345, 358, 433n55-56
World War I, America's Entry into 305-306
World War II 33, 68, 80, 87, 113, 176, 195, 199, 217, 238-239, 268, 275, 293, 295-297, 343, 411n7, 420n47
World-System 115-116, 133
Wouk, Herman 203
Wudi Han 10, 35-36, 38-42, 221, 302-303, 305-306, 407n3
Xerxes 226
Yakir, Yona Emmanuilovich 293
Yannai, Alexander 325
Yassif, Eli 334
Year of Disaster (Rampjaar), Dutch 104
Yehudah HaNassi 228
Yerushalmi, Yoseph Chaim 170
Yiddish 7, 216-218, 263, 291, 293
Yishuv 236, 296
Young Turk Revolt 99, 358
Yu (Emperor) 40
Yuan Shizu (Emperor) 290

Z
Zealot 228
Zedekiah 308
Zevi, Sabbatai see Sabbatai Zevi
Zhang Qian 302-303
Zhang Qianhong xii, 407n1
Zimmermann, Arthur 305-306
Zionism, Jewish Orthodox Opposition to 170, 178, 217
Zionism, Zionist 71, 96, 126-129, 147, 170, 181, 200-201, 216-218, 235-241, 247, 255, 286, 292-293, 295-296, 311-312, 323-324, 339-340, 360, 371-372
Zionist Federation of America 236
Zlotogora, Joel 424n35
Zobel, Moritz 420n47

CPSIA information can be obtained at www.ICGtesting.com
Printed in the USA
BVOW03s0044110214

344222BV00008BA/12/P